ECONOMIC SANCTIONS RECONSIDERED

Economic Sanctions Reconsidered:

GARY CLYDE HUFBAUER and JEFFREY J. SCHOTT
assisted by KIMBERLY ANN ELLIOTT

History and
Current Policy

INSTITUTE FOR INTERNATIONAL ECONOMICS
Washington, DC 1985

Gary Clyde Hufbauer is a Senior Fellow at the Institute for International Economics. He was formerly Deputy Director of the International Law Institute at Georgetown University, Deputy Assistant Secretary for International Trade and Investment Policy of the US Treasury, Director of the International Tax Staff at the Treasury, and Professor of Economics at the University of New Mexico. He is counsel to the Washington law firm of Chapman, Duff & Paul. Dr. Hufbauer has published numerous studies on international trade, investment, and tax issues.

Jeffrey J. Schott, now a Research Associate, completed this book while a Visiting Fellow at the Institute for International Economics. He was formerly a Senior Associate at the Carnegie Endowment for International Peace, where he carried out his initial work on this study; an international economist at the US Treasury Department; and a member of the research staff of The Brookings Institution.

Kimberly Ann Elliott is a Research Assistant at the Institute for International Economics. She is a graduate of the Johns Hopkins School of Advanced International Studies.

INSTITUTE FOR INTERNATIONAL ECONOMICS
C. Fred Bergsten, *Director*
Kathleen A. Lynch, *Director of Publications*
Michele McCord, *Business Manager*

The Institute for International Economics was created, and is principally funded, by the German Marshall Fund of the United States.

The views expressed in this publication are those of the authors. The publication is part of the research program of the Institute, as endorsed by its Board of Directors, but does not necessarily reflect the views of individual members of the Board or the Advisory Committee.

Library of Congress Cataloging in Publication Data
Hufbauer, Gary Clyde.
  Economic sanctions reconsidered.

  Bibliography: p. 93
  1. Economic sanctions. I. Schott, Jeffrey J., 1949– . II. Elliott, Kimberly Ann, 1960– . III. Title.

HF1413.5.H85 1985   382'.3   84–3755
ISBN 0–88132–017–X

To George P. Shultz

Judicious controller of "light switch diplomacy"

INSTITUTE FOR INTERNATIONAL ECONOMICS
11 Dupont Circle, NW, Washington, DC 20036
(202) 328–0583 Telex: 248329 CEIP

C. Fred Bergsten, *Director*

Preface

This book presents a comprehensive analysis of the use of economic sanctions for foreign policy purposes. It does so by reviewing over one hundred cases in which sanctions have been employed, mostly by the United States but by a number of other countries as well, throughout this century. The authors attempt to judge the effects of these efforts by scoring them against a constant set of criteria. They then draw policy conclusions from the historical record in an effort to inform the debate on whether and how to use sanctions in future episodes.

To achieve the Institute's objective of making its work available quickly and to a wide audience, we published in October 1983 a summary of the major analytical conclusions and policy recommendations of this study entitled *Economic Sanctions in Pursuit of Foreign Policy Goals*. That presentation, in our POLICY ANALYSES IN INTERNATIONAL ECONOMICS series, briefly summarized much of the technical analysis underlying the findings and conclusions of the research. The analysis has been updated and is largely included as chapters one through five of this volume. The detailed case studies, the complete methodology used, and a full presentation of the underlying data appear in the appendices. This technique of publishing a shorter policy-oriented version and a longer, more detailed version of the same study follows the approach previously developed in our work on *IMF Conditionality, Trade Policy in the 1980s,* and *International Debt: Systemic Risk and Policy Response.*

The Institute for International Economics is a private, nonprofit, nonpartisan research institution for the study and discussion of international economic policy. Its purpose is to analyze important issues in that area, and to develop and communicate practical new approaches for dealing with them.

The Institute was created in November 1981 through a generous commitment of funds from the German Marshall Fund of the United States. Financial support is being received from a number of private foundations and corporations, and the Institute is now broadening and diversifying its financial base. It wishes to thank the Carnegie Endowment for International Peace for assistance in carrying out this project.

The Board of Directors bears overall responsibility for the Institute and gives general guidance and approval to its research program—including identification of topics that are likely to become important to international economic policymakers over a period of one to three years. The Director of the Institute, working closely with the staff and an outside Advisory Committee, is responsible for the development of particular projects and makes the final decision to publish an individual study.

The Institute hopes that its studies and other activities will contribute to building a stronger foundation for international economic policy around the world. Comments as to how it can best do so are invited from readers of these publications.

C. FRED BERGSTEN
Director
June 1985

Acknowledgments

The authors are particularly grateful to C. Fred Bergsten and Robert Gilpin for reviewing the entire manuscript. They also benefited from comments by George W. Ball, Richard N. Cooper, Klaus Knorr, Stanley J. Marcuss, Joseph S. Nye, Jr., Lionel H. Olmer, Richard N. Perle, and Richard E. Pipes. A number of other scholars provided critiques of specific case studies.

Typing numerous drafts of the manuscript required the skilled and dedicated effort of the Institute's support staff, especially Gloria Quinlan, Patricia Taylor, Maren Hesla, Wendy Berg, Diane Wheeler, and Carol Trimble. Kathleen A. Lynch, Michelle K. Smith, and Samuel Sharkey carefully edited the final draft.

We appreciate the assistance of all who contributed to this book on its way to publication.   G.C.H.   J.J.S.   K.A.E.

Contents

Text Tables

Introduction

The US grain embargo against the Soviet Union and US restrictions on the Soviet-European gas pipeline rekindled a heated international debate over the use of economic sanctions in pursuit of foreign policy goals. This debate continues to rage today in the context of proposals to expand sanctions against the South African policy of apartheid. Advocates regard such measures as an important weapon in the arsenal of economic warfare. Skeptical observers question whether sanctions are an effective instrument of foreign policy and whether the costs of sanctions are worth the benefits derived.

To put these issues in perspective, we have delved into the rich history of the use of sanctions by a number of countries in the twentieth century in order to identify circumstances in which economic sanctions can "succeed" in attaining foreign policy goals. We believe it is useful to look beyond actions taken in the context of East–West relations; while the Soviet cases are important, they do not tell the whole story. Indeed, sanctions have been imposed in the East–West context (broadly defined) in only about 20 percent of the cases we have studied. The large majority of episodes involve either low political stakes or small target countries. Generalizations about the use of economic sanctions must give appropriate weight to these cases, since they constitute the "natural domain" of economic diplomacy.

Our study concentrates on three central questions: What factors in a sanctions episode—both political and economic—usually result in the achievement of foreign policy goals? What are the costs of sanctions to both target and sender[1] countries, and to what extent do they influence policy decisions? What lessons can be drawn from this experience to guide the policymaker on the use of sanctions in the future?

---

[1] We use the term "sender" to denote the country whose foreign policy goals are being pursued at least in part through the threat or imposition of economic sanctions. A synonymous term often found in the literature is "sanctioner."

1

Lessons Drawn from Case Studies

Much has been written about the use of economic sanctions in the conduct of foreign policy, and most of the literature takes the form of case studies. In this study we attempt to extract propositions of general validity from that literature.

The starting point for our analysis is the list shown in table 1.1 (at the end of this chapter) of 103 cases of economic sanctions, beginning with the economic blockade of Germany in World War I. Abstracts of those 103 cases make up the bulk of this book. The abstracts summarize the key events, goals, responses, economic costs, and assessments of each case. Because each abstract cites sources, we have minimized source notes in the analytic chapters. A bibliography of general references follows chapter 5. Moreover, because our abstracts summarize each episode, and because detailed narratives can be found in the literature, we deliberately refrain from extensive descriptions of the events of individual episodes in our analysis.

The cases listed in table 1.1 plainly do not include all instances since World War I of economic leverage applied by one sovereign state to try to change the conduct of another. Boundaries must be drawn to distinguish economic sanctions from other economic instruments and to separate foreign policy goals from other goals at home and abroad. Our boundaries may be described in the following way.

We define economic sanctions to mean the deliberate government-inspired withdrawal, or threat of withdrawal, of "customary" trade or financial relations. "Customary" does not mean "contractual"; it simply means levels that would probably have occurred in the absence of sanctions. Generally we exclude instances where economic incentives are used to achieve foreign policy goals. However, when incentives are closely connected with economic sanctions ("carrot-and-stick" diplomacy), they are covered in our abstracts and analysis.

We define foreign policy goals to encompass changes actually and purportedly sought by the sender state—the country imposing sanctions—in the political behavior of the target state. We rely on public statements of officials of the sender country, supplemented by the assessment of historians of each particular episode, for a definition of the foreign policy goals sought through the use of sanctions.

We exclude from foreign policy goals the normal realm of objectives sought in banking, commercial, and tax negotiations between sovereign states. However, many of our cases deal with attempts to settle expropriation disputes using economic leverage. Many expropriation episodes harbor political disputes that go beyond compensation issues, and those are the episodes we seek to cover.

Sanctions also serve important domestic political purposes in addition to whatever change they may bring about in the behavior of foreign states. As

David Lloyd George remarked in the celebrated League of Nations foray in 1935 against Italy, "[Sanctions] came too late to save Abyssinia, but they are just in the nick of time to save the [British] Government."[2]

The same is true today. What president—or Kremlin leader for that matter—has not been obsessed with the need to demonstrate leadership, to take initiatives to shape world affairs, or at least to react forcefully to adverse developments? And what president—or Kremlin leader—wants to go to war to make his point? The desire to be seen acting forcefully, but not to precipitate bloodshed, can easily overshadow specific foreign policy goals. Indeed, one suspects that in some cases domestic political goals were the motivating force behind the imposition of sanctions. Such measures often serve to distract attention from domestic ills and to galvanize public support for the government, either by inflaming patriotic fever (illustrated by US sanctions against Japan prior to World War II) or by quenching the public thirst for action (illustrated by US sanctions against Qaddafi's adventurism in northern Africa). However, we have left to others the arduous task of unearthing the domestic side of the story and determining whether sanctions in fact satisfy domestic political purposes.

In this study we make no attempt to evaluate the merits of foreign policy goals pursued through the use of sanctions. We have opinions on those goals, but we doubt that many readers are eager to discover the collective wisdom of Hufbauer, Schott, and Elliott on the merits, for example, of destabilizing the Trujillo government in 1960–61. Similarly we do not explore the fascinating international law questions raised by the imposition of sanctions, in particular the definition and proper limitation of "extraterritorial" measures. Much literature is devoted to these questions and we could not usefully contribute to the legal debate (see, for example, Marcuss and Richard, 1981; Rosenthal and Knighton, 1982; Moyer and Mabry, 1983; Marcuss and Mathias, 1984).

Table 1.1 probably omits many uses of sanctions imposed between powers of the second and third rank. These cases are often not well documented in the English language, and we did not have adequate resources to study source material in foreign languages. Also, we may have overlooked instances where sanctions were imposed by major powers in comparative secrecy to achieve relatively modest goals. To the extent of these omissions, our generalizations will not adequately reflect the experience of the twentieth century.[3]

---

[2] Peter Rowland, *David Lloyd George: A Biography* (New York: Macmillan, 1975), p. 723.

[3] Richard James Ellings has written a Ph.D. thesis in which he lists 107 instances of the use of economic sanctions since World War II. Our table 1.1 contains some cases not in his work; others in his list do not fit our definition of sanctions. In some instances, he has broken down lengthy episodes into two or more cases. See "Strategic Embargoes, Economic Sanctions, and the Structure of World Politics: Lessons from American Foreign Policy" (University of Washington, 1983).

Historical Overview

Economic sanctions entered the diplomatic armory long before World War I. Indeed the technique was used in ancient Greece. The most celebrated occasion was Pericles' Megarian decree, enacted in 432 BC, in response to the kidnapping of three Aspasian women. Thucydides accords the decree only minor notice; by contrast, Aristophanes in the *Archarnians* (lines 530–43), assigns the Megarian decree a major role in triggering the Peloponnesian War:

Then Pericles the Olympian in his wrath / thundered, lightened, threw Hellas into confusion,/ passed laws that were written like drinking songs / [decreeing] the Megarians shall not be on our land, in our market,/ on the sea or on the continent. //Then the Megarians, since they were starving little by little, begged the Lacedaemonians to have the decree / arising from the three strumpets withdrawn./ But we were unwilling, though they asked us many times. Then came the clash of the shields./ Someone will say it was not right. But say, then, what was. /Come, if a Lacedaemonian sailed out in a boat /and denounced and confiscated a Seriphian puppy, /would you have sat still?[4]

Despite the rich history of episodes from ancient Greece through the nineteenth century, we start with World War I both because earlier episodes are less well documented and because lessons from the distant past may seem less relevant to today's problems. However, by way of historical perspective, table 1.2 (at the end of this chapter) lists selected pre-World War I instances of economic sanctions. Most of these episodes foreshadowed or accompanied warfare. Only after World War I was extensive attention given to the notion that economic sanctions might substitute for armed hostilities.

Through World War II, the objectives sought with the use of sanctions retained a distinctive martial flavor. Sanctions were usually imposed to disrupt military adventures or to complement a broader war effort. Of the 11 cases we have identified in table 1.1 between 1914 and 1940, all but 2 are linked to military action. Four of the cases involved League of Nations attempts, through collective action, to settle disputes. These efforts had varied results: from the successful threat of economic sanctions that led Greece to back down from its incursion into Bulgaria in 1925, to the League's celebrated failure at persuading Italy to withdraw from Abyssinia in the mid-1930s.

In the period following World War II, other foreign policy motives became increasingly common, but sanctions were still deployed to force a target country to withdraw its troops from border skirmishes, to abandon plans of territorial acquisition, or to desist from other military adventures. In most instances in

---

[4] See Charles Fornara, "Plutarch and the Megarian decree," 24 *Yale Classical Studies* (1975).

the postwar period where economic pressure was brought to bear against the exercise of military power, the United States played the role of international policeman. For example, the United States was able to coerce the Netherlands into backing away from its military efforts in 1948–49 to forestall the Indonesian federation; in 1956, the United States pressed the French and British into leaving the Suez; and in the early 1960s, the United States persuaded Egypt to withdraw its troops from Yemen and the Congo by withholding development and PL 480 food aid.

More recent attempts have not been as successful. Turkish troops continue to be stationed in Cyprus over a decade after the invasion and in spite of US economic pressure in the mid-1970s. The grain and Olympic boycott of the USSR did not discourage the Soviet occupation of Afghanistan. Indeed, major powers have never been able to deter the military adventures of other major powers simply through the use of economic sanctions.

Closely related to military adventure cases are the episodes where sanctions are imposed to impair the economic capability of the target country, thereby limiting its potential for military activity. This was an important rationale for the broad-based multilateral controls on strategic trade that the United States instituted against the USSR and China in the late 1940s, and was cited by US officials in defense of recent sanctions against the USSR following the invasion of Afghanistan and the crisis in Poland. It is doubtful whether these cases have yielded positive results, not least because it is difficult to hamper the military capabilities of a major power with marginal degrees of economic deprivation.

In this book we do not evaluate the narrowly defined national security issues that arise in cases where sanctions are deployed to deprive the USSR and other countries of access to goods and technologies with direct military applications. While attempts to impair the military potential of an adversary usually entail narrowly defined national security controls—identifying military hardware and "dual use" technologies that can be denied the adversary—the sender country often seeks to limit the foreign policy options of the target state as well. In our view, the COCOM and CHINCOM controls[5] were aimed both at restricting strategic exports to the USSR and China to prevent technological advances in weaponry, and at impairing the ability of the Soviet and Chinese economies to support an expanded military machine. The latter goal—to inhibit potential

---

[5] *United States and COCOM v. USSR and COMECON* (1948–), and *United States and CHINCOM v. China* (1949–70). COCOM, the Coordinating Committee for Multilateral Export Controls, is an informal group of NATO countries (minus Iceland, plus Japan) which attempts to limit the shipment of strategic goods (broadly and narrowly defined) to the Soviet Union. CHINCOM, a parallel but smaller group of countries controlling exports to China, was disbanded in 1958, at which time China came under COCOM controls. COMECON, the Council for Mutual Economic Assistance, is an organization established in 1949 to facilitate economic cooperation between the USSR and its satellites.

Soviet and Chinese foreign policy responses by limiting the national capability to support a military machine—is the reason why these cases are included in our analysis.

Sanctions have also been deployed in pursuit of a number of other foreign policy goals. Especially noteworthy is the frequent resort to sanctions to help destabilize foreign governments, usually in the context of a foreign policy dispute involving other issues. Destabilization episodes have often found a superpower pitted against a smaller country. The United States has engaged in destabilization efforts 14 times, often against neighboring countries in the hemisphere such as Cuba, the Dominican Republic, Nicaragua, Brazil, and Chile. Sanctions contributed at least in part to the overthrow of Trujillo in 1961, Goulart in 1964, and Allende in 1973; on the other hand, Castro's Cuba and the Sandinistas in Nicaragua have not succumbed to US pressure, in large measure due to compensating aid from the USSR.

The USSR has also picked on its neighbors, though less successfully. Every time the USSR used sanctions in an effort to topple a government of the socialist bloc, it failed (Yugoslavia in 1948, China in 1960, and Albania in 1961); the only success story came when the USSR coerced Finland into adopting a more pliant attitude toward Soviet policies during the "Nightfrost Crisis" of 1958. Finally, the United Kingdom also has participated in the destabilization game through the use of economic sanctions to topple hostile or repressive regimes in areas where Britain once exercised colonial influence—Iran in 1951–53, Rhodesia in 1965–79, and Uganda in 1972–79.

Since the early 1960s, sanctions have been deployed in support of numerous other foreign policy goals, most of them relatively modest compared to the pursuit of war, peace, and political destabilization. For example, sanctions have been used on behalf of efforts to protect human rights, to halt nuclear proliferation, to settle expropriation claims, and to combat international terrorism. Here again, the United States has played the dominant role as guardian of its version of global morality.

Following a series of congressionally inspired initiatives beginning in 1973, human rights became a "cause célèbre" of the Carter administration. In the early phase, country-specific riders were attached to military aid bills requiring the Nixon and Ford administrations to deny or reduce assistance to countries found abusing human rights. In the later phase, President Carter adopted the congressional mandate as his own guiding light. Eventually, many countries in Latin America and elsewhere became targets of US sanctions.

Sanctions were also frequently used, by both the United States and Canada, to enforce compliance with nuclear nonproliferation safeguards. In 1974, Canada acted to prevent Pakistan from acquiring nuclear explosive capability, and tried to control the reprocessing of spent fuel in both India and Pakistan to guard against weapons production. The United States joined the Canadians in applying financial pressure on South Korea to forestall its purchase of a nuclear reprocessing plant. Subsequently, the United States imposed sanctions on shipments of nuclear fuel and technology to South Africa, Taiwan, Brazil, Argentina, India, and Pakistan in similar attempts to secure adequate multilateral surveillance of nuclear facilities.

Since World War II, the United States has used sanctions nine times in its efforts to negotiate compensation for property expropriated by foreign governments. In almost all the cases, the United States hoped to go beyond the claims issue and resolve conflicting political philosophies. This was true the first time the US pressured Iran—seeking the overthrow of the Mussadiq regime—and was behind US efforts to undermine Castro in Cuba, Goulart in Brazil, and Allende in Chile.

Antiterrorism has been another of the modest (but important) policy goals sought by the United States through the imposition of economic sanctions. A wave of international plane hijackings in the 1960s and 1970s, and the massacre of Israeli athletes at the Munich Olympics in 1972, focused world attention on terrorism. The hijacking problem was greatly reduced through international hijacking agreements—including one signed in 1973 by the United States and Cuba. Lethal terrorist raids, often funded by radical, oil-rich countries, have proven much harder to control. In 1980, following a congressional directive, the US State Department branded four countries—Libya, Syria, Iraq, and South Yemen—as international outlaws because of their support of terrorist activities. The United States soon imposed sanctions on Libya and Iraq in an attempt to limit their ability as suppliers of military equipment to terrorist groups.

This brief historical review illustrates the important role that economic sanctions have played since World War I in the conduct of US foreign policy. Of the 103 cases documented in table 1.1, the United States, either alone or in concert with its allies, has deployed sanctions 68 times. Other significant users have been the United Kingdom (21 instances, often in cooperation with the League of Nations and the United Nations); the Soviet Union (10 uses, usually against recalcitrant satellites); and the Arab League and its members (4 uses of its new-found oil muscle).

This overview also demonstrates that sanctions have been deployed more frequently with each passing decade. Table 1.3 summarizes the record: first, the number of sanctions episodes initiated in each five-year period beginning with 1911–15; second, the total cost imposed on target countries every fifth year beginning with 1915 (expressed as an annualized figure in current US dollars); and third, for comparison, the value of world exports (expressed in current US dollars). The summary in table 1.3 indicates that the quinquennial level of new episodes has increased from under 5 in the pre-1945 period to approximately 10 to 15 in the post-1960 period. The annual cost imposed on target countries was quite high in 1915, on account of World War I; it fell markedly thereafter, and has since risen from very low levels in the 1920s and 1930s to some $1.5 billion and higher in the post-1965 period. The aggregate cost of sanctions peaked in 1980, with almost $5.7 billion of costs imposed on target countries.

While sanctions activity has grown, particularly in recent decades, it has not kept pace over the long haul with the very buoyant growth of world trade. The level of world trade (expressed in current dollars) expanded more than a hundred times between 1915 and 1980. Compared to total world trade flows, the cost imposed on target countries is barely a ripple.

The Cyclical Popularity of Sanctions

Like other fashions, economic sanctions wax and wane in popularity. After World War I, great hopes were held out for the "economic weapon," with President Woodrow Wilson the leading advocate. Speaking in Indianapolis in 1919 he said:

A nation that is boycotted is a nation that is in sight of surrender. Apply this economic, peaceful, silent, deadly remedy and there will be no need for force. It is a terrible remedy. It does not cost a life outside the nation boycotted, but it brings a pressure upon the nation which, in my judgment, no modern nation could resist.[6]

The League of Nations enjoyed minor success with the use of sanctions against smaller powers in the 1920s and 1930s. But with the failure of the League's campaign against Italy, the reputation of the "economic weapon" correspondingly sank. Scholars were quick to point out that sanctions had not in fact been used decisively against Italy, but the public at large simply concluded that sanctions were not equal to the task.

The reputation of the "economic weapon" was somewhat rehabilitated by the contribution of the naval blockade of Europe and the preemptive buying of strategic materials by the Allies to the ultimate defeat of Germany and Japan during World War II. Sanctions were used frequently and with some success in the late 1940s and 1950s, but they did not again attract public notice until the US campaign against Cuba and the UK/UN campaign against Rhodesia in the 1960s. Overoptimistic British pronouncements in the Rhodesian case and the considerable success of Cuba—with massive aid from the Soviet Union—in withstanding economic pressure again fostered disillusion. Disillusion grew progressively more fashionable with the extensive American reliance on sanctions, and a series of conspicuous failures, in the 1970s and early 1980s.

---

[6] See Saul K. Padover, ed., *Wilson's Ideals* (Washington: American Council on Public Affairs, 1942), p. 108.

Have we reached the bottom of the current wave of disfavor over the use of sanctions? Perhaps so.[7] But we would suggest that the "economic weapon" will not regain its respectability until a few episodes have passed in which sanctions were deployed judiciously and successfully.

Whatever the cycle of fashion, our purpose in this study is to distinguish between circumstances in which economic sanctions make some contribution to the pursuit of foreign policy goals, and circumstances in which sanctions achieve very little.

Sender Countries and Their Motives

Sanctions are part and parcel of international diplomacy, a tool to coerce target governments into particular avenues of response. The use of sanctions presupposes the sender country's desire to "interfere in the internal affairs" of the target government.

Among the cases we have documented, the countries that impose sanctions generally are large nations that pursue an active foreign policy. To be sure, there are instances of neighborhood fights (*Indonesia v. Malaysia*, 1963–66; *Spain v. United Kingdom*, 1954–84). But in the main, sanctions have been used by big powers—precisely because they are big and can seek to influence events on a global scale. Instances of the collective use of sanctions—the League of Nations against Italy in 1935–36, the United Nations against Rhodesia in 1965–79, the Alliance powers against Germany and Japan, 1939–45—are in fact usually episodes of major powers enlisting their smaller allies.

"Demonstration of resolve" has often supplied the driving force behind the imposition of sanctions. This is particularly true for the United States, which frequently has deployed sanctions to assert its leadership in world affairs. US presidents seemingly feel compelled to dramatize their opposition to foreign misdeeds, even when the likelihood of changing behavior in the target country seems remote. In these cases sanctions often are imposed because the cost of inaction—in lost confidence at home and abroad in the ability or willingness of the US to act—is seen as greater than the cost of the sanctions. Indeed, such action is often expected by the international community—to demonstrate moral outrage and to reassure the alliance that the United States will stand by its international commitments. The impact of such moral and psychological factors on the decision to impose sanctions should not be underestimated, even if it is hard to document.

---

[7] A leading scholar, David A. Baldwin, is writing a book that seeks to rehabilitate the use of economic diplomacy as a tool of statecraft. See *Economic Statecraft: Theory and Practice*, forthcoming.

"Deterrence" is another frequently cited reason for sanctions: supposedly a sender country can discourage future objectionable policies by increasing the associated costs. In many cases, such as *United States v. USSR* over Afghanistan from 1980 to 1981, it is difficult, if not impossible, to determine whether sanctions are an effective deterrent against future misdeeds.

Finally, sanctions are used as a surrogate for other measures. A diplomatic slap on the wrist may not hit where it hurts. More extreme measures, such as covert action or military measures, may be excessive. Sanctions provide a popular middle road: they add "teeth" to international diplomacy—even if the bark is worse than the bite.

In a sense, the imposition of sanctions conveys a triple signal: to the target country it says the sender does not condone your actions; to allies, it says that words will be supported with deeds; to domestic audiences it says the sender's government will act to safeguard the nation's vital interests.

The parallels between the motives for sanctions and the three basic purposes of criminal law are unmistakable: to punish, to deter, and to rehabilitate. Countries that impose sanctions, like states that incarcerate criminals, may find their hopes of rehabilitation unrealized, but they may be quite satisfied with whatever punishment and deterrence are accomplished. Nevertheless, in judging the success of sanctions, we confine our examination to changes in the policies and capabilities of the target country.

Limitations on the Use of Sanctions

Sanctions often do not succeed in changing the behavior of foreign countries. One reason for failure is plain: the sanctions imposed may simply be inadequate to achieve the objectives sought—the goals may be too elusive, the means too gentle, or cooperation from other countries, when needed, too tepid.

A second reason for failure is that sanctions may create their own antidotes. In particular, economic sanctions may unify the target country both in support of the government and in search of commercial alternatives. This outcome was evident in a number of episodes; for example, a nationalistic reaction seems to have plagued the League of Nations actions against Italy in 1935–36, USSR sanctions against Yugoslavia in 1948–55, US measures against Indonesia in 1963–66, and UN actions against Rhodesia in 1965–79. As Mussolini put the matter in 1935: "To sanctions of an economic character we will reply with our discipline, with our sobriety, and with our spirit of sacrifice."[8]

---

[8] Robin Renwick, *Economic Sanctions*, Harvard Studies in International Affairs No. 45 (Cambridge, Mass.: Harvard University Center for International Affairs, 1981), p. 18.

A third reason for the unsuccessful application of economic pressure is that sanctions may prompt powerful allies of the target country to lend support, largely offsetting whatever deprivation results from the sanctions themselves. In the period since World War II, offsetting compensation has occurred most conspicuously in episodes where the big powers were caught up in ideological conflict over the policies of a smaller nation: *USSR v. Yugoslavia* (1948–55), *United States v. Cuba* (1960–), *USSR v. Albania* (1961–65), and the *United States v. Nicaragua* (1981–). Another example, with different historical origins, is the Arab League campaign against Israel, a campaign that has helped ensure a continuing flow of public and private assistance to Israel from the United States and Western Europe.

A fourth reason for failure is that economic sanctions create their own backlash, abroad and at home. Allies abroad may simply not share the goals of the sender country. As a result, they may, in the first instance, ask exasperating questions about the probability of a successful outcome; in the second instance, they may refuse to take stern measures against the target country, thereby making the sender's own initiatives seem all the more futile; finally, they may revolt and enforce national antisanctions laws, such as the US antiboycott provisions and the British Protection of Trading Interests Act, to counteract the impact of sanctions on their own foreign policy and economic interests. The protective legal barrier is a relatively new development, but one that has spread to a number of countries—France, Denmark, Australia and others—where firms have been victimized by the often errant aim of a sender state imposing sanctions.

The backlash from the sender's allies may be exacerbated if attempts are made to enforce the sanctions on an extraterritorial basis, as was done in the recent pipeline case. The Europeans refused to cooperate with the United States; indeed, they wondered who the "real" target of the sanctions was: the target *country* subject to sanctions, or their own *firms*, whose trade was being hit by the measures. The internecine feud that ensued between the United States and Europe undercut the economic and psychological force of the sanctions, rendering the action ineffective.

Business firms at home may experience severe losses when sanctions interrupt trade and financial contacts. Moreover, they may lose their reputation for reliability. Outcries from US business against both the grain embargo and the pipeline sanctions arose as much from the fear of future competitive weakness as "unreliable suppliers" as from the immediate sacrifice of grain, pipelayer, and gas turbine sales to the Soviet Union. After the first flush of patriotic enthusiasm, such complaints can undermine a sanctions initiative.

These assorted pitfalls are well known to most policy officials, and they can hardly escape the briefing memoranda prepared for world leaders. Why then are sanctions so frequently used? In the first place, sanctions have not been, on balance, nearly so unsuccessful as recent episodes directed against the USSR would suggest. Chapters 3, 4, and 5 attempt to provide a rounded view of success and failure, measured in foreign policy terms. In the second place, world leaders often find the most obvious alternatives to economic sanctions—military action or diplomatic protest—too massive or too meager. Sanctions can provide a satisfying theatrical display, yet avoid the high costs of war. This is not to say that sanctions are costless. Our purpose is to suggest conditions in which sanctions are most likely to achieve a positive benefit at a bearable cost.

Plan of the Book

In chapter 2, we examine the components of a sanctions episode. In a simple and crude way, we attempt to quantify a number of dimensions. We explain our definition of "success," our scheme for distinguishing objectives, our scale of international cooperation, and our measurement of economic costs. In chapter 3, we assess sanctions episodes in terms of their political variables. In chapter 4, we summarize the economic variables in a sanctions episode, and relate economic costs to the measure of success achieved. In chapter 5, we derive general lessons from the cases studied and suggest a list of nine commandments that sender countries might follow to improve their prospects for achieving foreign policy goals. Appendix A sets forth our multiple regression analysis of the factors that explain a successful sanctions episode. Appendix B explains how we calculate economic costs to the target country. Finally, the case abstracts in appendix C give details on each of the 103 cases that we examined.

Table 1.1 Chronological summary of economic sanctions for foreign policy goals, 1914–84

Case number	Principal sender	Target country	Active years	Goals of sender country
14–1	United Kingdom	Germany	1914–18	Military victory
17–1	United States	Japan	1917	(1) Contain Japanese influence in Asia (2) Persuade Japan to divert shipping to Atlantic
18–1	United Kingdom	Russia	1918–20	(1) Renew support for Allies in World War I (2) Destabilize Bolshevik regime
21–1	League of Nations	Yugoslavia	1921	Block Yugoslav attempts to wrest territory from Albania; retain 1913 borders
25–1	League of Nations	Greece	1925	Withdraw from occupation of Bulgarian border territory
32–1	League of Nations	Paraguay and Bolivia	1932–35	Settle the Chaco War
33–1	United Kingdom	USSR	1933	Release two British citizens
35–1	United Kingdom and League of Nations	Italy	1935–36	Withdraw Italian troops from Abyssinia
38–1	United Kingdom and United States	Mexico	1938–47	Settle expropriation claims
39–1	Alliance Powers	Germany, later Japan	1939–45	Military victory
40–1	United States	Japan	1940–41	Withdraw from Southeast Asia
44–1	United States	Argentina	1944–47	(1) Remove Nazi influence (2) Destabilize Perón government
46–1	Arab League	Israel	1946–	Create a homeland for Palestinians
48–1	United States	Netherlands	1948–49	Recognize Republic of Indonesia
48–2	India	Hyderabad	1948	Assimilate Hyderabad into India

Table 1.1   Chronological summary of economic sanctions for foreign policy goals, 1914–84 *(continued)*

Case number	Principal sender	Target country	Active years	Goals of sender country
48–3	USSR	United States, United Kingdom, and France	1948–49	(1) Prevent formation of a West German government (2) Assimilate West Berlin into East Germany
48–4	USSR	Yugoslavia	1948–55	(1) Rejoin Soviet camp (2) Destabilize Tito government
48–5	United States and COCOM	USSR and COMECON	1948–	(1) Deny strategic materials (2) Impair Soviet military potential
49–1	United States and CHINCOM	China	1949–70	(1) Retaliation for Communist takeover and subsequent assistance to North Korea (2) Deny strategic and other materials
50–1	United States and United Nations	North Korea	1950–	Withdraw attack on South Korea
51–1	United Kingdom and United States	Iran	1951–53	(1) Reverse the nationalization of oil facilities (2) Destabilize Mussadiq government
54–1	USSR	Australia	1954	Repatriate a Soviet defector
54–2	India	Portugal	1954–61	Assimilate Goa into India
54–3	Spain	United Kingdom	1954–84	Gain sovereignty over Gibraltar
54–4	United States and South Vietnam	North Vietnam	1954–	(1) Impede military effectiveness of North Vietnam (2) Retribution for aggression in South Vietnam
56–1	United States	Israel	1956–83 (intermittent episodes)	(1) Withdraw from Sinai (2) Implement UN Resolution 242 (3) Push Palestinian autonomy talks

Case number	Principal sender	Target country	Active years	Goals of sender country
56–2	United Kingdom, France, and United States	Egypt	1956	(1) Ensure free passage through Suez Canal (2) Compensate for nationalization
56–3	United States	United Kingdom and France	1956	Withdraw from Suez
56–4	United States	Laos	1956–62	(1) Destabilize Prince Souvanna Phouma government (2) Destabilize General Phoumi government (3) Prevent Communist takeover
57–1	Indonesia	Netherlands	1957–62	Control of West Irian
57–2	France	Tunisia	1957–63	Halt support for Algerian rebels
58–1	USSR	Finland	1958–59	Adopt pro-USSR policies
60–1	United States	Dominican Republic	1960–62	(1) Cease subversion in Venezuela (2) Destabilize Trujillo government
60–2	USSR	China	1960–70	(1) Retaliation for break with Soviet policy (2) Destabilize Mao government
60–3	United States	Cuba	1960–	(1) Settle expropriation claims (2) Destabilize Castro government (3) Discourage Cuba from foreign military adventures
61–1	United States	Ceylon	1961–65	Settle expropriation claims
61–2	USSR	Albania	1961–65	(1) Retaliation for alliance with China (2) Destabilize Hoxha government
61–3	Western Allies	German Democratic Republic	1961–62	Berlin Wall
62–1	United States	Brazil	1962–64	(1) Settle expropriation claims (2) Destabilize Goulart government

Table 1.1   Chronological summary of economic sanctions for foreign policy goals, 1914–84 *(continued)*

Case number	Principal sender	Target country	Active years	Goals of sender country
62–2	United Nations	South Africa	1962–	(1) End apartheid (2) Grant independence to Namibia
62–3	USSR	Romania	1962–63	Limit economic independence
63–1	United States	United Arab Republic	1963–65	(1) Cease military activity in Yemen and Congo (2) Moderate anti-US rhetoric
63–2	Indonesia	Malaysia	1963–66	Promote "Crush Malaysia" campaign
63–3	United States	Indonesia	1963–66	(1) Cease "Crush Malaysia" campaign (2) Destabilize Sukarno government
63–4	United States	South Vietnam	1963	(1) Ease repression (2) Remove Nhu (3) Destabilize Diem
63–5	United Nations and Organization for African Unity	Portugal	1963–74	Free African colonies
64–1	France	Tunisia	1964–66	Settle expropriation claims
65–1	United States	Chile	1965–66	Roll back copper price
65–2	United States	India	1965–67	Alter policy to favor agriculture
65–3	United Kingdom and United Nations	Rhodesia	1965–79	Majority rule by black Africans
65–4	United States	Arab League	1965–	Stop US firms from implementing Arab boycott of Israel
67–1	Nigeria	Biafra	1967–70	End civil war
68–1	United States	Peru	1968	Forego aircraft purchases from France
68–2	United States	Peru	1968–74	Settle expropriation claims
70–1	United States	Chile	1970–73	(1) Settle expropriation claims (2) Destabilize Allende government

Case number	Principal sender	Target country	Active years	Goals of sender country
71–1	United States	India and Pakistan	1971	Cease fighting in East Pakistan (Bangladesh)
S–1	United States	Countries supporting international terrorism	1972–	Overview
72–1	United Kingdom and United States	Uganda	1972–79	(1) Retaliation for expelling Asians (2) Improve human rights (3) Destabilize Amin government
S–2	United States	Countries violating human rights	1973–	Overview
73–1	Arab League	United States and Netherlands	1973–74	(1) Retaliation for supporting Israel in October war (2) Restore pre-1967 Israeli borders
73–2	United States	South Korea	1973–77	Improve human rights
73–3	United States	Chile	1973–	Improve human rights
S–3	United States and Canada	Countries pursuing nuclear weapons option	1974–	Overview
74–1	United States	Turkey	1974–78	Withdraw Turkish troops from Cyprus
74–2	Canada	India	1974–76	(1) Deter further nuclear explosions (2) Apply stricter nuclear safeguards
74–3	Canada	Pakistan	1974–76	(1) Apply stricter safeguards to nuclear power plant (2) Forego nuclear reprocessing
75–1	United States and Canada	South Korea	1975–76	Forego nuclear reprocessing
75–2	United States	USSR	1975–	Liberalize Jewish emigration

Table 1.1 Chronological summary of economic sanctions for foreign policy goals, 1914–84 *(continued)*

Case number	Principal sender	Target country	Active years	Goals of sender country
75–3	United States	Eastern Europe	1975–	Liberalize Jewish emigration
75–4	United States	South Africa	1975–82	(1) Adhere to nuclear safeguards (2) Avert explosion of nuclear device
75–5	United States	Kampuchea	1975–79	(1) Improve human rights (2) Deter Vietnamese expansionism
76–1	United States	Uruguay	1976–81	Improve human rights
76–2	United States	Taiwan	1976–77	Forego nuclear reprocessing
76–3	United States	Ethiopia	1976–	(1) Settle expropriation claims (2) Improve human rights
77–1	United States	Paraguay	1977–81	Improve human rights
77–2	United States	Guatemala	1977–	Improve human rights
77–3	United States	Argentina	1977–83	Improve human rights
77–4	Canada	Japan and EC	1977–78	Strengthen nuclear safeguards
77–5	United States	Nicaragua	1977–79	(1) Destabilize Somoza government (2) Improve human rights
77–6	United States	El Salvador	1977–81	Improve human rights
77–7	United States	Brazil	1977–84	Improve human rights
78–1	China	Albania	1978–83	Retaliation for anti-Chinese rhetoric
78–2	United States	Brazil	1978–81	Adhere to nuclear safeguards
78–3	United States	Argentina	1978–82	Adhere to nuclear safeguards
78–4	United States	India	1978–82	Adhere to nuclear safeguards
78–5	United States	USSR	1978–80	Liberalize treatment of dissidents (e.g., Shcharansky)
78–6	Arab League	Egypt	1978–83	Withdraw from Camp David process

Case number	Principal sender	Target country	Active years	Goals of sender country
78–7	China	Vietnam	1978–79	Withdraw troops from Kampuchea
78–8	United States	Libya	1978–	(1) Terminate support of international terrorism (2) Destabilize Qaddafi government
79–1	United States	Iran	1979–81	(1) Release hostages (2) Settle expropriation claims
79–2	United States	Pakistan	1979–80	Adhere to nuclear safeguards
79–3	Arab League	Canada	1979	Retaliation for planned move of Canadian Embassy in Israel from Tel Aviv to Jerusalem
79–4	United States	Bolivia	1979–82	(1) Improve human rights (2) Deter drug trafficking
80–1	United States	USSR	1980–81	(1) Withdraw Soviet troops from Afghanistan (2) Impair Soviet military potential
80–2	United States	Iraq	1980–82	Terminate support of international terrorism
81–1	United States	Nicaragua	1981–	(1) End support for El Salvador rebels (2) Destabilize Sandinista government
81–2	United States	Poland	1981–84	(1) Lift martial law (2) Free dissidents (3) Resume talks with Solidarity
81–3	United States	USSR	1981–82	(1) Lift martial law in Poland (2) Cancel USSR-Europe pipeline project (3) Impair Soviet economic/military potential
81–4	European Community	Turkey	1981–82	Restore democracy
82–1	United Kingdom	Argentina	1982	Withdraw troops from Falkland Islands

Table 1.1   Chronological summary of economic sanctions for foreign policy goals, 1914–84 *(continued)*

Case number	Principal sender	Target country	Active years	Goals of sender country
82–2	Netherlands and United States	Suriname	1982–	(1) Improve human rights (2) Limit alliance with Cuba and USSR
82–3	South Africa	Lesotho	1982–83	Return refugees suspected of antistate activities
83–1	Australia	France	1983–	Stop nuclear testing in the South Pacific
83–2	United States	USSR	1983	Retaliation for downing of Korean airliner
83–3	United States	Zimbabwe	1983–84	Temper opposition in United Nations to United States foreign policy
83–4	United States and Organization of Eastern Caribbean States	Grenada	1983	Destabilize Bishop/Austin regime

Table 1.2 Selected pre-World War I episodes of economic sanctions for foreign policy goals

Sender country	Target country	Active years	Background and objectives	Resolution	Source
Athens	Megara	circa 432 BC	Pericles issued the Megarian decree limiting entry of Megara's products into Athenian markets in retaliation for Megara's attempted expropriation of territory and the kidnapping of three women.	The decree contributed to the Peloponnesian War between Athens and Sparta.	de Ste. Croix 252–60; Fornara 222–26
American colonies	Britain	1765	England passed Stamp Act as a revenue measure; colonies boycotted English goods.	Britain repealed the Stamp Act in 1766.	Renwick 5
American colonies	Britain	1767–70	England passed Townshend Acts to cover salaries of judges and officials; colonies boycotted English goods.	Britain repealed the Townshend Acts except on tea; the tea tax gave pretext for the Boston Tea Party of 1774 and calling of the Continental Congress.	Renwick 5
Britain France	France Britain	Napoleonic Wars: 1793–1815	British goal: contain French expansion and eventually defeat Napoleon; French goal: deprive Britain of grain through the Continental System, and eventually defeat England.	"The experience of economic warfare during this period is inconclusive as to its possible effects when applied with more systematic organization." One result of sanctions was French development of beet sugar cultivation, anticipating development of substitutes in later war.	Jack 1–42

Table 1.2 Selected pre-World War I episodes of economic sanctions for foreign policy goals *(continued)*

Sender country	Target country	Active years	Background and objectives	Resolution	Source
United States	Britain	1812–14	United States embargoed British goods in response to British Naval Acts limiting US trade with France. The total embargo, which evolved out of the Non-Intercourse Acts of 1809, followed an ineffective embargo imposed from 1807–9.	The Orders in Council which the United States had protested were revoked, but the United States, not knowing of the revocation, declared war two days later. The War of 1812 ensued.	Knorr 101–2
Britain/ France	Russia	Crimean War: 1853–56	Britain and France blockaded the mouth of the Danube River so that the Russian army could not receive supplies by sea.	Russia was defeated and the partition of Turkey prevented.	Oppenheim 514
US North	Confederate states	Civil War: 1861–65	"In seapower, railroads, material wealth and industrial capacity to produce iron and munitions the North was vastly superior to the South. This disparity became even more pronounced as the ever tightening blockade gradually cut off the Confederacy from foreign imports."	The South lost: "Attrition and blockade had scuttled the Confederate capacity. . . ."	Leckie 513; Matloff 192
France	Germany	Franco-Prussian	France declared war on Germany to	The German army prevailed despite	Oppenheim 515

Sender country	Target country	Active years	Background and objectives	Resolution	Source
		War: 1870–71	prevent emergence of a unified German state. France block-aded the German coast and even blockaded three of their own ports which had been occupied by the Germans.	supply problems.	
France	China	Indochina War: 1883–85	At war with China over the Vietnamese territory of Annam, France declared rice to be contraband be-cause of its impor-tance to the Chinese population.	China ceded to France control over the Annamese terri-tory.	Oppenheim 554
United States	Spain	Spanish-American War: 1898	"To the extent the United States had a strategy for conduct of the war against Spain in the Carib-bean, it consisted of maintaining a naval blockade of Cuba while native insur-gent forces carried on a harassing cam-paign against Span-ish troops on the is-land." A companion blockade of the Phil-ippines was in-tended to deny Spain revenues from that colony.	The United States obtained independ-ence for Cuba and, after occupying the Philippines and Puerto Rico, forced Spain to cede those territories and Guam to the United States for $20 million.	Matloff 324–26; Leckie 566

Table 1.2   Selected pre-World War I episodes of economic sanctions for foreign policy goals *(continued)*

Sender country	Target country	Active years	Background and objectives	Resolution	Source
Britain	Dutch South Africa	Boer War: 1899–1902	The British denied articles of contraband to the Boers.	The Boers were eventually overwhelmed and South Africa added to the British Empire.	Jack 73
Russia	Japan	Russo-Japanese War: 1904–5	Russia declared rice, all types of fuel, and cotton as contraband.	Following military defeat, Russia ceded portions of its own territory to Japan and recognized Korea as within Japan's sphere of influence.	Oppenheim 454
Italy	Turkey	1911–12	Italy used a limited blockade as part of its campaign to acquire Libya	Italy acquired Libya from the Ottoman Empire.	Dupuy and Dupuy 926

Bibliography, table 1.2:

Dupuy, R. Ernest, and Trevor N. Dupuy. 1970. *The Encyclopedia of Military History.* New York: Harper & Row.

De Ste. Croix, G. E. M. 1972. *The Origins of the Peloponnesian War.* London: Duckworth.

Fornara, Charles. 1975. "Plutarch and the Megarian decree." 24 *Yale Classical Sudies.*

Jack, D. T. 1941. *Studies in Economic Warfare.* New York: Chemical Publishing Co.

Knorr, Klaus. 1977. "International Economic Leverage and Its Uses." In *Economic Issues and National Security,* ed. Klaus Knorr and Frank N. Traeger. Lawrence, Kan.: Regents Press.

Leckie, Robert. 1968. *The Wars of America.* New York: Harper & Row.

Matloff, Maurice, ed. 1969. *American Military History.* Washington: GPO.

Oppenheim, L. 1921. "War & Neutrality." In *International Law: A Treatise,* ed. Ronald F. Roxburgh. Vol. 2, 3d ed. London: Longmans, Green.

Renwick, Robin. 1981. *Economic Sanctions.* Harvard Studies in International Affairs, no. 45. Cambridge, Mass.: Harvard University Center for International Affairs.

Table 1.3 Comparison of number of sanctions episodes initiated, aggregate cost of sanctions to target countries, and world exports, 1915–84

	Number of episodes initiated in past five years[a]	Aggregate annual cost each 5th year[b] (billion dollars)	Total world exports[c] (billion dollars)
1915	1	0.84	15[d]
1920	2	—	n.a.
1925	2	—	25[e]
1930	0	—	32
1935	3	0.09	n.a.
1940	3	0.78	25[f]
1945	1	0.03	50
1950	8	0.85	55
1955	5	1.03	85
1960	10	1.55	115
1965	16	2.02	165
1970	4	1.65	285
1975	13	2.18	795
1980	24	5.65	1,870
1984	11	1.55	1,660[g]

n.a. Not available.

Sources: Tables 1.1 and 4.1 through 4.5; P. Lamartine Yates, *Forty Years of Foreign Trade* (London: George Allen & Unwin, 1959); United Nations, *Yearbook of International Trade Statistics,* various issues; International Monetary Fund, *International Financial Statistics,* various issues.

a. The counts are based on table 1.1; the figure for 1975, for example, represents cases initiated in 1971–75.

b. The figures represent the net annualized cost (after offsets) to target countries of outstanding cases, based on abstracts of 103 cases summarized in tables 4.1 through 4.5. All figures are in current dollars, rounded to the nearest $10 million.

c. Based on P. Lamartine Yates for 1915 to 1940; UN for 1945; *International Financial Statistics* for 1950 to 1984. All figures are in current dollars, rounded to the nearest $5 billion.

d. Extrapolated from 1913 data ($21.0 billion).

e. Extrapolated from average of 1926–29 data ($31.8 billion).

f. Extrapolated from 1938 data ($22.7 billion).

g. 1983 data.

2

Anatomy of a Sanctions Episode

The case abstracts provide the data base for our analysis. The narrative portion of each abstract sets out what happened and—in the view of actual participants and case historians—why. Each abstract also contains statistical information on the economy of the target country and economic relations between the target and sender countries. This information underlies our evaluation of motives and outcomes.

This chapter describes our definitions and methods. It may be skipped by readers who are eager to turn to the results.

Senders and Targets

We use the term "sender" to designate the principal author of the sanctions episode. More than one country may be engaged in the campaign, but usually a single country takes the lead and brings others along. The leader may enlist support through bilateral consultations or, less frequently, through an international organization—the League of Nations, the United Nations, or the Organization of American States. In a few instances, two countries, or a country and an international organization, may share leadership, and in these cases both are listed as "sender countries" in table 1.1. Our abstracts concentrate on the motives and actions of the sender country, with separate mention made of the supporting cast.

We use the term "target" to describe the immediate object of the episode. On occasion, sanctions may be aimed at two or more countries, for example the COCOM sanctions directed against the USSR and its East European allies. The lessons of a sanctions episode can also be intended for countries that might be silently contemplating objectionable policies, for example, imprisoning political opponents, undertaking a nuclear weapons program, or embarking on a military adventure. However, our abstracts and analysis necessarily concentrate on the response of the immediate targets.

Type of Sanctions

There are three main ways a sender country tries to inflict costs on the target country: first by limiting exports; second by restricting imports; third by impeding finance, including the reduction of aid. Most of the cases we have studied involve some interruption of trade. Such measures engender costs to the target country in terms of lost export markets, denial of critical imports, lower prices received for embargoed exports, and higher prices paid for substitute imports.

In over one-third of the cases, both export and import controls have been employed. In instances where only one or the other is invoked, export controls are almost always preferred to restrictions on imports. Exports have been manipulated in such highly publicized cases as the Arab oil embargo of 1973–74 and President Carter's cut-off of grain shipments to the USSR. One of the few examples of the use of import controls alone was the USSR embargo on wool imports from Australia in 1954 in an unsuccessful attempt to force the return of a defected Soviet diplomat.

Why have import controls been used less often? There seem to be two explanations: first, target countries usually can find alternative markets or arrange triangular purchase arrangements to circumvent the sender country's import controls. Indeed, for many products—especially bulk commodities such as oil and grains—it is hard to verify the origin of goods entering customs. Secondly, some important sender countries do not have the legal authority to impose import controls for foreign policy reasons. The United States, for example, can only impose import limitations pursuant to a national security finding or a presidential declaration of national emergency under section 232 of the Trade Expansion Act of 1962 or under the International Emergency Economic Powers Act. Both avenues are unwieldy administratively; as a result, the United States rarely has imposed import sanctions, the most notable cases being against Iran and Libya (for oil imports), pursuant to a 1975 national security finding under section 232.[1]

Target countries are often hurt through the interruption of commercial and official finance. The interruption of commercial finance will usually require the target country to pay a higher interest rate to alternative creditors. The same happens when official finance is turned off. In addition, when a poor country is the target, the grant component of official financing may provide further leverage. The United States, for example, manipulated food and economic aid in the 1960s to great effect with the United Arab Republic (UAR), India, and

---

[1] A major issue in the Export Administration Act debate of 1983–84 was whether to grant the president the authority to control imports as a means of achieving foreign policy goals. Curiously, the Reagan administration did not want this additional authority, fearing that the forces of protection would champion its misuse.

Chile, and used the carrot-and-stick approach with military aid in the 1970s, possibly improving the human rights situation in Brazil, but failing to move Turkey out of Cyprus.

The ultimate form of financial and trade control is a freeze of the target country's assets. A freeze not only stops financial flows; it also directly and indirectly impedes trade. The US freeze of Iranian assets in late 1979 played an important role in the eventual resolution of the hostage crisis. The UK freeze of Argentine assets made a modest contribution to the British victory in the Falklands in 1982.

Foreign Policy Goals

We have found it useful to divide the episodes into five categories, classified according to the major foreign policy objective sought by the sender country:

☐ Change target country policies in a relatively modest way (modest in the scale of national goals, but often of burning importance to participants in the episode), illustrated by the human rights and nuclear nonproliferation cases.

☐ Destabilize the target government (including, as an ancillary goal, change the target country policies), illustrated by the US campaign against Castro, and the Soviet campaign against Tito.

☐ Disrupt a minor military adventure, illustrated by the UK sanctions against Argentina over the Falkland Islands.

☐ Impair the military potential of the target country, illustrated by World Wars I and II and the COCOM sanctions against the USSR and its allies.

☐ Change target country policies in a major way (including the surrender of territory), illustrated by the UN campaign against South Africa over apartheid and control of Namibia.

An episode may have more than one objective. Such cases are classified according to the most difficult objective, except in a few instances where two objectives are judged to be equally important; in those few instances the cases are cross-listed. For example, in the US campaign against Cuba, the principal objective shifted from settlement of expropriation claims, to destabilization, to an attempt to disrupt military adventurism. Destabilization usually presupposes a lesser goal, in this instance settlement of the expropriation dispute. Hence, we submerge the expropriation dispute within the destabilization category. However, we cross list the *United States v. Cuba* case as a disruption of military adventure case as well as a destabilization episode because both objectives seemed equally important—and equally elusive.

Other examples of multiple policy goals are the cases of *United States v. Argentina* (1944–47: Perón) and *United States v. UAR* (1963–65: Yemen and Congo). In the Argentine case, the United States was initially preoccupied with ending the love affair between Argentina and fascism; later senior US officials began to view Juan Perón as an exponent of fascism and therefore a target for removal from office. We have listed this case solely as a destabilization episode, although it had another important goal, namely ridding Argentina of fascist tendencies. In the UAR case, the United States wanted to convince Nasser both to moderate his anti-American rhetoric and to cease military operations in Yemen and the Congo. Since the two goals were equally important, but quite different, this case has been listed both as a disruption of military adventure case and as a modest policy goal case.

Attempts to impair the military power of an adversary usually encompass an explicit or implicit goal—however elusive—of destabilizing the target country's government. Hence, we do not list these cases under the destabilization heading. Where appropriate, however, these cases are cross-listed under the disruption of military adventure category when the conflict is less than a major war. An example is *United States and CHINCOM v. China* (1949–70).

To summarize, even though the goals of destabilization and impairment of military potential usually encompass other policy disputes, the cases are not cross-listed under those headings. However, if a case also entails disruption of a military adventure, it is listed under that heading as well.

Sender countries do not always announce their goals with clarity. Indeed, obfuscation is the rule in destabilization cases. The USSR never directly said it wished to overthrow Tito or Hoxha; the United States was equally circumspect in its public statements about Castro, Allende, and the Sandinistas. Moreover, goals may change during the course of an episode. Here, as elsewhere in this study, we must rely on newspaper accounts and other secondary sources in assigning episodes to categories.

Overview of the Variables

Whether to impose sanctions—and if so, how—is influenced by a whole host of factors, both domestic and international, which constrain the actions a sender country can take in pursuit of its foreign policy goals. For example, conflicting pressures within the sender government often lead to an indecisive response, which neither emits the desired political signal nor imposes arduous costs on the target country.

The classic example of confused signals was the League of Nations sanctions against Italy in 1935–36. The major powers in the League (Britain and France) were torn between their desire to stop the Italian advance in Abyssinia and their fear of upsetting the political balance in Europe. With an eye on upcoming national elections, efforts were made to keep the peace in Europe; thus, even while sanctions were being considered by the League Council, attempts were made to appease the Italians by ceding some territory in Abyssinia.

Clearly, there are a number of underlying elements that may influence the outcome of a sanctions episode. The factors that influence a specific episode are described in the abstracts of each case. We have divided these, somewhat artificially, into two clusters: a group of "political" variables and a group of "economic" variables. The political variables that we have scored (by no means an exhaustive list) include:

- companion policies used by the sender country, namely covert maneuvers (identified by a J), quasi-military activity (identified by a Q), and regular military activity (identified by an R)

- the number of years economic sanctions were in force

- the extent of international cooperation in imposing sanctions, scaled from 1 (no cooperation) to 4 (significant cooperation)

- the presence of international assistance to the target country (indicated by an A)

- the political stability and economic health of the target country, scaled from 1 (a distressed country) to 3 (a strong and stable country)

- the warmth of prior relations (i.e., before the sanctions episode) between the sender and target countries, scaled from 1(antagonistic) to 3 (cordial).

The economic variables that we have scored (again not an exhaustive list) include:

- the cost imposed on the target country, expressed in absolute terms, and as a percentage of its gross national product (GNP)

- commercial relations between the sender and target countries, measured by the flow of trade between them as a percentage of the target country's total trade

- the respective economic size of the countries, measured by the ratio of their GNP values

- the type of sanctions, namely whether it involved an interruption of finance (identified by an F), an interruption of exports from the sender country (identified by an X), or an interruption of imports to the sender country (identified by an M)

☐ the cost to the sender country, expressed as an index scaled from 1 (net gain to sender) to 4 (major loss to sender).

In this chapter, we describe our approach to distilling and quantifying "success," and then discuss each of the underlying political and economic variables. In chapter 3, we discuss the connection between success and political variables. In chapter 4, we examine the relationship between success and economic variables. Finally, in chapter 5, we summarize our findings and draw policy conclusions.

The Success of an Episode

The "success" of an economic sanctions episode—as viewed from the perspective of the sender country—has two parts: the extent to which the policy outcome sought by the sender country was in fact achieved, and the contribution made by sanctions to a positive outcome. In determining whether the episode was "successful," we confine our examination to changes in the policies, capabilities, or government of the target country.

Policy outcomes are judged against the *stated* foreign policy goals of the sender country. As noted earlier, domestic political motives may overshadow concerns about changing foreign behavior. Unfortunately, the literature on individual economic sanctions episodes seldom evaluates the role of domestic political objectives nor indicates whether they were satisfied.

Our conclusions regarding both the achievement of the foreign policy goals and the contribution of sanctions to the outcome are heavily influenced by the qualitative conclusions reached by previous scholars of the particular episodes, as summarized in the abstracts. We recognize that such assessments entail a good deal of subjective evaluation. Indeed, since foreign policy objectives often come in multiple parts, since objectives evolve over time, and since the contribution of sanctions to the policy outcome is often murky, judgment plays an important role in assigning a single number to each element of the "success equation." However, by relying on the consensus views of other analysts of the cases, we believe we have minimized the bias resulting from our personal views. This method of critical assessment works better when the case has been examined by two or more scholars. Fortunately, the major cases have usually been studied by several.

We have devised a simple index system, scaled from 1 to 4, to score each element. Our index system is described as follows:

Policy Result

(1) failed outcome, illustrated by the USSR attempt to destabilize Tito in the period 1948–55

32 ECONOMIC SANCTIONS RECONSIDERED

(2) unclear but possibly positive outcome, illustrated by the Arab League's long campaign against Israel which, to some extent, has isolated Israel in the international community

(3) positive outcome, that is to say, a somewhat successful result, illustrated by US efforts to prevent a communist takeover of the Laotian government during the period 1956–62

(4) successful outcome, illustrated by the joint efforts of the United Kingdom and United States to overthrow Idi Amin in Uganda in the late 1970s.

Sanctions Contribution

(1) zero or negative contribution, illustrated by the US campaign against Ethiopia from 1976 to the present

(2) minor contribution, illustrated by the USSR withdrawal of assistance from China in the 1960s

(3) modest contribution, illustrated by the withdrawal of Dutch economic aid to Suriname since 1982

(4) significant contribution, illustrated by the US success in destabilizing the Trujillo government in the Dominican Republic in 1960–61.

By multiplication, the two elements are combined into a "success score" that ranges in value from 1 to 16. We characterize a score of 9 or higher as a "successful" outcome. Successful does not mean that the target country was vanquished by the denial of economic contacts or even that the sanctions decisively influenced the outcome. Success is defined against more modest standards. A score of 9 means that sanctions made a modest contribution to the goal sought by the sender country and that the goal was in part realized; a score of 16 means that sanctions made a significant contribution to a successful outcome. By contrast, a score of 1 indicates that the sender country clearly failed to achieve its goals; indeed sanctions may even have left the sender country worse off than before the measures were imposed.

Companion Policy Measures

"War is nothing but the continuation of politics with the admixture of other means."[2] The same could be said of economic sanctions. Indeed, sanctions frequently serve as a junior weapon in a battery of diplomatic artillery aimed at the antagonistic state. Leaving aside the normal means of diplomatic protest—exemplified by recalling an ambassador or canceling a cultural mission—we

---

[2] Carl von Clausewitz, *Vom Kriege* (1832), cited in *The Oxford Dictionary of Quotations*, 3d ed. (Oxford: Oxford University Press, 1979), p. 152.

distinguish three types of companion policies: covert action; quasi-military action; and regular military action.

Covert action, mounted by the intelligence forces, often accompanies the imposition of economic sanctions when the destabilization of a target government is sought. In destabilization cases and in other episodes where major policy changes are sought, the sender state may also invoke quasi-military force—for example, massing troops at the border, or stationing war vessels off the coast. Finally, sanctions may precede or accompany armed hostility.

Length of Sanctions

The life of a sanctions episode is not often defined with the precision of college matriculation and graduation. In the early phases, the sender country may take pains to conceal and even deny that it is imposing sanctions. This seems to have been the case when the United States first began its campaigns against Chile in 1970 and against Nicaragua in 1981. In other cases, the whole episode may pass with hardly an official word, as in the US actions against the United Kingdom and France in the Suez episode of 1956. In still other cases, the ending may be misty rather than sharp, as in the USSR campaigns against Albania and China.

Our approach in dating episodes is to start the episode with the first recorded sanctions threat from official sources or the first recorded sanctions event—whichever comes earlier. We stop the episode when the sender or target country changes its policies in a significant way, or when the campaign simply withers away. Because exact dates of the onset and termination of sanctions episodes are often indistinct, we have made an arbitrary decision to calculate the length of sanctions episodes by rounding to the nearest whole year, disregarding the beginning and ending month, with a minimum of one year. For example, an episode that began in January 1981 and ended in November 1983 would be counted as lasting two years (1983 *minus* 1981 *equals* 2).

International Cooperation

In high profile cases, such as the two world wars, the League of Nations foray against Italy, and the series of US sanctions against the USSR, much emphasis has been placed on achieving international cooperation in order to deny the target country the supplies or markets of its principal trading partners. In fact, the degree of cooperation realized has usually disappointed the lead country. Even in World Wars I and II, when the Allies ultimately achieved a high degree of cooperation, Germany was able to draw on supplies from Eastern Europe and adjacent neutral powers. The following statement, taken not from a lament of President Reagan's advisors at the Versailles or Williamsburg summits, but from a commentary on World War I, describes the problem:

... all attempts in this direction [of a permanent inter-Allied organization] had been wrecked by the contradictory nature of the commercial interests of the Allied nations, which were only kept in touch with one another by means of intermittent conferences. . . .[3]

While a complete economic blockade is seldom achieved, there are substantial differences from episode to episode in the degree of cooperation realized. We have used an index scaled from 1 to 4 to grade the extent of cooperation:

(1) no cooperation: a single sender country imposes sanctions, and usually seeks no cooperation; illustrated by the *United States v. Brazil* (1962–64: Goulart)
(2) minor cooperation: the sender country enlists verbal support and possibly token restraints from other countries; illustrated by the *United States v. USSR* (1981–82: Poland)
(3) modest cooperation: the sender country obtains meaningful restraints—but limited in time and coverage—from some but not all the important trading partners of the target country, illustrated by the *United States v. Cuba* (1960–   :Castro) and *United States v. Iran* (1979–81: Hostages)
(4) significant cooperation: the important trading partners make a major effort to limit trade, although leakages may still exist through neutral countries, illustrated by the two world wars, and the early years of COCOM.

The many efforts and inevitable failures in building watertight economic barriers have led, we think, to an overemphasis on the role played by cooperation in determining the success or failure of a sanctions episode. Proponents of economic sanctions often engage in an "if only" form of argument.[4] "If only" the Europeans and the United States would impose a financial freeze on Argentina. "If only" the United States would stop all new investment in South Africa. "If only" the Europeans would restrict their commerce with the Soviet Union.

From the standpoint of the sender country, it is almost axiomatic that more cooperation is better than less. But other variables are also at play. A critical variable is the nature of the objective. The inspiring words of Browning seem

---

[3] Louis Guichard, *The Naval Blockade, 1914–1918* (New York: Appleton, 1930), p. 67.
[4] As an example of the "if only" argument in the Rhodesian context, see C. Lloyd Brown-John, *Multilateral Sanctions in International Law: A Comparative Analysis* (New York: Praeger, 1975), p. 378.

written for sender countries: "A man's reach should exceed his grasp, or what's a heaven for?" The pursuit of more ambitious objectives accompanied by much fanfare often goes hand in hand with efforts to enlist international cooperation. After all, other countries are not likely to rally in support of modest goals; and the grasp of ambitious objectives usually remains beyond the reach of sender countries, even when those countries are assisted by a large measure of international cooperation.

International Assistance to the Target Country

The mirror image of international cooperation with the sender country is the degree to which the target country receives support from neighbors and allies. Target countries are seldom cut off from alternative markets or financing sources when sanctions are imposed; trade and financial channels usually remain open, even though at a higher cost. For this reason, we do not count evasive and covert trade as "assistance." Such transactions are part and parcel of every episode. Rather we are concerned with overt economic or military aid to the target country.

If a target country can rely on its friends to compensate for the burdens imposed by sanctions, the impact can be reduced. Indeed, in several cases, target countries have turned sanctions to their economic advantage, coaxing opponents of the sender country to provide new or additional funds in order to "make a stand" against the policy excesses of the rival power. The US and its allies came to the rescue of Yugoslavia in the early postwar period when Tito was threatened by Stalin. The USSR in similar fashion joined forces with Colonel Mengistu in war torn Ethiopia to deflect US attempts to foster human rights and gain compensation for expropriated property. In both cases, the amount of aid provided to the target more than offset the economic impact of the sanctions. In addition, there are many episodes—such as the USSR against Albania and the ongoing case of the United States against Nicaragua—where assistance from a major foreign power provided welcome moral support to the target. We do not attempt to scale the degree of international assistance. Instead we simply identify those cases where significant assistance was given to the target country.

Economic Health and Political Stability

The atmosphere in the target country is critical to the outcome of a sanctions episode. An analogy with rainmaking is appropriate. If storm clouds are overhead, rain may fall without man's help. If moisture laden clouds are in the sky, chemical seeding may bring forth rain. If the skies are clear and dry, no amount of human assistance will produce rain. Similarly, sanctions may be redundant, productive, or useless in pursuing foreign policy goals depending on the economic health and political stability of the target country.

It is no simple matter to summarize the complex of events that describe a country's economy and politics at a point in time. Our task is made more difficult because we wish to know the target country's health and stability in the absence of sanctions over a period of time. Consider, for example, the problem of assessing health and stability in the context of a successful destabilization case. At the beginning of the episode, the target country might be experiencing significant problems; shortly before its downfall, the target government might well have reached a crisis stage, quite apart from the pressure imposed as a result of sanctions. We have heroically put these difficulties to one side in devising an index with values of 1, 2, and 3 to describe the overall political and economic health of the target country, throughout the period of the sanctions episode, and in the hypothetical absence of sanctions:

(1) distress: a country with acute economic problems, exemplified by high unemployment and rampant inflation, coupled with political turmoil bordering on chaos, illustrated by Chile at the time of Allende and Uganda in the later years of the Amin regime
(2) significant problems: a country with severe economic problems, such as a foreign exchange crisis, coupled with substantial internal dissent, illustrated by Ceylon under P. M. Bandaranaike
(3) strong and stable: a country with the government in firm control (even though dissent may be present) and an economy experiencing only the normal range of inflation, unemployment, and similar ills, illustrated by India during the nuclear nonproliferation campaigns of the 1970s and the USSR at the time of the Afghanistan invasion.

Prior Relations Between Sender and Target

Sanctions are imposed against friends and foes alike. Against belligerent countries, forceful sanctions may be needed to coerce the target government into yielding, especially since the domestic political consequences of "backing down" can be damaging. On the other hand, a friendly country will often consider the importance of its overall relations with the sender country before fashioning a response to economic sanctions. Such considerations led South Korea and Taiwan to accede to mild US pressure and to forego construction of nuclear reprocessing plants in the mid-1970s. With friends, subtle sanctions may succeed.

To reflect the role of prior relations in determining the outcome of a sanctions episode, we have constructed an index, scaled from 1 to 3, to classify the cases according to the state of political relations between the sender and target countries before the imposition of sanctions:

(1) antagonistic: the sender and target countries are in opposing camps; illustrated by most East–West cases, US-Japan relations prior to World War II, and Arab-Israeli relations.

(2) neutral: the sender country does not have strong ties to the target, but there is a workable relationship without antagonism; illustrated by Canadian relations with India and Pakistan in the 1970s, and relations between Spain and the UK, despite centuries of dispute over Gibraltar.

(3) cordial: the sender and target countries are close friends and allies; illustrated by ties between the Arab League and Egypt prior to the Camp David accords and relations between the US, UK, and France before the Suez crisis of 1956.

Estimating the Costs

Sanctions are designed to penalize the target country for its unwanted behavior. In theory, the target country will weigh the costs imposed by the sanctions against the benefits derived from its continuing policies—the higher the cost, the more likely that the target country will alter its policies. The cost that sanctions impose on a target country cannot, however, be viewed as an abstract number: a cost of $100 million means more to Chile than to the USSR. We have, therefore, related the cost figures to the gross national product of the target country. Our methodology for estimating the cost to the target country is explained in detail in appendix B.

We have not attempted to calculate the actual costs of sanctions to sender countries. Nor have we attempted to measure the political costs visited on the sender as a result of flexing its economic "muscle." Instead, we have drawn from the case abstracts a rough sense of the trade or financial loss incurred by the sender from the imposition of sanctions, and we have related this loss to the sender country's total external trade. Illustrations of our approach are provided in chapter 4. The following index reflects our judgment as to the relative cost to the sender country:

(1) net gain to sender: usually cases where aid is withheld, illustrated by the US suspension of aid to Turkey in 1974

(2) little effect on sender: cases where a trivial dislocation occurs, illustrated by the US export controls on nuclear fuel shipments to Taiwan in 1976

(3) modest loss to sender: some trade is lost, but neither the size nor the

concentration of the loss is substantial, illustrated by the League of Nations campaign against Italy in 1935–36

(4) major loss to sender: large volumes of trade are adversely affected, illustrated by the two world wars against Germany.

Country Size and Trade Links

Quite apart from the magnitude of costs that the sender imposes on the target, the outcome of a sanctions episode may be influenced by the relative size of the two countries and the trade links between them. The imposition of even minor sanctions carries the implicit threat of more drastic action. Whether that threat looms large or small depends very much on respective country sizes and trade flows. Hence, we include among our economic variables a ratio between sender country and target country GNP levels, and figures on trade between target and sender expressed as a percentage of the target country's total trade.

Analytic Methods

In the following chapters, we focus on relations between individual explanatory variables and the outcomes—successful or otherwise—of the various groups of episodes. In addition, we have performed multiple regression analysis, relating the case success scores to all the variables simultaneously. The full multiple regression results are set forth in appendix A. Reference is made to the multiple regression results as appropriate in the narrative.

On to the Results

With these methodological issues out of the way, the road is now clear for us to examine "success" in terms of the underlying political and economic variables.

3

Political Variables

In evaluating "success," the first step is to distinguish between types of foreign policy objectives sought in different sanctions episodes. The nature of the objective may be the most important political variable of all: sanctions cannot stop a military assault as easily as they can free a political prisoner. Accordingly, our discussion is organized around five major groups of objectives, namely: modest changes in policy, destabilization of the target government, disruption of military adventures, impairment of military potential, and other major policy changes. As mentioned in chapter 2, in classifying cases the more ambitious goal takes precedence over the less ambitious goal. Thus, destabilization cases usually involve, as ancillary goals, the search for modest or even major policy changes. Only occasionally are cases cross-listed under two objectives.

Modest Changes in Policy

Sanctions have been frequently threatened or deployed in pursuit of relatively modest changes in the policies of target countries. Modest changes are not trivial changes. Changes that we have labeled "modest" may have seemed overwhelmingly important at the time of confrontation to the target or sender country. But in the grander scale of events, the settlement of an expropriation dispute, or the improvement of human rights on a limited scale, does not compare with stopping a military adventure or destabilizing a government.

Illustrative of these episodes is the case of *United States and Canada v. South Korea* (1975–76), where South Korea was dissuaded from procuring a nuclear reprocessing plant from France as a result of the threat of financial sanctions from the US and Canada. The objective was quite specific, and the sender states

41

had a great deal of leverage due to Korea's "sensitivity . . . to a slight hardening in Canadian and American financial terms [for nuclear transactions]."[1]

The United States is particularly active in the pursuit of modest policy goals, accounting for 33 of the 44 cases listed in table 3.1 (the United States was a co-sender in 4 of the 33 cases). This lopsided US weight may partly reflect our omission of contests between second and third rank powers over modest policy goals.

Of the 44 modest change cases listed in table 3.1, there are some 20 cases where we scored the outcome as positive (score 3) or successful (score 4). (All tables appear at the end of this chapter.) In 22 of 44 cases, we conclude that sanctions made a contribution to the outcome ranging from modest (score 3) to significant (score 4). The combined result is that, in 18 of the 44 cases, we obtain a success score of 9 or higher. Thus, by our analysis, in not quite half of the modest policy change cases, the sender country made some progress in achieving its goals through the use of economic sanctions. This, we think, is a significant finding. As often as not, the pursuit of modest goals with economic sanctions is likely to be rewarded with at least modest success—a better batting average than the current wave of skepticism might suggest. However, even · these results should be further qualified: in the last 11 years, the failure rate has been much higher than before 1973.

In their quest for modest policy changes, sender countries usually do not employ covert force, neither do they engage in quasi-military measures, or regular military action. Rather, in this group of cases, sanctions tend to stand alone as the policy instrument.

Because of the narrow scope of objectives sought in this category, target countries do not rally supporters to help counter the sanctions. The threat generally is small in political terms; both sender and target countries treat the policy dispute as a bilateral affair.

For the same reasons, international cooperation with the sender is generally minor or nonexistent. Indeed, it is usually not sought. In part, this is because sanctions were imposed against friendly or neutral countries. Only 6 of the 44 cases (14 percent) are directed against hostile target countries. A look at table 3.1 reveals that there is little correlation between the extent of international cooperation and the contribution of sanctions to the policy outcome.

In the 18 cases for which the success score was 9 or higher, the average sanctions period was 2.9 years. In the 26 cases with success scores of 8 or lower, the average sanctions period was 3.9 years, and in 5 of these unsuccessful cases, sanctions are still in effect. Shorter is better.

---

[1] Albert Wohlstetter, "Spreading the Bomb Without Quite Breaking the Rules," 25 *Foreign Policy* (Winter 1976/1977), p. 168.

The average score for the economic health and political stability of the target country in successful cases was 2.2. By comparison, the health and stability score in less successful episodes was 2.3. There is little difference between these values.

Destabilizing a Government

Destabilization episodes usually spring from conflicts over other issues. In some instances, the underlying dispute involves modest changes in target country policies, for example expropriation (*United States v. Brazil*, 1962–64), terrorism (*United States v. Libya*, 1978–), or human rights (*United States v. Nicaragua*, 1977–81). In other instances, destabilization is sought because the target government has adopted a hostile attitude in its overall relations with the sender country. This category of cases has a decided East–West flavor—for example, in episodes involving Yugoslavia, Finland, and Albania, the USSR found its smaller allies wandering from its socialist sphere; in cases involving Cuba, Brazil, and Chile, the United States found its neighbors stealing away from the capitalist camp. Over half the cases involve attempts to overthrow the regimes of former friends.

When another goal underlies or accompanies a destabilization case, we have generally listed these cases only in the destabilization group. (After all, a destabilization attempt presupposes policy disputes as well as personality differences.) We make an exception, however, when the sender country seeks both to destabilize a government and to disrupt a military adventure; such cases are cross-listed under both headings.

Table 3.2 summarizes 19 destabilization cases. Our research suggests that sanctions, coupled with other policies, are surprisingly successful in destabilizing governments. In over half of the destabilization cases, the success score is 9 or greater, and in 2 of the remaining cases (*United States v. Libya*, 1978– ; and *United States v. Nicaragua*, 1981–) the outcome remains in doubt. This high success rate contrasts sharply with the skepticism expressed in the literature, and compares positively with results obtained in applying sanctions to obtain other foreign policy goals.

A word of caution: it must be emphasized that economic sanctions seldom achieve destabilization unassisted by companion measures. Covert action and quasi-military operations regularly play a role in destabilization cases; indeed, companion policies were present in all but five of the episodes. On the other hand, international cooperation is not an important ingredient of successful destabilization episodes. In two cases the Soviet Union was supported by its East European allies; and the United States enjoyed some international coop-eration in its efforts to isolate Cuba. But in each of these instances the target country received considerable material and moral support from an opposing major power, and that support compensated for the impact of the sanctions on the target country and led to low success scores.

In the ten cases with a success score of 9 or higher the average sanctions period was 4.0 years; in the nine other cases (including the two which are still in doubt) the average sanctions period was 5.9 years. Sanctions that have an immediate impact are those that are most effective. If an episode drags on, this probably indicates that the government was more resistant to erosion.

The average index of economic health and political stability for target governments that succumbed to destabilization was only 1.3. By contrast, the average index for target regimes that resisted destabilization was 1.9. Prosaic but true: governments in distress are more easily destabilized.

Disrupting Military Adventures

At the end of World War I the classic rationale offered for economic sanctions was to persuade hostile countries to abandon their military adventures. Lord Curzon, speaking in 1918, suggested that the sure application of sanctions might have averted the outbreak of a lesser conflict than World War I:

[Sanctions] did not, it is true, succeed in preventing the war; they have not, at any rate at present curtailed its duration, but I should like to put it this way. I doubt very much whether, if Germany had anticipated when she plunged into war the consequences, commercial, financial, and otherwise, which would be entailed upon her by two, three, or four years of war, she would not have been eager to plunge in as she was. Remember this. Though possibly we have not done all we desired, we have done a great deal, and we could have done a great deal more if our hands had not been tied by certain difficulties. It is naturally a delicate matter for me to allude to this. A good many of them have been removed by the entry of the United States of America into the war, but we have always the task of handling with great and necessary delicacy the neutral states, and this difficulty still remains with us.[2]

Apparently influenced by the arguments of spokesmen such as Lord Curzon and President Wilson, British and American policy officials came increasingly to use sanctions as an explicit substitute for military action or as a key component of an overall effort to disrupt unwelcome military adventures.

Table 3.3 identifies 18 military adventure cases. We define a military adventure as an action on a less grand scale than the Napoleonic Wars or the two world wars. The classic instance is the *League of Nations v. Italy* (1935–36); other

---

[2] D. Mitrany, *The Problem of International Sanctions* (London: Oxford University Press, 1925), p. 36.

instances include *United States v. Japan* (1940–41); *United States v. Cuba* (1960–); and *United Kingdom v. Argentina* (1982). There are few ambiguous cases in this group: when sanctions succeeded, they did so decisively; when they failed, they flopped. In 6 of these cases, a success score of 9 or higher was reached. In the remaining 12 cases, sanctions failed to deter the target country's martial ambitions.

The presence of companion measures—covert interference and military and quasi-military action—was not decisive in distinguishing between success and failure cases. In only one case, *United Kingdom v. Argentina* (1982), were companion policies used to good effect. But in six other instances, companion policies did not materially advance the desired outcome.

International cooperation was of marginal significance. The average degree of cooperation in the six success cases was 2.3; the average degree of cooperation in the nine failure cases was 2.2. In the success episodes, the sanctions period on average lasted 1.2 years. In the failure episodes, the average sanctions period was 3.2 years.

Target countries that engage in military adventures are usually not in acute distress. At most they have significant internal problems—for example, malfunctioning economies in Egypt in the mid-1970s and in Turkey in 1974. However, the weaker the national condition, the more likely that sanctions will succeed. The average health and stability index for target countries was 2.0 in success cases and 2.3 in failure cases.

An additional feature that helps distinguish between success and failure episodes is the prior relations index. Success more often (but not invariably) resulted when the target country was either an ally or at least neutral, and on friendly terms with the sender country prior to the episode: *League of Nations v. Greece* (1925); *United States v. Netherlands* (1948–49); *United States v. UK and France* (1956); *United States v. United Arab Republic* (1963–65). By contrast, in cases where a background of hostility preceded the use of sanctions, success proved elusive: *United States v. Japan* (1940–41); *United States and CHINCOM v. China* (1949–70); *United States v. USSR* (1980–81). The average prior relations index for target countries was 2.3 in success cases and 2.1 in failure cases.

Impairing Military Potential

The immediate purpose of practically every economic sanctions episode is to diminish the potential power of the target country. Nevertheless, we can distinguish between the imposition of short-term economic measures to achieve defined political goals, and the conduct of a long-term campaign to weaken a major adversary. Table 3.4 lists ten episodes where weakening the target's economy became an end in its own right. These episodes usually involve contests between major powers, often in wartime or in the shadow of war.

In neither World War I nor II, nor in the Korean War, did the Allies believe that sanctions would decisively contribute to the outcome. Instead, they hoped and expected that economic denial would marginally limit the adversary's military capabilities. Economic sanctions became a minor adjunct to a major war effort, and "trading with the enemy" was labeled an offense in its own right, quite apart from calculations of cost and benefit. These features distinguish the impairment episodes from the disruption of military adventure cases. Similarly, for more than three decades, the United States has sought to limit the economic underpinnings of the Soviet military machine, initially through COCOM, and more recently through denial measures associated with the Afghanistan invasion and the Polish crisis.

Apart from the two world wars, we assign these episodes low success scores. With the exception of North Korea and Vietnam, the target countries are economically healthy and politically stable. With the exception of North Korea, Vietnam, and Israel, the targets are major powers. It is unreasonable to expect that sanctions that disrupt a modest amount of trade or finance can significantly detract from the economic strength of a major power.

It is not surprising that the two successes were associated with major wars. But even in wartime, as subsequent studies of defeated Germany showed, it was hard to find key economic links which—when destroyed by sanctions or by bombing—would cripple the war machine. Instead, the contribution of sanctions was a contribution of attrition.

Other Major Policy Changes

Under this heading, we put cases that are not already covered by the destabilization and impairment groupings. Examples include the *United Nations v. South Africa* (1962–   ), over apartheid and Namibia; and the *Arab League v. United States and Netherlands* (1973–74), over support of Israel.

As table 3.5 shows, in only 3 of the 17 cases was a success score of 9 or better reached. Two of these cases involved civil wars: the submission of Hyderabad by India and the defeat of Biafra by Nigeria. In these two cases, the success of sanctions was clearcut. The borderline success case was the *Arab League v. United States and Netherlands*. The sudden rise in the price of oil in 1973–74 from $2.59/bbl. to $11.65/bbl. gave the Organization of Petroleum Exporting Countries (OPEC) instant and spectacular wealth. In our judgment, the sanctions were more an occasion than a cause of the price leap. However, the threat to withhold oil from diplomatic adversaries contributed to a shift in West European and Japanese policies on the Palestinian question. Accordingly, we conclude that sanctions made a positive contribution to the diplomatic achievements of the OPEC group. We recognize that other observers might ascribe a less important role to sanctions in this episode.

To mention just a few of the failures, there is no evidence that UN sanctions have materially affected South African attitudes on apartheid, or that the Arab League boycott has moved Israel on the question of establishing a Palestinian homeland, or that sanctions helped Indonesia prevent the consolidation of neighboring territory into the nation of Malaysia. It is noteworthy that the target countries in this group generally enjoy high levels of economic health and political stability, and that the failure cases on average lasted 8.1 years.

Table 3.1 Modest changes in target country policies: political variables

Case[a]	Sender and target	Policy result[b] (index)	Sanctions contribution[c] (index)	Success score[d] (index)
33–1	UK v. USSR	4	3	12
38–1	US, UK v. Mexico	3	3	9
54–1	USSR v. Australia	1	1	1
56–2	US, UK, France v. Egypt	3	3	9
61–1	US v. Ceylon	4	4	16
62–3	USSR v. Romania	1	1	1
63–1	US v. UAR[k]	4	4	16
64–1	France v. Tunisia	3	3	9
65–1	US v. Chile	3	4	12
65–2	US v. India	4	4	16
68–1	US v. Peru	1	1	1
68–2	US v. Peru	3	4	12
73–2	US v. South Korea	2	2	4
73–3	US v. Chile	2	3	6
74–2	Canada v. India	2	2	4
74–3	Canada v. Pakistan	2	2	4
75–1	US, Canada v. South Korea	4	4	16
75–2	US v. USSR	2	2	4
75–3	US v. Eastern Europe	3	4	12
75–4	US v. South Africa	2	2	4
76–1	US v. Uruguay	3	2	6
76–2	US v. Taiwan	4	4	16
76–3	US v. Ethiopia	1	1	1
77–1	US v. Paraguay	2	3	6

a. The *case* refers to the identification system used in table 1.1.

b. The *policy result,* on an index scale of 1 to 4, indicates the extent to which the outcome sought by the sender country was achieved. Key: (1) failed outcome; (2) unclear but possibly positive; (3) positive outcome; (4) successful outcome.

c. The *sanctions contribution,* on an index scale of 1 to 4, indicates the extent to which the sanctions contributed to a positive policy result. Key: (1) zero or negative contribution; (2) minor contribution; (3) modest contribution; (4) significant contribution.

d. The *success score* is an index on a scale of 1 to 16, found by multiplying the index of policy result by the index of sanctions contribution.

e. *Companion policies* refer to covert action (J); quasi-military operations (Q); and regular military action (R).

f. The extent of *international cooperation with sender,* on an index scale of 1 to 4, indicates the degree of assistance received by the principal sender country in applying sanctions. Key: (1) no cooperation; (2) minor cooperation; (3) modest cooperation; (4) significant cooperation.

Companion policies[e]	International cooperation with sender[f] (index)	International assistance to target[g]	Sanctions period[h] (years)	Health and stability[i] (index)	Prior relations[j] (index)
—	1	—	1	2	1
—	2	—	9	3	2
—	1	—	1	3	1
R	2	—	1	2	2
—	1	A	4	2	2
—	4	—	1	3	3
—	1	—	2	2	2
—	1	—	2	2	3
—	1	—	1	2	2
—	1	—	2	2	2
—	1	—	1	2	2
—	1	—	6	2	2
—	1	—	4	2	3
—	1	—	11+	1	2
—	2	—	2	3	2
—	2	—	2	2	2
—	2	—	1	3	3
—	1	—	9+	3	1
—	1	—	9+	3	1
—	2	—	7	3	2
—	1	—	5	2	2
—	1	—	1	3	3
—	2	A	8+	1	2
—	1	—	4	3	2

g. *International assistance to target*, indicated by an A, is judged to exist when another country (usually a major power) extends significant economic or military assistance to the target country. The mere transshipment of goods subject to sanction is not counted here as assistance.

h. The *sanctions period* represents the rounded number of years, from first official threat or event to conclusion. The minimum period is one year. A(+) indicates that the sanction is still in effect.

i. *Health and stability* is an index, scaled from 1 to 3, that represents the target country's overall economic health and political stability (abstracting from sanctions) during the sanctions episode. Key: (1) distressed country; (2) country with significant problems; (3) strong and stable country.

j. *Prior relations* is an index, scaled from 1 to 3, that measures the degree of warmth, prior to the sanctions episode, in overall relations between target and sender country. Key: (1) antagonistic; (2) neutral; (3) cordial.

k. This case is also listed under disruption of military adventures.

Table 3.1 Modest changes in target country policies: political variables *(continued)*

Case[a]	Sender and target	Policy result[b] (index)	Sanctions contribution[c] (index)	Success score[d] (index)
77–2	US v. Guatemala	2	2	4
77–3	US v. Argentina	3	2	6
77–4	Canada v. EC, Japan	3	3	9
77–6	US v. El Salvador	2	3	6
77–7	US v. Brazil	3	3	9
78–1	China v. Albania	1	1	1
78–2	US v. Brazil	2	2	4
78–3	US v. Argentina	2	2	4
78–4	US v. India	2	2	4
78–5	US v. USSR	1	1	1
79–1	US v. Iran	4	3	12
79–2	US v. Pakistan	2	2	4
79–3	Arab League v. Canada	4	3	12
79–4	US v. Bolivia	2	3	6
80–2	US v. Iraq	2	2	4
82–2	Netherlands, US v. Suriname	3	3	9
82–3	South Africa v. Lesotho	4	4	16
83–1	Australia v. France	2	1	2
83–2	US v. USSR	1	1	1
83–3	US v. Zimbabwe	2	2	4

Table 3.2 Destabilization of target governments: political variables

Case[a]	Sender and target	Policy result[b] (index)	Sanctions contribution[c] (index)	Success score[d] (index)
18–1	UK v. Russia	1	1	1
44–1	US v. Argentina	2	2	4
48–4	USSR v. Yugoslavia	1	1	1
51–1	UK, US v. Iran	4	3	12
56–4	US v. Laos	3	3	9
58–1	USSR v. Finland	4	4	16
60–1	US v. Dominican Republic	4	4	16
60–3	US v. Cuba[k]	1	1	1
61–2	USSR v. Albania	1	1	1

a.–j. See table 3.1.
k. These cases are also listed under disruption of military adventures.

Companion policies[c]	International cooperation with sender[f] (index)	International assistance to target[g]	Sanctions period[h] (years)	Health and stability[i] (index)	Prior relations[j] (index)
—	1	A	7+	2	2
—	1	—	6	2	2
—	1	—	1	3	3
—	1	—	4	1	2
—	1	—	7	2	2
—	1	—	5	3	3
—	1	—	3	2	2
—	2	—	4	2	2
—	2	—	4	3	2
—	2	—	2	3	1
Q	3	—	2	1	3
—	2	A	1	2	2
—	3	—	1	3	2
—	2	A	3	1	2
—	1	—	2	2	2
J	2	A	2+	1	3
Q	1	—	1	2	3
—	1	—	1+	3	3
—	4	—	1	3	1
—	1	—	1	2	2

Companion policies[c]	International cooperation with sender[f] (index)	International assistance to target[g]	Sanctions period[h] (years)	Health and stability[i] (index)	Prior relations[j] (index)
Q,R	4	—	2	1	1
—	2	—	3	2	2
Q	4	A	7	2	3
J	2	—	2	2	3
J	2	—	6	1	3
—	1	—	1	2	3
Q,J	3	—	2	1	3
Q,J	3	A	24+	2	3
J	4	A	4	2	3

Table 3.2 Destabilization of target governments: political variables (continued)

Case[a]	Sender and target	Policy result[b] (index)	Sanctions contribution[c] (index)	Success score[d] (index)
62–1	US v. Brazil	4	3	12
63–3	US v. Indonesia[k]	4	2	8
63–4	US v. South Vietnam	4	3	12
65–3	UK, UN v. Rhodesia	4	3	12
70–1	US v. Chile	4	3	12
72–1	UK, US v. Uganda	4	3	12
77–5	US v. Nicaragua	4	3	12
78–8	US v. Libya	2	2	4
81–1	US v. Nicaragua	2	2	4
83–4	US, OECS v. Grenada	4	2	8

Table 3.3 Disruption of military adventures (other than major wars): political variables

Case[a]	Sender and target	Policy result[b] (index)	Sanctions contribution[c] (index)	Success score[d] (index)
21–1	League v. Yugoslavia	4	4	16
25–1	League v. Greece	4	4	16
32–1	League v. Paraguay, Bolivia	3	2	6
35–1	League v. Italy	1	1	1
40–1	US v. Japan	1	1	1
48–1	US v. Netherlands	4	4	16
49–1	US, CHINCOM v. China[k]	1	1	1
56–3	US v. UK, France	4	3	12
57–2	France v. Tunisia	1	1	1
60–3	US v. Cuba[m]	1	1	1
63–1	US v. UAR[o]	4	4	16
63–3	US v. Indonesia[m]	4	2	8
71–1	US v. India, Pakistan	2	1	2
74–1	US v. Turkey	1	1	1
75–5	US v. Kampuchea	1	1	1
78–7	China v. Vietnam	1	1	1
80–1	US v. USSR (Afghanistan)[k]	1	1	1
82–1	UK v. Argentina	4	3	12

a.–j. See table 3.1.
k. These cases are also listed under impairment of military potential.
l. For this case, the length of the episode is linked to the Korean war period only.
m. These cases are also listed under destabilization of target governments.

Companion policies[c]	International cooperation with sender[f] (index)	International assistance to target[g]	Sanctions period[h] (years)	Health and stability[i] (index)	Prior relations[j] (index)
J	1	—	2	1	2
—	1	—	3	2	2
J	1	—	1	1	3
Q	4	A	14	2	3
J	1	—	3	1	2
—	2	—	7	1	2
—	1	—	2	1	3
Q,J	1	—	6+	3	1
Q,J	1	A	3+	2	2
R	3	—	1	1	2

Companion policies[c]	International cooperation with sender[f] (index)	International assistance to target[g]	Sanctions period[h] (years)	Health and stability[i] (index)	Prior relations[j] (index)
—	4	—	1	2	2
—	4	—	1	2	2
—	3	—	3	2	2
—	4	A	1	3	2
—	2	—	1	3	1
—	1	—	1	2	3
R,Q	3	A	4^l	3	1
—	1	—	1	3	3
R	1	A	6	2	3
Q,J	3	A	$9+^n$	3	3
—	1	—	2	2	2
—	1	—	3	2	2
Q	1	—	1	2	2
—	1	—	4	2	3
—	1	—	4	1	2
R	3	A	1	2	3
J	3	—	1	3	1
R	3	—	1	1	2

n. For this case, the length of the episode is linked to the deployment of Cuban troops in foreign countries (e.g., Angola).

o. This case is also listed under modest changes in target country policies.

Table 3.4 Impairment of military potential (including major wars): political variables

Case[a]	Sender and target	Policy result[b] (index)	Sanctions contribution[c] (index)	Success score[d] (index)
14–1	UK v. Germany	4	3	12
39–1	Alliance Powers v. Germany, Japan	4	3	12
46–1	Arab League v. Israel	2	2	4
48–5	US, COCOM v. USSR, COMECON	2	2	4
49–2	US, CHINCOM v. China[k]	1	1	1
50–1	US, UN v. North Korea	2	1	2
54–4	US, South Vietnam v. North Vietnam	1	1	1
60–2	USSR v. China	2	2	4
80–1	US v. USSR (Afghanistan)[k]	1	1	1
81–3	US v. USSR (Poland)	1	1	1

a.–j. See table 3.1.
k. These cases are also listed under disruption of military adventures.

Table 3.5 Other major changes in target country policies (including surrender of territory): political variables

Case[a]	Sender and target	Policy result[b] (index)	Sanctions contribution[c] (index)	Success score[d] (index)
17–1	US v. Japan	2	2	4
48–2	India v. Hyderabad	4	3	12
48–3	USSR v. US, UK, France	1	1	1
54–2	India v. Portugal	4	2	8
54–3	Spain v. UK	2	3	6
56–1	US v. Israel (intermittent episodes)	2	1	2
57–1	Indonesia v. Netherlands	4	2	8
61–3	Western Allies v. GDR	1	1	1
62–2	UN v. South Africa	1	1	1
63–2	Indonesia v. Malaysia	1	1	1
63–5	UN, OAU v. Portugal	4	2	8
65–4	US v. Arab League	2	3	6
67–1	Nigeria v. Biafra	4	3	12
73–1	Arab League v. US, Netherlands	3	3	9
78–6	Arab League v. Egypt	1	1	1
81–2	US v. Poland	3	2	6
81–4	EC v. Turkey	2	3	6

a.–j. See table 3.1.

Companion policies[c]	International cooperation with sender[f] (index)	International assistance to target[g]	Sanctions period[h] (years)	Health and stability[i] (index)	Prior relations[j] (index)
R	4	A	4	3	1
R	4	A	6	3	1
R	3	A	38+	3	1
—	4	A	36+	3	1
R,Q	3	A	21	3	1
R	4	A	34+	2	1
R	2	A	30+	2	1
Q	3	—	10	3	3
J	3	—	1	3	1
—	2	—	1	3	1

Companion policies[c]	International cooperation with sender[f] (index)	International assistance to target[g]	Sanctions period[h] (years)	Health and stability[i] (index)	Prior relations[j] (index)
—	1	—	1	3	2
R	1	—	1	2	3
Q	1	A	1	3	1
R	1	—	7	3	2
—	1	—	30	3	2
—	1	—	4	3	3
R	2	—	5	3	2
Q	3	A	1	3	1
—	3	—	22+	3	2
Q	1	—	3	2	2
—	3	—	11	2	2
—	2	—	19+	3	2
R	1	—	3	1	3
—	3	A	1	3	2
—	3	A	5	2	3
—	3	A	3	1	2
—	2	—	1	2	3

4

Economic Variables

The economic variables in a sanctions episode are summarized in tables 4.1 through 4.5 (the tables appear at the end of this chapter). As in chapter 3, we have grouped the cases according to the major foreign policy objective. However, in this chapter we organize the discussion according to economic variables.

Size of Sender and Target Countries

The economy of the sender country is usually very much larger than the economy of the target country. In most cases, the sender's GNP is over 10 times greater than the target's GNP, and in almost half the cases the ratio is over 50. Indeed, the GNP ratio exceeds 100 in over 70 percent of the destabilization cases. These figures reflect, on the one hand, the prominence of the United States, the United Kingdom, and the USSR as senders, and, on the other hand, the small size of the countries they usually try to influence with economic sanctions.

In many instances, when the GNP ratio is under 10, sanctions flounder. Cases that entail major policy changes often belong to this category of failures. These cases either involve big power confrontations, or sender countries that are not major powers. Examples are the two world wars, the series of US-USSR confrontations, and Canadian attempts to advance nuclear nonproliferation policies in the mid-1970s. In several instances, however, sanctions were successful even though the GNP ratio was less than 10: the two world wars; US efforts against the United Kingdom and France during the Suez crisis of 1956; the Arab oil embargo against the United States and the Netherlands in 1973–74 (in this case, the GNP ratio was less than one); and the British sanctions during the Falklands war of 1982. But in most of these instances military victory was critical to the success of the episode.

These latter cases may explain why the GNP ratio is the only variable we tested through multiple regression analysis that was not consistent with our conclusions. A higher GNP ratio was associated with a lower success index. We attribute this surprising result to two phenomena: the close correlation between the GNP ratio and the type of policy goal, as noted above; and the correlation between the GNP ratio and the costs imposed on the target country, expressed as a percentage of GNP, discussed below. When we ran a correlation between the GNP ratio and the success score, without reference to the type of policy goal or other variables, the results confirmed our view that sanctions used by large countries against much smaller countries more often succeed. The statistical analysis is discussed in greater detail in appendix A.

Trade Linkages

Since sender countries are generally very large countries, it is not surprising that the target's import and export trade with the sender usually accounts for over 10 percent of the target's total trade. In the cases we have scored as successes, the sender country accounts, on average, for about a quarter of the target country's total trade. Even when the sender country interrupts only a small portion of that trade, the interruption carries an important message to the target country: change your policies or risk a larger disturbance.

The trade ratios in cases involving modest policy goals vary greatly. Some cases were successful when only a small amount of bilateral trade was involved (for example, *United States v. Ceylon*, 1961–65: 9 percent of exports; 3 percent of imports). Many cases were unsuccessful even when a high proportion of trade was at stake, such as in the human rights episode of *United States v. Guatemala* (1977–), where over one-third of Guatemala's total trade was with the United States. In general, however, higher trade linkages are more closely associated with success episodes (average trade linkage of 27 percent) than with failure episodes (average trade linkage of 14 percent).

Due to the usual close proximity of senders and targets in destabilization cases, their trade linkages are generally strong. One exception is the case *United Kingdom and United States v. Uganda* (1972–79), over the atrocities of the Idi Amin regime. But in almost every case in this group, the sender takes more than 10 percent of the exports, and supplies over 10 percent of the imports, of the target country. Within this group, the extent of linkage appears somewhat greater for success cases (average 32 percent) than for failure cases (average 25 percent).

Trade linkage does not appear to play a major role in episodes involving the disruption of military adventure, impairment of military potential, and other major policy changes, listed in tables 4.3, 4.4, and 4.5. Some successful cases involve high trade dependencies (*League v. Greece*, 1925; *United States v. United Arab Republic*, 1963–65), while other successes occur when the bilateral trade relations are small (*United Kingdom v. Argentina*, 1982; in this case, however, the financial ties between the United Kingdom and Argentina were much stronger than the trade ties). Conversely, high levels of bilateral trade do not ensure success, as is evident in the UN sanctions against South Africa from 1962 on, and Soviet measures against China in the 1960s.

Type of Sanction

Success may depend, to some extent, on whether the sanctions hit a sensitive sector in the target country's economy. A $100 million cost may have quite different effects—at home and abroad—depending on whether it is imposed by way of export sanctions, import sanctions, or financial sanctions. Officials in the US State Department and other foreign ministries spend long hours tailoring their creations because they believe that the cut of a sanction matters a great deal.

The success of the Iranian asset freeze and the aid-denial cases of the 1960s involving Egypt, Brazil, India, and other countries, suggest that financial sanctions can be more effective than trade sanctions. Why? In the first place, if the financial sanctions entail a reduction in official aid or credits they are not likely to create the same backlash, from business firms at home and allies abroad, as the interruption of private trade. In the second place, private financiers who might provide an alternative source of credit must anticipate a long-term relationship with the target country, and long-term relations are unsettled when financial sanctions are in the air.[1] In the third place, the denial of finance can disrupt the well-laid plans of powerful government ministers. By contrast, pain resulting from the shortage of goods can often (but not always) be spread across the populace at large.

When trade weapons are deployed, sender countries more frequently use export controls than import controls. One reason is that sender countries usually enjoy a more dominant market position as suppliers of exports than as purchasers of imports. Hence, for a given interruption of trade, sender countries may inflict greater pain by stopping exports than by stopping imports. The dominant position of the United States as a manufacturer of military hardware and high technology equipment has particularly influenced US tactics. A second reason for the emphasis on export controls, peculiar to the United States, is that the Congress has given the president much greater flexibility to restrain exports than to slow imports. Exports may be stopped readily through the mechanisms of the Export Administration Act,[2] whereas imports can be slowed only by

---

[1] It should be noted that major capital projects, such as electric power plants, also involve long-term relations between countries.

[2] The 98th Congress failed to reauthorize the Export Administration Act. However, the substantive provisions of that act have been extended on an emergency basis through the invocation of the International Emergency Economic Powers Act.

invoking the more cumbersome International Emergency Economic Powers Act, the national security section (section 232) of the Trade Expansion Act of 1962, or pre-existing quota legislation (such as sugar or textile quotas).

It is worth pointing out, however, that export controls often result in a concentrated burden on individual companies in the sender country, whereas import controls usually spread the burden more widely. This is a good argument for devising statutes that make it equally easy (or equally hard) for the executive branch to impose import controls as export controls.[3]

The Cost of Sanctions

Sanctions are supposed to impose economic penalties in order to coerce the target country to alter its policies; if the sanctions impose no costs, they are unlikely to change foreign behavior. In short, according to the underlying rationale, the level of costs importantly determines the success or failure of a sanctions episode.

Costs To Targets

Some economists have constructed fairly elaborate theoretical models to suggest how the conditions of supply and demand for the sanctioned commodity might affect the level of costs incurred by the sender and imposed on the target, and how the balance of costs might affect the outcome of a sanctions episode. Unfortunately, the more elaborate the model the less likely that it is tarnished by economic data. In fact, few studies go beyond anecdotal accounts of the costs that economic sanctions impose on target countries. We have, therefore, developed a very simple analytical construct to guide our own rudimentary efforts to estimate the costs imposed on the target country. Our methodology is detailed in appendix B.

In order to calculate the cost of each sanctions episode to the target country, we have estimated the initial deprivation of markets, supplies, or finance, expressed on an annualized basis in current US dollars. To calculate the "welfare loss" to the target's economy, we then used our own judgment to estimate the "sanctions multiplier" that should be applied in the context of the particular

---

[3] GATT Article XXI enables a country to take "any action which it considers necessary for its national security interests. . . ." Notwithstanding this provision, Nicaragua challenged US sanctions on sugar imports as inconsistent with the GATT. A GATT Panel determined that these import controls, imposed for foreign policy purposes, do not fall within the purview of Article XXI.

episode. Some types of sanctions affect the target country more than others for a given amount of trade or finance. The welfare loss caused by reductions in aid may be 100 percent of the value of the aid; on the other hand, trade controls may cause less harm than the value of the shipments affected because of the availability of other markets or substitution for other goods.

We recognize that the third law of physics—for every action there is a reaction—seems to play a role in the course of a sanctions episode. The impact of sanctions on the target country may be partially or totally offset by the helping hand of another major power. There are several instances where the target has actually become better off, in economic terms, as a result of the sanctions. Soviet attempts to pressure Yugoslavia in 1948 failed miserably from Moscow's perspective, but yielded Tito an abundant harvest of Western aid and trade credits. In a similar fashion, American efforts to coerce Ethiopia on human rights and compensation issues helped push Colonel Mengistu into the waiting and generous arms of the Russians. In our cost estimates, we attempt to reflect these offsetting benefits.

A brief survey of three cases may help illustrate our calculations of economic costs.

LEAGUE OF NATIONS V. ITALY (1935–36: ABYSSINIA)

In a belated attempt to coerce Italy into withdrawing its troops from Abyssinia, the League agreed in late 1935 to a limited trade embargo and to restrictions on loans and credits to Italy. The sanctions did not include key commodities such as oil, nor were they applied by some League and non-League members (for example, the United States). Nonetheless, trade was sharply reduced from the presanction period. Financial conditions in Italy were also affected by the sanctions (and the cost of the war): the lira was devalued by 25 percent in November 1935, and Italy was forced to sell about $94 million in gold between November 1935 and June 1936 to bolster its dwindling reserves.

The sanctions caused a decline in both exports and imports, and forced a sale of gold reserves. During the six months when sanctions were in effect, exports dropped by $56 million and imports by $72 million from the previous year's levels. Yet, in analyzing this period, M. J. Bonn noted that "[s]tocks on hand, the practice of economies, the development of substitutes, and the purchase of goods with gold, foreign securities, emigrants' remittances and tourists' disbursements kept the country going without too severe a strain."[4] The "elasticity of substitution" was undoubtedly high. Accordingly, we estimated

---

[4] See M. J. Bonn, "How Sanctions Failed," 15 *Foreign Affairs* (January 1937), p. 360.

the welfare loss to the Italian economy at 30 percent of the value of interrupted trade, or $34 million and $43 million, respectively, for exports and imports, when calculated on an annualized basis. In addition, we estimated that Italy incurred a financial loss of $9 million because of forced gold sales, which we estimated to have been made at a 10 percent discount. In sum, we estimate that the sanctions led to an $86 million loss in welfare to the Italian economy, equal to 1.7 percent of GNP.

USSR V. YUGOSLAVIA (1948–55: NATIONALISM)

Stalin used economic pressure and threats of military intervention in an attempt to force Tito back into the Soviet fold. Almost all economic ties between Yugoslavia and the Soviet bloc were suspended by mid-1949. The sanctions led Yugoslavia to expand its trade and to seek military and economic aid from the West. Total trade flows were not reduced but there was a dramatic shift in the direction of trade: in 1948, over 50 percent of Yugoslav trade was with the Soviet Union and Eastern Europe; by 1954, over 80 percent of trade was with the United States and Western Europe.

Yugoslavia claimed it lost $400 million between 1948 and 1954 as a result of the Soviet sanctions. Our calculations are in the same ball park. We took the amount of Soviet credits offered to Yugoslavia at the end of the sanctions episode as a surrogate for the reduction in aid from the COMECON countries. The Soviet bloc offered $289 million in credits in 1955. Spreading the credits over a six-year period and estimating the welfare loss at 75 percent of the value of the aid yields an annualized cost of $36 million. The suspension of debt payments by COMECON countries also cost the Yugoslavs about $300 million over the period 1948–54, which, when valued at 70 percent of the lost revenues, led to a further loss of $35 million per year. The confrontation with the Soviet bloc also caused a sharp increase in military expenditures, which accounted for 22 percent of national income during 1950–54.[5] The increase in the military budget was directly attributable to the heightened tensions caused by the Soviet sanctions; accordingly, we also took account of increases in the Yugoslav military budget over the sanctions period. Annual military expenditures in 1950–54 ran about $162 million above the 1948 level; we estimated the annual welfare loss at 25 percent of the additional expenditures, or $40.5 million a year.

These various costs amounted to 3.6 percent of Yugoslav GNP in 1952. However, the costs were more than offset by compensating aid flows from the

---

[5] See R. Barry Farrell, *Yugoslavia and the Soviet Union 1948–1956* (Hamden, Conn.: Shoe String Press, 1956), pp. 27–30.

United States and Europe, and loans from the World Bank. From 1950–54, Yugoslavia received about $1 billion in military and economic aid from the West. Clearly, such funds would not have been forthcoming in the absence of a breach in the Soviet bloc. We estimated Yugoslavia's welfare gain as 75 percent of the transfers, or $187.5 million a year. As a result, there was an annual net welfare *gain* to the Yugoslav economy during this period of $76 million, equal to 2.5 percent of GNP.

UNITED STATES V. DOMINICAN REPUBLIC (1960–62: TRUJILLO)

The notorious abuses of Rafael Trujillo prompted the US, in 1960, to impose a limited trade embargo to destabilize the Trujillo regime. The embargo covered arms, petroleum products, trucks, and spare parts. In addition, the United States imposed a special two cents a pound entry fee for nonquota sugar imported from the Dominican Republic. While multilateral in nature, for all practical purposes the sanctions were imposed only by the United States.

The most costly measure was the US sugar fee. It has been estimated elsewhere[6] that this fee cost the Dominican Republic about $12.5 million per year. Imports of the sanctioned petroleum products fell by 25 percent, but limited product coverage and alternate sourcing in Europe softened the impact on the Dominican economy. Accordingly, we estimated the annual welfare loss at 30 percent of the trade affected by the sanctions, or only $0.7 million on an annual basis. Imports of trucks, buses, and parts were so small that the losses caused by the sanctions had a negligible impact. Nonetheless, in total the sanctions put the squeeze on an already shaky economy, and contributed both to a drop in per capita GNP from $293 in 1960 to $267 in 1961 and to a decline of $28 million in gold and foreign exchange reserves. We estimated that the drop in reserves resulted in a welfare loss of $2.8 million (based on 10 percent of the decline). Overall, the sanctions cost the Dominican Republic some $16 million, equal to 1.9 percent of GNP in 1960.

As these three examples show, we tried to err on the side of overestimating the economic impact of sanctions on target countries. Nevertheless, we uncovered few cases where sanctions inflicted a heavy cost relative to national income. Very seldom did the costs of sanctions (expressed on an annualized basis) reach even 1 percent of the target country's GNP. Of course, government officials fight very hard for policy changes that might change GNP by 1 percent; and elections are won or lost, and coups are staged, with the expenditure of far less money. Still, the numbers seem small.

---

[6] See C. Lloyd Brown-John, *Multilateral Sanctions*, p. 229.

Why don't sanctions impose a heavier cost on the target country? The most important reason is that sender countries encounter great difficulty in extending the scope of sanctions to cover a broad range of economic activity and a large number of trading partners. Even when allied governments embark on a joint sanctions effort, the obstacles are formidable. Sanctions create powerful incentives for evasion. It could be said that a sieve leaks like a sanction. Ingenious new trading relationships, devised by domestic and third-country firms, flower because it is difficult to trace the origin and destination of traded goods. In the 1980s, Iran and Argentina obtained spare military parts, and Libya marketed its oil in Europe—albeit at some cost and delay—thanks to triangular trade arrangements. Moreover, transshipments can be routed through friendly (or at least not antagonistic) countries: for many years, the lifeline for Rhodesia was its continuing trade with South Africa, Zambia, and Mozambique.

Despite these many leakages, sanctions do impose a cost. And when the costs of the sanctions are over 1 percent of GNP, sanctions often succeed. Destabilization episodes stand out as cases where the sender country is generally willing and able to turn the screws hard. In over 50 percent of the destabilization cases, the cost of sanctions equaled or exceeded 1 percent of GNP. By contrast, when a sender seeks modest policy goals, it seldom inflicts heavy costs—in only 20 percent of the cases listed in table 4.1 did the costs exceed 1 percent of GNP. Yet even sanctions that exert a modest impact relative to GNP can contribute to the successful achievement of foreign policy goals. The fear of deprivation can be just as important as deprivation itself. Moreover, policy decisions often turn on amounts that are quite small in GNP terms.

Costs To Senders

Foreign policy measures generally entail domestic costs, and sanctions episodes are no exception. Domestic firms pay an immediate price when trade, aid, or financial flows are disrupted. Moreover, sanctions increase the long-term uncertainty, and therefore the cost, of doing business abroad. All trading partners of the sender country, not just the target country, may be prompted to seek diversified sources of supply, alternative partners for joint ventures, and technologies not developed in the sender country.

There is a limited exception to the general rule that sanctions entail costs for the sender country. If the sender seeks to coerce the target by cutting aid or official credits, the sender may enjoy an immediate economic gain due to a reduction in budget expenditures. But even in these instances, the corollary loss of trade contacts may entail an economic burden—in the form of lost sales and jobs—on the sender country.

It is often said that the sender country in a sanctions episode should seek to maximize its political gains and to minimize its economic costs. Sometimes this advice is translated into the recommendation that the sender country should seek to maximize the ratio of costs inflicted to costs incurred. At best, these precepts are honored in the abstract. The domestic costs of a sanctions episode are rarely calculated—and almost never in advance—for two basic reasons.

First of all, it is just plain hard to quantify the costs to the sender country. Too many intangible factors are at play. If the green eyeshade staff of the Office of Management and Budget were ever asked to calculate the costs of imposing sanctions, they would be aghast. Hard data rarely exist. And many costs will only appear years later as a result of lost sales opportunities which befall firms branded with the tag of "unreliable supplier."

The second reason for not making advance calculations is that, for large countries, the overall impact on the sender's economy may be regarded as trivial. In most of the cases we have examined, the cost to the target is less than 1 percent of its GNP. The costs borne by sender countries, as a percentage of their GNP levels, usually will be very much less, since they have much larger economies. From the lofty perspective of the White House or 10 Downing Street, the costs may seem entirely affordable.

However, the recent US grain embargo and pipeline sanctions focused attention on the very different perspective of individual firms. Sanctions are paid for by the industries whose trade is most deeply affected. By contrast, most other foreign and defense policies are financed out of general treasury revenues.

Under present procedures, sanctions amount to a discriminatory, sector specific tax to finance foreign policy—an approach that seems entirely unfair. In many instances, sanctions restrict the sale of goods that are available from competitors in foreign countries, or require the cancellation of existing contracts, or both. The impact of sanctions may fall most heavily on a few firms that suffer lost sales and damaged reputations. This sort of lopsided burden-sharing can quickly arouse political opposition to the goals of the sender government.

To avoid these pitfalls, the sender government needs to address the problems of foreign availability and contract sanctity when crafting a sanctions policy. Both issues are difficult.

Unlike national security export controls, whose success depends on the prohibition of access to controlled goods (a modern form of contraband), the success of foreign policy sanctions does not entirely depend on restricting access to goods from other countries. However, the availability of goods from other sources lessens the impact of the sanctions, raises the level of international cooperation required to implement the sanctions, and increases the domestic political costs of maintaining the controls. It is clearly preferable to impose sanctions on goods not readily obtainable in foreign markets.

The contract sanctity issue cuts in two directions. On the one hand, sanctions are more likely to be effective when they are imposed abruptly and with maximum force. This argues for canceling existing contracts in spite of inevitable domestic dissatisfaction. On the other hand, if existing contracts are honored, domestic costs will be reduced, but the initial impact on the target country will be lessened, providing time for the target country to adjust and to attract compensating foreign assistance.

No absolute answers can resolve this dilemma. However, broken contracts do impose significant costs to firms in the sender country. When contracts are broken, the sender country should compensate workers and firms for their losses.

It may be useful to illustrate our construction of the cost-to-sender index through a review of two cases.

UNITED STATES V. SOUTH KOREA (1973–77: HUMAN RIGHTS)

Sanctions generally impose small costs on domestic economic interests—and generate little or no domestic political opposition—when they involve the closing of the bilateral aid spigot. This is clearly illustrated by US actions in support of human rights in South Korea following President Park's declaration of martial law in 1972. The average US citizen did not feel the pinch from the substantial cutback in economic aid (mostly PL 480 food aid) and military aid to South Korea; indeed, the US budget "profited" from the reduced expenditures, although the reduction of a few hundred million dollars in aid transfers had little impact on the US budget deficits that were run up during this period.

From 1974–78, average US economic and military aid to South Korea declined by over $450 million from the average level of the period 1970–73. While the cutbacks in PL 480 and military aid led to some increased costs for the US (for example, in storage and other incidental expenses for grain), the short-run impact on the US budget was minimal (about 1 percent of the deficit) but favorable. In this case, the cost to the sender was negative—the United States was actually slightly better off, in economic terms, as a result of the sanctions. This result illustrates those cases that we accorded a cost to sender index number of 1.

UNITED STATES V. USSR (1980–81: AFGHANISTAN)

Much has been written about the economic impact of the grain embargo on the US farm sector. When the Carter administration imposed the embargo in January 1980, it estimated that US farm income would be reduced by $2.0 billion to $2.25 billion as a result of a cut of 17 million tons in grain shipped to the Soviet Union. Corresponding measures were introduced to soften the blow on the US farmer, entailing purchases for the grain reserve and increases in loan, release, and call prices. These measures added an additional $2 billion to $3 billion to the federal deficit during FY 1980 and 1981.[7] The purchases for the grain reserve, which sopped up about $2.4 billion in grain that would have been dumped on the market after the embargo was announced, ended up costing the US taxpayer (according to estimates of the General Accounting Office) over $600 million in direct budgetary expenditures, including costs incurred in the purchase, storage, and resale of the grain.

The extent to which the embargo imposed a welfare loss on the US farm sector as a whole is more problematical. The Congressional Research Service noted that it took nine months for wheat, corn, and soybean prices to recover from the shock of the onset of the embargo;[8] at the same time, farm income plummeted, although how much of the fall was due to the embargo and how much to other factors (for example, high interest rates) is hard to quantify. In any event, US farmers lost a significant share of the Soviet market. Even though the US share of the world market actually grew by 2 percent in the 1980–81 marketing year compared to pre-embargo levels,[9] these lost sales to the USSR probably imposed a welfare loss to US farmers through their effect on prices and stunted trade opportunities.

The grain embargo was accompanied by export controls on high technology products and superphosphoric acid, affecting close to $500 million in prospective US exports. Using the same methodology that we employed to calculate the cost to the target country, we estimate the welfare loss to US producers, after account is made for substitution and price effects, as about 30 percent of the value of trade affected by the sanctions. This translates into $150 million for superphosphoric acid and high technology products and at least $600 million for farm goods. In sum, the sanctions against the USSR—while difficult to quantify—did inflict significant costs on US economic interests. In GNP terms, the costs to the United States were negligible; yet the sanctions did result in substantial trade diversion—and important losses for specific sectors of the US economy. These losses in turn created political problems for the administration. We have not based our cost-to-sender index on costs as a percentage of GNP; instead we only consider whether there has been a modest or substantial level of trade diversion which might be expected to create, as it did in this case, domestic political opposition to the sanctions. By this standard, the Afghanistan case was given an index number of 3 to reflect the cost-to-sender.

---

[7] *Weekly Compilation of Presidential Documents*, 28 January 1980, pp. 105ff.

[8] Congressional Research Service, *An Assessment of the Afghanistan Sanctions: Implications for Trade and Diplomacy in the 1980s* (Washington: GPO, 1981), pp. 45–46.

[9] US Congress, Office of Technology Assessment, *Technology and East-West Trade: An Update* (Washington, 1983), p. 54.

In about 40 percent of the cases involving modest policy goals listed in table 4.1, the sender country enjoyed a net gain (usually quite small) as a result of withholding aid and official credits. The only episode in the modest policy goals category where significant trade diversion occurred, with consequent losses to the firms in the sender country, was the case involving US efforts to release hostages held by Iran.

The successful destabilization cases listed in table 4.2, except for the Rhodesian sanctions episode, generally cost the sender country rather little. The average cost index number for the successful cases was 1.5. By contrast, the average for failed cases was 2.1, and some of the episodes were rather expensive to the sender. US traders have long since adjusted to the Cuban embargo, but the initial measures entailed losses of some consequence for particular US industries. In the Libyan case, some US oil companies were placed in a disadvantaged position. Exxon, for one, settled for a payment substantially less than the book-value of its Libyan assets.

In the successful cases involving disruption of military adventures, listed in table 4.3, the average cost to the sender was an index of just 1.7. For disruption cases with failed outcomes, the cost index was 1.9. Here again, the figures suggest that failed episodes were generally more costly to the sender—a finding that will come as no surprise to the farmers affected by the Soviet grain embargo.

When countries resort to sanctions in order to impair the military potential of target countries, or to pursue other major policy changes, not only are they distinctly unsuccessful (short of all-out war) but they also invariably accept a significant economic burden. In the success cases, the costs to the sender were understandably great in the two world war cases and in the case of *Nigeria v. Biafra* (1967–70). On the other hand, India prevailed over Hyderabad at relatively little cost, while the Arabs clearly gained from their oil embargo. However, this sample is too small to yield clear trends. The average cost-to-sender index in the failed, impaired military potential cases was 3.0; the average cost-to-sender index in the failed, other major policy change cases was 2.3. While small in GNP terms, the annualized cost figures probably run in the hundreds of millions of dollars and those losses are usually concentrated on relatively few firms.

To summarize: higher failure rates are associated with greater costs borne by the sender country. On the one hand, failed cases may entail intrinsically tougher objectives and the sender government may be willing to expend greater effort in achieving its goals; on the other hand, as costs mount, pressures may arise within the sender country to abandon the attempt, thereby contributing to the failure of the episode.

The costs of economic sanctions are not confined to the economic realm. A failed episode can impose heavy political costs on the sender country, particularly if the episode attracts public attention. US sanctions against the USSR (1981–82) over the pipeline and Poland badly disturbed the NATO alliance. Earlier celebrated episodes in which failure exacted large political costs include *United Kingdom and League of Nations v. Italy* (1935–36) and *United States v. Japan* (1940–41).

Even when a sanctions episode succeeds, it can impose political costs on the sender country. Such instances would include the *United States v. United Kingdom and France* (1956), where American diplomacy in response to the Suez invasion left a bitter taste in Europe for many years; *United States v. Chile* (1970–73), which gave the United States a reputation of using the CIA to accomplish "dirty tricks"; and *Canada v. Japan and EC* (1977), where Canadian insistence on nuclear safeguards (prompted by the "peaceful" Indian nuclear explosion) irked Canada's trading partners and allies.

We have not attempted to systematically assess the political cost of each episode to the sender country. All diplomacy has its political costs. In political terms, some episodes are dear and others are cheap. The political costs of economic sanctions may be lower or higher than the political costs of achieving the same diplomatic ends by different means. We leave these matters to thorough exploration by other scholars.[10]

---

[10] David A. Baldwin, in *Economic Statecraft: Theory and Practice* (forthcoming), explores these questions.

Table 4.1 Modest changes in target country policies: economic variables

Case[a]	Sender and Target	Success score[b] (index)	Cost to target[c] (million dollars)	Cost as percentage of GNP[d]
33–1	UK v. USSR	12	4	negl.
38–1	US, UK v. Mexico	9	2	0.2
54–1	USSR v. Australia	1	50	0.5
56–2	US, UK, France v. Egypt	9	138	3.4
61–1	US v. Ceylon	16	8.7	0.6
62–3	USSR v. Romania	1	—	—
63–1	US v UAR	16	54	1.4
64–1	France v. Tunisia	9	12	1.5
65–1	US v. Chile	12	0.5	negl.
65–2	US v. India	16	41	negl.
68–1	US v. Peru	1	33	0.7
68–2	US v. Peru	12	35	0.7
73–2	US v. South Korea	4	333	1.8
73–3	US v. Chile	6	36	0.4
74–2	Canada v. India	4	33	negl.
74–3	Canada v. Pakistan	4	13	0.1
75–1	US, Canada v. South Korea	16	—	—
75–2	US v. USSR	4	112	negl.
75–3	US v. Eastern Europe	12	39	negl.
75–4	US v. South Africa	4	2	negl.
76–1	US v. Uruguay	6	10	0.3
76–2	US v. Taiwan	16	17	0.1
76–3	US v. Ethiopia	1	(160)	(5.5)
77–1	US v. Paraguay	6	2	0.1
77–2	US v. Guatemala	4	21	0.4
77–3	US v. Argentina	6	62	0.1
77–4	Canada v. Japan, EC	9	115	negl.
77–6	US v. El Salvador	6	13	0.5
77–7	US v. Brazil	9	94	0.1
78–1	China v. Albania	1	43	3.3
78–2	US v. Brazil	4	5	negl.

Negl. indicates very small; — indicates none, because sanctions did not go beyond threat stage.

a. The *case* refers to the identification system used in table 1.1.

b. The *success score* is an index on a scale of 1 to 16, found by multiplying the index of policy result by the index of sanctions contribution (see tables 3.1 through 3.5).

c. The *cost to target* is expressed in terms of millions of current US dollars, as estimated in the abstracts. Parentheses around a cost figure indicate a gain to the target country.

d. The *cost as percentage of GNP* refers to the cost of sanctions to the target country as a percentage of its GNP. Parentheses indicate a gain.

Cost per capita	Trade linkage[e] (percentage)	GNP ratio:[f] sender to target	Type of sanction[g]	Cost to sender[h] (index)
negl.	13	1	M	2
0.11	69	75	F,M	2
5.56	3	18	M	2
5.87	22	160	F,X	2
0.86	6	375	F	1
—	40	24	—	2
1.93	14	153	F	1
2.67	47	106	F,M	2
0.06	37	98	F,M	2
0.08	24	13	F	1
2.60	9	186	F	1
2.72	9	186	F	1
9.60	29	78	F	1
3.53	18	187	F	1
0.06	2	2	F,X	2
0.18	1	14	X	2
—	32	87	—	2
0.44	3	2	F,M	2
0.54	1	5	F,M	1
0.08	12	43	X	2
3.57	10	452	F,X	1
1.01	31	100	X	2
(5.67)	21	592	F,M	1
0.71	13	959	F	1
3.17	36	355	F	1
2.38	13	38	F,X	2
0.31	2	0.1	X	2
3.02	31	685	F	1
0.84	18	12	F	1
16.54	34	249	F,X,M	2
0.04	22	11	X	2

e. The *trade linkage* equals the average of presanction target country exports to the sender country (as a percentage of total target country exports) and imports from the sender country (as a percentage of total target country imports).

f. The *GNP ratio* refers to the ratio of the sender country GNP to the target country GNP.

g. The *type of sanction* refers to the interruption of commercial finance, aid and other official finance (F), the interruption of exports from the sender country to the target country (X), and the interruption of imports by the sender country from the target country (M).

h. The *cost to sender* is an index number scaled from 1 to 4. Key: (1) net gain to sender; (2) little effect on sender; (3) modest welfare loss to sender; (4) major loss to sender.

Table 4.1 Modest changes in target country policies: economic variables
(continued)

Case[a]	Sender and Target	Success score[b] (index)	Cost to target[c] (million dollars)	Cost as percentage of GNP[d]
78–3	US v. Argentina	4	0.2	negl.
78–4	US v. India	4	12	negl.
78–5	US v. USSR	1	51	negl.
79–1	US v. Iran	12	3,349	3.8
79–2	US v. Pakistan	4	34	0.2
79–3	Arab League v. Canada	12	7	negl.
79–4	US v. Bolivia	6	48	1.7
80–2	US v. Iraq	4	22	0.1
82–2	Netherlands, US v. Suriname	9	84	8.2
82–3	South Africa v. Lesotho	16	19	3.6
83–1	Australia v. France	2	negl.	negl.
83–2	US v. USSR	1	negl.	negl.
83–3	US v. Zimbabwe	4	31	0.5

Table 4.2 Destabilization of target governments: economic variables

Case[a]	Sender and target	Success score[b] (index)	Cost to target[c] (million dollars)
18–1	UK v. Russia	1	446
44–1	US v. Argentina	4	29
48–4	USSR v. Yugoslavia	1	(76)
51–1	UK, US v. Iran	12	186
56–4	US v. Laos	9	5
58–1	USSR v. Finland	16	45
60–1	US v. Dominican Republic	16	16
60–3	US v. Cuba	1	114
61–2	USSR v. Albania	1	3
62–1	US v. Brazil	12	110
63–3	US v. Indonesia	8	110
63–4	US v. South Vietnam	12	9
65–3	UK, UN v. Rhodesia	12	130
70–1	US v. Chile	12	163
72–1	UK, US v. Uganda	12	36
77–5	US v. Nicaragua	12	22
78–8	US v. Libya	4	151
81–1	US v. Nicaragua	4	(50)
83–4	US, OECS v. Grenada	8	negl.

a.–h. See table 4.1.

Cost per capita	Trade linkage[c] (percentage)	GNP ratio:[f] sender to target	Type of sanction[g]	Cost to sender[h] (index)
negl.	14	34	X	2
0.02	12	18	X	2
0.19	3	2	X	2
90.51	13	28	F,X,M	3
0.43	9	114	F	1
0.30	2	1	F,X,M	2
8.73	22	562	F	1
1.71	5	69	X	2
212.66	37	2,565	F	1
13.57	100	103	X,M	2
negl.	negl.	0.3	X	2
negl.	2	2	M	2
4.08	7	462	F	1

Cost as percentage of GNP[d]	Cost per capita	Trade linkage[c] (percentage)	GNP ratio:[f] sender to target	Type of sanction[g]	Cost to sender[h] (index)
4.1	2.49	18	1	F,X,M	3
0.8	1.82	19	58	F,X	2
(2.5)	(4.47)	13	52	F,X,M	1
14.3	11.14	41	235	F,X,M	1
4.2	2.08	2	4,372	F	1
1.1	10.23	19	58	F,X,M	2
1.9	5.52	56	596	F,X,M	2
4.4	16.76	46	173	F,X,M	3
0.6	1.76	50	494	F,X,M	2
0.6	1.49	48	30	F	1
2.0	1.05	24	145	F	1
0.3	0.59	20	206	F	1
13.0	28.89	68	1,388	F,X,M	3
1.5	17.16	16	102	F	1
2.6	3.44	22	860	F,X,M	2
1.0	9.48	26	913	F,X	1
0.8	55.93	20	118	X,M	3
(3.6)	(18.52)	34	1,727	F,M	2
negl.	negl.	1	32,900	F,X,M	2

Table 4.3 Disruption of military adventures (other than major wars): economic variables

Case[a]	Sender and target	Success score[b] (index)	Cost to target[c] (million dollars)	Cost as percentage of GNP[d]
21–1	League v. Yugoslavia	16	—	—
25–1	League v. Greece	16	—	—
32–1	League v. Paraguay, Bolivia	6	4	3.0
35–1	UK, League v. Italy	1	86	1.7
40–1	US v. Japan	1	88	0.9
48–1	US v. Netherlands	16	14	0.2
49–1	US, CHINCOM v. China	1	106	0.5
56–3	US v. UK, France	12	167	0.3
57–2	France v. Tunisia	1	7	0.9
60–3	US v. Cuba	1	114	4.4
63–1	US v. UAR	16	54	1.4
63–3	US v. Indonesia	8	110	2.0
71–1	US v. India, Pakistan	2	117	0.2
74–1	US v. Turkey	1	77	0.2
75–5	US v. Kampuchea	1	42	6.8
78–7	China v. Vietnam	1	254	3.5
80–1	US v. USSR (Afghanistan)	1	525	negl.
82–1	UK v. Argentina	12	960	0.6

a.–h. See table 4.1.

Table 4.4 Impairment of military potential (including major wars): economic variables

Case[a]	Sender and target	Success score[b] (index)	Cost to target[c] (million dollars)
14–1	UK v. Germany	12	843
39–1	Alliance Powers v. Germany, Japan	12	688
46–1	Arab League v. Israel	4	258
48–5	US, COCOM v. USSR, COMECON	4	556
49–1	US, CHINCOM v. China	1	106
50–1	US, UN v. North Korea	2	8
54–4	US, South Vietnam v. North Vietnam	1	109
60–2	USSR v. China	4	287
80–1	US v. USSR (Afghanistan)	1	525
81–3	US v. USSR (Poland)	1	480

a.–h. See table 4.1.

Cost per capita	Trade linkage[e] (percentage)	GNP ratio:[f] sender to target	Type of sanction[g]	Cost to sender[h] (index)
—	26	37	—	2
—	36	56	—	2
1.03	74	224	X	2
1.98	16	6	F,X,M	3
1.21	31	11	F,X	3
1.43	9	45	F	1
0.20	38	13	F,X,M	3
3.25	9	7	F	2
1.75	65	76	F	1
16.76	46	173	F,X,M	3
1.93	14	153	F	1
1.05	24	145	F	1
0.18	19	16	F,X	1
1.92	12	42	F	1
6.27	negl.	2,523	F,X,M	1
5.20	12	41	F	1
2.00	3	2	X	3
34.16	4	3	F,X,M	2

Cost as percentage of GNP[d]	Cost per capita	Trade linkage[e] (percentage)	GNP ratio:[f] sender to target	Type of sanction[g]	Cost to sender[h] (index)
7.1	12.58	9	1	F,X,M	4
1.6	5.00	15	2	F,X,M	4
4.1	123.00	2	2	F,X,M	4
0.1	1.86	23	3	X	3
0.5	0.20	38	13	F,X,M	3
1.2	0.83	20	378	F,X,M	2
2.6	3.34	1	358	F,X,M	2
0.5	0.42	46	4	F,X,M	4
negl.	2.00	3	2	X	3
negl.	1.79	2	2	X	3

Table 4.5 Other major changes in target country policies (including surrender of territory): economic variables

Case[a]	Sender and target	Success score[b] (index)	Cost to target[c] (million dollars)
17–1	US v. Japan	4	23
48–2	India v. Hyderabad	12	18
48–3	USSR v. US, UK, France	1	258
54–2	India v. Portugal	8	negl.
54–3	Spain v. UK	6	5
56–1	US v. Israel (intermittent episodes)	2	16
57–1	Indonesia v. Netherlands	8	69
61–3	Western Allies v. GDR	1	—
62–2	UN v. South Africa	1	273
63–2	Indonesia v. Malaysia	1	29
63–5	UN, OAU v. Portugal	8	11
65–4	US v. Arab League	6	8
67–1	Nigeria v. Biafra	12	220
73–1	Arab League v. US, Netherlands	9	5,697
78–6	Arab League v. Egypt	1	(77)
81–2	US v. Poland	6	246
81–4	EC v. Turkey	6	300

a.–h. See table 4.1.

Cost as percentage of GNP[d]	Cost per capita	Trade linkage[e] (percentage)	GNP ratio:[f] sender to target	Type of sanction[g]	Cost to sender[h] (index)
0.8	0.44	20	13	X	2
2.0	1.10	99	22	F,X	2
0.1	1.05	1	0.4	X,M	3
negl.	negl.	negl.	13	F,X,M	2
negl.	0.10	1	0.2	X,M	2
0.1	4.13	22	217	F,X	2
0.7	6.27	2	0.2	F,X,M	2
—	—	12	40	—	2
2.8	15.08	77	130	F,X	3
1.0	3.14	6	2	X,M	4
0.3	1.25	14	10	F,X,M	2
negl.	0.06	9	31	F,X	2
15.2	14.67	50	3	F,X,M	3
0.4	25.55	2	0.04	X	1
(0.4)	(1.88)	4	16	F,X,M	3
0.1	6.83	4	17	F,X,M	2
0.5	6.47	34	40	F	1

5

Conclusions

A number of lessons can be abstracted from the sanctions episodes of the past seventy years. In this concluding chapter, we first assess the overall effectiveness of sanctions, based on the experience of 103 cases. We then group the lessons learned into a list of propositions—nine commandments—to guide governments in the use of economic sanctions.

First a word of caution. Forecasting the outcome of statecraft, like forecasting the stock market, is hazardous business. Idiosyncratic influences are often at play. Human personalities and plain luck may well determine the outcome of a sanctions episode. These simple truths are underscored by appendix A, which presents our multiple regression analysis. In this analysis, success scores were related to the variables catalogued in Chapters 3 and 4. As one might expect from a diverse collection of 103 cases, the statistical results are not always clearcut. Much depends on the personalities of national leaders, the kaleidoscope of contemporaneous world events, and other factors which are not captured by our variables. Hence our summary assessments and nine commandments must be read as general indicators, not infallible guideposts, in the fine art of statecraft.

Are Sanctions Effective?

Policymakers need to take a close look at the cost and effectiveness of sanctions when designing foreign policy strategy. In most cases, sanctions do not contribute very much to the achievement of foreign policy goals; however, in some instances—particularly situations involving small target countries and modest policy goals—sanctions have helped alter foreign behavior. Table 5.1 summarizes the score card. By our standards, success cases are those with a success score of 9 or higher; failure cases are those with a score of 8 or lower. We must emphasize that a score of 9 does not mean that economic sanctions achieved a foreign policy triumph. A score of 9 merely means that sanctions made a

Table 5.1 Success by type of policy goal

Policy goal	Success cases	Failure cases	Success ratio (percentage of total)
Modest policy changes	18	26	41
Destabilization	10	9	53
Disruption of military adventures	6	12	33
Military impairment	2	8	20
Other major policy changes	3	14	18
Totals[a]	39	69	36

a. The figures include five instances of cases included under two different policy goals: 49–1: US v. China; 60–3: US v. Cuba; 63–1: US v. UAR; 63–3: US v. Indonesia; and 80–1: US v. USSR (Afghanistan). Since these cases are generally failures, double counting them adds a small negative bias to the success ratio.

modest contribution to a goal that was partly realized (often at some political cost to the sender country).

Perhaps surprisingly, sanctions have been "successful"—by our definition—in 36 percent of the cases overall. However, the success rate importantly depends on the type of goal sought. Episodes involving destabilization succeed in half the cases, (usually against target countries that are small and shaky), while modest goals are attained in just over 40 percent of the cases. But attempts to disrupt military adventures, to impair a foreign adversary's military potential, or otherwise to change its policies in a major way, generally fail. Our multiple regression analysis indicates that, all other things equal, the success scores on average were 1.0 index points higher for destabilization and modest goal cases than for other categories.[1]

Success has proven more elusive in recent years than in earlier decades. This point is made in table 5.2. Taking the pre-1973 period as a whole, not quite half of the episodes succeeded. In the period 1973–84, the success rate was just over a quarter. The difference seems to reflect much poorer results in episodes entailing modest policy goals. While the number of these episodes ballooned, the success rate dropped markedly between the two periods, from 75 percent to 28 percent. The impression conveyed by table 5.2 is confirmed by our multiple regression analysis. The time trend is negative: with all other things equal, an episode launched in 1984 would, on average, have a success score 0.05 index points lower than the same episode launched just a year

---

[1] In this analysis, the two world wars were assigned to a separate category.

Table 5.2 Success by period

Policy goal	Pre-1973		1973–84	
	Success cases	Failure cases	Success cases	Failure cases
Modest policy changes	9	3	9	23
Destabilization	9	6	1	3
Disruption of military adventures	5	8	1	4
Military impairment	2	6	0	2
Other major policy changes	2	11	1	3
Totals	27	34	12	35

earlier. Put another way, over a 20-year period, the representative success score dropped by 1.0 index points ($0.05 \times 20 = 1.0$).

With the frequent use of economic sanctions (particularly by the US) to achieve modest goals, target countries may have become more immune to their impact. This immunity may derive from two factors: first, latter-day target countries are less dependent on trade with sender countries; and second, more nations are willing and able to play Sir Galahad to target countries. Ties between target and sender countries have become more remote: the average trade linkage fell from 26 percent to 15 percent in recent cases compared to the pre-1973 period. Many of the failures in recent years are connected with the widespread use of sanctions by the United States in support of human rights and nuclear nonproliferation campaigns against countries as remote as Pakistan and Argentina. Moreover, the growth in global economic interdependence and the East–West confrontation have made it easier for target countries to find alternate suppliers, markets, and financial backers to replace goods embargoed or funds withheld by the sender country. For these reasons, we conclude that sanctions are a decreasingly useful policy instrument.

Nine Commandments

From the summary in table 5.1, it is clear that sanctions occasionally bear fruit, but only when planted in the right soil and nurtured in the proper way. Nine propositions are offered for the statesman who would act as a careful gardener.

I. "DON'T BITE OFF MORE THAN YOU CAN CHEW."

Sanctions cannot move mountains nor can they force strong target countries into making fundamental changes. Countries often have inflated expectations of what sanctions can accomplish. This is especially true of the US today and the UK in an earlier era. At most, there is a weak correlation between economic deprivation and political willingness to change. The *economic* impact of sanctions may be pronounced, both on the sender and the target country, but other factors in the situational context almost always overshadow the impact of sanctions in determining the *political* outcome.

Sanctions are seldom effective in impairing the military potential of an important power, or in bringing major changes in domestic policies of the target country. In cases involving these "high" policy goals,[2] success was achieved in only 5 of the 27 cases, or only 19 percent of the time. Excluding the two world wars and the two civil wars, we have found only one case (*Arab League v. US and Netherlands*) where economic coercion was effective in changing major domestic policies. In this case, the Arab oil embargo helped accomplish two of its four objectives: it caused a significant shift, namely a more pro-Arab slant, in European and Japanese policies toward the Palestinian question; and it supported OPEC's decision to boost the world price of oil to OPEC's enormous economic benefit. But the embargo failed to get Israel to retreat behind its pre-1967 frontiers, and it failed to persuade the US to abandon its pro-Israel policy stance. The sanctions were an important factor in the attainment of results that, on balance, must be deemed at least marginally successful from the Arab viewpoint. In the other cases where impairment was sought and attempts were made to change major policies of target countries—ranging from the lifting of martial law in Poland to the ending of apartheid in South Africa—sanctions were ineffective.

To justify even a remote hope for success in military impairment and major change cases, sender countries would have to form a near monopoly over trading relations with the target country. This obvious precept, learned in the first and second world wars, was forgotten in the case of UN sanctions against South Africa and turned on its head in the recent case of US sanctions to block construction of the Soviet-European gas pipeline.

II. "THE WEAKEST GO TO THE WALL."

"Summing up all cases in the five groups, there seems to be a direct correlation between the political and economic health of the target country and its susceptibility to economic pressure. Our multiple regression analysis indicates that sanctions imposed on a "strong and stable" country on average are characterized by a success score that is 2.8 index points lower than sanctions imposed on a "distressed" country.

---

[2] We use the term "high" policy goals to refer only to military impairment and major policy change episodes. Some authors have used the same phrase to refer to destabilization and disruption of military adventure cases as well.

Table 5.3 Success, health and stability

	Average health and stability index	
Policy goal	Success cases	Failure cases
Modest policy changes	2.2	2.3
Destabilization	1.3	1.9
Disruption of military adventures	2.0	2.3
Military impairment	3.0	2.7
Other major policy changes	2.0	2.6
Totals	2.0	2.3

Table 5.3 clearly demonstrates that countries in distress or experiencing significant problems are far more likely to succumb to the policy objectives of the sender country. When specific goals are at issue, the health and stability of the target country is usually an important determinant in the success of the episode. This feature is most pronounced in destabilization cases, where successes generally came against weak regimes. The health and stability index was also lower in success cases than in failure cases when disruption of military adventures and other major policy changes were at stake. In cases involving modest policy goals and impairment of military potential, the health and stability of the target country seem to be less of a factor in determining success.

In the great majority of cases we have documented, the target country has been much smaller than the sender country. Thus, while sanctions typically involve only a small proportion of the trade or financial flows of the sender country, they can significantly affect the external accounts of the target country. The importance of size is illustrated by table 5.4. In cases involving modest goals, the sender's economy is on average more than 150 times larger than the target's economy, and in cases involving destabilization, the ratio exceeds 400.

For the disruption of military adventure, military impairment and other major policy change cases, the figures in table 5.4 indicate less of a size differential between sender and target. However, there is still a significant mismatch in economic clout: in 78 percent of the disruption of military adventure cases, in 30 percent of the military impairment cases and in 59 percent of the other major change cases, the sender country's GNP was over 10 times the size of the target country's GNP.

Our results indicate that the cases involving policy goals that exhibit the highest success scores (modest goals and destabilization) are also those that have the highest average GNP ratio. Surprisingly, our multiple regression results suggest that, when all other things are equal, cases that involve a low GNP ratio (10 and under) exhibit success scores that, on average, are 1.8 index

Table 5.4 The importance of size

Policy goal	Average GNP ratio: sender to target	Percentage of cases where the GNP ratio is:					
		0 to 10		11 to 100		101 and over	
		success	failure	success	failure	success	failure
Modest policy changes	155[a]	9	11	18	20	16	25
Destabilization	421[a]	0	5	11	11	42	32
Disruption of military adventures	62[a]	11	11	17	33	6	22
Military impairment	77	20	50	0	10	0	20
Other major policy changes	33	12	29	6	41	0	12
Totals	156[a]	9	17	13	23	15	23

a. The averages exclude four cases where the GNP ratio is over 2,000 (56–4: US v. Laos; 75–5: US v. Kampuchea; 82–2: Netherlands and US v. Suriname; and 83–4: US and OECS v. Grenada) because their inclusion would bias the results.

points higher than cases where the GNP ratio is over 100. Evidently, size alone is not the key factor. The relative size of the target economy is less important than other factors that come into play, such as trade linkage, the economic impact of the sanctions, and the warmth of relations between sender and target countries prior to the imposition of sanctions.

III. "ATTACK YOUR ALLIES, NOT YOUR ADVERSARIES."

Economic sanctions seem most effective when aimed against erstwhile friends and close trading partners. By contrast, sanctions directed against target countries that have long been adversaries of the sender country, or against targets that have little trade with the sender country, are generally less successful. These results are illustrated by table 5.5.

The higher compliance with sanctions by allies and trading partners reflects their willingness to bend on specific issues in deference to an overall relationship with the sender country. Such considerations may not be decisive in the calculus of an antagonistic target country, or a target country that has little economic contact with the sender. Sanctions may succeed more often against friends than foes, but a word of caution must be inserted: the preservation of political

Table 5.5   Success, prior relations, and trade linkage

Policy goal	Prior relations index		Average trade linkage (percentage of total trade)	
	Success cases	Failure cases	Success cases	Failure cases
Modest policy changes	2.3	2.0	27	14
Destabilization	2.7	2.1	32	25
Disruption of military adventures	2.3	2.1	16	28
Military impairment	1.0	1.2	12	17
Other major policy changes	2.7	2.1	50	15
Totals	2.4	2.0	27	19

alliances and economic ties should be equally important to prospective senders as to intended targets.

The warmth of pre-episode relations between sender and target countries is measured by an index scaled from 1 (antagonistic) to 3 (cordial). Table 5.5 indicates that, for most groups of sanctions, pre-episode relations were warmer in success cases than in failure cases. This result is confirmed by our multiple regression analysis, which suggests that a prior cordial relation between sender and target adds 2.5 index points to the predicted success score, by comparison with a prior antagonistic relation.

Likewise, the trade linkage data suggest that success is more often achieved when the target country conducts a large portion of its trade with the sender. Trade linkage is measured as the average of: (1) the target country's imports from the sender as a percentage of its total imports; and (2) the target country's exports to the sender as a percentage of its total exports. In most episodes involving modest policy goals or destabilization attempts, the trade linkage exceeds 20 percent; further, the trade linkage in success cases is generally higher than in failure cases. Cases involving disruption of military adventures also have trade linkages at the 20 percent level; in this category, failed cases exhibit a somewhat higher trade linkage than successes.

In the military impairment cases, the trade linkage is usually less than 20 percent. Although the trade linkage is perversely higher in failed cases, the distinction between successful cases and failures is not significant—the only successes in this category are sanctions applied during the two world wars. Similarly, in cases involving other major policy changes, the trade linkage is usually low, though in the three successful episodes the average trade linkage was high. Taking all categories together, success cases exhibit higher trade linkage (28 percent) than failure cases (19 percent).

Our multiple regression analysis confirms that trade linkage affects the chances of success. Twenty additional percentage points of trade linkage translate, on average, into an additional 0.6 index points in the success score.

IV. "IF IT WERE DONE, WHEN 'TIS DONE, THEN 'TWERE WELL IT WERE DONE QUICKLY."

A heavy, slow hand invites both evasion and the mobilization of domestic opinion in the target country. Sanctions imposed slowly or incrementally may simply strengthen the target government at home as it mobilizes the forces of nationalism. Moreover, such measures are likely to be undercut over time either by the sender's own firms or by foreign competitors. Sanctions generally are regarded as a short-term policy, with the anticipation that normal commercial relations will be reestablished after the resolution of the crisis. This explains why, even though popular opinion in the sender country may welcome the introduction of sanctions, public support for sanctions often dissipates over time.

The cases we have documented show a clear association, summarized in table 5.6, between the duration of sanctions and the waning prospects of success. It is not the passage of time alone that undermines economic sanctions. Indeed our multiple regression analysis indicates that, when all other things are equal, the length of a sanctions episode has no significant bearing on the outcome. The reason is that other factors are correlated with the length of an episode. Episodes between erstwhile allies are generally short, to the point, and often successful. Further, the target country is more likely to receive assistance from another major power if the episode continues for a number of years. Finally, the greater the latent likelihood of success, the shorter the sanctions period necessary to achieve results.

In any event, the inverse relationship between success and sanctions period argues against a strategy of "turning the screws" on a target country, slowly applying more and more economic pressure over time until the target succumbs. Time affords the target the opportunity to adjust—to find alternative suppliers, to build new alliances, and to mobilize domestic opinion in support of its policies.

V. "IN FOR A PENNY, IN FOR A POUND."

Cases that inflict heavy costs on the target country are generally successful. As shown in table 5.7, the average cost for all success cases was over 2 percent of GNP; by contrast, failed episodes barely dented the economy of the target country, averaging well under 1 percent of GNP. Both averages reflect the heavy costs imposed in destabilization cases which counterbalance the generally minor impact of sanctions in cases involving modest policy changes. Our

Table 5.6 Success and length of sanctions

Policy goal	Length of episode (in years)	
	Success cases	Failure cases[a]
Modest policy changes	2.9	3.9
Destabilization	4.0	5.9
Disruption of military adventures	1.2	3.2
Military impairment	5.0	21.4
Other major policy changes	1.7	8.1
Totals	2.9	6.9

a. The periods for the failure cases are biased on the low side because several cases are still ongoing.

multiple regression analysis indicates that, when a cost of 4 percent of GNP is imposed on the target country, the associated success score is 0.7 index points higher than when the cost imposed is zero.

The seeming perverse result in cases involving disruption of military adventures, where the average costs of failed cases are much higher than for successes, reflects the experience of the early League of Nations sanctions against Yugoslavia and Greece. In these two episodes, the *threat* of sanctions succeeded in forcing the invading armies to withdraw, and therefore no costs were imposed on the target country.

Table 5.7 Success and costs to the target

Policy goal	Costs as percentage of GNP	
	Success cases	Failure cases
Modest policy changes	1.3	0.1[a]
Destabilization	4.0	1.7[a]
Disruption of military adventures	0.4	2.0
Military impairment	4.3	1.1
Other major policy changes	5.9	0.4
Totals	2.3	0.7[a]

a. In some cases, there is a net gain to the target country, resulting from offsetting trade or aid flows. A large offset in the US v. Ethiopia case accounts for the low average cost for modest policy changes, which otherwise would be 0.4 percent. Similarly, offsets in USSR v. Yugoslavia and US v. Nicaragua deflate the destabilization average from 1.8 percent to 1.7 percent. As a result of offsets, the average cost for all failed outcomes drops from 1.0 percent to 0.7 percent of GNP.

Table 5.8 The price of success

| | Cost to sender index | |
Policy goal	Success cases	Failure cases
Modest policy changes	1.7	1.6
Destabilization	1.5	2.1
Disruption of military adventures	1.7	1.9
Military impairment	4.0	3.0
Other major policy changes	2.0	2.3
Totals	1.8	2.0

A conclusion can be drawn from these findings: if sanctions can be imposed in a comprehensive manner, the chances of success improve. Sanctions that bite are sanctions that work. A corollary to this conclusion is equally important: sanctions that attract offsetting support from a major power may cost the target country very little and are less likely to succeed.

VI. "IT YOU NEED TO ASK THE PRICE, YOU CAN'T AFFORD THE YACHT."

The more it costs a sender country to impose sanctions, the less likely it is that the sanctions will succeed. This conclusion finds support in table 5.8: the cost to sender index is generally lower in success cases than failure cases. Our multiple regression analysis indicates that an episode that entails a "net gain to sender" is associated with a success score 1.9 index points higher than an episode that entails a "modest welfare loss" to the sender country.

The costs imposed on domestic firms in the sender country are generally higher in cases that fail than those that succeed. The exceptions arise in the case of the two world wars. In most other instances, the cost to the sender country in successful episodes is insignificant, and often the short-term result is a net gain.

The basic conclusion from table 5.8 and the regression analysis is clear: a country should shy away from deploying sanctions when the economic costs to itself are high. Countries that shoot themselves in the foot may not mortally wound their intended targets. Although we did not attempt to measure the political costs of sanctions episodes to sender country, we believe this conclusion would apply with equal force to episodes that entail high political costs.

The results suggest that sender governments should design sanctions so as not to impose unduly concentrated costs on particular domestic groups. One example of actions to avoid is the retroactive application of sanctions to cancel existing contracts. Such actions not only leave the affected firms "high and dry" with unsold inventories and excess capacity, but they also sour chances

Table 5.9   Success and companion policies

Policy goal	Incidence of companion policies (percentage of cases)	
	Success cases	Failure cases
Modest policy changes	22	0
Destabilization	70	78
Disruption of military adventures	17	50
Military impairment	100	75
Other major policy changes	67	36
Totals	41	35

of competing for future business. If the sender government believes that retroactive application is essential to the success of an episode, then it might do well to compensate affected domestic firms.

Sanctions episodes that are least costly to the sender are often those that make use of financial leverage—manipulating aid flows, denying official credits, or, at the extreme, freezing assets—rather than trade controls. The multiple regression analysis suggests that financial controls are marginally more successful than export controls, but that import controls are the most successful of all types.

VII. "MORE IS LESS."

Economic sanctions are often deployed in conjunction with other measures directed against the target: covert action, quasi-military measures, or regular military operations. As shown in table 5.9, these companion measures are used most frequently in episodes involving destabilization and impairment of military potential. By contrast, companion policies are seldom used in cases involving modest policy changes, and are used in less than half the disruption and major policy change cases. On balance, there is little evidence that covert and military actions, when used in parallel with economic sanctions, tip the scales in favor of success. Indeed, our multiple regression coefficients, while statistically insignificant, suggest that the presence of covert action or military force are associated with marginally lower success scores.

VIII. "TOO MANY COOKS SPOIL THE BROTH."

The greater the number of countries needed to implement the denial measures, the less likely sanctions will be effective. Contrary to conventional wisdom, multilateral sanctions are not frequently associated with success.

Table 5.10 Success and international cooperation

Policy goal	International cooperation index	
	Success cases	Failure cases
Modest policy changes	1.4	1.6
Destabilization	1.8	2.6
Disruption of military adventures	2.3	2.2
Military impairment	4.0	3.0
Other major policy changes	1.7	1.9
Totals	1.8	2.0

In a sense, the importance of international cooperation is over-played. Basically, a country looks to its allies for help because its goals are ambitious; in cases involving more modest goals, such cooperation is not needed. These conclusions are borne out in table 5.10. On average, the degree of international cooperation is somewhat *less* in success cases than in failed cases.

Without significant cooperation from its allies, a sender country stands little chance of achieving success in cases involving "high" policy goals. However, international cooperation does not guarantee success even in these cases, as evidenced from the long history of the US and COCOM strategic controls against the USSR and COMECON, and the Arab League's futile boycott of Israel.

In successful episodes involving the first three types of policy goals, the index of international cooperation was generally lower than in failed episodes. When a sender country thought it necessary to seek and obtain cooperation from other countries, it was probably pursuing a sufficiently difficult objective that the prospects for ultimate success were not bright. Indeed, our multiple regression coefficients indicate that "significant" international cooperation is associated with a success score 0.5 index points lower than "no" cooperation.

To be sure, international cooperation serves three useful functions: it increases the moral suasion of the sanction; it helps isolate the target country from the global community; and it preempts foreign backlash, thus minimizing corrosive friction within the alliance. These observations, together with our statistical analysis, suggest that forced international "cooperation" brought about by the heavy hand of extraterritorial controls will seldom yield desirable results. Sanctions should be either deployed unilaterally—because the impact on one's allies is slight—or they should be designed in cooperation with one's allies in order to reduce backlash and evasion.

This last point is significant. Too many cooks *opposing* sanctions can also spoil the sender's broth. Adversaries of the sender country may be prompted by a sanctions episode to assist the target nation. Such opposition frequently occurs

Table 5.11 Success and international assistance to the target country

| | Incidence of international assistance (percentage of cases) | |
Policy goal	Success cases	Failure cases
Modest policy changes	11	15
Destabilization	10	44
Disruption of military adventures	0	42
Military impairment	100	62
Other major policy changes	33	29
Totals	15	32

in episodes which provoke East–West rivalry. Assistance extended by a major power not only offsets the economic cost inflicted on the target country; it also bolsters the target government's standing at home and abroad.

Table 5.11 indicates that external assistance to the target country erodes the chances of success, particularly in cases where the policy goal is destabilization of the target government or disruption of a military adventure. Our multiple regression analysis confirms the general result: the presence of international assistance reduces the predicted success score by 3.0 index points.

IX. "LOOK BEFORE YOU LEAP."

The sender government should think through its means and objectives *before* taking a final decision to deploy sanctions. Leaders in the sender country should be confident that their goals are within their grasp, that they can impose sufficient economic pain to command the attention of the target country, that their efforts will not simply prompt offsetting policies by other major powers, and that the sanctions chosen will not impose insupportable costs on their domestic constituents and foreign allies. These conditions will arise on only infrequent occasions, and even then the odds of success are not great. The prudent leader will weigh carefully the costs and benefits of economic sanctions before resorting to their use in foreign policy ventures.

Do's and Don'ts

Bearing in mind that economic sanctions are often an unsuitable tool of diplomacy, here is our short list of "do's and don'ts" for the architects of a sanctions policy:

(1) Don't bite off more than you can chew.

(2) Do pick on the weak and helpless.

(3) Do pick on allies and trading partners; but remember, good friends are hard to come by and even harder to lose.

(4) Do impose the maximum cost on your target.

(5) Do apply sanctions decisively and with resolution.

(6) Don't pay too high a price for sanctions.

(7) Don't suppose that, where sanctions will fail, covert maneuvers or military action will necessarily succeed.

(8) Don't exaggerate the importance of international cooperation with your policies and don't underestimate the role of international assistance to your target.

(9) Do plan carefully: economic sanctions may worsen a bad situation.

"FOREWARNED IS FOREARMED."

General Bibliography

Note: This bibliography lists only general reference works. A detailed bibliography accompanies the abstract of each episode.

Abbott, Kenneth W. 1981. "Linking Trade to Political Goals: Foreign Policy Export Controls in the 1970s and 1980s." 65 *Minnesota Law Review.*

Adler-Karlsson, Gunnar. 1968. *Western Economic Warfare, 1947–1967: A Case Study in Foreign Economic Policy.* Stockholm: Almqvist and Wiksell.

Alting von Geusau, Frans A. M., and Jacques Pelkmans. 1982. *National Economic Security: Perceptions, Threats and Policies.* Tilburg, The Netherlands: John F. Kennedy Institute.

Ayubi, Shaheen, Richard E. Bissell, Nana Amu-Brafih Korsah, and Laurie A. Lerner. 1982. *Economic Sanctions in U.S. Foreign Policy.* Philadelphia Policy Papers. Philadelphia: Foreign Policy Research Institute.

Baer, George W. 1967. *The Coming of the Italo-Ethiopian War.* Cambridge, Mass.: Harvard University Press.

Baldwin, David A. 1971. "The Power of Positive Sanctions." 24 *World Politics* (October).

———. 1984. "Economic Sanctions as Instruments of Foreign Policy." Atlanta: International Studies Association, March.

———. Forthcoming. *Economic Statecraft: Theory and Practice.* Dartmouth College.

Ball, George W. 1968. *The Discipline of Power: Essentials of a Modern World Structure.* Boston: Little, Brown & Co.

Barber, James. 1979. "Economic Sanctions as a Policy Instrument." 55 *International Affairs.*

Bayard, Thomas O., Joseph Pelzman, and Jorge Perez-Lopez. 1983. "Stakes and Risks in Economic Sanctions." 6 *The World Economy* (March).

Bienen, Henry, and Robert Gilpin. 1979. "Evaluation of the Use of Economic Sanctions to Promote Foreign Policy Objectives." Boeing Corp., unpublished, 2 April.

Blechman, Barry M., and Stephen S. Kaplan. 1978. *Force without War: U.S. Armed Forces as a Political Instrument.* Washington: Brookings Institution.

Brown-John, C. Lloyd. 1975. *Multilateral Sanctions in International Law: A Comparative Analysis.* New York: Praeger.

"Conference on Extraterritoriality for the Businessman and the Practicing Lawyer." 1983. 15 *Law and Policy in International Business.*

Daoudi, M. S., and M. S. Dajani. 1983. *Economic Sanctions: Ideals and Experience.* London: Routledge and Kegan Paul.

DeKieffer, Donald E., ed. 1983. "Incentives: Economic and Social." 15 *Case Western Reserve Journal of International Law* (Spring).

Doxey, Margaret P. 1980. *Economic Sanctions and International Enforcement.* 2d ed. New York: Oxford University Press for Royal Institute of International Affairs.

———. 1983. "International Sanctions in Theory and Practice." 15 *Case Western Reserve Journal of International Law* (Spring).

———. 1983. "International Sanctions: Trials of Strength or Tests of Weakness." 12 *Millenium* (May).

Export Controls: Reconciling National Objectives. 1984. Selected presentations from academy industry program seminar, Washington, 14 February. Washington: National Academies of Science and Engineering.

Finney, Lynne Dratler. 1983. "Development Assistance—A Tool of Foreign Policy." 15 *Case Western Reserve Journal of International Law* (Spring).

Freedman, Robert Owen. 1970. *Economic Warfare in the Communist Bloc: A Study of Soviet*

Economic Pressure Against Yugoslavia, Albania, and Communist China. New York: Praeger.

Galtung, Johan. 1967. "On the Effects of International Economic Sanctions: With Examples from the Case of Rhodesia." 19 *World Politics* (April).

Guichard, Louis. 1930. *The Naval Blockade: 1914–1918.* New York: D. Appleton & Company.

Highley, Albert E. July 1938. *The First Sanctions Experiment: A Study of League Procedures.* Geneva: Geneva Research Centre.

Hirschman, Albert O. 1945. *National Power and the Structure of Foreign Trade.* Berkeley: University of California Press.

International Institute for Strategic Studies. 1982. *Strategic Survey 1982–83.* London.

Jack, D. T. 1941. *Studies in Economic Warfare.* New York: Chemical Publishing Company.

Knorr, Klaus. 1977. "International Economic Leverage and Its Uses." In *Economic Issues and National Security,* ed. Klaus Knorr and Frank Traeger. Lawrence, Kan.: Regents Press.

———. 1975. *The Power of Nations: The Political Economy of International Relations.* New York: Basic Books.

Leyton-Brown, David, ed. 1985. *The Utility of Economic Sanctions.* London: Croom Helm. Forthcoming.

Lillich, Richard B. 1975. "Economic Coercion and the International Legal Order." 51 *International Affairs* (July).

Losman, Donald L. 1979. *International Economic Sanctions: The Cases of Cuba, Israel, and Rhodesia.* Albuquerque: University of New Mexico Press.

Marcuss, Stanley J., and D. Stephen Mathias. 1984. "U.S. Foreign Policy Export Controls: Do They Pass Muster Under International Law?" 2 *International Tax and Business Lawyer* (Winter).

Marcuss, Stanley J., and Eric L. Richard. 1981. "Extraterritorial Jurisdiction in United States Trade Law: the Need for a Consistent Theory." 20 *Columbia Journal of Transnational Law.*

Medlicott, W. N. 1952. *The Economic Blockade.* 2 vols. London: Longmans, Green.

Mitrany, D. 1925. *The Problem of International Sanctions.* London: Oxford University Press.

Moyer, Homer E., Jr., and Linda A. Mabry. 1983. "Export Controls as Instruments of Foreign Policy: The History, Legal Issues, and Policy Lessons of Three Recent Cases." 15 *Law and Policy in International Business* 1–171.

Nincic, Miroslav, and Peter Wallensteen, eds. 1983. *Dilemmas of Economic Coercion: Sanctions in World Politics.* New York: Praeger.

Olson, Richard Stuart. 1979. "Economic Coercion in World Politics: With a Focus on North-South Relations." 31 *World Politics* (July).

Perlow, Gary H. 1983. "Taking Peacetime Trade Sanctions to the Limit." 15 *Case Western Reserve Journal of International Law* (Spring).

Renwick, Robin. 1981. *Economic Sanctions.* Harvard Studies in International Affairs No. 45. Cambridge, Mass.: Harvard University Center for International Affairs.

Rosenthal, Douglas E., and William M. Knighton. 1983. *National Laws and International Commerce: The Problem of Extraterritoriality.* Chatham House Papers, no. 17. London: Routledge & Kegan Paul for the Royal Institute of International Affairs.

Schreiber, Anna P. 1973. "Economic Coercion as an Instrument of Foreign Policy: U.S. Economic Measures Against Cuba and the Dominican Republic." 25 *World Politics* (April):387–413.

Shultz, George P. Speech delivered 14 October 1978. Reprinted in *Washington Post,* 29 August 1982.

US Congress. Office of Technology Assessment. 1983. *Technology and East-West Trade: An Update.*

US General Accounting Office. 1983. *Administration Knowledge of Economic Costs of Foreign Policy Export Controls*. Report to Senator Charles H. Percy. Washington.

Wallensteen, Peter. 1968. "Characteristics of Economic Sanctions." *5 Journal of Peace Research* 248–67.

Walters, Francis P. 1952. *A History of the League of Nations*. 2 vols. London: Oxford University Press.

Weintraub, Sidney, ed. 1982. *Economic Coercion and U.S. Foreign Policy: Implications of Case Studies from the Johnson Administration*. Boulder, Colo.: Westview Press.

Wu, Yuan-Li. 1952. *Economic Warfare*. New York: Prentice Hall.

Appendices

A Statistical Analysis of the Effectiveness of Sanctions

Multiple regression analysis was used to explain success scores in terms of the various explanatory variables set forth in chapters 3 and 4.[1] The corrected R-squared value of the multiple regression equation was only 0.210. This means that some 21 percent of the variance in success scores can be explained by the factors we have measured. While the multiple regression equation is significant at the 1 percent confidence level, it obviously leaves a great deal of unexplained variance. Nevertheless, the regression results serve to indicate the influence of selected variables whose T-statistics are significant (i.e., greater than one).

Our preferred equation, chosen after experimentation, appears below. T-statistics appear in parentheses below the coefficients.

Index of success (scaled from 1 to 16) =

$+12.231$
(3.222)

$-0.054 \times$ (time trend, represented by the last two digits of the year
(-1.596) in which the episode began)

$+1.044 \times$ (dummy variable that takes the value one if the episode
(0.938) involves a modest policy change or destabilization; otherwise zero)

$+10.262 \times$ (dummy variable that takes the value one for World War
(2.596) I and World War II; otherwise zero)

---

[1] On February 4, 1985, Spain lifted its blockade of Gibraltar; in return, Britain agreed to discuss Spain's claim to sovereignty. In light of that development we raised the success score from 1 to 6, 2 on policy result, and 3 for sanctions contribution. This change is not reflected here; however, any resultant change in the statistical analysis would be insignificant. See Case 54-3 *Spain v. United Kingdom* (1954–84).

-0.459 × (dummy variable that takes the value one if covert action
(-0.317) is employed in the episode; otherwise zero)

-0.388 × (dummy variable that takes the value one if quasi-
(-0.333) military force or regular military force is employed in
    the episode; otherwise zero)

-0.168 × (index of international cooperation, scaled from 1 to 4)
(-0.314)

-2.957 × (dummy variable that takes the value one if the target
(-2.249) country receives significant support from third countries;
    otherwise zero)

$+1.266$ × (index of prior relations between sender and target
(1.539) countries, scaled from 1 to 3)

-0.024 × (length of sanctions episode in years)
(-0.341)

-1.425 × (index of political and economic health and stability of
(-1.785) the target country scaled from 1 to 3)

$+0.178$ × (cost of sanctions to the target country, expressed as a
(0.942) percentage of GNP)

$+0.031$ × (presanction trade linkage between target and sender
(1.100) countries, expressed as a percentage of the target coun-
    try's total trade)

$+1.758$ × (dummy variable that takes the value one if the sender
(1.077) country's GNP is up to 10 times greater than the target
    country's GNP; otherwise zero)

$+0.510$ × (dummy variable that takes the value one if the sender
(0.403) country's GNP is between 10 and 100 times greater than
    the target country's GNP; otherwise zero)

-1.519 × (dummy variable that takes the value one if the sender
(-1.254) country imposes export controls; otherwise zero)

$+0.730$ × (dummy variable that takes the value one if the sender
(0.615) country imposes import controls; otherwise zero)

-0.262 × (dummy variable that takes the value one if the sender
(-0.206) country imposes financial controls; otherwise zero)

-0.942 × (index of the cost of sanctions to the
(-0.955) sender country, scaled from 1 to 4)

Number of observations	108
R-bar squared	0.210
F-statistic (20,87)	2.420
Durbin-Watson statistic	2.009
Standard error of the regression	4.571

Individual regression coefficients are discussed in chapter 5. A few general points may be noted here.

First, 108 observations were included in the analysis—one for each case listed in tables 3.1 through 3.5. In this listing, five cases are counted twice, because the sender country sought multiple goals that were classified under more than one category.

Second, a dummy variable was used to capture the exceptional nature of the two world wars, namely the successful use of sanctions in inauspicious circumstances, but accompanied by total and victorious warfare waged by the sender countries.

Third, in certain instances, two explanatory variables were represented by a single dummy variable when they captured similar effects and when prior experimentation showed no significant difference between their coefficients. For example, quasi-military and regular military operations were combined. Likewise, modest policy change and destabilization cases were pooled because they displayed generally higher success scores than other case categories.

Fourth, the explanatory power of the regression equation is not high, as shown by the low value of *R*-bar squared. This value, 0.210, indicates that about 21 percent of the variance in success scores is explained by the enumerated independent variables. The rest of the variance must be attributed to unidentified factors. The unidentified factors include idiosyncratic elements in each episode, such as the personalities of national leaders, the balance of political forces in the sender and the target country, and the kaleidoscope of contemporaneous world events that affect the urgency of the episode to each party. Statecraft remains an art, not a science.

Fifth, the regression equation as a whole is statistically significant at the one percent confidence level, as shown by the *F*-statistic (20, 87) of 2.420. In other words, even though the regression equation explains less than a quarter of the variance in success scores, the equation is significant in what it does explain.

Sixth, many of the estimated coefficients are not significantly different from zero, in the sense that their standard errors exceed their estimated values (their *T*-statistics are less than one). This is true of 10 of the estimated coefficients. The remaining 8 coefficients are statistically significant.

Finally, the regression equation has a standard error of 4.57 success score points. This suggests that the equation usually predicts whether the underlying factors in a sanctions episode point to outright failure (success score of 1 or 2) or good success (success score of 12 or higher). But the equation can not distinguish between circumstances that lead to marginal failures (success score of 6 or 8) and circumstances that produce marginal successes (success score of 9).

B Estimating the Cost of Sanctions: Methodology

This appendix sets forth the basic analytical model we have used to guide our efforts to estimate the costs of sanctions to both target and sender countries. The following discussion focuses solely on the costs imposed on the target country, but parallel analysis also is relevant for the calculation of the welfare costs to the sender country. Our methodology is illustrated by figure B.1.

In figure B.1, supply and demand curves are shown for a hypothetical good or service (e.g., bank credit) exported from the sender country to the target country. The presanction equilibrium price, $P(1)$, and quantity, $Q(1)$, are shown by the intersection of the supply and demand schedules at $e(1)$. In the first instance, the sender and its allies deprive the target country of supplies in the amount dQ. Since the sender country and its allies are ordinarily not the only suppliers of the good or service, overall supply availability does not decline by the full amount dQ. Instead, the supply curve facing the target country shifts from $S(1)$ to $S(2)$. The horizontal shift from $S(1)$ to $S(2)$ corresponds to the removal of the amount dQ from the pool of supplies available to the target country. Other suppliers, responding to the abandoned market and potentially higher prices, provide an additional quantity indicated by x to the target country. As a result, the net quantity supplied to the target country declines by the amount y. The postsanction equilibrium of price and quantity is $e(2)$; and the post-sanction price is $P(2)$, which is higher than the initial price of $P(1)$ by the amount dP.

How much does the target country lose from this sequence of events? In order to answer that question, we must start with a concept used to describe the gains that purchasers enjoy from engaging in market transactions, namely "consumers' surplus." A word on terminology: the concept of consumers' surplus applies with equal force to spare parts, capital goods, and food. It might better be called "purchasers' surplus" than "consumers' surplus." Consumers' surplus is measured by the difference between the total amount actually paid for the quantity consumed (price times quantity) and the total amount that

Figure B.1   Illustration of welfare loss from the imposition of export sanctions

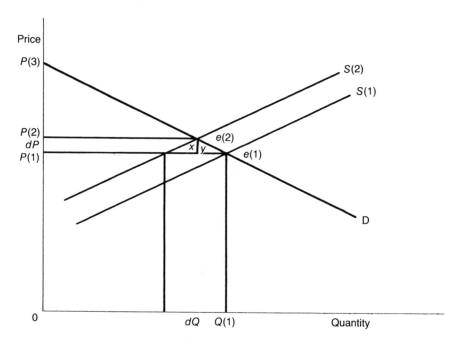

consumers would hypothetically be willing to pay if the market could be segregated and each consumer were charged his demand schedule price.

In figure B.1, the level of consumers' surplus before the imposition of sanctions is shown by the triangular area bounded by $P(1)$, $P(3)$, and $e(1)$. When sanctions are imposed, and the supply curve shifts from $S(1)$ to $S(2)$, the trapezoidal area bounded by $P(1)$, $P(2)$, $e(1)$, and $e(2)$ is subtracted from the previous level of consumers' surplus. This loss of consumers' surplus represents the cost that export sanctions impose on the target country. By inspection, it is intuitively obvious that the steeper the slope of the demand curve in the neighborhood of the initial equilibrium price (i.e., the more "essential" the item to the target country and the smaller the range of substitute products), and the steeper the slope of the supply curve (i.e., the smaller the range of available alternatives) the greater will be the deprivation experienced by the target country.

The loss of consumers' surplus is customarily referred to as a "welfare loss." The area of the trapezoid representing lost consumers' surplus approximately equals the rectangle denoted by $Q(1)dP$. Hence, as a first approximation, we may write:

(1) $Q(1)dP$ = welfare loss

With the use of some algebra, the change in price, dP, can be expressed in terms of the elasticity of supply, Es, and the elasticity of demand, Ed. The elasticity of supply is defined as the ratio between the percentage change in quantity supplied, to a rough approximation denoted as $x/Q(1)$, and the percentage change in price, denoted as $dP/P(1)$. Similarly, the elasticity of demand is defined as the ratio of the percentage change in quantity demanded, denoted as $y/Q(1)$, and the percentage change in price, denoted as $dP/P(1)$. These elasticities can be represented by the following equations:

(2) $\quad (x/Q(1))/(dP/P(1)) = Es.$

(3) $\quad (y/Q(1))/(dP/(P(1)) = Ed.$

As noted earlier, supply and demand curves that are more steeply sloped in the neighborhood of the initial equilibrium price are characterized by smaller elasticities of supply and demand.

As a further element in our algebraic exercise, we note that:

(4) $\quad x + y = dQ$

We thus have three equations, (2), (3), and (4), and three unknowns, x, y, and dP. By algebraically solving these three equations it can be shown that:

(5) $\quad dP = [P(1)dQ]/[(Ed + Es)(Q(1)]$

Substituting this expression for dP in equation (1), the result follows:

(6) $P(1)dQ/(Ed] + Es) = $ welfare loss.

In equation (6), $P(1)dQ$ represents the face value of the reduction in supply from the sender and its allies, before the price paid by the target country rises and other suppliers partly fill the gap.

To summarize, in this simple construct, the welfare loss inflicted on the target country depends on the size of the initial deprivation, the elasticity of supply, and the elasticity of demand. Table B.1 gives some hypothetical values of demand and supply elasticities and the resulting values of the expression $1/(Es + Ed)$. This expression is, in a sense, the "sanctions multiplier," a number applied to the initial deprivation of supplies experienced by the target country in order to calculate the welfare loss.

By a similar analysis, it can be shown that equation (6) also describes the welfare loss imposed when the sender country closes its markets, and the target country initially loses sales in the amount dQ. In this case, however, the welfare loss represents a reduction in producers' surplus, not consumers' surplus. That is to say, the welfare loss represents a burden on the producers in the target country—a deduction of part of the difference between the market price producers actually receive for the product and the price producers would hypothetically receive if the market could be segregated and each supplier were paid his supply schedule price.

Table B.1 Relation between elasticities of supply and demand and
the sanctions multiplier

(Es + Ed)	1/(Es + Ed)
0.5	2.00
1.0	1.00
2.0	0.50
4.0	0.25
10.0	0.10

In order to calculate the cost of each sanctions episode to the target country, we first estimate the initial deprivation of markets or supplies, expressed on an annualized basis in current US dollars. We then use our own judgment to estimate the "sanctions multiplier" that should be applied in the context of the particular episode. As a general proposition, we have tried to err on the side of overestimating the appropriate "sanctions multiplier." To illustrate, we apply a multiplier of 1.00 to most reductions in aid, and a multiplier between 0.10 and 0.50 to most reductions in the supply or demand for goods. In a war context, we may apply a multiplier as high as 2.00. The estimates are generous because, in most contexts, the combined supply and demand elasticities would ordinarily exceed 5.0, simply because the target country is likely to be a small factor in world markets. A combined elasticity greater than 5 would correspond to a sanctions multiplier less than 0.2.

C Case Abstracts

Case 14–1   UK v. Germany

(1914–18: World War I)

CHRONOLOGY OF KEY EVENTS

August–October 1914	Following outbreak of war against Germany, UK publishes successively longer lists of absolute contraband and conditional contraband (i.e., contraband if destined for an enemy port), narrows privileges of neutral vessels. (Jack 83–86)
26 December 1914	US lodges first in series of protests concerning British restrictions on US trade. (Jack 87)
1914–15	US exports of key raw materials to neutral states increase significantly; for example, oil to Scandinavia, 0.7 million gallons, September–October 1913, vs. 1.6 million gallons, September–October 1914. (Jack 90–91)
4 February 1915	Germany declares waters surrounding British Isles a war zone, announces that safety of neutral ships in zone cannot be assured. (Jack 91)
11 March 1915	Britain institutes complete blockade of Germany as declared reprisal for submarine warfare. Invoking extended version of doctrine of "continuous voyage," Britain intercepts shipments to and from Germany even via neutral countries, ignores US protests. Britain establishes navicert system—documentation of neutral destination issued at source—to administer blockade. (Jack 94–97; Doxey 17–18; Guichard 258–59)
May 1915	German submarine sinks Lusitania, claiming 114 American lives; subsequent incidents further inflame American opinion. (Jack 104–6)

107

| July 1916 | Britain restricts trade with neutrals to prewar levels; blacklists persons and firms in neutral countries with connection to Axis; denies bunker and port facilities to ships engaged in enemy trade; ignores US protests. (Jack 100–101; Doxey 18) |

| Early 1917 | Germany intensifies submarine attacks, warns neutrals that they enter war zone at their own risk; Britain tightens blockade by establishing rebuttable presumption that ships traveling to and from neutral ports adjacent to Germany are engaged in trade with Germany. US severs diplomatic relations with Germany and enters war. (Jack 99–100; 106) |

| 29 May 1918 | Sweden agrees to restrict exports to Central Empires, stopping important shipments of iron ore to German steel industry. However, agreement comes too late to affect German wartime production. (Guichard 271–72) |

| 11 November 1918 | Armistice is agreed to, war ends. (Pratt 488) |

GOALS OF SENDER COUNTRY

Louis Guichard
"[In late 1916], Great Britain regarded the blockade from a commercial point of view; it had seemed natural to her during the first two years of the war to try to take Germany's place in several neutral markets, to sell her manufactured goods there, and to take agricultural produce in exchange. France had a more legal conception of the blockade: she was ready to sacrifice her trade interests in their entirety to the complete isolation of the Central Empires." (Guichard 68)

D. T. Jack
"Apart from the traditional use of the methods of blockade and contraband, the efforts of the belligerents to cripple their opponents by curtailing their economic resources were reinforced by other practices. . . . On the British side, new devices were evolved with the object of preventing supplies from reaching enemy destinations through adjacent neutral territory." (Jack 108)

RESPONSE OF TARGET COUNTRY

January 1915
"[T]he economic life of Germany . . . had only been slightly affected; she knew, however, that as the months went by Allied action would become intensified; she was aware of the increasing severity of control exercised by the Allied navies . . . she was still breathing normally but was haunted by fears of suffocation; she beheld herself as it were a fortress, already beset, a state of mind which was itself becoming an obsession. This obsession was one of the reasons which impelled Germany to embark systematically upon the adventure of submarine warfare." (Guichard 39)

4 February 1915
Germany declares that "any hostile merchant ship encountered in British or Irish waters would be destroyed without regard for crew or passengers." (Guichard 39–41)

October 1916
Germany embarks on policy of unrestricted submarine warfare. Chief of the Naval Staff writes to the Emperor: "In a word, unrestricted submarine warfare is the best and only means of bringing the war to a victorious conclusion." (Guichard 94)

27 April 1918
Article 55 C of German Ordinance is issued with supplementary clause that in effect extends submarine warfare to all foreign ships. Purpose is to terrorize neutral shipping, force acceptance of strict German conditions that aimed "to disorganize radically the maritime trade of the Allies." (Guichard 120–21)

ATTITUDE OF OTHER COUNTRIES

United States
In 1914, US proposes that Declaration of London of 1909 be applied to shipping rights of neutrals; UK rejects proposal because it regards contraband rules as too lax; proposal is accepted by Germany. Between 1914 and 1916, US lodges series of protests against British restrictions. On 20 February 1915, US proposes new rules concerning use of mines and designation of contraband, but proposals are rejected by Britain and Germany. (Jack 87, 90–93, 100–101)

In 1917, after entering war, US cooperates with Britain in enforcing blockade, uses export controls as bargaining lever against neutrals. (Doxey 18)

France
"From June 1915 onwards the French government had never ceased requesting that the blockade should be conducted by means of a permanent inter-Allied organisation. But all attempts in this direction on the part of ministers, especially those of M. Clemenceau who was the moving spirit at the earlier inter-Allied economic conferences, had been wrecked by the contradictory nature of the commercial interests of the Allied nations, which were only kept in touch with one another by means of intermittent conferences and by the fact that members of the diplomatic body could sit upon the various national committees." (Guichard 67)

Adjacent neutrals
In April 1917, trading organizations are formed in Netherlands, Denmark, Sweden, and Norway that certify destination of imports to the satisfaction of the British authorities. (Jack 109–10)

Later in 1917, Germany threatens to stop coal exports to Netherlands (then subject to a British blockade) unless it increases credits, foodstuff exports, transit rights to Germany. Netherlands agrees. (Jack 109–10)

LEGAL NOTES

Rules of blockade and contraband as established by practice in Napoleonic Wars, Declaration of Paris of 18 April 1856, and unratified Declaration of London of 26 February 1909:

Blockade

☐ A blockade to be binding must be effective in the sense that a ship attempting to run the blockade would be captured.
☐ Only a belligerent can establish a blockade.
☐ A blockade must be duly declared and notified as to exact geographical limits.
☐ The blockade must be limited to the ports and coasts of the enemy.

Contraband

☐ A belligerent can declare goods he considers "contraband of war."
☐ The goods so declared must be suitable for belligerent use and they must have an enemy destination.
  1. "Absolute contraband"—items "susceptible exclusively to military use"—may be seized when the ultimate destination is the enemy, even though an intermediate destination is a neutral country under the doctrine of "continuous voyage."
  2. "Conditional contraband"—items "susceptible of use both for military and civil purposes"—may be seized only if the immediate destination is an enemy port.
  3. The unratified Declaration of London lists 11 articles of "absolute contraband," 14 articles of "conditional contraband," with the understanding that a belligerent could add to these lists in the course of war; and a "free list" of 17 items that could never be declared contraband.

☐ A belligerent may search private neutral vessels, but not warships, and seize "contraband of war."
☐ The belligerent must be prepared to defend the seizure in a Prize Court.

Enemy Goods and Neutral Goods

☐ A belligerent can seize enemy goods aboard an enemy vessel, but neutral goods, with the exception of contraband of war, are immune from capture.
☐ A belligerent cannot seize enemy goods with the exception of contraband of war, aboard a neutral vessel.

Ambiguities surrounding US attitude toward neutral and belligerent rights were not solved by US entry into World War I, or discussions during interwar period, particularly regarding: doctrine of continuous voyage for seizure of contraband; bunker control and blacklisting; hovering off 3-mile limit. (Medlicott 4–5, 9–10; Guichard 8–13)

ECONOMIC IMPACT

Observed Economic Statistics

German exports to Great Britain in 1913 totaled £57 million, imports £40 million. (Guichard 257)

German trade (million marks†)

	Exports	Imports
1913	10,900	11,600
1915	3,100	7,100
1916	3,800	8,400
1917	3,400	8,100
1918	3,000	5,900

† 1 mark = 23.8¢.
Source: Jack 128–29.

Receipts from German customs, which amounted to 850 million marks in 1913, fell to only 133 million marks in 1918. (Guichard 261)

In 1918, German ration of cereals fell to 64 percent of prewar consumption; meat to 18 percent, fats to 12 percent. "[However], the Allied blockade was only a contributory cause of this shortage." (Jack 129)

German petroleum supplies were met by Austria-Hungary and Romania, whose combined annual output of 3.0 million tons was able to cover annual German import needs of about 1.3 million tons. (Guichard 275)

Prewar German imports of 1.73 million tons of oleaginous grain were entirely cut off by end of 1914. Oil from this grain was replaced from other domestic sources, but at cost of 90 percent cut in output of leather and soap industries (because of cutback in supply of fats to these industries from 430,000 tons to 40,000 tons). (Guichard 276)

Price of kilogram of rubber in Germany rose from 4 marks in January 1914 to 45 marks in December 1914, 150 marks by 1917. (Guichard 278)

British coal and cotton exports to all destinations, valued at £175 million in 1913, fell by one-half during war. (Jack 119)

By weight, UK imports from all sources declined from 55 million tons in 1913 to 35 million tons in 1918. (Jack 114)

During first five months of 1915, US shipments of cotton to Scandinavia were 17 times normal. Cotton was essential for manufacture of explosives, but as concession to the US, cotton was left off conditional contraband list. (Medlicott 9–10)

Calculated Economic Impact

	Annual cost to target country
Reduction in German trade during 1915–18 from prewar levels; welfare loss estimated at 60 percent of drop in total trade.	$843 million

Relative Magnitudes

Gross indicators of German economy	
German GNP (1913)	$11.9 billion
German population (1913)	67 million
Annual effect of sanctions related to gross indicators	
Percentage of GNP	7
Per capita	$12.58
German trade with UK as percentage of total trade	
Exports (1913)	11
Imports (1913)	7
Ratio of UK GNP (1913: $15.9 billion) to German GNP (1913: $11.9 billion)	1

ASSESSMENT

D. T. Jack
"The interception of supplies to the Central Powers was far from complete before 1917 and the turning point may be associated with the entry of the United States into the Allied coalition." (Jack 82)

Lord Curzon, member of the war cabinet
Speaking in 1918, in context of debate about the future League of Nations: "[Sanctions] did not, it is true, succeed in preventing the war; they have not, at any rate at present curtailed its duration, but I should like to put it this way. I doubt very much whether, if Germany had anticipated when she plunged into war the consequences, commercial, financial, and otherwise, which would be entailed upon her by two, three, or four years of war, she would not have been eager to plunge in as she was. Remember this. Though possibly we have not done all we desired, we have done a great deal, and we could have done a great deal more if our hands had not been tied by certain difficulties. It is naturally a delicate matter for me to allude to this. A good many of them have been removed by the entry of the United States of America into the war, but we have always the task of handling with great and necessary delicacy the neutral states, and this difficulty still remains with us." (Mitrany 35)

Margaret P. Doxey
"The Allied blockade was undoubtedly a factor in Germany's eventual defeat. Shortages of essential materials such as copper, tin, rubber, and cotton became acute, particularly as Germany had not expected and was, therefore, inadequately prepared for a war lasting several years. The German government was driven to extreme lengths to conserve supplies of those materials and to develop artificial substitutes, but lack of food may have been a more powerful factor in the German defeat than lack of raw materials." (Doxey 18, see also Tryon)

Louis Guichard
"Germany was shaken and enfeebled by the steady pressure of the Allies; in 1917, however, when the encirclement was about to become effective, such a breach was made in the East by the defection of Russia that none but a bold man would affirm that in the event hostilities having been prolonged any more definite results would have been achieved by the economic war." (Guichard 306)

AUTHORS' SUMMARY

Overall assessment	Assigned scores
☐ Policy result, scaled from 1 (failed) to 4 (success)	4
☐ Sanctions contribution, scaled from 1 (none) to 4 (significant)	3
☐ Success score (policy result *times* sanctions contribution), scaled from 1 (outright failure) to 16 (significant success)	12

Political and economic variables

☐ Companion policies: J (covert), Q (quasi-military), or R (regular military)	R

	Assigned scores
Political and economic variables (continued)	
□ International cooperation with sender, scaled from 1 (none) to 4 (significant)	4
□ International assistance to target: A (if present)	A
□ Sanctions period (years)	4
□ Economic health and political stability of target, scaled from 1 (distressed) to 3 (strong)	3
□ Presanction relations between sender and target, scaled from 1 (antagonistic) to 3 (cordial)	1
□ Type of sanction: X (export), M (import), F (financial)	F, X, M
□ Cost to sender, scaled from 1 (net gain) to 4 (major loss)	4

BIBLIOGRAPHY

Clark, Evans, ed. 1932. *Boycotts and Peace: A Report by the Committee on Economic Sanctions.* New York: Harper & Brothers.

Doxey, Margaret P. 1971. *Economic Sanctions and International Enforcement.* London: Oxford University Press for Royal Institute of International Affairs.

Guichard, Louis. 1930. *The Naval Blockade: 1914–1918.* New York: D. Appleton & Company.

Jack, D. T. 1941. *Studies in Economic Warfare.* New York: Chemical Publishing Company.

Medlicott, W. N. 1952. *The Economic Blockade,* vol. 1. London: Longmans, Green.

Mitrany, D. 1925. *The Problem of International Sanctions.* London: Oxford University Press.

Pratt, Julius W. 1955. *A History of United States Foreign Policy.* New York: Prentice Hall.

Tryon, F. G. 1932. "How Germany Met the Raw Materials Blockade 1914–1918." In *Boycotts and Peace: A Report by the Committee on Economic Sanctions,* ed. Evans Clark. New York: Harper & Brothers.

Case 17–1   US v. Japan

(1917–18: Contain Japan)

CHRONOLOGY OF KEY EVENTS

1912–17   Chinese Revolution and outbreak of war in Europe open door for greater Japanese involvement in China in competition with US interests. War also leads to boom in Japanese shipping: the "Japanese merchant fleet almost doubled in size as freight rates soared to fabulous levels." (Safford 441–49; Lockwood 534, 545)

3 May 1915   State Department warns Japan against actions that might impair "the Treaty rights of the United States and its citizens in China, the political or territorial integrity of the Republic of China, or the international policy relative to China commonly known as the Open Door Policy." (Toynbee 423)

Spring 1917   War demands cause England to curtail steel shipments to Japan. US supplies steel to Japan but conditions shipments "on the proper employment in the interest of the Allies of Japanese shipping." (Safford 441)

May 1917   Congress authorizes President to embargo "exports vital to the war interests of the nation . . . when deemed expedient." (Safford 441)

9 July 1917   President Woodrow Wilson classifies steel, iron, other items as "war essentials," thus subject to immediate embargo. (Safford 441)

September 1917   Export Administration Board (later War Trade Board), sole issuer of export licenses, decrees that US steel will be released to Japan only in exchange for immediate delivery of ships for Atlantic war effort. (Safford 445–46)

Fall 1917   M. A. Oudin, founder of National Foreign Trade Council, recommends immediate use of economic leverage against Japanese: "In the present embargo the United States has the most powerful leverage that it has ever possessed to deal with Far Eastern questions." (Safford 443)

November 1917   US Secretary of State Robert Lansing exchanges notes with Viscount Kikujiro Ishii, special Japanese ambassador, committing Japan to maintain China's territorial integrity while recognizing Japan's special interests in area. "Lansing, perhaps the only ranking American official realistic enough to appraise correctly the weakness of the American position in China and its contiguous areas, molded what was in effect a delicate compromise. Recognition of Japan's 'special interests' was granted in return for a Japanese pledge to prohibit discriminatory acts against foreign commerce in areas [on the Chinese mainland] under Tokyo's control." (Safford 444)

January 1918   A member of War Trade Board (WTB) reports that "one or two large shipbuilding firms in Japan had run out of steel and were willing to do business on the United States' terms." (Safford 447)

March 1918   US State Department circumvents WTB, directs Ambassador Roland S. Morris to negotiate agreement with Japanese under which US will charter 150,000 tons of Japanese shipping for six months to be used solely in Atlantic war trade. Later in month, State Department pressures WTB into exchanging 250,000 tons of American steel for purchase of 45 steel cargo carriers. (Safford 449)

GOALS OF SENDER COUNTRY

Jeffrey J. Safford
"From the time of American entry into the war in 1917, an embargo on raw materials constituted a major weapon by which Washington sought to strengthen a generally weak American stand for Chinese integrity and the Open Door. Given Japan's serious lack of steel and iron, the State Department and Shipping and War Trade Boards attempted to block Tokyo's commercial and territorial expansion by limiting its access to these materials, particularly those that could be used in maritime construction." (Safford 440)

"From an American standpoint there was ample reason to justify such a denial. By 1917, Japan's exploitation of the war-caused shipping shortage in the Pacific was viewed by the United States as an ominous threat to American economic interests and ambitions in that area." (Safford 440)

The Shipping and War Trade Boards "were primarily concerned with the prompt and effective containment of Japan's maritime expansion, regardless of whether ships were secured for the Atlantic war effort. . . . The embargo would be used at the expense of Japan's vital shipping industry and no consideration would be given as to time of peace or war." (Safford 445–46)

E. T. Williams, head of Department of State's Division of Far Eastern Affairs
[Williams] "warned that the Japanese had taken advantage of the situation to 'promote their own commerce at the expense of Europe and America's and argued forcefully that the embargo had to be maintained until a sufficient proportion of the Japanese merchant fleet was diverted to the Atlantic war effort." (Safford 442)

RESPONSE OF TARGET COUNTRY

July 1917
After Wilson's announcement of the embargo: "The Japanese Minister for Foreign Affairs quickly protested that all industrial enterprises and particularly the current construction

of ships would be 'enormously' affected; he added that if Japan 'should be shut off from the markets of this country . . . her foundries and factories would be shut down and great loss would ensue.' An American official in Tokyo reported that 'the greatest apprehension is now felt by shipbuilding and dockyard companies' and warned that the move was interpreted as a 'weapon to force Japan to send ships to the Atlantic.'" (Safford 442)

"Ironically, the embargo had forced Japan to reconsider its lack of resources and to begin developing its own supplies of iron and steel." Japan attempted to expand its own capacity and to seek out and control any iron ore deposits in China. (Safford 447)

ATTITUDE OF OTHER COUNTRIES

United Kingdom
"The use of economic leverage received strong British endorsement in the spring and summer of 1917. England's interest in containing the advances of Japan's economic empire was long-founded and, as Stanley Hornbeck, American Far Eastern expert, noted, 'The value to her of the Open Door in China is greater in its immediate aspect than it is to us.' Tokyo made every use of the Anglo-Japanese alliance to secure steel from England in exchange for policing the Pacific. Japan also managed to keep its vessels out of the Allied war shipping pool and instead used them for purposes of trade aggrandizement at English expense." (Safford 441)

In the fall of 1917, "The British added their pressure, maintaining that the Japanese were falsifying their need for vessels in essential trades and were 'employing their tonnage purely in their own interest and with a view to commercial expansion.' They further suggested that the State Department consider the embargo a valuable postwar economic weapon. Moreover, London declared it would strengthen the American hand in the negotiations by abandoning its own efforts to acquire Japanese tonnage." (Safford 443)

ECONOMIC IMPACT

Observed Economic Statistics

By 1917 Japan had gained 55 percent of carrying trade in Pacific, US only 2 percent. (Safford 441)

Steel trade 1913 (million metric tons)

	Exports	Imports	Percentage of world trade
UK	2.74	n.a.	22.8
US	2.54	n.a.	21.1
World total	12.02	n.a.	100.0
Japan	n.a.	0.56	4.7

n.a. Not applicable.
Source: Maizels 246, 255.

In September 1917, US steel prices were $2.90/100 lbs. for bars; $3.00/100 lbs. for shapes; and $3.25/100 lbs. for plates. (Litman 281)

Japanese merchant fleet (steam vessels) totaled 1.5 million tons in 1913, rose to 2.84 million tons by 1919. "[W]ith the help of construction subsidies, they were turning out ships at an average rate (1909–13) of about 100 steam vessels totaling 50,000 tons a year." However, Japanese shipyards "were still largely dependent on imported materials." (Lockwood 23–24, 39)

"Launchings of steam vessels rose from 52,000 tons in 1909–13 to 646,000 tons in 1919. The earlier subsidy scheme was replaced in 1917 with measures to encourage the steel industry, mainly through bounties on the use of Japanese steel in ship construction." (Lockwood 547)

"[N]et shipping income of the Empire rose from 41.2 million yen in 1914 to 381.4 million yen in 1919." (Lockwood 39)

Share of Japanese trade carried in Japanese bottoms rose from 57 percent in 1914 to more than 80 percent in 1919. (Lockwood 39)

In 1913, Japan produced 255,000 tons of steel, supplying one-third of its domestic consumption. Total rose to more than 500,000 tons by 1919, or 45 percent of consumption. (Lockwood 24; Beasley 216)

Calculated Economic Impact

	Annual cost to target country
Embargo of US steel shipments to Japan from mid-1917 to spring 1918; welfare loss estimated at 125 percent of value of reduced steel trade (assuming import shortfall to be 50 percent of prewar import levels or 280,000 tons on annualized basis).	$23 million

Relative Magnitudes

Gross indicators of Japanese economy	
Japanese GNP (1913)	$2.93 billion
Japanese population (1913)	51.9 million
Annual effect of sanctions related to gross indicators	
Percentage of GNP	0.8
Per capita	$0.44
Japanese trade with US as percentage of total trade	
Exports (1913)	26
Imports (1913)	15
Ratio of US GNP (1913: $36.7 billion) to Japanese GNP (1913: $2.93 billion)	13

ASSESSMENT

Jeffrey J. Safford
"It is questionable whether the embargo did much more than temporarily stunt the phenomenal increase in Japan's maritime strength. Despite its inability to obtain American steel, Japan still managed in 1918 to double the previous year's tonnage production. In fact, Japan reached the zenith of its ship construction that year, and related industries were stimulated to a growth and output never before conceived. This, and the additional prospect of an embargo in peacetime, was sufficient to steel Japan's determination never to be deprived of its mainland interests . . . the steel embargo, originally directed by members of the Wilson war administration to restrict Japan's imperial growth and to support Chinese integrity, had backfired. . . . Japan, convinced that it could not become a ranking industrial and military power until it could secure unimpeded access to steel and iron, had been furnished with a prime 'motive for territorial expansion.'" (Safford 450–51)

AUTHORS' SUMMARY

Overall assessment	Assigned scores
☐ Policy result, scaled from 1 (failed) to 4 (success)	2
☐ Sanctions contribution, scaled from 1 (none) to 4 (significant)	2
☐ Success score (policy result *times* sanctions contribution), scaled from 1 (outright failure) to 16 (significant success)	4

Political and economic variables

☐ Companion policies: J (covert), Q (quasi-military), or R (regular military)	—
☐ International cooperation with sender, scaled from 1 (none) to 4 (significant)	1
☐ International assistance to target: A (if present)	—
☐ Sanctions period (years)	1
☐ Economic health and political stability of target, scaled from 1 (distressed) to 3 (strong)	3
☐ Presanction relations between sender and target, scaled from 1 (antagonistic) to 3 (cordial)	2
☐ Type of sanction: X (export), M (import), F (financial)	X
☐ Cost to sender, scaled from 1 (net gain) to 4 (major loss)	2

BIBLIOGRAPHY

Beasley, W. G. 1963. *The Modern History of Japan.* New York: Praeger.
Litman, Simon. 1920. *Prices and Price Controls in Great Britain and the United States during the World War.* New York: Carnegie Endowment for International Peace.
Lockwood, William W. 1968. *The Economic Development of Japan.* Princeton, NJ: Princeton University Press.

Maizels, Alfred. 1963. *Industrial Growth and World Trade*. Cambridge: Cambridge University Press.

Safford, Jeffrey J. 1970. "Experiment in Containment: The United States Steel Embargo and Japan, 1917–1918." 39 *Pacific Historical Review* 439–51.

Toynbee, Arnold J. 1925. *Survey of International Affairs: 1920–1923*. London: Oxford University Press.

Case 18–1   UK v. Russia

(1918–20: Anti-bolshevism)

CHRONOLOGY OF KEY EVENTS

3 March 1918	Treaty of Brest-Litovsk ends war between Germany, Russia. (Ullman 2: 6)
Spring–Summer 1918	Allies send troops to Russia in effort to reconstitute Eastern Front against Germany; Allied forces begin undeclared war against Soviet units; US, UK, Japanese troops land in Siberia. (Ullman 2: 6–9)
11 November 1918	Allies and Germany sign Armistice; blockade of Germany is maintained, extended to Russia to keep up pressure on Germany to sign and ratify Treaty of Versailles. (Ullman 2: 59, 287)
9 July 1919	Germany ratifies Treaty of Versailles, ending World War I, removing legal basis for maintaining blockade of Russia, which nonetheless is continued into 1920. (Ullman 2: 287–93)
29 September 1919	Allies ask neutral countries to follow their lead by imposing: controls on trade and finance with Russia; travel restrictions, controls on mail and telegraphic communications to and from Bolshevik Russia. (Ullman 2: 292)
20 November 1919	British cabinet decides not to redeploy British warships in Baltic to enforce blockade after spring thaw. (Ullman 2: 293)
16 January 1920	Allies lift blockade. (Ullman 2: 330)

GOALS OF SENDER COUNTRY

John Albert White

"The British position was based on the belief that victory in the war would be out of the question should Germany gain access to the raw materials of Russia. The blockade would be nullified. Even a military victory on the Western Front would be nullified. . . . " (White 219)

British Foreign Secretary Lord Balfour
" . . . new anti-Bolshevik administrations have grown up under the shelter of Allied forces. We are responsible for their existence and we must endeavor to support them." (Ullman 2: 16)

RESPONSE OF TARGET COUNTRY

November 1918
Russian government proposes to British a general armistice, initiation of peace talks. (Ullman 2: 87)

December 1918
Foreign Minister Georgi Vasilievich Chicherin in letter to President Woodrow Wilson: "[The Soviet government is] prepared to go to any length of concessions . . . if they can secure thereby conditions enabling them to work out peacefully their social schemes." (Ullman 2: 87)

ATTITUDE OF OTHER COUNTRIES

Germany
In response to Allied request in October 1919 to neutrals to adhere to its sanctions policy: " . . . while [the German government] was anxious to combat Bolshevism, it nevertheless felt that restrictions on trade would only drive the remaining democratic elements in Russia into the Soviet camp and therefore serve to strengthen just those groups which such measures were designed to cripple." (Ullman 2: 292)

France
"Among the three Western Allies the French were the most insistent upon an intervention particularly after the signing of the Treaty of Brest-Litovsk." (White 217)

According to British Prime Minister David Lloyd George, in December 1919, French Premier George Clemenceau "was much more concerned about future danger from Germany than he was about the spread of Bolshevism, either by force or subversion, from Russia. . . . [He wanted] to restore Russia as a counterweight against Germany. To this end, Clemenceau advocated a strong Poland in order to dam up the Russian flood and to provide a check to Germany." (Ullman 2: 313–14)

United States
"[T]he United States took part in the embargo by refusing to grant export licenses to those intending to do business in Russian territory under Bolshevik control and by refusing clearance papers to ships bound for Soviet ports." (White 324)

ECONOMIC IMPACT

Observed Economic Statistics

Cost to British treasury of intervention in Russia from Armistice to 31 July 1919, was £69 million. Later Sir Winston Churchill, secretary of war, admitted costs had soared to

£94.8 million (including £47 million worth of "nonmarketable stores"). (Ullman 2: 211, 304)

Before war, Russia supplied UK with much of its imports of wheat and flax. (Ullman 2: 317)

Russian exports and imports in 1913 totaled 1,520 million rubles and 1,374 million rubles, respectively. (Nove 68)

UK exports to and imports from Russia in 1913 totaled £27.7 million and £40.3 million respectively, accounting for 4.4 percent and 5.2 percent of total British exports and imports. (Ullman 3: 436)

Germany was Russia's leading trading partner in 1913, exporting £44 million to Russia and importing £71 million in return. (Keynes 183)

Per capita Russian national income in 1913 was 101 rubles, or only a little more than a fifth of Britain's per capita GNP. (Nove 14)

Calculated Economic Impact

	Annual cost to target country
Suspension of trade as result of blockade and civil war; welfare loss estimated at 50 percent of value of prewar trade with UK and Germany.	$446 million

Relative Magnitudes

Gross indicators of Russian economy	
Russian GNP (1913)	$10.9 billion
Russian population (1914)	178.9 million
Annual effect of sanctions related to gross indicators	
Percentage of GNP	4.1
Per capita	$2.49
Russian trade with UK as percentage of total trade	
Exports (1913)	21
Imports (1913)	16
Ratio of UK GNP (1913: $15.9 billion) to Russian GNP (1913: $10.9 billion)	1

ASSESSMENT

Richard H. Ullman
"Never could the Allies fully admit that they were at war with the Soviet government. Instead, they allowed the rigid categories of international law, which were not intended

to function in the shadowy area between war and peace, to impede for months their efforts to apply the sanctions they thought necessary." (Ullman 2: 293)

Manchester Guardian (17 January 1920)
"The decision [to lift the blockade] implied an even more basic decision to make peace finally with Moscow. . . . Obviously, they cannot at the same time open up trade relations with Russia and go on hitting her." (Ullman 2: 338)

Winston Churchill, secretary of war (14 February 1920)
"The Great Allied Powers will, each of them and all of them, learn to rue the fact that they could not take more decided and more united action to crush the Bolshevist peril at its center before it had grown too strong." (Ullman 2: 347)

AUTHORS' SUMMARY

Overall assessment	Assigned scores
□ Policy result, scaled from 1 (failed) to 4 (success)	1
□ Sanctions contribution, scaled from 1 (none) to 4 (significant)	1
□ Success score (policy result *times* sanctions contribution), scaled from 1 (outright failure) to 16 (significant success)	1

Political and economic variables

□ Companion policies: J (covert), Q (quasi-military), or R (regular military)	Q, R
□ International cooperation with sender, scaled from 1 (none) to 4 (significant)	4
□ International assistance to target: A (if present)	—
□ Sanctions period (years)	2
□ Economic health and political stability of target, scaled from 1 (distressed) to 3 (strong)	1
□ Presanction relations between sender and target, scaled from 1 (antagonistic) to 3 (cordial)	1
□ Type of sanction: X (export), M (import), F (financial)	F, X, M
□ Cost to sender, scaled from 1 (net gain) to 4 (major loss)	3

BIBLIOGRAPHY

Keynes, John Maynard. 1920. *The Economic Consequences of the Peace.* London: Macmillan.
Nove, Alec. 1969. *An Economic History of the USSR.* London: Penguin Press.
Ullman, Richard H. 1968. *Anglo-Soviet Relations, 1917–1921.* Vol. 2, *Britain and the Russian Civil War;* vol. 3, *The Anglo-Soviet Accord.* Princeton, NJ: Princeton University Press.
White, John Albert. 1950. *The Siberian Intervention.* Princeton, NJ: Princeton University Press.

Case 21-1 League of Nations v. Yugoslavia

(1921: Border Dispute)

CHRONOLOGY OF KEY EVENTS

17 May 1913   In aftermath of Balkan War of 1912, Turkey and Balkan allies agree to arbitration of frontiers of Albania. Conference of Ambassadors from major European powers convenes in London to demarcate borders between Albania and Greece, Serbia, and Montenegro. (Toynbee 343)

17 December 1913   Albania and Greece agree on common border; "the delimitation of the Albano-Serbian and Albano-Montenegrin sectors [is] prevented by the outbreak of the War of 1914." (Toynbee 343)

1914   Italy occupies island of Sasseno and port of Valona, which controls access to Adriatic Sea. Italian forces are not withdrawn until August 1920. (Gathorne-Hardy 91)

1920–21   Both Yugoslavia and Greece, seeking hegemony over parts of Albania, demand revision of 1913 frontier. League of Nations receives complaints about alleged Yugoslav incursions into Albania. (Gathorne-Hardy 91)

2 November 1921   Yugoslav troops invade Albania; League calls a special session of Council for November 16 to review situation. (Toynbee 345)

7 November 1921   British request that Council "take immediate steps . . . to consider the situation and to agree upon measures to be taken under Article 16 in the event of the Serb-Croat-Slovene Government refusing or delaying to execute their obligations under the Covenant." (Toynbee 345)

9 November 1921   Conference of Ambassadors agrees to retain 1913 frontier. Article 1 of pact recognizes Albania "as a sovereign and independent state." (Gathorne-Hardy 92; Toynbee 346)

14 November 1921   Yugoslavia informs Conference of Ambassadors that it will withdraw its troops from Albania "in order to avoid the dangerous consequences of nonacceptance." (Toynbee 346)

GOALS OF SENDER COUNTRIES

G. M. Gathorne-Hardy
League of Nations and Conference of Ambassadors sought end to Yugoslav military incursions into Albania and to preserve territorial integrity of Albania as defined by boundaries agreed to in 1913. (Gathorne-Hardy 91–92)

RESPONSE OF TARGET COUNTRY

14 November 1921
Yugoslav note to Conference of Ambassadors: "The Conference of Ambassadors has . . . summoned [the Yugoslav government] to evacuate without delay the territory assigned to Albania . . . and threatens it with the application of extreme measures such as those provided for in Article 16 of the Covenant of the League of Nations. By this action a threatening situation has been created resembling that arising out of an ultimatum. Placed in this position the Royal Government states with the greatest regret, and under protest, that it bows to the decision of the Conference of Ambassadors in order to avoid the dangerous consequences of nonacceptance." (Toynbee 346)

Note: For the text of Article 16 of the League of Nations Covenant, see Case 35–1 UK and League of Nations v. Italy (1935–36: Abyssinia).

ECONOMIC IMPACT

Observed Economic Statistics

Yugoslav trade with all countries (1921): exports, $58.3 million; imports, $97.7 million.

Calculated Economic Impact

None, since sanctions never went beyond threat stage.

Relative Magnitudes

Gross indicators of Yugoslav economy	
Yugoslav GNP (1913)	$680 million
Yugoslav population (1913)	13 million
Annual effect of sanctions related to gross indicators	
Percentage of GNP	nil
Per capita	nil
Yugoslav trade with selected League members (UK, Italy) as a percentage of total trade	
Exports (1921)	26
Imports (1921)	27

Ratio of selected League members' GNP (1913: UK, France, and Italy, \$24.9 billion) to Yugoslav GNP (1913: \$680 million)	37

ASSESSMENT

Albert E. Hindmarsh
"Jugo-Slavia frankly admitted that the possibility of economic pressure left open no other course [but to withdraw its troops from Albania]." (Hindmarsh 131)

Arnold J. Toynbee
". . . the British Government's action [calling for League sanctions] had brought Jugoslavia to terms by imperilling the prospects of a Jugoslav loan on the London market and causing a fall in the dinar exchange, and it had stimulated the Conference of Ambassadors into performing their function." (Toynbee 345)

AUTHORS' SUMMARY

Overall assessment	Assigned scores
□ Policy result, scaled from 1 (failed) to 4 (success)	4
□ Sanctions contribution, scaled from 1 (none) to 4 (significant)	4
□ Success score (policy result *times* sanctions contribution), scaled from 1 (outright failure) to 16 (significant success)	16

Political and economic variables

□ Companion policies: J (covert), Q (quasi-military), or R (regular military)	—
□ International cooperation with sender, scaled from 1 (none) to 4 (significant)	4
□ International assistance to target: A (if present)	—
□ Sanctions period (years)	1
□ Economic health and political stability of target, scaled from 1 (distressed) to 3 (strong)	2
□ Presanction relations between sender and target, scaled from 1 (antagonistic) to 3 (cordial)	2
□ Type of sanction: X (export), M (import), F (financial)	—
□ Cost to sender, scaled from 1 (net gain) to 4 (major loss)	2

BIBLIOGRAPHY

Gathorne-Hardy, G. M. 1950. *A Short History of International Affairs 1920–1939*. London: Oxford University Press.

Hindmarsh, Albert E. 1933. *Force in Peace; Force Short of War in International Relations.* Cambridge, Mass.: Harvard University Press.

Toynbee, Arnold J. 1925. *Survey of International Affairs: 1920–1923.* London: Oxford University Press.

Case 25-1   League of Nations v. Greece

(1925: Border Skirmish)

CHRONOLOGY OF KEY EVENTS

19 October 1925   Border skirmishes occur between Bulgaria and Greece. (Barros 1; Walters 311)

21 October 1925   Greece issues ultimatum to Bulgaria to cease military actions, apologize, pay indemnity of 6 million drachmas. Note indicates that "orders had been issued to the military commander to repulse the invasion by taking all measures that we will judge *a propos* for the integrity of the national territory and its security, until satisfaction is given." (Barros 6, 12)

23 October 1925   Bulgarian government announces entry of Greek armed forces 10 kilometers into Bulgaria, requests immediate meeting of League of Nations Council under Article 11. League Council demands halt to fighting, withdrawal to frontiers; Bulgaria agrees, Greece resists. (Walters 311–13)

26–28 October 1925   League Council hints of naval demonstration, economic sanctions against Greece under Article 16; Greece agrees to evacuate Bulgarian territory; League sends Commission of Inquiry (composed of British, French, Italian military attachés) to scene to monitor compliance. (Walters 313; Barros 81–82)

7 December 1925   Commission of Inquiry reports findings; recommends troop withdrawal to frontiers, assesses damages of £45,000 against Greece. Report is accepted by both parties, payment is made in full in March 1926. (Walters 313–14; Gathorne-Hardy 94).

GOALS OF SENDER COUNTRIES

James Barros
"The desire to consolidate the new European *status quo*, legalized by the Locarno settlement, and make sure that no action by any state jeopardize this settlement, drove all the powers to act in unison and with dispatch." (Barros 119)

128

League Council President Aristide Briand of France
"'If the leak were not stopped up at once, there might be a flood.' . . . If Greece's attitude were to continue, 'it was essential for the Council to act at once and to act strongly.'" (Barros 79)

RESPONSE OF TARGET COUNTRY

Greek Prime Minister General Theodoros Pangalos
" . . . unless the 'Bulgarian aggression were dealt with promptly and with a strong hand,' the Greek refugees from Asia Minor, who had been settled near the Bulgarian frontier and were already nervous, would flee to Salonika and the entire refugee problem would be greatly complicated." (Barros 5)

James Barros
"Diplomatically isolated and with the threat of sanctions looming on the horizon, the Greek Government was in no position to resist. After receipt of the Council's resolution, [Athens] confirmed its previous instructions to the Greek military to evacuate Bulgarian territory." (Barros 81)

ECONOMIC IMPACT

Observed Economic Statistics

"Economically, Greece was reeling under the impact of more than a million refugees. . . . Politically, the country was seething with unrest as a result of the dictatorial government of General Pangalos." (Barros 119)

"[In late 1925] the Athens government had no cash at its disposal beyond such amounts as were required for current administrative expenses and supplies of immediate necessity. Payments in all fields had been deferred and fiscal obligations disregarded." (Barros 96)

Calculated Economic Impact

None, since sanctions did not go beyond threat stage.

Relative Magnitudes

Gross indicators of Greek economy	
Greek GNP (1929)	$533 million
Greek population (1920)	5.5 million
Annual effect of sanctions related to gross indicators	
Percentage of GNP	nil
Per capita	nil

Greek trade with selected League members (UK, France, Italy) as percentage of total trade	
Exports (1925)	39
Imports (1925)	33
Ratio of selected League members' GNP (1929, UK and France: $30 billion) to Greek GNP (1929: $533 million)	56

ASSESSMENT

James Barros
" . . . the most important consideration [in the Greek decision to obey the Great Powers] was its military weakness and susceptibility to naval blockade and harassment. Similarly, a demilitarized, friendless, and isolated Bulgaria was more than happy to comply with any and all requests made by the Great Powers. The fact that neither nation was tied to one of the Great Powers in any alliance, formal or informal, expedited the task of the powers and made collective action possible." (Barros 119)

"The League Council's success as an organ of international coercion had been due to a unique combination of factors which would never occur again in the years that were to follow." (Barros 115)

Francis P. Walters
"Amongst the keen supporters of the League, and indeed in the Council itself, its achievement was described in exaggerated language. . . . Yet . . . the settlement of the Greco-Bulgar affair was a notable event." (Walters 315)

G. M. Gathorne-Hardy
" . . . war was only stopped by the intervention of the League of Nations, whose supporters rightly claim this episode as perhaps the most strikingly successful instance of the efficacy of its machinery for the preservation of peace." (Gathorne-Hardy 94)

AUTHORS' SUMMARY

Overall assessment	*Assigned scores*
☐ Policy result, scaled from 1 (failed) to 4 (success)	4
☐ Sanctions contribution, scaled from 1 (none) to 4 (significant)	4
☐ Success score (policy result *times* sanctions contribution), scaled from 1 (outright failure) to 16 (significant success)	16

Political and economic variables

☐ Companion policies: J (covert), Q (quasi-military), or R (regular military)	—
☐ International cooperation with sender, scaled from 1 (none) to 4 (significant)	4

Political and economic variables (continued)	Assigned scores
□ International assistance to target: A (if present)	—
□ Sanctions period (years)	1
□ Economic health and political stability of target, scaled from 1 (distressed) to 3 (strong)	2
□ Presanction relations between sender and target, scaled from 1 (antagonistic) to 3 (cordial)	2
□ Type of sanction: X (export), M (import), F (financial)	—
□ Cost to sender, scaled from 1 (net gain) to 4 (major loss)	2

BIBLIOGRAPHY

Barros, James. 1970. *The League of Nations and the Great Powers.* Oxford, England: Clarendon Press.

Gathorne-Hardy, G. M. 1950. *A Short History of International Affairs 1920–1939.* London: Oxford University Press.

Walters, Francis P. 1952. *A History of the League of Nations.* 2 vols. London: Oxford University Press.

Case 32–1   League of Nations
v. Paraguay and Bolivia

(1932–35: Chaco War)

CHRONOLOGY OF KEY EVENTS

1928   Skirmishes break out between Paraguay and Bolivia over the Chaco, area of about 100,000 square miles. Conference of American States establishes Neutral Commission to mediate, with Colombia, Cuba, Mexico, Uruguay, US as members. (Walters 527; Conference Report 45)

1928–32   Bolivia, Paraguay stock up on munitions; skirmishes continue. (Walters 528)

2 August 1932   American republics call for peaceful settlement; Neutral Commission asks League of Nations to stand aside. (Walters 528)

September–
December 1932   Argentina, Brazil, Chile stand aloof from Neutral Commission, take no steps to limit arms shipments; League Council urges Commission of Inquiry. (Walters 529)

25 February 1933   Britain, France call upon League Council to organize arms embargo; President Herbert Hoover urges similar action by US Congress; US Senate rejects proposal, which then dies. (Walters 529)

April 1933   Bolivia presses forward in field; Neutral Commission abandons efforts, turns problem over to League. (Walters 530)

May 1933   Paraguay declares war in vain hope of stopping flow of munitions through Chile, Peru to Bolivia; Argentina stops export of arms, foodstuffs to Bolivia and "at a later stage this decision was to cost Bolivia dear." League proposes Commission of Inquiry, which both parties accept. (Walters 530–31)

July–November
1933   Paraguay, Bolivia ask delay in Commission of Inquiry while they attempt, without success, to settle dispute. Commission of Inquiry arrives in November 1933. (Walters 532)

December 1933   After sweeping military victory, Paraguay proposes armistice; Commission invites meeting of parties. (Walters 533)

February 1934   Paraguay rejects settlement proposals that do not concede its military successes; Commission recommends arms embargo to League Council. (Walters 534)

May 1934	Under leadership of Anthony Eden (Britain) and Castillo Najera (Mexico), League makes fresh appeal for arms embargo; US Congress gives president power to block arms sales; President Franklin D. Roosevelt acts immediately. By August 1934, arms embargo is enforced by virtually all League members. (Walters 534)
November 1934	Assembly Committee of Latin American members (formed by League in summer 1934) proposes peace treaty, which Paraguay rejects; Assembly Committee then recommends that arms sanctions be applied to Paraguay only; Paraguay announces its intent to withdraw from League. (Walters 535)
December 1934– July 1935	Paraguay suffers military reversals resulting from overextended supply lines. As result of mutual military exhaustion, armistice is reached along lines of Assembly Committee plan. (Walters 536)
July 1938	Peace formally signed. Paraguay obtains two-thirds of disputed territory, Bolivia gains Puerto Suarez, an outlet on Paraguay River. (Walters 536; Thomas 335)

GOALS OF SENDER COUNTRIES

League of Nations
May 1933: "The Council decided to send out a League Commission [of Inquiry], not to affix the responsibility for the conflict but to attempt to bring it to an end." (Zimmern 427)

RESPONSE OF TARGET COUNTRIES

Bolivia
In response to declaration of 3 August 1932 of Neutral Commission, Bolivian government replies: "We wish to terminate the Chaco question, the country being resolved to make bloody sacrifices in defense of its territory. The nation needs to break the barrier which prevents access to its banks on the Paraguay River in order to have communication with the world. That is one of the bases for a solution which must be required for Paraguay to insure the peace of America." (Insfran 22)

Paraguay
President Eusebio Ayala sets following conditions for peace talks: "immediate cessation of hostilities"; safeguards against resumption of fighting; arbitration of boundary dispute; "investigation of the responsibilities of the war in order to apply sanctions." (Insfran 31)

ATTITUDE OF OTHER COUNTRIES

Colombia, Cuba, Mexico, Uruguay, and United States
Participate in Neutral Commission, chaired by US, in attempt to mediate settlement terms from spring 1931 to 27 June 1933, when it is dissolved. (Conference Report 5)

Neutral Commission
3 August 1932: Members declare they "will not recognize any territorial arrangement of this controversy which had not been obtained by peaceful means nor the validity of any territorial acquisitions through occupation or conquest by force of arms." (Insfran 22)

Argentina, Brazil, Chile, Peru
Try to mediate peace settlement in fall 1933; later form mediatory group with Uruguay, US in 1935 to negotiate cessation of hostilities. (Conference Report 5–8)

United States
Letter of President Roosevelt to Col. Germán Busch, president of Bolivia, on 25 May 1938: "The Government of the United States has cooperated loyally and actively . . . in seeking a just and definitive settlement of the Chaco controversy. It has a vital interest, in common with its sister republics of the Americas, in perserving peace in our hemisphere." (Conference Report 135–36)

LEGAL NOTES

Bolivia
Claims the Chaco (territory between Bahia Negra and Pilcomay River) based on terms of Audiencia of Charcas and by virtue of principle of *uti possidetis*. (Conference Report 3)

Paraguay
Disputes Bolivian rights under Audiencia, counters that it had held the territory throughout colonial period. (Conference Report 3)

ECONOMIC IMPACT

Observed Economic Statistics

Bolivian exports dropped from more than $50 million in 1929 to $10 million in 1932 while imports shrank from $25 million to under $5 million. (Thomas 433)

In 1930, Bolivia's foreign debt reached $60 million; annual interest payments of $6 million severely strained total government revenues of $16 million. (Thomas 434)

Foreign investment in Bolivia (mostly in oil and tin) totaled about $150 million by 1929. (Thomas 433)

Bolivian and Paraguayan trade (million dollars)

	Exports		Imports	
	Bolivia	*Paraguay*	*Bolivia*	*Paraguay*
1932	10.4	7.5	4.7	3.8
1933	15.0	6.9	8.2	5.0
1934	31.2	8.3	16.0	7.6
1935	34.9	7.5	16.7	7.6

Source: Foreign Commerce Yearbook.

Food and clothing accounted for 33 percent of Bolivian imports in 1930 and 54 percent of Paraguayan imports in 1933. (*Foreign Commerce Yearbook*)

Calculated Economic Impact

	Annual cost to target country
Reduction in imports of foodstuffs and military equipment (estimated to be 30 percent of total imports) in 1934–35 by Bolivia and Paraguay; welfare loss estimated at 75 percent of value of trade.	$4 million

Relative Magnitudes

Gross indicators of Paraguayan and Bolivian economies	
Paraguayan and Bolivian GNP (1929 est.)	$134 million
Paraguayan and Bolivian population (1933)	3.9 million
Annual effect of sanctions related to gross indicators	
Percentage of GNP	3.0
Per capita	$1.03
Paraguayan and Bolivian trade with selected League members (UK, France, Italy, and Argentina) as percentage of total trade	
Exports (1933)	85
Imports (1933)	63
Ratio of selected League members' GNP (1929, UK, France: $30 billion) to Paraguayan, Bolivian GNP (1929: $134 million)	224

ASSESSMENT

Alfred Barnaby Thomas
Until 1934, "Neither side had difficulty in purchasing war materials, since the great industrial countries were glad to find an active market in the doldrums of the Depression." (Thomas 435–36)

"Both the Bolivian and Paraguayan governments, still uncertain of their capacity to prevent revolt at home, sought arbitration from the League, a step which set aside the League's authority to enforce the arms embargo. The war therefore continued for another year." (Thomas 436)

Alfred Zimmern
"[The cease-fire] was not due to any outside efforts but simply to weariness and financial exhaustion." (Zimmern 425)

"In the Chaco War both belligerents profited by [confusion caused by numerous mediation efforts], which enabled them and their respective backers to pursue operations without any effective restraint on the part of the League." (Zimmern 425–26)

AUTHORS' SUMMARY

Overall assessment	Assigned scores
☐ Policy result, scaled from 1 (failed) to 4 (success)	3
☐ Sanctions contribution, scaled from 1 (none) to 4 (significant)	2
☐ Success score (policy result *times* sanctions contribution), scaled from 1 (outright failure) to 16 (significant success)	6

Political and economic variables

☐ Companion policies: J (covert), Q (quasi-military), or R (regular military)	—
☐ International cooperation with sender, scaled from 1 (none) to 4 (significant)	3
☐ International assistance to target: A (if present)	—
☐ Sanctions period (years)	3
☐ Economic health and political stability of target, scaled from 1 (distressed) to 3 (strong)	2
☐ Presanction relations between sender and target, scaled from 1 (antagonistic) to 3 (cordial)	2
☐ Type of sanction: X (export), M (import), F (financial)	X
☐ Cost to sender, scaled from 1 (net gain) to 4 (major loss)	2

BIBLIOGRAPHY

Insfran, Pablo Max, ed. 1950. *The Epic of the Chaco: Marshal Estigarribia's Memoirs of the Chaco War, 1932–35.* Austin: University of Texas Press.
Thomas, Alfred Barnaby. 1956. *Latin America: A History.* New York: Macmillan.
US Department of Commerce. *Foreign Commerce Yearbook.* Various years. Washington.
US Department of State. 1940. *The Chaco Peace Conference.* Report of the US Delegation to the Peace Conference held in Buenos Aires 1 July 1935–23 January 1939. Washington.
Walters, Francis P. 1952. *A History of the League of Nations.* 2 vols. London: Oxford University Press.
Zimmern, Alfred. 1936. *The League of Nations and the Rule of Law 1918–1935.* London: Macmillan.

Case 33–1   UK v. USSR

(1933: Release of British Citizens)

CHRONOLOGY OF KEY EVENTS

16 April 1930	UK, USSR sign commercial pact; British firms ship about £15 million of manufactures during Russia's first five-year plan (1928–33) as result of improved trade relations. (Beloff 34)
17 October 1932	UK renounces 1930 trade agreement after Imperial Conference in Ottawa. UK frustrated because Soviets will not buy more British goods in order to diminish British trade deficit with USSR. (Beloff 35; Strang 117)
March 1933	Six British employees of Metropolitan-Vickers Ltd. are arrested; initially charged with wrecking three large electrical stations. Accusations of economic espionage and bribery are added later. (Beloff 35; Strang 81, 89)
20 March 1933	Britain suspends commercial negotiations with Russia. British Ambassador to Moscow, Sir Esmond Ovey, presses for stronger measures including immediate embargo on imports from USSR and possible severance of diplomatic relations. (Beloff 35; Strang 84)
27 March 1933	Ovey per instructions from London informs Soviet Foreign Minister Maxim Litvinov that action would be taken against Soviet imports unless word were received by 29 March that a trial would not be held. Litvinov responds that evidence is sufficient and a trial will be held. (Strang 87)
30 March 1933	Ovey leaves Moscow for consultations in London. (Strang 87)
April 1933	Parliament passes statute enabling government to embargo Russian imports. (Beloff 35)
12 April 1933	Trial opens. (Strang 99)
19 April 1933	Five of six British subjects are convicted, two are sentenced to two and three years in prison respectively while the others are expelled from USSR. London had decided previous day to bar Soviet imports

19 April 1933	if imprisonment decreed. British government authorizes far-reaching
(continued)	embargo on April 19 to go into effect in seven days. Moscow retaliates
	against British imports and recalls head of trade mission in London.
	(Strang 110; Beloff 35)

26 June 1933   British Foreign Secretary Sir John Simon and Litvinov begin talks in London on release of British citizens. (Beloff 35; Strang 114)

1 July 1933   Russia releases the two British prisoners, both embargoes are withdrawn. (Beloff 35; 114–16)

GOALS OF SENDER COUNTRY

Lord Strang, embassy counsellor and acting ambassador from April through October 1933
Immediately after arrests, "the British Government were absolutely convinced that there could be no justification for the charges. The future of Anglo-Soviet commercial relations and indeed of diplomatic relations was at stake. The best thing would be for the investigating authorities to discover that there was insufficient evidence and to release the prisoners." (Strang 84)

After trial began, Strang and others in Moscow Embassy felt that "unless preparation or apology were exacted, or some sanction applied, the Soviet authorities would have been allowed to organise a gigantic frame-up of these six completely innocent British subjects. . . . The Government took a calmer view and which in the cool light of retrospect, I would now recognize to have been a juster view, more in keeping with the facts of international life. If there were to be an embargo, this would only be if there were sentences which were in fact carried out." (Strang 99)

Following enactment of the embargo on 26 April, government informed Parliament that, "the embargo could be removed, and would be removed, as soon as the two prisoners returned safely to Britain. . . ." (Strang 112)

RESPONSE OF TARGET COUNTRY

Max Beloff
At World Economic Conference in London, "the Soviet delegation proposed a mutual withdrawal of all discriminations against the trade of particular countries . . . and Litvinov again elaborated his idea of an economic nonaggression pact." (Beloff 54)

Maxim Litvinov
In response to initial British request for release of its citizens, "Litvinov maintained . . . that British subjects could not be exempt from Soviet law; but that the authorities, and in particular his own department, were stretching points so as to be as helpful to us as possible. . . . " (Strang 84)

According to Tass, in Ovey's 27 March meeting with him, "Litvinov had said that the decision to hold a trial had been taken and could not be changed whatever the British Government might do. Methods of diplomacy by gross external pressure might be successful in Mexico but were doomed to failure in the Soviet Union." (Ovey had served in Mexico City before coming to Moscow.) (Strang 87)

Lord Strang
"Our act of economic discrimination against the Soviet Government raised a point of vital principle for them, and they would be bound to delay a settlement until they could demonstrate their capacity to make compensating arrangements with other countries, which they now proceeded to do with no great success." (Strang 113)

ECONOMIC IMPACT

Observed Economic Statistics

Soviet trade with UK (million pounds sterling)

	Exports	Imports
1932	19.7	10.6
1933	17.4	4.3
1934	17.3	7.5
1935	21.8	9.7
1936	18.9	13.3
1937	29.1	19.5
1938	19.5	17.4

Source: Beloff 111.

In 1930s UK was leading market for Soviet exports, taking 27 percent of total Russian exports in 1930, 24 percent in 1932, only 17.5 percent and 16.6 percent in 1933 and 1934, but rebounding to 23.5 percent, 26.6 percent, 32.7 percent, and 28.2 percent in following years. (Beloff 41, 111)

"Soviet foreign indebtedness rose from 415 million roubles in October 1929 to . . . 975 million in June 1932. (From 1933 the return to an active trade balance, coupled with increasing gold production, rapidly diminished the outstanding indebtedness.)" (Beloff 30)

Calculated Economic Impact

	Annual cost to target country
Reduction in exports to UK for 2½ months in 1933; welfare loss estimated at 35 percent of value of trade affected by embargo.	$4 million

Relative Magnitudes

Gross indicators of USSR economy	
USSR GNP (1930)	$18.1 billion
USSR population (1932)	165.7 million

Gross indicators of USSR economy (continued)	
Annual effect of sanctions related to gross indicators	
Percentage of GNP	negl.
Per capita	negl.
USSR trade with UK as percentage of total trade	
Exports (1933)	17
Imports (1933)	9
Ratio of UK GNP (1930: $19.4 billion) to USSR GNP (1930: $18.1 billion)	1

ASSESSMENT

Lord Strang

"The strong reaction of the British Government and the deep anger of the British people were not foreseen . . . the Soviet authorities were constrained to modify in some degree the normal pattern of examination, trial, and sentence in cases of this nature. The early release of [two prisoners], the subsequent release of three of their colleagues on bail . . . the perfunctoriness of the action against some of the prisoners, the relatively decorous staging of the trial, the lightness of the sentences—all these were undoubtedly attributable to powerful intervention from London. . . . As for foreign opinion in Moscow, it unreservedly recognized that the British Government had in the end had their way." (Strang 118–20)

AUTHORS' SUMMARY

Overall assessment	Assigned scores
□ Policy result, scaled from 1 (failed) to 4 (success)	4
□ Sanctions contribution, scaled from 1 (none) to 4 (significant)	3
□ Success score (policy result *times* sanctions contribution), scaled from 1 (outright failure) to 16 (significant success)	12

Political and economic variables

□ Companion policies: J (covert), Q (quasi-military), or R (regular military)	—
□ International cooperation with sender, scaled from 1 (none) to 4 (significant)	1
□ International assistance to target: A (if present)	—
□ Sanctions period (years)	1
□ Economic health and political stability of target, scaled from 1 (distressed) to 3 (strong)	2
□ Presanction relations between sender and target, scaled from 1 (antagonistic) to 3 (cordial)	1
□ Type of sanction: X (export), M (import), F (financial)	M
□ Cost to sender, scaled from 1 (net gain) to 4 (major loss)	2

BIBLIOGRAPHY

Beloff, Max. 1947. *The Foreign Policy of Soviet Russia: 1929–1941.* Vol. 1 (1929–36). London: Oxford University Press for Royal Institute of International Affairs.

Hoover, Calvin B. 1931. *The Economic Life of Soviet Russia.* New York: Macmillan.

Strang, William. 1956. *Home and Abroad.* London: A. Deutsch.

Case 35–1   UK and League of Nations v. Italy

(1935–36: Abyssinia)

CHRONOLOGY OF KEY EVENTS

5 December 1934	Italian, Abyssinian (Ethiopian) forces clash at Wal-Wal over disputed border between Abyssinia, Italian Somaliland. (Doxey 46; Zimmern 436)
December 1934–October 1935	France, UK seek solution within Abyssinian context using Anglo-French-Italian Treaty of 1906 as framework. (Doxey 46)
3 January 1935	Abyssinia appeals to League Council under Article 11 concerning Wal-Wal incident; issues are submitted to arbitration under Italian-Abyssinian treaty of 1928 without results. (Highley 107; Doxey 46)
17 March 1935	Chancellor Adolph Hitler introduces conscription in Germany, violating Treaty of Versailles. (Doxey 47)
September 1935	League appoints Committee of Five (UK, France, Poland, Spain, Turkey) under Article 15:3 to investigate Abyssinian complaint. French Prime Minister Pierre Laval insists in private meetings with British that no measures that might lead to war should be taken. This position is known to Italy by 12 October 1935. (Highley 10, 100)
5 October 1935	Italy invades Abyssinia. (Highley 10)
7 October 1935	League of Nations Committee of Six (appointed 5 October 1935) finds Italy guilty of violating Article 12. (Highley 10)
11 October 1935	League approves Proposal No. 1, embargoing supply of arms to Italy. (Renwick 12; Highley 14)
19 October 1935	League approves Proposal No. 2, prohibiting loans and credits to government of Italy and quasi-public organizations; Proposal No. 3 (effective 18 November 1935) prohibiting imports from Italy; Proposal No. 4 (effective 18 November 1935) embargoing limited range of exports to Italy, including rubber, certain minerals, transport animals, but *not* including coal, oil, or steel (moreover, extensive exemptions

are provided for fulfilling contracts when goods are partly paid for); Proposal No. 5, providing vague mutual assistance measures for countries disrupted by sanctions. (Renwick 12; Highley 78–92)

2 November 1935   League considers Proposal No. 4A, adding coal, oil, pig iron, steel to embargoed exports; Laval requests and obtains deferral of decision. League approves Proposal No. 4B obligating members to survey their trade, control abnormal increases in traffic with Italy through third countries. (Renwick 13–14)

7 December 1935   British Foreign Secretary Sir Samuel Hoare and Laval meet secretly in Paris to work out agreement for partial cession of Abyssinia to Italy; proposals are leaked, causing scandal in UK; Hoare resigns 18 December 1935. (Renwick 16)

12 February 1936   Estimates circulate that oil sanctions would require 12 to 14 weeks to be effective provided US participated; however, Hoare-Laval proposal of 7 December 1935 (above) undercut possibility of US participation. (Renwick 16)

2 March 1936   Hoare's successor, Sir Anthony Eden, advocates oil sanctions in Sanctions Committee; cabinet colleagues and French block idea for fear of starting major European war. "[The British government] inquired of [Italian dictator Benito] Mussolini whether he would object to his oil being cut off; when told that he would, they successfully resisted oil sanctions in Geneva." (Renwick 17–18; Hoffman 144–45; Taylor 127)

7 March 1936   Hitler denounces Locarno Treaty; German troops occupy Rhineland. (Renwick 17)

15 April 1936   League addresses "supreme appeal" to Italy to cease hostilities, but Italian delegation insists on *de facto* recognition of military position. (Highley 110, 117)

5 May 1936   Italian troops enter Addis Ababa. (Renwick 17)

4 July 1936   League of Nations discontinues sanctions by vote of 44 to 1 (Abyssinia). (Renwick 18)

GOALS OF SENDER COUNTRIES

August–October 1935
According to statements in British cabinet, "psychological effect on Signor Mussolini and the Italian people cannot fail to be very great." (Renwick 12)

Late 1935
"There was strong resistance within the international banking community to more drastic action. Italy's large outstanding foreign debt rendered the creditor countries anxious to avoid precipitating a repudiation." (Renwick 19)

2 December 1935
Cabinet statement of British Prime Minister Stanley Baldwin concerning efficacy of oil sanctions: "The object of an oil sanction was to stop the war. If war could be stopped by making the peace, that would be better." (Renwick 16)

29 May 1936
Cabinet statement of Baldwin: Keeping sanctions in force would not likely have any effect on Mussolini "except to make matters worse. . . . The difficulty was one of face-saving and public opinion in this country." (Renwick 17)

26 June 1936
Winston Churchill: "First, the Prime Minister had declared that sanctions meant war; secondly, he was resolved there must be no war; and thirdly, he decided upon sanctions." (Renwick 23)

1935–36
"[N]one of the leading politicians (from Eden to Litvinov) were especially interested in Ethiopia. What they wanted was both to preserve the principles and keep Italy as an ally. Italy and the 'principles' were then intended to be used in the political campaign against Germany." (Hoffman 142)

RESPONSE OF TARGET COUNTRY

2 October 1935
Speech by Mussolini: "At the League of Nations, they dared to speak of sanctions. To sanctions of an economic character we will reply with our discipline, with our sobriety, and with our spirit of sacrifice. To sanctions of a military character we will reply with orders of a military character." However, Mussolini later told Hitler privately that if League had followed Eden and imposed oil sanctions, Italy would have had to withdraw. (Renwick 18, 108–9)

November 1935
Fascist Grand Council states its "implacable resistance" to sanctions and its determination to "reveal to the world the Roman virtue of the Italian people in the year 14 of the Fascist era." Sir Eric Drummond, British ambassador to Italy, is duly persuaded of Italian intransigence: "In their present mood, Signor Mussolini and the Italian people are capable of committing suicide if this seems the only alternative to climbing down." (Highley 106; Renwick 24)

24 November 1935
Le Temps: "Authoritative opinion has it that the Italian ambassador warned of the danger to Franco-Italian relations which would result from application of Proposal IVA, and that, in consequence, M. Laval suggested to Sir George [Clerk] the postponement of the proposed meeting of the Committee of Eighteen." Proposal 4A, which would have extended sanctions to oil, coal, and steel, was never implemented. (Highley 107)

1935–36
Summary by Highley of Italian attitude: "Mussolini, confident that war would be avoided by members of the League at any cost and emboldened by M. Laval's voeu that the most severe economic measures be withheld until Italy checked new efforts at conciliation, was enabled to ward off increased sanctions by threats of war or hints of a conciliatory

attitude." According to Walters: "Political and economic measures were instituted (by Italy), including controls over foreign exchange, and an intensive propaganda campaign mounted." (Highley 101, 105; Doxey 107; Walters 650–51)

February 1936
Italian delegate to League, Renato Bova-Scoppa, warns Pierre Etienne Flandin, French delegate, that oil sanctions might cause Italy to withdraw from League and denounces military agreement that was corollary to Franco-Italian pact of 7 January 1935. (Highley 113)

ATTITUDE OF OTHER COUNTRIES

50 members of League of Nations
Approve sanction measures on 12 October 1935 and 19 October 1935; report progress toward implementation by 31 October 1935. (Renwick 12)

Austria, Hungary, Albania (League members)
Refuse to apply sanctions for political and security reasons. (Highley 75–76)

Switzerland (League member)
Refuses to apply Proposal 3 for neutrality reasons but gives assurances that trade will not exceed 1934 levels. (Highley 75–76, 90)

Ecuador, Paraguay (League members)
Refuse to put measures in force. (Highley 75–76)

Yugoslavia (League member)
Applies sanctions, incurs severe trade losses; UK grants partial relief via duty-free entry of poultry and large bacon quota. (Highley 36)

Argentina, Guatemala, Honduras, Nicaragua, Panama, El Salvador, Uruguay, Venezuela (League members)
Accept some or all of measures "in principle" only. (Highley 75–76)

Germany (non-League member, gave notice of withdrawal from League in October 1933, effective October 1935)
Does not support sanctions but states that it will not increase exports at expense of countries applying sanctions. (Highley 97).

United States (non-League member)
President Franklin D. Roosevelt's response is constrained by First Neutrality Act of August 1935. On 5 October 1935, Roosevelt administration embargoes arms to both belligerents; asks traders not to profiteer and not to trade with Italy in excess of "normal peacetime levels." Nevertheless, US supplies 6.5 percent of Italian oil imports before embargo, and 17 percent by end of 1935. (Highley 95; Renwick 15)

Egypt (non-League member)
Applies sanctions. (Highley 95)

Brazil, Saudi Arabia, Costa Rica (non-League members)
Give dilatory responses or refuse to apply sanctions. (Highley 95)

LEGAL NOTES

Legal basis for League of Nations action—Article 16
"Should any Member of the League resort to war in disregard of its Covenants under Articles 12, 13 or 15, it shall *ipso facto* be deemed to have committed an act of war against all other Members of the League, which hereby undertake immediately to subject it to the severance of all trade or financial relations, the prohibition of all intercourse between their nationals and the nationals of the Covenant-breaking state, and the prevention of all financial, commercial or personal intercourse between the nationals of the Covenant-breaking state and the nationals of any other state, whether a Member of the League or not."

Legal basis for national action
In order to implement League measures, 17 states enact special legislation; 29 states act under preexisting legislation and constitutional provisions. (Highley 66–68)

Bilateral most-favored-nation treaty clauses
League suggests that bilateral benefits based on initial concessions to Italy (now withdrawn) could also be withdrawn but that they should be left in place as matter of mutual support; League also suggests that special favors granted under mutual support provisions need not be extended on MFN basis. (Highley 62–63)

Commercial rights of Italian nationals
League pronounces that commercial rights of Italian nationals are overridden by League action. (Highley 63)

ECONOMIC IMPACT

Observed Economic Statistics

Italian trade with principal partners (million dollars)

	Exports	Imports
Presanction		
November 1934–June 1935	161.4	236.2
Postsanction		
November 1935–June 1936	105.4	163.9

Source: Renwick 98.

Miscellaneous
Italy devalues lira by 25 percent in November 1935. (Renwick 19)

Italian net gold sales are $93.8 million in period November 1935–June 1936. (Renwick 98)

In 1935–36, foreign banks restrict credit to Italy out of prudential concerns. (Renwick 19)

Calculated Economic Impact

	Annual cost to target country
Reduction of merchandise exports by $56 million over 6 months; welfare loss estimated at 30 percent of face value of trade.	$34 million
Reduction of merchandise imports by $72 million; welfare loss estimated at 30 percent of face value of trade.	43 million
Forced sale of gold reserves of $93.8 million; welfare loss estimated at 10 percent of face value.	9 million
Total	$86 million

Relative Magnitudes

Gross indicators of Italian economy	
Italian GNP (1937)	$5 billion
Italian population (1937)	43.4 million
Annual effect of sanctions related to gross indicators	
Percentage of GNP	1.7
Per capita	$1.98
Italian trade with UK and France as percentage of total trade	
Exports (1935)	17
Imports (1935)	15
Ratio of UK and French GNP (1937: $32 billion) to Italian GNP (1937: $5 billion)	6

ASSESSMENT

Sir Anton Bertram, expressing a pre-Abyssinian view of the League
"The economic weapon, conceived not as an instrument of war but as a means of peaceful pressure, is the great discovery and the most precious possession of the League." (Bertram 169)

David Lloyd George on sanctions
"They came too late to save Abyssinia, but they are just in the nick of time to save the Government." (Rowland 723)

M. J. Bonn
"Stocks on hand, the practice of economies, the development of substitutes, and the purchase of goods with gold, foreign securities, emigrants' remittances and tourists' disbursements kept the country going without too severe a strain." (Bonn 360)

"The financial boycott did not imply much more than the moral sanctification of a prudent businesslike attitude." (Bonn 354)

Neville Chamberlain, chancellor of the exchequer, speaking on 10 June 1936
Sanctions "failed to prevent war, failed to stop war, failed to save the victims of aggression." Continuance of sanctions was "the very midsummer of madness." (Renwick 18)

Foreign Minister Anthony Eden speaking to the House of Commons on 18 June 1936
"The fact has to be faced that sanctions did not realize the purpose for which they were imposed." (Renwick 18)

AUTHORS' SUMMARY

Overall assessment	Assigned scores
□ Policy result, scaled from 1 (failed) to 4 (success)	1
□ Sanctions contribution, scaled from 1 (none) to 4 (significant)	1
□ Success score (policy result *times* sanctions contribution), scaled from 1 (outright failure) to 16 (significant success)	1

Political and economic variables

□ Companion policies: J (covert), Q (quasi-military), or R (regular military)	—
□ International cooperation with sender, scaled from 1 (none) to 4 (significant)	4
□ International assistance to target: A (if present)	A
□ Sanctions period (years)	1
□ Economic health and political stability of target, scaled from 1 (distressed) to 3 (strong)	3
□ Presanction relations between sender and target, scaled from 1 (antagonistic) to 3 (cordial)	2
□ Type of sanction: X (export), M (import), F (financial)	F, X, M
□ Cost to sender, scaled from 1 (net gain) to 4 (major loss)	3

BIBLIOGRAPHY

Bertram, Sir Anton. 1932. "The Economic Weapon as a Form of Peaceful Pressure." 17 *Transactions of the Grotius Society.*
Bonn, M. J. 1937. "How Sanctions Failed." 15 *Foreign Affairs* 350–61.
Brown-John, C. Lloyd. 1975. *Multilateral Sanctions in International Law: A Comparative Analysis.* New York: Praeger.
Doxey, Margaret P. 1980. *Economic Sanctions and International Enforcement.* 2d ed. New York: Oxford University Press for Royal Institute of International Affairs.
Highley, Albert E. 1938. *The First Sanctions Experiment.* Geneva: Geneva Research Centre, July.

Hoffmann, Fredrik. 1967. "The Functions of Economic Sanctions: A Comparative Analysis." 4 *Journal of Peace Research* 140–60.

Renwick, Robin. 1981. *Economic Sanctions*. Harvard Studies in International Affairs No. 45. Cambridge, Mass.: Harvard University Center for International Affairs.

Rowland, Peter. 1975. *David Lloyd George, A Biography*. New York: Macmillan.

Taylor, A. J. P. 1965. *The Origins of the Second World War*. Hammondsworth, England: Penguin.

Walters, Francis P. 1952. *A History of the League of Nations*. 2 vols. London: Oxford University Press.

Zimmern, Alfred. 1936. *The League of Nations and the Rule of Law 1918–1935*. London: Macmillan.

Case 38–1   UK and US v. Mexico

(1938–47: Expropriation)

CHRONOLOGY OF KEY EVENTS

1917   Article 27 of Mexican constitution of 1917 defines nation's ownership of subsoil resources. (Bermúdez 23)

18 March 1938   Mexico expropriates foreign oil companies; forms Petróleos Méxicanos (PEMEX). (Bermúdez 23)

7 May 1938   Mexico reaches understanding with Sinclair group for compensation of $8.5 million plus sale to Sinclair of 20 million barrels (bbls.) of oil at favorable prices, ranging from $0.60/bbl. to $0.90/bbl. (Bermúdez 24–25)

1938   UK breaks diplomatic relations with Mexico over expropriation. (Bermúdez 175)

US Under Secretary of State Sumner Welles publicly accepts Mexican claims of sovereignty over natural resources (thereby distressing US oil industry) but continues to press for compensation for Standard Oil of New Jersey, other US groups, not including value of oil in ground. (Engler 194–95; Bermúdez 17)

1938–42   International oil companies boycott PEMEX products, deny PEMEX access to tetraethyl lead; major tanker fleets avoid Mexican ports; US delays Export–Import Bank loan for Mexican refining facilities; US companies attempt, without success, to persuade US government to reduce import quotas on oil from Mexico, cut silver purchases. (Engler 195)

December 1940   Mexico amends Article 27 of constitution of 1917 to cancel all oil concessions. (Bermúdez 23)

17 April 1942   Standard Oil group claims are satisfied by Cooke-Zevada agreement between US State Department and Mexican foreign office, calling for payment of $24 million of principal. (Bermúdez 25–26)

17 April 1942   Cities Service negotiates compensation of $1.1 million for two members of its group. In 1948, $1 million settlement is reached with four other companies in group. (Bermúdez 26)

1943	State Department supports bid of major US oil firms to reenter Mexico; reportedly blocks independent firm's efforts to build Mexican refinery. (Engler 196)
	Eximbank provides $10 million for construction of new Azcapotzalco refinery. (Bermúdez 176)
29 August 1947	Agreement reached with Royal Dutch/Shell group, which had represented about 70 percent of industry before expropriation, calling for compensation of $81.3 million plus interest at 3 percent from 1938. (Bermúdez 26–27)
1950	Eximbank lends Mexico $150 million, which is on-loaned to PEMEX. (Bermúdez 180–81)

GOALS OF SENDER COUNTRIES

George Philip
"[T]he US government took so dim a view of [PEMEX's] future that it sought only to contain the agency in the expectation that it would eventually die an almost natural death." (Philip 329)

RESPONSE OF TARGET COUNTRY

George Philip
"The Mexican nationalization resulted above all from the claim to effective national sovereignty. Discontent on the part of the Mexican government with particular aspects of company behavior, while important, was subordinate to a greater discontent with the status claimed by the companies themselves." (Philip 225)

ECONOMIC IMPACT

Observed Economic Statistics

Mexican oil industry

	Average daily production (1,000 bbl.)	Average daily exports (1,000 bbl.)	Average daily exports (million dollars)
1936	112	—	—
1937	129	—	—
1938	105	25	8.8

Mexican oil industry (*continued*)

	Average daily production (1,000 bbl.)	Average daily exports (1,000 bbl.)	Average daily exports (million dollars)
1939	118	45	13.0
1940	120	51	11.9
1941	118	43	13.7
1942	95	17	6.8
1943	96	16	8.0
1944	104	13	7.7
1945	119	22	9.8
1946	135	26	13.7
1947	154	38	24.9
1948	160	36	34.9

— Zero or negligible.
Source: Bermúdez 215, 222, 248.

Before 1947, PEMEX had banking relations only with Chemical Bank and Trust Company. By 1958, PEMEX had established relations with 7 large US banks, involving revolving credits of $54 million. (Bermúdez 181–83)

Calculated Economic Impact

	Annual cost to target country
Delay in Eximbank loan for Mexican refinery; welfare loss estimated at 10 percent of value of loan.	$1 million
Reduction in export revenues in 1938 resulting from boycott by international oil companies; welfare loss estimated at 40 percent of lost earnings.	2 million
Offset	
Gain from delay in compensation for expropriated oil companies; welfare gain estimated at 3 percent interest on value of assets.	($1 million)
Total	$2 million

Relative Magnitudes

Gross indicators of Mexican economy	
Mexican GNP (1938)	$1.2 billion
Mexican population (1938)	18.7 million

Gross indicators of Mexican economy (continued)

Annual effect of sanctions related to gross indicators	
Percentage of GNP	0.2
Per capita	$0.11

Mexican trade with US, UK as percentage of total trade	
Exports (1938)	77 (US: 67)
Imports (1938)	62 (US: 58)

Ratio of UK, US GNP (1938: $90 billion) to Mexican GNP (1938: $1.2 billion)	75

ASSESSMENT

Antonio J. Bermúdez

"However, it was natural that during its earlier period (1938–1942) the national corporation would be viewed from abroad with misgivings, and from certain quarters with open hostility. During those years, international markets for Mexican oil were practically cut off, as were most sources of material and equipment." (Bermúdez 175)

"Fortunately the Government under President Miguel Valdés Alemán was able, in 1947, to settle the question of indemnities for the expropriated English companies. This settlement and the desire of foreign manufacturers and suppliers of the vast amount of heavy material, equipment, and services to do business with Mexico, were two of the most important steps in establishing the corporation's importance and trustworthiness. . . . " Shortly thereafter PEMEX was able to purchase on terms other than cash in advance or on very short terms. (Bermúdez 177)

"One of the most important results of the settlement concluded with the British companies was the increase in international prestige of Mexico and Petróleos Méxicanos which in turn brought about ā notable influx of credit." (Bermúdez 27)

George Philip

"The birth of Pemex was not easy and the prospects of the infant were not generally regarded highly . . . most of the senior technical and administrative staff were foreign and left at the time of the expropriation. To add to this there was the effect of the boycott which had been successfully mounted by the oil companies on Mexican oil exports and on supplies of capital goods to Pemex." (Philip 329)

AUTHORS' SUMMARY

Overall assessment	Assigned scores
□ Policy result, scaled from 1 (failed) to 4 (success)	3
□ Sanctions contribution, scaled from 1 (none) to 4 (significant)	3
□ Success score (policy result *times* sanctions contribution), scaled from 1 (outright failure) to 16 (significant success)	9

Political and economic variables	Assigned scores
☐ Companion policies: J (covert), Q (quasi-military), or R (regular military)	—
☐ International cooperation with sender, scaled from 1 (none) to 4 (significant)	2
☐ International assistance to target: A (if present)	—
☐ Sanctions period (years)	9
☐ Economic health and political stability of target, scaled from 1 (distressed) to 3 (strong)	3
☐ Presanction relations between sender and target, scaled from 1 (antagonistic) to 3 (cordial)	2
☐ Type of sanction: X (export), M (import), F (financial)	F, M
☐ Cost to sender, scaled from 1 (net gain) to 4 (major loss)	2

BIBLIOGRAPHY

Bermúdez, Antonio J. 1963. *The Mexican National Petroleum Industry: A Case Study in Nationalization.* Stanford, Calif.: Stanford University, Institute of Hispanic American and Luso-Brazilian Studies.

Cline, Howard F. 1953. *The United States and Mexico.* Cambridge, Mass.: Harvard University Press.

Engler, Robert. 1961. *Politics of Oil.* Chicago: University of Chicago Press.

Philip, George. 1982. *Oil and Politics in Latin America.* Cambridge: Cambridge University Press.

US Congress. Senate Committee on Naval Affairs. 1946. *Nomination of Edwin W. Pauley for Appointment as Under Secretary of the Navy.* 79 Cong., 2 sess., vol. 12: 1974–88.

Case 39–1 Alliance Powers v. Germany and Japan

(1939–45: World War II)

CHRONOLOGY OF KEY EVENTS

Also see Case 40–1 US v. Japan (1940–41: Withdrawal from Southeast Asia)

1936–39 Britain formulates plans for economic warfare against Germany, including as major elements: Trading with the Enemy Act to control trade with enemy government, its residents, its controlled corporations, and designated sympathetic neutrals; distinction between "adjacent neutrals" and "overseas neutrals" (i.e., US) with stricter trade controls such as "forcible rationing" applied to "adjacent neutrals," limiting imports to peace-time requirements less stocks on hand; blacklisting suspect neutrals as to sales of goods, provision of shipping facilities, and extension of credit. (Medlicott 1:18–22)

Summer 1939 Britain, France lay joint plans for controlling contraband, regulating trade with neutrals. J. M. Keynes proposes "policy of temptation" be followed—making available to Germany goods that are least likely to help in wartime—coupled with policy of preemptive buying; proposals are rejected as impractical. (Medlicott 1:36–39)

3 September 1939 Britain declares state of war with Germany, following invasion of Poland; establishes Ministry of Economic Warfare. According to prewar plans, "The aim of economic warfare is so to disorganize the enemy's economy as to prevent him from carrying on the war." (Medlicott 1:1)

November 1939 British Ministry of Economic Warfare imposes complete blockade on seaborne German exports, which are reduced by 80 percent in a few months. German imports are limited by several measures: compulsory navicerts (as in World War I), supplemented by ship warrants, required for all neutrals trading with Britain; blacklisting of ships and firms suspected of buying on behalf of Germany; preemptive buying of essential materials; rationing of exports to neutral countries; a reprisals order to justify seizure of German exports in neutral ships. (Medlicott 1:43, 58)

155

September 1939– June 1940	During "phony war," Britain takes cautious line against important neutrals—Japan, US, USSR—and does not implement forcible rationing, preemptive buying, or bombing of industrial targets in Germany. (Medlicott 1:44–45)
September 1939– March 1940	Meanwhile, Britain and France consider methods of denying Swedish and Norwegian iron ore to Germany; both countries reject démarches and plan is dropped. Similarly, plans to deny Germany use of Russian and Romanian oil supplies by strategic bombing and other means are explored and abandoned. (Medlicott 1:44–45)
17 January 1940	R. H. Cross, minister of economic warfare, overoptimistically declares that Germany is in same difficult straits as after first two years of World War I. (Medlicott 1:44)
8 April 1940	Britain mines Norwegian waters as way of stopping ships; Germany occupies Norway, then Denmark. As result, UK freezes assets of those countries under its Trading with the Enemy Act. (Medlicott 1:46, 59)
30 July 1940	Following fall of France, UK institutes: compulsory navicerts (with US acquiesence); ship warrants, issued only to vessels that comply with navicerts, as passport to use of British-controlled shipping facilities; compulsory rationing. (Medlicott 1:422)
August 1940	UK Commercial Corporation undertakes aggressive preemptive buying in "adjacent" neutral states. (Medlicott 1:424–25)
February 1941	US undertakes preemptive buying in cooperation with UK, directed against Japan as well as Germany. Eventually joint program covers wool, rubber, iodine, platinum, beryllium, industrial diamonds, wolfram, molybdenum, and mercury. (Medlicott 1:426)
June 1941	Germany invades Soviet Union; UK almost immediately pledges assistance to USSR, as does US. (*Keesing's* 4667, 4739)
December 1941	With attack on Pearl Harbor, US embargo of Japan merges with UK embargo of Germany. (Medlicott 2:119)
Winter 1941–Fall 1942	"[A]llied military prospects gave no leverage to economic warfare. The German sweep into Russia and Allied disasters at Pearl Harbor and in Southeast Asia left few counterpressures to German demands on the neutrals." (Acheson 49)
1943	"Combined Bomber Offensive" begins in spring with American bombers making daylight precision raids on German industry with goal of destroying German aircraft, ball bearing, and oil industries. "Loss of any one could be fatal to the Nazis." British RAF carries out massive "area strikes" at night targeted at industrial centers, with additional objective of undermining civilian morale. (Sunderman 170–73)

19 May 1945   Germany unconditionally surrenders, thus ending war in Europe. (*Keesing's* 7191)

1 September 1945   Japan surrenders, thus ending war in Asia. (*Keesing's* 7397)

GOALS OF SENDER COUNTRIES

W. N. Medlicott

☐ Drastically limit German imports from non-European sources.
☐ Create encirclement neurosis.
☐ Hamper Axis armament efforts through raw material shortages.
☐ Indirectly hamper Axis economy.
☐ Strengthen neutral resistance to Axis powers both by economic aid and by threats of retaliation. (Medlicott 2:659)

"In its widest application the term 'economic warfare' covered three means of defeating the German economic effort—blockade, counterproduction, and attack behind the enemy's fighting front. . . . At no stage of the war was Germany decisively weakened by shortages due to the blockade alone. That it was not a negligible factor in the Allied war effort is equally certain." (Medlicott 2:630–31)

RESPONSE OF TARGET COUNTRIES

Margaret P. Doxey
In 1930s, Germany instituted self-sufficiency program. During war, Germany assiduously cultivated neutrals, obtaining, for example, wolfram from Spain and Turkey; ball bearings from Sweden. (Doxey 20)

Admiral Erich Raeder, commander in chief of the Navy
In August 1942, advised Chancellor Adolph Hitler that: "(1) It is urgently necessary to defeat Russia and thus create a *Lebensraum* which is blockade-proof and easy to defend. Thus we could continue to fight for years;" and "(2) The fight against the Anglo-Saxon sea powers will decide both the length and the outcome of the war, and could bring England and America to the point of discussing peace terms." (Medlicott 2:646)

ATTITUDE OF OTHER COUNTRIES

Overseas neutrals
In December 1939, US, Argentina, Uruguay, Brazil subscribe to UK navicert system, i.e., "commercial passports" for noncontraband cargo. (Medlicott 1:54)

In 1941, US establishes Board of Economic Warfare (BEW) for purpose, inter alia, of collaborating with UK Ministry of Economic Warfare. (Medlicott 1:502)

In February 1941, British Ambassador Lord Halifax asks US support in limiting supplies to Japan; President Franklin D. Roosevelt exhibits caution. (Medlicott 2:74–75)

Adjacent neutrals
In 1939–40, UK negotiates War-Trade Agreements with adjacent neutrals precluding reexport, limiting shipments to normal prewar levels: Sweden, Belgium (December 1939);

Norway, Holland, Denmark (early 1940). However, no agreements are reached with South European, Baltic, or Balkan states, or USSR. In May 1940, agreement is reached with Spain. (Medlicott 2:55–56)

In December 1940–January 1941, UK, Netherlands agree on quotas for shipments from Netherlands East Indies to Japan covering tin, rubber, nickel ore, other materials. (Medlicott 2:81–82)

In 1943–44, adjacent neutral states yield to Allied pressure to limit shipments to Germany: Sweden (ball bearings); Switzerland (various manufactured goods); Turkey (chrome); Spain and Portugal (wolfram). (Medlicott 2:639)

Spain
In 1940, Hitler pressures Spain to enter war on Axis side; Generalissimo Francisco Franco narrowly avoids doing so after haggling over territorial spoils in Africa. (Medlicott 2:541)

In 1941, Britain lends Spain funds to purchase phosphates, manganese, wheat. (Medlicott 2:545)

In 1942, Hitler offers 100,000 tons of grain and part of Africa for Spanish participation in war. (Medlicott 2:541–42)

In 1942, Britain buys oranges and mercury from Spain in exchange for wheat and rubber. (Medlicott 2:295–96)

In 1943, Hitler offers high-quality war matériel to Spain. (Medlicott 2:549)

In June 1943, Franco puts out feelers to Allies. US, UK provide 100,000 tons of cotton (normal Spanish requirements) and 541,000 tons of petroleum (60 percent of normal needs); buy Spanish goods at rising prices. (Medlicott 2:557–76)

In 1944, US halts petroleum shipments until Spain agrees to recall its division from Eastern front, expel Axis agents, reduce exports to Germany, release certain Italian ships for Allies to capture. Spain acquiesces. (Medlicott 2:557–76)

ECONOMIC IMPACT

Observed Economic Statistics

Germany
During war, more than half of German oil supplies are cut off; 85 percent of manganese; 96 percent of molybdenum; 92 percent of tungsten; 85 percent of nickel; 77 percent of copper. (Medlicott 2:633)

Occupation of France, Norway, Denmark brings perhaps 2.0 million metric tons (mmt) of captured oil, compared to 1940 German consumption of 5.9 mmt. Russian campaign adds little to German oil supplies; however, synthetic oil technology yields good results by 1942. (Medlicott 2:651–53)

In May 1944, Allied bombing destroys 90 percent of German fuel capacity; Albert Speer, minister of armaments and production, views war as lost at that point. (Medlicott 2:640)

Iron ore imports from Sweden: 10.3 million tons, 1943; 4.5 million tons, 1944; drop caused in large part by British pressure. However, while decline hurts steel production, it comes too late to affect war outcome. (Medlicott 2:658–59)

After significant drop in 1939–41, German grain imports are replaced by supplies from occupied territories. These imports average 3.6 mmt annually 1939–44 compared with normal prewar imports of 3.8 mmt. Meat consumption in Germany declines 37 percent but overall grain consumption is maintained, in part by food requisitioned from occupied territory. (Medlicott 2:648–49)

Japan
By 1944, imports of essential materials drop sharply from 1940 levels: scrap iron and steel, down from 1.4 mmt to 0.074 mmt; coking coal, 1.4 mmt down from 3.3 mmt; iron ore, 1.7 mmt as compared to 5.1 mmt in 1940; crude oil and products, down to 5.0 million barrels from 37.2 million barrels. (Cohen 116–34)

During period 1939–41, average annual Japanese exports and imports are ¥3,288 million and ¥3,085 million respectively; during 1942–44 these totals drop to ¥2,851 million and ¥2,902 million. (Cohen 13, 69)

Calculated Economic Impact

	Annual cost to target country
Reduction in Japanese trade 1942–44; welfare loss valued at 200 percent of decline.	$288 million
Reduction in German trade with US, UK 1940–44; welfare loss valued at 100 percent of decline.	400 million
Total	$688 million

Relative Magnitudes

Gross indicators of German and Japanese economies	
German and Japanese GNP (1939)	$43.6 billion
German and Japanese population (1937)	137.6 million
Annual effect of sanctions related to gross indicators	
Percentage of GNP	1.6
Per capita	$5.00
German and Japanese trade with US/UK as percentage of total trade	
Exports (1939)	12
Imports (1939)	18
Ratio of US/UK GNP (1939: $95.9 billion) to German and Japanese GNP (1939: $43.6 billion)	2

ASSESSMENT

Germany

W. N. Medlicott
"If Germany be no Achilles with a single vital spot, she is vulnerable and can be bled to

death if dealt sufficient wounds. This may be said to have remained the basic assumption of the Ministry throughout the war, although the search for Achilles' heel . . . was never abandoned." (Medlicott 1:47)

"[I]n spite of the cutting off of overseas supplies, Germany could hope, with her natural resources, her considerable measure of self-sufficiency, her stocks, and her access to Swedish and Balkan supplies, to withstand economic pressure in a war with the Western European powers for a considerable period; the estimate of a period of 15 to 18 months before Allied pressure began to have an effect was not, in the circumstances, unduly pessimistic." (Medlicott 1:35)

"It is in fact one of the broad paradoxes of this story that as the effectiveness of economic weapons increased their reputation declined." (Medlicott 1:43)

"'Blockade and bombing' played a leading part in the grand strategy of [1940–41], and throughout the war it continued to be assumed that they would play an appreciable part in 'softening up' the enemy. But in fact . . . the most characteristic achievements in the economic war for the next three years lay in a remarkable development of the contraband-control system, based on control at source and preemption with American help." (Medlicott 2:636–37)

"[T]here could be no final certainty that a trickle of smuggled goods was not reaching Germany (through Spain). But with this reservation, it can be said that the control of contraband from overseas to Europe after 1942 was complete." (Medlicott 2:639)

"In general then it can be said that fear of the consequences of blockade played a part in drawing Germany into the Russian adventure and the two-front war which ultimately proved so disastrous for her; perhaps one can say that in this sense the fear of blockade may have been more important than blockade itself in bringing her to ultimate defeat." (Medlicott 2:646)

" . . . by the summer of 1944 the German economy was on the verge of decline both absolutely and relative to the mounting Allied output. This really means that 'economic warfare' measures had fulfilled their purpose, if we take this to be the weakening of the enemy's production for war purposes to an extent which would give the Allied forces the advantage in equipment and resources at the decisive moment." (Medlicott 2:647)

Klaus Knorr

"Economic warfare hardly caused the downfall of Germany and Japan, although it contributed to their eventual collapse. And the contribution it did make surely resulted overwhelmingly from *military* measures of economic warfare, from naval blockade, and especially in the case of Germany, from aerial bombardment." (Knorr 140)

Dean Acheson

"The denial of materials for enemy war production was much less successful and important [than procurement of materials for allies]. Until the latter part of 1944 it was marginal everywhere. From then on it was more successful in Sweden than elsewhere.

"A good case can be made for the argument that economic measures resulted in stopping important exports for military needs from Sweden to Germany about six months before military measures would have done so. Exports from Switzerland and the Iberian Peninsula probably moved in minimum necessary quantities until military measures stopped them.

"However such economic measures as raising prices and preclusive buying reduced all other exports from all neutral sources to the injury of the enemy." (Acheson 62)

Margaret P. Doxey
"But although the Allied effort in economic warfare undoubtedly had its effect in weakening Germany's war potential and capacity and contributed to her eventual defeat, it is not contended, or generally considered that it was a decisive factor at any stage." (Doxey 20)

Economist
"In the second world war, too, the Germans demonstrated that they could find substitutes for almost any product of which they were deprived—including oil. The head of Bomber Command was assured that the destruction of a molybdenum mine in Norway would have a serious effect on German output. It was destroyed on two occasions, but this had no perceptible impact on Germany." (*Economist* [London], 2 October 1982, 102)

Japan

W. N. Medlicott
"The economic-warfare problem was an infinitely simpler one [in the Pacific] than in Europe; in the Pacific area there was virtually no neutral screen, and the enemy could not exist for long without his overseas supplies. . . . In the Pacific area, far more than in Europe, the softening-up function of a maritime blockade might ensure the substance of victory. In the end, Japan was brought to unconditional surrender without an invasion of her home islands, and after devastating and expensive air attack; there seems every reason to think that the same result could have been achieved more economically by blockade alone." (Medlicott 2:126–27)

"After 1942 the economic isolation of Japan became almost entirely a matter of action by submarines and aircraft against supply ships trying to make the long and vulnerable passage from Southeast Asia to the home islands." (Medlicott 2:661)

Margaret P. Doxey
"The case of Japan was rather different [from Germany's]. Lacking adjacent neutrals from whom she could draw supplies and, like Britain, vulnerable to interference with her shipping routes by air and sea attacks, she was seriously affected by traditional blockade tactics. In particular, shortages of minerals which resulted from the Allied blockade all but halted Japanese industries engaged in war production which were not, in any case, able to compete with Allied output." (Doxey 20–21)

Jerome B. Cohen
". . . in large measure Japan's economy was destroyed twice over, once by cutting off of imports and secondly by air attack." (Cohen 107)

AUTHORS' SUMMARY

Overall assessment	Assigned scores
☐ Policy result, scaled from 1 (failed) to 4 (success)	4
☐ Sanctions contribution, scaled from 1 (none) to 4 (significant)	3
☐ Success score (policy result *times* sanctions contribution), scaled from 1 (outright failure) to 16 (significant success)	12

Political and economic variables	Assigned scores
☐ Companion policies: J (covert), Q (quasi-military), or R (regular military)	R
☐ International cooperation with sender, scaled from 1 (none) to 4 (significant)	4
☐ International assistance to target: A (if present)	A
☐ Sanctions period (years)	6
☐ Economic health and political stability of target, scaled from 1 (distressed) to 3 (strong)	3
☐ Presanction relations between sender and target, scaled from 1 (antagonistic) to 3 (cordial)	1
☐ Type of sanction: X (export), M (import), F (financial)	F, X, M
☐ Cost to sender, scaled from 1 (net gain) to 4 (major loss)	4

Comments

Allied success in World War II was essentially a *military* victory but economic blockade of Germany, Japan played modest role in final outcome. Because of geography, blockade had greater impact on Japan; but even in Germany, particularly by 1944, it did affect production of war matériel. If, as Medlicott suggests, the threat of Allied blockade helped turn Hitler's attention eastward to Russia, then its contribution was more than modest.

BIBLIOGRAPHY

Acheson, Dean. 1969. *Present at the Creation.* New York: W. W. Norton & Co.

Cohen, Jerome B. 1949. *Japan's Economy in War and Reconstruction.* Minneapolis: University of Minnesota Press.

Doxey, Margaret P. 1971. *Economic Sanctions and International Enforcement.* London: Oxford University Press for Royal Institute of International Affairs.

Keesing's Contemporary Archives. 1940–43, 1943–45.

Knorr, Klaus. 1975. *The Power of Nations: The Political Economy of International Relations.* New York: Basic Books.

Medlicott, W. N. 1952. *The Economic Blockade.* 2 vols. London: Longmans, Green.

Sunderman, James F., ed. 1981. *World War II in the Air: Europe.* New York: Van Nostrand Reinhold Co.

Case 40–1   US v. Japan
(1940–41: Withdrawal from Southeast Asia)

CHRONOLOGY OF KEY EVENTS

April 1940   Japan bombs rail link between Indochina and China that France used to move munitions to China. (Feis 66)

6 June 1940   Government of Netherlands East Indies gives assurances, demanded by Japan, of continued supply of oil. (Feis 68)

15 June 1940   President Franklin D. Roosevelt suggests he would stop export of scrap iron to Japan once he had legislative authority; Congress quickly passes National Defense Act containing such authority. (Feis 72)

17 June 1940   France asks Germany for armistice. The next day, Japan demands that France cease all military shipments from Indochina to China and accept posting of Japanese observers in Indochina; France accedes on 20 June 1940. (Feis 66)

2 July 1940   Roosevelt issues first presidential order under National Defense Act, licensing exports of: arms, ammunition, implements of war; aluminum, magnesium; airplane parts, optical instruments, metalworking machinery. Order conspicuously omits controls on oil and scrap iron at insistence of Secretary of State Cordell Hull. (Feis 74)

12 July 1940   Britain agrees, at Japanese insistence, to close overland transport routes for war materials, including oil and trucks, from Burma and Hong Kong to China. (Feis 71)

18–20 July 1940   Cabinet Secretaries Henry Morgenthau, Jr., Treasury; Henry L. Stimson, War; and Frank Knox, Navy, together with British Ambassador Lord Lothian, formulate sweeping plan to deprive Germany and Japan of oil, entailing bombing synthetic fuel plants in Germany; destroying oil wells in Netherlands East Indies; imposing complete US embargo on Japan; carrying out preemptive buying elsewhere in world. Morgenthau plan is presented to Roosevelt. Acting Secretary of State Sumner Welles prepares less sweeping embargo order that would limit only aviation fuel and lubricants and high-quality iron scrap, contending that complete ban would precipitate Japanese

18–20 July 1940 *(continued)*	action against Indies and Britain. Morgenthau then prepares alternative order that would license all oil and all scrap metal, leave the extent of embargo for later determination. (Feis 89–91)
25 July 1940	Roosevelt signs Treasury (Morgenthau) version; State Department protests; British and Dutch governments, sharing State Department fears, urge prudent course against Japan; president then substitutes less restrictive State Department version. (Feis 93–94)
26–27 July 1940	Cabinet of Prime Minister Prince Fumimaro Konoye adopts diplomatic policy that stresses: quick end to conflict in China; solving "problem" in Southeast Asia by means that would not lead to war with "other powers" (namely, US and Britain). (Feis 84–85)
16 August 1940	US government urges private oil companies operating in Indies (Standard Vacuum and Dutch Shell) to drive hard commercial bargain with Japan and not sell large amounts of aviation fuel. (Feis 98–99)
13 September 1940	Japan asks Indies to supply three million tons of oil annually for five years, five-fold increase. Dutch delay, ask US not to embargo oil while talks are in progress. (Feis 104–5)
24 September 1940	Japanese army enters Indochina in limited fashion with quasi-consent of Vichy government. (Feis 98, 106)
26 September 1940	Roosevelt embargoes all grades of iron, steel scrap to Japan; says nothing about oil; Gallup poll reveals 88 percent of Americans approve US embargo. (Feis 106, 122)
27 September 1940	Tripartite Pact secretly concluded in Berlin, recognizes primacy of Germany and Italy in Europe, of Japan in Greater East Asia. Article 3 provides that powers "undertake to assist one another with all political, economic and military means when one of the three Contracting Parties is attacked by a power [i.e., US] at present not involved in the European War or in the Sino-Japanese Conflict." (Feis 111)
12 November 1940	Private oil companies in East Indies agree to provide Japan with 1.8 million tons of oil annually, instead of 3.1 to 3.7 million tons demanded. (Feis 131)
November–December 1940	US, British naval officers confer on joint measures to protect Singapore and Atlantic route, presaging closer military cooperation in succeeding months. Britain asks US to take its oil tankers out of Japanese routes, urges concerted pressure on private companies to reject Japanese oil demands in Indies. (Feis 133–44, 158)
28 December 1940	Morgenthau proposes freeze on all foreign assets in US as means of controlling trade with Japan; Hull blocks proposal. (Feis 143)
February–March 1941	Hull yields to pressure from British and Morgenthau, agrees to control exports of drums and storage tanks, keeps US-controlled tankers out of Japanese routes. (Feis 159)

13 April 1941	Japanese-Soviet neutrality pact signed, paving way for further Japanese expansion to south. (Feis 187–89)
14 May 1941	Foreign Minister Yosuke Matsuoka complains to Ambassador Joseph C. Grew that pro-British US activities are provoking Germany and that, if war came, Japan would be compelled to fight. (Feis 202)
27 May 1941	Roosevelt declares "unlimited national emergency" for purpose of providing assistance to Britain. (Feis 204)
28 May 1941	US Congress extends Section 6 of National Defense Act to cover US territories and dependencies; Roosevelt applies it to embargo exports of iron, chrome ore and manganese, copper, copra, abaca from Philippines. (Feis 205–6)
17 June 1941	Japan breaks off talks with Indies on increased access to raw materials; receives less than half its requests for rubber, tin. (Feis 207)
20 June 1941	Domestic scarcity prompts Roosevelt to embargo oil exports from eastern US ports to Japan while maintaining shipments to British Empire; he rejects advice to suspend all oil shipments to Japan as endangering peace in Pacific. (Feis 206)
22 June–2 July 1941	Germany invades Russia; Foreign Minister Matsuoka urges Japan to join attack but Konoye cabinet at Imperial Conference decides against war with USSR, instead determines to consolidate control of Indochina. By code interception, US learns of Imperial Conference decision to move farther in the south. (Feis 210–14)
10 July 1941	Acting Secretary of State Welles informs British Ambassador Lord Halifax that US would impose economic and financial embargoes if Japan takes overt steps to acquire alien territories in Far East. (Feis 227)
24 July 1941	Roosevelt tells Japanese Ambassador Kichisaburo Nomura that danger of war could be averted "if the Japanese Government would refrain from occupying Indochina. . . ." Nevertheless, Japan proceeds with occupation plans; Japanese warships appear off Camranh Bay, troop transports move south. (Feis 236–38)
26 July 1941	President issues Executive Order 8832 freezing Japanese assets. US licensing policy limits Japan to "usual or prewar quantities" (i.e., 1935–36) of low-grade gasoline, crude oil, and lubricants; adopts posture that licenses may be issued in individual cases. In fact no licenses are issued. (Feis 238–39, 247–48)
July 1941	Great Britain, Dominions, and Empire freeze Japanese funds, renounce trade treaties with Japan. (Feis 245)
28 July 1941	Netherlands East Indies, adopting new posture of firmness, imposes licensing system limiting all exports to Japan; embargoes exports of tin, rubber. (Feis 246–47)

6 August 1941	Ambassador Nomura links Japanese withdrawal from Indochina with settlement of China war, recognition of Japan's preeminent role in Southeast Asia, restoration of normal trade; proposes Roosevelt-Konoye meeting, idea Roosevelt rebuffs. (Feis 249, 257–58)
6 September 1941	Japan Imperial Conference determines to seek US, British acquiescence by diplomacy, and if diplomacy does not bear fruit by October, to prepare for war. Declining oil stocks plus threat of bad weather after December prompt imperial army, navy to force early decision; Konoye is rebuffed again in attempt to meet with Roosevelt. (Feis 261–70)
16 October 1941	Konoye cabinet falls; General Hideki Tojo becomes prime minister. (Feis 277–87)
26 November 1941	Hull rejects Tokyo proposals that US recognize Japanese primacy in China and Southeast Asia, offering instead "comprehensive basic proposal." Roosevelt anticipates invasions in Thailand, Malaya, Dutch Indies, "possibly" Philippines. (Feis 295, 320)
7 December 1941	Japan attacks Pearl Harbor, Southeast Asia. US embargo becomes appendage to World War II. (Medlicott 2:119)

GOALS OF SENDER COUNTRY

May 1939
US Ambassador to Tokyo Grew warns Roosevelt that " . . . if we cut off Japanese supplies of oil . . . and she cannot obtain sufficient oil from other commercial sources to ensure her national security, she will probably send her fleet down to take the Dutch East Indies." (Maechling 12)

Early October 1940
State Department adopts view that no US measures will restrain or appease Axis group and that US cannot afford to permit Japan to seize Indies or Singapore. Hull urges delay in tightening export controls because US admirals report that fleet is not ready to fight Japan. (Feis 123)

October–November 1940
Roosevelt, in reelection campaign, reaffirms support for Britain but denies any intention to engage American forces abroad. "I have said this before, but I shall say it again and again and again: Your boys are not going to be sent into any foreign wars." (Feis 128, 133)

19 July 1941
US Navy War Plans Division, in "Study of the Effect of the Embargo on Trade between the United States and Japan" concludes: "7(c). An embargo would probably result in a fairly early attack by Japan on Malaya and the Netherlands East Indies, and possibly would involve the United States in early war in the Pacific. . . . 8. *Recommendation*—That trade with Japan not be embargoed at this time." Admiral Richard K. Turner, war plans

officer, and Admiral Harold R. Stark, chief of naval operations, endorse these conclusions. (Feis 232)

24 July 1941
Roosevelt asks Japan to "refrain from occupying Indochina." Two days later, when Japanese troop transports move south, he freezes Japanese assets, effectively stops all trade in petroleum products in retaliation for aggression. (Feis 236–39)

RESPONSE OF TARGET COUNTRY

July 1940
"The Konoye Cabinet read no lesson in the orders about oil and scrap. . . . It still felt itself free to push on with the program for the New Order in East Asia, despite the injunction contained in the resolution of the Imperial Conference of July 26–27 'to solve the problem of the South within such scope as would not lead to war with other powers.'" (Feis 95)

September 1940
Few in Japan "were in the mood to draw what would have been the saving conclusion or dared to do so: that Japan should give up aims that would bring her into war against the United States. . . . The embargo failed as a lesson, since it was taken as a challenge." (Feis 109)

July 1941
"Events were to show that the freezing order shook the Japanese rulers. But they did not change their course. They were soon to decide to rush full speed ahead, lest they not have enough oil to reach those distant ports which were marked on the Imperial chart." (Feis 239)

1941
"Drastic civilian economies in the use of motor gasoline cut consumption from 6.3 mmb [million metric barrels] in 1940 to 1.5 mmb in 1941. This was done to meet the Anglo-American–Dutch embargo and to permit greater military stockpiling." (Cohen 25)

2 December 1941
A Japanese ambassador noted that "the Japanese people believe that economic measures are a more effective weapon of war than military measures; that . . . they are being placed under severe pressure by the United States to yield to the American position; and that it is preferable to fight rather than to yield to pressure." (Acheson 64–66)

LEGAL NOTES

Section 6, Act to Expedite the Strengthening of the National Defense (1940)
"Whenever the President determines that it is necessary in the interest of national defense to prohibit or curtail the exportation of any military equipment or munitions, or component parts thereof, or machinery, tools, or material or supplies for the manufacture, servicing or operation thereof, he may by proclamation prohibit or curtail such exportation, except under such rules or regulations as he shall prescribe." (Feis 73)

ECONOMIC IMPACT

Observed Economic Statistics

Japanese trade (million yen)

	Exports	Imports
1938	2,690	2,663
1939	3,576	2,918
1940	2,656	3,453
1941	2,651	2,899

Source: Cohen 13.

Civilian oil consumption in 1940 is cut from 6 million to 7 million barrels/year to 1.6 million; dependence on US supplies is reduced from 80 percent to 60 percent. (Maechling 13)

Japanese imports of US crude oil and products

Million barrels	Crude	Products	Total
August–December 1939	6.7	4.9	11.6
August–December 1940	5.2	6.1	11.3
August–December 1941	0.1	0.3	0.4
Million dollars			
1939	20.9	23.8	44.7
1940	15.9	35.3	51.2
1941	6.9	21.1	28.0

Source: Feis 268–69; Wilkins 374.

Miscellaneous

Japan imports 2.4 million metric tons (mmt) of scrap iron, steel in FY 1937, 1.4 mmt in 1938, 2.6 mmt in 1939, 1.4 mmt in 1940, and 0.2 mmt in 1941. US exports to Japan average 1.8 mmt for period 1937–39 before sanctions are imposed. (Cohen 118; Feis 108)

US exports of scrap iron, steel to Japan 1937–40 total $37.4 million, $21.7 million, $32.5 million, and $17.0 million, respectively. (Wilkins 372)

In 1940 Japanese iron and steel scrap imports total 1.4 million tons, equal to 32 percent of consumption; iron ore imports total 5.7 million tons, equal to 82 percent of consumption. (Medlicott 2:108)

Japan's stockpile of 5.8 mmt of scrap iron in 1939 is reduced by more than 20 percent during 1940–41. (Feis 109; Cohen 48)

Estimates in August 1941 indicate that Japanese stocks of several key commodities (nickel, zinc, lead, antimony, wolfram, tin, copper) are 12 months' usage or less. Oil stocks are 5.7 million tons in December 1941, down from peak of 7 million tons in 1939. (Cohen 134; Medlicott 2:119–20)

At time of asset freeze, Japanese holdings in UK are £1.6 million; in rest of sterling area (mostly India) additional £2.6 million is held. (Medlicott 2:108)

Calculated Economic Impact

	Annual cost to target country
Reduced shipments to Japan of crude oil and products; welfare loss estimated at 125 percent of value of trade.	$60 million
Blocking of Japanese assets in the US, UK, British Empire, valued at 100 percent.	17 million
Reduction in Japanese imports of iron and steel scrap; welfare loss estimated at 40 percent of reduced trade.	11 million
Total	$88 million

Relative Magnitudes

Gross indicators of Japanese economy	
Japanese GNP (1940)	$9.3 billion
Japanese population (1940)	72.5 million
Annual effect of sanctions related to gross indicators	
Percentage of GNP	0.9
Per capita	$1.21
Japanese trade with US as percentage of total trade	
Exports (1938)	20
Imports (1938)	42
Ratio of US GNP (1940: $100 billion) to Japanese GNP (1940: $9.3 billion)	11

ASSESSMENT

Secretary of the Treasury Henry Morgenthau, Jr.
"My own opinion is that the time to put pressure on Japan was before she went into Indo-China and not after and I think it's too late and I think the Japanese and the rest of the dictators are just going to laugh at us. The time to have done it was months ago and then maybe Japan would have stopped, looked, and listened." (Feis 106)

Herbert Feis
"My own best surmise is that stronger and earlier action would not have caused Japan to slow up, then desist from its course. More probably, I think, it would have caused it to move farther and faster." (Feis 107)

"The embargo failed as a lesson, since it was taken as a challenge. Japan had already engaged herself in a combination with the prime purpose of deterring the United States from bringing its power to bear." (Feis 109)

W. N. Medlicott
"What is incontestable is that the almost complete suspension of exports to Japan from so many vital sources would have compelled her to abandon her whole policy of expansion if she had not been prepared to face the risks of war." (Medlicott 2:119)

AUTHORS' SUMMARY

Overall assessment	Assigned scores
☐ Policy result, scaled from 1 (failed) to 4 (success)	1
☐ Sanctions contribution, scaled from 1 (none) to 4 (significant)	1
☐ Success score (policy result *times* sanctions contribution), scaled from 1 (outright failure) to 16 (significant success)	1

Political and economic variables

☐ Companion policies: J (covert), Q (quasi-military), or R (regular military)	—
☐ International cooperation with sender, scaled from 1 (none) to 4 (significant)	2
☐ International assistance to target: A (if present)	—
☐ Sanctions period (years)	1
☐ Economic health and political stability of target, scaled from 1 (distressed) to 3 (strong)	3
☐ Presanction relations between sender and target, scaled from 1 (antagonistic) to 3 (cordial)	1
☐ Type of sanction: X (export), M (import), F (financial)	F, X
☐ Cost to sender, scaled from 1 (net gain) to 4 (major loss)	3

BIBLIOGRAPHY

Acheson, Dean. 1969. *Present at the Creation*. New York: W. W. Norton & Co.
Cohen, Jerome B. 1949. *Japan's Economy in War and Reconstruction*. Minneapolis: University of Minnesota Press.
Feis, Herbert. 1950. *The Road to Pearl Harbor*. Princeton, NJ: Princeton University Press.
Herzog, James H. 1973. *Closing the Open Door*. Annapolis, Md.: Naval Institute Press.
Maechling, Charles. 1979. "The First Energy War." *Foreign Service Journal* (August): 11–13, 29–31.
Medlicott, W. N. 1952. *The Economic Blockade*. 2 vols. London: Longmans, Green.
Wilkins, Mira. 1973. "The Role of US Business." In *Pearl Harbor as History*, ed. Dorothy Borg and Shumpei Okamoto. New York: Columbia University Press.

Case 44–1 US v. Argentina

(1944–47: Destabilize Perón)

CHRONOLOGY OF KEY EVENTS

January 1942   At meeting of American states in Rio de Janeiro, US pressures all Latin American states to break diplomatic relations with Axis powers. Although many already had done so and several had declared war on Axis, Argentina authors successful resolution that merely recommends breaking relations rather than making break mandatory. (Frank 4–6)

May 1942   US Secretary of the Treasury Henry Morgenthau, Jr., urges freezing Argentine assets in US. Secretary of State Cordell Hull opposes recommendation as detrimental to Good Neighbor Policy initiated by President Franklin D. Roosevelt. Hull opposes same suggestion when Morgenthau reiterates it in June 1943 following overthrow of Argentine President Ramón S. Castillo. "This blatant approach, Hull insisted, would have a reverse effect and only strengthen the military because of the 'supersensitivity of the Argentines to any suggestion of outside pressure.'" (Frank 19–20)

Spring 1943–early 1944   Argentine military is concerned by growing power of Brazil, which is receiving arms from US through Lend-Lease program. When Castillo fails to get US arms for Argentina, military overthrows him. When new leaders also fail, they secretly send envoy to Germany. His capture by British and revelation of his mission in January, along with disclosure in Buenos Aires that Axis espionage ring has been operating there, prompt Argentina to break diplomatic relations with Axis powers 24 January 1944. (Frank 24–26)

Spring 1944   Pedro P. Ramírez, who had succeeded Castillo, is ousted as President and Vice President Edelmiro J. Farrell succeeds him. US does not recognize new government. Behind scenes is Col. Juan Perón, who acquires positions of acting minister of war, head of Secretariat of Labor and Social Welfare. In June 1944 he becomes vice president. Perón had been neutralist opposed to the rupture of relations with the Axis and refused to comply with Ramírez's promises to provide US with information on Axis intelligence operations in Argentina;

Spring 1944 (continued)	to ban telecommunications with Germany and Japan; to implement economic sanctions against enemy; and to cease Argentina's "cryptic activities in neighboring countries." (Frank 50)
June–October 1944	US, angered by Argentina's refusal to take action against Axis, recalls its ambassador, freezes Argentina's gold deposits in New York, prohibits American vessels from calling on Argentine ports. Third action "did not exist for more than a few months." Assistant Secretary of State Dean Acheson terms actions, "using a club to kill a mosquito." (Frank 20–21; Alexander 1951, 207)
October 1944	Perón proposes meeting of foreign ministers of Latin American countries be held "to resolve the problems between the United States and Argentina." US is opposed, particularly as State Department leadership is in transition from Hull to Edward R. Stettinius, Jr., but finally accepts idea in spirit of "inter-American solidarity." (Frank 54)
February 1945	Inter-American Conference on Problems of War and Peace convenes in Mexico City. "Though the question of Argentina was not officially included on the agenda, all the delegations were in agreement as to the resolution of the problem. The Argentines would first declare war on the Axis powers and move to eliminate their considerable activities in Argentina. Moreover, the military government was to comply with the principles set forth in the Act of Chapultepec relative to individual liberty and democratic standards. The United States would then relax its coercive policy, remove its economic sanctions, recognize the military rulers, and attempt to bring about Argentina's entrance into the United Nations. To these benefits would be added the very real prospect of Argentina receiving military equipment." (Frank 54)
March 1945	Argentina declares war on Germany, Japan. Perón begins to hint constitutional rule may be restored. (Frank 55)
May 1945	New US Ambassador, Spruille Braden, arrives in Buenos Aires. Braden "maintained that Perón's adherence to the Chapultepec agreement was simply 'cynical opportunism'. One must handle Perón in tough fashion," he thought. British Ambassador Sir David Kelly felt that Braden arrived in Argentina "with the notion that 'he had been elected by Providence to overthrow the Farrell-Perón regime.'" (Frank 56–57)
30 June 1945	In response to Braden's press campaign to undermine him, Vice President Perón warns Braden that he can no longer guarantee safety of members of American press and those who associate with them (Braden) from "fanatics" loyal to Perón who believe press is part of plot to overthrow government. Braden cables Washington about confrontation, suggests offering reporters asylum in embassy and use of its communication facilities to send stories by code. He acknowledges "[t]heir courageous reporting has been of utmost utility in weakening Perón." (Frank 66–69)

6 August 1945	Perón, in effort to demonstrate his commitment to democratic solution, lifts state of siege imposed by President Castillo in December 1941. "The month of August became a memorable one in Argentine history for violence in the streets." Perón "fell back on repression." (Frank 79)
11 September 1945	US Foreign Economic Administration announces that Argentina (and several other countries named as Axis collaborators) will not benefit from postwar relaxation of export restrictions. (*New York Times*, 13 September 1945, A13)
Late September 1945	Braden is recalled to Washington to become assistant secretary of state for Latin American affairs, following Nelson Rockefeller's resignation. Shortly after Braden's departure, Perón reinstates a state of siege in response to attempted coup. Crackdown leads US to announce it will undertake full review of its relations with Argentina, will consider both diplomatic and economic actions. (Frank 86–88; *New York Times*, 28 September 1945, A5)
3 October 1945	Dean Acheson, as acting secretary of state, denounces Argentina for not living up to obligations under Chapultepec agreement, among them "the control of enemy property and persons, observing democratic principles, doing away with war restrictions, permitting freedom of the speech and of the press. . . . " As result of this failure, Acheson announces US will not associate with Argentina in "multilateral military alliance for the Western hemisphere," will ask for postponement of Pan-American conference scheduled to negotiate alliance in Rio de Janeiro 20 October 1945. (*New York Times*, 4 October 1945, A1)
9 October 1945	Perón is forced to resign all three of his positions under pressure from military. On 13 October he is arrested but is released, restored to power four days later following massive demonstration in Buenos Aires by more than 200,000 laborers threatening general strike. (Frank 92–93)
12 February 1946	In move interpreted by many as intended to block Perón's presidential candidacy, Braden and State Department release so-called Blue Book that alleges collaboration between military government of Argentina and Nazis. Braden denies defeat of Perón is his goal. (Frank 102)
24 February 1946	Perón is elected president by "a record 56 percent of the Argentine people." (Frank 108)
27 March 1946	Braden rejects breaking diplomatic relations with and economic sanctions against Argentina as options in US policy. He characterizes "any attempt to impose sanctions as futile, because neither France nor Britain would back us, nor would we in this country want to assume the responsibility of depriving the starving of Europe of the food Argentina could supply." (*New York Times*, 28 March 1946, A1)

25 *June 1946*	Argentine Foreign Minister Juan A. Bramuglia announces that US, at request of its new ambassador, George Messersmith, has agreed to unfreeze Argentina's gold assets held at Federal Reserve Bank in New York. (*Keesing's* 8010)
July 1946	Braden continues to insist, with President Harry S Truman's support, that arms embargo—by potential European as well as American suppliers—remain in effect until Argentina demonstrates "full compliance with its Chapultepec commitments to act against Axis interests and agents." (Potash 68)
May 1947	Despite US objections, UK approves some £20 million in contracts to supply aircraft, naval vessels to Argentina. (Potash 77)
3 June 1947	Truman announces he is satisfied with Argentine compliance with Chapultepec agreement and "long-deferred Rio conference [for discussing a mutual defense pact] could now be scheduled." "Rio Treaty" is signed on 2 September 1947. (Potash 78–79)
4 June 1947	Braden resigns from State Department; Argentina, US resume "normal diplomatic relations." (Frank 111)
October 1947– *October 1948*	Perón obtains antiaircraft guns from US and within a year "formal military mission agreement" is signed between the countries. (Potash 81–82)
May 1950	With economic situation "beginning to approach a crisis," Argentine banks receive $125 million loan from US Export–Import Bank. Coming just before Argentina's ratification of Rio Treaty, many Argentines interpret loan as "payoff" but other observers disagree. Perón's attacks on US policy diminish. (Alexander 1979, 73; Potash 120)

GOALS OF SENDER COUNTRY

January 1942
Prior to Rio conference, meeting is held in Washington between Hull and members of US delegation headed by Under Secretary of State Sumner Welles: "It was agreed that supreme emphasis should be placed on inducing all Latin American nations to sever diplomatic relations with the Axis. . . . The severance of diplomatic relations with the enemy was deemed a fundamental requirement of American security. The United States was convinced that Axis consulates throughout Latin America were actively reporting on ship movements and preparations for defense. Most American nations were also aware that Axis diplomatic missions were engaged in subversive activity dedicated to undermining Latin governments friendly to the Allies." (Frank 3–4)

January 1944
Following Argentina's break of relations with Germany and Japan: "The State Department, of course, wanted a good deal more at this point than simply a rupture in relations. Ambassador [Norman] Armour insisted the Argentines take strong measures against the Axis powers." (Frank 25)

Summer 1945
"[P]erón's principal concern with the Ambassador, at least initially, was the company Braden kept. Virtually all of Braden's numerous Argentine friends were avowed enemies of the military regime. . . . Braden's appointment and demonstrated unwillingness to seek action presented them with a golden opportunity. With little reluctance and great clamor, they joined Braden in an effort to topple the military. . . . Domestic opposition continued to mount and Braden sought to accelerate it even more." (Frank 58)

July 1945
Braden, in interview with Perón: "Your government's failure to deal effectively with German and Japanese firms still operating in Argentina is a source of great concern to the Allies. If you demonstrated a larger desire to assist the United States, you could gain a great deal of international prestige. Perhaps, too, the United States might be less of an obstacle to your eventual presidential candidacy." (Frank 73)

February 1946
Following release of Blue Book: "The State Department insisted that its true purpose was to inform the Latin American governments, as well as the United States' citizens, that Argentina had assisted the enemy and violated its pledges of cooperation." (Frank 104)

May 1946
"It is presumably the policy of the United States and Great Britain not to rearm Argentina until all Nazi influence has been eliminated here and until there are practical assurances against any Argentine policy of expansionism." (*New York Times*, 12 May 1946, A29)

RESPONSE OF TARGET COUNTRY

June 1944
Following rupture of US-Argentine relations: "Perón, in a successful effort to achieve greater internal support, cleverly exploited the natural indignation of the Argentine nation." (Frank 51)

Summer 1945
Perón, in response to suggestion by Braden that greater cooperation with US would lessen American opposition to his quest for presidency: "At that price I prefer to remain unknown because if I accepted everyone in Argentina would call me a son-of-a-bitch." (Frank 73)

ATTITUDE OF OTHER COUNTRIES

United Kingdom
In summer 1944, after freezing of gold assets and blockade of ports: "The British were reluctant to join these punitive designs. They had always taken a more relaxed view with regard to Argentine neutrality and her flirtation with the Axis. Great Britain understandably felt that the need for Argentine beef and wheat during the war surpassed any other consideration. They were also forced to consider the extensive nature of their investments in Argentina and the possibility of retaliation." (Frank 20–21)

In January 1947, UK informs US that it plans "henceforth to treat Argentina in all respects on the same footing as other Latin American countries." In essence, this is notification that UK no longer will be bound by "gentlemen's agreement" under which US had extended arms embargo against Argentina to European suppliers. (Potash 77)

Latin America
In June–July 1944, all American states except Chile, Paraguay, and Bolivia break relations with Argentina at urging of US. (Alexander 1951, 201)

ECONOMIC IMPACT

Observed Economic Statistics

"Before it was clear that she would not cooperate, the Argentine navy was put down for a tidy $20 million [in Lend-Lease aid], which, of course, was subsequently cancelled." (Whitaker 385)

Argentina decides to repatriate its gold from US in November 1943 when US relations began to deteriorate seriously because of Argentina's refusal to break diplomatic relations with Axis. At that time, $212 million in Argentine gold is estimated to be in US; in August 1944, when free flow of the gold is prohibited, unofficial figures show $45 million had been repatriated. Minister of Finance Cesar Ameghino does not consider measure very serious "since it did not alter Argentina's free disposition of her gold but merely prevented the exportation of gold to Argentina." (*New York Times*, 17 August 1944, A1)

The next day Ameghino reports that since November 1943, Argentine gold in US has *increased* by $270 million and $53 million has actually been repatriated, leaving balance of $429 million. (*New York Times*, 18 August 1944, A7)

Only about 3.5 percent of ships arriving in Argentine ports are American and about 6 percent of total tonnage arrives in US ships. (*New York Times*, 27 September 1944, A1)

"For some time after the war, most of the world's shipping continued to be regulated by the Anglo-American bodies set up for the purpose while the conflict was going on. The Argentines maintained that the curtailment of shipping to them was greatly in excess of the actual shipping shortage. Furthermore, the Argentine government, and Perón himself on various occasions, claimed that the Argentines found it impossible to purchase needed vehicles and other machinery which was available to other countries, but not to Argentina." (Alexander 1951, 207)

"The country had acquired large foreign exchange reserves during World War II. European agriculture was for the time being in ruins, and the demand there and elsewhere for the meat and grain which Argentina produced was exceedingly strong." (Alexander 1979, 54)

Argentina builds up $1,608 million reserve of hard currencies and gold during war. (Whitaker 385)

Argentine trade with US (million dollars)

	Exports	Imports
1938	40.7	86.8
1939	61.9	70.9

Argentine trade with US (*continued*)

	Exports	Imports
1940	83.3	106.9
1941	166.6	109.3
1942	150.0	71.9
1943	n.a.	n.a.
1944	177.0	29.0
1945	169.0	38.7
1946	194.4	191.1
1947	154.6	679.9
1948	180.0	380.9
1949	97.5	129.1

n.a. Not available.
Source: Statistical Abstract, 1944–1945, 550, 554; 1950, 858–59.

Calculated Economic Impact

	Annual cost to target country
Ban on repatriation of Argentine gold reserves held in US; welfare loss for the two-year duration of the freeze is estimated at 5 percent of the value of the reserves.	$11 million
Denial of Lend-Lease aid; welfare loss estimated at 90 percent of proposed transfers.	18 million
Total	$29 million

Relative Magnitudes

Gross indicators of Argentine economy	
Argentine GNP (1944)	$3.6 billion
Argentine population (1946)	15.9 million
Annual effect of sanctions related to gross indicators	
Percentage of GNP	0.8
Per capita	$1.82
Argentine trade with US as percentage of total trade	
Exports (1944)	26
Imports (1944)	13
Ratio of US GNP (1944: $210.6 billion) to Argentine GNP (1944: $3.6 billion)	58

ASSESSMENT

Gary Frank
Following President Ramírez's breaking of relations with Axis under pressure from US: "The move was hardly greeted with enthusiasm by the Argentine people. Even those who were sympathetic to the Allied cause recognized that Ramírez had collapsed under excessive pressure. His subservience to the United States would result in national condemnation and loss of office." (Frank 26)

Arthur P. Whitaker
"[S]ecretary of State Hull made Argentina front page news time and again in his effort to oust the recalcitrant Farrell-Perón regime by a combination of nonrecognition, the blocking of funds, and a rhetorical campaign. . . . Hull's effort failed dismally for lack of the only element that could have enabled it to succeed, which was British cooperation in an embargo on trade with Argentina." (Whitaker 382)

New York Times
"It may be argued that whatever concessions Argentina has made to the United Nations were not made freely but under compulsion, and were, moreover, made with a notable lack of good grace. This undoubtedly is so. This very fact serves to emphasize, however, that it has been an uphill fight to wrest from Argentina even a partial abandonment of her policy of strict neutrality. The State Department handling of the Argentine situation, despite the charges of maladroitness leveled at it from more than one quarter, has certainly produced results." (*New York Times*, 8 October 1944, IV, 4)

Robert J. Alexander
"As a result of this situation [acceptance of the Export–Import Bank loan], [Perón] was no longer in a position to offer general leadership to the other Latin American countries in presenting their grievances against Uncle Sam. Although his representatives often continued to be critical of the United States in international gatherings . . . the Perón government no longer conducted a consistent campaign of attack on the United States." (Alexander 1951, 73)

AUTHORS' SUMMARY

Overall assessment	Assigned scores
□ Policy result, scaled from 1 (failed) to 4 (success)	2
□ Sanctions contribution, scaled from 1 (none) to 4 (significant)	2
□ Success score (policy result *times* sanctions contribution), scaled from 1 (outright failure) to 16 (significant success)	4

Political and economic variables

□ Companion policies: J (covert), Q (quasi-military), or R (regular military)	—
□ International cooperation with sender, scaled from 1 (none) to 4 (significant)	2
□ International assistance to target: A (if present)	—
□ Sanctions period (years)	3

	Assigned scores
Political and economic variables (continued)	
□ Economic health and political stability of target, scaled from 1 (distressed) to 3 (strong)	2
□ Presanction relations between sender and target, scaled from 1 (antagonistic) to 3 (cordial)	2
□ Type of sanction: X (export), M (import), F (financial)	F, X
□ Cost to sender, scaled from 1 (net gain) to 4 (major loss)	2

BIBLIOGRAPHY

Alexander, Robert J. 1951. *The Perón Era.* New York: Columbia University Press.

———. 1979. *Juan Domingo Perón: A History.* Boulder, Colo.: Westview Press.

Frank, Gary. 1980. *Juan Perón vs. Spruille Braden: The Story Behind the Blue Book.* Boston: University Press of America.

Keesing's Contemporary Archives. 1946–48.

Potash, Robert A. 1980. *The Army and Politics in Argentina: 1945–1962.* Stanford, Calif.: Stanford University Press.

US Department of Commerce. 1944–45, 1950. *Statistical Abstract of the United States.* Washington.

Whitaker, Arthur P. 1976. *The United States and the Southern Cone.* Cambridge, Mass.: Harvard University Press.

Case 46–1   Arab League v. Israel

(1946–   : Palestine)

CHRONOLOGY OF KEY EVENTS

1920s–30s   Arab leaders call for boycott of Jewish businesses in Palestine. (Dewitt 1; Stanislawski 1–2)

1944   Arab League founded; among its stated objectives is "to frustrate Jewish economic development by means of a boycott against Zionist produce." (Losman 47)

1946   Arab League forms Permanent Boycott Council; establishes Central Boycott Office (CBO); endorses laws prohibiting sale of Arab lands to Zionists. (Losman 49; Stanislawski 2)

May 1948   State of Israel created; Arab states attack Israel; Egypt closes Suez Canal to Israeli ships and vessels of all other flags carrying goods to or from Israel; Egypt maintains restrictions despite UN Security Council resolution calling for their termination. (Doxey 21)

1949   CBO moved from Cairo to Damascus with branches in individual Arab states. Over next three years, CBO widens boycott from primary to secondary and tertiary boycotts, covering dealings with firms and individuals that do business with, or sympathize with, Israel. (Steiner 1367–70; Stanislawski 2; Dewitt 1)

December 1963   Boycott list names 605 firms including 167 in US. By 1976, 1,500 American firms and individuals are on list. "Since the upsurge in oil prices began in late 1973, the number of boycott requests and the general vigor of the boycott has increased substantially." (Losman 60)

1967   Six Day War; Israel substantially enlarges her territory at expense of neighboring Arab states. (*Keesing's* 22099–22103)

1973   October 1973 war, ensuing OPEC success in raising oil prices strengthens hand of Arab League, opening new phase in boycott, with increasing "voluntary" compliance by business firms. (Dewitt 2, 4)

March 1979   Following President Jimmy Carter's initiatives at Camp David, Israel and Egypt sign peace treaty; Arab League imposes economic sanctions against Egypt. Also see Case 78–6 Arab League v. Egypt (1978–83: Peace Treaty with Israel). (Doxey 23)

GOALS OF SENDER COUNTRIES

1944

Arab League is established via Protocol of Alexandria signed by Egypt, Jordan, Syria, Lebanon, Saudi Arabia, Iraq, Yemen, and delegates from Palestinian Arabs. One stated objective: "To frustrate further Jewish economic development in Palestine by means of a boycott against Zionist produce." (Losman 47)

1946

Arab League establishes Permanent Boycott Committee, adopts Resolution No. 16: "Products of Palestinian Jews are to be considered undesirable in Arab countries. They should be prohibited and refused as long as their production in Palestine might lead to the realization of Zionist political aims." (Losman 49)

1954

"The interpretation given by the League is that the boycott will bring about the eventual economic collapse of the state of Israel and will reveal that it is not economically viable in the midst of a hostile world." (Boutros-Ghali 421)

June 1966

King Faisal of Saudi Arabia: "Unfortunately Jews support Israel and we consider those who provide assistance to our enemies as our own enemies." This rationale is invoked to justify worldwide boycott of Jewish firms. (Losman 60)

RESPONSE OF TARGET COUNTRY

1960

Israel opens antiboycott office. (Doxey 22)

January 1965

Israel announces that firms complying with Arab demands will be subject to discriminatory treatment. (Losman 65)

1966

Israel warns seven companies to stop doing business through dummy firms. All seven accede. "Of considerably greater significance however, have been the efforts of various domestic groups in non-Arab nations that have aroused a negative public reaction against firms acceding or appearing to accede to the boycott." (Losman 65)

1971

Israel closes antiboycott office on ground that boycott is ineffective. (Doxey 22)

September 1975

Israel reestablishes antiboycott office as the Authority Against Economic Warfare. (Doxey 22; Dewitt 4)

ATTITUDE OF OTHER COUNTRIES

United States
Beginning in 1965, Congress in legislation often enacted over administration protests, takes progressively more critical view of US firms' cooperation with boycott. Also see Case 65–4 US v. Arab League (1965–   :Antiboycott Measures).

Canada
Beginning with statement by Prime Minister Pierre Trudeau before House of Commons on 8 May 1975, Canadian government takes an increasingly critical attitude toward Canadian business compliance with boycott. (Stanislawski 26–44; Doxey 22)

European Community
Israel requests associated state status with EC; EC rejects request for fear that associated status would harm cordial European relations with Arab world. As substitute, EC grants tariff, quota concessions to Israel. (Losman 71)

LEGAL NOTES

Paraphrased text of Unified Law in Boycott of Israel, adopted by Council of Arab League, Resolution No. 849, 11 December 1954:

☐ All persons within the enacting country are forbidden to conclude any agreement or transaction, directly or indirectly, with any person or organization situated in Israel; affiliated with Israel through nationality; or working for or on behalf of Israel, regardless of place of business or residence.
☐ Importation into the enacting country is forbidden for all Israeli goods, including goods manufactured elsewhere containing ingredients or components of Israeli origin or manufacture.
☐ Foreign companies with offices, branches, or general agencies in Israel shall be considered prohibited corporations for purposes of the prohibition on agreements or transactions.
☐ All goods destined for Israel, directly or indirectly or for persons prohibited by the preceding paragraphs, are considered Israeli goods and therefore subject to the ban on exports as well as transit.
☐ The Central Boycott Office shall maintain blacklists of firms that license their trademarks or patents in Israel; banks that finance Israeli projects; and ships that call at an Arab and Israeli port on the same voyage. Prohibition against dealing with blacklisted firms is enforced by a self-certification process by firms doing business in the Arab League countries. (Lowenfeld 26–27)

ECONOMIC IMPACT

Observed Economic Statistics

Some 20 percent of Palestine imports in period 1936–39 come from Middle East, 12 percent of exports are sold to Middle East. (Losman 54)

Between 1957 and 1960, US Navy uses "Haifa clause" in oil tanker contracts: Navy could cancel contract if vessel was denied access to Arab ports because it had called on

Haifa. US Army Corps of Engineers excludes Jewish personnel from Saudi Arabian projects. (Losman 62)

Between 1948 and 1956, Egypt blockades Gulf of Aqaba. Beginning in 1956, Egypt excludes Israeli-bound goods from Suez Canal. (Losman 62)

Lebanon, Jordan each sell more than 60 percent of their exports in 1957–62 to other Middle Eastern countries; Israel sells only 5 percent (to Cyprus and Turkey); Israel obtains from Middle East only 1 percent of her total imports; Jordan and Lebanon import 27 percent and 22 percent, respectively. (Losman 69)

In 1967, Israel pays $100 million more for oil supplies than from its previous source, Iraq. For many years, Haifa refinery is operated at under 50 percent of capacity because high-cost petroleum precludes export markets. (Losman 67–68)

Various highly publicized boycott compliance and refusal cases occur from late 1950s to mid-1970s; for example:

1957–59
Air France is blacklisted by Arab League for planned lease arrangement with El Al. (Doxey 21–22)

1961
Renault is threatened with boycott if it establishes assembly plant in Israel. (Doxey 21)

1961
Norwich Union, British insurance firm, is threatened with boycott because it has a Jewish director, Lord Mancroft (who subsequently resigns). (Doxey 21)

1965
Imperial Chemical Industries (ICI) and its subsidiaries are boycotted for three months for alleged dealings with Israel. (Doxey 21)

1966
Ford Motor is blacklisted for negotiating with Israeli dealer for assembly of trucks and tractors. (Losman 58)

1966
Coca-Cola refuses to franchise Israeli bottler; following storm of protest in US, awards Israel franchise to Arab banker; Central Boycott Office blacklists Coca-Cola, Arab sales dry up. (Losman 59)

1969
Of US firms surveyed, 57 percent report little or no boycott effect; 20 percent, insignificant effect; 1.5 percent, moderately or highly significant effects. (Losman 65)

Calculated Economic Impact

	Annual cost to target country
Reduction in Israeli exports resulting from Arab boycott; welfare loss valued at 15 percent of estimated lost sales.[†]	

Calculated Economic Impact (*continued*)

	Annual cost to target country
1951–60 $25 million	
1961–72 $69 million	
1973–80 $667 million	
Annual average, 1951–80	$214 million

Reduction in Israeli imports caused by Arab boycott; welfare loss valued at 15 percent of estimated lost trade.†

1951–60 $16 million	
1961–72 $12 million	
1973–80 $127 million	
Annual average, 1951–80	$44 million
Total annual average 1951–80	$258 million

Note: In 1953, Gardner Patterson estimates boycott cost to Israel at $25 million–$30 million annually. (Patterson 321) In 1957, Harry Ellis estimates cost to Israel at $40 million annually. (Ellis 162)

† Assumes potential Israeli trade with Arab League would be same share of total trade as Lebanon once enjoyed. In 1957–62, Lebanon sells about 60 percent of exports, takes 22 percent of imports from other Mideast countries; in 1968–72, figures are 44 percent and 6 percent, respectively.

Relative Magnitudes

Gross indicators of Israeli economy	
Israeli GNP (average 1951–60)	$1,796 million
Israeli population (average 1951–60)	1.6 million
Israeli GNP (average 1973–80)	$13,415 million
Israeli population (average 1973–80)	3.6 million
Annual effect of sanctions (1951–60) related to gross indicators	
Percentage of GNP	2.3
Per capita	$25.62
Annual effect of sanctions (1973–80) related to gross indicators	
Percentage of GNP	5.9
Per capita	$220.56
Israeli trade relations with Arab League as percentage of total trade	
Exports (1951)	1
Imports (1951)	4
Ratio of Arab League GNP (1951: $3.3 billion†) to Israeli GNP (1951: $1.94 billion)	2
Ratio of Arab League GNP (1973: $58.3 billion††) to Israeli GNP (1973: $8.9 billion)	7

† Lebanon, Iraq, Egypt.

†† Based on OAPEC membership.

ASSESSMENT

David B. Dewitt
"In summary, Israel's domestic economic development continues, while economic exchanges expand in both dollar value and diversity of partner. This is not to say that the Arab boycott efforts have not had effect on Israeli development. There is no doubt that they have introduced additional constraints, impeded the free flow of goods and services, and placed in jeopardy Israel's ability to gain secure access to strategic resources and markets. But the record seems to indicate a resiliency and adaptability that has undercut the intent of the boycott leaders." (Dewitt 9)

Ephraim Davrath, deputy director general for international affairs of Israeli Ministry of Finance
"[T]here is no doubt that trade and other fields of economic cooperation would have expanded at a much faster pace, and that Israel's chronic deficit would have been lower, had it not been for the effect of the Arab boycott." (Ministry of Finance, Government of Israel, press release, 11 January 1982)

AUTHORS' SUMMARY

Overall assessment	*Assigned scores*
☐ Policy result, scaled from 1 (failed) to 4 (success)	2
☐ Sanctions contribution, scaled from 1 (none) to 4 (significant)	2
☐ Success score (policy result *times* sanctions contribution), scaled from 1 (outright failure) to 16 (significant success)	4

Political and economic variables

☐ Companion policies: J (covert), Q (quasi-military), or R (regular military)	R
☐ International cooperation with sender, scaled from 1 (none) to 4 (significant)	3
☐ International assistance to target: A (if present)	A
☐ Sanctions period (years)	38 +
☐ Economic health and political stability of target, scaled from 1 (distressed) to 3 (strong)	3
☐ Presanction relations between sender and target, scaled from 1 (antagonistic) to 3 (cordial)	1
☐ Type of sanction: X (export), M (import), F (financial)	F, X, M
☐ Cost to sender, scaled from 1 (net gain) to 4 (major loss)	4

BIBLIOGRAPHY

Boutros-Ghali, B. Y. 1954. "The Arab League: Ten Years of Struggle." *International Conciliation* (May): 387–448.
Chill, Dan S. 1976. *The Arab Boycott of Israel: Economic Aggression and World Reaction.* New York: Praeger.

Dewitt, David B. 1985. "The Arab Boycott of Israel." In *The Utility of Economic Sanctions,* ed. David Leyton-Brown. London: Croom Helm. Forthcoming.

Doxey, Margaret P. 1980. *Economic Sanctions and International Enforcement.* 2d ed. New York: Oxford University Press for Royal Institute of International Affairs.

Ellis, Harry. 1957. *Israel and the Middle East.* New York: Ronald Press Co.

Keesing's Contemporary Archives. 1967–68.

Losman, Donald L. 1979. *International Economic Sanctions: The Cases of Cuba, Israel, and Rhodesia.* Albuquerque: University of New Mexico Press.

Lowenfeld, Andreas F. 1977. "'. . . Sauce for the Gander:' The Arab Boycott and United States Political Trade Controls." 12 *Texas International Law Journal* 25–39.

Nelson, W. H., and T. Prittie. 1977. *The Economic War Against the Jews.* New York: Random House.

Patterson, Gardner. 1954. "Israel's Economic Problems." 32 *Foreign Affairs* (January): 310–22.

Stanislawski, Howard. 1985. "The Impact of the Arab Economic Boycott of Israel on the United States and Canada." In *The Utility of Economic Sanctions,* ed. David Leyton-Brown. London: Croom Helm. Forthcoming.

Steiner, Henry J. 1976. "International Boycotts and Domestic Order: American Involvement in the Arab-Israeli Conflict." 54 *Texas Law Review* 1353–1437.

Case 48–1   US v. Netherlands

(1948–49: Indonesian Federation)

CHRONOLOGY OF KEY EVENTS

17 August 1945	President Ahmed Sukarno and Vice President Mohammad Hatta proclaim Republic of Indonesia. (Taylor xxiii)
November–December 1945	Netherlands, Republic begin talks, with encouragement from US, UK. (Taylor xxiii)
February–March 1946	Netherlands calls for "Commonwealth of Indonesia"; lands nine battalions; envisages Republic rule in Java, separate governments in other islands. (Taylor xxiii)
June 1946	Republic calls for international recognition of its *de facto* authority over Java, Madura, and Sumatra. (Taylor xxiv)
15 November 1946	Republic, Netherlands initial Linggadjati agreement under which Dutch agree to recognize *de facto* Republic authority over Java, Sumatra; Indonesians agree to federal form of government for proposed United States of Indonesia. (McMahon 133–34)
Early February 1947	Netherlands promulgates new export-import laws that "imposed a virtual embargo on all Republican trade." (McMahon 153)
March–April 1947	US, UK accord *de facto* recognition to Republic following ratification of Linggadjati agreement. (Taylor xxiv; McMahon 151–52)
20 July 1947	Netherlands launches first "police action" in Java, Sumatra. (Taylor xxiv)
August 1947	UN Security Council calls for cease-fire and peaceful settlement; establishes Good Offices Committee (GOC) composed of Belgium, Australia, US. Netherlands ceases operations only when its major military objectives have been attained. (Taylor xxiv–xxv; McMahon 190)
10–17 January 1948	US Secretary of State George C. Marshall pressures Netherlands to accept so-called "six principles" advanced by GOC as integral part of political settlement. (Taylor 316)

| 17–19 January 1948 | Agreement reached on USS Renville between Netherlands and Republic on guiding political principles for settlement, including "six principles" advanced by GOC. Netherlands accepts compromise only after US representatives warn that failure to do so "would prevent American assistance in financing Indonesian reconstruction and would endanger Dutch participation in the European Recovery Program (ERP)." (Taylor xxv; McMahon 203) |

Spring 1948 — US authorizes $506 million in ERP aid for Netherlands; $84 million of total is earmarked for "reconstruction of the Netherlands Indies." State Department intelligence report points out that, "[t]he practical effect of ECA [Economic Cooperation Administration] aid on the political conflict is to strengthen the political, economic, and military position of the Netherlands in Indonesia. . . ." (McMahon 228)

July–December 1948 — Dutch-Republic relations deteriorate. (Taylor xxiv)

6 November 1948 — US representative to GOC, H. Merle Cochran, frustrated by Dutch unwillingness to compromise, wires Secretary of State Marshall recommending that Dutch be informed that "no more financial aid of any sort will be forthcoming if police action taken against Republic and as long as Netherlands fails [to] consummate settlement through GOC. . . ." Cochran repeats suggestion following month when negotiations break down, police action appears imminent. On 7 December, US State Department sends aide mémoire to Netherlands government implying the suspension of Marshall Plan aid if second police action occurs. (McMahon 245–49)

19 December 1948 — Netherlands launches second "police action"; interns political leaders, including Sukarno. US, Australia call for active role by UN Security Council to replace GOC efforts. (Taylor xxvi, 171, 396)

21 December 1948 — ECA Administrator Paul Hoffman announces suspension of further Marshall Plan aid to Netherlands Indies "pending clarification of current developments." Move is "largely symbolic" since all but 20 percent of money appropriated for Indonesia had been distributed already. (McMahon 255)

22 December 1948 — Philip Murray, president of CIO, and others call on State Department to take "every feasible step in the realm of diplomacy and economics to help terminate the Dutch aggression in Indonesia." (Taylor 171; McMahon 257–58)

23 December 1948 — Director of State Department Office of UN Affairs Dean Rusk rejects use of ERP aid as lever against the Netherlands in telegram to UN Ambassador Philip C. Jessup. "The most effective leverage that the United States could bring to bear on the Netherlands, of course, was the suspension of all Marshall Plan aid. . . . Such action was categorically rejected by leading State Department and ECA officials. As [Walter] Butterworth [director of State Department far eastern affairs office] explained to Sir Benegal Rama Rau, Indian ambassador to the United Nations, 'A resort to unilateral punishment of Holland by cancellation of ECA would establish a dangerous precedent of attempting to achieve solutions to world problems by direct individual nation approach and of employing economic aid to achieve political goals.'" (McMahon 259, 267)

24 December 1948	UN Security Council calls for cease-fire, release of political prisoners; repeats resolution 28 December. (Taylor xxvi; McMahon 265)
2 January 1949	Indian Prime Minister Jawaharlal Nehru calls for a conference of Asian nations to condemn Dutch actions in Indonesia. (McMahon 268)
11 January 1949	Jessup speech before UN signals US shift to firmer policy. For first time, US "condemned outright the Netherlands police action and subsequent flouting of the Security Council's cease-fire resolution." (McMahon 271)
28 January 1949	UN Security Council resolution calls for restoration of Republican government, transfer of sovereignty by 1 July 1950. (Taylor xxvi)
11 February 1949	E. J. Sassen, Dutch minister for overseas territories, resigns following rejection of his policy of "total noncompliance" with UN Security Council resolution of 28 January. "The path toward a compromise settlement now appeared open." Subsequent compromise settlement proposed by Dutch, however, is still unacceptable to Indonesians as it excludes participation of Republican leaders. (McMahon 281–85)
February–March 1949	US Congress criticizes Dutch position; US administration threatens to withhold Marshall aid to Netherlands. (Taylor 396; McMahon 277–79)
31 March 1949	Dutch Foreign Minister Dirk Stikker meets with Secretary of State Dean Acheson in Washington; Acheson warns that unless Dutch offer "prompt tangible evidence" of willingness to conclude just agreement in Indonesia, it is unlikely Congress will authorize funds "for military supplies to the Netherlands." (McMahon 292–93)
7 May 1949	After little over three weeks of negotiations, compromise agreement is "formally accepted by the Dutch and Republican delegations." (McMahon 295)
11 August 1949	Cease-fire goes into effect in Java, in Sumatra four days later. (McMahon 298)
17 August 1950	Unitary Republic of Indonesia proclaimed under leadership of President Sukarno. (Taylor xxviii)

GOALS OF SENDER COUNTRY

Alastair M. Taylor
Throughout the episode, US goal was to keep Indonesia an ally in free world yet not alienate Netherlands in collective security endeavors in Europe. (Taylor 395–96)

Abbott Moffatt, head of State Department's Southeast Asia division in memorandum 8 July 1947
"The objective of the United States is to secure a settlement of the present Indonesian situation which will meet the natural aspirations of Indonesian nationalism and, at the same time, preserve so far as possible for the Netherlands the economic strength which she derives from association with the Indies." (McMahon 164)

Paul G. Hoffman, Economic Cooperation Administration administrator
"In an explanatory statement, . . . Hoffman said that pending a determination of the actual state of affairs in Indonesia it was impossible to say whether the United States aid could be distributed efficiently there or contribute to economic recovery there or in Europe. He said that without such assurance ECA aid had no legal basis." (*New York Times*, 23 December 1948, A1).

Robert J. McMahon
"This, again, was the classic dilemma that had been haunting the United States since the closing years of World War II: it could not risk alienating its traditional European allies by pursuing an anticolonial policy, but neither could it afford to abandon America's historical identification with the principles of self-determination and thereby forfeit the respect and support of Asian and African nationalist movements." (McMahon 182)

RESPONSE OF TARGET COUNTRY

Spring 1948
Following authorization of ERP aid: "The Dutch press in Holland and in the Indies suggested that the European Recovery Program indicated that the United States had reversed its previous position of withholding financial aid until a political settlement had been reached; this reversal, it suggested, was due to Washington's realization that Dutch economic recovery was closely tied to the economic recovery of Indonesia." (McMahon 228)

December 1948
Upon receipt of December aide mêmoire pertaining to collapse of negotiations: "Dutch authorities deeply resented this pointed American message. . . . the Dutch cabinet was 'unanimously bitter' about Washington's intervention; Stikker [Dutch foreign minister] later wrote that 'the United States did not understand that this type of action always has the opposite effect from what is intended.'" (McMahon 248)

ATTITUDE OF OTHER COUNTRIES

Ceylon, India, Pakistan
In December 1948, these nations close their harbors and airports to ships and aircraft transporting "troops or war materials intended for use against the Indonesians." (McMahon 253)

United Nations
In January 1949, Security Council adopts resolution calling on Netherlands to restore Republican government, transfer sovereignty by 1 July 1950. (Taylor xxvi)

Arab League
In December 1948 Arab League condemns Netherlands. (McMahon 253)

Australia, Burma, India

Following second police action these countries call on US to reconsider its economic assistance to Netherlands. (McMahon 257)

Indonesia

In aftermath of second Dutch police action, Sumitro Djojohadikusomo, acting head of Indonesian delegation to UN, calls on US to halt ERP aid to Holland: "In view of the fact that the present Dutch military campaign is an act of war in Indonesia, a threat to peace and stability in Southeast Asia and dangerously impairing implementation of the European Recovery Program, furthermore, in view of the fact that the Netherlands are diverting ERP dollars for the purpose of waging a colonial war against freedom-loving people, we respectfully but urgently request the United States Government to discontinue rendering American dollars to the Netherlands under the European Recovery Program or otherwise." (McMahon 256)

"[M]ost Indonesians believed, understandably, that the Dutch would have been unable to launch their second police action had it not been for the considerable economic assistance provided by the Marshall Plan." (McMahon 257)

ECONOMIC IMPACT

Observed Economic Statistics

Late 1945–47, US Lend-Lease aid to Netherlands totals $100 million. (McMahon 103)

Post-World War II non-ERP aid to Netherlands: Eximbank credits of $300 million; $130 million in credits for surplus military supplies; $190 million in civilian supplies as military relief. (McMahon 256)

Cutoff of US aid in December 1948 does not affect $54 million in purchases already under contract. Of remaining $69 million still to be allocated, $14.1 million is withheld as result of sanctions. (*New York Times*, 23 December 1948, A1)

ERP aid ($298 million) allocated directly to Netherlands is unaffected. (McMahon 255)

Amount of Marshall Plan aid to Dutch in 1948 "was almost identical to the [sum] spent by the Dutch government to sustain its military effort against the Indonesian Republic." (McMahon 288)

Calculated Economic Impact

	Annual cost to target country
Reduction in US aid; welfare loss estimated at 100 percent of reduced transfers.	$14 million

Relative Magnitudes

Gross indicators of Dutch economy	
Dutch GNP (1948)	$5.7 billion
Dutch population (1948)	9.8 million

Gross indicators of Dutch economy (continued)	
Annual effect of sanctions related to gross indicators	
Percentage of GNP	0.2
Per capita	$1.43
Dutch trade with US as percentage of total trade	
Exports (1949)	3
Imports (1949)	15
Ratio of US GNP (1948: $257.6 billion) to Dutch GNP (1948: $5.7 billion)	45

ASSESSMENT

Robert J. McMahon
"Direct American pressure on the Dutch in the spring of 1949, as much as any other single factor, compelled the Netherlands to grant independence to its rich colony. . . .'" (McMahon 12)

"American displeasure with The Hague's intransigence was particularly instrumental in prompting . . . reconsideration of policy. Dutch policy makers were well aware of the overwhelming importance of ERP assistance to the postwar recovery of their nation. It was 'not a question of whether you were in favor of it,' Stikker later recalled, 'because it was absolutely a must—you couldn't do without it.'" (McMahon 280)

Dean Acheson, US secretary of state
"Withholding help and exhorting the ally or its opponent can be effective only when the ally can do nothing without help, as was the case in Indonesia." (McMahon 294)

AUTHORS' SUMMARY

Overall assessment	Assigned scores
☐ Policy result, scaled from 1 (failed) to 4 (success)	4
☐ Sanctions contribution, scaled from 1 (none) to 4 (significant)	4
☐ Success score (policy result *times* sanctions contribution), scaled from 1 (outright failure) to 16 (significant success)	16

Political and economic variables

☐ Companion policies: J (covert), Q (quasi-military), or R (regular military)	—
☐ International cooperation with sender, scaled from 1 (none) to 4 (significant)	1
☐ International assistance to target: A (if present)	—
☐ Sanctions period (years)	1
☐ Economic health and political stability of target, scaled from 1 (distressed) to 3 (strong)	2

Political and economic variables (continued)	Assigned scores
☐ Presanction relations between sender and target, scaled from 1 (antagonistic) to 3 (cordial)	3
☐ Type of sanction: X (export), M (import), F (financial)	F
☐ Cost to sender, scaled from 1 (net gain) to 4 (major loss)	1

BIBLIOGRAPHY

Grieve, Muriel J. 1968. "Economic Sanctions: Theory and Practice." 3 *International Relations* (October): 431–43.

McMahon, Robert J. 1981. *Colonialism and Cold War: The United States and the Struggle for Indonesian Independence, 1945–49.* Ithaca, NY: Cornell University Press.

Taylor, Alastair M. 1960. *Indonesian Independence and the United Nations.* Ithaca, NY: Cornell University Press.

Case 48–2   India v. Hyderabad

(1948: Political Integration)

CHRONOLOGY OF KEY EVENTS

12 June 1947   Hyderabad officials announce state will not join either Indian or Pakistani Union, will remain independent when power is transferred by Great Britain. Hindus constitute majority of Hyderabad population but government of the ruling Nizam [native leader of state] is dominated by Muslims. (*Keesing's* 8667, 9421)

August 1947   Negotiations begin between Hyderabad, India with "aim of reaching a final settlement of the future political relationship" between the two. (*Keesing's* 9421)

November–December 1947   "Standstill" agreement that maintains political *status quo* for year is signed in late November. Shortly thereafter, Indian government accuses Hyderabad of violating several provisions. Hyderabad takes provocative actions, including restricting exports of precious metals to India, declaring Indian currency no longer legal tender, extending loan in form of Government of India securities to Pakistan, announcing intention of appointing agents in foreign countries. (Menon 339)

January 1948   Hyderabad denies actions are intended to harm Indian economy; justifies currency decision as needed to popularize state's own currency; characterizes restriction on minerals exports as not ban but simply requirement for prior approval for such sales; asserts decision on Pakistan loan was made before standstill agreement was signed. As "countercharge," it accuses India of slowing imports to Hyderabad from abroad. (Menon 339)

7 April 1948   Indian Prime Minister Jawaharlal Nehru meets with Sir Walter Monckton, constitutional adviser to Nizam, assures him that India has no intention of either blockading or invading Hyderabad but that India could not control actions of private merchants. (Menon 351)

17 June 1948   Nehru announces negotiations breakdown following Nizam's rejection of draft agreement. Nizam accuses India of unwillingness to compromise, complains unofficial blockade of Hyderabad has denied its people "the necessities of life, including salt and medical supplies." (*Keesing's* 9421)

July 1948	India imposes series of financial and other economic sanctions against Hyderabad in response to initial attempts by Pakistan to cash some of bank securities. These include freeze on transfer of Indian government securities held by Nizam, his government, or Hyderabad state bank; ban on export of gold, silver, jewelry, and Indian currency, and halt in Indian air service. Clashes occur on border; on 24 July, Indian troops occupy village in Hyderabad territory following attack on their convoy. (*Keesing's* 9422; Menon 371)
17 August 1948	Nizam's representative, Prime Minister Mir Laik Ali, informs Nehru that Hyderabad is taking case to UN and accuses India of imposing total economic blockade and its soldiers of repeatedly violating Hyderabad territory. (Menon 373)
13 September 1948	Indian forces invade Hyderabad with expressed intent of restoring order that had been disrupted by "rampaging" Razakars (essentially a "private army of the Muslim party in Hyderabad"). (*Keesing's* 10401)
17 September 1948	Hyderabad forces surrender, Nizam declares immediate cease-fire. Nizam accedes to Indian demands to disband Razakars, allow Indian troops to be stationed in Secunderabad, drop appeal in UN. (*Keesing's* 10401)
24 November 1949	Nizam issues declaration "implying the State's accession to the Indian Union." "It was officially stated in Hyderabad on November 26 that the Nizam had not signed an instrument of succession, but that acceptance of the Indian Constitution was regarded as tantamount to accession and that Hyderabad had thus become integrated into the Union." (*Keesing's* 10401).

GOALS OF SENDER COUNTRY

Prime Minister Jawaharlal Nehru
Press conference on 1 May 1948: "Hyderabad is in the heart of India, surrounded on all sides. The Indian Union cannot possibly tolerate that any part of Indian territory, inside or on its borders, should be potentially capable to being made a foreign base. No foreign power can tolerate that. The existence of such a foreign power would endanger our security, and there would be constant and ceaseless conflict. Hyderabad cannot possibly remain independent in that way and must, therefore, necessarily form part of the Indian Union." (*Keesing's* 9422)

Keesing's
In the negotiations, Indian representatives insist on three points: no recognition of Hyderabad as independent state; introduction of "responsible government" in Hyderabad; and immediate suppression of Razakars. (*Keesing's* 9421)

RESPONSE OF TARGET COUNTRY

Keesing's

Nizam proposes plebiscite be conducted under supervision of impartial body to determine will of the people on accession to Indian Union. However, in his words: "The Government of India demanded that the substance of accession should be conceded immediately, irrespective of what the decision of the plebiscite might be. This was obviously unfair and amounted to prejudicing the popular will." (*Keesing's* 9421)

In proposing conflict be brought before UN in mid-August 1948, Prime Minister Mir Laik Ali claims Hyderabad has been subjected to: " . . . violent intimidation and threats of invasion [and to] a crippling economic blockade which has inflicted cruel hardships on the people of Hyderabad and which is intended to coerce Hyderabad into a renunciation of its independence." (*Keesing's* 9523)

V. P. Menon

"The Nizam's advisers, it was reported to [Menon], had assured him that if India resorted to any economic blockade it was not likely to be effective, as Hyderabad could easily stand on its own legs for the next few months during which time public opinion in the world could be organized in its favour." (Menon 348)

ECONOMIC IMPACT

Observed Economic Statistics

"[Hyderabad] had been entirely dependent on India for its railways, its postal, telegraphic, and telephonic services, and its air communications." (Menon 387)

Calculated Economic Impact

	Annual cost to target country
Currency and other financial/trade controls on imports and financial transactions with Hyderabad; welfare loss estimated at 2 percent of Hyderabad's gross income.	$18 million

Relative Magnitudes

Gross indicators of Hyderabad's economy	
Hyderabad's GNP (1947)	$893 million†
Hyderabad's population (1947)	16.3 million
Annual effect of sanctions related to gross indicators	
Percentage of GNP	2
Per capita	$1.10
Hyderabad's trade with India as percentage of total trade†	
Exports (1947)	99
Imports (1947)	99

Gross indicators of Hyderabad's economy (continued)

Ratio of Indian GNP (1950: $19.8 billion) to Hyderabad's GNP (1950: $893 million)	22

† Authors' estimates, based on assumption that per capita income is same in India and Hyderabad and that almost all Hyderabad's trade is with India.

AUTHORS' SUMMARY

Overall assessment	*Assigned scores*
☐ Policy result, scaled from 1 (failed) to 4 (success)	4
☐ Sanctions contribution, scaled from 1 (none) to 4 (significant)	3
☐ Success score (policy result *times* sanctions contribution), scaled from 1 (outright failure) to 16 (significant success)	12

Political and economic variables

☐ Companion policies: J (covert), Q (quasi-military), or R (regular military)	R
☐ International cooperation with sender, scaled from 1 (none) to 4 (significant)	1
☐ International assistance to target: A (if present)	—
☐ Sanctions period (years)	1
☐ Economic health and political stability of target, scaled from 1 (distressed) to 3 (strong)	2
☐ Presanction relations between sender and target, scaled from 1 (antagonistic) to 3 (cordial)	3
☐ Type of sanction: X (export), M (import), F (financial)	F, X
☐ Cost to sender, scaled from 1 (net gain) to 4 (major loss)	2

Comments

Indian goal of incorporating Hyderabad into union is achieved. Although military force was decisive factor, economic blockade served to undermine Nizam's authority and weaken resistance, thus contributing in modest way to successful outcome.

BIBLIOGRAPHY

Keesing's Contemporary Archives. 1946–48, 1948–50.
Menon, V. P. 1956. *The Story of the Integration of the Indian States*. New York: Macmillan.

Case 48–3 USSR v. US, UK, and France

(1948–49: Berlin Blockade)

CHRONOLOGY OF KEY EVENTS

10 March 1948	Soviet Military Administration (SMA) in Berlin imposes restrictions on Germans traveling from East German zone to Berlin. (Smith 364)
30 March 1948	Soviets impose rail, highway restrictions on Allied traffic between Western zones and Berlin. "Little airlift" begins. (Smith 364)
3 April 1948	Soviets close freight routes to Berlin from Munich, Hamburg. On 9 April, USSR announces that all trains on remaining Berlin-Helmstadt line will require individual clearances from Soviet Kommandatura in Berlin. (Smith 364)
20 April 1948	SMA imposes additional restrictions on barge traffic to and from Berlin. (Smith 364)
9 June 1948	Travel restrictions imposed March 10 are tightened. (Smith 364)
11–13 June 1948	Soviets block all rail traffic between West German zones and Berlin; on 12 June, close Elbe River bridge for repairs. (Smith 368)
18 June 1948	Western powers announce currency reform for all Western sectors of Germany but Berlin. Soviets respond next day with suspension of all passenger traffic into Berlin. (Smith 365)
23–25 June 1948	Soviets order currency reform in Eastern zone and Berlin; Western powers implement their own currency reform in West Berlin. On 24 June, Soviets impose complete blockade on traffic into Berlin, interrupt electrical power, mail, parcel post services to West Berlin. On 25 June, airlift begins in earnest. General Lucius D. Clay, US military governor, halts all shipments of goods between West Berlin and Soviet zone. (Smith 127, 365)
4 July 1948	Western powers suspend reparations deliveries to Soviet Union. (Smith 365)

September 1948	US, UK prohibit shipment of goods manufactured in their zones of Germany to Soviet zone, halt all rail traffic from non-German countries to Soviet zone through US and UK zones. (Smith 128, Davison 155)
4 February 1949	West tightens "counterblockade," stops all truck traffic to Soviet zone. (Smith 267)
20 March 1949	Western powers announce West mark will be only legal tender in West Berlin. (Smith 367)
25 April–1 May 1949	East Berlin government expropriates all houses, land, banks, insurance companies in East Berlin. (Smith 367)
4 May 1949	Four-power representatives to UN Security Council announce agreement to end blockade. (Smith 367)
8 May 1949	West German government created. (Smith 133)
12 May 1949	Blockade lifted. (Smith 367)
8 July 1949	SMA closes all main crossing points between East and West zones, limits traffic to one autobahn. (Smith 367)
14 July 1949	Soviets lift travel restrictions. (Smith 368)
30 September 1949	Berlin airlift terminated. (Smith 368)

GOALS OF SENDER COUNTRY

W. Phillips Davison
"The objective of the Berlin Blockade was to prevent West German economic recovery and formation of a West German government or, failing this, to incorporate the population and resources of West Berlin into East Germany, thus depriving the democracies of a valuable outpost behind the iron curtain and invaluable prestige throughout the world." (Davison xi)

On 3 July 1948, General Clay and British and French military governors approached Marshal Vassily Sokolovsky, their Soviet counterpart, about compromise on currency issue so normal traffic could be resumed. "According to General Clay's account, 'Sokolovsky interrupted to state blandly that the technical difficulties would continue until we had abandoned our plans for West German government.' It was the first time that an official Soviet source had given this as the reason for the blockade. Sokolovsky did not even wish to discuss the currency issue." (Davison 123)

RESPONSE OF TARGET COUNTRIES

General Lucius D. Clay
In April 1948, following Soviet restrictions on freight movements to and from Berlin, General Clay states his reasons for remaining in city: "We have lost Czechoslovakia. Norway is threatened. We retreat from Berlin. When Berlin falls, Western Germany will

be next. . . . To hold Europe against communism we must not budge. . . . If we withdraw, our position in Europe is threatened. . . . I believe the future of democracy requires us to stay. . . ." (Smith 105)

W. Phillip Davison
"No Allied agency ever attempted a systematic study of the actual or potential effects of the counterblockade while it was in progress or after it was over." (Davison 277)

ECONOMIC IMPACT

Observed Economic Statistics

Cost to US: $252.5 million; to UK: £10.3 million; population (West Berlin): 2.2 million. (*Keesing's* 10321)

1949–50: West Berlin's ordinary budget is 2 billion marks, extraordinary expenditure is 950 million marks. (*Keesing's* 10160)

"The ten months of the blockade prevented all but the most essential commerce from taking place [in Berlin]. Food and fuel took priority on the incoming aircraft, and without raw materials Berlin's industries stood idle." (Smith 138)

Airlift accidents cost lives of 48 British and American airmen; 7 British and 17 American planes lost. (Davison 273)

In 1947, trade between East and West Germany is estimated at 496 million marks; this drops to 357 and 432 million marks, respectively, in 1948 and 1949, years affected by blockade. "In 1950, the figure jumped to 807 million payment units [a device used because of the difference in value of the East and West marks], but it sank back to 365 million payment units in 1951 and 293 in 1952." (Davison 277)

Swedish Social Democrats donate 25,000 Swedish crowns to West German SPD to buy food for Berlin in early July 1948. Finance Committee of West German Landerrat receives recommendation that 20 million DM be placed at disposal of West Berlin government at about same time. One West German state donates 100,000 tons of coal. (Davison 119, 124)

Calculated Economic Impact

	Annual cost to target country
Cost of airlift of supplies to Berlin; welfare loss estimated at 90 percent of costs incurred.	$253 million
Reduction in trade between East and West Germany; welfare loss estimated at 30 percent of reduced trade.	7 million
Offset	
Suspension of reparation payments to USSR; welfare gain estimated at 10 percent of deferred transfers.	($2 million)
Total	$258 million

Relative Magnitudes

Gross indicators of US, UK, French economies	
Allied GNP (1950)	$352.3 billion
Allied population (1950)	244.6 million
Annual effect of sanctions as percentage of gross indicators	
Percentage of GNP	0.1
Per capita	$1.05
Allied trade with USSR as percentage of total trade	
Exports (1948)	0.4
Imports (1948)	1
Ratio of USSR GNP (1950: $148.3 billion) to Allied GNP (1950: $352.3 billion)	0.4

ASSESSMENT

Jean Edward Smith
"Thereafter [13 September 1948] the counterblockade was gradually tightened until soon, only a small trickle of goods was arriving in Eastern Germany from the West. Since most of East Germany's manufactured goods at this time came from the West, the counterblockade now began to hurt the Soviet Union more than the blockade of Berlin was hurting the Allies." (Smith 128)

General Lucius D. Clay
"It was certain that our counterblockade would be more harmful to East Germany than to West Germany. East Germany lacked coking coal and steel and could not obtain these materials from behind the iron curtain, where the available quantities did not suffice. . . . While we could not obtain accurate statistical information, we did know that the economy of Eastern Germany was at a standstill during a period in which the productive output of West Germany was increasing at a more rapid rate than anywhere else in Europe. The consistent attempt to purchase goods in West Germany to be smuggled into East Germany was in itself proof of the need. We had every reason to believe that if economic life in East Germany was not deteriorating it had ceased to progress. In the spring of 1949 there were many rumors that economic conditions would result in early lifting of the blockade." (Clay 389)

W. Phillips Davison
"Berlin's ability to hold during the blockade seems to have been based on a combination of four factors. First, the will to resist was widely shared throughout the population. . . . Second, Berlin had a corps of able political leaders who were willing to run personal risks and refused to be intimidated by Soviet threats. Third, these leaders controlled efficient political institutions. . . . Finally, a material basis for resistance was provided by airlifted supplies. The four factors were closely interrelated, and the absence or insufficiency of any one of them could easily have made the other three ineffective, thus precipitating the fall of Berlin." (Davison xiv)

"The most important programs of the Western powers in Europe during this period were the Marshall Plan, the establishment of a West German government, and the formation of defensive alliances. Though not specifically directed against the blockade, they probably played a much more important part in bringing it to an end than did the counterblockade." (Davison 251)

"No one knows the precise extent to which the sharpened counterblockade hampered the East German economy, but reports in the West Berlin press mentioned a number of factories that had been forced to lay off workers or curtail their working hours because of it." (Davison 265)

". . . postwar trade between East and West Germany was relatively small, irrespective of the blockade. . . . It is difficult to believe, therefore, that economic considerations played more than a minor role in the Soviet decision to lift the blockade." (Davison 277)

Philip C. Jessup
February 1949: "[The US Administration] felt there was some basis for the supposition that the Soviets wanted to end the blockade. The airlift was a daily triumph for the West, and the counterblockade was pinching the East European economies. The Soviets had failed to push us out of Berlin, and the US was moving forward steadily with plans for the establishment of a West German government." (Jessup 380)

"The original institution of the Western mark was a brilliant success in its effect on the economic situation in West Berlin, which became a showcase of prosperity in contrast to the bleak conditions in the Soviet zone. The Soviet government naturally wanted to level this difference, but as the blockade was met by the West's counterblockade, the damage to the Eastern bloc's economy by this restriction on trade was probably a more important factor than the institution of the mark in persuading Moscow that the effort to impose its will on the West was a failure. Even more persuasive must have been the daily realization of the impressive impact on world opinion of the unprecedented success of the airlift." (Jessup 396)

AUTHORS' SUMMARY

Overall assessment	Assigned scores
☐ Policy result, scaled from 1 (failed) to 4 (success)	1
☐ Sanctions contribution, scaled from 1 (none) to 4 (significant)	1
☐ Success score (policy result *times* sanctions contribution), scaled from 1 (outright failure) to 16 (significant success)	1

Political and economic variables

☐ Companion policies: J (covert), Q (quasi-military), or R (regular military)	Q
☐ International cooperation with sender, scaled from 1 (none) to 4 (significant)	1
☐ International assistance to target: A (if present)	A
☐ Sanctions period (years)	1
☐ Economic health and political stability of target, scaled from 1 (distressed) to 3 (strong)	3

	Assigned
Political and economic variables (continued)	*scores*
☐ Presanction relations between sender and target, scaled from 1 (antagonistic) to 3 (cordial)	1
☐ Type of sanction: X (export), M (import), F (financial)	X, M
☐ Cost to sender, scaled from 1 (net gain) to 4 (major loss)	3

BIBLIOGRAPHY

Clay, Lucius D. 1950. *Decision in Germany*. Garden City, NY: Doubleday.

Davison, W. Phillips. 1958. *The Berlin Blockade*. Princeton, NJ: Princeton University Press.

Jessup, Philip C. 1972. "Park Avenue Diplomacy—Ending the Berlin Blockade." 87 *Political Science Quarterly* 377–400.

Keesing's Contemporary Archives. 1948–50.

Smith, Jean Edward. 1963. *The Defense of Berlin*. Baltimore: Johns Hopkins University Press.

US Congress. Senate Committee on Foreign Relations. 1961. *Documents on Germany, 1944–1961*. 87 Cong., 2 sess.

Case 48–4 USSR v. Yugoslavia

(1948–55: Nationalism)

CHRONOLOGY OF KEY EVENTS

December 1947	Soviet dictator Joseph Stalin tries to curb Prime Minister Tito's political independence by delaying negotiations on trade agreement to replace one expiring in April 1948. (Freedman 24)
Early 1948	Stalin, Foreign Minister Vyacheslav M. Molotov denounce Tito and Central Committee of Yugoslav Communist Party for "boundless ambition, arrogance, and conceit" and "having broken the international traditions of the Communist Party of Yugoslavia and taken the road to nationalism." (Farrell 2)
3 January 1948	Tito meets with US Ambassador Cavendish Cannon, is "considerably friendlier" than previously. Tito proposes $20 million of Yugoslav gold held in US be reserved for adjudication of US claims against Yugoslavia. He suggests remaining $30 million be released for Yugoslav purchase of machinery, industrial equipment in US. Secretary of State George C. Marshall rejects proposal. (Freedman 24)
Late February 1948	Soviet officials inform Yugoslav trade delegation that no agreement for exchange of goods in 1948 can be concluded, say only that further negotiations may be resumed much later that year. Tito calls special Central Committee meeting. While recognizing "pernicious effects of the delay . . . for Yugoslavia's five-year plan," a majority agree that country must "'endure the pressure' for the sake of its independence." (Freedman 25)
18–19 March 1948	Stalin orders withdrawal of all military, technical advisers, charging Yugoslavia with "a lack of hospitality and a lack of confidence. . . . It is difficult to overestimate the consequences of this withdrawal to an economy as lacking in skilled managers, planners, and workers as the Yugoslav." (Freedman 28)
28 June 1948	Bucharest Resolution contains open appeal to Yugoslav Party to overthrow Tito. (Farrell 2; Freedman 27)
4 July 1948	US agrees to unfreeze most of $50 million in gold held in US. Washington officials deny timing of decision has any "bearing

whatsoever on Yugoslavia's quarrel with the Cominform [Communist Information Bureau]." (Freedman 28)

August 1948   Tourists from Cominform countries stop visiting Yugoslavia; Romania delays shipment of oil derivatives. In September other exports—mainly cotton, oil, and coke—from Eastern Europe to Yugoslavia are delayed. (Freedman 29)

Late 1948   "[T]hat the growing Cominform economic pressure was having some effect" is demonstrated by Tito's efforts to lure skilled Yugoslav workers from abroad and to find alternate suppliers in West. In November, Tito states that consumer goods will have to be sacrificed to industrialization. In December, some pressure is relieved when $120 million trade agreement is signed with UK. (Freedman 29)

Late 1948   Tito attempts to patch up relations with Stalin; protests that Yugoslavia will never accept aid from "imperialist camp"; London and Washington observe quarrel with detached amusement. (Farrell 8–9)

27 December 1948   USSR signs trade agreement with Yugoslavia "but for a very sharply reduced amount of goods." Tass communiqué states that, "Owing to the hostile policy of the Yugoslav government towards the Soviet Union . . . [the] exchange of goods will be reduced by eight times as compared with 1948." (Freedman 29)

February 1949   Stalin abrogates long-term capital aid agreement signed with Yugoslavia in 1947, rejects Tito request to join recently formed Council for Mutual Economic Assistance (COMECON). (Freedman 30)

24 April 1949   Yugoslavia announces agreement with US firm to exchange raw materials for capital equipment. (Freedman 31)

June 1949   Economic blockade of Yugoslavia is imposed as "one Cominform nation after another denounce[s] its trade agreement with Yugoslavia." Embargo follows Tito's overture to World Bank and request that US representative take "friendly attitude" toward loan application. (Freedman 31–32)

4 August 1949   Yugoslavia signs trade agreement with Italy to obtain raw materials, industrial machinery. (Freedman 33)

September 1949   US Export–Import Bank approves $20 million loan to Yugoslavia. "This was to be the first in a long series of US loans and grants. Loans from France, England, and West Germany were also soon forthcoming." (Freedman 35)

1949   East European troops mass on Yugoslav borders with Albania, Bulgaria, Hungary, Romania; Yugoslavia reports 1,453 military border incidents by end of 1950; borders are sealed; various East European leaders are tried and executed for Titoist tendencies; Yugoslav children in East European schools are not allowed to return home; radio broadcasts from Eastern Europe call for revolt against Tito. (Farrell 10; Doxey 34)

1950	Drought hits Yugoslavia. Combination of natural and political adversity prompts nation to initiate extensive trade relations with Western Europe, US; over four-year period US, Western Europe, World Bank extend military and economic aid estimated at $1 billion. (Farrell 27; Doxey 34)
November 1950	Congress approves Yugoslavia Emergency Relief Act that authorizes $50 million in aid, primarily economic, consisting mostly of food to relieve drought effects. (Calvocorressi 457)
Spring 1952	US, UK extend $40 million in emergency aid to Yugoslavia for raw materials to keep factories operating. At same time, US, UK essentially agree that long-term loan of $400 million to $500 million will be necessary to avert collapse of Yugoslavia's economy. (Calvocorressi 460)
5 March 1953	Stalin dies.
25 October 1954	Marshall Tito signals "a great relaxation" in Yugoslav-USSR relations, stemming "from a changed Soviet foreign policy." (Farrell 3)
26 May 1955	Joint communiqué issued during visit by Soviet leaders Nikita Khrushchev, Nikolai Bulganin to Yugoslavia stresses rapprochement with USSR. (Farrell 3, 42)
29 July 1955	Yugoslavia waives claims stemming from Cominform break; USSR forgives counterclaims; trade, credits resumed. (Farrell 43)
17 April 1956	Yugoslavia becomes participating member of COMECON. (Farrell 1; Doxey 35)
2 June 1956	Khrushchev warmly receives Tito on state visit to Moscow, telling him: "The entire Soviet people greet you." Molotov, a Tito foe, is replaced as USSR foreign minister by D. T. Shepilov. US Congress speaks of reappraisal of relations with Yugoslavia. (Farrell 1, 48–52)
Fall 1956	Yugoslav-Soviet relations begin to deteriorate as Khrushchev comes to regard Tito as "too much of a divisive force in Eastern Europe." Relations further deteriorate when Tito criticizes Soviet suppression of Hungarian revolt. (Freedman 43)
1957	In attempt to further Yugoslavia's reconciliation with USSR, Tito recognizes government of East Germany. In so doing, however, he further alienates Yugoslavia from West without preventing increasing deterioration in relations with USSR. (Freedman 43)
1958	Again responding to Tito's independent line, USSR suspends aid to Yugoslavia; trade declines. Total embargo is not imposed, however, and other East European countries continue to trade with Yugoslavia. (Freedman 43–44)
1960	USSR seeks rapprochement with Yugoslavia to improve Soviet position vis-à-vis China. Increased aid, trade result. (Freedman 46)

GOALS OF SENDER COUNTRY

1948
Common theories in Belgrade as to Soviet strategy: Cominform denunciation would lead Yugoslav Central Committee to overthrow Tito; or denunciation would spark civil war between diverse nationalities in Yugoslavia, provide pretext for neighboring USSR satellites to invade Yugoslavia, overthrow Tito. (Farrell 7)

1949–50
Stalin becomes deeply concerned about Tito's "bad example," outbreak of nationalist tendencies elsewhere in Eastern Europe. USSR instigates overthrow, trial, imprisonment of several leaders in Eastern Europe, including Koci (Albania), Gomulka (Poland), Kostov (Bulgaria), Slansky (Czechoslovakia), Rajk (Hungary). (Farrell 7–10)

RESPONSE OF TARGET COUNTRY

Early 1948
"Tito had evidently not given up hope of acquiring the United States as an alternate supplier, and he continued his behind-the-scenes work to arrange for the release of the US-held gold. Significantly, on April 2, it was officially announced that Yugoslavia had engaged the prestigious Washington law firm of Penie and Lesser . . . to act as its agent in the United States for this purpose." (Freedman 26)

1948–54
Yugoslav military expenditures and reparations of $438 million in 1948 rise to 1950–54 average of $600 million, about 22 percent of national income. (Farrell 29–30)

1949
Tito arrests approximately 53,000 Yugoslavs suspected of pro-Stalinist tendencies. (Farrell 18)

August 1949
Yugoslavia applies for $25 million Eximbank loan. (Farrell 27)

1950–54
Yugoslavia receives US and European (largely British) military, economic aid estimated at $1 billion. (Farrell 27)

1952–53
Yugoslav theoreticians denounce Stalin as exponent of "state capitalism" by contrast with "workers' democracy" in Yugoslavia. (Farrell 13–15)

1954
Tito: "The United States imposed no conditions [when providing aid] which would violate our sovereignty and independence." (Farrell 29)

December 1954–January 1955
Tito visits India, Burma, arranges to visit President Gamal Abdel Nasser in Egypt; associates Yugoslavia with nonalignment, coexistence themes. (Farrell 40–41)

December 1954
External Yugoslav debt of $400 million, coupled with more liberal policies of Khrushchev

after death of Stalin, prompts Yugoslavia to renew economic ties with Eastern Europe. (Farrell 30)

ECONOMIC IMPACT

Observed Economic Statistics

In 1948, more than 50 percent of Yugoslav trade is with Cominform nations while trade with Western Europe, US is negligible. By 1952, 19 percent of Yugoslav imports are from US, 20 percent from West Germany; 14 percent of Yugoslav exports go to US, 20 percent to West Germany. By 1954, more than 80 percent of Yugoslav trade is with US, Europe. (Farrell 27; Doxey 34)

Yugoslav military expenditures increase sharply, from $438 million in 1948 to $665 million in 1952, reaching 22.3 percent of national income. Between 1949 and 1954 Yugoslavia spends more of its GNP on military than any non-Communist country in Europe. (Farrell 33–34)

Yugoslavia suffers drought, poor harvests in 1950–52; value of agricultural production: 452 billion dinars (average postwar figure); 333 billion dinars, 1950; 308 billion dinars, 1952. (Farrell 29)

US, West European aid 1950–54 amounts to $1 billion. In 1955, US economic aid falls to $43.8 million; in 1956, again in 1957, administration requests only $30 million. (Farrell 44; Doxey 34)

Yugoslavia claims impact of Cominform economic sanctions is $400 million for period 1948–54. (Farrell 29)

Trade, credit protocol signed with USSR in September 1955 provides: $54 million credit repayable over 19 years at two percent interest with 3-year grace period; $30 million hard currency loan, repayable over 10 years at two percent interest; project financing of about $110 million, repayable over 10 years at two percent interest. In 1956 Poland extends $20 million credit, Czechoslovakia $75 million. Total Soviet bloc "reconciliation" credits thus amount to $289 million. (Farrell 44–45)

Calculated Economic Impact

	Annual cost to target country
Increase in Yugoslav military budget as result of military threat from Cominform countries; welfare loss estimated at 25 percent of additional expenditures.	$40.5 million
Reduction in economic assistance from Cominform countries; annual welfare loss estimated at 75 percent of value of credits provided to Yugoslavia in 1955, spread over six years.	36 million
Suspension of payments by Cominform countries of estimated $300 million in obligations to Yugoslavia over six	35 million

	Annual cost to target country
years (1948–54); welfare loss estimated at 70 percent of lost receipts per year.	
Offset	
Increase in economic, military aid from US, Europe, World Bank; welfare gain estimated at 75 percent of transfers of $250 million per year.	($187.5 million)
Total (gain)	($76 million)

Relative Magnitudes

Gross indicators of Yugoslav economy	
Yugoslav GNP (1952)	$3.1 billion
Yugoslav population (1952)	17 million
Annual effect of sanctions related to gross indicators	
Percentage of GNP (gain)	(2.5)
Per capita (gain)	($4.47)
Yugoslav trade with USSR as percentage of total trade	
Exports (1948)	15
Imports (1948)	11
Ratio of USSR GNP (1952: $162 billion) to Yugoslav GNP (1952: $3.1 billion)	52

ASSESSMENT

Robert Owen Freedman
"Thanks to . . . aid from the West, the Yugoslav economy was kept afloat and Yugoslavia did not crumble before Russian economic, military and political pressure." (Freedman 36)

"[A] continual shortage of raw materials, coupled with Yugoslavia's other economic problems, such as its chronic balance of payments difficulties, helped make Tito amenable to the rapprochement overtures of the post-Stalin leadership of the USSR. Even a partial return to the pre-1948 trade pattern would alleviate some of Yugoslavia's balance of payments problem by enabling it to obtain a number of vital imports without spending scarce foreign exchange to acquire them." (Freedman 37)

"All-in-all, the post-Stalin rapprochement with Yugoslavia seemed by June, 1956, to have borne major dividends for the Soviet Union. Whereas Stalin had attempted to crush the Tito regime by preying on its economic weaknesses, Khrushchev exploited Yugoslavia's economic weakness in order to bring Tito into closer alliance with the Soviet Union." (Freedman 42)

Margaret P. Doxey
"Political survival proved possible after 1948 in spite of ruthless external pressure; the force of national feeling was amply demonstrated, and the leadership of Marshal Tito was strengthened and unchallenged. Practical assistance from the West tided the Yugoslav economy over the worst period, and in this instance the Soviet Union evidently judged it unwise to resort to force." (Doxey 35)

AUTHORS' SUMMARY

Overall assessment	Assigned scores
□ Policy result, scaled from 1 (failed) to 4 (success)	1
□ Sanctions contribution, scaled from 1 (none) to 4 (significant)	1
□ Success score (policy result *times* sanctions contribution), scaled from 1 (outright failure) to 16 (significant success)	1

Political and economic variables

□ Companion policies: J (covert), Q (quasi-military), or R (regular military)	Q
□ International cooperation with sender, scaled from 1 (none) to 4 (significant)	4
□ International assistance to target: A (if present)	A
□ Sanctions period (years)	7
□ Economic health and political stability of target, scaled from 1 (distressed) to 3 (strong)	2
□ Presanction relations between sender and target, scaled from 1 (antagonistic) to 3 (cordial)	3
□ Type of sanction: X (export), M (import), F (financial)	F, X, M
□ Cost to sender, scaled from 1 (net gain) to 4 (major loss)	1

BIBLIOGRAPHY

Calvocorressi, Peter. 1951. *Survey of International Affairs*. London: Oxford University Press.
Doxey, Margaret P. 1971. *Economic Sanctions and International Enforcement*. London: Oxford University Press for Royal Institute of International Affairs.
Farrell, R. Barry. 1956. *Yugoslavia and the Soviet Union 1948–1956*. Hamden, Conn.: Shoe String Press.
Freedman, Robert Owen. 1970. *Economic Warfare in the Communist Bloc: A Study of Soviet Economic Pressure Against Yugoslavia, Albania, and Communist China*. New York: Praeger.
United Nations. 1954. *Economic Survey of Europe in 1953*. Geneva.
Yugoslavia. 1951. *White Book on Aggressive Activities by the Governments of the USSR (and others) towards Yugoslavia*. Belgrade: Ministry of Foreign Affairs.

Case 48–5 US and COCOM v. USSR and COMECON

(1948–   : Technology Controls)

CHRONOLOGY OF KEY EVENTS

15 January 1948   US Department of Commerce requires licenses for all commercial shipments to Europe after 1 March 1948. (Adler-Karlsson 22)

Late March 1948   Congress inserts requirement in foreign aid bill that European recipients assure that goods deemed "strategic" by US will not be reexported to Eastern bloc. However, controls are laxly enforced: "The impression that is gained . . . is that at least up till October 1948, the enforcement of the US export regulations was more or less in a mess, with many loopholes to circumvent the existing laws." (Adler-Karlsson 25)

1948–49   US begins informally to enlist West European cooperation in coordinated embargo against Communist bloc. Efforts are stimulated by Berlin crisis, Communist leader Mao Tse-tung's triumph in China, explosion of first Soviet atomic bomb, break between Soviet leader Joseph Stalin and Marshal Tito followed by COMECON embargo against Yugoslavia. (OTA 1979, 153)

28 February 1949   Congress enacts Export Control Act of 1949. (Woolcock 8)

22 November 1949   Under US leadership, Consultative Group and Coordinating Committee for Multilateral Export Controls (COCOM) are secretly formed, eventually consist of 15 NATO countries (all NATO except Iceland and Spain) plus Japan. Consultative Group is policy-guiding group at ministerial level that rarely meets. COCOM is permanent working group that implements policy. Under COCOM procedures, items on embargo list and exceptions to list must be agreed unanimously. Europeans are less enthusiastic about COCOM than US because: they historically had engaged in more East-West trade and are less convinced about balance of pain and benefit resulting from sanctions; they are less sure than US that technical problems could be resolved

22 November *1949 (continued)*	adequately; they place less emphasis on Soviet economic dependence as fulcrum of leverage; and they resent pressure to restrict commercial ties. (Wolf 53; OTA 1979, 153; Adler-Karlsson 6)
1 January 1950	COCOM begins operation with membership consisting of US, Great Britain, France, Italy, Benelux countries. Later that year, Norway, Denmark, Canada, West Germany join. (OTA 1979, 153)
September 1950	Congress passes Cannon amendment to 1951 Supplemental Appropriations Act forbidding US aid to any nation that exports "strategic" goods, as designated by US, to Communist bloc; however, legislation contains presidential waiver authority. (Adler-Karlsson 27)
January 1952	Congress passes Battle Act requiring nations to comply with US export regulations in order to receive aid. This objective is largely achieved by COCOM. (Adler-Karlsson 27)
1952	Portugal, Japan join COCOM. Most of COCOM nations combine to form China Committee (CHINCOM) to limit trade with China. (Adler-Karlsson 52)
1953	Greece, Turkey join COCOM. COCOM secrecy is loosened somewhat, though lists themselves are classified. Stalin's death, liberalization in USSR are followed by shortening of COCOM lists in period 1954–58. (OTA 1979, 153)
August 1957	Eisenhower administration relaxes controls on trade with Poland following Wladyslaw Gomulka's rise to power there. (Garson 64)
1958	Second major revision of COCOM lists: "after 1958, almost all observers agree that the COCOM lists (as they still existed in 1967) mainly include goods which are conventionally understood as having a 'strategic importance'." US, however, unilaterally continues to maintain stricter embargo, based on old list. (Adler-Karlsson 8)
1963	US accepts view of European allies that "nonstrategic Western trade with the Soviet bloc, or the denial thereof, cannot affect basic Soviet military capability. . . . That capability is independently based on the Soviet's own advanced weapons-technology and military production." (Garson 14, citing Battle Act Report of 1963)
July 1964	COCOM controls relaxed on trade with Romania because of its perceived desire for independence from USSR. (Garson 64)
September 1966	US administration spokesman: "[the US welcomes] increased trade in nonstrategic goods with Eastern European countries to weaken their ties with what was once a monolithic Soviet bloc." (Garson 64)
1969	Congress passes Export Administration Act that essentially switches US "from a policy of economic denial to a more narrow strategic embargo." Three reasons are cited for switch: National Security Adviser Henry A. Kissinger's "web of interdependence"; "our policy

of maintaining a broad trade embargo on the Soviet Union clearly had not significantly retarded Soviet economic growth or inhibited Soviet foreign policy"; Allies increasingly refuse to cooperate in broad policy of denial. (Bingham 896)

1972 US begins normalization of relations with Peking, drops "China differential," namely, tighter restrictions on exports to China than to Eastern Europe. (Meese 23)

July 1981 At Ottawa summit, Western leaders support US initiative for high-level review of COCOM controls. (Woolcock 3)

11 January 1982 NATO ministers agree to "reflect on longer term East-West economic relations, particularly energy, agricultural commodities and the export of technology" in order to "protect [NATO's] competitive position in the field of military and technological capabilities." (Woolcock 70)

21 January 1982 At US urging, COCOM holds Deputy Minister meeting (first at that high a level in 23 years); Reagan administration pushes for tighter controls on high technology items, puts forward proposals to add 100 items to COCOM list, including robots, large dry docks (USSR is using Japanese dry dock to build aircraft carrier), computers, microprocessors. US also proposes "no exceptions" policy on computers. (Woolcock 68; *Wall Street Journal*, 19 January 1982, 33; *New York Times*, 20 January 1982, A8)

November 1982 Britain, France, Germany refuse to appoint permanent subcommittee of military experts to aid COCOM in decisions about military significance of certain "dual use" (i.e., both civilian, military) items put forward by US at January meetings. (*Financial Times* [London], 13 November 1982, 2)

November 1982 Senate Subcommittee on Investigations charges Commerce Department with lax enforcement of export controls. Report states that Soviets have major program underway for acquiring Western technology by any means available. (*Washington Post*, 15 November 1982, A1).

December 1982 US, France agree on series of projects designed to strengthen Western control over trade with East. (*Washington Post*, 15 December 1982, A1)

March 1983 President Ronald Reagan approves National Security Decision Directive 75, which sets policy of using economic pressure to limit resources, foreign policy and military options open to Soviet Union. (*Washington Post*, 21 March 1983, A3)

January 1984 It is reported that: "Nearly 100 Soviet officials were expelled from Western countries last year, chiefly for attempted or successful industrial espionage." (*Financial Times*, 24 January 1984, 10)

12 July 1984 COCOM members agree to extend restrictions on large computers,

12 July 1984 *(continued)*	some types of software and sophisticated telecommunications equipment. Restrictions on "many varieties of commonly available desktop computers" are removed. Pentagon official says, "There's a red line on the high end and more decontrol on the low end, which satisfies business interests all around." (*Washington Post*, 17 July 1984, A1)
January 1985	COCOM announces plans to hold a high-level meeting in February to discuss streamlining embargo exceptions procedure in order to facilitate trade with China. 70 percent–80 percent of exceptions requests being filed concerns sales to China. In 1984, US alone filed 3,122 applications for embargo exceptions, 89 percent of them for sales to China. US companies complain of delays of six to eight months in getting export licenses for China. US, however, opposes simply shortening lists for China because of loss in flexibility if relations deteriorate; also fears such preference might offend Soviets at a time when US is seeking to improve relations. US wants COCOM to speed up exceptions approval by allowing more of them to be subject to "national discretion" rather than subject to unanimous COCOM approval. Another proposal, likely to be readily approved, is to subject embargo lists to continuous review rather than only updating them once every three years. (*Financial Times*, 10 January 1985, 4)

GOALS OF SENDER COUNTRIES

Klaus Knorr
"Thus, after World War II, the United States placed an embargo on the export of a wide range of 'strategic goods' to the Soviet Union. The object then was not to coerce Russia to do something or other, but to obstruct the growth of her military strength." (Knorr 1975, 5)

"Although motivations were mixed, ranging from a sheer desire to express righteous antagonism to the idea of waging comprehensive economic warfare against the Communist bloc, the main purpose came to be that of maintaining Soviet, and later Chinese, military inferiority, presumably in the interest of curbing their capacity for aggression. . . . The intent was to weaken, not coerce." (Knorr 1975, 142)

Gunnar Adler-Karlsson
"By the end of 1949 the control machinery was being used almost exclusively to keep out of the hands of Russia and her satellites items that might contribute to their military strength." (Adler-Karlsson 25)

Stephen Woolcock
In early 1970s US adopts linkage policy based on "web of constructive relationships," believing that increased trade and economic links—fostered by a carrot-and-stick approach using trade credits and sanctions—could contribute to improved East-West relations. (Woolcock 13)

Lawrence J. Brady, assistant secretary of commerce
"The basic US aim is for the West to maintain its 'qualitative' advantage over the Soviet

Union. The United States wants to avoid a repeat of the 1970s when the Soviets narrowed their technology gap with the West, thanks largely to acquisitions—legally and illegally— of Western technology." (*Journal of Commerce*, 4 October 1982, 1A)

Lionel H. Olmer, under secretary of commerce for international trade
"Our national security export control system serves a similar protective function by enabling the West to preserve its lead over the USSR in technology relevant to military purposes. The control system, though cumbersome and sometimes inefficient, is very much like a fisherman's net. Sometimes the holes in the net are opened more widely. Sometimes they are drawn more closely. We have an ongoing series of consultations with the Allies and US business over the spacing of these holes. But it would be extremely shortsighted to argue that the net should be taken away or that mutual security would be enhanced by an unimpeded flow of technology from West to East." (Olmer 12)

McGeorge Bundy
"When I first encountered this question of the definition of exports that would be helpful to the Soviet Union, it was in 1948 when I was a very junior person in the Economic Cooperation Administration, the Marshall Plan, and was assigned briefly to that issue. And one of the items that was proposed for embargo by the Defense Department was baseball bats. When we asked why that was, the answer was that baseball bats were issued to troops and were helpful to morale. . . . There is a recurrent tendency, I think, when there is tension between us and the Soviet Union for people to put quite a lot of pressure on. The general feeling in such times is that if the Defense Department says no, or indeed if some section of the Defense Department says no, we better be very careful." (*Trade and Technology* 21)

RESPONSE OF TARGET COUNTRIES

Gunnar Adler-Karlsson
"Several politicians in both the East and the West also believe that Stalin *did* exploit [the embargo] to his own advantage. Not only did he try to sow the seeds of disunity inside the West by making the businessmen of each country believe that their competitors in the other Western nations could trade much less restricted by the embargo than themselves. More important may be that the embargo policy, being a very evident and forceful example of Western hostility, could be used by Stalin to push the bloc together in a harsh manner, blaming the harshness of a policy he anyway had intended to realize, on the Western embargo actions." (Adler-Karlsson 7)

"The Soviet response to the embargo policy had mainly two forms. On the one hand it sought to influence the West Europeans to keep the restrictions down as much as possible; on the other it had to find ways and means to circumvent those restrictions that did come into existence." (Adler-Karlsson 78)

Central Intelligence Agency
"The combination of past Soviet acquisition practices and projected Soviet military needs indicates that the United States and its Allies are likely to experience serious counterintelligence and related industrial security and export control problems over the next five to ten years." (CIA 12)

ATTITUDE OF OTHER COUNTRIES

Sweden, Switzerland, Iceland, Austria, Finland
These countries choose not to compromise their neutrality by joining COCOM. Sweden and Switzerland are seen as major alternative suppliers of items on COCOM list. Their relationship with COCOM is informal, their cooperation "unpredictable." (OTA 1979, 153)

Federal Republic of Germany, United Kingdom, France
"Originally all three countries (UK, FRG, France) adhered to COCOM because they believed it was in their own political and economic self-interest and because they were concerned about the Soviet threat. They were dependent on the US for their economic recovery and for their defense against the USSR." (Yergin 10)

"With the passage of time, all to some degree, have come to regard COCOM . . . as an American instrument for controlling and limiting European competition. The unpredictability of American policy and its repeated changes of direction regarding trade controls have made the Europeans doubly suspicious of American motives." (Yergin 3–5)

"The United States and the FRG converged in their view of trade in the 1950s and 1960s, but today they increasingly diverge over the politics of East-West trade. The FRG believes that East-West trade can be a stabilizing force, creating interdependencies that may serve to moderate Soviet behavior." (Yergin 26)

"[France] has never officially recognized COCOM's existence, has consistently maintained that security controls should be decided nationally and has led the opposition to any formal treaty establishing COCOM, as sought by the United States on various occasions." (Woolcock 61)

Japan
In anticipation of March 1983 COCOM meetings, Japanese government announces: "it basically cannot agree to the expanding of the COCOM restriction framework, going beyond the scope of military materials . . . the Japanese side fears that 'if restrictions are expanded in order to prevent the Soviet Union's acquisition of foreign currencies, it may even lead to the denial of East-West trade, as a whole, in the end,' and it intends to assert reversely that 'the development of East-West trade will increase the degree of the Soviet economy's dependence on the nations of the West, and this will reversely have big plus effects on security." (*Nihon Keizai*, 16 March 1983, 1)

LEGAL NOTES

Office of Technology Assessment
"The formulation of the framework of [COCOM] . . . is thus shrouded in secrecy. It is, in fact, doubtful whether any written understanding has ever existed; most likely a gentleman's agreement was undertaken, members agreeing to follow the licensing rules laid down by unanimous decisions among the group.

"Because it is an informal and voluntary organization, COCOM has no power of enforcement. It is based neither on treaty nor executive agreement." (OTA 1979, 153)

ECONOMIC IMPACT

Observed Economic Statistics

COCOM control lists have several parts:

☐ munitions list, including all military items
☐ atomic energy list, including sources of fissionable materials and nuclear reactors and their components
☐ industrial/commercial list, composed of:
1. International List I: embargoed items
2. International List II: quantitatively controlled items
3. International List III: exchange of information and surveillance items.

List I items of the industrial/commerical list cannot be exported to Communist bloc nations without an exception. List II items may be exported but only in specified quantities. Amounts above specified total require special exception. List III items may be sold but must be reported to COCOM and their end use tracked. "Most of the dual use items that pose the greatest problems for export controls are contained in List I. . . ." (OTA 1979, 155)

In November 1949, COCOM embargo list had 86 items; total rose to 270 by November 1951 before dropping to 170 in August 1954, 118 in July 1958. It then rose again to 161 by August 1965, has declined slowly since. (OTA 1979, 156)

Annual average of USSR imports of all goods from developed West: $676 million (1950–59); $2,730 million (1960–70); $11,602 million (1970–80). (Knorr 1975, 154; Portes 89)

Industrial world's high tech exports to USSR, Eastern Europe, 1970–81 (million dollars)

	USSR	Eastern Europe	Total high tech exports[†]	Total mfg. exports	High tech exports as percentage of total mfg. exports
1970	403	414	817	4,971	16.4
1972	582	619	1,201	7,168	16.8
1974	1,036	1,223	2,259	15,978	14.1
1976	1,627	1,525	3,152	20,607	15.3
1977	2,003	1,741	3,744	21,306	17.6
1979	2,371	2,360	4,731	27,445	17.2
1980	2,330	2,194	4,524	29,252	15.5
1981	1,735	1,721	3,456	25,475	13.6

[†] Annual average 1970–81: $2,985.
Source: Commerce 7, 13; OTA 1983, 51.

Calculated Economic Impact

	Annual cost to target country

Reduction in high technology exports, estimated to have accounted, in absence of controls, for additional 5 percentage point share of total USSR and Eastern Europe imports of manufactured goods; welfare loss valued at 125 percent of difference between actual imports and potential high tech imports.

1950–59	$69 million
1960–69	$280 million
1970–81	$1,191 million

Total annual average 1950–81	$556 million

Relative Magnitudes

Gross indicators of COMECON economies	
COMECON GNP (1950)[†]	$148.3 billion
COMECON population (1948–50)	245 million
COMECON GNP (1970)	$688 billion
COMECON population (1970)	346 million
Annual effect of sanctions (1950–59) related to gross indicators	
Percentage of GNP	negl.
Per capita	$0.28
Annual effect of sanctions (1970–81) related to gross indicators	
Percentage of GNP	0.2
Per capita	$3.44
COMECON trade with COCOM as percentage of total trade	
Exports (1948)	32
Imports (1948)	31
Exports (1970)	15
Imports (1970)	15
Ratio of COCOM GNP (1950: $447 billion) to COMECON GNP (1950: $148.3 billion)	3
Ratio of COCOM GNP (1970: $2,204 billion) to COMECON GNP (1970: $688 billion)	3

† Based on USSR only.

ASSESSMENT

Stephen Woolcock
"Although it seems clear that Western technology has been of importance to the Soviet economy, it is impossible to say whether or not it is of such importance that the threat of denial would influence Soviet policy. Recent research . . . suggests that the impact of Western exports depends on the ability of the Soviet economy to absorb and thus reproduce Western technological know-how." (Woolcock 32)

Gunnar Adler-Karlsson
"It is today impossible to maintain the original embargo motives, that the American restrictions over East-West trade to an appreciable extent can slow down the growth of the Soviet economy or of the military sector of that economy." (Adler-Karlsson 8)

Rand Report for US Department of Defense
"[Export controls] 'would not halt Soviet economic or military development and will only slow it slightly. . . . As export controls move away from areas in which the USA stands to make 'near-term military gains,' toward 'technologies that afford the Soviets longer term industrial gains . . . , the benefits of export controls become more diffuse and uncertain, while the costs of trying to enforce them become progressively greater.'" (Woolcock 46)

Lionel H. Olmer, testifying at congressional hearing, March 1983
Because "very, very slow progress" has been made in harmonizing US, Western Europe, and Japanese export controls, "American business is taking a hosing in a number of specific areas." (*New York Times*, 2 March 1983, D2)

AUTHORS' SUMMARY

Overall assessment	Assigned scores
□ Policy result, scaled from 1 (failed) to 4 (success)	2
□ Sanctions contribution, scaled from 1 (none) to 4 (significant)	2
□ Success score (policy result *times* sanctions contribution), scaled from 1 (outright failure) to 16 (significant success)	4

Political and economic variables

□ Companion policies: J (covert), Q (quasi-military), or R (regular military)	—
□ International cooperation with sender, scaled from 1 (none) to 4 (significant)	4
□ International assistance to target: A (if present)	A
□ Sanctions period (years)	36 +
□ Economic health and political stability of target, scaled from 1 (distressed) to 3 (strong)	3
□ Presanction relations between sender and target, scaled from 1 (antagonistic) to 3 (cordial)	1
□ Type of sanction: X (export), M (import), F (financial)	X
□ Cost to sender, scaled from 1 (net gain) to 4 (major loss)	3

Comments

Our success scores do not address utility of national security controls that seek to limit exports of technology and goods directly relevant to military uses. Rather, they assess success of COCOM in using broader measures of economic denial to limit resources available for the Soviet defense establishment. Although quantitative estimates cannot be made, most observers believe COCOM controls had little impact on Soviet economic growth or defense spending. Any potential impact was undermined by intense, often successful Soviet effort to acquire restricted technology by covert means. We judge that the policy result of economic denial was, at best, marginally achieved, and that the sanctions, at best, made a small contribution to that achievement.

BIBLIOGRAPHY

Adler-Karlsson, Gunnar. 1968. *Western Economic Warfare, 1947–67: A Case Study in Foreign Economic Policy.* Stockholm: Almqvist and Wiksell.
Bingham, Jonathan B., and Victor C. Johnson. 1979. "A Rational Approach to Export Controls." 58 *Foreign Affairs* (Spring): 894–920.
Drabek, Zdenek. 1983. "The Impact of Technological Differences on East-West Trade." 119 *Weltwirtschaftliches Archiv.* 630–48.
Garson, John R. 1971. "The American Trade Embargo Against China." In *China Trade Prospects and US Policy,* ed. Alexander Eckstein. New York: Praeger.
Knorr, Klaus. 1973. *Power and Wealth: The Political Economy of International Power.* New York: Basic Books.
———. 1975. *The Power of Nations: The Political Economy of International Relations.* New York: Basic Books.
Meese, Sally A. 1984. "Export Controls to China: An Emerging Trend for Dual-Use Exports." 7 *The International Trade Law Journal* (Fall): 20–37.
Portes, Richard. 1983. *Deficits and Detente.* Background paper for report of international conference on balance of trade in COMECON countries. New York: Twentieth Century Fund.
US Central Intelligence Agency. 1982. *Soviet Acquisition of Western Technology.* Washington.
US Congress. Office of Technology Assessment. 1979. *Technology and East-West Trade.*
———. 1983. *Technology and East-West Trade: An Update.*
———. Senate Committee on Banking, Housing, and Urban Affairs. Subcommittee on International Finance. 1980. *Hearings on Trade and Technology, Part 2, East-West Trade and Technology Transfer.* 96 Cong., 1 sess., 28 November 1979.
———. Senate Committee on Foreign Relations. Subcommittee on International Policy. 1982. *Hearings on Economic Relations with the Soviet Union.* Testimony of Lionel H. Olmer, under secretary of commerce for international trade. 97 Cong., 2 sess., 30 July.
US Department of Commerce. International Trade Administration. 1983. "Quantification of Western Exports of High Technology Products to Communist Countries." Washington.
Wickens, Justin H. 1984. *Technology Transfer Controls: Theory and Practice.* Paper prepared for Executive Seminar in National and International Affairs, Foreign Service Institute, 26 sess. Washington.
Wolf, Thomas. A. 1973. *US East-West Trade Policy.* Lexington, Mass.: Lexington Books.
Woolcock, Stephen. 1982. *Western Policies on East-West Trade.* Chatham House Papers, no. 15. London: Royal Institute of International Affairs.
Yergin, Angela Stent. 1980. *East-West Technology Transfer: European Perspectives.* The Washington Papers, no. 75. Beverly Hills and London: Sage Publications.

Case 49–1   US and CHINCOM v. China

(1949–70: Communist Control of China and Korean War)

CHRONOLOGY OF KEY EVENTS

October 1949   Communist forces push south in China; US imposes selective trade controls under Export Control Act of 1949. (Garson 7)

March 1950   Peking adopts "Lean to One Side" policy. US, other members of Coordinating Committee (COCOM) make their controls on China trade coextensive with controls on USSR, East European trade they instituted in January 1950. (Garson 7; Evans 4)

25 June 1950   Following outbreak of Korean War, COCOM lists are expanded to cover 350 strategic items. US goes further, imposes total embargo on trade with North Korea; in July 1950, US revokes all existing licenses for export to China of items that were put under control by March 1950 action. (Garson 7; Evans 4)

August 1950   At US State Department request, US oil companies with overseas facilities embargo petroleum shipments to China. (Garson 7)

3 December 1950   US Commerce Department, invoking Export Control Act of 1949, requires license for export of any item to China. (*New York Times*, 7 December 1950, A1)

16 December 1950   President Harry S Truman declares national emergency in connection with Korean War; Secretary of the Treasury John W. Snyder issues Foreign Assets Control Regulations under authority of Trading with the Enemy Act of 1917. All imports from China are banned, Chinese assets in US are frozen, US financing of third-country trade in Chinese goods is prohibited, similar regulations are applied to North Korea. US Congress withdraws most-favored-nation (MFN) status of imports from Communist countries, a redundant restriction with respect to China trade. (Note: US imports of goods from countries without MFN status are charged Smoot-Hawley tariff.) (Garson 16–18, 25–27)

| September 1952 | China Committee (CHINCOM) is formally established as parallel organization to COCOM. CHINCOM embargo on some 500 items is more extensive than COCOM embargo, covering, for example, rubber tubing, paraffin wax, trucks and tractors, barbed wire. (Evans 5) |

1953   Korean war ends.

1958   CHINCOM is abolished; COCOM carries out remaining multilateral trade controls. US continues total embargo against China unilaterally. (Evans 12–13)

1967   US Commerce Department announces willingness to license drugs to fight epidemic in China; Chinese newspaper headlines story "God of Plague Peddles Vaccine," accuses US of spreading false rumors about epidemic. (Garson 70)

1968   US Treasury Department authorizes RCA to pay $600,000 to China for telecommunications services; China refuses payment. (Garson 70)

July 1969   US State Department announces that returning American tourists can bring back up to $100 of Chinese merchandise for personal use. (Garson 3)

December 1969   US State Department removes $100 ceiling, extends importing privilege to tax-exempt organizations such as museums; US Treasury allows foreign subsidiaries of US firms to trade in Chinese goods, other than for import to US. Thus, after 1969, remaining controls reflect general strategic policy rather than lingering resentment of Chinese Communist government or Korean War. (Garson 3, 40; Meese 23)

1970   Ambassadorial talks progress in Warsaw, ultimately leading to Nixon's visit to Peking and US recognition of China. (*New York Times*, 28 February 1972, A1)

1979   US Treasury Secretary W. Michael Blumenthal travels to China, negotiates settlement of US asset claims; agreement signed March 1. (*New York Times*, 2 March 1979, A1)

January 1985   COCOM announces plans to hold a high-level meeting in February to discuss streamlining embargo exceptions procedure in order to facilitate trade with China. 70 percent–80 percent of exceptions requests being filed concerns sales to China. In 1984, US alone filed 3,122 applications for embargo exceptions, 89 percent of them for sales to China. US companies complain of delays of six to eight months in getting export licenses for China. US, however, opposes simply shortening lists for China because of loss in flexibility if relations deteriorate; also fears such preference might offend Soviets at a time when US is seeking to improve relations. US wants COCOM to speed up exceptions approval by allowing more of them to be subject to "national discretion" rather than subject to unanimous COCOM approval. (*Financial Times* [London], 10 January 1985, 4)

GOALS OF SENDER COUNTRIES

1950

US Department of State announces barriers will last "as long as a willful group of Chinese Communist leaders are willing to subvert their national interests and the welfare of the Chinese people to the designs of international Communist imperialism. If the Chinese Communists choose to withdraw their forces of aggression and act in conformity with United Nations principles, this Government will be prepared promptly to consider removing restrictions and restoring normal trade relations." (Eckstein 131)

1950–60

"At the risk of undue simplification, it is possible to distinguish what might be labelled a 'minimalist' and a 'maximalist' view of the objectives of sanctions. The minimalist view, often associated with the British position, accepted the need for restricting exports to Communist countries, including China, of goods that were of direct military significance. In time of war the extent of the restrictions could be broadened for strategical and psychological purposes, but the general objective was to minimize controls as far as feasible and reestablish free trade as quickly as possible. . . . The maximalist conception embraced a much broader range of objectives and political goals. The first was to punish the Communist leadership in Peking for past and future aggression. . . . Second was the goal of slowing China's industrial growth by creating dislocations, bottlenecks, and shortages in vulnerable sectors of the Chinese economy. This related to the recurrent hope that external pressures, including economic ones, might lead to the overthrow of the regime. Third, it was hoped that even sanctions on strategic goods alone would retard Chinese aggregate growth by demanding that scarce Chinese resources be diverted from other tasks. Fourth, arguments were made that even ineffective sanctions were an important contribution to the containment of an aggressive and expansionist Chinese Communist regime. . . . Finally, the position was taken, most often in the U.S. Congress, that restrictions on trade with China and even its abolition were moral ends in themselves whether or not they served other political purposes." (Evans 15–16)

1953

US Secretary of State John Foster Dulles states: "We ought to do everything possible to subject China to a maximum of economic strain in order to penalize her for her aggression, and make her repent her ways and to give up her aggression." (Garson 70)

January 1961

President John F. Kennedy indicates US would gladly consider Chinese request for food; Foreign Minister Chen Yi replies that China will never "stoop to beg for food from the United States." (Cohen 137)

Early 1966

Assistant Secretary of State William P. Bundy remarks: "Every time the subject [of trade with China] is seriously mentioned in this country, it is shot down immediately in Peking." (Cohen 137–38)

1980

"As the 1970s drew to a close, serious strains appeared in the American relationship with the Soviet Union. In response, United States export control policy began an unofficial 'tilt' toward China in the 1980's that has resulted in allowing China greater access to high-technology items than any other Communist country. The Soviet invasion of Afghanistan had the effect of making this unofficial 'tilt' the new policy—a policy that might be termed a 'China Preferential.'" (Meese 20)

RESPONSE OF TARGET COUNTRY

October 1949
Chairman Mao Tse-tung: "We want to do business, quite right, business will be done. We are against no one except the domestic and foreign reactionaries who hinder us from doing business. . . ." (Cohen 128)

December 1950
Following freeze of Chinese assets in US, China seizes American assets in China but does not take legal steps to restrict trade. (Cohen 129)

May 1951
China characterizes UN embargo resolution as "shameful," "slander," and illegal but does not retaliate with her own embargo. (Cohen 129)

April 1952
Nan Han-ch'en, head of Chinese delegation to International Economic Conference, Moscow: "The present standstill in trade between China and the United States is entirely due to the blockade and embargo against China imposed by the US Government. . . . The results are a loss of a broad, permanent, and reliable market of some 500 million people. . . ." (Cohen 130)

1953
China-Finland trade agreement prohibits US vessels from carrying Sino-Finnish cargo; similar clauses appear in 1967 Sino-Italian and Sino-Japanese trade agreements. (Cohen 143)

1955
Premier Chou En-lai initiates talks with US on repatriation of nationals, opening of trade; US refuses to negotiate end of embargo. (Cohen 132)

September 1960
China changes tack; claims attempts to address side issues with US have failed; declares no progress will be made on trade, tourism, culture or other questions until fundamental issue of Taiwan is settled. Ensuing Cultural Revolution is marked by spy mania, and China rigidly restricts travel by foreigners. (Cohen 133–49)

May 1964
Chen Ming, director of Chinese trade with Western Europe: "When the United States withdraws from Taiwan, gives up its scheme to create two Chinas, lifts its embargo policy against China, adopts a friendly attitude toward China, and when normal relations are established between our two countries, *then* it will be possible to carry out normal trade." (Cohen 135)

January 1965
Lin Hai-yun, vice minister of foreign trade: "The US imperialists are going to great lengths in their efforts to obstruct and sabotage such trade, but just as their blockade and embargo and other policies of trade discrimination against China went bankrupt, so their new conspiracies are meeting and are bound to meet ignominious defeat." (Cohen 139)

ATTITUDE OF OTHER COUNTRIES

Pre-COCOM cooperation
In 1949, three international control lists secretly take shape vis-à-vis China: total embargo on arms, implements of war, atomic materials; quantitative control list on certain machine tools, raw materials, equipment; surveillance list covering wide variety of goods. (Eckstein 184)

COCOM controls
In July 1950 following outbreak of Korean War, COCOM nations (NATO countries less Iceland, and Japan) secretly agree to embargo items on the three lists devised in 1949, plus 200 additional items. "China differential" results from stricter controls on shipments to China than to USSR, Eastern Europe. In August 1954, COCOM list is shortened, thus widening China differential further. "Differential" persists until 1957. (Garson 62; Eckstein 184)

CHINCOM
In September 1952 CHINCOM is established; Japan joins both CHINCOM and COCOM. Control list applied multilaterally to China is expanded; Japan follows US lead (until 1954), restricts even more trade with China. New Zealand, South Africa, Australia adopt restrictions that parallel COCOM lists. (Evans 5; Meese 23)

US reaction to third-country trade with China
In Summer 1950 Senator James P. Kem (R–Mo.), supported by Senator Kenneth Wherry (R–Ohio), proposes to cut US aid to countries that ship strategic goods to Communist nations: "It is entirely possible, even probable, that many of the shipments of iron and steel from Marshall Plan countries to Russia went into building those very same guns and tanks now killing our boys." Truman administration, sensitive to Alliance reaction, advocates cooperative embargo approach; claims cooperation has prevented $150 million of shipments in past two years. Senate defeats Kem proposals. (Garson 12–13)

Eventually, in August 1951, with Truman administration support, and after bitter congressional debate, Battle Act (US Mutual Defense Assistance Control Act of 1951) is passed, providing: mandatory termination of aid to countries shipping "arms, ammunition, and implements of war" to Communist nations; discretionary termination of aid to countries shipping "petroleum, transportation materials of strategic value, and items used in the production of arms, ammunition, and implements of war" to Communist nations; discretionary cut-off of aid to countries not cooperating with US in limiting exports of lesser strategic significance. Battle Act is violently opposed by Senator Kem, 16 Republican colleagues because of its discretionary character. (Note: Battle Act was applied, in its only use, to Ceylon for delivery of rubber to China, and that application was rescinded in 1956.) (Garson 22–23; Evans 7–8)

United Nations
In February 1951 UN adopts resolution branding China "aggressor nation." On 18 May 1951, at US urging, UN General Assembly adopts resolution (47 to 0, 8 abstentions, Soviet bloc not participating) recommending that each member state embargo shipments to China, North Korea of: "arms, ammunition and implements of war, atomic energy materials, petroleum, transportation materials of strategic value, and items useful in the production of arms, ammunition and implements of war." By June 1951 most UN members report implementation of resolution. (Garson 9–10; Evans 5)

Hong Kong, UK, France, Switzerland, OAS
In 1951, under US pressure, largely flowing from congressional criticism, Hong Kong bans rubber shipments to China; UK, France enlarge their lists of banned strategic goods; OAS imposes controls on trade that parallel COCOM restrictions; Switzerland is sealed off as transshipment point. (Garson 16–20; Evans 5)

UK action leading to abolition of CHINCOM
In May 1956, UK government announces it will use CHINCOM exceptions procedures to increase shipments to China. In May 1957, over US objections, UK announces it will conform its approach to CHINCOM and COCOM. All countries, with exception of US, Canada, and Turkey, follow UK lead. CHINCOM is abolished in 1958; embargo reverts to COCOM standard. (Garson 62–64; Evans 9–11)

Canada
Prior to 1957, Canada generally supported controls through its brand of "quiet diplomacy." In 1957 Ford Motor Canada proposes sale of 1,000 trucks to China but US Treasury blocks sale via directive to Ford Motor US; when it becomes public, this incident severely strains US-Canada relations. (Garson 40; Evans 11–14)

West Germany
In 1966, US pressures West Germany to refuse official guarantee on $87.5 million credit for China steel mill. (Garson 66)

LEGAL NOTES

Authority to embargo US exports
Controls are initiated under Export Control Act of 1949, which expired 31 December 1969, and was replaced by Export Administration Act of 1969. The 1969 act removes reference to "economic potential" of Communist nations as reason for controls, instead refers to military potential of target country, makes foreign availability of similar goods paramount consideration. (Garson 44–59)

Authority to embargo US imports, freeze Chinese assets, prevent foreign subsidiaries of US firms from dealing with China
Authority flows from Trading with the Enemy Act (TWEA) of 1917, Section 5b, triggered when president declares national emergency. Truman declares national emergency relating to Korean War but since US already is in national emergency this step is legally superfluous. Regulations issued in December 1950 extend jurisdiction of TWEA to "any partnership, association, corporation, or other organization wheresoever organized or doing business that is owned or controlled by [US citizens, residents, persons actually within US, domestic corporations]." This jurisdictional sweep causes severe criticism by US allies, notably Canada, France. (Garson 7, 26)

Extraterritorial application of US restrictions on trade with China
In October 1964, Fruehauf-France, 70 percent owned by Fruehauf-US, tenders to supply semitrailers to Beirut, which contracts to export them to China. US Treasury instructs Fruehauf-US to cancel contract; France protests. At request of French directors, French Commercial Court appoints temporary administrator to implement Beirut contract. US Treasury concedes Fruehauf-France no longer is under control of Fruehauf-US, waives sanctions against parent. This decision overlooks important language in US Foreign Assets Control Regulations that subjects companies "*owned* or controlled" (emphasis supplied)

by US firms to regulations. Subsequently, Rhodesian Transactions Regulations are applied only to firms controlled by US firms. (Hermann 33)

ECONOMIC IMPACT

Observed Economic Statistics

US congressional committee in 1963 estimates value of expropriated American investments in China, as of 1949, at $56 million; other estimates range to $100 million; private claims filed with US Foreign Claims Settlement Commission total $300 million. (Cohen 142–143, citing US House Committee on Foreign Affairs; *New York Times*, 30 December 1950, A3)

Chinese merchandise trade (million dollars)

	Exports		Imports	
	Non-Communist countries	*Total*	*Non-Communist countries*	*Total*
1950	486	697	483	876
1954	336	1,197	286	1,307
1958	685	1,985	768	1,777
1962	628	1,562	600	1,085
1966	1,615	2,172	1,410	1,905

Source: Garson 276–77.

"More surprising, Sino-American trade skyrocketed, rising faster than any American estimates had projected, from about $5 million (two-way) in 1971 to almost $934 million in 1974. By 1973, the United States, to everyone's surprise, was China's second largest trading partner—principally because of Peking's imports of U.S. agricultural commodities." (Barnett 202)

Calculated Economic Impact

	Annual cost to target country
Decline in exports to non-Communist countries, estimated at $150 million annually 1950–54; welfare loss estimated at 30 percent of reduced trade.	$45 million
Decline in imports from non-Communist countries, estimated at $197 million annually 1950–54; welfare loss estimated at 30 percent of reduced trade.	59 million
Freeze of about $80 million of Chinese assets in US; welfare loss valued at 10 percent of assets.	8 million

Calculated Economic Impact *(continued)*

	Annual cost to target country
Offset	
Estimated annual gain from seizure of $56 million of US assets in China, valued at 10 percent of assets.	($6 million)
Total	$106 million

Relative Magnitudes

Gross indicators of Chinese economy	
Chinese GNP (1949)	$19.7 billion
Chinese population (1949)	537.9 million
Annual effect of sanctions related to gross indicators	
Percentage of GNP	0.5
Per capita	$0.20
China trade with US as percentage of total trade	
Exports (1948)	25
Imports (1948)	51
Ratio of US GNP (1949: $258.3 billion) to Chinese GNP (1949: $19.7 billion)	13

ASSESSMENT

John R. Garson in 1970
"In 1967, the non-Communist world exported $1.5 billion worth of goods to China, and it is unlikely that the embargo has any significant impact on the volume of China's imports or its choice of goods. . . . The embargo has a very limited effect on the Chinese economy and on China's war-making potential." (Garson 69, 71)

Robert F. Dernberger in 1971
"[L]iberalization of trade with China is unlikely to cause a significant reorientation of either country's foreign trade or a significant flow of short-term capital in either direction. . . . There are, of course, advocates . . . who believe that, by offering the Chinese massive economic aid, we could 'buy' their friendship and cooperation. It is highly unlikely, however, that this policy would succeed for the 'capitalistic' and 'imperialistic' United States, after it had failed for the 'socialistic' and 'friendly' Soviet Union." (Dernberger 270, 273)

Gunnar Adler-Karlsson on role of CHINCOM in US domestic politics
COCOM-CHINCOM gave executive branch tool with which "to blur the picture for interested right-wing congressmen, and may also have diffused the responsibility for actual decisions taken, so as to provide the President with an excuse for not going as far as Congress wanted." (Adler-Karlsson 37)

Alexander Eckstein in 1966
"The practical consequences of the U.S. embargo and allied trade controls were negligible."
However, Western strategic embargo, coupled with Soviet sanctions in 1960, caused "a
marked deterioration in the equipment of the Chinese Communist armed forces" and
"postponed the acquisition of a nuclear capability by at least two years." (Eckstein 247,
265)

AUTHORS' SUMMARY

Overall assessment	Assigned scores
□ Policy result, scaled from 1 (failed) to 4 (success)	1
□ Sanctions contribution, scaled from 1 (none) to 4 (significant)	1
□ Success score (policy result *times* sanctions contribution), scaled from 1 (outright failure) to 16 (significant success)	1

Political and economic variables

□ Companion policies: J (covert), Q (quasi-military), or R (regular military)	R, Q
□ International cooperation with sender, scaled from 1 (none) to 4 (significant)	3
□ International assistance to target: A (if present)	A
□ Sanctions period (years)	21
□ Economic health and political stability of target, scaled from 1 (distressed) to 3 (strong)	3
□ Presanction relations between sender and target, scaled from 1 (antagonistic) to 3 (cordial)	1
□ Type of sanction: X (export), M (import), F (financial)	F, X, M
□ Cost to sender, scaled from 1 (net gain) to 4 (major loss)	3

BIBLIOGRAPHY

Adler-Karlsson, Gunnar. 1968. *Western Economic Warfare, 1947–1967*. Stockholm: Almqvist and Wiksell.
Barnett, A. Doak. 1981. *China's Economy in a Global Perspective*. Washington: Brookings Institution.
Cohen, Jerome Alan, Robert F. Dernberger, and John R. Garson. 1971. "Chinese Law and Sino-American Trade." In *China Trade Prospects and US Policy*, ed. Alexander Eckstein. New York: Praeger.
Dernberger, Robert F. 1971. "Prospects for Trade between China and the United States." In *China's Trade Prospects and US Policy*, ed. Alexander Eckstein. New York: Praeger.
Eckstein, Alexander. 1966. *Communist China's Economic Growth and Foreign Trade*. New York: McGraw-Hill.
Evans, Paul. 1985. "Sanctions Against the People's Republic of China." In *The Utility of Economic Sanctions*, ed. David Leyton-Brown. London: Croom Helm. Forthcoming.

Garson, John R. 1971. "The American Trade Embargo Against China." In *China Trade Prospects and US Policy,* ed. Alexander Eckstein. New York: Praeger.

Gittings, John, ed. 1964. *The Sino-Soviet Dispute 1956–1963: Extracts from Recent Documents.* Chatham House Memorandum. London: Royal Institute of International Affairs.

Haight, James T. 1965. "United States Controls over Strategic Transactions." *University of Illinois Law Forum.* Special vol. 337.

Hermann, A. H. 1982. *Conflicts of National Laws with International Business Activity: Issues of Extraterritoriality.* London: British North American Committee. August.

Meese, Sally A. 1981–82. "Export Controls to China: An Emerging Trend for Dual-Use Exports." 7 *The International Trade Law Journal* (Fall–Winter): 20–37.

US Congress. House Committee on Foreign Affairs. 1963. *Expropriation of American-Owned Property by Foreign Governments in the Twentieth Century.* 88 Cong., 1 sess.

US Mutual Defense Assistance Control Act Administrator. 1957. *The Strategic Trade Control System, 1948–1956,* 9th Report to Congress. Washington.

Young, Kenneth T. 1968. *Negotiating with the Chinese Communists: The United States Experience, 1953–67.* New York: McGraw-Hill.

Case 50–1   US and UN v. North Korea

(1950–   : Korean War)

CHRONOLOGY OF KEY EVENTS

Also see Case 49–1 US and CHINCOM v. China (1949–70: Communist Control of China and Korean War)

25 June 1950	North Korean forces cross demilitarized zone, invade South Korea. (Evans 4)
30 June 1950	President Harry S Truman orders naval blockade of Korean coast, imposes total trade embargo against North Korea. (*World Today* 330; Evans 4)
Fall–Winter 1950	Chinese forces sporadically appear in Korea before intervening massively in late November to turn back General Douglas MacArthur's "final offensive." (Dulles 99)
16 December 1950	Truman declares national emergency in connection with Korean War, invokes Trading with the Enemy Act to terminate all US economic contacts with North Korea. Truman also imposes embargo against China, freezes Chinese assets in US. Freeze also affects North Korean assets but these are thought to be negligible. (Garson 16–18, 25–27; *New York Times*, 17 December 1950, A1)
February 1951	UN resolution labels North Korea, China as aggressors in Korea. (Evans 5)
18 May 1951	UN General Assembly adopts resolution 47 to 0, with eight abstentions (Afghanistan, Egypt, Burma, India, Indonesia, Pakistan, Sweden, Syria, with Soviet bloc countries not participating) recommending that member countries impose arms embargo against North Korea, China. Items covered are: arms, ammunition, implements of war, and items useful in their production; atomic energy materials; petroleum; transportation materials of strategic value. (*New York Times*, 19 May 1951, A3)
15 July 1951	Of 55 replies to UN concerning implementation of May resolution, 35 nations, including five nonmembers (West Germany, Italy, Spain,

15 July 1951
(continued) Vietnam, Laos), pledge complete support; eight Soviet bloc representatives (from the three Soviet republics plus Czechoslovakia,
Poland, Romania, Albania, Hungary) reject resolution as illegal. (*New
York Times*, 17 July 1951, A4)

September 1952 NATO (less Iceland but plus Japan) establishes CHINCOM (parallel
organization to COCOM); embargo is imposed on all exports of
industrial equipment, raw materials; additional restrictions apply to
shipping, bunkering. (Doxey 17)

27 July 1953 Korean armistice is reached. US continues to prohibit all US economic
contacts with North Korea in line with general strategic controls
against China, Soviet bloc. (Dulles 137)

GOALS OF SENDER COUNTRIES

25 June 1950, excerpts from UN resolution
The Security Council, "Noting with grave concern the armed attack upon the Republic
of Korea by forces from North Korea,

"Determines that this action constitutes a breach of the peace,

"1. Calls for the immediate cessation of hostilities; and calls upon the authorities of
North Korea to withdraw forthwith their armed forces to the thirty-eighth parallel.
"2. Requests the United Nations Commission on Korea (a) to communicate its fully
considered recommendations on the situation with the least possible delay; (b) to
observe the withdrawal of the North Korean forces to the thirty-eighth parallel; (c)
to keep the Security Council informed on the execution of the resolution.
"3. Calls upon all members to render every assistance to the United Nations in the
execution of this resolution and to refrain from giving assistance to the North Korean
authorities." (*New York Times*, 26 July 1950, A4)

30 June 1950
White House "stated that 'in keeping with the Security Council's request for support to
the Republic of Korea in repelling the North Korean invaders President Truman had (1)
authorized the U.S. Air Force to 'conduct missions on specific targets in Northern Korea
. . . wherever militarily necessary'; (2) ordered a naval blockade of the entire Korean
coast; and (3) authorized General MacArthur to use certain supporting ground units in
Korea. . . . The President . . . had emphasized that the U.S.A. was 'not at war' but was
engaged in 'police action against a bunch of bandits.'" (*Keesing's* 10807)

1953
"With the Korean cease-fire the justification for a large-scale embargo became less
compelling in the eyes of most but not all of the participants. American officials, for
example, claimed that the cessation of hostilities did not mean the war was at an end or
the need for vigilance less precipitous." (Evans 9)

Authors' note
Complete US embargo on trade with North Korea has continued to the present, unaffected
even by loosening of controls on trade with China in past decade.

RESPONSE OF TARGET COUNTRY

3 July 1950
North Korean foreign minister sends note to UN accusing US government of "barefaced aggression" aimed at "imperialist domination" in Far East. Note reiterates North Korean contention that forces of South Korean President Syngman Rhee had been first to violate 38th parallel and that North Korean forces had crossed it only in "throw[ing] back the enemy." (*Keesing's* 10810)

ATTITUDE OF OTHER COUNTRIES

Soviet bloc nations
These countries deny validity of UN General Assembly arms embargo resolution, claiming motions of that sort can originate only in Security Council. (*New York Times*, 19 May 1951, A3)

ECONOMIC IMPACT

Observed Economic Statistics

North Korean trade and national income (million dollars)

	Exports	Imports	National income (index)
1946	n.a.	n.a.	100
1949	76.3	106.0	209
1953	31.0	42.0	145
1954	29.0	39.3	n.a.
1955	45.0	60.3	n.a.
1956	65.8	74.5	319
1957	100.0	114.8	n.a.

n.a. Not available.
Source: Chung 105, 146–47.

". . . during the Korean War . . . normal foreign trade activities either nearly ceased or slowed down considerably. . . ." (Chung 104)

Impact of war on North Korean economy is illustrated by fact that by end of conflict "the output of steel and rolled steel was only 2.5 and 3.0 percent, respectively, that of 1949." (Chung 106)

Until mid-1960s, USSR and China were North Korea's principal trading partners, accounting for about 90 percent of total trade. "Since the mid-1960s the proportion has been gradually declining owing to expanding North Korean trade with the non-Communist world, especially with Japan and Western Europe." (Chung 108)

USSR extends credit of 212 million rubles (repayable at 2 percent interest starting in 1952) to North Korea to cover Soviet imports from 1949–52. (Chung 118)

"According to an agreement concluded in September 1953, North Korea received a grant totaling 1 billion rubles (U.S. $250 million) from the Soviet Union for the express purpose of aiding North Korea's efforts to reconstruct. . . . The full amount of the grant was to be received within a two-year period. . . ." (Chung 118)

North Korea, China sign treaty in 1953 in which Chinese write off North Korean war debts (about $114 million), agree to provide North Korea about $325 million in reconstruction aid, 1954–57. (Chung 122)

In 1949–62 North Korea receives total of $1.37 billion in grants and loans from USSR ($557 million), China ($517 million), other Communist countries ($296 million). (Chung 142)

Calculated Economic Impact

	Annual cost to target country
Decline in North Korean GNP; welfare loss estimated at 20 percent of drop in GNP, 1949–53.	$42 million
Offsets	
Forgiveness of North Korean war debts to China; welfare gain valued at 80 percent of total debts written off.	($30 million)
Soviet trade credits to North Korea, 1949–52; welfare gain estimated at 20 percent of face value of credits.	(4 million)
Total	$8 million

Relative Magnitudes

Gross indicators of North Korean economy	
North Korean GNP (1949 est.)	$684 million
North Korean population (1949)	9.6 million
Annual effect of sanctions related to gross indicators	
Percentage of GNP	1.2
Per capita	$0.83
North Korean trade with US as percentage of total trade	
Exports (1949) (authors' estimate)	20
Imports (1949) (authors' estimate)	20
Ratio of US GNP (1949: $258.3 billion) to North Korean GNP (1949: $684 million)	378

ASSESSMENT

Joseph Sang-hoon Chung
" . . . the trade embargo imposed by the United States and other Western nations which went into effect during the Korean War had severely curtailed North Korean trade with some of the important potential trade nations of the non-Communist world including Japan." (Chung 109)

AUTHORS' SUMMARY

Overall assessment	Assigned scores
☐ Policy result, scaled from 1 (failed) to 4 (success)	2
☐ Sanctions contribution, scaled from 1 (none) to 4 (significant)	1
☐ Success score (policy result *times* sanctions contribution), scaled from 1 (outright failure) to 16 (significant success)	2

Political and economic variables

☐ Companion policies: J (covert), Q (quasi-military), or R (regular military)	R
☐ International cooperation with sender, scaled from 1 (none) to 4 (significant)	4
☐ International assistance to target: A (if present)	A
☐ Sanctions period (years)	34+
☐ Economic health and political stability of target, scaled from 1 (distressed) to 3 (strong)	2
☐ Presanction relations between sender and target, scaled from 1 (antagonistic) to 3 (cordial)	1
☐ Type of sanction: X (export), M (import), F (financial)	F, X, M
☐ Cost to sender, scaled from 1 (net gain) to 4 (major loss)	2

BIBLIOGRAPHY

Chung, Joseph Sang-hoon. 1974. *The North Korean Economy: Structure and Development.* Stanford, Calif.: Hoover Institution Press.
Doxey, Margaret P. 1980. *Economic Sanctions and International Enforcement.* 2d ed. New York: Oxford University Press for Royal Institute of International Affairs.
Dulles, Foster Rhea. 1972. *American Policy Toward Communist China.* New York: Thomas Y. Crowell Company.
Evans, Paul M. 1985. "Sanctions Against the People's Republic of China." In *The Utility of Economic Sanctions*, ed. David Leyton-Brown. London: Croom Helm. Forthcoming.
Garson, John R. 1971. "The American Trade Embargo Against China." In *China Trade Prospects and US Policy*, ed. Alexander Eckstein. New York: Praeger.
Keesing's Contemporary Archives. 1950–52.
"Korea: A Chronology of Principal Events, 1945–50." 6 *World Today* (August 1950): 319–30.

Case 51–1   UK and US v. Iran

(1951–53: Expropriation)

CHRONOLOGY OF KEY EVENTS

1949–50 Shah Mohammad Reza Pahlavi travels to US seeking economic aid but returns to Iran "empty handed." "When the United States finally extended economic aid to Iran, it was only a $25 million credit from the Export–Import Bank; the shah had hoped for at least six times that amount. The U.S. ambassador, Henry F. Grady, believed that had the United States 'come in quickly and with adequate amounts,' the oil nationalization crusade which was already under way by 1951 would have been averted." (Ramazani 13)

1951 Iranian Prime Minister Mohammad Mussadiq nationalizes Anglo-Iranian Oil Co. (*New York Times*, 16 March 1951, A18; Engler 202)

1951–53 Anglo-Iranian Oil mounts legal campaign to prevent third-country purchases of oil from its erstwhile properties; little or no oil is exported for three years. (Engler 202–3)

17–23 October 1952 UK, Iran break diplomatic relations; Anglo-Iranian employees are evacuated from Abadan. (*New York Times*, 17 October 1952, A1; 23 October, A4)

July 1953 US withholds aid to Iran. (*New York Times*, 10 July 1953, A4; Engler 205)

August 1953 Mussadiq is overthrown; shah is restored to power; CIA plays key role. (Engler 205)

1954 New company formed to exploit Iranian fields; Anglo-Iranian (later British Petroleum) owns 40 percent, five US giants 40 percent, Shell 14 percent, Compagnie Française des Pétroles 6 percent. Profits are split 50–50 between oil companies and Iran. (Engler 69, 207)

1955 Iran joins Baghdad Pact. (*New York Times*, 13 October 1955, A1)

GOALS OF SENDER COUNTRIES

R. K. Ramazani
"Washington perceived the situation increasingly from the perspective of the Cold War. During the early phase of the oil nationalization dispute, the US and British positions had been dissimilar. Washington pursued the path of mediation and negotiation, advised against the show of force by Britain, insisted on the AIOC's [Anglo-Iranian Oil Company] acceptance of the principle of a 50–50 profit-sharing, and invited Mussadiq to the White House for discussions. London opposed the takeover of the oil industry, sued the purchasers of Iranian oil, and imposed an 'economic blockade' on Iran. But as the Iranian internal economic situation deteriorated, as the Tudeh party gained strength, and as Mussadiq insisted on a 100 percent implementation of the acts of nationalization, the US concern with Iranian domestic politics grew." (Ramazani 16)

President Dwight D. Eisenhower
Commenting on 10 July 1953: "It would not be fair to the American taxpayers for the United States Government to extend any considerable amount of economic aid to Iran so long as Iran could have access to funds derived from the sale of its oil and oil products if a reasonable agreement were reached with regard to compensation. . . ." (Engler 205)

RESPONSE OF TARGET COUNTRY

1953
"[Mussadiq] was unable to compromise. To him and his supporters, the absolute control of the oil industry was a moral duty. They struggled, in effect, for Iranian 'self-determination' as they saw the dispute with Britain." (Ramazani 16)

ECONOMIC IMPACT

Observed Economic Statistics
US aid to Iran: 1946–48—$25.8 million (economic); 1949–52—$16.5 million (economic) and $17.2 million (military).

Iranian trade with UK (million dollars)

	Exports	*Imports*
1948	233.9	35.8
1949	128.0	114.6
1950	133.5	54.4
1951	92.4	49.1
1952	8.9	19.4
1953	7.2	13.0
1954	7.0	19.9

Source: IMF.

Calculated Economic Impact

	Annual cost to target country
Loss of oil export income, 1951–53, from reduced shipments of about 30 million tons per year valued at $13.60/ton; Iranian loss estimated at 50 percent of reduced export earnings.	$136 million
Reduction in US aid (per Engler); welfare loss estimated at 100 percent of value of reduced transfers.	50 million
Total	$186 million

Relative Magnitudes

Gross indicators of Iranian economy	
Iranian GNP (1947)	$1.3 billion
Iranian population (1951)	16.7 million
Annual effect of sanctions related to gross indicators	
Percentage of GNP	14.3
Per capita	$11.14
Iranian trade with UK, US as percentage of total trade	
Exports (1950)	28
Imports (1950)	55
Ratio of combined UK, US GNP (1949: $305 billion) to Iranian GNP (1947: $1.3 billion)	235

ASSESSMENT

Robert Engler
"The [US oil] industry received full backing in its economic blockade of Iran throughout the struggle. This meant government sanction for the private pricing and marketing controls governing the world supply. Oilmen had an assurance of immunity from antitrust action. . . ." (Engler 204)

R. K. Ramazani
"The overthrow of the Mussadiq government was followed immediately by the move to settle the oil nationalization dispute between Iran and Britain. The Shah's government was relatively powerless. Economically, the country was nearly bankrupt. The virtual closing down of the Iranian oil industry during the nationalization dispute, the inability of the Mussadiq government to sell Iranian oil in the cartel-controlled world markets, the refusal of the Eisenhower Administration to give the Mussadiq government any financial aid, and the British economic boycott against Iran meant that the Shah's

government was in no real position to bargain effectively with the Western governments and their oil companies on an equal footing. . . . The [new] consortium in effect controlled oil production and prices as had the Anglo-Iranian Oil Company during the previous decades." (Ramazani 21–23)

AUTHORS' SUMMARY

Overall assessment	Assigned scores
□ Policy result, scaled from 1 (failed) to 4 (success)	4
□ Sanctions contribution, scaled from 1 (none) to 4 (significant)	3
□ Success score (policy result *times* sanctions contribution), scaled from 1 (outright failure) to 16 (significant success)	12

Political and economic variables

□ Companion policies: J (covert), Q (quasi-military), or R (regular military)	J
□ International cooperation with sender, scaled from 1 (none) to 4 (significant)	2
□ International assistance to target: A (if present)	—
□ Sanctions period (years)	2
□ Economic health and political stability of target, scaled from 1 (distressed) to 3 (strong)	2
□ Presanction relations between sender and target, scaled from 1 (antagonistic) to 3 (cordial)	3
□ Type of sanction: X (export), M (import), F (financial)	F, X, M
□ Cost to sender, scaled from 1 (net gain) to 4 (major loss)	1

BIBLIOGRAPHY

Engler, Robert. 1961. *Politics of Oil*. Chicago: University of Chicago Press.
International Monetary Fund. *Direction of Trade Statistics*. Various issues.
Ramazani, R. K. 1982. *The United States and Iran: The Patterns of Influence*. New York: Praeger.

Case 54–1   USSR v. Australia

(1954: Petrov Defection)

CHRONOLOGY OF KEY EVENTS

13 April 1954 Australian Prime Minister Robert G. Menzies reports defection by Vladimir Petrov, third secretary and consul at the USSR Embassy, reveals information about Soviet spy ring, appoints Royal Commission to probe espionage charges that implicate Australian officials. (*New York Times*, 14 April 1954, A1)

14 April 1954 Petrov's wife charges he was kidnapped, allegation backed by USSR officials. (*New York Times*, 15 April 1954, A1)

19 April 1954 Petrov's wife asks for asylum after discovering her husband is not dead; subsequently, USSR aide is charged with kidnapping her. (*New York Times*, 20 April 1954, A1)

21–22 April 1954 USSR demands Petrov's return, saying he is thief and forger; Australia rejects demand. (*New York Times*, 22 April 1954, A2; 23 April 1954, A5)

23 April 1954 USSR breaks diplomatic relations with Australia. (*New York Times*, 24 April 1954, A1)

24 April 1954 USSR prevents departure of Australian staff from Moscow, embargoes Australian wool imports. (*New York Times*, 25 April 1954, A1)

19 October 1955 Australian opposition leader, Dr. Herbert V. Evatt, charges so-called "espionage" papers were fake and "the nation suffered heavy loss in trade and rupture of diplomatic relations with a great power." He accuses Menzies of manipulating Petrov affair for election purposes. Menzies denies charge in parliamentary debate, defends importance of Petrov's contribution. Menzies claims "Petrov had supplied more information than any previous single defector about the espionage activities at the M. V. D., and much of it had been confirmed by information held abroad." (*New York Times*, 20 October 1955, A26; *Keesing's* 14524)

Summer 1959 Australia, USSR reestablish diplomatic relations. (*New York Times*, 29 May 1959, A3)

GOALS OF SENDER COUNTRY

23 April 1954
Note from Soviet government to Australian chargé d' affaires in Moscow announcing that Soviet ambassador in Canberra and staff would be withdrawn: "The provocatory hullabaloo created by the Australian Government around the person of the criminal Petrov, the kidnapping of Mrs. Petrov, the assault of Soviet diplomatists and diplomatic couriers, and the search of diplomatic couriers by Australian police, carried out with bodily force, form the most brutal violations of generally accepted norms of international law, and are inadmissable under normal diplomatic relations between states. The Soviet government lodges a determined protest against this lawlessness, for which the entire responsibility rests with the Australian Government. It insists that the Australian Government hand over directly to the Soviet Union the criminal Petrov, return the kidnapped member of the Soviet Embassy in Canberra, Mrs. Petrov, and severely punish all those responsible for the above-mentioned acts of violence." (*Keesing's* 13541)

RESPONSE OF TARGET COUNTRY

23 April 1954
"The Australian Acting Minister of External Affairs [Sir Philip McBride] presented a note to the Soviet Embassy on the same day [April 23] repudiating the Soviet Government's note as a falsification of the facts, 'stating that facilities would be given for the departure of M. Generalov and his staff from Canberra, and asking for similar facilities to enable Australian diplomats to leave Soviet territory.'" (*Keesing's* 13541)

ECONOMIC IMPACT

Observed Economic Statistics

Australian wool exports (million Australian dollars)†

	Value	Price index††	Volume index††
1952	733	103	91
1953	869	120	93
1954	712	109	84
1955	709	92	97
1956	754	96	100

† A$1 = US $1.12.
†† 1975 = 100.
Source: IMF.

"The break with the Soviet Union could have economic consequences of some significance. The Soviet Union has been an important customer for Australian wool this season. Its purchases this year of Australian commodities, of which wool is the most important, are at the rate of about £30 million in Australian currency ($67.5 million) for the year. . . .

"The effects upon industry of the Soviet withdrawal may go much further than the mere loss of a market for wool. Soviet competition at wool auctions has had a steadying effect on prices. The fall of about 15 percent in the level of the market several months ago resulted almost entirely from a sudden Soviet withdrawal, ordered from Moscow when a Tass agency message from Australia reported that Russian buyers were bidding recklessly." (*New York Times*, 25 April 1954, A1)

Calculated Economic Impact

	Annual cost to target country
Decline in Australian wool export earnings; USSR embargo estimated to account for 50 percent of drop in total value of wool exports, from 1952–53 average (A$801 million) to 1954 level (A$712 million).	$50 million

Relative Magnitudes

Gross indicators of Australian economy	
Australian GNP (1954)	$10 billion
Australian population (1954)	9.0 million
Annual effect of sanctions related to gross indicators	
Percentage of GNP	0.5
Per capita	$5.56
Australian trade with USSR as percentage of total trade	
Exports (1954)	4.5
Imports (1954)	0.8
Ratio of USSR GNP (1954: $178 billion) to Australian GNP (1954: $10 billion)	18

AUTHORS' SUMMARY

Overall assessment	Assigned scores
☐ Policy result, scaled from 1 (failed) to 4 (success)	1
☐ Sanctions contribution, scaled from 1 (none) to 4 (significant)	1
☐ Success score (policy result *times* sanctions contribution), scaled from 1 (outright failure) to 16 (significant success)	1

Political and economic variables

☐ Companion policies: J (covert), Q (quasi-military), or R (regular military)	—
☐ International cooperation with sender, scaled from 1 (none) to 4 (significant)	1

	Assigned
Political and economic variables (continued)	*scores*
□ International assistance to target: A (if present)	—
□ Sanctions period (years)	1
□ Economic health and political stability of target, scaled from 1	3
(distressed) to 3 (strong)	
□ Presanction relations between sender and target, scaled from 1	1
(antagonistic) to 3 (cordial)	
□ Type of sanction: X (export), M (import), F (financial)	M
□ Cost to sender, scaled from 1 (net gain) to 4 (major loss)	2

Comments

Soviet ban on wool imports had no discernible effect on Australian policy. Petrov and his wife remained in Australia, and supplied valuable information against Soviet intelligence activities in West.

BIBLIOGRAPHY

International Monetary Fund. 1981. *International Financial Statistics Yearbook.*
Keesing's Contemporary Archives. 1952–54, 1955–56.

Case 54–2   India v. Portugal

(1954–61: Surrender Goa)

CHRONOLOGY OF KEY EVENTS

1947 UK grants India independence but French and Portuguese enclaves remain on subcontinent. (Rubinoff 48)

1949 India establishes legation in Portugal in attempt to negotiate status of Goa, Portuguese colony in subcontinent. (Rubinoff 48)

27 February 1950 India proposes initiation of talks on Goa with Portugal but is rebuffed. (Rubinoff 49)

Early 1953 India closes Portuguese bank in Bombay, claiming discriminatory treatment against Indian banks in Goa. (Rubinoff 49)

11 June 1953 India closes legation in Lisbon following Portuguese refusal to discuss Goa. Portugal retains legation in New Delhi "on the grounds of promoting good relations. . . ." (Rubinoff 49)

March 1954 Following further deterioration in relations, India restricts movement of Goan officials in India in retaliation for alleged similar restrictions in Goa. (Rubinoff 49)

Summer 1954 Consular relations between India and Portugal are broken, not reestablished until January 1955. (Rubinoff 51)

August 1954 In response to increased tensions, India prohibits transfer of Indian currency through mail to Goa. Action is serious because Goa is highly dependent on remittances from Goan workers in India. India also restricts sums of cash allowed for visitors from Goa. Sanctions are lifted in few days "because of resentment by hard-pressed Goans. . . ." (Rubinoff 51–52)

August 1955 Following suspension of rail traffic earlier in summer, dockworkers in Bombay, Calcutta, Madras refuse to handle ships headed to or from Goa. At this point, there is essentially no sea, air, or land traffic to Goa, one of "least accessible places in Asia." Deaths of some 20 Indian protesters on Goan border spur India to break all diplomatic ties with Portugal. (Rubinoff 55–60)

Fall 1955	Travel restrictions are lifted and telegraph service (cut in September) is restored to appease Goan people. Indian officials hope that "with the relaxation of domestic pressure the Indian government could feign a campaign to win the support of the Goan people." (Rubinoff 61)
28 February 1961	Indian government announces limited trade with Goa will be allowed as of April 1. (Rubinoff 61)
15 October 1961	"Money order remittances" from India to Goa are allowed to resume. (Rubinoff 61)
November 1961	Tensions heighten when two Indian sailors are shot, allegedly by Portuguese soldiers. (Rubinoff 85)
18 December 1961	Indian military forces invade Goa. They face little resistance from Portuguese contingent depleted by unrest in Portugal's African colonies. (Rubinoff 92–93)
14 March 1962	Goa is incorporated into Indian Union. (*Keesing's* 18856)

GOALS OF SENDER COUNTRY

Arthur Rubinoff
"For the Indians, foreign possession of Goa was not only an attack upon their honor but also a reminder of an unhappy colonial past not completely ended." (Rubinoff 30)

Prime Minister Jawaharlal Nehru
"[He] pursued peaceful methods for fourteen years because he believed that the restraint he showed over Goa would not alienate Portugal's NATO allies. He deemed this course to be more important than the approval a display of force would bring from the Communist and neutral nations. Thus he believed he was helping to mitigate tensions in the cold war." (Rubinoff 45)

RESPONSE OF TARGET COUNTRY

Arthur Rubinoff
"It was obvious the Portuguese knew they could not remain indefinitely. It appears they were determined to embarrass the Indian Government by forcing Prime Minister Nehru to abandon his adherence to nonviolent methods." (Rubinoff 110)

ATTITUDE OF OTHER COUNTRIES

United Kingdom
"The British were caught between supporting a former colony and Commonwealth partner, India, and an ally of such long standing as Portugal." (Rubinoff 62)

United States
Secretary of State John Foster Dulles referring to Goa in December 1955: "As far as I

know all the world regards it as a Portuguese province." He added, however, that the US government "took no position on the merits of the issue." (Rubinoff 68)

Portugal's African colonies
"They maintained the occupation of Goa by Indian forces would not be a small step in aiding their revolution. Rather they regarded such an event as a key, for it was alleged that the Portuguese empire in Africa would collapse once Goa fell." (Rubinoff 82)

ECONOMIC IMPACT

Observed Economic Statistics

By late 1955 when India lifted travel restrictions against Goa it had become "clear that Goa's changing economy made the Portuguese less dependent on India and that country's transportation facilities. In addition, India's economic sanctions were beginning to alienate the lower class Goans. . . ." (Rubinoff 61)

Indian trade with Portugal averaged $1.5 million per year over period 1952–63. (IMF)

Calculated Economic Impact

Negligible, since isolation of Goa did not result in significant increases in aid from Portugal.

Relative Magnitudes

Gross indicators of Portuguese economy	
Portuguese GNP (1953)	$1.7 billion
Portuguese population (1953)	8.5 million
Annual effect of sanctions related to gross indicators	
Percentage of GNP	negl.
Per capita	negl.
Portuguese trade with India as percentage of total trade	
Exports (1953)	negl.
Imports (1953)	negl.
Ratio of Indian GNP (1960: $31.8 billion) to Portuguese GNP (1960: $2.5 billion)	13

ASSESSMENT

Arthur Rubinoff
"[Nehru in October 1961] frankly admitted that the policy pursued by the Government of India toward Portugal had been a failure. . . . 'We have been forced into thinking afresh by the Portuguese to adopt other methods to solve the problem.'" (Rubinoff 83)

AUTHORS' SUMMARY

Overall assessment	Assigned scores
☐ Policy result, scaled from 1 (failed) to 4 (success)	4
☐ Sanctions contribution, scaled from 1 (none) to 4 (significant)	2
☐ Success score (policy result *times* sanctions contribution), scaled from 1 (outright failure) to 16 (significant success)	8

Political and economic variables

☐ Companion policies: J (covert), Q (quasi-military), or R (regular military)	R
☐ International cooperation with sender, scaled from 1 (none) to 4 (significant)	1
☐ International assistance to target: A (if present)	—
☐ Sanctions period (years)	7
☐ Economic health and political stability of target, scaled from 1 (distressed) to 3 (strong)	3
☐ Presanction relations between sender and target, scaled from 1 (antagonistic) to 3 (cordial)	2
☐ Type of sanction: X (export), M (import), F (financial)	F, X, M
☐ Cost to sender, scaled from 1 (net gain) to 4 (major loss)	2

BIBLIOGRAPHY

International Monetary Fund. *Direction of Trade Statistics.* Various issues.
Keesing's Contemporary Archives. 1961–62.
Rubinoff, Arthur. 1971. *India's Use of Force in Goa.* Bombay: Popular Prakashan.

Case 54–3   Spain v. UK

(1954–84: Gibraltar)

CHRONOLOGY OF KEY EVENTS

13 July 1713   Spain yields Gibraltar to Britain by Article X of Treaty of Utrecht. Dispute begins within few years concerning extent of British sovereignty over Gibraltar. (Hills 222)

19 January 1954   Spain delivers diplomatic protest against visit by Queen Elizabeth II of England to Gibraltar. (Hills 443)

19 April 1954   Spain prohibits Spaniards, other than those with work permits, from visiting Gibraltar; stops issuing new permits; limits holders of British passports to one-day trip through La Línea; forbids tourists of other nationalities from passing through La Línea. Spanish visitors to Gibraltar, 144,000 in 1953 (largely for purchase of duty-free goods), dwindle to zero. (Hills 443, 447)

31 July 1963   UK offers Spain "package deal": cooperation in preventing contraband traffic in exchange for relaxation of border restrictions. Spain refuses. (Hills 448)

11 September 1963   UN Committee of Twenty-four begins consideration of British, Spanish claims to Gibraltar. (Hills 449)

March 1964   UK proposes reorganization of governance of Gibraltar; Spain protests that reorganization bears parallel to progress of Britain's former colonies toward independence. (Hills 451)

16 October 1964   UN Committee of Twenty-four, in terms favorable to Spain, recommends that UK, Spain reach "negotiated solution." Spain welcomes report, Britain rebuffs it. (Hills 452)

Late October 1964   Spanish authorities impose strict, time-consuming customs checks at La Línea; all applications to export fresh food, building materials, etc., from Spain to Gibraltar are referred to Madrid. (Hills 453)

March 1965   Spain refuses to recognize passports issued "on behalf of the Government of Gibraltar"; accordingly, 600 to 1,000 non-Spanish residents of the Campo (area of Spain adjacent to Gibraltar) who work in Gibraltar must change their place of residence or work. Spain suspends the export of building materials to Gibraltar. (Hills 453–59)

18 May 1966   Spanish Foreign Minister Fernando Maria Castiella offers three proposals: cancel Article X of Utrecht, return Gibraltar to Spain; draft new Anglo-Spanish agreement on use of Gibraltar as British military base; provide international guarantees of Gibraltarian "personal status." UK responds with proposals for relaxation of border traffic controls, Spanish recognition of British sovereignty over entire area of Gibraltar. (Hills 456)

20 July 1966   Spain bans British overflights. (Hills 461)

August–October 1966   Spain prohibits female workers from exiting at La Línea, bars vehicular traffic to and from Gibraltar. (Hills 461)

October 1966   UK proposes that legal issues on Gibraltar status be decided by International Court of Justice. Spain rejects proposal on ground that UN resolutions obligate Britain to decolonize Gibraltar. (Hills 461–62)

17 November 1966   UN Committee of Twenty-four states that termination of colonial status should not be delayed. (Hills 461)

11 April 1967   Spain prohibits all aircraft in area around Algeciras, severely limiting use of Gibraltar airfield. (Hills 463)

14 June 1967   UK announces referendum to be held in Gibraltar as to whether it should pass under Spanish sovereignty or retain its link with Britain. (Hills 463–64)

1 September 1967   UN Committee of Twenty-four condemns referendum, calls upon UK to decolonize Gibraltar in accordance with UN Resolution 1514 (XV) para. 6—i.e., by returning Gibraltar to Spain. (Hills 465)

10 September 1967   Referendum held: out of 12,762 qualified electors, 12,182 vote—12,138 of them for continued association with Britain, 44 for association with Spain. (Hills 465)

19 December 1967   UN General Assembly declares referendum violates UN resolutions; endorses Committee of Twenty-four recommendation for decolonization. (Hills 466)

18 December 1968   UN General Assembly calls on UK "to terminate the colonial situation in Gibraltar no later than 1 October 1969." (Hills 466)

May 1969   UK abolishes term "colony" in reference to Gibraltar, uses "dominion." (Hills 466)

June 1969   Spain closes gate at La Línea, deprives Gibraltar of 4,778 Spanish workers; suspends Algeciras-Gibraltar ferry service. (Hills 466–67)

1980	Spain, UK agree to periodic meetings to discuss Gibraltar's future. (*New York Times*, 15 December 1982, A3)
9 December 1982	Spanish Foreign Minister Fernando Morán, British Foreign Secretary Francis Pym agree to renew talks in spring 1983. (*New York Times*, 15 December 1982, A3; *Washington Post*, 8 December 1982, A14)
15 December 1982	Spain opens gate at La Línea as "humanitarian gesture" to divided families; passage limited to Spanish and Gibraltarian pedestrians on once-daily basis. (*New York Times*, 15 December 1982, A3)
November 1984	Spain, UK agree to reopen border at Gibraltar "as a means of uniting families and reviving a ravaged economy. . . . The agreement . . . is designed to end 15 years of bristling Spanish-British relations and win Prime Minister Margaret Thatcher's approval of Spain's application to join the European Economic Community. For the first time Britain also agrees to begin talks over the sovereignty of Gibraltar. . . ." (*New York Times*, 30 November 1984, A2)
4 February 1985	Border blockade is completely lifted. Two countries also lift respective bans on ownership of property and businesses by Spaniards in Gibraltar and Gibraltarians in Spain. UK, although agreeing to discuss Spanish claim of sovereignty, reiterates determination to respect wishes of citizens of Gibraltar. "But many Gibraltar residents, mindful of the accommodation reached by Britain and China last year over the status of Hong Kong, fear what they think will be an eventual sellout by Britain." (*Washington Post*, 5 February 1985, A1)

GOALS OF SENDER COUNTRY

May 1966
Spanish proposals to UK for resolving Gibraltar issue:

"(1) The cancellation of Article X of Utrecht, that is the return of Gibraltar to Spain.
"(2) An Anglo-Spanish agreement on the use thereafter of Gibraltar as a British military base.
"(3) A 'personal status' for the Gibraltarian fully protecting, under international guarantee, all his rights and his particular cultural, social, and economic interests in Gibraltar or anywhere else in Spain." (Hills 456)

February 1985
Foreign Minister Morán states that "if Gibraltar were handed to him on a plate against the will of the Gibraltarians, 'I would not want it.'" However Morán also says that "there should be 'no misunderstanding' over Spain's long-term aim—the recovery of national sovereignty—but he said Spain had no intention of abolishing Gibraltar's institutions or forcing Spanish citizenship on Gibraltarians. 'There is room for a restoration of our territorial integrity, whenever that might be, and for the maintenance of Gibraltarian citizenship and a self-governing status for The Rock.'" (*Washington Post*, 5 February 1985, A1)

RESPONSE OF TARGET COUNTRY

April 1965
From conclusion of British White Paper on Gibraltar: "Great Britain has at no time renounced her title to Gibraltar or failed to defend her position there, and will not do so now. She has no desire to quarrel with Spain, but she will stand by the people of Gibraltar in their present difficulties and take whatever measures may be necessary to defend and sustain them. At the same time, and having regard to the consensus of the [UN] Committee of 24 and to their recent communications to the Spanish Government [recommending a negotiated settlement], H. M. Government will remain ready to entertain proposals by Spain for conversations, but cannot do so as long as an abnormal situation on the frontier continues." (*Keesing's* 20949)

February 1985
"Britain's assurances that it will uphold the wishes of the people of Gibraltar mean, in effect, that London has to maintain the costly, as well as politically embarrassing, colonial presence at a time when the strategic importance of Gibraltar has declined sharply. . . . In private, British officials concede that it would be preferable if the inhabitants of The Rock were to shift their affections toward Spain." (*Washington Post,* 5 February 1985, A1)

LEGAL NOTES

Excerpt from Article X, Treaty of Utrecht (1713)
"The Catholic King does hereby, for Himself, His heirs and successors, yield to the Crown of Great Britain the full and intire propriety of the Town and Castle of Gibraltar, together with the port, fortifications, and forts thereunto belonging. . . . But that abuses and frauds may be avoided by importing any kinds of goods, the Catholic King wills, and takes it to be understood, that the above named propriety be yielded to Great Britain without any territorial jurisdiction, and without any open communication by land with the country round about. . . ." (Hills 222)

ECONOMIC IMPACT

Observed Economic Statistics

With imposition of strict customs controls, Gibraltar reexports of manufactures, tobacco decline from £3.0 million in 1964 to £0.6 million in 1966. UK allocates £1 million in 1965 for housing for residents of Spain who can no longer commute to Gibraltar to work, provides £100,000 budget supplement for Gibraltar (population about 25,000). (Hills 453–55)

Britain provides development grant of £600,000 for period 1967–70, £4.1 million in aid in 1970–72, agrees in principle to £8 million in 1972–76. (*Keesing's* 21843; Hills 472)

Britain announces capital aid of £7.7 million for three-year development program beginning in 1974, allocates £14 million for development aid for April 1978–March 1981. (*Keesing's* 26890, 30296)

Calculated Economic Impact

	Annual cost to target country
UK subsidies to Gibraltar economy; welfare loss estimated at 100 percent of UK aid.	
1965–70	$ 1 million
1970–81	7 million
Annual average total 1965–81	$5 million

Relative Magnitudes

Gross indicators of UK economy	
UK GNP (1954)	$50.7 billion
UK population(1954)	51.1 million
Annual effect of sanctions related to gross indicators	
Percentage of GNP	negl.
Per capita	$0.10
UK trade with Spain as percentage of total UK trade	
Exports (1954)	1
Imports (1954)	1
Ratio of Spanish GNP (1954: $8.7 billion) to UK GNP (1954: $50.7 billion)	0.2

ASSESSMENT

New York Times
"Franco closed the border in 1969 in an attempt to starve the British off what is known to both sides as the Rock. . . . But it is this Spanish border town [La Línea] that appears to have suffered the most. . . . 'In the fight to vindicate the state, people were forgotten,' the town's Socialist Mayor, Antonio Díaz Lara, said. . . . 'We were abandoned, the only town in Spain to feel the consequences. If the border closing had been necessary, it would have been all right, but the agreement is proof that the closure did not accomplish anything.'" (*New York Times*, 30 November 1984, A2)

Spanish Prime Minister Felipe González, however, is claiming Britain's willingness to discuss Gibraltar's sovereignty "as a diplomatic victory of his own." (*New York Times*, 30 November 1984, A2)

Washington Post
"The Geneva negotiation process [on the status of Gibraltar] has been prompted by the need to solve the dispute and to normalize British-Spanish relations in view of Spain's

present membership in NATO and the Madrid government's planned accession to the European Community next year." (*Washington Post*, 5 February 1985, A1)

AUTHORS' SUMMARY

Overall assessment	Assigned scores
□ Policy result, scaled from 1 (failed) to 4 (success)	2
□ Sanctions contribution, scaled from 1 (none) to 4 (significant)	3
□ Success score (policy result *times* sanctions contribution), scaled from 1 (outright failure) to 16 (significant success)	6

Political and economic variables

□ Companion policies: J (covert), Q (quasi-military), or R (regular military)	—
□ International cooperation with sender, scaled from 1 (none) to 4 (significant)	1
□ International assistance to target: A (if present)	—
□ Sanctions period (years)	30
□ Economic health and political stability of target, scaled from 1 (distressed) to 3 (strong)	3
□ Presanction relations between sender and target, scaled from 1 (antagonistic) to 3 (cordial)	2
□ Type of sanction: X (export), M (import), F (financial)	X, M
□ Cost to sender, scaled from 1 (net gain) to 4 (major loss)	2

Comments
British willingness to discuss sovereignty following lifting of blockade represents uncertain but possibly positive outcome. High political and economic costs of sanctions seem to have played modest role in British decision to change position.

BIBLIOGRAPHY

Hills, George. 1974. *Rock of Contention: A History of Gibraltar.* London: Robert Hale.
Keesing's Contemporary Archives. 1965–66, 1967–68, 1980.

Case 54–4   US and South Vietnam
v. North Vietnam

(1954–   : Vietnam War and Its Aftermath)

CHRONOLOGY OF KEY EVENTS

Summer 1954   Representatives of US, UK, France, USSR, China, Vietminh, and Bao Dai regime (headquartered in Saigon) meet in Geneva to arrange political solution in Vietnam and withdrawal of French forces. Under agreement, 17th parallel becomes temporary demarcation line, with Vietminh forces withdrawn to North, French and South Vietnamese to South. Accord calls for free elections in two years. Agreement is left unsigned because of US opposition.

"[South Vietnamese Prime Minister Ngo Dinh] Diem at once abrogated the Geneva agreement's provision for free trade between the two zones, thus depriving the North of the South's rice surplus it had always depended on for sustenance, and ended the right of movement between the zones." Diem also cuts off all other relations with northern zone, including postal service. At same time, US suspends all export licenses for North. (Kendrick 88–93, 97)

12 April 1955   Postal agreement is signed by the two zones. (Fall 336)

July 1956   Deadline set in Geneva for plebiscite on reunification of Vietnam passes without action. Three months later South Vietnam promulgates its own republican constitution. (Fall 316)

1961–63   In late 1961 President John F. Kennedy sends White House advisers Walt W. Rostow and General Maxwell Taylor to South Vietnam on fact-finding mission. As result of their gloomy assessment, American military advisers are increased from 700 to 2,400 within few weeks. By Kennedy's death in November 1963, number has risen to more than 16,000. (Ball 365–69, 504)

5 May 1964   US classifies North Vietnam as "designated" country under section 5B of foreign assets control regulations. Effect of action is to prohibit Americans from conducting commercial and financial transactions with North Vietnam and to freeze "any assets which might be in the U.S." (*Keesing's* 20066)

Late 1964	President Lyndon B. Johnson sends "peace feelers" to Hanoi indicating that if it "abide[s] by the Geneva agreements, keeping its troops inside its borders and sending no military supplies south," US will supply economic aid to "both Vietnams" and "create a new TVA in the Mekong and Red River deltas." However, there is implied threat that "[i]f Hanoi did not stop the NLF [National Liberation Front], the United States would retaliate with the 'greatest devastation' against North Vietnam." (Kendrick 173)
February–March 1965	US initiates "Rolling Thunder" bombing campaign against North Vietnam; in early March, two battalions of Marines land at Danang. (*Pentagon Papers*, II, 295–96)
August 1965	In response to series of naval incidents off North Vietnamese coast in Tonkin Gulf, US Congress adopts resolution giving president "carte blanche" in Vietnam. (Kendrick 179)
23 January 1973	Peace agreement is initialed by Henry A. Kissinger, US national security adviser, and Le Duc Tho, North Vietnamese representative. It is signed 27 January by foreign ministers of US, North and South Vietnam, and South Vietnamese Provisional Revolutionary Government (PRG). Agreement provides for: cease-fire, effective 28 January; withdrawal of American forces; return of American prisoners of war (POWs); establishment of council to arrange for elections. At press conference 24 January, Kissinger indicates economic reconstruction of Indochina pledged in accords will be discussed after implementation of agreements is "well advanced." (*Keesing's* 25781, 25789)
27 March 1973	All US forces are withdrawn, most American POWs returned. US–North Vietnamese economic discussions begin with establishment of joint economic committee (JEC). (*Keesing's* 25885)
July 1973	JEC talks are suspended by US because of cease-fire violations and continuing war in Cambodia. Later that summer, reconstruction aid is tied to release of information on American servicemen missing in action (MIA). (Zasloff 11–12)
30 April 1975	Saigon falls to North Vietnamese forces. (*Washington Post*, 30 April 1975, A1)
16 May 1975	President Gerald R. Ford extends trade embargo applied against North Vietnam to South Vietnam as well. "Some $70–$75 million" in Vietnamese assets in US, "mostly official bank accounts," are frozen. (Zasloff 17)
March–November 1976	Under pressure from Montgomery Committee (select House Committee on Missing Persons in Southeast Asia) and congressional legislation to partially lift trade embargo against Vietnam "as an inducement to Hanoi," Ford administration indicates willingness to normalize relations with Hanoi regime if satisfaction is obtained on MIA issue. During 1976, however, Congress attaches amendment to

| March–November | Foreign Assistance Act prohibiting aid or "reparations" for Vietnam. |
| *1976 (continued)* | (Zasloff 12–13, 23) |

2 July 1976   Vietnam is reunified as Socialist Republic of Vietnam. (*Keesing's* 27917)

March–May 1977   In March, President Jimmy Carter states he would "respond well" to suggestion of US aid to Vietnam in context of normalization of relations. In May, talks resume on MIAs and normalization of relations. (Zasloff 19; *Keesing's* 28912)

Summer 1977   Congress forbids US economic aid to Vietnam, either direct or indirect. In October, House of Representatives revokes ban on indirect aid following Carter's issuance of instructions to US representatives at multilateral development banks to vote against loans to Vietnam. (*Keesing's* 28912)

January 1979   Vietnamese forces invade Kampuchea, assist in overthrowing Premier Pol Pot and establishing pro-Vietnamese government in Phnom Penh. EC countries and Japan cut off aid to Vietnam, US refuses to consider granting aid until Vietnamese forces are withdrawn from Kampuchea. Also see Case 78–7 China v. Vietnam (1978– : Regional Influence). (*Keesing's* 29614–16)

GOALS OF SENDER COUNTRIES

1957

In response to North Vietnamese proposal for negotiations on issues leading to reunification: "The South Vietnamese Government replied that it could 'examine no proposal of the Vietminh Communists without proof and guarantee that they place the supreme interests of the nation above the interests of Communist imperialism' and that the subjection of the North to the Communist system was a fundamental obstacle to reunification." (*Keesing's* 16276)

1964

Following US classification of North Vietnam as "designated country," which put it in same category with China, North Korea, and Cuba, "US officials explained that at one time the United States had sought to treat Vietnam differently from Communist China in the hope that the regime in Hanoi would maintain some degree of independence; now, however, it was believed that the Hanoi regime appears to be coming under the domination of Peking." (*Keesing's* 20066)

Authors' note

With the widening conflict, economic sanctions became adjunct to war itself. After fall of Saigon in 1975, economic sanctions were seen as punitive response to North Vietnamese military force. In 1977, economic sanctions were tied to satisfactory resolution of MIA question. And in 1979, economic sanctions were further justified by Vietnamese invasion of Kampuchea.

RESPONSE OF TARGET COUNTRY

1956–58

As regards overtures of Prime Minister Pham Van Dong of North Vietnam to Diem aimed at improving economic relations: "This was not simply a matter of basic goodness for the North Vietnamese; but more than ever before, they needed South Vietnamese rice and they hoped to sell such cash items as coal and cement." (Fall 336)

1977

Following Carter's expression of willingness to offer aid if relations are normalized, Pham Hien, Vietnamese deputy foreign minister, responds that "the US contribution to healing the wounds of war and to postwar reconstruction of Vietnam is an 'undeniable duty.'" (*Keesing's* 28912)

ATTITUDE OF OTHER COUNTRIES

France

French government faces "grave dilemma" in relations with Vietnam after division under Geneva accords: "Her vast economic and other interests in Vietnam north of the 17th parallel did not permit her to ignore the Hanoi regime; on the other hand, her remaining properties in the South and the presence of about 15,000 of her citizens there give the Saigon regime a near stranglehold over French relations with any part of Vietnam." (Fall 191)

French government maintains "commercial attaché" in Hanoi until 1966 when President Charles De Gaulle extends full recognition following Saigon's closing of French Embassy. (Kendrick 99)

ECONOMIC IMPACT

Observed Economic Statistics

North Vietnamese population, 1956: 15.0 million (Fall 336); 1960: 16.9 million (Fall 151).

"When the DRVN [Democratic Republic of Vietnam] assumed control of Vietnam north of the 17th parallel in 1954, it inherited an area that had been ravaged twice in less than a decade: its land plundered by the Japanese and Chinese and its communications bombed by the U.S. Air Force in 1944–45; literally plowed under by French tanks and devastated by Vietminh saboteurs and guerrillas from 1946 until the cease-fire. In addition, the sudden exodus of 860,000[†] inhabitants of the Red River Delta to South Vietnam created a production shortfall in some of North Vietnam's key food-producing provinces; only a Russian financed 'crash' program of importing Burmese rice (about 150,000 tons in 1955) staved off a famine that would have been about as disastrous as that with which the Vietminh had inaugurated its regime in 1945." (Fall 152–53)

[†] Of these, 600,000 were Catholics, 65 percent of total Catholic population in the North before 1954.

In some ways, exodus to South relieves rural crowding and food shortage problems in North. "Thus, it is no exaggeration to say that the mass flight of refugees—which the West encouraged—gave the Vietminh its best boost toward control of the North Vietnamese countryside." (Fall 153–54)

"With the progressive destruction of the North Vietnamese communications infrastructure through aerial bombardment in 1965–66, followed by the bombing of major electricity plants and oil-storage areas and the evacuation of nonessential population from the major cities . . . the DRVN had to face up to the reality of the certain collapse of much of its economy." (Fall 168)

". . . There is one 'act-of-God' factor that operates in favor of the North's industrialization: the preponderance of Vietnam's mineral resources, by geological accident, happens to be located North of the 17th parallel. . . ." (Fall 170)

Soviet bloc aid to Hanoi regime 1955–61 is estimated to have totaled more than $1 billion, with USSR contributing $365 million, Eastern Europe $38 million, China $662 million. North Vietnamese nonmilitary imports from Soviet Union in 1961 are estimated at $80 million, exports to that country only $25 million. (Fall 125)

After 1965, US begins blacklisting vessels engaged in trade with North Vietnam. In 1966, only 233 free world ships call on North Vietnamese ports, compared to 542 year before. (Fall 194)

"Saigon's economic boycott compounded [North Vietnam's] problems, chief among them hunger. Any timetable Ho Chi Minh might have had for systematic development of a planned economy was shortcircuited by emergency." (Kendrick 107)

Following fall of South Vietnam in 1975 and subsequent interruption of commercial relations: "[T]he trade embargo and the freezing of assets in the United States were not of great commercial consequence to the United States. The chief losers were US oil companies, two of which had obtained leases from the [Nguyen Van] Thieu government in 1973 and 1974 for exploration of offshore tracts." (Zasloff 17)

In January 1977, International Monetary Fund (IMF) announces its first loan of $35.8 million to Vietnam following acceptance of its membership previous September. (Zasloff 17)

Average annual Vietnamese trade, 1955–61: exports, $69 million; imports, $246 million. Average annual trade, 1975–81: exports, $32 million; imports, $194 million. (IMF)

Calculated Economic Impact

	Annual cost to target country
Period I: 1955–61	
Reduction in trade 1955–61 from average levels of 1953–54; welfare loss estimated at 40 percent of value of trade (assumes North Vietnam bore entire loss recorded in aggregate Vietnamese trade statistics).	$62 million

Calculated Economic Impact (*continued*)

	Annual cost to target country
Offset	
Increased aid to North Vietnam from Soviet bloc; welfare gain valued at 80 percent of transfers.	($122 million)
Period II: 1962–74	
Reduction in economic production in North Vietnam as result of bombing, shipping blacklisting, blockades; welfare loss estimated as 10 percent shortfall in GNP.	221 million
Period III: 1975–81	
Freeze of Vietnamese assets in US; welfare loss estimated at 20 percent of face value of assets.	15 million
Reduction in trade with US from pre-1975 levels; welfare loss estimated at 15 percent of average annual value of trade 1971–75.	55 million
Average annual total, 1955–74 (Period I and Period II)	$123 million
Average annual total, 1975–81 (Period III)	$70 million
Average annual total, 1955–81	$109 million

Relative Magnitudes

Gross indicators of North Vietnamese economy	
North Vietnamese GNP (1961)	$1.1 billion
North Vietnamese population (1961)	16.4 million
Vietnamese GNP (1976)	$7.2 billion
Vietnamese population (1976)	48.8 million
Annual effect of sanctions related to gross indicators[†]	
Percentage of GNP	2.6
Per capita	$3.34
North Vietnamese trade with US as percentage of total trade	
Exports (1976)	2.0
Imports (1976)	0.2

[†] Scarcity of data over entire period required averaging of GNP and population figures from 1961 and 1976.

Ratio of US GNP (1961: $524.6 billion) to North Vietnamese GNP (1961: $1.1 billion)	477
Ratio of US GNP (1976: $1,718 billion) to Vietnamese GNP (1976: $7.2 billion)	239

ASSESSMENT

Alexander Kendrick
"By aiding the Diem regime and cutting off the North, the United States altered the pattern of Vietnam's economy and constrained Hanoi to more dependence on Peking and Moscow. North Vietnam became, in fact, part of the 'World Communist Conspiracy' that the United States had engaged itself against, a classic example of the creation of a condition which, if it did not exist, had to be invented." (Kendrick 93)

AUTHORS' SUMMARY

Overall assessment	*Assigned scores*
☐ Policy result, scaled from 1 (failed) to 4 (success)	1
☐ Sanctions contribution, scaled from 1 (none) to 4 (significant)	1
☐ Success score (policy result *times* sanctions contribution), scaled from 1 (outright failure) to 16 (significant success)	1

Political and economic variables

☐ Companion policies: J (covert), Q (quasi-military), or R (regular military)	R
☐ International cooperation with sender, scaled from 1 (none) to 4 (significant)	2
☐ International assistance to target: A (if present)	A
☐ Sanctions period (years)	30+
☐ Economic health and political stability of target, scaled from 1 (distressed) to 3 (strong)	2
☐ Presanction relations between sender and target, scaled from 1 (antagonistic) to 3 (cordial)	1
☐ Type of sanction: X (export), M (import), F (financial)	F, X, M
☐ Cost to sender, scaled from 1 (net gain) to 4 (major loss)	2

BIBLIOGRAPHY

Ball, George W. 1982. *The Past Has Another Pattern.* New York: W. W. Norton & Co.
Fall, Bernard B. 1967. *The Two Viet-Nams: A Political and Military Analysis.* New York: Praeger.
International Monetary Fund. 1980. *International Financial Statistics Yearbook.*

Keesing's Contemporary Archives. 1957–58, 1963–64, 1973, 1976, 1978, 1979.

Kendrick, Alexander. 1974. *The Wound Within: America in the Vietnam Years, 1945–1974.* Boston: Little, Brown & Co.

The Pentagon Papers: The Defense Department History of United States Decisionmaking on Vietnam. 1971. Ed. Mike Gravel. Vol. 2. Boston: Beacon Press.

Zasloff, Joseph J., and MacAlister Brown. 1978. *Communist Indochina and U. S. Foreign Policy: Postwar Realities.* Westview Special Studies in International Relations. Boulder, Colo.: Westview Press.

Case 56–1   US v. Israel

(1956–83: Palestinian and Border Questions)

CHRONOLOGY OF KEY EVENTS

1948   Creation of State of Israel leads to first diaspora of Palestinian people. (Ball 238)

October–   Israel, in collaboration with French and British forces, attacks Suez.
November 1956   Following occupation of Sinai, Prime Minister David Ben-Gurion asserts that Sinai is historically part of Israel and 1949 armistice boundaries are "dead and buried and will never be resurrected." Ben-Gurion grudgingly retreats from most of Sinai but stands fast on Gaza, Sharm-el-Shaikh. (Ball 232)

Early 1957   President Dwight D. Eisenhower privately threatens to suspend economic aid, tax incentives for investment in Israel unless Israel withdraws. Attempts of American Jewish community to sway Eisenhower fail. (Ball 232–33)

16 March 1957   Ben-Gurion angrily yields to Eisenhower's threats; withdraws all Sinai troops. (Ball 233)

Early 1960s   President John F. Kennedy embraces Israel as ally, approves Israeli purchase of Hawk missiles in response to growing reliance by President Gamal Abdel Nasser of Egypt on Soviet arms. (Ball 234)

Mid-1960s   President Lyndon B. Johnson seeks to rectify military balance between Israel, Arab states. US becomes Israel's sole source of arms after Six Day War. (Ball 235)

Spring 1967   Nasser occupies Sinai, closes Gulf of Aqaba; Israel launches Six Day War without consulting US. King Hussein of Jordan enters war as Nasser ally, enabling Israel to seize East Jerusalem, occupy West Bank, make territorial gains in Sinai, Gaza, Golan Heights. As result, Israel controls 1.2 million Palestinians, leading to second diaspora. (Ball 236)

December 1967   UN Security Council passes Resolution 242, requiring Israeli withdrawal from occupied territories. Arabs refuse to negotiate with Israel, which hardens attitude toward retention of occupied territories. (Ball 236)

1969–70   On two occasions, administration of President Richard M. Nixon delays shipments of military equipment to Israel as means of exerting leverage but administration ultimately yields to domestic pressure to support Israel. (Ball 237)

October 1973   Egypt attacks in Sinai; massive US airlift aids Israel in thwarting advances. (Ball 237–38)

1974–75   US Secretary of State Henry A. Kissinger focuses on negotiating separate peace between Israel and Egypt dealing with Sinai; puts Jerusalem, Gaza, Palestinian issues on back burner. (Ball 240)

March 1975   Israeli-Egyptian negotiations over Sinai break down, in Kissinger's view owing to Israeli intransigence. President Gerald R. Ford slows delivery of arms to Israel. (Ball 240)

21 May 1975   Pro-Israeli lobby mobilizes 76 senators to urge that Ford reconsider his tactics, "be responsive to Israel's urgent military and economic needs." In summer of 1975, Senate, again at urging of Israeli lobby, blocks Ford-Kissinger attempt to sell Hawk missiles to Jordan. (Ball 240)

September 1975   US, Egypt, and Israel conclude Sinai agreement entailing massive US military, financial aid to Israel and commitment that US not deal directly with Palestine Liberation Organization (PLO): "In a sense, the Sinai II agreement of September 1975 amounted to a vast real estate deal in which the United States bought a slice of the Sinai Desert from Israel for a huge financial and political consideration and then paid Egypt for accepting it." (Ball 241)

September 1978   Camp David accord secures peace between Egypt and Israel but makes little progress toward Palestinian solution. Subsequently, Israel narrows scope of promised "autonomy plan." (Ball 242–43)

5 June 1982   Israel invades Lebanon; US considers various means of retaliation. (*Washington Post*, 9 June 1982, A23)

18 November 1982   *New York Times* editorial asserts that Israeli opponents of Prime Minister Menachem Begin's West Bank and Gaza policies urge "sharp cuts" in US nonmilitary aid to Israel as means to "topple the Begin Government." Israeli government denounces suggestion as "a satanic act." (*New York Times*, 18 November 1982, A10)

1 December 1982   US Secretary of State George P. Shultz attempts to discourage Senate Appropriations Committee from exceeding recommended administration levels of aid to Israel. Nevertheless, committee votes (without dissent) $910 million of FY 1983 economic aid ($125 million more than administration request) and conversion of $350 million of military loans to grants. Total aid package to Israel is $2.6 billion, of

1 December 1982 *(continued)*	which $1.7 billion is military grants and loans. (*Washington Post*, 4 December 1982, A1, A17)
4 December 1982	Israeli Foreign Minister Yitzhak Shamir accuses administration of President Ronald Reagan of "clearly violating" past pledge not to link economic and military aid to Israel to political issues. Deputy Foreign Minister Yehuda Ben-Meir accuses US of "trying to appease the Arabs." (*Washington Post*, 4 December 1982, A1, A17)
1 April 1983	Reagan publicly announces that he is withholding formal approval of sale of 75 F-16 fighters to Israel until all its troops are out of Lebanon. Administration aides point out that release of planes would be against "spirit of the law," not letter of the law. Shamir terms Reagan statement "regrettable pronouncement." (*New York Times*, 2 April 1983, A2)
6 May 1983	Israel, Lebanon reach peace agreement along lines proposed by Shultz, with withdrawal of Israeli forces contingent on parallel withdrawal by Syria and PLO. (*Washington Post*, 7 May 1983, A1; *New York Times*, 17 May 1983, A12)
19 May 1983	Reagan releases 75 F-16 jet fighters withheld since Israel's invasion of Lebanon. (*Washington Post*, 20 May 1983, A1)
25 May 1983	Reagan administration switches positions, announces support for increased military and economic grants to Israel totaling some $400 million. (*New York Times*, 26 May 1983, A13)

GOALS OF SENDER COUNTRY

Fall 1956
Eisenhower declares Israeli refusal to withdraw would "impair the friendly cooperation between our two countries." (Ball 232)

1960s and later
During Johnson administration and after Six Day War, "the issues in American-Israeli relations were largely conditioned by the American objective—largely derived, in turn, from a preoccupation with Soviet policy in the region—of a political settlement of that conflict. This very objective made it difficult for the United States, despite substantial differences with Israel, to use arms transfers to influence Israeli policy." (Pollock 19)

1973 and later
During and after 1973 Middle East War: "Already during the war itself, Kissinger took the initiative in delaying supplies in order to secure Israeli acceptance of two proposed cease-fires in place. Then, in the two years of shuttle diplomacy which followed, Kissinger again used a carrot-and-stick approach to arms supplies in extracting Israeli territorial concessions for disengagements in Sinai and on the Syrian front." (Pollock 298)

Late 1970s
US policy vis-à-vis Israel in later years of administration of President Jimmy Carter is

concerned primarily with restraining Israeli military operations in Lebanon, expansion of settlements in West Bank. (Pollock 302)

April 1983
In explaining his position on sale of F-16s to Israel, Reagan says, "we are forbidden by law to release those planes" while Israeli troops occupy Lebanon. Aides clarify explaining it would be against "spirit" rather than "letter" of law to release aircraft. (*New York Times*, 2 April 1983, A2)

RESPONSE OF TARGET COUNTRY

1958–present
Mindful of Suez episode, Israel builds powerful lobby in US. "Not only do Israel's American supporters have powerful influence with many members of the Congress, but practically no actions touching Israel's interests can be taken, or even discussed, within the executive branch without it being quickly known to the Israeli government." (Ball 233)

Following Six Day War
"On these procedural issues [getting Arab-Israeli negotiations started], the Israeli government did indeed respond [to 'high level American requests'] with a number of small diplomatic gestures involving increasingly explicit, though still qualified acceptance of both Resolution 242 and indirect negotiations." (Pollock 439)

1968, 1971–72
"[T]here were several occasions on which Israeli gestures of diplomatic flexibility were linked, in one form or another, with American approval of a pending Israeli request to purchase arms." (Pollock 294)

1978
"Even when the [Carter] administration proposed selling Israel only about one half the requested F-16s and F-15s in February 1978, Israeli government protests on that score were few and muted. . . . Of greater concern to the Israeli government and its American supporters were the long-run political-military implications of the package, in which the above sales to Israel were tied to sales of F-15s to Saudi Arabia and F-5s to Egypt." (Pollock 301)

August 1982
Senior Israeli official warns that US sanctions against Israel would backfire and that reaction would make siege of Beirut "look like peanuts." (*Washington Post*, 7 August 1982, A1)

ATTITUDE OF OTHER COUNTRIES

Palestine Liberation Organization and Soviet Union
In August–September 1982, PLO and USSR call for UN sanctions against Israel. (*Washington Post*, 17 August 1982, A13; *Financial Times* [London], 20 September 1982, 3)

European Community
In November 1982, EC delays $40 million concessionary credit to Israel in response to Israeli occupation of Lebanon, intransigence toward PLO. (*Wall Street Journal*, 16 November 1982, 32)

France
From 1950 to 1967, France provides bulk of military aid to Israel and nuclear reactor at Dimona. Following 1967 war, however, President Charles de Gaulle, mindful of oil and other French interests, halts flow of arms to Israel. (Ball 234)

ECONOMIC IMPACT

Observed Economic Statistics

US aid to Israel (million dollars)

Fiscal year	Economic	Military
1953–61 av.	56.4	0.1
1962–68 av.	47.7	23.1
1969	36.7	85.0
1970	41.1	30.0
1971	55.8	545.0
1972	104.2	300.0
1973	109.8	307.5
1974	51.5	2,482.7[tt]
1975	353.1	300.0
1976 + TQ[t]	793.0	1,700.0
1977	742.0	1,000.0
1978	791.8	1,000.0
1979	790.1	4,000.0
1980	786.0	1,000.0
1981	764.0	1,400.0
1982	785.0	1,400.0

[t] Transitional quarter: beginning of US fiscal year changed from June to October.
[tt] Yom Kippur War.
Source: AID.

Calculated Economic Impact

	Annual cost to target country
Welfare loss associated with slowdown in military, economic flows; estimated as time cost of 5 percent of	$16 million

	Annual cost to target country

transfers, namely in 1956 and 1957, $56 million; 1969, $85 million (military only); 1970, $30 million (military only); in 1975, $200 million (military only); in 1982, $1,400 million (military only). Total figure thus derived is divided by six to average it over number of occasions involving slowdowns.

Note: Sometimes delay resulted in loans being forgiven and turned into outright grants; moreover, each year after threatening to withhold shipments, US increased economic, military aid.

Relative Magnitudes

Gross indicators of Israeli economy	
Israeli GNP (1956)	$1.4 billion
Israeli population (1956)	1.8 million
Israeli GNP (1980)	$19.6 billion
Israeli population (1980)	3.87 million
Annual effect of sanctions related to gross indicators	
Percentage of GNP (1980)	0.1
Per capita (1980)	$4.13
Israeli trade with US as percentage of total trade	
Exports (1956)	18
Imports (1956)	31
Exports (1980)	18
Imports (1980)	21
Ratio of US GNP (1956: $422 billion) to Israeli GNP (1956: $1.4 billion)	301
Ratio of US GNP (1980: $2,633 billion) to Israeli GNP (1980: $19.6 billion)	134

ASSESSMENT

1980
George Ball calls for economic sanctions in event that Israel fails to move toward self-determination for Palestine: "In short . . . Israeli-American relations must either become much closer—with Israel accepting the essential changes in its present position—or they must become much looser, with the United States resuming its freedom of action on all forms of aid to Israel, so long as Israel sticks to its present course." (Ball 255)

Authors' note

By implication, apart from 1956–57 episode, US attempts at using economic sanctions to modify Israeli policy had failed up to 1980. However, 1982–83 sanctions apparently helped achieve Israeli agreement on conditional withdrawal from Lebanon.

AUTHORS' SUMMARY

Overall assessment	Assigned scores
☐ Policy result, scaled from 1 (failed) to 4 (success)	2
☐ Sanctions contribution, scaled from 1 (none) to 4 (significant)	1
☐ Success score (policy result *times* sanctions contribution), scaled from 1 (outright failure) to 16 (significant success)	2

Political and economic variables

☐ Companion policies: J (covert), Q (quasi-military), or R (regular military)	—
☐ International cooperation with sender, scaled from 1 (none) to 4 (significant)	1
☐ International assistance to target: A (if present)	—
☐ Sanctions period (years)†	4
☐ Economic health and political stability of target, scaled from 1 (distressed) to 3 (strong)	3
☐ Presanction relations between sender and target, scaled from 1 (antagonistic) to 3 (cordial)	3
☐ Type of sanction: X (export), M (import), F (financial)	F, X
☐ Cost to sender, scaled from 1 (net gain) to 4 (major loss)	2

† Due to intermittent imposition of sanctions, only the "active" period when sanctions were in force is counted.

Comments

US may have influenced Israeli policy at various times over past 30 years. But it appears that whatever degree of influence US achieved resulted more from overall importance of relationship than from specific threats concerning aid, arms sales.

BIBLIOGRAPHY

Agency for International Development. *Overseas Loans and Grants*. Various issues.

Ball, George W. 1979–80. "The Coming Crisis in Israeli-American Relations." 58 *Foreign Affairs* (Winter): 231–56.

Pollock, David. 1982. *The Politics of Pressure: American Arms and Israeli Policy Since the Six Day War*. Westport, Conn.: Greenwood Press.

Case 56–2   US, UK, and France v. Egypt

(1956: Nationalization of Suez Canal)

CHRONOLOGY OF KEY EVENTS

26 July 1956   Egyptian President Gamal Abdel Nasser issues decree nationalizing Suez Canal (Law 285 of 1956). Nasser's announced reasons: to end Western imperialist exploitation and domination; to collect full revenues from canal. Nasser asserts additional revenues would be used to finance Aswan Dam without Western aid. (Note: US Secretary of State John Foster Dulles had announced week earlier that US was withdrawing its offer to assist in financing Aswan Dam. Dulles announcement appears to have triggered nationalization move. According to Anthony Nutting, minister of state in British Foreign Office, Nasser wanted "to show Egypt was not going to be pushed around by the West.") (Bowie 1, 13; Nutting 45)

28 July–1 August 1956   UK, France, US freeze Egyptian assets under their respective jurisdictions. On 30 July, UK bans export of war matériel to Egypt. French, British also order shipping companies under their respective flags to pay canal dues "to the former company's account in London or Paris and refuse to pay anything to the new Egyptian Canal Authority." British Prime Minister Anthony Eden telegraphs President Dwight D. Eisenhower "that economic pressures alone were 'unlikely to attain our objectives' and that he and his colleagues were 'convinced that we must be ready, in the last resort to use force to bring Nasser to his senses.'" (Nutting 48–50)

2 August 1956   Anglo-French military organizations begin planning for invasion of Egypt, reinforce troop concentrations in Mediterranean. Eisenhower expresses grave misgivings. (Bowie xvi; Nutting 48)

Early August 1956   After three days of talks, UK, France, US agree to call conference in London of 24 "concerned maritime powers" to devise international arrangement that will ensure continuity of canal operation. Egypt, Greece refuse to attend. Of the nations present, 18 agree on proposal for international use (USSR, India oppose it) which is submitted to Egypt by committee of five (Australia, Ethiopia, Iran, Sweden, US) headed by Australian Prime Minister Sir Robert Menzies. Nasser

Early August 1956 (continued)	rejects proposal as infringing on Egyptian sovereignty. (Bowie 36–42)
4 September 1956	Dulles proposes formation of Suez Canal Users' Association (SCUA) to deal with Nasser on nationalization issue. SCUA is formed on 1 October but has little impact. (Bowie 43)
15 September 1956	European pilots on canal are withdrawn from Egypt. Canal continues to operate smoothly. (Bowie 57)
23 September 1956	UK, France refer Suez problem to UN Security Council, both for domestic political reasons and to avoid alienating US. Council begins deliberations 5 October. (Bowie xvi)
Late September 1956	US orders ships under its flag to pay canal dues to SCUA account rather than to Nasser's new Canal Authority. US refuses, however, to order large number of US-owned ships flying Liberian, Panamanian flags to do so as well. (Nutting 68)
Mid-October 1956	In Security Council meetings on canal issue, Egypt demonstrates unexpected willingness to compromise. "In sum, Egypt [is] now willing to negotiate an agreement which [gives] the maritime powers substantially all that they were asking." Nutting attributes this generosity to, "in ascending order of importance . . . economic pressure . . . Indian influence . . . and political pressures by other Arab states, fearful lest a row over the Canal should endanger this vital outlet for their oil shipments to Western markets." (Nutting 72–77)
29 October 1956	Israeli army attacks Egyptian forces in Sinai. UK, French forces become involved later, using justification that their troops are needed to separate combatants, enforce a cease-fire. Also see Case 56–3 US v. UK and France (1956: Suez). (Bowie 73–75)

GOALS OF SENDER COUNTRIES

United Kingdom
"As for Eden himself, this [the nationalization] was, of course, the challenge for which he had been waiting. Now at last he had found a pretext to launch an all-out campaign of political, economic, and military pressures on Egypt and to destroy forever Nasser's image as the leader of Arab nationalism." (Nutting 47)

United States
Secretary of State Dulles, on visit to London, "lost no time in saying that he was in full agreement with Eden's statement in the House of Commons that no arrangements for the Suez Canal's future would be acceptable 'which would leave it in the unfettered control of a single power which could exploit it for purposes purely of national policy.'" (Nutting 52)

France
"[Foreign Minister Christian] Pineau stated that France would not accept the unilateral action of Colonel Nasser. Prime Minister [Guy] Mollet went even further in the days

ahead and called Nasser an 'apprentice dictator' whose methods were similar to [Adolph] Hitler's . . . [Mollet] announced that France had decided upon 'an energetic and severe counterstroke.'" (Neff 280)

RESPONSE OF TARGET COUNTRY

Anthony Nutting
Following Franco-British orders concerning payment of canal fees, which they hoped would precipitate "unwise" response: "Nasser was not to be led into their carefully baited trap, and throughout the next three months, until the Canal was blocked following the Israeli invasion of Sinai, British, French and other shipping continued to pass without let or hindrance between Port Said and Suez." (Nutting 50)

When presented with August conference proposal to create international board to oversee canal operation: "Nothing would induce [Nasser] to consider any solution which derogated from Egypt's absolute right to run the Canal as an Egyptian national undertaking. The Eighteen-Power proposal challenged that right and sought to reimpose foreign domination over Egypt, and he would have none of it." (Nutting 54–55)

Donald Neff
In explaining why he had not attended August conference, Nasser charged UK, France, US with conspiring "'to starve and terrorize the Egyptian people. The three powers immediately froze Egyptian assets and funds in their banks. Britain and France mobilized their reserves and officially announced that their troops and fleets were on the move. The Egyptian government strongly deplores these measures, and regards them as a threat to the Egyptian people to make them surrender part of their territory and sovereignty to an international body, which in fact is international colonialism.'" (Neff 296)

New York Times
"Egypt declared today [18 September 1956] a policy of virtual trade boycott against the West and in favor of business with the East. . . . The declaration was viewed as a defensive one forced upon Egypt by the economic squeeze the West had imposed on her as a result of the Suez Canal crisis." (*New York Times*, 19 September 1956, A1)

ATTITUDE OF OTHER COUNTRIES

Iraq
". . . [T]he Iraqis were, not surprisingly, nettled that Nasser should have failed to consult any fellow Arab state, even any of the oil-producing states, before embarking on a course of action that was bound to have serious political and economic repercussions on the whole Arab world. Inevitably, therefore, their reaction was more angry than cautious and Nuri [es-Said, prime minister], in particular, expressed the hope that Britain would respond resolutely to Nasser's act of defiance." (Nutting 47)

Israel
Given Egypt's refusal to allow ships bound for Israeli ports through canal, "[Israel's] obvious interests lay in control of the Canal and of the terminal ports of Suez and Port Said being taken out of Nasser's hands." (Nutting 49)

Arab nations
All the Arab states, even pro-British Iraq in the end, officially "endorsed Nasser's nationalization." (Neff 297)

India, Soviet Union
At London conference: "In the diplomatic thrust and parry that continued until August 23, when the Conference finally ended, India's V. K. Krishna Menon [acting foreign minister] was the main combatant for Egypt, with the Soviet Union acting as his second." (Neff 297)

ECONOMIC IMPACT

Observed Economic Statistics

Before nationalization, annual dues from operation of canal had been averaging $100 million per year, of which Egypt was receiving only $3 million. (Nutting 44–45)

"With the French and ourselves [the British] and most of the other principal Canal users, except the Americans, paying our dues to the former company's account in London and Paris, Nasser was being denied some 65 percent of the income which he had hoped to gain by nationalization." (Nutting 59)

"The economic pressures imposed by the Western Powers had largely destroyed the basis of Egypt's triangular trade with Western Europe and India and the Far East. In the past this had been sustained by covering deficits in trade with the former by credits with the latter and drawing on sterling reserves to bridge the gap. But now, with her sterling balances frozen, Egypt's trade with Europe had fallen to a mere fraction of its pre-July figure. Against this, however, she was able to draw $15,000,000 from her deposits with the [IMF], and a Chinese credit of 1,600,000 in Swiss francs was made available to her in Zurich. India had also offered to pay for her imports in rupees, while Japan agreed to accept deferred payment." (Nutting 74)

Estimates of Egyptian assets frozen: UK: $420 million in sterling deposits and $310 million arising from World War II debts which were being paid out at a rate of $56 million/year; US: $46 million; France minimal. (*New York Times*, 5 August 1956, IV, 3; 1 January 1957, A1; 2 March 1957, A1)

"The freezing of Egyptian sterling accounts in Britain and of other accounts in France and the restrictions on all but current dollar accounts in the United States have made it almost impossible for Egypt to buy anything for more than a month from her traditional Western markets." (*New York Times*, 19 September 1956, A1)

Egyptian trade (million dollars)

	Exports		Imports	
	US	*UK/France*	*US*	*UK/France*
1955	26.0	57.9	62.0	113.3
1956	13.5	43.5	71.7	90.4
1957	22.3	9.5	47.1	13.8
1958	12.1	20.0	51.4	36.4
1959	5.9	21.2	86.0	61.0
1960	28.6	24.1	114.8	64.3

Source: IMF.

Calculated Economic Impact

	Annual cost to target country
Freeze of Egyptian assets in US, UK, France; welfare loss estimated at 20 percent of face value of assets.	$93 million
Reduction in Egyptian trade with US, UK, France in 1956; welfare loss estimated at 40 percent of value of reduced trade from 1955 levels.	16 million
Reduction in operating revenues from Suez Canal from diversion to SCUA account; welfare loss estimated at 100 percent of reduced earnings.	63 million
Offsets	
Increased aid from China; welfare gain valued at 90 percent of SF 1.6 million credit.	(negl.)
Realized Suez Canal revenue in excess of prenationalization rental ($3 million).	($34 million)
Total	$138 million

Relative Magnitudes

Gross indicators of Egyptian economy	
Egyptian GNP (1960)	$4.0 billion
Egyptian population (1956)	23.5 million
Annual effect of sanctions related to gross indicators	
Percentage of GNP	3.4
Per capita	$5.87
Egyptian trade with US, UK, and France as percentage of total trade	
Exports (1956)	15
Imports (1956)	30
Ratio of US, UK, French GNP (1960: $641 billion) to Egyptian GNP (1960: $4 billion)	160

ASSESSMENT

Anthony Nutting

"[M]ore aggravating for those who wanted to settle with Nasser by the use of force rather than by negotiation, these economic sanctions, combined with growing political pressures from Egypt's Arab League associates, succeeded three months later in inducing Nasser to concede terms which Selwyn Lloyd [British foreign secretary] was to describe as offering an acceptable compromise. But because neither Eden nor Mollet then wanted any compromise and because they insisted on using force, these terms were to become a dead letter." (Nutting 50)

AUTHORS' SUMMARY

Overall assessment	Assigned scores
□ Policy result, scaled from 1 (failed) to 4 (success)	3
□ Sanctions contribution, scaled from 1 (none) to 4 (significant)	3
□ Success score (policy result *times* sanctions contribution), scaled from 1 (outright failure) to 16 (significant success)	9

Political and economic variables

□ Companion policies: J (covert), Q (quasi-military), or R (regular military)	R
□ International cooperation with sender, scaled from 1 (none) to 4 (significant)	2
□ International assistance to target: A (if present)	—
□ Sanctions period (years)	1
□ Economic health and political stability of target, scaled from 1 (distressed) to 3 (strong)	2
□ Presanction relations between sender and target, scaled from 1 (antagonistic) to 3 (cordial)	2
□ Type of sanction: X (export), M (import), F (financial)	F, X
□ Cost to sender, scaled from 1 (net gain) to 4 (major loss)	2

Comments

Egypt's willingness to compromise in UN talks in October 1956 reflected pressure sanctions were exerting on its economy—but because UK, France had broader goals than operation of canal, they did not take Nasser up on his offer. Sanctions worked for a specific goal but failed to undermine Nasser's domestic political support.

BIBLIOGRAPHY

Bowie, Robert R. 1974. *Suez 1956: International Crisis and the Role of the Law*. New York: Oxford University Press.
International Monetary Fund. *Direction of Trade Statistics*. Various issues.
Neff, Donald. 1981. *Warriors at Suez*. New York: Linden Press/Simon & Schuster.
Nutting, Anthony. 1967. *No End of a Lesson: The Story of Suez*. London: Constable.

Case 56–3   US v. UK and France

(1956: Suez)

CHRONOLOGY OF KEY EVENTS

26 July 1956   Egyptian President Gamal Abdel Nasser nationalizes Suez Canal. (Bowie 1; Nutting 45)

2 August 1956   UK, France reinforce troops stationed in Mediterranean, begin planning for military action against Egypt. (Bowie xvi)

August–September 1956   Nasser rejects proposal for international oversight of operation of canal, which continues to run smoothly. (Bowie 36–42)

23 September 1956   UK, France refer Suez problem to UN Security Council. Deliberations begin 5 October. (Bowie xvi)

29 October 1956   Israeli army attacks Egyptian forces in Sinai. Next day, UK, France deliver ultimatum to Israel, Egypt to withdraw from canal, allow British, French troops to occupy canal sites temporarily. They expect Egypt to reject ultimatum, thereby providing excuse to intervene. On 31 October, UK, France begin bombing Egyptian airfields. US calls for emergency meeting of UN Security Council but UK, France move first. They veto US proposal for immediate unconditional cease-fire, saying it would be ineffective. (Bowie 66)

3 November 1956   Israel completes occupation of Gaza and Sinai, accepts UN General Assembly proposal for cease-fire. (Bowie 73–75)

4 November 1956   Egypt accepts cease-fire. It announces canal has been blocked by ships sunk at Port Said and Lake Timseh and by blowing up of bridge at El Ferdan. Shortly thereafter, portions of oil pipeline from Iraq to Tripoli, Lebanon, are sabotaged by Syrian engineers; Saudis impose oil embargo against French, British. (Bowie 73–75; *Keesing's* 15185; Nutting 133)

5 November 1956   After pressuring Israel into revoking its agreement to cease-fire, UK, France drop paratroops into Egypt with stated objective of separating belligerents, enforcing the cease-fire. (Bowie 73–75)

275

| 7 November 1956 | All military operations in Egypt are halted after US refuses to permit UK access to dollar credits to pay for oil imports from dollar zones of North and South America. (Bowie 75) |

| November 1956 | "There was no indication when or whether the US intended to implement its emergency plans for increasing the quota of Western hemisphere oil available to the Europeans. . . . In Washington, it was hoped that this continued uncertainty might hasten a British and French decision to evacuate their forces from Egypt." (Bowie 82) |

| 3 December 1956 | British Foreign Secretary Selwyn Lloyd announces that UK, French forces will be withdrawn from Egypt. Evacuation is completed by 22 December. On same day, President Dwight D. Eisenhower announces "he had authorized American oil companies to work together to supply oil to Europe." (Bowie xvii; Nutting 156) |

GOALS OF SENDER COUNTRY

Robert R. Bowie
"US policy in the Suez Crisis was largely dominated by the effort to resolve the dispute by peaceful means and prevent resort to force. That objective reflected various considerations, but a major factor was Eisenhower's strong commitment to the UN Charter obligations against resort to force." (Bowie 29)

US fears that failure to oppose intervention by British and French forces will: undermine UN; appear as act of imperialism, thereby alienating Third World states; provide cover for Soviet actions in Hungary; and possibly create situation so explosive it could lead to nuclear war between US, USSR. (Bowie 61–63)

". . . the President sought to pursue a consistent course throughout the crisis in support of the principles of the UN as he understood them. That support was not merely verbal; it included severe pressure on Allied states led by personal friends." However, Eisenhower did not employ all possible pressure: "On 5 November 1956, when an aide talked to him of halting oil supplies to Britain and France, Eisenhower said, 'Good lands! I'm a friend of theirs. I'm not going to make life too complicated for them.'" (Bowie 65)

RESPONSE OF TARGET COUNTRIES

United Kingdom
Prime Minister Sir Anthony Eden is explicit about his objectives in a private conversation more than four months before Suez crisis. "But what's all this nonsense about isolating Nasser and 'neutralizing' him, as you call it? I want him destroyed, can't you understand? I want him removed. . . ." Thus, subsequent British actions have dual aim: placing Suez Canal under international control; destabilizing Nasser. From beginning, UK makes known to US its willingness to use force if necessary. (Bowie 22)

"The blockage of the Canal, the disruption of oil shipments and other commerce, as well as the invasion, put severe strains on the limited British monetary reserves. As the Chancellor of the Exchequer, Harold Macmillan, commented, the strain was greater than the economy could bear. . . . The need for US assistance for the pound and for oil was too great to resist." (Bowie 64)

France
Like Britain, France also is interested in destabilizing Nasser. French motivation is to stop his support for rebels in Algeria. (Bowie 26)

ATTITUDE OF OTHER COUNTRIES

Soviet Union and Arab states
"As for the Russians and the Arab World, the hostility of the latter was a foregone conclusion and the former, who were currently engaged in the bloody business of suppressing rebellion which had broken out against Russian rule in Hungary, were only too anxious to see Britain and France sharing the 'dock' with them at the United Nations." (Nutting 120)

Commonwealth nations
". . . the Commonwealth had joined the ranks of our opponents. India had condemned us, [UK, France, Israel] in the strongest terms, Canada had expressed her profound regret at our action, New Zealand had said the same in slightly less frigid terms; and although she and Australia were later to give us their reluctant support in the United Nations General Assembly, the Australian delegation had voted against us in the Security Council." (Nutting 120)

Baghdad Pact
Representatives of Iraq, Turkey, Iran, Pakistan, deliberately excluding British representative, adopt resolution on 7 November calling for immediate withdrawal of French, British forces from Egypt. (Nutting 146)

ECONOMIC IMPACT

Observed Economic Statistics

"On 5 November, the Bank of England alone had spent $300 million to maintain the exchange rate." (Bowie 75)

"In the month of November, Britain lost $279 million from its total gold and dollar reserves." UK had lost $141 million in previous two months. (Bowie 64; Nutting 145)

Blockage of canal, damage to oil pipeline force UK to turn to "dollar areas of North and South America" for oil imports. This alternative also is blocked, however, by lack of dollar reserves caused by recent run on pound, US refusal to extend credits. Rationing eventually has to be imposed in UK, France. (Nutting 133, 151)

Calculated Economic Impact

	Annual cost to target country
Cost of British support for pound; welfare loss valued at 5 percent of reduction in official gold and dollar holdings in month of November 1956, annualized to a 12-month basis.	$167 million

Relative Magnitudes

(Note: Sanctions are applied only against UK, even though British and French act in tandem in Suez invasion. For this reason, relative magnitudes reflect only US/UK relations.)

Gross indicators of British economy	
UK GNP (1956)	$58.7 billion
UK population (1956)	51.4 million
Annual effect of sanctions related to gross indicators	
Percentage of GNP	0.3
Per capita	$3.25
British trade with US as percentage of total trade	
Exports (1956)	8
Imports (1956)	11
Ratio of US GNP (1956: $421.7 billion) to UK GNP (1956: $58.7 billion)	7

ASSESSMENT

Robert R. Bowie
From late October through early November, UK's oil reserves are nearly depleted and serious run on the pound threatens its financial position. US blocks attempts by UK to draw on its IMF reserves, refuses to provide financial assistance to support pound unless UK accepts UN recommendations, promises Eden $1 billion loan as soon as British troops are withdrawn from Suez. "Totally beaten, Eden capitulated at noon on 6 November." (Bowie 75–76)

"The British government was determined, however, to see definite arrangements for clearing the canal before ordering more than a token withdrawal of allied forces. Even intense American pressure could not spur the British government to an unequivocal undertaking to withdraw from Egypt promptly without independent assurances that UNEF [UN Emergency Force] would be more than simply an Egyptian vehicle for getting rid of foreign troops. Finally, pressure from Washington and the likelihood of castigation by the General Assembly forced a definite British commitment to withdraw." (Bowie 82–83)

AUTHORS' SUMMARY

Overall assessment	Assigned scores
☐ Policy result, scaled from 1 (failed) to 4 (success)	4
☐ Sanctions contribution, scaled from 1 (none) to 4 (significant)	3
☐ Success score (policy result *times* sanctions contribution), scaled from 1 (outright failure) to 16 (significant success)	12

Political and economic variables	Assigned scores
☐ Companion policies: J (covert), Q (quasi-military), or R (regular military)	—
☐ International cooperation with sender, scaled from 1 (none) to 4 (significant)	1
☐ International assistance to target: A (if present)	—
☐ Sanctions period (years)	1
☐ Economic health and political stability of target, scaled from 1 (distressed) to 3 (strong)	3
☐ Presanction relations between sender and target, scaled from 1 (antagonistic) to 3 (cordial)	3
☐ Type of sanction: X (export), M (import), F (financial)	F
☐ Cost to sender, scaled from 1 (net gain) to 4 (major loss)	2

BIBLIOGRAPHY

Bowie, Robert R. 1974. *Suez 1956: International Crisis and the Role of the Law.* New York: Oxford University Press.
Keesing's Contemporary Archives. 1955–56.
Neff, Donald. 1981. *Warriors at Suez.* New York: Linden Press/Simon & Schuster.
Nutting, Anthony. 1967. *No End of a Lesson: The Story of Suez.* London: Constable.

Case 56–4 US v. Laos

(1956–62: Prevent Communist Takeover)

CHRONOLOGY OF KEY EVENTS

21 March 1956   Prince Souvanna Phouma, neutralist and half-brother of Communist Pathet Lao leader Prince Souphanouvong, becomes prime minister of Laos, pledging reconciliation of all factions. (Stevenson 334)

1 August 1956   Prince Souvanna initiates talks with Souphanouvong in attempt to unite Laos under coalition government despite US opposition to involvement of Pathet Lao in Laotian government. (Stevenson 334)

Fall 1956   "Mixed committees" of neutralist, rightist, Pathet Lao representatives, set up as result of August discussions, agree to establish diplomatic relations with "consenting neighbors" and accept aid "given unconditionally by any nation." US, viewing this as prelude to opening of relations with USSR, China (PRC), suspends aid in December on pretext of corruption in import program. Aid is resumed after a month when pledges are received that US right to approve import licenses will be honored. (Stevenson 43)

November 1957   Agreement is reached on coalition government that includes two Pathet Lao members; calls for integration of Pathet Lao forces into Royal Laotian Army, return of two Pathet Lao–controlled provinces to central government administration, and holding of elections next year. Thailand temporarily closes border with Laos in protest against inclusion of Communists in government. Closure "could have brought serious economic dislocation to Laos because most of its trade with the outside world transits Thailand. In 1957 this was a gesture to show Thailand's displeasure and was not enforced for any length of time. . . ." (Stevenson 335; Neuchterlein 145)

4 May 1958   Pathet Lao and allies receive 32 percent of vote, win 13 of 21 seats in National Assembly. Three days later US Congress holds hearings to investigate allegations of corruption in Laos aid program. (Stevenson 59, 336)

1 July 1958	US suspends monthly aid payments, insisting that devaluation of Laotian currency (kip) is necessary to end corruption and speculation in commodity import program. US-backed rightist party, Committee for the Defense of National Interests (CDNI), forces parliamentary crisis; on 23 July Souvanna resigns after losing vote of confidence on currency issue. (Hilsman 118; Stevenson 59)
Summer/Fall 1958	Rightist Phoui Sananikone is made prime minister in August. In September Laos establishes relations with Republic of Vietnam and Taiwan, thereby rejecting neutralist policy followed by Souvanna. In October, kip is devalued; US aid is resumed shortly thereafter. (Stevenson 59, 336)
1959	Fighting breaks out between Royal Laotian forces and Pathet Lao forces allegedly supported by Vietminh. US increases aid to Laos. In late December, Prime Minister Phoui resigns under pressure from army led by General Phoumi Nosavan. (Stevenson 337–39)
Early 1960	Phoumi, staunch anti-Communist strongly backed by CIA, becomes primary source of power behind government. (Stevenson 339)
August 1960	Kong Le, captain in Royal Laotian Army, conducts successful bloodless coup, asks Souvanna to form centrist and neutralist government. Souvanna opens negotiations with rightists under Phoumi, leftists under Souphanouvong in attempt to create coalition government. Phoumi moves to Savannakhet, establishes a "countercoup" committee in opposition to Souvanna and Kong Le forces. Thailand imposes a blockade on Vientiane, Laotian capital. (Neuchterlein 174; Stevenson 340)
Early Fall 1960	Souvanna requests airlift of oil and rice from US but is turned down after being told operation would be too costly. In late September Souvanna announces he will allow Soviets to open embassy in Laos. US suspends aid in early October, uncertain of which faction to back, but resumes it two weeks later when compromise is worked out with Souvanna. Under agreement, US continues monthly budget support payments to government in Vientiane but at same time ships military assistance directly to Phoumi, with caveat that it cannot be used against government in Vientiane or Kong Le's forces but only against Pathet Lao. (Neuchterlein 174; Hilsman 150; Stevenson 340; Dommen 159)
Late Fall 1960	When it becomes obvious Phoumi has no intention of keeping bargain and is, in fact, marching with his troops toward Vientiane, Souvanna asks US to halt shipments of military equipment. Such transfers are halted on November 30. On 4 December, USSR begins airlift to Laotian capital pursuant to agreement reached in late October. Soviet aid is too late. On 9 December, Prince Souvanna goes into voluntary exile in Cambodia while Kong Le joins his forces with those of Pathet Lao. On 14 December, Phoumi takes Vientiane; next day, his ally, Prince Boun Oum, is named prime minister. On 19 December, US military aid to Phoumi is resumed. (Dommen 160–67; Stevenson 341)

1961	Military conflict between rightist, leftist forces continues sporadically despite conclusion of cease-fire in May. Concomitant efforts to find compromise solution, form unified coalition government also continue. US policy shifts under President John F. Kennedy from goal of pro-West, anti-Communist Laos to willingness to accept genuinely neutralist, nonaligned Laos. This shift includes willingness to accept Prince Souvanna as coalition leader. Administration of President Dwight D. Eisenhower had considered Souvanna "soft on communism." (Stevenson 342–44; Hilsman 150–70; Dommen 180)
January 1962	US suspends monthly aid payment in order to pressure rightist faction to negotiate with centrist, leftist factions about formation of coalition government. Boun Oum agrees to meet with Princes Souvanna Phouma and Souphanouvong despite his skepticism about successful outcome. Two days later US aid is resumed. (Stevenson 169)
February 1962	Following reports of outbreak of fighting and under pressure from president's special envoy in area, W. Averell Harriman, US again suspends aid payments. However, cut-off affects only cash-grant aid, not shipments of military equipment. CIA reportedly counteracts suspension by supplying its own funds to Phoumi's forces. (Stevenson 170)
6 May 1962	Pathet Lao forces defeat Phoumi's, capture Royal Lao Army outpost at Nam Tha in first major violation of cease-fire. "For Phoumi . . . the combination of Harriman's unrelenting pressure and the defeat at Nam Tha was too much; it broke his will. On June 11, 1962, Souvanna announced that an agreement had been reached on the composition of a government of national union." Three days later, US aid to Laos is resumed again. (Hilsman 151; Stevenson 178)
23 July 1962	"The foreign ministers of the fourteen nations at a Geneva Conference [essentially the same group that in 1954 arranged for independence of Indochina] initial the 'Declaration on the Neutrality of Laos.'" In subsequent months, US, USSR withdraw all advisers to opposing factions in Laos in compliance with Geneva agreement. (Dommen 224)
1963–75	Geneva accord marks end of period of intense, direct US interest in Laos. In words of Secretary of State Dean Rusk: "After 1963 Laos was only the wart on the hog of Vietnam." In April 1963, the tripartite coalition government falls apart when Pathet Lao representatives pull out. Military situation remains stalemated until 1969 when Pathet Lao goes on offensive in effort that results in Communist control of nearly 80 percent of Lao territory. In 1973, US persuades Vientiane government to accept cease-fire in conjunction with cease-fires in neighboring Vietnam, Cambodia. A year later another coalition government is formed but lasts only a year before Pathet Lao takes complete control, forms Lao Democratic People's Republic. At that time US cuts off all economic and military aid. (Stevenson 180–81; Stuart-Fox preface)

GOALS OF SENDER COUNTRY

Charles A. Stevenson
"Opposition to a coalition government in Laos was a basic feature of American policy during the Eisenhower administration. Politically, the Republicans could not tolerate the 'loss' of further territory to Communist domination. . . ." (Stevenson 41)

"Although the chief policymakers were agreed on the desirability of a neutral government headed by Souvanna Phouma, they wanted to avoid the impression of being defeated militarily by the Communists." (Stevenson 170)

Arthur J. Dommen
Assistant Secretary of State for Far Eastern Affairs J. Graham Parsons is sent to Laos during fall 1960 crisis. In conversations with government officials, "he made it unmistakably clear that resumption of American cash-grant aid to Souvanna Phouma's government depended on the attitude Souvanna Phouma took toward pending political questions, most urgent of which was the negotiations with the Pathet Lao that had commenced the previous day."

Parsons' objectives were: to terminate negotiations with Pathet Lao; to open negotiations with General Phoumi; to move capital to Luang Prabang, presumably to enhance conservative influence of King Savang Vatthana who resides there. (Dommen 159)

Arthur M. Schlesinger, Jr.
Under President Kennedy, goal in Laos shifts: "As [Kennedy] thought aloud, it was evident that he hoped to steer the course between intervention and retreat and end up somehow with neutralization." (Schlesinger 310)

RESPONSE OF TARGET COUNTRY

Thai blockade
"Prince Souvanna's decision to open diplomatic relations with the Soviet Union and his subsequent request for a Soviet airlift of rice and fuel, as well as for other badly needed supplies, to Vientiane, was partially the result of Thailand's refusal to permit the transport of these goods across its soil." (Neuchterlein 173)

1960 aid cut-off
On 14 October "Prince Souvanna Phouma, premier of Laos, told the United States . . . that he would not change his policy of neutrality and that if the United States did not like the policy he would have to seek assistance elsewhere. 'Elsewhere' was taken to mean the Soviet Union." (*New York Times*, 15 October 1960, A1)

Neutrality
"Laos was too weak and divided to oppose all comers. The only alternative lay in joining forces with one or another foreign power. Under these circumstances, all attempts at neutrality were doomed to failure." (Stuart-Fox 5)

ATTITUDE OF OTHER COUNTRIES

Soviet Union
USSR decides to make airlift in winter of 1960 demonstration of friendship, does not require any payment. (Neuchterlein 175)

USSR declares in note on 13 December 1960: "The United States Government . . . makes extensive use of Thailand, its ally in the military SEATO pact, which makes the territory of its country available for active military operations against the Government units and effects a brutal blockade of Laos. . . . All this is a glaring violation by the Government of the United States of Article 12 of the Final Declaration of the Geneva Conference on Indochina. . . ." (Dommen 173)

In 1961–62: "There still remained the thin hope that the Russian interest sprang less from a desire to get in themselves than to get the Chinese out and that they might eventually accept the policy of neutralization." (Schlesinger 309)

Thailand
"During the 1950s Thailand's policy toward Laos changed from a desire to reestablish Thai control to a determination to prevent Laos from falling prey to any hostile country. Thailand was convinced by 1954 that the greatest threat to its security was from Communist China and North Vietnam . . . it was, therefore, imperative for Thailand that Laos be preserved as a buffer zone between the Communist and non-Communist areas of Southeast Asia." (Neuchterlein 139)

Following Kong Le's coup in August 1960: "The Thai government never officially refused the requests of the Vientiane government to permit food to flow freely across the Mekong, but it found a number of pretexts to avoid reopening the border. . . ." (Neuchterlein 173)

"[The blockade] was a product of Marshal Sarit's [Thanarat, distant relative of General Phoumi and prime minister of Thailand] opposition to Souvanna Phouma's government, which he feared would make a deal with the Communists and outflank him." (Dommen 155)

ECONOMIC IMPACT

Observed Economic Statistics

Structure of US aid program: "Each month the United States Government made a multimillion-dollar deposit in a New York bank account in the name of the Royal Lao Government. The latter then placed in circulation the equivalent value in kip, which was officially pegged at 35 to the dollar. The dollars were used to pay for hard goods that were then imported into Laos by commercial importers under a licensing system operated by the Lao Government." (Dommen 103)

Magnitude of aid program: "Exact amounts of aid given in this first five-year period (1955–59) are almost impossible to determine. Three different sources, all supposedly drawing upon the same information supplied by the foreign aid agency, provide inexplicably differing figures. . . . Some of these variations may come from distinctions between obligations and actual expenditures or from changing definitions of what constitutes each category. Even if the published figures could be reconciled, the picture would still be incomplete, for the Central Intelligence Agency spent large sums for its activities in Laos." (Stevenson 38)

Most sources estimate that $300 million in assistance is transferred to Laos from 1955–59. Of this, one source contends only $7 million is for technical cooperation, economic development. Another source estimates that $18.7 million is delivered as "project assistance" but that half of this is spent on militarily related projects such as improving roads and airports, only $1.3 million on agricultural projects. (Schlesinger 304; George 38; Stevenson 37)

Officially, US economic and military aid to Laos 1955–61 is $267.1 million and $91.4 million, respectively. In 1962 economic aid dips to $29.4 million while military aid soars to $43.1 million. (AID)

Summer 1962: "The spread between the official kip rate of 80 to the dollar and the black market rate was steadily growing. At the end of 1961, the black market rate stood at 120 to the dollar. Then, following the cutoff of US cash-grants (in February 1962), Boun Oum placed in circulation large quantities of paper money not backed by dollar deposits in the United States. By the summer of 1963, the progressive reduction in dollar backing of the kip notes in circulation (which had increased in the same period from 2.7 billion kip to 6.1 billion kip) had pushed the black market rate to 360 to the dollar." (Stevenson 169)

Vientiane Consumer Price Index—1959: 100; 1961: 115; 1963: 268. (Stevenson 169)

In response to January 1962 temporary aid suspension, Lao government stops selling foreign currency, imposes wage and price controls. (Stevenson 169)

Calculated Economic Impact

	Annual cost to target country
Suspension of US aid for one month in 1956, four months in 1958, one month in 1960, four months in 1962 (nonmilitary aid only); welfare loss valued at 100 percent of reduced transfers—annual costs calculated as average of aggregate cutbacks during 1956–62.	$5 million

Relative Magnitudes

Gross indicators of Lao economy	
Lao GNP (1961)	$120 million
Lao population (1961)	2.4 million
Annual effect of sanctions related to gross indicators	
Percentage of GNP	4.2
Per capita	$2.08
Lao trade with US as percentage of total trade	
Exports	negl.
Imports	4
Ratio of US GNP (1961: $524.6 billion) to Lao GNP (1961: $120 million)	4,372

ASSESSMENT

Roger Hilsman

"Many of the Lao leaders themselves were reluctant [to have the US support its army]—and they might have been even more reluctant if they had fully realized how much power the United States would acquire in internal Lao affairs through financing the army. For by merely withholding the monthly payment to the troops, the United States could create the conditions for toppling any Lao Government whose policies it opposed. As it turned out, in fact, the United States used this weapon twice—to bring down the government of one Lao leader and to break the will of another." (Hilsman 111)

Charles A. Stevenson

On 1956 aid suspension: "The aid was resumed after a month; its suspension had not had a significant impact on the Laotian economy or politics . . . [L]acking much leverage with its aid program or its embassy's importunings, the United States increased its direct, but covert, intervention in Laotian political affairs." (Stevenson 43)

On 1958 suspension that led to Prince Souvanna's resignation: "The aid suspension and American opposition were too much [for Souvanna] to overcome." (Stevenson 66)

Barry M. Blechman and Steven S. Kaplan

On 1962 suspension of aid to General Phoumi: "Under the combined pressure of military defeat [the fall of Nam Tha], continued economic and political pressure from the Kennedy administration, and a clear signal that US troops in Thailand would not assist the Lao army, Phoumi capitulated to US demands that he join the proposed Laotian coalition government on terms dictated by Souvanna Phouma." (Blechman 162)

Arthur J. Dommen

On effect of Thai blockade: "Souvanna Phouma's difficulties were measurably increased by Thailand's imposition of an unofficial blockade on Vientiane. . . . By far the greater portion of Vientiane's supplies came across the Mekong from Thailand so that cutting off this traffic soon had a drastic effect on the capital's economy. The railhead in the Thailand town of Nong Khai was particularly important in the supplying of petroleum products which accounted for 26 percent of the value of Laos' total imports. Insofar as it affected the movement of rice and vegetables, the blockade was not completely effective. . . . Although rice prices on the Vientiane market nearly doubled during the blockade, no serious shortages ever developed." (Dommen 155)

AUTHORS' SUMMARY

Overall assessment	Assigned scores
☐ Policy result, scaled from 1 (failed) to 4 (success)	3
☐ Sanctions contribution, scaled from 1 (none) to 4 (significant)	3
☐ Success score (policy result *times* sanctions contribution), scaled from 1 (outright failure) to 16 (significant success)	9

Political and economic variables

☐ Companion policies: J (covert), Q (quasi-military), or R (regular military)	J

Political and economic variables (continued)	*Assigned scores*
☐ International cooperation with sender, scaled from 1 (none) to 4 (significant)	2
☐ International assistance to target: A (if present)	—
☐ Sanctions period (years)	6
☐ Economic health and political stability of target, scaled from 1 (distressed) to 3 (strong)	1
☐ Presanction relations between sender and target, scaled from 1 (antagonistic) to 3 (cordial)	3
☐ Type of sanction: X (export), M (import), F (financial)	F
☐ Cost to sender, scaled from 1 (net gain) to 4 (major loss)	1

Comments

By manipulating aid flows, on which Laotian government was highly dependent, US achieves modest success during period 1956–62 in its goals, initially of minimizing Communist influence in Laos and, later of stabilizing and neutralizing country.

BIBLIOGRAPHY

Agency for International Development. *Overseas Loans and Grants*. Various issues.

Blechman, Barry M., and Stephen S. Kaplan. 1978. *Force without War: U.S. Armed Forces as a Political Instrument*. Washington: Brookings Institution.

Dommen, Arthur J. 1971. *Conflict in Laos: The Politics of Neutralization*. Rev. ed. New York: Praeger.

Fall, Bernard B. 1969. *Anatomy of a Crisis: The Laotian Crisis 1960–61*. Garden City, NY: Doubleday.

George, Alexander L., David K. Hall, and William E. Simons. 1971. *The Limits of Coercive Diplomacy: Laos, Cuba, and Vietnam*. Boston: Little, Brown & Co.

Hilsman, Roger. 1967. *To Move a Nation: The Politics of Foreign Policy in the Administration of John F. Kennedy*. Garden City, NY: Doubleday.

Neuchterlein, Donald E. 1965. *Thailand and the Struggle for Southeast Asia*. Ithaca, NY: Cornell University Press.

Schlesinger, Arthur M., Jr. 1965. *A Thousand Days*. Boston: Houghton Mifflin.

Stevenson, Charles A. 1972. *The End of Nowhere: American Policy Toward Laos Since 1954*. Boston: Beacon Press.

Stuart-Fox, Martin, ed. 1982. *Contemporary Laos*. New York: St. Martin's Press.

Case 57–1 Indonesia v. Netherlands

(1957–62: West Irian)

CHRONOLOGY OF KEY EVENTS

December 1949 — Netherlands transfers sovereignty over territory of Dutch East Indies to Republic of the United States of Indonesia. Territory of West New Guinea (West Irian) is excluded because of difficulties of administering "a wild, sparsely populated jungle inhabited by some 800,000 primitive Papuans." Indonesia expects Dutch control of area to be temporary. It is agreed that meeting will be held within a year, with Dutch expecting to discuss *whether* sovereignty over West Irian will be transferred, Indonesians expecting to discuss *how*. (Jones 175)

1950 — Meetings between Indonesians, Dutch in March and December fail to produce agreement on West Irian. (Jones 176–77)

November 1951 — Dutch parliament accepts constitutional amendment in which West New Guinea is defined geographically as being part of Kingdom of the Netherlands. (Jones 177)

1954–57 — Indonesia submits West Irian issue four times to UN but cannot muster two-thirds support necessary to pass resolution on it. (Jones 177)

Summer 1957 — President Ahmed Sukarno threatens "drastic action" if Indonesian resolution in UN General Assembly aimed "at a renewal of discussion between the two contesting parties" is rejected. (Jones 184)

November 1957 — Indonesian resolution does not pass. In December, Sukarno forces Dutch business out of country; this action affects some 40,000 Dutch citizens, more than $2 billion in property. (Jones 184–85)

14 April 1960 — Indonesia bans all Dutch ships from its ports after 6 June either for picking up or for delivering passengers or goods. The minister of sea communications, Dr. Abdulmutalib, says action is "a further consequence of the Indonesian campaign for the liberation of West Irian from Dutch colonial domination." (*Keesing's* 17433)

| 17 August 1960 | Indonesia breaks diplomatic relations with Netherlands, implies that, since all other efforts have failed, military force may be tried next. (Jones 188) |

| Winter 1960–61 | After US turndown on assistance, General Abdul Haris Nasution, defense minister, travels to USSR in search of assistance, is "given the red-carpet treatment." (Jones 189–90) |

| 19 December 1961 | Sukarno issues his "Trikora Command" calling for "total mobilization for the purpose of regaining West Irian." In January, Dutch, Indonesian naval vessels clash in waters between Indonesia, West Irian; Indonesian paratroopers are "dropped into the inhospitable jungles of New Guinea." Netherlands then indicates willingness to reopen negotiations without previous insistence that self-determination be prior condition. (Jones 204) |

| 15 August 1962 | Agreement finally is reached under which Indonesia will undertake administrative control of West Irian as of 1 May 1963. (Jones 212) |

| 13 March 1963 | UN Secretary General U Thant announces Indonesia and Netherlands have agreed to resumption of diplomatic relations. (*Keesing's* 19308) |

| 4 July 1963 | Indonesia announces lifting of 1960 ban on Dutch shipping in its waters in order to improve direct trade relations between the countries. (*Keesing's* 19591) |

GOALS OF SENDER COUNTRY

Robert C. Bone, Jr.
"For Indonesia, so long as the Dutch flag flies over West Irian the national revolution is not fulfilled, brother Indonesians yet remain under colonial rule and the former colonial rulers still hold a base for possible subversive activities at the nation's very door step." (Bone ix)

Howard P. Jones
"It was a nationalistic issue to which all Indonesians reacted alike. It was a nation-building issue; it brought Indonesians together. Finally, it was a powerful political weapon for Sukarno, allowing him to consolidate power in his own hands." (Jones 188)

RESPONSE OF TARGET COUNTRY

1957
Following ejection of Dutch businesses from Indonesia ". . . the Dutch continued adamant, unwilling even to discuss the matter with the Indonesians." (Jones 188)

1961
"As [the Dutch] saw it, Sukarno, after all, had driven over 40,000 Dutchmen out of Indonesia and confiscated property estimated at upwards of two billion dollars in an effort to force them to turn over West Irian. They had not yielded then; they were not about to do so now." (Jones 201)

ATTITUDE OF OTHER COUNTRIES

Soviet Union, People's Republic of China
"For more than a decade, the West Irian issue constituted Sukarno's measure of the friendship of foreign powers. Soviet Russia and Communist China early appreciated and exploited this by giving vigorous public support to Indonesia's claim to West Irian." (Jones 174)

Following General Nasution's visit to USSR in January 1961, Indonesia receives some $400 million in arms from Soviets. "Their total arms assistance to Indonesia would reach more than $1 billion before they were through." (Jones 190)

United States
". . . American government sympathies were with the Dutch. We would support what the Dutch wanted to the extent consistent with our public position of neutrality on the issue." (Jones 178)

"In sum, we [the US] had sufficient foresight to realize it was out of the question for us to take a position in support of Dutch, or any other nation's retention of a colony. In the view of John Foster Dulles and most other men in the administration in 1957–58, however, it was not the job of American diplomacy to pass on the question of right or wrong in the issue of sovereignty over West Irian. American policy therefore followed what seemed a sound and pragmatic course in remaining neutral about an issue in which right and wrong were somewhat obscure and the national interest seemed not to be directly concerned." (Jones 181)

ECONOMIC IMPACT

Observed Economic Statistics

"The mass confiscation of Dutch estates, banks, shipping firms and other institutions resulted in an immediate and serious deterioration of the Indonesian economic situation. . . . [On 11 December 1957] President Sukarno warned the Indonesian people that they would have to face shortages of food, clothing and other vital commodities in the 'struggle for West Irian.'" (*Keesing's* 15931)

Seventy percent of estate production and inter-island shipping were in Dutch hands at time of nationalization. (*Keesing's* 15931)

Under Dutch, those estates yield 28 percent of Indonesian exports. Netherlands takes 19 percent of total Indonesian exports. (*Keesing's* 15931)

Dutch trade with Indonesia (million dollars)

	Exports	*Imports*
1955	68.0	97.0
1956	83.0	115.9
1957	72.0	119.5
1958	29.2	81.0
1959	25.7	71.5
1960	26.3	62.1
1961	13.0	40.5

Dutch trade with Indonesia *(continued)*

	Exports	Imports
1962	4.1	19.2
1963	8.7	15.3
1964	11.9	95.1
1965	32.6	110.5
1966	33.1	97.6
1967	45.8	97.9

Source: IMF.

Calculated Economic Impact

	Annual cost to target country
Reduction in trade with Indonesia; welfare loss valued at 30 percent of reduced trade from average levels of 1955–57.	$36 million
Expropriation of Dutch assets in Indonesia; welfare loss estimated at 25 percent of value, amortized over 15 years.	33 million
Total	$69 million

Relative Magnitudes

Gross indicators of Dutch economy	
Dutch GNP (1957)	$9.3 billion
Dutch population (1957)	11 million
Annual effect of sanctions related to gross indicators	
Percentage of GNP	0.7
Per capita	$6.27
Dutch trade with Indonesia as percentage of total trade	
Exports (1957)	2
Imports (1957)	3
Ratio of Indonesian GNP (1967: $5.4 billion) to Dutch GNP (1967: $22.7 billion)	0.2

ASSESSMENT

J. A. C. Mackie
"A combination of diplomacy, threats, bluff and infiltrations of regular and irregular forces was utilized to stretch the resources of the enemy to the limit. . . . In December

1961 the campaign to recover West Irian was dramatically intensified after a decade of unsuccessful pressure to induce the Dutch to discuss the Indonesian claim. . . . By late 1961 Sukarno was beginning to threaten open military action to regain the territory if the Dutch would not negotiate." (Mackie 99)

AUTHORS' SUMMARY

Overall assessment	Assigned scores
□ Policy result, scaled from 1 (failed) to 4 (success)	4
□ Sanctions contribution, scaled from 1 (none) to 4 (significant)	2
□ Success score (policy result *times* sanctions contribution), scaled from 1 (outright failure) to 16 (significant success)	8

Political and economic variables

□ Companion policies: J (covert), Q (quasi-military), or R (regular military)	R
□ International cooperation with sender, scaled from 1 (none) to 4 (significant)	2
□ International assistance to target: A (if present)	—
□ Sanctions period (years)	5
□ Economic health and political stability of target, scaled from 1 (distressed) to 3 (strong)	3
□ Presanction relations between sender and target, scaled from 1 (antagonistic) to 3 (cordial)	2
□ Type of sanction: X (export), M (import), F (financial)	F, X, M
□ Cost to sender, scaled from 1 (net gain) to 4 (major loss)	2

BIBLIOGRAPHY

Bone, Robert C., Jr. 1958. *The Dynamics of the Western New Guinea Problem.* Monograph series, Modern Indonesia Project. Ithaca, NY: Cornell University.

International Monetary Fund. *Direction of Trade Statistics.* Various issues.

Jones, Howard P. 1971. *Indonesia: The Possible Dream.* New York: Harcourt Brace Jovanovich.

Keesing's Contemporary Archives. 1957–58, 1959–60, 1963–64.

Mackie, J. A. C. 1974. *Kronfrontasi: The Indonesia-Malaysia Dispute 1963–66.* London: Oxford University Press.

Case 57–2 France v. Tunisia

(1957–63: Halt Aid to Algerian Rebels)

CHRONOLOGY OF KEY EVENTS

Fall 1956   Tunisian President Habib Bourguiba visits Paris, proposes that France recognize Algeria's "right to independence" in order to stop bloodshed there. In late October Bourguiba releases joint statement with Sultan of Morocco expressing their "entire solidarity with the Algerian people in their efforts to obtain their freedom." (*Keesing's* 15329)

22 October 1956   Five Algerian nationalist leaders, on Moroccan plane en route to Tunis, are intercepted, arrested by French authorities. Bourguiba denounces French actions, recalls Tunisian ambassador in Paris. Diplomatic relations are restored in December. (*Keesing's* 15329–31)

4–6 January 1957   Bourguiba speech in support of Algerian nationalists prompts French Secretary of State for Foreign Affairs, Maurice Faure, to postpone a planned trip to Tunis. (*Keesing's* 15376)

April 1957   Economic agreement is signed in which France agrees to provide $34.6 million to Tunisia in several installments. (*Keesing's* 15885; *New York Times*, 23 May 1957, A1)

20 May 1957   France decides to withhold first aid payment of $5.8 million "because of Tunisia's present attitude." Tunisia responds that such action releases it from its obligations under Franco-Tunisian economic and financial convention signed in June 1955. (*Keesing's* 15885; *New York Times*, 23 May 1957, A1; *Times* [London], 23 May 1957, 12)

Late May 1957   French, Tunisian troops clash on Tunisian-Algerian border. Tunisia indicates desire to open negotiations on withdrawal of French forces. (*Keesing's* 15885)

Summer 1957   France announces it has right to pursue fleeing Algerian rebels into Tunisian territory, exercises that "right" for first time in early September. (*Keesing's* 15886)

August 1957   France refuses Tunisian request for arms, fearing they would end up in Algeria. Following hints by Bourguiba that he might turn to Soviets, US, UK provide arms to Tunisia. (*Keesing's* 15883)

| 8 February 1958 | French forces bomb small Tunisian village on Algerian border following antiaircraft attacks against French planes believed to have originated in that area. Raid toll is 69 dead, 130 wounded. Bourguiba recalls ambassador from France, forbids all French troop movements, demands evacuation of French forces, and appeals to UN Security Council. (*Keesing's* 16203–4) |

June 1958 Newly installed French Prime Minister, Charles de Gaulle, exchanges conciliatory notes with Bourguiba. Shortly thereafter, agreement is reached on withdrawal of some French forces in Tunisia, and diplomatic relations are restored. (*Keesing's* 16304)

27 February 1961 Bourguiba visits de Gaulle in France to discuss Algerian problem. (*Keesing's* 18091)

6 July 1961 Tunisia asks France to enter negotiations leading to evacuation of French forces from naval base at Tunisian port of Bizerte. This is one of four main bases for French. (*Keesing's* 18341)

17 July 1961 Tunisia announces Bizerte base will be blockaded. (*Keesing's* 18341)

19 July 1961 France refuses to negotiate under pressure, sends reinforcements to Bizerte. Violent clashes follow; French forces occupy most of town. (*Keesing's* 18341)

20 July 1961 Tunisia appeals to UN Security Council and breaks diplomatic relations with France. Security Council is unable to agree on cease-fire resolution. (*Keesing's* 18344)

21 August 1961 France boycotts UN General Assembly special meeting convened to discuss "Bizerte crisis." (*Keesing's* 18346)

29 September 1961 French, Tunisian officials reach agreement on withdrawal of French forces to positions held prior to outbreak of fighting on 19 July. Negotiations on eventual evacuation of all French forces at Bizerte continue into 1962. (*Keesing's* 18349; 18609)

20 July 1962 Resumption of Franco-Tunisian relations is announced in Paris. "Tension between the two countries had been eased by the French Government's decision to evacuate the base installations at Menzel-Bourguiba which were formally handed over to Tunisia on June 30, and subsequently by the cease-fire in Algeria and the achievement of Algerian independence." (*Keesing's* 18948)

9 August 1963 France agrees to resume economic aid to Tunisia, pledges £14 million for current year, half in long-term loans, half in export credits. (*Keesing's* 19696)

GOALS OF SENDER COUNTRY

French Foreign Ministry communiqué
Suspension of economic aid: ". . . had, however, 'once again brought to the Tunisian Government's notice the inadmissible character of the assistance which it was giving or

allowing to be given to the Algerian rebellion. In particular, it had been emphasized that it was 'inconceivable that French aid to Tunisia should directly or indirectly assist France's enemies. . . . '" (*Keesing's* 15885)

RESPONSE OF TARGET COUNTRY

Official Tunisian statement
Following cut-off of economic aid: "When speaking of assistance given to the Algerians, and demanding Tunisia's neutrality, the French Government fails to take into account that its own troops stationed in Tunisian territory use the country as an operational base, contrary to the wishes of the government of Tunisia. The economic and financial convention between France and Tunisia signed on June 3, 1955, stipulated that aid from France was an inseparable counterpart of the economic concessions freely agreed to by Tunisia. As a French Government has considered it unnecessary to carry out its commitments in this matter, Tunisia is released from the obligations which she had accepted as a counterpart." (*Keesing's* 15885)

ATTITUDE OF OTHER COUNTRIES

United States
"A statement issued in Washington on November 14 [1957] said that Tunisia, as a free and independent member of the UN, had the right to provide for her internal security and self-defense. Tunisia had freely chosen to identify herself with the West, and Western nations should provide her with an opportunity to purchase arms from Western sources." (*Keesing's* 15883)

United Kingdom
"In a statement on November 27 [1957] to the House of Commons, [Prime Minister Harold] Macmillan said that Britain [in discussions in Paris] had given no assurances that no further arms would be supplied to Tunisia, but had expressed the hope that they would normally be supplied by France." (*Keesing's* 15884)

ECONOMIC IMPACT

Observed Economic Statistics

In 1957 France ". . . cut off the financial subsidy of 12 billions [francs] provided for under the 1955 convention, leaving Tunisia without resources and undoubtedly in the worst imbroglio of her history. . . ." (Rossi 66)

"The crisis of 1959 was surmounted because the Tunisian people's courage was supplemented by the invaluable American contribution, which replaced the help which the former protecting power had cut off: it amounted to 5.7 million dinars in 1957, 9.2 million in 1958 and 14 million dinars in 1959." (Rossi 68)

Exchange rate: (dinars per US dollar) 1957: 0.36; 1958: 0.42; 1959: 0.42.

Tunisian trade with France (million dollars)

	Exports	Imports
1955	58.7	136.0
1956	61.9	134.3
1957	90.3	122.3
1958	95.0	110.4
1959	72.0	100.2
1960	62.5	113.5
1961	60.6	113.1
1962	61.3	113.4

Source: IMF.

Calculated Economic Impact

	Annual cost to target country
Suspension of French aid to Tunisia from May 1957 to August 1963; welfare loss estimated at 90 percent of lost transfers.	$31 million
Offset	
Increase in US economic aid to Tunisia; welfare gain valued at 90 percent of average annual transfers from 1957–59.	(24 million)
Total	$7 million

Relative Magnitudes

Gross indicators of Tunisian economy	
Tunisian GNP (1960)	$798 million
Tunisian population (1957)	4 million
Annual effect of sanctions related to gross indicators	
Percentage of GNP	0.9
Per capita	$1.75
Tunisian trade with France as percentage of total trade	
Exports (1957)	61
Imports (1957)	70
Ratio of French GNP (1960: $60.9 billion) to Tunisian GNP (1960: $798 million)	76

ASSESSMENT

Wilfred Knapp
". . . the common cause of North African independence linked Tunisia to the Algerian national movement in an alliance which the Tunisians would not sacrifice for the sake of commercial agreements with France." (Knapp 175)

AUTHORS' SUMMARY

Overall assessment	Assigned scores
□ Policy result, scaled from 1 (failed) to 4 (success)	1
□ Sanctions contribution, scaled from 1 (none) to 4 (significant)	1
□ Success score (policy result *times* sanctions contribution), scaled from 1 (outright failure) to 16 (significant success)	1

Political and economic variables

□ Companion policies: J (covert), Q (quasi-military), or R (regular military)	R
□ International cooperation with sender, scaled from 1 (none) to 4 (significant)	1
□ International assistance to target: A (if present)	A
□ Sanctions period (years)	6
□ Economic health and political stability of target, scaled from 1 (distressed) to 3 (strong)	2
□ Presanction relations between sender and target, scaled from 1 (antagonistic) to 3 (cordial)	3
□ Type of sanction: X (export), M (import), F (financial)	F
□ Cost to sender, scaled from 1 (net gain) to 4 (major loss)	1

BIBLIOGRAPHY

International Monetary Fund. *Direction of Trade Statistics*. Various issues.
Keesing's Contemporary Archives. 1957–58, 1961–62, 1963–64.
Knapp, Wilfred. 1970. *Tunisia*. London: Thames and Hudson.
Rossi, Pierre, and Ronald Matthews, trans. 1967. *Bourguiba's Tunisia*. Tunis: Éditions Karia.

Case 58–1 USSR v. Finland
(1958–59: Nightfrost Crisis)

CHRONOLOGY OF KEY EVENTS

April 1948   Soviet-Finnish Treaty of Friendship, Cooperation and Mutual Assistance obligates Finland to maintain "friendly" relations with USSR. (Forster 147)

1948–58   Finnish President J. K. Paasikivi advances doctrine that his country will "do nothing in conflict with the interests of the Soviet Union." Consistent with Paasikivi line, Finland accepts no Marshall Plan aid, holds only observer status in Nordic Council until 1955. (Garfinkle 26–27)

1958   Finnish imports from USSR decline (autos, in particular, drop from 7,960 in 1957 to 1,200 in 1958) as Finland enlarges trade with Western Europe. Finland asks USSR for partial hard currency settlement of ruble surplus. (Forster 148)

July 1958   Parliamentary elections lead to formation of cabinet by Social Democratic Prime Minister Karl August Fagerholm, which is criticized immediately in Soviet press. (Vayrynen 100)

October 1958   USSR lodges official protest against political cartoonist's portrayal of Nikita Khrushchev, first secretary of the Communist party; requests Finland block publication of memoirs of an anti-Soviet Finnish Communist. (Forster 148)

Late 1958   USSR recalls ambassador from Helsinki; delays signing of fishing rights agreement for Gulf of Finland; suspends discussions on ruble credit; walks out of talks on lease of Saimaa Canal; suspends planning for power plant in USSR to serve Finland; cancels scientific, technical, trade meetings; suspends imports from Finland; postpones payment of 23 million-ruble debt to Finland. (Garfinkle 34)

4 December 1958   Prime Minister Fagerholm, *"persona non grata* with the Russians," resigns. (Forster 149)

January 1959 President Urho Kekkonen visits Leningrad, further assures Khrushchev of Finland's "good neighborliness." Trade negotiations, commerce resume. (Forster 149)

GOALS OF SENDER COUNTRY

Raimo Vayrynen
"The Soviet Union *perceived* that Finland was moving away from her traditional foreign policy line (the so-called Paasikivi line) through the Nordic customs union into the arms of NATO states." (Vayrynen 95)

RESPONSE OF TARGET COUNTRY

Adam M. Garfinkle
As conciliatory gesture, in late 1958 Finland agrees to purchase additional 450,000 tons of Soviet petroleum. (Garfinkle 34)

President Kekkonen
Radio address in mid-December 1958: "I am compelled to state—after weighing each word carefully—that recently the foundations of the policy of good neighborliness between Finland and the Soviet Union have been undermined in different ways." He calls for strict adherence to Paasikivi line. (Forster 149)

ECONOMIC IMPACT

Observed Economic Statistics

In September 1957 Finland devalues mark by 39 percent, removes compulsory licensing requirements on imports from West. (Vayrynen 97)

In winter 1958, Finnish unemployment reaches record 100,000; unemployment relief becomes largest item in Finnish budget. (Forster 149; Vloyantes 97)

"The cost of the [Soviet] boycott to Finland was altogether 1.9 billion marks, or 4 percent of Finland's total exports to the Soviet Union in that year." (Vayrynen 106)

Finnish trade (million dollars)

	Exports		Imports	
	World	*USSR*	*World*	*USSR*
1957	838	169	901	159
1958	775	143	729	138
1959	835	149	835	157

Source: IMF.

Calculated Economic Impact

	Annual cost to target country
Suspension of exports to USSR for about 2 months; welfare loss estimated at 30 percent of trade (payment in nonconvertible rubles).	$45 million

Relative Magnitudes

Gross indicators of Finnish economy	
Finnish GNP (1958)	$4 billion
Finnish population (1958)	4.4 million
Annual effect of sanctions related to gross indicators	
Percentage of GNP	1.1
Per capita	$10.23
Finnish trade with USSR as percentage of total trade	
Exports (1958)	19
Imports (1958)	19
Ratio of USSR GNP (1958: $234 billion) to Finnish GNP (1958: $4 billion)	58

ASSESSMENT

Raimo Vayrynen
"Conditions in Finnish foreign trade were quite exposed to the effective influence of economic sanctions." (Vayrynen 108)

". . . the Soviet Union used means of influence quite selectively, let us say instrumentally. She began with discontinuance of negotiations, went on with the recall of her ambassador and terminated with the selective economic boycott. . . . Finland was also at that time to some extent, at least psychologically, isolated." (Vayrynen 119–20)

". . . the resignation of the Fagerholm cabinet and the obvious political effects of sanctions offered the Soviet Union a clear sign of her success. . . ." (Vayrynen 118)

AUTHORS' SUMMARY

Overall assessment	Assigned scores
☐ Policy result, scaled from 1 (failed) to 4 (success)	4
☐ Sanctions contribution, scaled from 1 (none) to 4 (significant)	4
☐ Success score (policy result *times* sanctions contribution), scaled from 1 (outright failure) to 16 (significant success)	16

Political and economic variables	Assigned scores
☐ Companion policies: J (covert), Q (quasi-military), or R (regular military)	—
☐ International cooperation with sender, scaled from 1 (none) to 4 (significant)	1
☐ International assistance to target: A (if present)	—
☐ Sanctions period (years)	1
☐ Economic health and political stability of target, scaled from 1 (distressed) to 3 (strong)	2
☐ Presanction relations between sender and target, scaled from 1 (antagonistic) to 3 (cordial)	3
☐ Type of sanction: X (export), M (import), F (financial)	F, X, M
☐ Cost to sender, scaled from 1 (net gain) to 4 (major loss)	2

BIBLIOGRAPHY

Forster, Kent. 1960. "The Finnish-Soviet Crisis of 1958–1959." 15 *International Journal* (Spring): 147–50.

Garfinkle, Adam M. 1978. *"Finlandization": A Map to a Metaphor*. Foreign Policy Research Institute Monograph 24. Philadelphia: FPRI.

International Monetary Fund. *Direction of Trade Statistics*. Various issues.

Vayrynen, Raimo. 1969. "A Case Study of Sanctions: Finland–The Soviet Union in 1958–59." In *International Sanctions: Theory and Practice*, ed. Peter Wallensteen. Department of Peace and Conflict Research, report no. 1. Uppsala, Sweden: Uppsala University.

Vloyantes, John N. 1975. *Silk Glove Hegemony: Finnish-Soviet Relations, 1944–1974*. Kent, Ohio: Kent State University Press.

Case 60–1   US v. Dominican Republic
(1960–62: Trujillo)

CHRONOLOGY OF KEY EVENTS

16 August 1930	Rafael Trujillo assumes power as president, establishes a regime of oppression and terror. (Brown-John 181; Rodman, chaps. 9, 10)
1950–59	Trujillo builds "network of terror" to eliminate opposition exiles abroad; incidents include notorious Galindez case in which an exile is kidnapped from New York City, allegedly murdered in Dominican Republic (DR), perhaps by Trujillo himself. (Brown-John 179; Rodman 154)
1959–60	World recession severely affects Latin America. DR sugar earnings decline 15 percent; coffee, cacao exports drop 25 percent. DR military spending of $80 million to $100 million consumes about two-thirds of budget, straining economy and starving traditional sectors. (Brown-John 183–86)
31 January 1960	Roman Catholic pastoral letter calls upon Trujillo to make internal reforms, signifying break between church, government. (Brown-John 189; Rodman 156)
1 April 1960	Trujillo formally withdraws from DR politics in favor of Joaquín Balaguer as president but maintains control of government. (Brown-John 167)
24 June 1960	Capping two decades of mutual animosity, Trujillo unsuccessfully attempts to have President Rómulo Betancourt of Venezuela assassinated. (Brown-John 197–200)
21 August 1960	In response to assassination attempt, and prompted by US, Organization of American States (OAS), acting under Rio Treaty Articles 6 and 8, recommends following measures: break diplomatic relations with DR; immediately suspend arms trade, study feasibility of suspending other trade; terminate sanctions when DR no longer threatens hemispheric peace and security. (Doxey 33; Brown-John 203–4)

| September 1960 | US revokes Cuban sugar quota of 2.42 million tons for 1960, reallocates quota principally to Latin American countries, some 322,000 tons of it to DR. Administration of President Dwight D. Eisenhower seeks legislation to enable him to withhold this windfall from DR. Prompted by well-lubricated DR lobby in Washington, House refuses to enact legislation, on grounds that: this sanction exceeds those approved by OAS; Trujillo government is stable and anti-Communist; US investments in DR might be jeopardized. As compromise, DR is permitted to ship nonquota, but authorized, sugar to US, subject to 2¢ per pound "entry fee." This costs DR some $22 million to $28 million in 1960–61. (Brown-John 170, 208, 219–29; Doxey 33; Rodman 155) |

4 January 1961   OAS votes, by bare two-thirds majority, to extend trade embargo to petroleum, trucks, spare parts. Cuba, Brazil, other countries dissent. (Brown-John 205)

30 May 1961   Trujillo is assassinated with apparent CIA involvement. Trujillo relatives, secret police direct campaign of torture and death against Trujillo's assassins, other enemies. (Doxey 34; Brown-John 167; Rodman 152–58)

19 November 1961   US fleet appears off Santo Domingo in support of Balaguer's efforts against Trujillo's brothers and son. Trujillo relatives go into exile. (Brown-John 167; Doxey 34)

17 December 1961   In response to street rioting and widespread opposition, Balaguer forms seven-member Council of State, with himself as president, announces intention to resign when OAS lifts sanctions. On 29 December, DR congress approves constitutional amendment allowing Council of State to function as provisional government; Council of State sworn in 1 January 1962. (Brown-John 171–73)

4–6 January 1962   OAS sanctions removed; US resumes diplomatic relations with DR, restores sugar quota, thereby removing 2¢/lb. "entry fee." (Brown-John 173)

22 January 1962   US extends $25 million emergency balance of payments support to DR. (Brown-John 172; Doxey 34)

GOALS OF SENDER COUNTRY

1960
Publicly proclaimed goal of US, other OAS members in August 1960 is to punish Trujillo government for intervening in affairs of Venezuela, culminating in attempted assassination of Betancourt. (Brown-John 203–4)

US also has private goals: "Thus beginning in mid-1960, the United States attempted to force major changes in the Trujillo regime, if not actually to bring it down." (Slater 1964, 273–74)

By late 1960, US has second thoughts: ". . . it appears reasonable to suggest that at some point [in US government deliberations preceding 4 January 1961 sanctions] a transition was made from effective economic sanctions to acceptable economic sanctions. The intermediary in this process was probably the US State Department [reflecting growing Latin American opposition to extension of sanctions]." (Brown-John 217)

1961
Following May 1961 assassination of Trujillo, US escalates its goals: "In order to remove all members of the Trujillo family from governmental positions, President [John F.] Kennedy promised that the economic sanctions should be withdrawn the moment the Trujillos left the country. This was paralleled by a coup in the Dominican Republic. When the Trujillo family actually left the country and elections were scheduled for 1962, President Kennedy delivered a speech on the 'most encouraging development' in the Dominican Republic and sanctions were lifted." (Wallensteen 251)

RESPONSE OF TARGET COUNTRY

Jerome Slater
"In the last year or so of his rule Trujillo had retaliated against the US sanctions by allowing increased Communist activity in the Dominican Republic. . . ." (Slater 1978, 293)

ATTITUDE OF OTHER COUNTRIES

Organization of American States
Resolution of August 1960 meets stiff resistance in OAS Council. Resulting sanctions, while collective in form, are essentially unilateral on part of US. (Brown-John 209, citing Slater 1964, 273–74)

United Nations
UN Security Council, on request from DR, takes divided view on propriety of OAS action without prior UN authorization. (*New York Times*, 10 September 1960, A1)

Europe
". . . the European states were apparently prepared, if the fourth quarter [of 1960] is any indication, to fill the vacuum created by a US suspension of [manufactures] trade. . . . In any case, whatever the reasons, the European states were clearly in a position to fill any gaps that might be left by an American suspension of trade in petroleum." (Brown-John 213, 215)

ECONOMIC IMPACT

Observed Economic Statistics

DR 1960 imports of trucks, buses, and parts from US decline from quarterly average of $193,000 first three quarters to $105,000 fourth quarter. DR imports from other sources increase from $125,000 quarterly average first three quarters to $175,000 fourth quarter. (Brown-John 212)

DR 1960 imports of petroleum oil, lubricants from all countries decline from quarterly average of $2.4 million, first three quarters to $1.8 million fourth quarter. Noticeable switch in sourcing from Caribbean colonies (Netherlands Antilles, Trinidad, and Tobago) to European mother countries (Netherlands, UK). (Brown-John 213)

DR per capita GNP drops from $293 in 1960 to $267 in 1961, suggesting that, at most, sanctions directly and indirectly reduced per capita income by $26. (Brown-John 242)

DR gold, foreign exchange reserves fall from approximately $35 million in 1959 to about $7 million beginning 1961. (Brown-John 238)

Calculated Economic Impact

	Annual cost to target country
Entry fee on sugar, valued at 100 percent.	$12.5 million
Decline in total DR petroleum oil, lubricants imports from quarterly average of $2.4 million to $1.8 million, valued at 30 percent of annualized decline.	0.7 million
Decline in gold, foreign exchange reserves of $28 million valued at 10 percent of decline.	2.8 million
Decline in DR imports of trucks, buses, parts from US, valued at 30 percent of decline.	negl.
Total	$16 million

Relative Magnitudes

Gross indicators of DR economy	
DR GNP (1960)	$850 million
DR population (1960)	2.9 million
Annual effect of sanctions related to gross indicators	
Percentage of GNP	1.9
Per capita	$5.52
DR trade with US as percentage of total trade	
Exports (1959)	53
Imports (1959)	59
Ratio of US GNP (1960: $506.5 billion) to DR GNP (1960: $850 million)	596

ASSESSMENT

C. Lloyd Brown-John
"Given the extent of bilateral trade relations between the United States and the Dominican Republic, a general trade embargo by the Americans would have had dreadful short-term consequences for the Dominicans, but the commodities sanctioned did not constitute a general trade embargo, nor did they encompass commodities for which the United States was realistically the major supplier." (Brown-John 216–17)

"Although sanctions cannot be credited exclusively with either Trujillo's or the Trujilloists' collapse, they were a significant element. They fulfilled two roles. First, they served to increase pressure upon an already troubled regime by adding to domestic difficulties and then by providing an excuse for Dominicans to blame Trujillo and Trujilloists for many more ills than could have been attributed under more usual circumstances. Second, after Trujillo's assassination, sanctions acquired an importance to Dominican political opposition groups greatly out of proportion to any identifiable economic impact." (Brown-John 251)

Peter Wallensteen
"To estimate the importance of sanctions during these confused six months [May–November 1961] is not easy, but it seems as if they had some impact on the situation and contributed to the changes in the Dominican government." (Wallensteen 251)

Jerome Slater
". . . by making the US economic pressures part of the official peacekeeping functions of an international organization, the OAS gave the Dominican opposition leaders—whose strategy was to bring to bear a maximum of external as well as internal pressures on the Balaguer regime—a degree of maneuver that nationalistic pride might otherwise have denied them. It was one thing for the Dominicans—[Juan] Bosch, [Viriato] Fiallo, [leaders of major opposition parties], and others—to plead repeatedly with the OAS to maintain sanctions against their own nation and against the wishes of their government, but it might have been quite another if they had been forced to communicate their appeals directly to the United States without the OAS screen." (Slater 1978, 299)

"In the short run US policy was remarkably successful. As a direct result of its combined economic leverage and military threats the US government was able to induce all the major Dominican actors to conform to its objectives. . . . It seems reasonable to suppose that one show of force and the accompanying threats to use it if necessary were crucial to the achievement of US objectives during the November and January crises. The economic pressures undoubtedly helped, but even though the Trujilloistas . . . understood full well that those pressures would continue if they attempted to reassert their rule, they were apparently prepared to ignore them ruthlessly, for in each case coups were averted or reversed only after the military displays." (Slater 1978, 299)

AUTHORS' SUMMARY

Overall assessment	Assigned scores
□ Policy result, scaled from 1 (failed) to 4 (success)	4
□ Sanctions contribution, scaled from 1 (none) to 4 (significant)	4

Overall assessment (continued)	*Assigned scores*
☐ Success score (policy result *times* sanctions contribution), scaled from 1 (outright failure) to 16 (significant success)	16

Political and economic variables

☐ Companion policies: J (covert), Q (quasi-military), or R (regular military)	Q, J
☐ International cooperation with sender, scaled from 1 (none) to 4 (significant)	3
☐ International assistance to target: A (if present)	—
☐ Sanctions period (years)	2
☐ Economic health and political stability of target, scaled from 1 (distressed) to 3 (strong)	1
☐ Presanction relations between sender and target, scaled from 1 (antagonistic) to 3 (cordial)	3
☐ Type of sanction: X (export), M (import), F (financial)	F, X, M
☐ Cost to sender, scaled from 1 (net gain) to 4 (major loss)	2

BIBLIOGRAPHY

Brown-John, C. Lloyd. 1975. *Multilateral Sanctions in International Law: A Comparative Analysis*. New York: Praeger.

Connell-Smith, Gordon. 1966. *The Inter-American System*. New York: Oxford University Press for Royal Institute of International Affairs.

Doxey, Margaret P. 1980. *Economic Sanctions and International Enforcement*. 2d ed. New York: Oxford University Press for Royal Institute of International Affairs.

Kurzman, Dan. 1965. *Santo Domingo: Revolt of the Damned*. New York: G. B. Putnam's Sons.

Macdonald, R. St. John. 1964. "The Organization of American States in Action." 15 *University of Toronto Law Journal* 359–429.

Rodman, Selden. 1964. *Quisqueya: A History of the Dominican Republic*. Seattle: University of Washington Press.

Schrieber, Anna P. 1973. "Economic Coercion as an Instrument of Foreign Policy: U.S. Measures against Cuba and the Dominican Republic." 25 *World Politics* (April): 387–413.

Slater, Jerome. 1964. "The United States, the Organisation of American States, and the Dominican Republic, 1961–63." 18 *International Organization* (Spring): 268–91.

———. 1970. *Intervention and Negotiation: The United States and the Dominican Republic*. New York: Harper & Row.

———. 1978. "The Dominican Republic, 1961–1966." In *Force without War: U.S. Armed Forces as a Political Instrument*, ed. Barry M. Blechman and Stephen S. Kaplan. Washington: Brookings Institution.

Wallensteen, Peter. 1968. "Characteristics of Economic Sanctions." 5 *Journal of Peace Research* 248–67.

Case 60–2   USSR v. China

(1960–70: Ideology and Nationalism)

CHRONOLOGY OF KEY EVENTS

1954–56   Chairman Mao Tse-tung of China criticizes Nikita Khrushchev, first secretary of Soviet Communist party, for embracing revisionist policies, exemplified by reconciliation with Tito, pursuit of improved relations with US, criticism of Stalin. (Ellison xvii)

November 1957   Following USSR occupation of Hungary, Mao states: "The socialist camp must have one head and that head can only be the USSR."

In previous month, the two nations had signed agreement on "new technology for national defense" that Chinese claimed committed Soviets "to supply them with a sample atomic bomb and technical information relating to its manufacture." "In agreeing to give the Chinese a sample atomic bomb, the Russians made a major contribution to the Chinese economy by enabling the Chinese to avoid a lengthy and costly research and development process that would have consumed large amounts of scarce Chinese resources." (Ellison xvii; Talbott 254; Freedman 115)

1958   Moscow criticizes Chinese Great Leap Forward; takes detached attitude toward Quemoy crisis; limits economic, military aid. Tension mounts on Sinkiang border. (Ellison xvii; Griffith xi)

June 1959   USSR cancels Sino-Soviet agreement on atomic cooperation, seemingly as accommodation to US, and because Chinese refuse to accede to Soviet demands for some control over their nuclear weapons program. In September Khrushchev visits US; USSR remains neutral in Sino-Indian border incident. (Ellison xvii, xviii; Griffith xi; Freedman 118)

April–June 1960   Chinese launch series of sharp polemical attacks against Soviet policies, charging USSR has "strayed from the true path of Leninism." This event, according to Soviets, "marked the turning point in Sino-Soviet relations." (Freedman 124)

July 1960   USSR abruptly withdraws all technicians, blueprints for plant installations; cancels aid, credits to China. (Eckstein 144–45, 153; Doxey 20)

November 1960   At Moscow meeting of Communist parties, Moscow attacks Albanian "dogmatism," China criticizes Yugoslavian "revisionism"; attacks reflect mutual Sino-Soviet ideological conflict. Nevertheless, China signs Moscow Declaration, basically backing Soviet ideological position. In spring of 1961, "a number of economic agreements are worked out." (Ellison xviii; Freedman 127)

November 1961   Premier Chou En-lai of China walks out of 22d CPSU Congress, following Khrushchev attack on Albania. USSR-China relations steadily deteriorate from 1961 to 1964. (Ellison xviii; Griffith xi)

October 1962   China denounces USSR as "adventurist" for sending missiles to Cuba and as "capitulationist," for withdrawing them. In same month, USSR initially supports China, then reverts to neutral stance in Sino-Indian border dispute. In November 1962, Eastern European Communist parties attack China. (Gittings 74; Griffith xi)

Fall 1963   In attempt to quiet China's polemics over border disputes and reverse its economic turn toward West, USSR offers to resume technical assistance, increase trade with China. "The Chinese answer to Khrushchev's offer, however, was contemptuous in tone." (Freedman 135)

Late 1964   Temporary improvement in Sino-Soviet relations follows Khrushchev's fall from power, succession of Leonid Brezhnev as Communist first secretary. (Freedman 150)

1965–69   After slight increase in trade in 1965, economic, political relations deteriorate precipitously following purge of pro-Soviet members of Chinese leadership, expulsion of Soviet diplomats during "Great Proletarian Cultural Revolution." (Freedman 151)

1966   China expels Soviet students, diplomats; USSR expels Chinese students. (Ellison xviii)

August 1968   USSR invades Czechoslovakia under banner of Brezhnev Doctrine; China denounces invasion, doctrine. (Ellison xviii–xix)

March 1969   USSR, China engage in border conflicts at confluence of Amur and Ussuri rivers. (Ellison xviii)

1970   USSR, China exchange ambassadors, sign new trade agreement, resume border negotiations. (Ellison xix)

July 1971   Henry A. Kissinger, US national security adviser, secretly flies to Peking to arrange for President Richard M. Nixon's visit; China embarks on new diplomacy of repairing fences. (Ellison xix)

GOALS OF SENDER COUNTRY

1960

Following summer 1960 disruption of economic relations: "Khrushchev's move, coming at a time of severe economic crisis in China, was a naked use of Soviet economic power to coerce the dissident camp member into obedience." (Freedman 125)

Soviet explanation for withdrawal of technicians was that Chinese first had ignored their advice, later tried to "subvert" them. (Freedman 126)

September 1963

"[T]he Soviet government issued a statement attacking the Chinese leaders for their stand on the partial nuclear test ban treaty, for their invasion of India, and for such 'dangerous experiments' as the communes and the 'Great Leap Forward'. . . . In the middle of October, however, there was an apparent change in Soviet policy toward China. Khrushchev, perhaps realizing that he would not be able to secure a sufficiently strong majority at a proposed international Communist conference either to force the Chinese to capitulate or else to excommunicate them from the international Communist movement, decided to take a more conciliatory position. . . . Part of the Soviet offer [of renewed economic assistance] may have been tied to a quid pro quo whereby the Chinese would end their polemics over the border areas acquired by the czars from China. . . . There may, however, have been another reason for this striking change in Khrushchev's policy. By August 1963, the Chinese economy had recovered sufficiently for the Chinese to place a number of orders for complete plants in the West. . . . Given Peking's economic turn to the West (and its potential political turn, as well), Khrushchev may have decided to make his offer of renewed technical aid and increased trade to arrest this development." (Freedman 132–35)

RESPONSE OF TARGET COUNTRY

Fall 1959

"The tearing up of the agreement on new technology for national defense by the leadership of the CPSU and its issuance of the statement on the Sino-Indian border clash on the eve of Khrushchev's visit to the United States were ceremonial gifts to President Dwight D. Eisenhower so as to curry favor with US imperialists and create the so-called 'Spirit of Camp David.'" (Freedman 119)

1962

"In apparent retaliation for the cut in Soviet deliveries, the Chinese ordered the closing of the Soviet consulates in Shanghai, Darien, Harbin, Urumchi, Inim in September, 1962." (Freedman 131)

1963

Anonymous Chinese spokesman, in fall of 1963: "Now you [the Soviets] have again suggested sending experts to China. To be frank, the Chinese people cannot trust you. They have just healed the wounds caused by your withdrawal of experts. . . . We would like to say in passing that, basing ourselves on the internationalist principle of mutual assistance among countries in the socialist camp, we are very concerned about the present economic situation in the Soviet Union. If you should feel the need for the help of Chinese experts in certain fields, we would be glad to send them." (Freedman 135)

ECONOMIC IMPACT

Observed Economic Statistics

In February 1950, USSR-China treaties provide for $300 million credit to China at 1 percent interest, repayable over 10 years. USSR subsequently builds 50 plants. (Eckstein 138)

First formal trade agreement between USSR, China in April 1950 sets format for subsequent agreements: bilateral trade deficits limited to 6 million rubles, any excess to be financed by long-term credits. (Eckstein 140)

Total Soviet credits 1950–55 (including unpublicized credits) amount to about $1,325 million. USSR promises total of 211 plants (later reduced to 166); target completion date of 1959. (Eckstein 142–43, 181)

After 1954 USSR refuses to grant any further capital aid to Chinese. (Freedman 111)

China completely exhausts Soviet credits by 1957; Mao's visit to Moscow produces no new credits. (Eckstein 144)

". . . without the Soviet supplies, it is doubtful whether China could have achieved the industrial production levels it reached in 1957. According to Soviet statistics, by 1957, the USSR had exported [$1.5 billion] worth of machinery and equipment to China, of which [$786 million] worth was in the form of complete plants. The willingness of the USSR to supply China with complete factories together with the technicians who knew how to set them up was unquestionably the major factor in the success of China's first five-year plan (1953–57)." (Freedman 121)

"Although in August, 1958, the USSR agreed to *sell* China another 47 plants and the necessary technical assistance to put them in operation, this was still not the economic assistance the Chinese economy needed; and although Soviet exports to China rose sharply in 1958, Chinese exports to the Soviet Union rose even more sharply as the Chinese continued to pay back previous Soviet aid." (Freedman 115)

"Between 1950 and 1960, the Soviet Union supplied China with some 10,000 technicians." (Freedman 122)

"Soviet economic pressure against China during the Khrushchev era was not restricted to the withdrawal of specialists and the gradual curtailment of trade. Other Soviet policies have included a sharp increase in trade and economic assistance to India—China's main Asian enemy—and a curtailment of economic assistance and military aid to North Korea, which was China's main Asian ally in the Sino-Soviet conflict." (Freedman 124)

In April 1961, Soviets agreed to five-year moratorium on $320 million that Chinese owed them. (Freedman 130)

Chinese trade (million dollars)

	Exports				Imports			
	USSR	Eastern Europe	Non-Communist countries†	All countries	USSR	Eastern Europe	Non-Communist countries†	All countries
1959	1,100	354	632	2,211	954	325	651	2,011
1963	412	154	712	1,699	182	89	699	1,271

† Adjusted for reexports.
Source: Eckstein 94.

China trade with USSR: imports largely capital goods, petroleum, certain metals; exports largely foodstuffs, soybeans, oilseeds, other agricultural products. (Eckstein 149)

According to F. H. Mah (cited by Eckstein 171–72) USSR exports to China are "overpriced" by 30 percent compared to USSR shipments to Eastern Europe, entailing "loss" to China of $940 million 1955–59. This interpretation is questioned by Eckstein (172–73).

In 1960, approximately 66 percent of China's external trade is conducted with Communist world; by late 1960s, that is down to only 20–25 percent. (Cohen xix, xx)

Calculated Economic Impact

	Annual cost to target country
Reduction in exports to USSR and Eastern Europe; welfare loss estimated at 20 percent of face value of trade (Note: Some of loss was offset by increased exports to West).	$44 million
Reduction in imports from USSR, Eastern Europe; welfare loss estimated at 30 percent of face value of trade.	76 million
Reduction in Soviet credits to China from levels granted during 1950–55; welfare loss estimated at 90 percent of reduced transfers less allowance for rescheduling of $320 million loan to China in 1961 (valued at annual saving of 10 percent of loan amount).	167 million
Total	$287 million

Relative Magnitudes

Gross indicators of Chinese economy	
Chinese GNP (1961)	$56 billion
Chinese population (1961)	701 million
Annual effect of sanctions related to gross indicators	
Percentage of GNP	0.5
Per capita	$0.42
Chinese trade with USSR as percentage of total trade	
Exports (1960)	42
Imports (1960)	50
Ratio of USSR GNP (1960: $247 billion) to Chinese GNP (1960: $56 billion)	4

ASSESSMENT

Robert Owen Freedman
At time of his policy shift in fall of 1963, "it seems that Khrushchev, having finally realized that his policy of economic pressure had not forced [China] to renounce its 'anti-Soviet' position, wished to prevent relations between China and Soviet bloc countries from being completely destroyed."

"Thus, although Soviet trade with China diminished, Soviet bloc trade gradually increased and, despite increasingly poor political relations, economic relations were maintained, and the Chinese did not become entirely dependent on trade with the West." (Freedman 138)

AUTHORS' SUMMARY

Overall assessment	Assigned scores
□ Policy result, scaled from 1 (failed) to 4 (success)	2
□ Sanctions contribution, scaled from 1 (none) to 4 (significant)	2
□ Success score (policy result *times* sanctions contribution), scaled from 1 (outright failure) to 16 (significant success)	4

Political and economic variables

□ Companion policies: J (covert), Q (quasi-military), or R (regular military)	Q
□ International cooperation with sender, scaled from 1 (none) to 4 (significant)	3
□ International assistance to target: A (if present)	—
□ Sanctions period (years)	10
□ Economic health and political stability of target, scaled from 1 (distressed) to 3 (strong)	3
□ Presanction relations between sender and target, scaled from 1 (antagonistic) to 3 (cordial)	3
□ Type of sanction: X (export), M (import), F (financial)	F, X, M
□ Cost to sender, scaled from 1 (net gain) to 4 (major loss)	4

BIBLIOGRAPHY

Borisov, O. B., and B. T. Koloskov. 1975. *Sino-Soviet Relations 1945–1973.* Moscow: Progress Publishers.
Cohen, Jerome Alan, Robert F. Dernberger, and John R. Garson. 1971. "Chinese Law and Sino-American Trade." In *China Trade Prospects and US Policy,* ed. Alexander Eckstein. New York: Praeger.
Doxey, Margaret P. 1980. *Economic Sanctions and International Enforcement.* 2d ed. New York: Oxford University Press for Royal Institute of International Affairs.

Eckstein, Alexander. 1966. *Communist China's Economic Growth and Foreign Trade*. New York: McGraw-Hill.

Ellison, Herbert J. 1982. *The Sino-Soviet Conflict*. Seattle: University of Washington Press.

Freedman, Robert Owen. 1970. *Economic Warfare in the Communist Bloc: A Study of Soviet Economic Pressure Against Yugoslavia, Albania, and Communist China*. New York: Praeger.

Gittings, John. 1968. *Survey of the Sino-Soviet Dispute*. London: Oxford University Press.

Griffith, William E. 1964. *The Sino-Soviet Rift*. Cambridge, Mass.: MIT Press.

Mah, F. H. October 1963. *Communist China's Foreign Trade, Price Structure and Behavior 1955–1959*. Rand Research Memorandum 3825–RC. Santa Monica, Calif.: The Rand Corp.

Perkins, Dwight. 1982. "The Economic Background and Implications for China." In *The Sino-Soviet Conflict*, ed. Herbert J. Ellison. Seattle: University of Washington Press.

Talbott, Strobe, ed. 1974. *Khrushchev Remembers: The Last Testament*. Boston: Little, Brown & Co.

Case 60–3   US v. Cuba

(1960–   : Castro)

CHRONOLOGY OF KEY EVENTS

7 January 1959 ✗ US recognizes government of President Fidel Castro. (Schreiber 390)

1960 ✗ On advice of US State Department, US oil firms in Cuba stop refining oil purchased from USSR; Cuba nationalizes refineries; President Dwight D. Eisenhower cancels most of Cuban sugar quota (prior to 1960, sales to US were 3 million tons annually, half of Cuban crop). Cuba then expropriates all US property, valued at about $1 billion, discriminates against imports of US products. (Newfarmer 128; Schreiber 386)

August 1960 ✗ US imposes partial embargo on exports to Cuba; raises Cuban issue in OAS, obtains weak general declaration. (Doxey 35)

19 October 1960 US imposes total embargo on exports to Cuba (except medicine, ✗ food), extends embargo to foreign subsidiaries of US firms, reduces Cuban sugar quota in US market to zero, blacklists vessels carrying cargo to and from Cuba from carriage of US government-financed cargo. (Doxey 35; Losman 21, 26; Lowenfeld 33)

1961 Castro acknowledges Marxist-Leninist affiliation, describes revolution ✗ as socialist, anti-imperialist. (Newfarmer 128)

January 1961 US-Cuban diplomatic relations severed. (Newfarmer 128)

April 1961 US launches unsuccessful Bay of Pigs invasion. (Schreiber 393)

January 1962 OAS declares 20 to 1 (Cuba) that adherence to Marxist-Leninist ideology is incompatible with inter-American system; two-thirds majority votes that Cuba has "voluntarily" placed itself outside OAS system. (New York Times, 31 January 1962, A1)

February–May In successive steps, US bans virtually all imports from Cuba. (Schreiber 1962 386)

| July 1962 | OAS votes 16 to 1 (4 abstentions) to suspend trade with Cuba in military goods. Cuba urges UN Security Council to suspend OAS measures; UN takes no decision. (Doxey 35; Schreiber 389) |

July 1962   OAS votes 16 to 1 (4 abstentions) to suspend trade with Cuba in military goods. Cuba urges UN Security Council to suspend OAS measures; UN takes no decision. (Doxey 35; Schreiber 389)

October 1962   US enabling legislation permits President John F. Kennedy to withhold foreign aid from countries that allow their flag ships to carry goods to or from Cuba. (Schreiber 387)

23 October 1962   In wake of missile crisis, OAS unanimously supports US "quarantine" of Cuba, authorizes members to take measures, including armed force, to ensure hemispheric security. With resolution of missile crisis, quarantine is lifted on 20 November 1962. (Doxey 36)

February 1963   Kennedy encourages maritime unions to boycott ships named on US government blacklist because of their trade with Cuba. (Lowenfeld 33; Schreiber 387)

July 1963   Invoking Trading with the Enemy Act, US freezes all Cuban assets (about $33 million). Under US pressure, NATO countries agree to embargo military items but continue economic trade with Cuba. (Doxey 37; Schreiber 388)

July 1964   Following discovery of arms cache of Cuban origin in Venezuela, and led by US and Venezuela, OAS calls for: mandatory sanctions covering all trade except food, medicine (then about $18 million annually); severing of diplomatic relations (Chile, Bolivia, Uruguay, Mexico dissent). (Doxey 37; Schreiber 389)

July 1975   OAS lifts collective sanctions; thereafter, US follows policy of licensing foreign subsidiaries of US firms to trade with Cuba. (Lowenfeld 32)

Late 1975   Cuba deploys 36,000 combat troops in Angola; US threatens military action if Cuba sends troops elsewhere, makes withdrawal of troops from Angola precondition for normalizing economic relations. (Newfarmer 129)

1977   Some Cuban troops withdraw from Angola; President Jimmy Carter proposes fishing agreement with Cuba; diplomatic interests sections opened in Havana, Washington; discussions opened on broad range of issues. (Newfarmer 129)

1978   Cuba deploys 20,000 troops in Ethiopia, MIG-23 fighter planes at home; Katangan rebels, inspired by Cuba, attack Zaire troops. (Newfarmer 129)

1979   Soviet "combat brigade" observed in Cuba. (Newfarmer 130)

1980   Flotilla of Cuban refugees from port of Mariel arrives in Florida. (Newfarmer 130)

1981   Administration of President Ronald Reagan initiates tighter economic embargo; proposes Radio Martí (anti-Castro information radio); sees Cuba as instigator of Marxist control in Nicaragua, supporter of El Salvador insurgents; characterizes Grenada as "virtual surrogate" of

Cuba; attempts to obtain Latin American cooperation against Castro. (Newfarmer 132; *Newsweek*, 11 November 1982, 49; Enders 2; *Washington Post*, 27 February 1983, A1; Shultz 1983, 37)

May 1982 US bans business, tourist travel to Cuba. (Newfarmer 33; *New York Times*, 26 February 1983, A23)

August 1982 US Senate passes resolution (69 to 27) urging president to use any means "including the use of arms" to limit extension of Cuban influence in Western Hemisphere. (*San Francisco Chronicle*, 12 August 1982, 2)

September 1982 Cuba declares inability to repay principal on external debt, estimated at $10.5 billion to $11 billion, including hard currency debt of about $3 billion. (*Wall Street Journal*, 2 September 1982, 1; *Financial Times* [London], 1 September 1982, 1)

May 1983 Assistant Secretary of State Thomas O. Enders lists several options, including "surgical removal" of Cuban transmitting antennas, if Cuba jams US radio stations in retaliation for broadcasts from proposed Radio Martí. (*New York Times*, 7 May 1983, A5)

June 1983 Cuba announces continued inability to repay principal due on some $1.3 billion of debt to Western banks. ". . . the Reagan Administration has let it be known that it would disapprove of too generous terms being conceded to Cuba by Washington's allies." (*Financial Times*, 1 June 1983, 4)

February 1985 Following Angola's announcement of willingness to phase out Cuban troop presence in return for South African withdrawal from Namibia, Castro expresses support for US mediation effort in the region. Also says number of Cuban troops in Ethiopia has fallen to "symbolic" level. Comments hint at "substantial lowering of Cuban military ambitions in Africa" as popular support for involvement wanes. (*Washington Post*, 6 February 1985, A1)

GOALS OF SENDER COUNTRY

Early 1960
Following expropriations, anti-US rhetoric, there is widespread public demand in US for retaliation against Cuba. (Schreiber 389)

October 1960
President Eisenhower bans exports to Cuba, partly to assist Richard M. Nixon's presidential bid; Kennedy, in response, promises "to do something about Fidel Castro." Initial purpose of sanctions thus is "to destabilize the Castro regime, causing its overthrow, or, at a minimum, to make an example of the regime by inflicting as much damage on it as possible." (Barber 369; Newfarmer 128–29)

23 April 1964
Under Secretary of State George Ball reformulates purpose of economic sanctions against Cuba: to reduce Castro's ability to export subversion; to show Cuban people that Castro

cannot serve their interests; to demonstrate that Communism has no future in Western Hemisphere; to raise cost to USSR of maintaining Communist outpost. Ball: "[E]conomic denial is a weapon that must be used with great selectivity. It can never be more effective than the economic circumstances of the target country." (Doxey 37; Roca 4; Bender 29)

15 December 1981
Assistant Secretary of State Thomas O. Enders: Reagan administration is "tightening the economic embargo" against Cuba in response to Cuban promotion of leftist revolution in Central America, especially El Salvador. (*Washington Post*, 15 December 1981, A6)

1983
"The objectives pursued by the US in 22 years of economic warfare against Cuba, despite variations in design and scope, can be classified under two major headings: overthrow and containment." (Roca 2)

RESPONSE OF TARGET COUNTRY

1963
Cuba negotiates long-term agreement for sugar sales to USSR at 6¢ per pound, obtains substantial economic aid from USSR. Castro publicly states willingness to reach compensation agreement with US, conditional on US reparations for damage caused by trade embargo and Bay of Pigs invasion. (Newfarmer 138; Doxey 39)

September 1975
Cuba supports independence for Puerto Rico. (Losman 44)

1975
Cuba begins supporting Marxist factions in Ethiopia, Angola. (Newfarmer 128)

ATTITUDE OF OTHER COUNTRIES

Soviet Union
In 1960, USSR begins extensive program of shipping goods, extending credits to Cuba; program lasts into 1980s. (Newfarmer 128)

Canada, Mexico, and Europe
Continue their commercial relations with Cuba, extensively transship US goods to Cuba. (Losman 29)

Organization of American States
In 1964, 21 of 22 members of OAS (excluding Mexico) suspend all trade and shipping with Cuba. "Every possible effort has been made [by US] to isolate Cuba economically." (Losman 43)

In early 1970s, selected OAS members (Peru, Argentina, Jamaica, Guyana, Barbados) reestablish commercial ties with Cuba; Argentina extends credits to Cuba. (Losman 44)

In July 1975, OAS ends sanctions, with approval of 16 countries, including US. (*New York Times*, 30 July 1975, A1)

LEGAL NOTES

1960

US Trading with the Enemy Act classifies as a "US affiliate" a foreign firm owned to extent of 10 percent of equity by US parent; subjects such affiliates to embargo. Embargo applies to direct contracts, subcontracts. (Hermann 33)

1975

Amendments to Canadian Combines Investigation Act give Canadian Restrictive Trade Practices Commission power to prohibit implementation of foreign judgments, laws, etc., "which would adversely affect [Canadian] competition, efficiency or trade." (Hermann 33)

"[The Fruehauf case (see Legal Notes in 49–1, US and Chincom v. China)] should establish the assumption, to be respected by courts of law, that no parent company has the power to compel its foreign subsidiary to disregard local laws." (Hermann 35)

1976

US announces virtually automatic approval will apply to all trade in nonstrategic goods by Canadian subsidiaries of US firms. In practice, long delays in granting licenses cause US firms to discourage Canadian subsidiaries from soliciting Cuban business. (Hermann 33)

ECONOMIC IMPACT

Observed Economic Statistics

Ship blacklisting policy increases Cuban freight costs, circa 1963, by $50 million annually. (Losman 28)

"One-quarter of the island's buses were out of operation for want of spare parts late in 1961. Only one-half of Cuba's 1,400 railroad passenger cars were functioning in 1962. . . . The sugar industry was particularly affected, especially by the failure of the transport system and mill breakdowns. . . . By 1965 nine sugar mills had been cannibalized. Of the 161 mills existing in 1969, Mesa-Lago reports that only 115 still functioned in April 1972. . . ." (Losman 34)

In 1959, Cuba imposes import controls; imports from Western countries decline by 44 percent, 1957–62. US supplied 70 percent of Cuba's imports in 1958, 68 percent in 1959, only 4 percent in 1961. (Losman 21)

In February 1960, USSR agrees to buy 2.7 million tons of Cuban sugar, extend long-term credit of $100 million, first step in aid program that entails Soviet assistance to Cuba of about $3.6 billion in next decade, corresponding Cuban trade deficit to USSR of $100 million to $300 million annually. (Doxey 37–40)

Estimated Cuban external debt, late 1960s, $4 billion. (Losman 26)

Estimated debt service (principal and interest) 1971, $131 million. (Losman 43, citing *Economist Intelligence Unit*)

Cuba experiences negative growth of 1.2 percent per year, 1960–71 period. (Losman 37, citing *World Bank Atlas*, 1973)

Cuba estimates cost of trade embargo at $9 billion. (*Financial Times*, 1 September 1982, 1)

In 1983, USSR is said to pay up to five times world price for Cuban sugar. "Such guaranteed Soviet purchases, along with 16 million metric tons of oil at $16 a barrel, help lift Soviet aid to a level Western economists put at about $4 billion this year, about a quarter of the Cuban gross national product. Cuban officials have told Western bankers that none of the Soviet aid goes for arms, which they said Moscow gives for free." (*Washington Post*, 4 June 1983, A15)

Cuban trade (million dollars)

	Exports		Imports	
	Socialist share	*Total*	*Socialist share*	*Total*
1959	14	638	2	675
1960	150	618	119	638
1961	458	625	492	703
1962	427	521	629	759
1963	366	544	704	867
1964	422	714	687	1,019
1965	538	686	657	865
1966	482	592	739	926
1967	581	715	783	990

Source: Losman 25.

Calculated Economic Impact

	Annual cost to target country
Increased freight costs caused by US ship blacklisting policy, diversion of trade to East-bloc nations; welfare loss estimated at 50 percent of increased costs (50 percent borne by trading partners).	$25 million
Reduction in purchasing power associated with shift in trade to countries with nonconvertible currencies; welfare loss estimated at 30 percent of total trade with those countries.	341 million
Offset	
Compensatory aid flows from USSR; welfare gain estimated at 70 percent of transfers.	($252 million)
Total	$114 million

Note: Losman calculates impact of sanctions as 2 percent reduction of growth per year throughout 1960s, assuming 3:1 capital/output ratio, 6 percent normal depreciation, 12 percent depreciation on account of cannibalization. (Losman 36)

Note: If *Washington Post* estimate (4 June 1983, A15) of $4 billion of direct and disguised USSR economic aid in 1983 is correct, current level of offsets far exceeds cost of sanctions.

Relative Magnitudes

Gross indicators of Cuban economy	
Cuban GNP (1958)	$2.6 billion
Cuban population (1960)	6.8 million
Annual effect of sanctions related to gross indicators	
Percentage of GNP	4.4
Per capita	$16.76
Cuban trade with US as percentage of total trade	
Exports (1960)	58
Imports (1960)	35
Ratio of US GNP (1958: $449.7 billion) to Cuban GNP (1958: $2.6 billion)	173

ASSESSMENT

Margaret P. Doxey
"The OAS policy of economic denial has retarded, though it cannot entirely prevent, Cuba's economic development. More important still—and is this perhaps its main justification now?—it has made more difficult the export of revolution. . . ." (Doxey 40, citing 'Viator' 320–21)

David L. Losman
In 1977 Secretary of State Cyrus Vance states that sanctions against Cuba are "failure." (Losman 44)

"In summary, the embargo has been quite economically damaging, although much of its incidence has been shifted to the socialist bloc. Its political results, on the other hand, have been questionable." (Losman 46)

AUTHORS' SUMMARY

Overall assessment	*Assigned scores*
□ Policy result, scaled from 1 (failed) to 4 (success)	1
□ Sanctions contribution, scaled from 1 (none) to 4 (significant)	1
□ Success score (policy result *times* sanctions contribution), scaled from 1 (outright failure) to 16 (significant success)	1

Political and economic variables	Assigned scores
☐ Companion policies: J (covert), Q (quasi-military), or R (regular military)	Q, J
☐ International cooperation with sender, scaled from 1 (none) to 4 (significant)	3
☐ International assistance to target: A (if present)	A
☐ Sanctions period (years)	24+
☐ Economic health and political stability of target, scaled from 1 (distressed) to 3 (strong)	2
☐ Presanction relations between sender and target, scaled from 1 (antagonistic) to 3 (cordial)	3
☐ Type of sanction: X (export), M (import), F (financial)	F, X, M
☐ Cost to sender, scaled from 1 (net gain) to 4 (major loss)	3

Comments

US imposed significant costs on Cuban economy with trade, financial embargo. Because USSR was willing to assume large portion of those costs, however, embargo may have exerted counterproductive effect on Castro, and may have helped consolidate his position in Cuba.

BIBLIOGRAPHY

Barber, James. 1979. "Economic Sanctions as a Policy Instrument." 55 *International Affairs* (July): 367–84.

Bender, Lynn D. 1975. *The Politics of Hostility: Castro's Revolution and United States Policy.* Hato Rey, PR: Inter-American Press.

Bonsal, Philip. 1971. *Cuba, Castro and the United States.* Pittsburgh: University of Pittsburgh Press.

Doxey, Margaret P. 1980. *Economic Sanctions and International Enforcement.* 2d ed. New York: Oxford University Press for Royal Institute of International Affairs.

Enders, Thomas O. 1981. "Tasks for US Policy in the Hemisphere." US Department of State, *Current Policy* no. 282, 3 June. Washington.

Hermann, A. H. 1982. *Conflicts of National Laws with International Business Activity: Issues of Extraterritoriality.* London: British–North American Committee.

Losman, David L. 1979. *International Economic Sanctions: The Cases of Cuba, Israel, and Rhodesia.* Albuquerque: University of New Mexico Press.

Lowenfeld, Andreas F. 1977. " . . . 'Sauce for the Gander': The Arab Boycott and United States Political Trade Controls." 12 *Texas International Law Journal* 25–39.

Mesa-Lago, Carmelo, ed. 1971. *Revolutionary Change in Cuba.* Pittsburgh: University of Pittsburgh Press.

Newfarmer, Richard, ed. 1982. "Relations with Cuba." In *From Gunboats to Diplomacy: New Policies for Latin America.* Papers prepared for the Democratic Policy Committee, US Senate, June.

Roca, Sergio. 1985. "Economic Sanctions Against Cuba." In *The Utility of Economic Sanctions*, ed. David Leyton-Brown. London: Croom Helm. Forthcoming.

Schreiber, Anna P. 1973. "Economic Coercion as an Instrument of Foreign Policy: U.S. Economic Measures Against Cuba and the Dominican Republic." 25 *World Politics* (April): 387–413.

Shultz, George P. 1983. "Strengthening Democracy in Central America." US Department of State, *Current Policy* no. 468, 16 March. Washington.

Szulc, Tad, and Karl E. Meyer. 1962. *The Cuban Invasion: Chronicle of a Disaster.* New York: Praeger.

"Viator." 1970. "Cuba Revisited after Ten Years of Castro." 48 *Foreign Affairs* (January): 312–21.

Case 61–1   US v. Ceylon

(1961–65: Expropriation)

CHRONOLOGY OF KEY EVENTS

1956   S.W.R.D. Bandaranaike leads socialist coalition to victory, becomes prime minister of Ceylon. (Olson 206)

1959   Bandaranaike assassinated; succeeded as prime minister by his widow, Sirimavo Bandaranaike. (Olson 206)

January 1961   Prime Minister Bandaranaike introduces bill to create Ceylon Petroleum Corporation, expropriate assets of US, UK oil companies: Standard Vacuum Oil, joint subsidiary of Socony-Mobil, Standard Oil of New Jersey (about $2.3 million); CALTEX, subsidiary of Texaco, Standard Oil of California (about $2.3 million); Royal Dutch Shell Group (about $7 million). (Olson 207)

Anglo-American diplomatic protest warns that expropriation will deter private investment in Ceylon. Ceylon dismisses objection on grounds that private capital has shown no interest in Ceylon and that USSR will sell oil to Ceylon at 25 percent below world market price and on soft terms. (Olson 207–8)

April–June 1962   Ceylon Petroleum Corporation expropriates about 20 percent by number, 50 percent by value, of private company service stations; concludes deal for favorable oil supplies from USSR, Romania, UAR. (Olson 208)

7 July 1962   US Ambassador Francis Willis warns Ceylon "aid from Washington might be stopped if American oil companies are not quickly compensated." (Olson 208)

1 August 1962   Hickenlooper amendment (PL 87–565), barring aid to countries that expropriate US property, is signed by President John F. Kennedy. In floor debate, Senator Bourke B. Hickenlooper (R–Iowa) refers to expropriations in Cuba, Brazil, Ceylon, possible expropriations in Honduras, Panama, Chile, Peru as inspiration for his measure. (Olson 207–9)

11 January 1963	US warns Ceylon of possible suspension of aid under Hickenlooper amendment unless progress is made on compensation agreement. (Olson 209–10)
February 1963	US AID director David Bell suspends aid to Ceylon. Ceylon, in retaliation, imposes low ceiling price on imported oil, warns companies that failure to maintain supplies will result in complete nationalization. (Olson 210)
1 January 1964	Following halt in shipments of petroleum products to Ceylon by private oil companies, Ceylon expropriates remaining retail outlets. However, Ceylon Petroleum Corporation continues to purchase products from Esso, CALTEX, Shell. (Olson 210)
April 1964	Minister of Trade T. B. Ilangaratne orders Ceylonese compensation tribunal to work as quickly as possible since "Ceylon was losing aid because of the delay in settling the claims for compensation." However, tribunal work proceeds slowly. (Olson 217)
March 1965	Bandaranaike government falls to conservative United National party (UNP). In general election campaign, UNP had claimed it would settle dispute with oil companies "within 24 hours." (Olson 217)
27 March 1965	UNP reaches preliminary compensation agreement. Final agreement, 23 June 1965, provides for $7 million to Shell, $2.3 million each to Esso, CALTEX. (Olson 217)

GOALS OF SENDER COUNTRY

Richard Stuart Olson
"By sanctioning Ceylon, Kennedy (and then President Lyndon B. Johnson) could quiet conservatives in the US with minimal damage to their foreign policy images. Ceylon's isolation and inaction on the diplomatic front and impotence on the economic front made this an attractive course of action for the US especially in view of the complex ongoing expropriation dispute with Brazil. . . . Ceylon was thus extremely useful as a political whipping boy to spike criticism that the administration was being soft on all those leftist governments which were expropriating American property. . . ." (Olson 222)

RESPONSE OF TARGET COUNTRY

Richard Stuart Olson
"Given its leftist orientation, the Bandaranaike government probably was not overly concerned about the reaction of the US and Great Britain to the proposed shift to Soviet bloc oil." (Olson 208)

"Since the Ceylonese government never appreciated the gravity with which the US viewed its action, it was continually puzzled by the severity of the American response." (Olson 209)

ATTITUDE OF OTHER COUNTRIES

United Kingdom

"The British government maintained a relatively low profile throughout the dispute" although UK net long-term loans declined markedly. UK interests in Ceylon extended well beyond oil (unlike US interests), and UK was anxious not to jeopardize those interests. (Olson 222–23)

ECONOMIC IMPACT

Observed Economic Statistics

US aid authorizations to Ceylon decline from $17.7 million in 1959 to $3.9 million in 1965. Following loss of control by Bandaranaike in 1965, aid increases to $14.0 million in 1966. (Olson 211)

Following $15.0 million loan in 1961, Ceylon is deemed by World Bank as "no longer creditworthy" pursuant to internal policy memoranda that bank will not lend to countries that expropriate without compensation. (Olson 212, citing Hayter 31)

Ceylon receives no World Bank loans from 1962–67, $4 million in 1968, $4.9 million in 1969, $43.5 million in 1970. (*IBRD/IDA Annual Reports*)

USSR net long-term loan flows to Ceylon rise from $0.4 million in 1959 to $4.8 million in 1965, decline to $1.7 million in 1967. (Olson 214)

Ceylon's international reserves drop from $236 million in 1956 to $144 million in 1959 to $73 million in 1965. Thus, limitations on flow of official assistance exacerbate precarious external position. Agricultural output also drops, from index of 114 in 1960 to 100 in 1963. (Olson 214–15)

Following election of UNP and compensation agreement with oil companies, Ceylon external debt increases from $102 million (1965) to $266 million (1970).

Calculated Economic Impact

	Annual cost to target country
Suspension of US aid from 1963–65; welfare loss estimated at 90 percent of reduced transfers.	$2.5 million
Suspension of multilateral loans from IBRD; welfare loss estimated at 60 percent of annual loans extended in 1968, 1969, 1970 (average $17.5 million) after lifting of ban.	10.5 million
Offsets	
Increased transfers from USSR; welfare gain estimated at 90 percent of aid.	($4 million)

	Annual cost to target country
Gain from expropriated assets, estimated at 10 percent of value of settlement, amortized over four years.	(0.3 million)
Total	$ 8.7 million

Relative Magnitudes

Gross indicators of Ceylonese economy	
Ceylonese GNP (1961)	$1.4 billion
Ceylonese population (1961)	10.1 million
Annual effect of sanctions related to gross indicators	
Percentage of GNP	0.6
Per capita	$0.86
Ceylonese trade with US as percentage of total trade	
Exports (1961)	9
Imports (1961)	3
Ratio of US GNP (1961: $524.6 billion) to Ceylonese GNP (1961: $1.4 billion)	375

ASSESSMENT

Richard Stuart Olson
"The coerciveness of the sanctions against Ceylon lay in the intensification of the economic decline and, most critically, in the withholding of that help which the Ceylonese saw as the only way of arresting the deterioration of their economy. Thus, in the absence of a clearly formulated radical alternative . . . desperation induced compliance." (Olson 225)

AUTHORS' SUMMARY

Overall assessment	Assigned scores
☐ Policy result, scaled from 1 (failed) to 4 (success)	4
☐ Sanctions contribution, scaled from 1 (none) to 4 (significant)	4
☐ Success score (policy result *times* sanctions contribution), scaled from 1 (outright failure) to 16 (significant success)	16

Political and economic variables

☐ Companion policies: J (covert), Q (quasi-military), or R (regular military) —

Political and economic variables (continued)	*Assigned scores*
☐ International cooperation with sender, scaled from 1 (none) to 4 (significant)	1
☐ International assistance to target: A (if present)	A
☐ Sanctions period (years)	4
☐ Economic health and political stability of target, scaled from 1 (distressed) to 3 (strong)	2
☐ Presanction relations between sender and target, scaled from 1 (antagonistic) to 3 (cordial)	2
☐ Type of sanction: X (export), M (import), F (financial)	F
☐ Cost to sender, scaled from 1 (net gain) to 4 (major loss)	1

BIBLIOGRAPHY

Hayter, Teresa. 1971. *Aid as Imperialism*. Baltimore: Penguin.
International Bank for Reconstruction and Development. *IBRD/IDA Annual Report*. Various years.
Olson, Richard Stuart. 1977. "Expropriation and International Economic Coercion: Ceylon and the 'West' 1961–65." 11 *Journal of Developing Areas* (January): 205–25.

Case 61-2   USSR v. Albania

(1961-65: Destabilization)

CHRONOLOGY OF KEY EVENTS

March 1960   Relations between USSR, Albania become strained as result of attempts by Nikita Khrushchev, Soviet Communist leader, to improve relations with President Tito's Yugoslavia, Albania's arch enemy. In reprisal for failure of Albanian President Enver Hoxha to show up at special Warsaw Pact Consultative Conference, USSR threatens to alter the terms of scholarship agreement under which it pays 60 percent of tuition, and upkeep for Albanians studying in USSR. (Freedman 71; Steele 99–100)

June 1960   Albania supports China on several key issues at meeting of Communist party leaders in Bucharest. Khrushchev responds by trying to split Albanian Communist party, oust Hoxha. Khrushchev refuses to ship 50,000 tons of wheat to Albania when it experiences serious grain shortage later in summer. China then provides needed wheat. "Thus, a united Albanian leadership, strengthened by the knowledge that the Chinese would give it concrete assistance, was able to stand up to Khrushchev." (Freedman 73)

January 1961   USSR, Albania conclude one-year trade agreement for 1961, with no extension of credit. Later in month, USSR announces withdrawal of Soviet technical assistance to Albanian oil industry. Subsequent reports allege sabotage of oil installations by Soviet technicians before departure. (Freedman 77)

February 1961   China-Albania long-term trade agreement provides for Chinese shipment of Canadian wheat, Chinese grain, steel, fertilizer, and other goods to Albania; Albanian shipment of copper, chrome ore, petroleum, tobacco to China. (Doxey 32; Freedman 77)

March 1961   USSR stops all aid, technical assistance to Albania; on same day, USSR announces agreement with Yugoslavia for exchange of foreign ministers. (Freedman 78; Doxey 31–32)

August 1961   Soviet ambassador leaves Albania; scholarships of Albanian students in USSR are revoked. (Freedman 78)

Diplomatic, trade relations between Soviet Union, Albania are broken, Albania is excluded from participation in Council for Mutual Economic Assistance (CMEA). (Freedman 79)

1965   USSR, after Khrushchev's removal from office, attempts to improve relations with Albania, even hinting at renewed trade, assistance. Albania shows no interest. (Freedman 90)

1978–83   Following Albania's break with China in 1978, "Moscow [begins] calling for the normalization of relations with Tirana." Albania responds with "stinging editorial" in party newspaper that rejects possibility of restoring ties with Moscow. Nevertheless, in November 1982 ". . . Pravda assured the Albanians that Russia was ready to restore normal relations. . . . That offer was turned down flat." USSR continues to attempt to woo Albania back into Soviet camp after Brezhnev dies and Yuri Andropov assumes leadership. (Doxey 32; *Economist* [London], 23 April 1983, 48; *Wall Street Journal*, 18 May 1983, 38)

GOALS OF SENDER COUNTRY

1960
"Khrushchev tried to bully the Albanians back into line. In the middle of a food shortage caused by drought that summer, he suddenly cut back on Soviet aid. He encouraged a pro-Soviet faction within the Albanian leadership to attempt a coup d'état. The move failed." (Steele 101)

April 1961
In letter terminating assistance to Albania, Soviet First Deputy Premier Aleksei Kosygin says "After weighing all the circumstances, the Soviet Government is obliged to reexamine the question of future relations with the Albanian People's Republic. . . . The Soviet Union deems it necessary henceforth to establish its relations with Albania on a new basis, taking into account the unfriendliness of its leadership toward the Soviet Union and the other socialist countries, and USSR aid to Albania, these will depend entirely on the attitude adopted by the Albanian party." (Freedman 78)

1964
"Following the fall of Khrushchev, the new Soviet leaders attempted to improve relations with Albania. Unlike the case of Yugoslavia where Stalin's successors, through certain ideological concessions and the agreement to resume trade, had effected a rapprochement, the new Soviet leaders were unwilling to make major ideological concessions although they were willing to resume trade relations with Albania." (Freedman 91)

RESPONSE OF TARGET COUNTRY

Robert Owen Freedman
"As the Soviet Union increased pressure on Albania, the Balkan nation was consolidating its alliance with China still further." (Freedman 75)

According to Albanian publication: "The Albanian people and the Party of Labor of

Albania will firmly march along the correct road of Socialist construction in defense of our Socialist homeland. Temporary difficulties will not stop us on our road. We are sure of our future. The tasks of the third five-year plan will be fulfilled and overfulfilled regardless of the obstacles that N. Khrushchev and his followers are trying to raise before us." (Freedman 82)

Enver Hoxha
October 1960, in preparation for Moscow meeting: "We say without reservation that all the evils that are apparent in the socialist camp today have their source in the errors of the present Soviet leadership. This is our view, which they cannot make us change, even with the threats that will be made toward us to the effect that 'Albania is an encircled country, it has economic needs,' etc. But let those gentlemen who speak in this way know that Albania and the Albanian communists do not sell themselves either for rubles, for wheat, or for dollars." (Hoxha 157)

At meeting of Communist parties in Moscow in November 1960: ". . . our only 'crime' is that we are a small and poor country which, according to Comrade Khrushchev, should merely applaud and approve but should express no opinion of its own. But this is neither Marxist nor acceptable. Marxism-Leninism has given us the right to have our say and we will not give up this right for anyone, neither on account of political and economic pressure nor on account of the threats and epithets that they might hurl at us. . . ." (Steele 104–5)

ATTITUDE OF OTHER COUNTRIES

Eastern Europe
East European countries cut off aid, technical assistance to Albania but USSR does not compel them to break off all trade. Thus, while East European exports to Albania drop in 1962 to 68 percent of 1961 level, in 1963 they rebound to 98 percent. Imports from Albania decline very little. (Freedman 81)

China
"In a speech delivered at the reception [given by the Albanian ambassador in Peking in 1961], [Premier] Chou En-lai assured the Albanians that they could expect to receive aid from China, and he expressed appreciation for the 'powerful support' China had received from the Albanian people." (Freedman 75)

Subsequently, in 1978, Albania accuses China of collaboration with American imperialism; China terminates economic, military aid. In spring 1983, Chinese delegation visits Albania to explore the possibility of resuming trade relations. Delegation reportedly discusses "new purchases of Albanian chrome in exchange for industrial spares, cotton, and such staples as rice and cooking oil." (*Washington Post*, 2 June 1983, A23; *Wall Street Journal*, 18 May 1983, 38)

ECONOMIC IMPACT

Observed Economic Statistics
In 1959, Albania receives a $13.75 million loan from China for third five-year plan (1961–65), $75 million developmental credit, promise of $8.75 million loan from Soviet

Union, $25 million loan from Czechoslovakia, $16 million credit from East Germany. (Freedman 62)

"Soviet aid, although not as extensive as the Albanians might have wished, had nonetheless provided the basis for Albania's economic advancement." (Freedman 66)

Albanian commodity trade with USSR (million new rubles)

	Exports	Imports
1955	5.5	15.1
1956	8.2	18.2
1957	14.1	32.7
1958	14.1	44.3
1959	13.3	44.0
1960	21.8	39.2
1961	19.6	81.3
1962	0	0

Source: Freedman 68.

In 1959, USSR receives 45 percent of Albania's exports, supplies 56 percent of its imports. Albanian trade with all of Eastern Europe, including Soviet Union, accounts for 94 percent of its exports, 93 percent of its imports. (Freedman 70)

As part of Albanian-Chinese trade and assistance agreement signed in early 1961, Chinese agree to extend $123 million credit to Albania for construction of "25 major industrial projects" during third five-year plan. That is $118 million more than amount promised by Soviet Union. China also buys 60,000 tons of Canadian wheat, has it shipped to Albania. (Freedman 77)

"To compensate for the absence of Soviet supplies, there was a major change in the nature of Albanian imports. Instead of having a large percentage of its imports in the form of machinery and equipment, the Albanians now began to concentrate on the import of semimanufactures such as rolled steel for conversion into finished products in Albania." (Freedman 84)

"Since most of the Albanian students (numbering approximately 4,500) who were studying in Soviet bloc schools were preparing themselves to be scientists and engineers, the cancellation of their scholarships and their abrupt return to Albania has unquestionably hurt Albania's economic development." (Freedman 86)

"Between the early 1960s when Albania sided with the Chinese against Russia, and 1978, when it quarreled with them but remained hostile to Russia, it had received some $5 billion worth of Chinese aid." (*Economist*, 23 April 1983, 48)

Wall Street Journal also mentions $5 billion figure but refers to it as debt accumulated by Albania to China since 1960. (*Wall Street Journal*, 18 May 1983, 38)

Michael Ellman cites an estimate of $1.5 billion as the amount of aid which Albania has received from all sources in the period 1945–75. Soviet aid, when forthcoming, is estimated to have paid for more than half of Albania's imports. (Ellman 336)

"Albania has experienced rapid growth, but from a very low initial level. . . . The downswings in the rate of growth (for example, in the early 1960s and middle 1970s) have been caused by the end of relations with the hitherto main donor of aid." The average annual rate of growth in net material product was 11.2 percent in 1951–55, 7.0 percent in 1956–60, 5.8 percent in 1961–65, 9.1 percent in 1966–70. (Ellman 333–34)

"A pugnacious refusal to have much trade or other dealings with the outside world has left Albania as Europe's poorest and least developed country." (*Wall Street Journal*, 6 June 1983, 1)

"Although Albanian officials boast of steady growth in economic measures such as income, western diplomats here . . . have no doubt that the country is in serious trouble." (*Wall Street Journal*, 6 June 1983, 1)

Calculated Economic Impact

	Annual cost to target country
Reduction in trade with USSR; welfare loss estimated at 30 percent of average value of trade from 1958 to 1960.	$16 million
Reduction in USSR aid; welfare loss estimated at 90 percent of lost transfers.	15 million
Offsets	
Increase in Chinese economic aid to Albania; welfare gain valued at 90 percent of credits, 35 percent of loans. (Authors' note: Aid estimated from transfers made during third five-year plan; we are skeptical of $5 billion aid figure for 1961–78 period).	($23 million)
Delivery of 60,000 tons of wheat purchased by China; welfare gain of 100 percent of value of shipment.	(5 million)
Total	$3 million

Relative Magnitudes

Gross indicators of Albanian economy	
Albanian GNP (1961)	$0.5 billion
Albanian population (1961)	1.7 million
Annual effect of sanctions related to gross indicators	
Percentage of GNP	0.6
Per capita	$1.76

Albanian trade with USSR as percentage of total trade
Exports (1959)   45 (94)[†]
Imports (1959)   56 (93)[†]

Ratio of USSR GNP (1961: $247 billion) to Albanian GNP (1961: $0.5 billion)   494

[†] Albanian trade with USSR, other East European countries.

ASSESSMENT

Robert Owen Freedman
"Although China provided the bulk of Albania's trade during the 1962–64 period, the nations of Eastern Europe provided approximately 25 percent, including certain kinds of machinery and equipment that the Chinese were unable to supply. Although Albania no longer obtained credits from the region, the trade relations it continued to maintain were a valuable aid to its strained economy." (Freedman 80)

"There was a gradual increase in the level of economic pressure until trade relations were cut off. The gradualness of the increase not only provided the Albanians with time to readjust their economy; from the Soviet point of view, it also gave time for an Albanian change in policy. . . . By breaking trade relations but allowing the other East European nations to continue trading with Albania, Khrushchev kept the pressure on the Albanian leadership and yet did not fully exclude that nation from the Soviet bloc. By maintaining a constant stream of propaganda to Albania about the benefits of a good relationship with the USSR, Khrushchev kept open the possibility of an eventual rapprochement." (Freedman 91)

Jonathan Steele
"Khrushchev tried to bully the Albanians back into line. . . . The move failed." (Steele 101)

AUTHORS' SUMMARY

Overall assessment	*Assigned scores*
☐ Policy result, scaled from 1 (failed) to 4 (success)	1
☐ Sanctions contribution, scaled from 1 (none) to 4 (significant)	1
☐ Success score (policy result *times* sanctions contribution), scaled from 1 (outright failure) to 16 (significant success)	1

Political and economic variables

☐ Companion policies: J (covert), Q (quasi-military), or R (regular military)	J

Political and economic variables (continued)	Assigned scores
☐ International cooperation with sender, scaled from 1 (none) to 4 (significant)	4
☐ International assistance to target: A (if present)	A
☐ Sanctions period (years)	4
☐ Economic health and political stability of target, scaled from 1 (distressed) to 3 (strong)	2
☐ Presanction relations between sender and target, scaled from 1 (antagonistic) to 3 (cordial)	3
☐ Type of sanction: X (export), M (import), F (financial)	F, X, M
☐ Cost to sender, scaled from 1 (net gain) to 4 (major loss)	2

BIBLIOGRAPHY

Doxey, Margaret P. 1980. *Economic Sanctions and International Enforcement.* 2d ed. New York: Oxford University Press for Royal Institute of International Affairs.

Ellman, Michael. 1984. "Albania's Economy Today and Tomorrow." 7 *World Economy* (September): 333–40.

Freedman, Robert Owen. 1970. *Economic Warfare in the Communist Bloc: A Study of Soviet Economic Pressure Against Yugoslavia, Albania, and Communist China.* New York: Praeger.

Hoxha, Enver. 1976. *Albania Challenges Krushchev Revisionism* (materials from vol. 19 of *Works* [in Albanian]). New York: Gamma Publishing Co.

Kaser, M. 1967. *COMECON: Integration Problems of the Planned Economies.* 2d ed. London: Oxford University Press.

Steele, Jonathan, ed. 1974. *Eastern Europe Since Stalin.* New York: Crane, Russak, & Co.

Stolte, Stefan C. 1962. "Albania under Economic Pressure from Moscow." 9 *Bulletin* (Munich) 3: 25–34.

Case 61–3 Western Allies v. German Democratic Republic

(1961–62: Berlin Wall)

CHRONOLOGY OF KEY EVENTS

31 August 1960　US, UK, French commandants in Berlin protest USSR announcement of restrictions on free movement in Berlin for period 31 August–4 September 1960. On 5 September, German Democratic Republic (GDR) interferes with barge traffic to Berlin, on 8 September reimposes restrictions on entry of West Germans into East Berlin. (Committee 622)

1 October 1960　West Germany threatens trade ban against East Germany if harassment continues. "Almost overnight the situation in Berlin eased and for the next three months the GDR attempted no further moves against Western rights." (Smith 228, 373)

19 July 1961　President John F. Kennedy protests intention of Soviet leader Nikita Khrushchev to make a separate peace with GDR. (Committee 687)

2–11 August 1961　GDR clamps down on "border-crossers" in Berlin. (Smith 375)

13 August 1961　GDR restricts travel between East, West Berlin; erects barbed and chicken wire barricades, deploys GDR guards along border between Soviet, Western zones. Between 18 and 20 August, permanent wall is completed. West German Chancellor Konrad Adenauer threatens, but does not implement, trade embargo. (Committee 723; Smith 5, 375)

19–21 August 1961　Vice President Lyndon B. Johnson and General Lucius D. Clay, former US commandant in Berlin, go to Berlin to revive morale. American garrison is strengthened by 1,500 men. US State Department announces commercial air pact with Soviet Union will not be signed "in the light of the overall world situation." (Smith 286–93, 299)

23 August 1961　Further measures are imposed by GDR to divide East, West Berlin. Crossing points are reduced from 12 to 7. (Committee 953; Smith 375)

5 June 1962　Adenauer announces long-term credits of $1 billion to GDR will not be considered until freedom of movement is restored to Berlin. East German officials indicate they will withdraw request for credits. (*New York Times*, 6 June 1962, A2)

GOALS OF SENDER COUNTRIES

August 1961
Adenauer tells Dean Rusk, US secretary of state, that most effective threat for West Berlin would be total embargo on trade with Eastern Europe. "But a full-scale trade embargo, to be effective, had to be undertaken by all the NATO countries, and that was bound to take time. In the nature of things it was a long-term countermeasure, whereas this new challenge [dividing the city] was immediate." (Cate 289)

4 August 1961
US Department of State: "Now it is possible that if the Soviet Government continues its threatening attitude toward the vital interests of the US and its allies, we will be obliged to reconsider all aspects of our relations, including economic, with the USSR and the countries of the Soviet Bloc. However, we do not believe that our interests or the cause of world peace would be served at this time by the initiation of actions designed to interrupt or significantly modify current economic relations with these countries." (Committee 714)

14 August 1961
In campaign speech, Adenauer reiterates belief that West's most effective weapon against East is total trade embargo. However, other West Germans are not convinced that would be appropriate response: "Even the idea of a purely West German and selective embargo— aimed at depriving the GDR of certain vitally needed machines, chemicals, and other products—was [opposed by politicians both from within and outside the government]." (Cate 395)

14–15 August 1961
"Adenauer mentions that economic sanctions are being considered by the West." He says trade agreement with East Germany must be "'looked at in the light of the latest move on Berlin.'" British Foreign Office spokesmen, however, reveal that they oppose an "'economic embargo.'" (Smith 278)

RESPONSE OF TARGET COUNTRY

15 August 1961
GDR announces that any attempt to apply economic sanctions against it will be met by total blockade of all West German traffic to Berlin. Free Democratic Party in Bonn later announces it opposes embargo as it does not want to give GDR excuse to block access to Berlin. (Smith 279–80)

ECONOMIC IMPACT

Observed Economic Statistics

"It is remarkable that there was no change in the economic indices for the second and third quarters of 1961." (Dulles 50)

East German trade with FRG (million dollars)

	Exports	Imports
1961	219	182
1962	210	192
1963	242	192
1964	264	252
1965	291	256

Source: UN Yearbook of International Trade Statistics, 1966, 294.

Calculated Economic Impact

None, since sanctions did not go beyond threat stage. (Even West German threat to withhold credits was abandoned in 1960s.)

Relative Magnitudes

Gross indicators of GDR economy	
GDR GNP (1961)	$18.7 billion
GDR population (1961)	16.9 million
Annual effect of sanctions related to gross indicators	
Percentage of GNP	nil
Per capita	nil
GDR trade with US, UK, France, FRG as percentage of total trade	
Exports (1961)	11
Imports (1961)	13
Ratio of US, UK, French, FRG GNP (1961: $751 billion) to GDR GNP (1961: $18.7 billion)	40

ASSESSMENT

Jean Edward Smith

"For Nikita Khrushchev, the sealing of the East Berlin sector boundary represented a major triumph; the construction of the wall between East and West Berlin an even greater one. With free movement within the city now a thing of the past, the four-power status of the former German capital was over, and East Berlin passed almost unnoticed behind the Iron Curtain. . . .

". . . By successfully sealing the border between East and West Berlin, the ruinous [out]flow of East German refugees had been halted. The tottering East German government was bolstered and dissident elements within the Soviet zone could now be brought under control." Also because border closure was carried out by GDR, it forced at least de facto acceptance by West of regime of Walter Ulbricht, Communist party leader. (Smith 5, 6)

AUTHORS' SUMMARY

Overall assessment	Assigned scores
☐ Policy result, scaled from 1 (failed) to 4 (success)	1
☐ Sanctions contribution, scaled from 1 (none) to 4 (significant)	1
☐ Success score (policy result *times* sanctions contribution), scaled from 1 (outright failure) to 16 (significant success)	1

Political and economic variables

☐ Companion policies: J (covert), Q (quasi-military), or R (regular military)	Q
☐ International cooperation with sender, scaled from 1 (none) to 4 (significant)	3
☐ International assistance to target: A (if present)	A
☐ Sanctions period (years)	1
☐ Economic health and political stability of target, scaled from 1 (distressed) to 3 (strong)	3
☐ Presanction relations between sender and target, scaled from 1 (antagonistic) to 3 (cordial)	1
☐ Type of sanction: X (export), M (import), F (financial)	—
☐ Cost to sender, scaled from 1 (net gain) to 4 (major loss)	2

BIBLIOGRAPHY

Cate, Curtis. 1978. *The Ides of August: the Berlin Wall Crisis*. New York: M. Evans & Co.
Dulles, Eleanor Lansing. 1967. *Berlin, the Wall Is Not Forever*. Chapel Hill: University of North Carolina Press.
Keller, John W. 1964. *Germany, The Wall, and Berlin*. New York: Vantage Press.
Smith, Jean Edward. 1963. *The Defense of Berlin*. Baltimore: Johns Hopkins University Press.
US Congress. Senate Committee on Foreign Relations. 1961. *Documents on Germany, 1944–61*. 87 Cong., 1 sess.

Case 62–1   US v. Brazil

(1962–64: Goulart)

CHRONOLOGY OF KEY EVENTS

1955–60 Brazil's President Juscelino Kubitschek, promising "fifty years progress in five," pursues ambitious development program; inflation accelerates; external debt grows. (Olson 247–48)

11 May 1959 Governor of Rio Grande do Sul, Leonel Brizola, brother-in-law, adviser to João Goulart, future president, expropriates Companhia de Energia Eléctrica Riograndense, subsidiary of American and Foreign Power (AMFORP), with assets of $135 million, declares no compensation will be paid. (Olson 249–50)

7 September 1961 President Janio Quadros resigns after seven months; Vice President Goulart becomes president following passage, at military insistence, of Additional Act that limits presidential powers. (Parker 6)

16 February 1962 Governor Brizola expropriates Companhia Telefônica Nacional, subsidiary of ITT, with assets of $7 million to $8 million, offers compensation of $0.4 million. ITT President Harold Geneen, characterizing Brizola as anti-American, requests US State Department "to take immediate steps with the government of Brazil for a rescinding of the order of expropriation." (Olson 249–50)

17 February 1962 US State Department calls for "prompt, adequate, and effective compensation," says seizure "appears to be a step backward in the mobilization of available resources for the success of the Alliance for Progress." (Olson 250–51)

February 1962 Goulart, caught between leftist nationalism sparked by Governor Brizola and necessity of US financial support, seeks to soothe Washington, temporize on substantive issues. (Olson 251)

28 February 1962 US congressional bill that would cut off aid if Brazilian congress limits profit remittances of US companies attracts hostile press attention in Brazil. (Olson 252)

March 1962 Brazilian federal government reaches agreement for $7.3 million in compensation for ITT, most of which would be invested in another ITT subsidiary; settlement is implemented in February 1963. Brazilian state governors of Santos and Rio de Janeiro then announce plans to expropriate subsidiaries of Brazilian Power, Traction, and Light, in hope Brazilian federal government will be forced to pay compensation. To avoid chaos, Goulart blocks expropriation action by states. (Olson 252, 254)

5 April 1962　Joint communiqué following meeting between President John F. Kennedy and President Goulart states that nationalization of public utilities by Brazil will be accompanied by fair compensation, to be reinvested in other sectors. (Olson 252–53)

1 August 1962　Hickenlooper amendment (section 620(e) of Foreign Assistance Act of 1961), with retroactive effect to 1 January 1962 explicitly designed to encompass ITT case, is signed by Kennedy. In floor debate, Senator Bourke B. Hickenlooper (R–Iowa) indicates Brazil is among countries he has in mind. (Olson 253–54)

September 1962　Brazil passes strict profit remittance law over objections of foreign corporations, US Embassy. Goulart delays publication of implementing regulations. (Olson 254)

6 January 1963　US AID Administrator David Bell and Brazil's newly appointed Finance Minister, San Tiago Dantas, reach agreement providing stopgap assistance of $845 million, coupled with future assistance of $314 million conditioned on: long-term assistance from World Bank, IMF, and others; Brazilian austerity program. (Parker 38)

March–May 1963　Attempted implementation of Bell-Dantas agreement, coupled with simultaneous agreement to pay $135 million for 10 AMFORP subsidiaries, provokes strong reaction in Brazil, dooms both schemes. Ultimately, Brazil receives less than 25 percent of US stabilization loan. (Parker 40–41; Olson 249–55)

May 1963　Goulart abandons "positive left" in favor of Brizola faction; senior US officials accuse Goulart of "flirting with the Soviet Union." (Olson 255)

June 1963　Goulart dismisses entire cabinet; Bell-Dantas agreement collapses. (Parker 43)

November 1963　President Kennedy is assassinated. Lyndon B. Johnson becomes president, appoints Thomas Mann as assistant secretary of state for interamerican affairs, designates him administration's "one voice" on hemisphere matters (thereby depriving Kennedy men of control). (Parker 53)

Late 1963　USSR offers to provide transport planes to Brazilian air force; US government strongly discourages acceptance. (Parker 53)

January 1964　Goulart signs entire Profits Remittance Law, aimed against US

January 1964 (continued)	business interests, after assuring US Ambassador Lincoln Gordon he would veto most restrictive parts. (Parker 55–56)
February 1964	General Humberto Castelo Branco, army chief of staff, joins conspirators against Goulart, providing them enormous respectability. US is informed of conspiracies in progress; Ambassador Gordon urges additional US military support for Brazil. (Parker 58)
13 March 1964	Goulart expropriates privately owned oil refineries. (Parker 60)
18 March 1964	Mann announces US would not automatically punish military juntas that overthrow democratic regimes. (Parker 61–62)
27 March 1964	Gordon concludes Goulart is seeking dictatorial powers and that, if he prevails, Brazil probably will come "under full Communist control." Embassy staff develops two plans: to supply petroleum for military transportation, key civilian activities in case Goulart supporters destroy refineries during coup; to send US carrier task force to Brazil for symbolic presence and to evacuate US citizens. (Parker 64–68)
	Goulart grants amnesty to protesting sailors, thereby alienating military hierarchy. (Parker 70)
31 March 1964	General Mourão Filho, commander of Fourth Military Region in Minas Gerais, marches on Rio. US activates plans to send aircraft carrier, petroleum supplies but avoids overt action for fear it would "play into Goulart's hands." (Parker 71, 75–76, 78)
	Brazilian military deposes President Goulart. According to conventional view, US government was "exceptionally well-informed" about preparations for coup. (Olson 255)
1 April 1964	Goulart flies to Rio Grande do Sul; leader of Brazilian senate declares presidency vacant; interim President Paschoal Ranieri Mazzilli sworn in. Next day, US recognizes new government, offers significant economic aid. (Parker 79, 85; Olson 255)

GOALS OF SENDER COUNTRY

Assistant Secretary of State Thomas Mann
Speaking in April 1967: "when we assumed our duties [in January 1964] we were convinced that communism would rapidly erode the government of João Goulart in Brazil. Even before assuming our actual position, moreover, we already were following a policy destined to grant aid to certain state governments in Brazil. We did not furnish any money to support the balance of payments or the budget, nor did we take any measures that could directly benefit the central government of Brazil. . . . Now, after the replacement of Sr. Goulart, . . . we would be prepared to consider making appreciably more substantial funds available." (Parker 92–93)

Ambassador Lincoln Gordon
The policy amounted to concentrating aid on "islands of administrative sanity." (Parker 93)

Robert Wesson
"Up to mid-1963, the US policy had been in cautious cooperation with Goulart while warning of Communist or allegedly Communist penetration in unions and various state agencies (especially Petrobras) and encouraging reform while harping on the need to check inflation, which was getting even worse. But after July, the American authorities concluded that further aid to the Goulart government would be wasted, and no new commitments were made except for the supply of some surplus wheat and some projects for the impoverished Northeast." (Wesson 26)

RESPONSE OF TARGET COUNTRY

Phyllis R. Parker
"According to [Roberto] Campos [Brazil's ambassador to US], Goulart viewed the [Bell-Dantas] agreement as 'proof of US mistrust and that embittered him and further deviated him from the road of cooperation.'" (Parker 41)

Robert Wesson
"So far as Goulart leaned on those for whom anti-Americanism was valuable and a major means of influence, he was not to be influenced; the most that could be done, it seemed to American policymakers, was to endeavor to weaken him and counteract his policies." (Wesson 33)

ECONOMIC IMPACT

Observed Economic Statistics

No program loans are negotiated while Goulart is president. Bell-Dantas negotiation leads to release of $25.5 million in April 1963 from program loans negotiated during Quadros administration. (Parker 93)

During period 1962–64, military assistance fluctuates from $18 million to $99 million annually but without restrictive trend. Ambassador Gordon regards Brazilian military as "an essential factor in [the] strategy for restraining left-wing excesses of the Goulart government." (Parker 58)

In 1963–64, US concentrates aid on "islands of sanity" within Brazil, namely "sensible" state governments, the military. Economic aid authorizations drop from annual level of $304 million (during Quadros regime) to $174 million (in Goulart regime), rise to $337 million following military coup. (Olson 255–57)

New foreign investment in Brazil drops from $147 million in 1961, to $69 million in 1962, $30 million in 1963, $28 million in 1964. (Olson 257–59)

In June 1964, three months after the coup, US releases $50 million of emergency funds; previously authorized program loans of $475 million also are released, supplemented by more than $600 million over next four years. (Parker 93; Wesson 51)

US aid to Brazil (million dollars)

	Economic	Military
1961	304	24
1962–63	174	33
1964	337	41

Source: Olson 256.

Calculated Economic Impact

	Annual cost to target country
Decline in US economic aid; welfare loss estimated at 75 percent of reduced loans, grants.	$110 million

Relative Magnitudes

Gross indicators of Brazilian economy	
Brazilian GNP (1962)	$19 billion
Brazilian population (1962)	74 million
Annual effect of sanctions related to gross indicators	
Percentage of GNP	0.6
Per capita	$1.49
Brazilian trade with US as percentage of total trade	
Exports (1962)	62
Imports (1962)	35
Ratio of US GNP (1962: $565 billion) to Brazilian GNP (1962: $19 billion)	30

ASSESSMENT

Phyllis R. Parker
"The evidence does not suggest that US economic assistance caused the downfall of Goulart. There is evidence that US aid further weakened an already weak central government, not only by withholding assistance from Goulart's government which the US policymakers felt would not or could not handle the aid responsibly, but also by effectively bypassing that government through direct US dealings with and support of other groups, leaders, and institutions in the country, and by frequently aligning US assistance with those elements of Brazilian society that eventually overthrew Goulart." (Parker 99)

Robert Wesson
"So far as the US was influential, it was mostly in helping to create the atmosphere in

which the coup was gestated and emboldening the makers of it. The concrete actions taken seem to have been trivial in their effects. They were partly counterproductive so far as they became known at the time and subsequently as they were cited to discredit the regime that the US favored." (Wesson 48)

AUTHORS' SUMMARY

Overall assessment	Assigned scores
☐ Policy result, scaled from 1 (failed) to 4 (success)	4
☐ Sanctions contribution, scaled from 1 (none) to 4 (significant)	3
☐ Success score (policy result *times* sanctions contribution), scaled from 1 (outright failure) to 16 (significant success)	12

Political and economic variables

☐ Companion policies: J (covert), Q (quasi-military), or R (regular military)	J
☐ International cooperation with sender, scaled from 1 (none) to 4 (significant)	1
☐ International assistance to target: A (if present)	—
☐ Sanctions period (years)	2
☐ Economic health and political stability of target, scaled from 1 (distressed) to 3 (strong)	1
☐ Presanction relations between sender and target, scaled from 1 (antagonistic) to 3 (cordial)	2
☐ Type of sanction: X (export), M (import), F (financial)	F
☐ Cost to sender, scaled from 1 (net gain) to 4 (major loss)	1

BIBLIOGRAPHY

Olson, Richard Stuart. 1979. "Expropriation and Coercion in World Politics: A Retrospective Look at Brazil in the 1960s." 13 *Journal of Developing Areas* (April): 247–62.

Parker, Phyllis R. 1979. *Brazil and the Quiet Intervention, 1964.* Austin: University of Texas Press.

Skidmore, Thomas E. 1967. *Politics in Brazil 1930–1964: An Experiment in Democracy.* New York: Oxford University Press.

Wesson, Robert. 1981. *The United States and Brazil: Limits of Influence.* New York: Praeger.

Case 62–2   UN v. South Africa

(1962–   : Apartheid)

CHRONOLOGY OF KEY EVENTS

1948   Nationalist party assumes power in South Africa, applies apartheid on rigid basis. (David 215)

April 1960   Sixty-four Africans are killed by police at Sharpeville. Incident provokes worldwide condemnation of South African regime; UN Security Council passes Resolution S/4300, with UK, France abstaining, calling for end of apartheid. (Doxey 1972, 537; Doxey 1980, 61)

1961   African states demand political, economic sanctions against South Africa. South Africa withdraws from "new" commonwealth upon becoming a republic, subsequently is excluded from specialized UN agencies. (Doxey 1980, 61; David 217)

19 October 1962   Francis T. P. Plimpton, US representative to UN, criticizes efficacy, potential use of economic sanctions against South Africa; states US "will continue to oppose" specific sanctions. (David 217)

6 November 1962   UN General Assembly Resolution 1761 calls upon members "separately or collectively, in conformity with the charter": to break diplomatic relations with South Africa; to close ports to South African vessels; to forbid their flag vessels to enter South African ports; to boycott South African trade; and to suspend landing rights for South African aircraft. (Doxey 1972, 537; David 217)

June 1963   Organization of African States established; recommends economic sanctions against South Africa, termination of diplomatic links, denial of overflight rights; calls on US to choose between Africa, colonial powers. (Doxey 1980, 62; David 218)

2 August 1963   US ambassador to UN, Adlai E. Stevenson, speaking in opposition to total arms embargo: "The application of sanctions in this situation is not likely to bring about the practical result that we seek. . . . Punitive measures would only provoke intransigence and harden the existing situation. . . ." Nevertheless, US pledges to terminate all new sales of military equipment by the end of 1963. (David 218)

7 August 1963	UN Security Council, with US support, UK and France abstaining, adopts Resolution 181 calling on all states to cease shipment of arms to South Africa. (Doxey 1972, 537; Doxey 1980, 61; David 218–19)
4 December 1963	UN Security Council, with US, UK, French support, adopts Resolution 182 proscribing shipment of equipment, materials for arms manufacture. UK, France state they will distinguish between weapons for internal suppression, external defense. US, UK, France oppose economic sanctions. (Doxey 1980, 62; David 219)
December 1963	US attempts to negotiate stretchout of uranium purchases from South Africa, prepayment of US Export–Import Bank loans; South Africa requests permission to purchase military equipment. Negotiations end in standoff. (David 220)
April 1964	UN Group of Experts, appointed pursuant to Security Council Resolution 182, recommends examination of economic sanctions. Export Committee Report is issued 2 March 1965; members vote 6 to 4 against sanctions. (Doxey 1972, 537–38; Doxey 1980, 62)
1964	Eximbank terminates direct loans to South Africa; US uses voting power in IMF to block purchase of South African gold; US imposes capital restrictions on South Africa. (Chettle 6, 8)
October 1964	Newly elected British Labour government bans all arms exports to South Africa. (Doxey 1980, 62)
21 October 1966	UN General Assembly passes Resolution 2145, 114 to 2 (3 abstentions), to terminate South African mandate for Namibia, place territory under UN administration. (Doxey 1972, 538; Doxey 1980, 63)
February 1967	US aircraft carrier *Franklin Delano Roosevelt*, returning from Vietnam, plans four-day refueling, recreation stop at Capetown. Following congressional protest, US Navy forbids crew to disembark; US announces future passing warships will refuel at sea. (David 221)
June 1968	At US instigation, IMF refuses to purchase gold from South Africa at prices in excess of $35 per ounce. (de Vries 409–16)
30 January 1970	UN Security Council Resolution 276 ends South African trusteeship of Namibia. International Court of Justice upholds Resolution 276 in 1971. (Doxey 1980, 63)
23 July 1970	UN Security Council Resolution 282 extends existing arms embargo. (*New York Times*, 24 July 1970, A7)
November 1973	OAPEC imposes total oil embargo on South Africa. (Doxey 1980, 65)

1974	UN General Assembly votes 91 to 22 to reject South Africa's credentials; UK, France, US veto Security Council resolution to expel South Africa. (Doxey 1980, 63)
1976	Hundreds of blacks are killed in Soweto riots sparking intensified international condemnation of apartheid regime. (Doxey 1980, 64)
March 1977	Adoption of six principles espoused by Rev. Leon Sullivan, first black board member of GM, relating to equal opportunity in workplace is announced by 11 US multinationals, several black church leaders. Similar codes subsequently are drafted by EC (September 1977), Canada, some private institutions. (Chettle 65–66; Bissell 85–86)
4 November 1977	Primarily as result of Soweto riots and other disturbances in South Africa, UN Security Council adopts Resolution 418: arms trade with South Africa (not apartheid *per se*) is "threat to peace" under Article 39, therefore illegal; in August 1977, France had announced it would discontinue arms sales to South Africa. (Doxey 1980, 64)
13 December 1977	UN General Assembly approves recommendation to Security Council for mandatory oil embargo against South Africa; US, UK, France, other key countries abstain, rendering proposal moot. (Spandau 152–53)
22 February 1978	Regulations issued by administration of President Jimmy Carter deny export or reexport of any item to South Africa or Namibia if exporter "knows or has reason to know" item will be "sold to or used by or for" military or police in South Africa. (Chettle 17)
July 1978	Rev. Leon Sullivan publishes expanded version of original six principles, announces that 103 companies have committed themselves to apply them. (Bissell 86–88)
1979	US reduces staffs of US military attaché in Pretoria, South African military attaché in Washington; Evans amendment prohibits Eximbank loans to all South African government firms and to private firms with unsatisfactory labor practices. (David 223–24)
1 July 1979	South Africa Act comes into force in Sweden prohibiting "the formation of any new Swedish companies in South Africa or Namibia. Swedish-owned subsidiaries already operating in those countries are forbidden to make any further investments in fixed assets. . . ." (*Swedish Business* 24)
June 1983	Administration of President Ronald Reagan adopts policy of "constructive engagement" with South Africa, emphasizing diplomatic means of achieving Namibian independence, racial equality within South Africa. South African and US governments insist withdrawal of South African troops from Namibia be accompanied by withdrawal of Cuban troops from Angola. (*New York Times*, 24 June 1983, A1; 27 September 1983, A3; *Washington Post*, 25 August 1983, A1; 24 September 1983, A24)

September 1983	Six Democratic presidential candidates endorse bill by Congressman Stephen J. Solarz (D–NY), criticize Reagan administration policy of "constructive engagement." Solarz bill would bar US importation of gold coins (Krugerrands) from South Africa, forbid US bank loans to South African government, require US firms in South Africa to implement equal opportunity provisions of Sullivan principles. An amendment by Congressman William Gray (D–Pa.) would bar further private investment in South Africa. (*Washington Post*, 24 September 1983, A24; *Wall Street Journal*, 22 January 1984, 22)
December 1983	House passes Export Administration Act with Solarz bill attached. Sponsors of South Africa legislation indicate they will waive amendments in Senate and take it directly to conference where they hope to work out an acceptable compromise. (*Wall Street Journal*, 23 January 1984, 22)
6 December 1983– *8 January 1984*	South African forces mount successful campaign into Namibia to destroy SWAPO logistical base and prevent planned offensive. South African forces, however, face sophisticated Soviet-supplied weaponry and "analysts say it was only the superior training and motivation of South African military personnel that carried the day." Informed observers contend arms embargo has entailed high cost for South Africa and has prevented acquisition of "the most sophisticated hardware that defense strategists [in South Africa] believe they need. . . . [The] lesson of the operation 'is that they can't match the Soviet buildup that can occur in front-line states like Angola, and it scares the hell out of them.'" (*Washington Post*, 24 February 1985, A26; *Facts on File* 14)
11 October 1984	Despite appearance of having worked out a compromise in April, EAA dies when House Democrats refuse to compromise on, and key Senate Republicans refuse to accept, ban on loans to South African government. Provisions banning importation of krugerrands and limiting new investment had already been dropped in conference. (*Washington Post*, 13 April 1984, F1; *New York Times*, 12 October 1985, D1; *Wall Street Journal*, 19 October 1984, 26)
12 December 1984	As popular protests against South Africa grow in Washington and other US cities, 119 of approximately 350 US companies operating in South Africa agree to expansion of Sullivan principles, committing them "to press for broad changes in South African society, including the repeal of all apartheid laws and policies." Rev. Sullivan indicates he will monitor compliance and says, "This is the first time American companies have entered the political arena in South Africa and pushed for an end to apartheid." (*New York Times*, 13 December 1984, D1)
13 December 1984	UN Security Council reaffirms 1977 embargo of arms exports to South Africa and votes unanimously to request that "all states refrain from importing arms ammunition of all types and military vehicles produced in South Africa." (*Washington Post*, 14 December 1984, A46)

Late December 1984–early January 1985	Archbishop Desmond Tutu, on visit to Washington after accepting Nobel Peace Prize in Oslo, criticizes administration's "constructive engagement" policy and says US could end apartheid "tomorrow" by adopting get-tough policy. In his first public appearance after returning to South Africa, Bishop Tutu calls for campaign of "persuasive pressure" against South Africa in which companies would "attach conditions for reform to their investments for a test period of 18 months to two years." Tutu said he was not advocating divestment but that diplomatic, political, and economic pressure was necessary "to avert a blood-bath." (*Washington Post,* 24 December 1984, C1; *International Herald Tribune,* 4 January 1985, 1)
3 January 1985	Senator William Proxmire (D–Wis.) introduces bill requiring sanctions against South Africa, includes basic provisions of Solarz bill passed by House in December 1983. (*Congressional Record-Senate,* 3 January 1985, S-256)
7 January 1985	Coalition of six employer groups, claiming to represent 80 percent of South African workers, issues statement calling for significant changes in apartheid system: meaningful political participation for blacks; recognition of right of all groups to ownership of property and employment; universal citizenship; free, independent unions; equal justice; end to forced removal of people. Statement cautions that such changes can be made only in atmosphere of economic growth; thus opposes sanctions, disinvestment. (*Wall Street Journal,* 9 January 1985, 31)
7 March 1985	Group of liberal lawmakers introduce Anti-Apartheid Act of 1985 in both House and Senate. Legislation would prohibit new investments in or loans to South Africa, would ban importation of Krugerrands. (*Washington Post,* 7 March 1985, A13)

GOALS OF SENDER COUNTRIES

UN General Assembly
Goals are to: end apartheid, possibly leading to black majority rule; terminate South African presence in Namibia. (*Doxey* 1980, 60-65)

Vice President Walter Mondale
Speaking in South Africa, 20 May 1977: "Every citizen should have the right to vote and every vote should be equally weighted." (Chettle 11)

US National Security Council
Outlines "types of actions which [the South African] government might take to improve relations with the United States" on 22 February 1978:

☐ *Bilateral*: Eliminate various forms of discrimination applied to US nonwhites in South Africa, South African nonwhites in US.

☐ *Internal*: Eliminate job discrimination; recognize African unions; abolish pass laws; move toward franchise for nonwhites.

☐ *Regional and international*: Recognize UN responsibility for Namibia; withdraw support for Rhodesia; give generous customs treatment to Botswana, Lesotho, Swaziland. (Chettle 58–60)

RESPONSE OF TARGET COUNTRY

John H. Chettle
Response to Sullivan Code has been "measurable and sometimes impressive. A number of signers have taken tangible and often dramatic steps towards increasing opportunities for black workers." In addition, limited progress has been made over the years in race relations, for example, desegregation of some public facilities, permanent presence of Africans accepted in designated "white areas," free education and low-cost national health for blacks, race-neutral labor legislation, significant recognition of black trade unions. (Chettle 50–55, 65, 67–68)

Margaret P. Doxey
"South Africa developed close trading links with France and Japan; military equipment was obtained from France . . . and in return France became an important purchaser of South African uranium." (Doxey 1980, 109)

Arnt Spandau
"South Africa's dependence on the importation of raw materials, foodstuffs, and other industrial products is gradually decreasing. To a lesser extent this is also true of the importation of machines and industrial equipment. By contrast, imports of petroleum products have increased sharply, not least for strategic stockpiling purposes." (Spandau 125)

New York Times
"So far, Pretoria has managed to stay ahead by paying a premium and keeping details of oil purchases secret. Disclosure of oil transactions is punishable by large fines and long prison sentences. . . . To achieve a measure of energy security, the country has spent millions of dollars to build up an oil stockpile in disused coal mines and specially built tank farms. The supply is intended to cover consumption for six months to two years. . . . Government officials predict that the Sasol plants will meet more than 40 percent of South Africa's oil needs by the mid-1980s." (*New York Times*, 21 March 1983, D7; Bissell 83–85)

Richard E. Bissell
". . . the South Africans pursued a number of strategies designed to heighten their ability to withstand potential American pressures: (1) establishment of intense economic ties in other directions, as with Taiwan and Israel; (2) the pursuit of technological self-sufficiency; (3) maximizing the value of exports and capitalizing on good fortune like the skyrocketing price of gold in 1979–80; and (4) pointing out to the US and others the collateral damage that sanctions would wreak on nearby black states in southern Africa." (Bissell 93)

ATTITUDE OF OTHER COUNTRIES

State/local governments in US
Wisconsin (1978), Nebraska (1980), Connecticut (1980) adopt legislation calling for divestment of shares held by public institutions in US companies with investments in

South Africa. More recently, Maryland, Massachusetts, Michigan, and the cities of Philadelphia, Washington, Boston, and New York have passed laws forbidding the investment of municipal or state funds in companies which operate in South Africa. American firms fear the growing tide of protest in US may lead to many more states and cities passing such laws in 1985. (Chettle 106–8; *New York Times,* 28 October 1984, A18; *Los Angeles Times,* 25 December 1984, A1)

Europe and Japan
"[Europe and Japan] have been active in turning the US restrictions into strong points for their country's manufacturers." US market share of South African imports is reduced from 21 percent (1976) to 17.6 percent (1979). "US controls have seemingly furthered South Africa's determination to achieve economic self-sufficiency and independence from any one foreign supplier." (*Export Administration Annual Report* 138)

In September 1982, in show of opposition to apartheid, Netherlands parliament requires visas from visiting South Africans, calls on National Sports Federation to end athletic competition with South Africa. (*Financial Times* [London], 8 September 1982, 2)

United Kingdom
"British business and political leaders are concerned about not antagonizing their important trade partners in black Africa, but are not, under current circumstances, willing to reduce trade substantially with South Africa or to withdraw British investments. Avoiding this choice is a key objective of British policy." (Foreign Policy Study 303)

Federal Republic of Germany
"The German government does not support economic sanctions, trade boycotts, or prohibitions on investments." (Foreign Policy Study 305)

Sweden
Under South African Act, it seems that Swedish subsidiaries in South Africa "are supposed to 'hibernate' until the day the conditions for the black majority in South Africa have changed for the better. It is the wish of Swedish politicians that Swedish business interests in South Africa should not really flourish until the black majority control the country. Until then, Swedish industry must show restraint, but without actually going so far as to discontinue operations. The latter course would, in the eyes of the politicians, be unfortunate. Experiences and assessments from other countries indicate that, if a total withdrawal were made today, it would be extremely difficult to regain a foothold in the market in the future even if South Africa had majority rule by then." (*Swedish Business* 25)

Soviet Union
General Secretary Leonid Brezhnev to Somalian President Siad Barre, as quoted by Richard M. Nixon: "Our aim is to gain control of the two great treasure houses on which the west depends—the energy treasure house of the Persian Gulf and the mineral treasure house of Central and Southern Africa." (Nixon 23)

Organization of Petroleum Exporting Countries
"Members of the Organization of Petroleum Exporting Countries and other African and Asian countries have tried for almost a decade to keep oil from reaching South Africa." (*New York Times,* 21 March 1983, D7)

International Monetary Fund
In November 1982, IMF approves $1.1 billion loan to South Africa, drawing critical

notice from US Congress. Administration of President Ronald Reagan subsequently argues that political issues should not intrude on IMF decisions, opposes House Banking Committee amendment to IMF funding bill that would require US to oppose any IMF loan to country practicing apartheid. (*Wall Street Journal*, 5 May 1983, 1; 18 May 1983, 39)

Zimbabwe and Zambia
In 1983, Zimbabwean Prime Minister Robert Mugabe criticizes Reagan administration policy of "constructive engagement," saying it has encouraged South Africa "to become more aggressive" toward neighboring black-ruled nations. Zambian President Kenneth Kaunda earlier had called on West to pressure South Africa, asking, "Why action in [Poland] and no action in [South Africa]?" (*Washington Post*, 2 April 1983, A16; 19 August 1983, A14)

Organization of African Unity
"Since its formation in 1963, the OAU has provided the institutional framework for activity against South Africa by black African states. . . . [R]esolutions calling for commercial, diplomatic, and political sanctions against South Africa have been introduced regularly at the United Nations by the African states." (Foreign Policy Study 305)

LEGAL NOTES

International Court of Justice (ICJ)
In December 1966, ICJ holds that Ethiopia, Liberia do not have standing to challenge South African administration of Namibia. (Doxey 1980, 63)

In January 1971, ICJ upholds Security Council Resolution 276 that ends South African trusteeship of Namibia. (Doxey 1980, 63)

ECONOMIC IMPACT

Observed Economic Statistics

South Africa depends on oil for less than 20 percent of its energy (though oil provides 80 percent of energy needs of transport sector). Moreover, South Africa has stockpiled 2–10 years' supply and is completing two nuclear power plants, a third gas-oil plant. (Chettle 82; Spandau 153–55)

Cumulative arms imports (1964–73) from US, $24 million; UK, $87 million; France, $208 million. Total South African arms imports were $32 million in 1963. (ACDA)

". . . informed estimates are that markups for arms purchased on the international black market range between 20 and 100 percent." (*Washington Post*, 24 February 1985, A26)

Book value of US investment in South Africa, 1982: $2.6 billion. UK assets in South Africa, 1977: $5.1 billion in shares, $6.8 billion in direct investment. (Chettle 60, 62)

"Direct American investment in South Africa is estimated by the State Department at $2.3 billion down from the $2.8 billion calculated by the South African Institute of Race Relations for 1982. Other estimates put overall American investment, including loans and gold stocks, at $14 billion." (*New York Times*, 28 October 1984, 18).

"Foreign investment, both direct and indirect, has played a key role in the development of the South African economy, and remains an important factor in maintaining a high rate of economic growth. But foreign investment is heavily influenced both by current South African events and by international political pressures. Moreover, decisions made by South Africa affecting its major area of vulnerability, energy, are based as much on political factors as on economic ones. For example, the development of alternative energy sources, such as synthetic fuels, has been dictated primarily by the threat of an international oil embargo. . . . Because of its controversial status in the international community, South Africa has consciously tried to develop a self-sufficient economy." (Foreign Policy Study 128–29)

As of 1979, total foreign investment in South Africa was $26.3 billion, of which 80 percent was held by: US (20 percent), UK (40 percent), West Germany (10 percent), Switzerland (5 percent), France (5 percent). (Foreign Policy Study 134)

On potential impact of divestment: "Indeed, the paradox is that the withdrawal of foreign companies from South Africa, rather than affecting the country's foreign exchange balance, might actually be advantageous to it, at least in the short run. The Investors Responsibility Research Center has pointed out [that] for the last decade, companies have been repatriating in interest and dividends more foreign exchange than they have been investing in South Africa." (Chettle 81)

"The economic development program . . . calls for reduced reliance on foreign capital. This reflects concern that South Africa has been overly dependent on foreign investment in the past, making the economy vulnerable to the effects of domestic political and social unrest on outside investors. For example, the drop in foreign investment following the Sharpeville shootings in 1960 prolonged and deepened the recession of 1959–63, while the reaction of foreign investors to the Soweto riots of 1976 had a similar impact on the 1974–78 downturn." (Foreign Policy Study 134)

Calculated Economic Impact

	Annual cost to target country
Reduction in Eximbank loans to South Africa; welfare loss estimated at 70 percent of reduced transfers.	$9 million
Increased cost of arms imports resulting from diversion of purchases from US, UK suppliers; welfare loss estimated at 10 percent of 1963 imports.	3 million
Economic security cost of holding large oil stockpiles incurred since 1974; welfare loss estimated at 10 percent of the value of the stockpile.	261 million
Total	$273 million

Relative Magnitudes

Gross indicators of South African economy	
South African GNP (1964)	$9.8 billion
South African population (1964)	18.1 million
Annual effect of sanctions related to gross indicators	
Percentage of GNP	2.8
Per capita	$15.08
South African trade with OECD as percentage of total trade	
Exports (1964)	71
Imports (1964)	83
Ratio of OECD GNP (1964: $1,276 billion) to South African GNP	
(1964: $9.8 billion)	130

ASSESSMENT

George Ball
In dealing with South Africa, US had no "cohesive" or "fundamental" policy; yet objective as broad as ending apartheid would require more than "tangential" approach. (David 22; Ball 253)

US Senate, Committee on Foreign Relations (Clark Report)
"Collectively, US corporations operating in South Africa have made no significant impact on either relaxing apartheid or in establishing company policies which would offer a limited but nevertheless important model of multinational responsibility. Rather, the net effect of American investment has been to strengthen the economic and military self-sufficiency of South Africa's apartheid regime, undermining fundamental goals and objectives of US foreign policy." (Chettle 62–63, citing Clark Report 13)

John H. Chettle
"Since new investment from the US was only half of one percent of total investment in South Africa, its termination was likely to be of little consequence...." (Chettle 7; Marcuss 3)

Vernon Jordan, director, National Urban League
Summarizing talks with black leaders in South Africa: "to a person they were firm in their convictions that American companies should not withdraw." (Chettle 71)

Princeton Lyman, deputy assistant secretary of state for Africa
Legislation restricting US loans and investment in South Africa "would be regarded in South Africa as deliberately provocative and would produce a confrontational atmosphere. In this atmosphere our ability to encourage and support change would be hampered, not enhanced." (Lyman 3)

Export Administration Annual Report
Controls on trade with South Africa are being extended "because there has been no movement towards fundamental, social and political change in South Africa." (137)

C. Fred Bergsten, assistant secretary of the Treasury for international affairs
"If we decided to use investment as an instrument for imposing sanctions or even for making a symbolic statement, the hard fact is that South Africa has more cards to play than we do in this area." (Bergsten 6; also see Bissell 95–98)

US House of Representatives, Committee on Interior and Insular Affairs, Subcommittee on Mines and Mining
"The US and its Western allies are dependent upon South African mineral suppliers. Although this dependence is acute in the case of the European Community and Japan, the interrupted supply from South Africa would also directly disrupt strategic and nonstrategic sectors of the US economy. . . ." (Sub-Saharan Africa 19–20)

Margaret P. Doxey
"The probability of effective enforcement of economic sanctions against South Africa is particularly low. Embargoes which were not universally observed would be useless without a blockade, not only of South African ports but also of ports in Angola and Mozambique." Cost of blockade is estimated at $28 million per month. (Doxey 1972, 544, citing Leiss)

Rev. Leon Sullivan, in 1983 article
"Though progress is still limited in comparison to the enormous size of the problem, the [Sullivan] principles are beginning to work. . . . In my opinion, the voluntary support of the principles has been effective, but is not getting the desired results quickly enough. More enforcement is needed. As I have testified before congressional committees on several occasions: the full compliance with the principles by *all* American companies with operations in the Republic of South Africa should be made mandatory by the United States government, and backed up with embargoes, tax penalties, sanctions, loss of government contracts, and any other effective means." (Sullivan 1983)

Martin Bailey
An oil embargo on South Africa would have "enormously disruptive effect" and South Africa "could probably only survive for a maximum of two and a half years. . . ." (Bailey 5, 23)

Foreign Policy Study Foundation
"The available evidence indicates that South Africa's vulnerability to even an effective oil embargo is decreasing with time. The combination of stockpiles, rationing, conservation, and alternative fuels should be able to keep vital South African industries and essential security and administrative machinery functioning for years. An embargo implemented after the mid-1980s would probably have little chance of significantly damaging the country's economy." (Foreign Policy Study 143)

AUTHORS' SUMMARY

Overall assessment	Assigned scores
☐ Policy result, scaled from 1 (failed) to 4 (success)	1
☐ Sanctions contribution, scaled from 1 (none) to 4 (significant)	1
☐ Success score (policy result *times* sanctions contribution), scaled from 1 (outright failure) to 16 (significant success)	1

Political and economic variables	Assigned scores
☐ Companion policies: J (covert), Q (quasi-military), or R (regular military)	—
☐ International cooperation with sender, scaled from 1 (none) to 4 (significant)	3
☐ International assistance to target: A (if present)	—
☐ Sanctions period (years)	22+
☐ Economic health and political stability of target, scaled from 1 (distressed) to 3 (strong)	3
☐ Presanction relations between sender and target, scaled from 1 (antagonistic) to 3 (cordial)	2
☐ Type of sanction: X (export), M (import), F (financial)	F, X
☐ Cost to sender, scaled from 1 (net gain) to 4 (major loss)	3

Comments

South Africa has demonstrated remarkable skill over 20 years in circumventing and defying economic sanctions aimed at changing its system of apartheid. Most sanctions have been relatively mild, enforced only loosely. Most potentially damaging, oil embargo by Arab members of OPEC had been undercut until 1979 by Iran's willingness to sell oil to South Africa. In addition, at significant cost, South Africa has reduced reliance on imported oil through stockpiling and promotion of nuclear energy, synthetic fuels programs.

BIBLIOGRAPHY

Arms Control and Disarmament Agency. 1974. *World Military Expenditures and Arms Transfers 1963–73*.

Bailey, Martin. 1980. "Oil Sanctions: South Africa's Weak Link." *Note and Documents*. United Nations Department of Political and Security Council Affairs.

Ball, George W. 1968. *The Discipline of Power: Essentials of a Modern World Structure*. Boston: Little, Brown & Co.

Barber, James. 1973. *South Africa's Foreign Policy 1945–1970*. London: Oxford University Press.

Bergsten, C. Fred. 1978. Testimony before House Committee on International Relations, Subcommittee on Africa and on International Economic Policy and Trade. 95 Cong., 2 sess., 10 August.

Bissell, Richard E. 1982. *South Africa and the United States: The Erosion of an Influence Relationship*. New York: Praeger.

Cheng, B. 1967. "The 1966 South-West Africa Judgment of the World Court." 20 *Current Legal Problems* 181–212.

Chettle, John H. 1982. "The Divestment of South African Stock: Is it Practical, Desirable, or Constitutional?" Paper submitted to Georgetown University Law School, October.

David, Mark. 1982. "United States–South African Relations—1962–67." In *Economic Coercion and U.S. Foreign Policy: Implications of Case Studies from the Johnson Administration*, ed. Sidney Weintraub. Boulder, Colo.: Westview Press.

De Vries, Margaret Garritsen. 1976. *The International Monetary Fund 1966–71*. Vol. 2. Washington: International Monetary Fund.

Doxey, Margaret P. 1972. "International Sanctions: A Framework for Analysis with Special Reference to the UN and South Africa." 26 *International Organization* (Summer) 527–50.

———. 1980. *Economic Sanctions and International Enforcement*. 2d ed. New York: Oxford University Press for Royal Institute of International Affairs.

Foreign Policy Study Foundation, Inc. 1981. *South Africa: Time Running Out*. The Report of the Study Commission on U.S. Policy Toward Southern Africa. Berkeley: University of California Press.

Government of Canada. 1970. *Foreign Policy for Canadians. The United Nations*. Ottawa: Queen's Printer.

Grundy, K. W. 1973. *Confrontation and Accommodation in South Africa: The Limits of Independence*. Berkeley: University of California Press.

International Court of Justice. 1966. *Reports of Judgments, Advisory Opinions and Orders*.

Johnson, R. W. 1977. *How Long Will South Africa Survive?* New York: Oxford University Press.

Leiss, Amelia C., ed. 1965. *Apartheid and UN Collective Measures: An Analysis*. New York: Carnegie Endowment for International Peace.

Lyman, Princeton. 1981. Testimony before House Committee on Foreign Affairs, Subcommittee on Africa and on International Economic Policy and Trade. 97 Cong., 1 sess., 15 October.

Marcuss, Stanley J. 1978. Testimony before House Committee on International Relations, Subcommittee on Africa and on International Policy and Trade. 95 Cong., 2 sess., 10 August.

Myers, Desaix, III, et al. 1980. *US Business in South Africa*. Bloomington: Indiana University Press.

Nixon, Richard M. 1980. *The Real War*. New York: Warner Books.

Olson, Martha J. 1979. "University Investments with a South African Connection: Is Prudent Divestiture Possible?" 11 *New York University Journal of International Law and Politics* (Winter): 543–80.

Porter, Richard C. 1978. "The Potential Impact of International Sanctions on the South African Economy." Unpublished, University of Michigan, 1 October.

Schlesinger, Arthur M., Jr. 1965. *A Thousand Days*. Boston: Houghton Mifflin.

Sohn, L. 1966. "Expulsion or Forced Withdrawal from an International Organization." 88 *Harvard Law Review* 1381–1425.

Spandau, Arnt. 1979. *Economic Boycott against South Africa*. Cape Town: Juta and Company.

Sullivan, Leon H. 1983. "It's Time to Step Up the Pressure on South Africa." *Washington Post*, 10 May, A19.

Swedish Business and South Africa. 1983. Stockholm: International Council of Swedish Industry.

United Nations. 1965. Document S/6210, SCOR 20th Year, Special Supplement no. 2, 2 March.

US Congress. House Committee on Foreign Affairs, Subcommittee on Africa. 1966. *Hearings on United States–South African Relations*. 89 Cong., 2 sess.

———. House Committee on Foreign Affairs, Subcommittee on Africa. 1982. *Hearings on Enforcement of the United States Arms Embargo Against South Africa*. 97 Cong., 2 sess., 30 March.

———. House Committee on Interior and Insular Affairs, Subcommittee on Mines and Mining. 1980. *Sub-Saharan Africa: Its Role in Critical Mineral Needs of the Western World*. 96 Cong., 2 sess., July.

————. Senate Committee on Foreign Relations. 1978. *US Corporate Interests in South Africa* (Clark Report). S. Rept. No. 382–3, 95 Cong., 2 sess.

US Department of Commerce. 1981. *Export Administration Report 1980.* Washington.

US Department of State. 47 *Department of State Bulletin* 1221, 19 November 1962; 49, 1261–62, 26 August 1963. Washington.

US National Security Council. Interdepartmental Group for Africa. 1969. "Study in Response to National Security Study Memorandum 39: Southern Africa." 15 August. Washington.

Wouk, Jonathan. 1972. "US Policy toward South Africa 1960–67." Ph.D. diss., University of Pittsburgh.

Case 62–3   USSR v. Romania

(1962–63: Economic Independence)

CHRONOLOGY OF KEY EVENTS

1960   Romanian leader Gheorghe Gheorghiu-Dej submits report prepared by Central Committee of Romanian Workers' Party to Third Party Congress that calls for "rapid all-round industrialization" and socialization of agriculture in next six-year plan period. Plan calls for more Soviet aid and technical assistance than Nikita Khrushchev, first secretary of the Communist party, has indicated a willingness to provide, and implies that if it is not received, Romania will turn to West for aid in economic development. (Fischer-Galati 78; Floyd 56)

Spring 1961   Romanian delegation visits US to investigate "the possibilities for American economic assistance. Concurrently, a far-reaching, long-range economic agreement was concluded with Italy." (Fischer-Galati 83)

Early June 1962   Following meeting of Council for Mutual Economic Assistance (CMEA, later COMECON) in Moscow, communiqué is issued that embodies "the principle of subordination of national to bloc interests. . . ." Romanian reaction is "restrained" but only because communiqué is broad enough to allow some freedom of interpretation. "It has been generally recognized by students of CMEA and of Soviet-Rumanian relations that the basically anti-Rumanian decisions adopted in Moscow and the Rumanian reaction to them constitute the formal beginning of the 'independent course'." (Fischer-Galati 87)

Late June 1962   Khrushchev visits Romania, fails to settle differences of opinion on development strategy. (Fischer-Galati 88)

August 1962   Khrushchev attempts to strengthen COMECON, further integrate its member nations by setting up supranational executive body. Proposal advocates "international specialization" among COMECON nations; Khrushchev hints that those not adopting strategy, i.e., Romania, may not "benefit from the proposed common investment fund." (Floyd 72)

September 1962	Gheorghiu-Dej travels to India, Indonesia in effort to promote closer economic ties. (Fischer-Galati 89)
October 1962	"Cuban missile crisis" takes place. (Fischer-Galati 90)
25 November 1962	Romanian officials announce Anglo-French consortium will build planned steel plant at Galati, "the focal point of the Soviet-Rumanian dispute on industrialization." This decision "left no doubt as to the Rumanians' determination to develop heavy industry regardless of Soviet objections." (Fischer-Galati 91)
July 1963	COMECON nations meet in Moscow. "This meeting ended in what appeared to be complete victory for the Rumanian point of view and the defeat of Khrushchev's plans." (Floyd 80)

GOALS OF SENDER COUNTRY

David Floyd
". . . the Russians' involvement in the expansion of their allies' industrial capacity was not entirely disinterested. They were happy to see the countries of Eastern Europe developing industries for which they had resources or which were of value to the Soviet economy, and they saw every reason for helping the expansion of industries which would also increase a country's dependence on the Soviet Union. But they were not interested in converting every one of their dependent states into a sturdy, independent industrial nation." (Floyd 57)

Stephen Fischer-Galati
" . . . Khrushchev left Rumania, [in June 1962] at the end of what was to be his last official visit to that country, determined to break Gheorghiu-Dej's resistance to Russia's plans for bloc integration. Gheorghiu-Dej's own determination to resist external interference in Rumanian affairs was, in turn, comparably strengthened." (Fischer-Galati 88)

RESPONSE OF TARGET COUNTRY

David Floyd
"[The Rumanians] knew that Khrushchev would not hesitate to exert economic pressure on them if they refused to yield. . . . The Rumanians were still very dependent on Russian aid and its withdrawal could gravely upset their plans.

"The Rumanian leaders therefore set out to seek alternative sources of raw materials and of financial aid. . . . In these and other ways the Rumanians were insuring themselves against Russian moves to coerce them and at the same time were letting the Russians know that such pressure would be ineffective." (Floyd 72)

"[I]t is clear that the Russians maintained their pressure throughout 1962 and into 1963. But Gheorghiu-Dej made it quite clear to the Rumanian Grand National Assembly on December 29, 1962, that he had no intention of abandoning his fight for Rumania's economic advancement." (Floyd 76)

Stephen Fischer-Galati
"During the winter of 1962–1963 the Rumanian leadership had intensified its drive to

rally the masses for a common national, and essentially anti-Russian effort. A sweeping amnesty to political prisoners was granted concurrently with the pursuit of a massive campaign for strengthening the 'socialist-patriotic' sentiments of the population at large in support of the party's programs." (Fischer-Galati 93)

ATTITUDE OF OTHER COUNTRIES

Eastern Europe
"For various reasons, both political and economic, the other East European leaders appear to have sided with the Russians against Rumanians. . . . " (Floyd 75)

ECONOMIC IMPACT

Observed Economic Statistics

"In 1960 Rumania's imports from Western Europe increased to 22.8 percent of its total imports compared with 15.1 percent in 1959, and exports to Western Europe rose from 16.4 percent to 22.1 percent. This was the beginning of a swing in the orientation of Rumania's foreign trade that was to continue and that was to cause friction with its Communist allies." (Floyd 60)

"In the early postwar years the proportion of the country's trade with Russia and the countries of Eastern Europe had been nearly 90 percent (87.4 percent in 1947). By 1960 this proportion had declined to 73 percent, while the figures for 1962 and 1963 were 68.7 percent and 67.9 percent respectively." (Floyd 92)

Romanian economy grew 16.9 percent in 1960, 14.7 percent in 1962, 12.5 percent in 1963; industrial production 1960–63 expanded average of 15 percent a year. (Floyd 101–2)

Calculated Economic Impact

None, since sanctions did not go beyond threat stage.

Relative Magnitudes

Gross indicators of Romanian economy	
Romanian GNP (1962)	$10.5 billion
Romanian population (1962)	18.7 million
Annual effect of sanctions related to gross indicators	
Percentage of GNP	nil
Per capita	nil

Romanian trade with USSR as percentage of total trade	
Exports (1962)	42
Imports (1962)	39

Ratio of USSR GNP (1962: $258 billion) to Romanian GNP (1962: $10.5 billion)	24

ASSESSMENT

David Floyd
"In 1962, Khrushchev committed himself publicly and personally to the integration of the countries of Eastern Europe with the Soviet Union. The chosen instrument of his policy was COMECON. By the end of the year it was clear that his plan had failed, and its failure was in no small part due to the stubborn opposition of the Rumanians." (Floyd 70)

Stephen Fischer-Galati
"Khrushchev's pronunciamento on 'Essential Questions in the Development of the World Socialist System,' in which he pressed his views on economic integration, implicitly criticized the Rumanians' 'autarchic tendencies' and 'trading on the side.' But the veiled threat of economic sanctions against nonconformists failed to impress Gheorghiu-Dej." (Fischer-Galati 89)

"It is an open question whether the Russians would have taken more drastic steps than verbal exchanges to coerce the Rumanians into accepting their formula had it not been for the Cuban confrontation. But in the immediate aftermath of that crisis, which resulted in an exacerbation of the Sino-Soviet conflict and exposed the comparative Russian weakness vis-à-vis the United States, the Kremlin was unprepared to take any action that would further jeopardize the unity of the bloc and of the socialist camp in general." (Fischer-Galati 90)

AUTHORS' SUMMARY

Overall assessment	*Assigned scores*
☐ Policy result, scaled from 1 (failed) to 4 (success)	1
☐ Sanctions contribution, scaled from 1 (none) to 4 (significant)	1
☐ Success score (policy result *times* sanctions contribution), scaled from 1 (outright failure) to 16 (significant success)	1

Political and economic variables

☐ Companion policies: J (covert), Q (quasi-military), or R (regular military)	—
☐ International cooperation with sender, scaled from 1 (none) to 4 (significant)	4
☐ International assistance to target: A (if present)	—

	Assigned scores
Political and economic variables (continued)	
☐ Sanctions period (years)	1
☐ Economic health and political stability of target, scaled from 1 (distressed) to 3 (strong)	3
☐ Presanction relations between sender and target, scaled from 1 (antagonistic) to 3 (cordial)	3
☐ Type of sanction: X (export), M (import), F (financial)	—
☐ Cost to sender, scaled from 1 (net gain) to 4 (major loss)	2

BIBLIOGRAPHY

Fischer-Galati, Stephen. 1967. *The New Rumania: From People's Democracy to Socialist Republic.* Cambridge, Mass.: MIT Press.

Floyd, David. 1965. *Rumania, Russia's Dissident Ally.* New York: Praeger.

Montias, John Michael. 1967. *Economic Development in Communist Rumania.* Cambridge, Mass.: MIT Press.

Case 63–1 US v. UAR

(1963–65: Yemen and Congo)

CHRONOLOGY OF KEY EVENTS

1963   UAR intervention in Yemen arouses US concern that subversion of Saudi Arabia might be goal. President John F. Kennedy threatens to terminate US aid unless UAR begins troop withdrawals by December 1963. (Kleeman 107)

Early 1964   UAR begins troop withdrawals; US suspends new development loans but leaves PL 480 (food aid) intact. President Gamal Abdel Nasser of Egypt denounces Libya for permitting US bases. Egyptian press criticizes assorted US "misdeeds." (Kleeman 107)

26 November 1964   John F. Kennedy Memorial Library in Cairo is burned. (Kleeman 110)

20 December 1964   Private US airplane is downed over UAR; US Ambassador Lucius Battle tells Egypt that aid discussions are not appropriate under circumstances. (Kleeman 110–11)

23 December 1964   Nasser confirms Egyptian assistance to Congolese rebels. (Kleeman 103, 111)

January 1965   US House passes Michel amendment (Congressman Robert Michel, R–Ill.) blocking PL 480 shipments to Egypt. After intense lobbying, Congress in October 1965 drops the Michel amendment, allows President Lyndon B. Johnson to continue aid with "national interest" finding. Meanwhile, administration withholds last $37 million of three-year PL 480 agreement. (Kleeman 103, 112)

January–April 1965   Nasser stops anti-US attacks in Egyptian press, halts aid to Congo rebels who in any event were losing. (Kleeman 112)

June 1965   Nasser withdraws military support from Arab Jordan River Project; US releases $37 million PL 480 shipment. (Kleeman 112)

July 1965   Johnson permits Egypt to purchase Commodity Credit Corporation (CCC) wheat (knowing that requisite bank guarantees cannot be

July 1965 (continued)	obtained). Nasser refuses Chinese request for North Vietnamese office in Cairo. Nasser offers peace proposal to Saudi Arabia on Yemen. (Kleeman 114)
August 1965	Nasser appoints moderate prime minister, Zakaric Mohieddin. (Kleeman 114)
December 1965	US announces six-month PL 480 package worth $55 million. UAR settles private claims, pays $500,000 for damage to Kennedy library; however, Jedda agreement for end of Yemen civil war breaks down. (Kleeman 115)
March 1966	Nasser requests $150 million PL 480 aid; Johnson instead offers $50 million CCC credit. (Kleeman 122)
Spring–Fall 1966	Nasser renews attacks on US role in Vietnam; announces end of "Arab coexistence" (i.e., between monarchies, republics); dismisses Prime Minister Mohieddin. (Kleeman 122)

GOALS OF SENDER COUNTRY

December 1964
US goals are enunciated in State Department cable to Egypt: end aid to Congolese rebels, disengage from Yemen, stop pressure on Libya; halt Arab Jordan River Project, keep Israel-Palestine questions in "ice box," stop anti-US campaign in UAR press. (Kleeman 117)

25 August 1965
Secretary of State Dean Rusk cautions President Johnson against explicit linkage between US aid, US political goals; suggests modification of UAR tactics is most that can be achieved. Short-lived settlement is reached in December 1965. (Kleeman 116)

RESPONSE OF TARGET COUNTRY

Robert Kleeman
Following downing of US civilian airplane and Ambassador Battle's comment that discussions on aid would "not be appropriate at that time," Nasser essentially says US can "jump in the lake" with its aid. A few weeks later, however, he stops anti-US attacks in press. They are resumed after release of PL 480 aid in June, "but the U.S. embassy in Cairo interpreted the attack[s] as due to 'pent up frustration for being forced to beg a full six months.'" (Kleeman 111–13)

ATTITUDE OF OTHER COUNTRIES

Soviet Union
From 1955 to 1965, Soviet Union gave about same amount of aid to Egypt as did US. Most of Soviet aid was for Aswan Dam, other development projects. In June 1965, when

Egyptians had only three-week supply of grain left and before US resumed PL 480 shipments, USSR diverted several shipments of Canadian wheat, intended for Soviet consumption, to Egypt. (Kleeman 104, 113)

ECONOMIC IMPACT

Observed Economic Statistics

Between 1955 and 1965, UAR saved about $1 billion between market value, cost of PL 480 food. By 1964, PL 480 supplied 15 percent of UAR food requirements, 50 percent of wheat; and UAR faced acute food shortages. (Kleeman 104)

Egypt had poor cotton harvests in 1961, 1964, 1965; this plus intervention in Yemen led to foreign exchange shortages. (Kleeman 105)

Calculated Economic Impact

	Annual cost to target country
Suspension of US development loans (excluding PL 480); welfare loss estimated at 90 percent of reduced transfers.	$39 million
Withholding of PL 480 aid; welfare loss estimated at 80 percent of value of shipments.	15 million
Total	$54 million

Relative Magnitudes

Gross indicators of Egyptian economy	
Egyptian GNP (1963)	$3.9 billion
Egyptian population (1963)	28.0 million
Annual effect of sanctions related to gross indicators	
Percentage of GNP	1.4
Per capita	$1.93
Egyptian trade with US as percentage of total trade	
Exports (1963)	4
Imports (1963)	25
Ratio of US GNP (1963: $596.7 billion) to Egyptian GNP (1963: $3.9 billion)	153

ASSESSMENT

Robert Kleeman
"The Johnson administration policies did work in 1965. . . . [But] Nasser had other reasons besides the food aid suspension to alter his policy. The Congolese aid program suffered from large inefficiencies, and the rebels themselves became relatively ineffective in their struggle. . . .

"The occasional and ephemeral reductions in anti-US attacks do seem to have been the result of the food aid suspension, as Nasser's actions during the Michel amendment incident in February indicate. . . .[However] [i]n less than one year, the gains of 1965 had been lost." (Kleeman 120–22)

AUTHORS' SUMMARY

Overall assessment	Assigned scores
☐ Policy result, scaled from 1 (failed) to 4 (success)	4
☐ Sanctions contribution, scaled from 1 (none) to 4 (significant)	4
☐ Success score (policy result *times* sanctions contribution), scaled from 1 (outright failure) to 16 (significant success)	16

Political and economic variables

☐ Companion policies: J (covert), Q (quasi-military), or R (regular military)	—
☐ International cooperation with sender, scaled from 1 (none) to 4 (significant)	1
☐ International assistance to target: A (if present)	—
☐ Sanctions period (years)	2
☐ Economic health and political stability of target, scaled from 1 (distressed) to 3 (strong)	2
☐ Presanction relations between sender and target, scaled from 1 (antagonistic) to 3 (cordial)	2
☐ Type of sanction: X (export), M (import), F (financial)	F
☐ Cost to sender, scaled from 1 (net gain) to 4 (major loss)	1

BIBLIOGRAPHY

Kleeman, Robert. 1982. "US Suspension of PL 480 Aid to UAR in 1965." In *Economic Coercion and U.S. Foreign Policy: Implications of Case Studies from the Johnson Administration*, ed. Sidney Weintraub. Boulder, Colo.: Westview Press.

Case 63–2   Indonesia v. Malaysia
(1963–66: "Crush Malaysia" Campaign)

CHRONOLOGY OF KEY EVENTS

Also see Case 63–3 US v. Indonesia (1963–66: Cease "Crush Malaysia")

1956	Malaya grants asylum to Indonesian rebels; Indonesia obstructs Malayan shipping in Strait of Malacca. (*Area Handbook* 260)
1961–62	Malayan Prime Minister Abdul Rahman proposes Federation of Malaya, Singapore, and three Borneo States of Brunei, Sabah, and Sarawak. In August 1962, Malayan, British officials set 31 August 1963 as date for formation of Malaysia. Initial Indonesian reaction is "cool but correct." Opposition grows more intense during 1962 under leadership of Indonesian Communist party (PKI). (*Area Handbook* 261; Jones 266–67)
December 1962	Revolt breaks out in Brunei against joining Malaysian Federation. Indonesian President Ahmed Sukarno uses revolt as excuse to further oppose formation of federation by claiming that it is not desire of people. (Jones 268)
13 February 1963	Sukarno announces at mass meeting in Djakarta, "I now declare officially that Indonesia opposes Malaysia." Following day, President John F. Kennedy reaffirms US support for Malaysia. (Jones 269)
26 July 1963	US Ambassador to Indonesia Howard Jones warns Sukarno that his failure to attend meeting in Manila with heads of state of Malaysia and Philippines to formulate compromise on Malaysia dispute may jeopardize US economic assistance. Sukarno attends meeting 30 July but in mass rally on 27 July he says, "If God wills it, I will leave for Manila the day after tomorrow to carry on our confrontation to oppose and eliminate the neocolonialist Malaysia." (Jones 281)
5 August 1963	Agreement reached in Manila is released to public. "Its key point was that Indonesia and the Philippines would welcome the formation of Malaysia if the UN Secretary General ascertained that the peoples of Sabah and Sarawak desired to be incorporated into Malaysia."

5 August 1963 (continued)	Methodology for this is to be "a scrutinizing of the recent elections in Sarawak and North Borneo, which had resulted in the choice of officials favorable to Malaysia, to determine if they had in fact represented the will of the people." (Jones 283)
29 August 1963	While UN mission is still at work, Malayan government announces that September 16 will mark inauguration of Federation of Malaysia. "Officials explain that the position that Malaysia has all along taken is that the ascertainment by the Secretary General is not a condition that will determine whether Malaysia should be formed or not." Indonesia views proclamation as violation of Manila accords. (Jones 287)
14–15 September 1963	UN Secretary General U Thant announces survey shows majority of population in both Sabah and Sarawak desires to join with Malaya, Singapore in greater Federation of Malaysia. Indonesia labels survey "farce"; Sukarno asks for new survey. On 15 September, Foreign Minister Subandrio says Indonesia will withhold recognition until UN makes "corrections" in surveys of North Borneo, Sarawak as to their desire to join Federation. (Jones 291–92)
16–17 September 1963	Federation of Malaysia proclaimed; Malaysia cuts diplomatic ties with Indonesia, Philippines. (*Area Handbook* 73)
18 September 1963	British Embassy in Indonesia is burned by demonstrators. (Jones 324; Mackie 188)
21 September 1963	Indonesia suspends all trade with Federation of Malaysia, launches "Crush Malaysia" campaign entailing support of guerrillas in Sabah, Sarawak. (*Area Handbook* 72–73)
22 September 1963	US announces temporary suspension of aid in response to Indonesia's attack on British Embassy, dispute with Malaysia. IMF also withholds credits; planned Development Assistance Committee (DAC) discussions on loan to Indonesia are cancelled. (Schenirer 81; Mackie 181)
Late November 1963	Following Kennedy assassination, President Lyndon B. Johnson undertakes policy of graduated aid reductions in attempt to force Indonesia to drop "crush Malaysia" campaign. (Schenirer 83)
1964	In January, US Attorney General Robert F. Kennedy negotiates temporary cease-fire in Borneo which includes withdrawal of Indonesian irregulars. Sukarno asserts only the tactics have changed, and confrontation will continue. Spring and summer are interspersed with unsuccessful attempts to settle dispute. "Initially, the economic thrust of confrontation seemed more purposeful and specific—the diversion of Indonesia's export trade away from Singapore, with the aim of strengthening the Indonesian economy and weakening Malaysia's. During 1964, however, the emphasis changed. Confrontation became an intensely political affair, its purpose far more 'expressive' than 'instrumental' so far as Sukarno and his government were concerned." (Mackie 200)

| 9 August 1965 | Expulsion of Singapore from Federation of Malaysia is announced following outbreaks of racial tension. (Mackie 297) |

| 1 October 1965 | Coup attempt against army linked to PKI, almost certainly with Sukarno's knowledge if not approval, is defeated by forces under General Suharto. Coup attempt, aftermath lead to violence in which at least 300,000 PKI supporters are killed. (Mackie 308; Jones 372) |

| 11 March 1966 | Following Sukarno's attempt to reassert his power by dismissing General Commander Abdul Haris Nasution as defense minister, General Suharto, commander of the army, forces Sukarno to transfer executive power to him. Suharto's authority is confirmed by People's Consultative Congress in July. (Mackie 317) |

| June 1966 | Indonesia, Singapore recognize one another, resume barter trade. (Mackie 321) |

| 28 July 1966 | Although Sukarno retains the title of president, new cabinet formed by Suharto more strongly supports his efforts to end confrontation with Malaysia. (Mackie 322) |

| 16 August 1966 | Malaysia, Indonesia sign normalization agreement. (*Area Handbook* 261) |

| March 1967 | Malaysia, Indonesia reestablish trade, commercial links; embark on joint program to suppress piracy in Strait of Malacca, Communists in Borneo; in August 1967, they restore diplomatic relations. (*Area Handbook* 261) |

GOALS OF SENDER COUNTRY

Howard P. Jones
"The various reasons [Indonesia] gave for opposition [to Malaysia] can be distilled into four:

"One, they were convinced that the Borneans wanted to be independent. Therefore, Indonesians would support them, true to the tradition of backing independence movements of colonies everywhere.

"Two, Sukarno believed that the formation of Malaysia was a British plot to encircle him and had no intention of permitting what he regarded as a hostile nation to be established on his northern border.

"Three, Sukarno scoffed at Britain's alleged decolonization plans, regarding them as 'recolonization' and pointing out that economic power and military defense of Malaysia would still be in British hands.

"Four, some prominent army leaders maintained that the reasons advanced for establishing Malaysia were specious. Instead of curtailing Communist opportunities, it would simply open up North Borneo to Communist penetration and ultimate subversion." (Jones 269)

J. A. C. Mackie
"To [Indonesia] the essential problem [in attaining economic independence] was to

liberate Indonesia's trade from the grip of the capitalist Singapore merchants who were hand in glove with the Nekolim [neocolonialist forces]. [The disruption of trade relations] was primarily a political act, demanding will power, sacrifices and reorganization within Indonesia. . . . It also offered a prospect of forcing Malaysia to her knees by disrupting Singapore's economy. . . . In any case, whatever the outcome of the struggle against Malaysia, Indonesia would increase in stature and self-confidence as a result of the trade break." (Mackie 217)

ATTITUDE OF OTHER COUNTRIES

United States
"The US opposed the Ganjung ["Crush Malaysia"] policy, it had supported the creation of Malaysia in the United Nations, and sought an end to the confrontation. Both Indonesia and Malaysia were important components of the US defense against communism in Southeast Asia. The US had been supplying Indonesia with economic aid for ten years, and attempted, through both the threat of aid termination and the promise of future aid, to coerce Sukarno into a peaceful settlement with Malaysia." (Schenirer 73)

United Kingdom
In response to Manila accord of August 1963: "To them, the Declaration represented intolerable concessions to Sukarno. . . . Duncan Sandys, minister for commonwealth relations, was outraged. His position was that the territories involved were British colonies and her disposition of them was her own business. Britain had not been a party to the Manila accords nor a participant at the conference that produced them. Sandys did not want to postpone the date for the formation of Malaysia, nor did he want the United Nations poking its nose into a British colony. But the three Southeast Asian heads of state had presented the British with a diplomatic fait accompli and the British, albeit with ill grace, bowed to it." (Jones 284)

ECONOMIC IMPACT

Observed Economic Statistics

"The Indonesians were cutting their own economic throat by halting trade with Singapore, the entrepôt through which some 20 to 30 percent of their trade flowed. In the early stages of the blockade, Indonesia had a serious problem as goods piled up in the ports of Sumatra with no ships to carry them. . . . Indonesia had products the world wanted; now it was cut off not only from warehousing, handling, and processing facilities for these products but, even more important, experience in marketing, finance, and insurance.

"Certainly no stabilization program could have succeeded under these conditions. . . . Plans that had envisaged some $400 million in financial assistance to Indonesia had to be scrapped. It would take years and a political cataclysm before another serious economic program would be mounted." (Jones 318)

By April 1965, "virtually all US economic assistance to Indonesia had been terminated, with the exception of four university technical assistance contracts." Military Assistance Program (MAP), begun in 1958 and providing $10 million–$20 million a year, had "practically ground to a halt." (Jones 318)

"The emancipation of Indonesia's trade from Singapore domination was almost forgotten and smuggling to Malaysia was gradually resumed in 1964." (Mackie 200)

Malaysian trade with Indonesia (million dollars)

	Exports	Imports
1962	16.1	108.0
1963	9.0	80.5
1964	1.3	17.5
1965	—	3.8
1966	0.7	6.4
1967	10.1	17.4
1968	10.3	61.7
1969	15.6	59.9

— Zero or negligible.
Source: IMF.

Calculated Economic Impact

	Annual cost to target country
Reduction in Malaysian trade with Indonesia from average level of 1962–63 of $106.8 million to average level of 1964–66 of $9.9 million; welfare loss valued at 30 percent of trade.	$29 million

Relative Magnitudes

Gross indicators of Malaysian economy

Malaysian GNP (1965)	$2.8 billion
Malaysian population (1965)	9.24 million

Annual effect of sanctions related to gross indicators
Percentage of GNP	1.0
Per capita	$3.14

Malaysian trade with Indonesia as percentage of total trade
Exports (1962)	2
Imports (1962)	11

Ratio of Indonesian GNP (1967: $5.5 billion) to Malaysian GNP (1967: $3.1 billion)	2

ASSESSMENT

Howard P. Jones
"Sukarno failed to crush Malaysia, but he succeeded in crushing the economy of his country already laboring under a load too heavy to bear." (Jones 318)

AUTHORS' SUMMARY

Overall assessment	Assigned scores
☐ Policy result, scaled from 1 (failed) to 4 (success)	1
☐ Sanctions contribution, scaled from 1 (none) to 4 (significant)	1
☐ Success score (policy result *times* sanctions contribution), scaled from 1 (outright failure) to 16 (significant success)	1

Political and economic variables

☐ Companion policies: J (covert), Q (quasi-military), or R (regular military)	Q
☐ International cooperation with sender, scaled from 1 (none) to 4 (significant)	1
☐ International assistance to target: A (if present)	—
☐ Sanctions period (years)	3
☐ Economic health and political stability of target, scaled from 1 (distressed) to 3 (strong)	2
☐ Presanction relations between sender and target, scaled from 1 (antagonistic) to 3 (cordial)	2
☐ Type of sanction: X (export), M (import), F (financial)	X, M
☐ Cost to sender, scaled from 1 (net gain) to 4 (major loss)	4

BIBLIOGRAPHY

Jones, Howard P. 1971. *Indonesia: The Possible Dream*. New York: Harcourt Brace Jovanovich.
Mackie, J. A. C. 1974. *Konfrontasi: The Indonesia-Malaysia Dispute 1963–1966*. London: Oxford University Press.
Shenirer, Jay. 1982. "The United States and Indonesia: A Study of Economic Pressure— September 1963–October 1965." In *Economic Coercion and U.S. Foreign Policy: Implications of Case Studies from the Johnson Administration*, ed. Sidney Weintraub. Boulder, Colo.: Westview Press.
United Nations. *Yearbook of International Trade Statistics*. Various issues.

Case 63–3   US v. Indonesia

(1963–66: Cease "Crush Malaysia")

CHRONOLOGY OF KEY EVENTS

Also see Case 63–2 Indonesia v. Malaysia (1963–66: "Crush Malaysia" Campaign)

1945	Future President Ahmed Sukarno: "Indonesia will not become secure unless the whole straits of Malacca is in our hands." (Schenirer 74–75)
8 January 1963	President Sukarno objects to prospective creation of Federation of Malaysia, particularly inclusion of Sabah, Sarawak (Borneo). (Schenirer 75)
13 February 1963	Sukarno announces at mass meeting in Djakarta, "I now declare officially that Indonesia opposes Malaysia." President John F. Kennedy reaffirms US support for Malaysia following day. (Jones 269)
25 July 1963	House Foreign Affairs Committee approves amendment to foreign aid bill that would cut off assistance to Indonesia unless president determines it is in national interest to continue. (Jones 279)
26 July 1963	US Ambassador to Indonesia Howard Jones warns President Sukarno that US economic assistance may be jeopardized by his threatened failure to attend conference in Manila, with heads of state of Malaysia, Philippines, to formulate compromise on Malaysia dispute. Sukarno attends meeting on 30 July but in a mass rally held on 27 July he says, "If God wills it, I will leave for Manila the day after tomorrow to carry on our confrontation to oppose and eliminate the neocolonialist Malaysia." (Jones 281)
5 August 1963	Agreement is reached in Manila calling on UN secretary general to ascertain whether "the peoples of Sabah and Sarawak" desire to be included in Federation of Malaysia. (Jones 283)
14–17 September 1963	On 14 September, UN Secretary General U Thant announces survey supports Malayan position. Indonesia calls survey a "farce," refuses to recognize new federation, which is proclaimed on 16 September.

14–17 September *1963 (continued)*	On 17 September, newly formed Federation of Malaysia breaks diplomatic relations with Indonesia, Philippines. (Jones 291–92; *Area Handbook* 73)
21 September *1963*	Indonesia suspends all trade with Malaysia, and launches "crush Malaysia" campaign entailing support of guerrillas in Sabah, Sarawak. (*Area Handbook* 72–73)
22 September *1963*	US announces temporary suspension of aid in response to Indonesia's attack on British Embassy 18 September, Indonesia's dispute with Malaysia. IMF credits also are withheld, planned Development Assistance Committee (DAC) discussions on loan to Indonesia are cancelled. (Schenirer 81; Mackie 181)
November 1963	US Congress adds section 620(i) to Foreign Assistance Act of 1963 calling for termination of aid to any country (i.e., Indonesia) "engaging in or preparing for aggressive efforts" against US aid recipient (i.e., Malaysia); Section 620(i) contains presidential "national interest" waiver. Tower amendment (Senator John Tower, R–Tex.), explicitly withholding all aid from Indonesia, is defeated in conference. (Schenirer 80)
19 November *1963*	Ambassador Jones, Assistant Secretary of State for Far Eastern Affairs Roger Hilsman urge Kennedy to consider accepting Sukarno invitation to visit Indonesia. Hilsman feels Sukarno places "so much importance on President Kennedy's visit to Indonesia that this possibility alone might bring him to recognize Malaysia where all other pressures fail." (Jones 295)
November– *December 1963*	Kennedy approves shipment to Indonesia of 40,000 tons of PL 480 (a food aid program) rice with no conditions, another 20,000 tons conditional on political progress. US denies export licenses for weapons to Indonesia. (Schenirer 81)
Early December *1963*	Following Kennedy's assassination, President Lyndon B. Johnson refuses to sign waiver that would authorize new aid to Indonesia. Shortly thereafter, he directs Secretary of Defense Robert S. McNamara to draw up, implement program of gradual, "progressive curtailment of aid" Indonesia was still receiving under previously authorized programs. (Jones 300)
27 December 1963	Ambassador Jones informs Sukarno: Indonesia should end support for Sarawak guerrillas; US then would provide 65,000 to 100,000 tons of rice in 1964, renew consideration of stabilization program; if tensions with Malaysia continue, US could not provide further assistance to Indonesia, would be called upon to honor Anzus Treaty. (Schenirer 83)
January 1964	Attorney General Robert F. Kennedy, after threatening "grave consequences" for US-Indonesia relations if hostilities continue, negotiates temporary cease-fire in Sarawak. However, cease-fire never is implemented fully because of Sukarno's refusal to withdraw Indonesian irregulars from Malaysian territory. (Schenirer 85; Jones 302)

3 March 1964	Jones warns pro-Western Indonesian military leaders Sukarno's course is playing into Communist party hands and Indonesia has no international support for prospective war with Britain over territorial integrity of Malaysia. (Schenirer 86)
28 March 1964	In response to Sukarno speech ("To hell with your aid"), Congressman Harold Ryan (D–Mich.), reflecting widespread congressional opinion, calls for Johnson to cut off all aid. (Schenirer 85)
May–July 1964	Assistant Secretary of State William P. Bundy publicly suggests US may have to eliminate all aid programs; Jones privately recommends continued US supply, training for Indonesian military, larger PL 480 shipments on "foot in the door" analysis. US continues making incremental cuts in aid. (Schenirer 89, 92)
23 July 1964	US announces agreement with Malaysia to undertake training of its military personnel, sale of $5 million in military equipment to Malaysia immediately after Prime Minister Abdul Rahman visits US. (Jones 345)
1965	US consulates in Medan, Surabaya are attacked, US Information Service libraries closed. Indonesia withdraws from UN, nationalizes Western oil companies, aligns with "anti-imperialist axis." (Schenirer 92)
1 October 1965	Coup attempt against army, linked to Indonesian Communist party (PKI) and almost certainly with Sukarno's knowledge if not approval, is defeated by forces under General Suharto. Coup attempt is followed by outburst of violence in which at least 300,000 PKI supporters are killed. (Mackie 308; Jones 372)
1966	General Suharto displaces Sukarno as de facto leader but allows him to retain title; soon thereafter settles Malaysian controversy. (Schenirer 94)
1967	US economic stabilization program provides $80 million to Indonesia in 1967, $55 million in 1968. (Schenirer 95)

GOALS OF SENDER COUNTRY

Ambassador Howard P. Jones
In meeting with Sukarno 26 July 1963, urging him to attend Manila conference: "There was another point he must consider: the effect his refusal would have on the economic program we had been working out together. If Sukarno failed to go to Manila, it would be a clear indication to all concerned that he was not interested in settling the Malaysia dispute, and I said I could not vouch for our continuing ability to assist Indonesia. I told him I knew President Kennedy wanted to help. I questioned whether it would be in Indonesia's interests to take actions that would make it politically impossible for Kennedy to carry out his intention expressed when the two heads of state met at the White House two years before, to provide economic assistance to Indonesia." (Jones 280)

Jay Schenirer
Initial US goals involved: settling Malaysian conflict through withdrawal of Indonesian support for guerrillas (publicly stated); demonstrating US support for Malaysia, alliance with UK (publicly stated); placating Congress with show of action (privately held). (Schenirer 80)

On 7 January 1964, after extensive review, President Johnson decides continued aid to Indonesia is essential to US national interests and US should "play out our hand as long as possible with Indonesia, i.e., by gradual cutoffs and private rather than public warnings." Thus, on 3 April 1964, Secretary of State Dean Rusk, following denunciation of US by Sukarno and call by Congressman Ryan to cut all aid states: "Some aid should be continued regardless of US-Indonesian political relations." (Schenirer 83, 88)

In April 1964, in response to elevation of Indonesia–North Korea relations to full diplomatic level, US warns Sukarno against appearance of North Korean "volunteers" in Malaysia. (Schenirer 89)

RESPONSE OF TARGET COUNTRY

January–February 1964
Indonesian unions take over British, US firms (Unilever, American Tobacco, Shell Oil, P&T Co.); Indonesian government takes over all supervisory posts in British firms; 1,500 students, escorted by Indonesian police, demonstrate in front of US Embassy. (Schenirer 85)

24 January 1964
Sukarno announces "confrontation" would continue, but that tactics might change; refuses to withdraw guerrilla leaders, military personnel from Borneo. (Schenirer 85)

25 March 1964
Sukarno to US: "To hell with your aid. We can do without aid, we'll never collapse: Indonesia is rich in natural resources, Indonesia is rich in manpower with 103 million inhabitants . . . not like Malaysia with its 10 million." (Schenirer 87)

9 April 1964
Sukarno: "If any nation offers aid with strings such as a condition that 'we cease confrontation,' I say go to hell with your aid!. . ." (Schenirer 89)

3–5 May 1964
Sukarno issues "action command" to "21 million volunteers" in fight to crush Malaysia, repeats "go to hell with your aid" statement. In private meeting with Ambassador Jones, Sukarno indicates it might be best if he no longer accepted US aid but Jones dissuades him from taking any action. Jones says, "The Indonesia reaction to Bundy's comment confirmed what I had been telling Washington, that the Indonesians would never yield to threats. . . ." (Schenirer 89; Jones 303)

17 August 1964
In response to Malaysian prime minister's visit to Washington and resultant joint communiqué, Sukarno, in annual independence day speech, attacks US, recognizes North Vietnam, North Korea. On 24 August, Sukarno reshuffles cabinet in way that strengthens Communists. In explaining moves to Jones, Sukarno says, "When your government

announced that it was going to give military aid to our enemy, Malaysia, this meant that you were joining Britain and Malaysia against us." (Jones 344, 347)

1966
After displacing Sukarno, General Suharto settles Malaysian controversy by withdrawing support from guerrilla forces. (Schenirer 94)

ECONOMIC IMPACT

Observed Economic Statistics

By one estimate, confrontation with Malaysia deprived Indonesia of more than $250 million in aid for its stabilization scheme. (Mackie 220)

Calculated Economic Impact

	Annual cost to target country
Reduction in PL 480 rice shipments; welfare loss estimated at 50 percent of value of reduced sales.	$3 million
Reduction in bilateral aid from US, loans from IMF; welfare loss estimated at 100 percent of reduced transfers.	107 million
Total	$110 million

Relative Magnitudes

Gross indicators of Indonesian economy	
Indonesian GNP (1967)	$5.5 billion
Indonesian population (1965)	105.1 million
Annual effect of sanctions related to gross indicators	
Percentage of GNP	2.0
Per capita	$1.05
Indonesian trade with US as percentage of total trade	
Exports (1963)	14
Imports (1963)	35
Ratio of US GNP (1967: $799.6 billion) to Indonesian GNP (1967: $5.5 billion)	145

ASSESSMENT

US State Department
In fall 1964, US State Department admits aid is "a frail lever in altering the course of basic Indonesian action." (Schenirer 92)

Jay Schenirer
"The major formal objective of US policy toward Indonesia was to bring sufficient pressure on President Sukarno to end the 'Crush Malaysia' policy. Toward this goal, the United States repeatedly threatened cuts in aid if Sukarno did not comply with US demands, and promised future aid and investments if Sukarno did comply. This policy failed. . . . In its objective of keeping Indonesia from becoming Communist, the United States was more successful although the reasons for success cannot be causally linked to US aid. . . . A third objective of US aid policy, maintaining a foot in the door for future contingencies, did succeed. However, neither this objective nor that of maintaining influence with the military was pursued through negative coercive techniques. The undisclosed objectives of mollifying both domestic and foreign pressures on the administration to take some form of action were really predetermined successes." (Schenirer 93–94)

J. A. C. Mackie
"Negotiations for a settlement of the dispute did not begin, therefore, until the Bangkok conference of February 1964, after the intervention of Robert Kennedy. It is arguable that the delay merely increased Indonesia's intransigence, for as time passed she became more confident that she could weather the economic perils of the new course she was embarked on and the alternatives left open to the advocates of moderation became fewer and fewer." (Mackie 194)

". . . economic dislocation did not greatly hamper the government in its campaign against Malaysia until late in 1964 (or even later) when the inflation began to accelerate and the shortage of foreign exchange became really acute. Even then, however, economic pressure did not force Soekarno to the conference table in 1965. Domestic political forces proved to be far more important than sheer economic necessity in determining the course of confrontation." (Mackie 201)

AUTHORS' SUMMARY

Overall assessment	Assigned scores
□ Policy result, scaled from 1 (failed) to 4 (success)	4
□ Sanctions contribution, scaled from 1 (none) to 4 (significant)	2
□ Success score (policy result *times* sanctions contribution), scaled from 1 (outright failure) to 16 (significant success)	8

Political and economic variables

□ Companion policies: J (covert), Q (quasi-military), or R (regular military)	—
□ International cooperation with sender, scaled from 1 (none) to 4 (significant)	1
□ International assistance to target: A (if present)	—

	Assigned scores
Political and economic variables (continued)	
☐ Sanctions period (years)	3
☐ Economic health and political stability of target, scaled from 1 (distressed) to 3 (strong)	2
☐ Presanction relations between sender and target, scaled from 1 (antagonistic) to 3 (cordial)	2
☐ Type of sanction: X (export), M (import), F (financial)	F
☐ Cost to sender, scaled from 1 (net gain) to 4 (major loss)	1

BIBLIOGRAPHY

American University. 1970. *Area Handbook for Indonesia.* Washington: GPO.

Jones, Howard P. 1971. *Indonesia: The Possible Dream.* New York: Harcourt Brace Jovanovich.

Mackie, J. A. C. 1974. *Konfrontasi: The Indonesia-Malaysia Dispute 1963–66.* London: Oxford University Press.

Schenirer, Jay. 1982. "The United States and Indonesia: A Study of Economic Pressure—September 1963–October 1965." In *Economic Coercion and U.S. Foreign Policy: Implications of Case Studies from the Johnson Administration,* ed. Sidney Weintraub. Boulder, Colo.: Westview Press.

Case 63–4   US v. South Vietnam

(1963: Diem)

CHRONOLOGY OF KEY EVENTS

(Note: The following chronology is almost verbatim condensation from The Pentagon Papers, 1971, 207–23)

8 May 1963	Government troops fire on Buddhist protest demonstration in Hue, killing 9, wounding 14. Incident triggers nationwide Buddhist protest, crisis of popular confidence in regime of President Ngo Dinh Diem. Government of South Vietnam (GVN) maintains the incident was act of Viet Cong (VC) terrorism.
18 May 1963	US Ambassador Frederick Nolting meets with Diem, outlines steps US wants him to take to redress Buddhist grievances, recapture public confidence. These include admission of responsibility for Hue incident, compensation of victims, reaffirmation of religious equality, nondiscrimination.
4 June 1963	US Chargé d'Affaires William Truehart meets with Secretary of State Nguyen Dinh Thuan, warns that US support for Diem regime could not be maintained if there were another bloody suppression of Buddhists.
11 June 1963	Thich Quang Duc, Buddhist monk, is immersed in gasoline, sets himself afire. His fiery protest suicide is photographed, becomes front page material in world's newspapers. Mme. Nhu, wife of Ngo Dinh Nhu, Diem's brother and chief political adviser, subsequently refers to event as a "barbecue."
12 June 1963	Truehart again protests to Diem over Buddhist problem and shock created by Quang Duc's suicide. Truehart warns that if Diem does not act, US will dissociate itself from him.
14 June 1963	Under US pressure, negotiations between Vice President Nguyen Ngoc Tho's specially appointed committee, Buddhist leadership reopen in apparent earnest.
16 June 1963	Joint GVN-Buddhist communiqué released as a product of negotia-

tions outlines elements of settlement but affixes no responsibility for 8 May incident in Hue.

27 June 1963   President John F. Kennedy, visiting in Ireland, announces appointment of Henry Cabot Lodge as new US ambassador to South Vietnam, effective in September.

3 July 1963   Vice President Tho's committee announces that preliminary investigation of 8 May incident has confirmed that deaths were result of act of VC terrorism.

11–19 July 1963   Nolting returns to Vietnam to make one last attempt to persuade Diem to conciliate Buddhists. Complying with letter of Nolting's request, Diem delivers brief radio address that makes only minor concessions to Buddhists, asks for support of government.

5 August 1963   Second Buddhist monk commits suicide by burning himself to death in continuing protest against Diem regime.

18 August 1963   Ten senior army generals decide they will ask Diem for declaration of martial law to permit them to return monks from outside Saigon to their own provinces and pagodas, thus reduce tensions in capital.

21 August 1963   Under cover of military martial law, forces loyal to Nhu and under his orders attack pagodas throughout Vietnam, arresting monks, sacking sacred buildings. More than 30 Buddhists are injured, more than 1,400 arrested. US State Department deplores raids as direct violation of Diem's assurances to Nolting. Initial intelligence reports place blame for raid on army, not Nhu.

24 August 1963   "August 24 cable" from US State Department to Ambassador Lodge acknowledges Nhu's responsibility for raids, says US no longer can tolerate his continuation in power. If Diem does not remove Nhu, generals are to be told that US will discontinue economic, military support to Diem but will provide assistance to them in any period of interim breakdown of GVN. Lodge's permission is requested for a Voice of America broadcast exonerating army of responsibility for August 21 raids.

26 August 1963   Voice of America in South Vietnam broadcasts press stories blaming Nhu for 21 August raids, absolving army. It also broadcasts press speculation that US is contemplating suspension of aid.

29 August 1963   General Duong Van Minh, a senior Army officer and coup leader, asks for clear evidence that US will not betray generals to Nhu. When asked what would constitute sign of support, Minh replies that US should suspend economic aid to regime.

31 August 1963   Minh calls off planned coup, citing inability to achieve favorable balance of forces in Saigon area, doubts as to whether US had leaked plans to Nhu. Future attempt is not ruled out.

2 September 1963   Kennedy, in TV interview with Walter Cronkite of CBS News,

2 September 1963 (continued)	expresses disappointment with Diem's handling of Buddhist crisis, concern that greater effort is needed by GVN to win popular support. This can be done, he feels, "with change in policy and perhaps with personnel. . . ."
8 September 1963	David Bell, director of US Agency for International Development (AID), expresses concern that Congress might cut aid to South Vietnam if Diem government does not change its repressive policies. Next day, Kennedy says he does not believe aid cut-off would be helpful in achieving American purposes in Vietnam at present.
10 September 1963	Representing Defense and State Departments, respectively, General Victor Krulak and Joseph Mendenhall return from Vietnam after four-day trip, report to National Security Council (NSC). Krulak stresses that war is being won and, while there is some dissatisfaction in military with Diem, no one would risk his neck to remove him. Continuation of present policies under Diem will yield victory. Mendenhall presents completely contradictory view: breakdown of civil administration, religious civil war are possible if Diem is not replaced; war certainly could not be won with Diem. Kennedy asks his two emissaries, "You two did visit the same country, didn't you?"
11 September 1963	Lodge reverses himself, suggests complete study of kinds of economic aid suspension that might be used to topple regime. Kennedy decides to hold economic aid renewal in abeyance pending complete examination of how it might be used to pressure Diem.
12 September 1963	With White House approval, Senator Frank Church (D–Idaho) introduces resolution condemning South Vietnamese government for repressive handling of Buddhist problem, calling for end to US aid unless repressions are abandoned.
14 September 1963	Lodge is informed that approval of $18.5 million commercial import program is deferred until basic policy decisions on Vietnam have been made.
16 September 1963	Martial law is ended throughout country.
17 September 1963	US considers alternative proposals for dealing with Diem. First would use escalating pressure to obtain his acceptance of US policy initiatives. Second would involve US acquiescence in recent GVN actions, recognition that Diem and Nhu are inseparable, attempt to salvage as much as possible from bad situation. Kennedy adopts first policy, sends Secretary of Defense Robert S. McNamara and General Maxwell Taylor, chairman of joint chiefs of staff, on fact-gathering mission.
2 October 1963	McNamara, Taylor return to Washington with compromise report. They confirm progress of war but warn of political turmoil, recommend pressure against Diem to bring changes. Militarily, they call for greater GVN effort in Delta and clear-and-hold operations, consolidation of strategic hamlet program. They propose announce-

ment of plans to withdraw 1,000 American troops by end of 1963. To put political pressure on Diem, they recommend selective aid suspension, end of support for special forces responsible for pagoda raids, continuation of Lodge's aloofness from regime. They recommend against a coup, but suggest alternative leadership be identified and cultivated. Kennedy promptly approves recommendations.

Statement following meeting reiterates US commitment to struggle against VC, announces 1,000-man troop withdrawal, dissociates US from Diem's repressive policies. It does not, however, announce aid suspension.

6 October 1963   Washington clarifies its views on coup by stating that US will not thwart move if it offers prospects of more effective fight against VC. Security and deniability of all contacts are paramount.

17 October 1963   Acting for Ambassador Lodge, General Stillwell informs Secretary of State Thuan that US aid for special forces units responsible for 21 August raids is being suspended until they are transferred to field, placed under Vietnamese Joint General Staff (JGS) command.

27 October 1963   Seventh Buddhist monk commits suicide by fire.

1 November 1963   First coup units begin to deploy in and around Saigon.

Coup committee convenes meeting of all senior Vietnamese officers except Generals Ton That Dinh, commander of the Saigon military region, and Huynh Van Cao at JGS. All support coup except Colonel Le Quan Tung, head of special forces in Saigon and loyal to Diem and Nhu. Their pledges of support are taped. Tung is taken into custody, later executed.

A CIA officer is invited to JGS, maintains telephone contact with US Embassy throughout coup. General Tran Van Don informs General Stillwell coup is under way. Generals go on radio, announce the coup, demand resignation of Diem and Nhu.

Diem calls General Don, surrenders unconditionally. He and Nhu are taken prisoner shortly thereafter, are murdered in back of armored personnel carrier en route to JGS.

3 November 1963   Generals Don and Le Van Kim call on Lodge, who promises immediate restoration of aid programs, assures generals of forthcoming US recognition. On 8 November, Lodge calls on new Foreign Minister, Pham Dang Lam, presents a note of US recognition.

GOALS OF SENDER COUNTRY

Geoffrey Warner
". . . on 11 September the Ambassador [Lodge] proposed 'that detailed consideration be given to ways in which nonmilitary aid suspension might be used as a sanction to topple the government.' He had reached the conclusion that the United States could not obtain

satisfaction from Diem 'and had to face up to the unpleasant task of forcing events.'" (Warner 6)

Pentagon Papers
September 1963: Policy reviews were held in Washington, Saigon to determine whether war effort was best advanced with or without Diem. "In the end, a third alternative was selected, namely to use pressure on Diem to get him to remove Nhu from the scene and to end his repressive policies." (*Pentagon Papers* 204)

"[The Taylor-McNamara report's] recommendations for aid suspensions and the announcement of US troop withdrawals were obviously designed as measures, short of a withdrawal of US support, that would create doubt within the Diem regime about US intentions and incentives for policy changes. The fact that these sanctions would be seen by the generals as a signal of our willingness to accept alternative leadership—i.e., a coup—does not seem to have figured in the recommendation, however, because elsewhere the report specifically rules out US encouragement of 'a change of government.' This is an important lapse in view of the generals' clear statement in August that they would regard an aid suspension as a coup signal." (*Pentagon Papers* 251)

RESPONSE OF TARGET COUNTRY

Pentagon Papers
Following suspension of Commodity Import Program, *The Times of Vietnam* (run by Nhu) carries article that "accused the US of subverting the war effort, and asserted that the cutoff had been decided in mid-September. Such fantastic pressure for petty reforms would jeopardize the entire revolutionary program of the government, it concluded." (*Pentagon Papers* 253)

"A CIA memorandum concluded that the GVN reaction to the new US policy, particularly the violent anti-US campaign in *The Times of Vietnam* and the surveillance and harassment of Americans and their employees, indicated that Diem and Nhu were preparing for a long fight and were unmoved by the new policy." (*Pentagon Papers* 253)

ECONOMIC IMPACT

Observed Economic Statistics

US aid to Vietnam (million dollars)

	Economic	Military
1962	156.0	204.2
1963	195.9	258.4
1964	222.4	181.8
1965	276.7	268.9

Source: AID.

Calculated Economic Impact

	Annual cost to target country
Deferral of $18.5 million in US aid in September 1983 for two months under commercial import program; welfare loss estimated at 50 percent of deferred resources.	$9 million

Relative Magnitudes

Gross indicators of South Vietnamese economy	
Vietnamese GNP (1963)	$2.9 billion
Vietnamese population (1963)	15.3 million
Annual effect of sanctions related to gross indicators	
Percentage of GNP	0.3
Per capita	$0.59
South Vietnamese trade with US as percentage of total trade	
Exports (1963)	2
Imports (1963)	38
Ratio of US GNP (1963: $596.7 billion) to South Vietnamese GNP (1963: $2.9 billion)	206

ASSESSMENT

Pentagon Papers
"Of the recommendations of the McNamara-Taylor mission, the proposal for the selective suspension of economic aid, in particular the suspension of the commercial import program, was the most significant both in terms of its effect, and as an example of the adroit use of denial of American assistance to achieve our foreign policy objectives. In this instance economic sanctions, in the form of selected aid suspensions in those programs to which the regime would be most sensitive but that would have no immediate adverse effect on the war effort, were used constructively to influence events rather than negatively to punish those who had violated our wishes, our usual reaction to coups in Latin America." (*Pentagon Papers* 205–6)

Roger Hilsman
"The trouble with these selective cuts was that they had no real leverage. Nhu could find other sources of income for his special forces and continue to use them against domestic opposition rather than the Viet Cong. The commodity imports would mean a sacrifice in semiluxuries and eventually inflation—although here, too, there were other ways to attack the problem of inflation. Selective cuts in the war effort, in other words, would not exert enough pressure to force Diem to change. But they did have considerable symbolic and psychological impact." (Hilsman 500)

AUTHORS' SUMMARY

Overall assessment	Assigned scores
□ Policy result, scaled from 1 (failed) to 4 (success)	4
□ Sanctions contribution, scaled from 1 (none) to 4 (significant)	3
□ Success score (policy result *times* sanctions contribution), scaled from 1 (outright failure) to 16 (significant success)	12

Political and economic variables

□ Companion policies: J (covert), Q (quasi-military), or R (regular military)	J
□ International cooperation with sender, scaled from 1 (none) to 4 (significant)	1
□ International assistance to target: A (if present)	—
□ Sanctions period (years)	1
□ Economic health and political stability of target, scaled from 1 (distressed) to 3 (strong)	1
□ Presanction relations between sender and target, scaled from 1 (antagonistic) to 3 (cordial)	3
□ Type of sanction: X (export), M (import), F (financial)	F
□ Cost to sender, scaled from 1 (net gain) to 4 (major loss)	1

BIBLIOGRAPHY

Agency for International Development. 1971. *Overseas Loans and Grants.*

Herring, George C. 1979. *America's Longest War: The United States and Vietnam 1958–1975.* New York: John Wiley & Sons.

Hilsman, Roger. 1967. *To Move a Nation: The Politics of Foreign Policy in the Administration of John F. Kennedy.* Garden City, NY: Doubleday.

The Pentagon Papers: The Defense Department History of United States Decisionmaking on Vietnam. 1971. Ed. Mike Gravel. Vol. 2. Boston: Beacon Press, pp. 201–76.

Warner, Geoffrey. 1975. "The United States and the Fall of Diem; Part 2: The Death of Diem." 29 *Australian Outlook* (April): 3–17.

Case 63–5 UN and OAU v. Portugal
(1963–74: African Colonies)

CHRONOLOGY OF KEY EVENTS

15 December 1960   UN General Assembly votes to classify Portugal's African colonies as "non-self-governing" territories, thus subject to provisions of UN Charter on decolonization of such territories. (Cervenka 214, n. 61)

1961–64   Armed rebellion breaks out in Angola (4 February 1961), Guinea-Bissau (3 April 1961), Mozambique (25 September 1964). By 1971, estimates of cost of war to Portugal range upwards of $400 million. (Cervenka 135)

1963   Organization of African Unity (OAU) adopts resolution declaring economic, diplomatic boycott of Portugal, calling on Western powers, particularly US, UK "to cease all direct and indirect support to Portugal." (Cervenka 138)

21 December 1965   By vote of 66 to 25, UN General Assembly calls for economic, arms boycott against Portugal until it frees its African colonies. Same resolution is reintroduced in every subsequent session until December 1973, continues to be approved by large margins. (*Keesing's* 21238; Doxey 59–60)

29 August 1970   OAU adopts resolution condemning US, UK, France, FRG for their "massive support" of Portugal. (*Keesing's* 24191)

14 December 1970   UN General Assembly adopts resolution requesting withdrawal of international support for Cabora Bassa project, a dam in Mozambique. Sweden had withdrawn in 1969, Italy by January 1971. Resolution states that project represents "plot designed to perpetuate the domination, exploitation and oppression of the peoples of this part of Africa by the Government of Portugal. . . ." (*Keesing's* 24667–8)

6 May 1971   Cabora Bassa project is opposed by State Department and anti-apartheid senators and congressmen. General Electric withdraws its application for Export–Import Bank loan relating to project. France, FRG continue their involvement. (*Keesing's* 24667–8)

| 22 May 1973 | UK, US veto Security Council resolution to extend trade sanctions already in effect against Rhodesia to South Africa and Portuguese territories in Africa. (*Facts on File* 507) |

21 November 1973   OAU Council of Ministers adopts "a resolution in which they unanimously appeal to all member-states of the organization and all friendly countries to 'impose a total economic embargo, and in particular an oil embargo, against Israel, Portugal, South Africa and the minority regime in Southern Rhodesia.'" (*Keesing's* 26246)

24 November 1973   At smaller meeting, OAU ministers threaten to take "diplomatic and economic measures" against US, some European countries if they continue to cooperate with white regimes. (*Keesing's* 26246)

28 November 1973   Arab chiefs of state, at conclusion of summit conference, announce embargo on oil exports to Portugal, Rhodesia, South Africa. (*Facts on File* 981)

April–May 1974   Portuguese army insurgents headed by General Antonio de Spinola overthrow government of Prime Minister Marcello Caetano, form civilian government, promising wide variety of reforms. (Cervenka 138–39)

27 July 1974   President Spinola announces Portugal will offer independence to overseas territories; Guinea-Bissau is granted independence in September 1974; Mozambique, Sao Tome and Principe, and Angola in 1975. (Graham 62; Cervenka 139)

GOALS OF SENDER COUNTRIES

Nzo Ekangaki, OAU secretary general
The 21 November 1973 embargo would "force the Portuguese colonialists and their racist allies to think again about their ability to go on opposing world opinion." (*Keesing's* 26246)

United Nations
General Assembly Resolution on Portugal's African colonies:

"(1) An affirmation of the right of the peoples of the Portuguese African territories to freedom and independence.

"(2) A condemnation of the colonial policy of Portugal and its persistent refusal to carry out the resolutions of the General Assembly and the Security Council.

"(3) An appeal to UN member states to take the following measures against Portugal: (a) the breaking off of diplomatic relations; (b) closing of their ports to Portuguese vessels; (c) refusal of landing or transit facilities for Portuguese aircraft; (d) a boycott on trade with Portugal.

"(4) An appeal to Portugal's NATO allies to ban the supply of sale of arms, ammunitions, and military equipment to Portugal.

"(5) An appeal to all UN specialized agencies, particularly to the World Bank and the IMF, to refrain from granting Portugal any financial, economic, or technical assistance so long as she failed to implement the General Assembly's resolution of 1960 on the ending of Portugal's colonial policy.

"(6) A request to the UN High Commissioner for Refugees, the specialized agencies concerned, and other international relief organizations, 'to increase their assistance to refugees from territories under Portuguese administration and to the people who have suffered from military operations.'

"(7) A request to the Security Council to consider putting into effect against Portugal the appropriate measures laid down in the Charter." (*Keesing's* 21238)

RESPONSE OF TARGET COUNTRY

Zdenek Cervenka
"Alone of the colonial powers, Portugal refused to consider granting independence to its overseas provinces, which it regarded as integral parts of Portugal whose future was therefore not negotiable with any international authority. This was maintained consistently by Portugal at the UN from the time it joined that organization in 1955 to the military coup in 1974." (Cervenka 135)

Keesing's
After passage of UN resolution 12 December 1966, "The Portugese Foreign Minister, Dr. Franco Nogueira, said in Lisbon that Portugal was not disquieted by the UN resolution, which he described as 'irresponsible' and characterized by 'aggressive verbosity'." (*Keesing's* 21869)

ATTITUDE OF OTHER COUNTRIES

United States
Explaining US veto on broadening sanctions against Rhodesia to include South Africa and Portuguese territories, Ambassador John Scali: "To pass resolutions which are clearly unenforceable would seriously damage the reputation and credibility of the United Nations and further erode public confidence in the United Nations to act in any meaningful way." (*Facts on File* 507)

North Atlantic Treaty Organization
" . . . The real power behind the Portuguese colonial wars in Africa which lasted 13 years was not Portugal itself but NATO, to which Portugal had been admitted in 1949. The main reason for this was the strategic importance of all Portugal's African territories. . . . At the same time, the economic potential of the Portuguese African possessions . . . represented vast raw-material resources for the industries of the NATO countries, so there was even more reason to give military support to Portugal despite the growing disapproval of public opinion in the NATO countries themselves." (Cervenka 135)

ECONOMIC IMPACT

Observed Economic Statistics

Portuguese oil imports (million metric tons)

	1973	1974
Quarter 1	1.06	1.59
Quarter 2	1.15	1.59
Quarter 3	1.25	1.40
Quarter 4	0.89	1.33

Source: OECD.

Calculated Economic Impact

	Annual cost to target country
Reduction in Portuguese oil imports in the 4th quarter of 1973 as a result of OPEC oil embargo; welfare loss estimated at 75 percent of value of trade.	$11 million
Reduction in support for Cabora Bassa dam in Mozambique by US, Sweden, Italy; welfare loss estimated at 70 percent of reduced aid.	negl.
Total	$11 million

(Pre-1973 UN and OAU embargo against Portugal had negligible impact on trade flows.)

Relative Magnitudes

Gross indicators of Portuguese economy	
Portuguese GNP (1965)	$3.8 billion
Portuguese population (1965)	8.8 million
Annual effect of sanctions related to gross indicators	
Percentage of GNP	0.3
Per capita	$1.25
Portuguese trade with Africa as percentage of total trade	
Exports (1972)	15
Imports (1972)	14
Ratio of African GNP (1976: $153.8 billion) to Portuguese GNP (1976: $15.7 billion)	10

ASSESSMENT

Margaret P. Doxey
"There was no evidence that these recommendations were carried out by United Nations members, or that Portuguese policy was modified as a result of them." (Doxey 60)

Peter Wallensteen
"In the case of Portugal, the OAU-imposed sanctions were terminated in 1975 following the successful coup that overthrew the Caetano regime. The OAU did not itself vigorously claim that its sanctions had, to a significant degree, contributed to this. Instead, most observers would agree that the liberation struggles in the Portuguese possessions of Angola, Guinea, and Mozambique were more instrumental in ousting the regime." (Wallensteen 94)

AUTHORS' SUMMARY

Overall assessment	Assigned scores
☐ Policy result, scaled from 1 (failed) to 4 (success)	4
☐ Sanctions contribution, scaled from 1 (none) to 4 (significant)	2
☐ Success score (policy result *times* sanctions contribution), scaled from 1 (outright failure) to 16 (significant success)	8

Political and economic variables

☐ Companion policies: J (covert), Q (quasi-military), or R (regular military)	—
☐ International cooperation with sender, scaled from 1 (none) to 4 (significant)	3
☐ International assistance to target: A (if present)	—
☐ Sanctions period (years)	11
☐ Economic health and political stability of target, scaled from 1 (distressed) to 3 (strong)	2
☐ Presanction relations between sender and target, scaled from 1 (antagonistic) to 3 (cordial)	2
☐ Type of sanction: X (export), M (import), F (financial)	F, X, M
☐ Cost to sender, scaled from 1 (net gain) to 4 (major loss)	2

BIBLIOGRAPHY

Cervenka, Zdenek. 1977. *The Unfinished Quest for Unity: Africa and the OAU.* New York: Africana Publishing Company.

Doxey, Margaret P. 1980. *Economic Sanctions and International Enforcement.* 2d ed. New York: Oxford University Press for Royal Institute of International Affairs.

Facts on File. 1973.

Graham, Lawrence S. 1975. *Portugal: The Decline and Collapse of an Authoritarian Order.* Beverly Hills, Calif.: Sage Publications.

Keesing's Contemporary Archives. 1965–66, 1967–68, 1969–70, 1971–72, 1973.

Organization for Economic Cooperation and Development. *Provisional Oil Statistics, by Quarters.* Various years.

Wallensteen, Peter. 1983. "Economic Sanctions: Ten Modern Cases and Three Important Lessons." In *Dilemmas of Economic Coercion: Sanctions in World Politics*, ed. Miroslav Nincic and Peter Wallensteen. New York: Praeger.

Case 64–1   France v. Tunisia

(1964–66: Expropriation)

CHRONOLOGY OF KEY EVENTS

October 1962   France, Tunisia open negotiations on transfer of French-owned agricultural land to government of Tunisia. (*Keesing's* 19320)

2 March 1963   Agreement is reached for transferring 370,000 acres of French-owned land to Tunisia, to be completed by September. Settlement requires Tunisia to pay $3.3 million for land, another $2.2 million for equipment, crops, livestock, etc. Another 120,000 acres are scheduled to change hands in 1964. (*Keesing's* 20152)

28 April 1964   Tunisian President Habib Bourguiba asks for drastic revision of March 1963 agreements lowering the amount Tunisia must pay for repatriated land. (*Keesing's* 20152)

2 May 1964   France suspends bilateral aid in response to Tunisia's proposal to reopen land question. (*Keesing's* 20152)

11 May 1964   Tunisia begins expropriating "virtually all remaining foreign-owned land" following passage of nationalization law by National Assembly. (*Keesing's* 20152)

13 May 1964   France cancels aid agreement signed with Tunisia in February that would have provided $9.2 million in 1964. (*Keesing's* 20152)

15 May 1964   Tunisia decides to raise compulsory "popular loan" based on income, repayable over 15 years, at 5 percent interest, to replace French aid. (*Keesing's* 20153)

10 June 1964   France denounces 1959 trade agreement with Tunisia (renewed in February 1964), imposes 5 percent duty on wine imports from Tunisia. (*Keesing's* 20153)

March 1966   Bourguiba, seeking improved relations with France, states at press conference that land nationalization was made necessary by Tunisia's dire economic circumstances. "This statement was regarded in Tunis as being intended to provide the kind of public 'gesture' reportedly

March 1966 (continued)	being sought by General [Charles] de Gaulle, president of France, from M. Bourguiba as a preliminary to renewed closer cooperation." (*Keesing's* 23616)
May 1966	France restores preferential tariffs for certain Tunisian products, in July allows quantity of wine to enter duty free. Net profit from wine transaction provides initial installment in compensation for French farmers displaced in 1964. Final agreement on compensation for expropriation is not reached but French-Tunisian relations steadily improve from this time. (*Keesing's* 23616)

GOALS OF SENDER COUNTRY

Quai d'Orsay, statement 12 May 1964
"Without waiting for the scheduled opening of negotiations, the Tunisian Government has unilaterally broken this agreement by deciding on the immediate recovery of all land belonging to foreigners. It then invited the French Government to start conversations on the *fait accompli*. The French Government obviously cannot accept such a summons." (*Keesing's* 20152)

RESPONSE OF TARGET COUNTRY

President Habib Bourguiba
April 1964: "France must understand that it is impossible for us to meet the whole payment of the sums due as compensation, since such a burden would impede achievement of our economic plans." (*Keesing's* 20152)

ATTITUDE OF OTHER COUNTRIES

Italy, United Kingdom, Switzerland
All protest Tunisian action on behalf of their nationals whose land has been affected. (*Keesing's* 20153)

ECONOMIC IMPACT

Observed Economic Statistics

At time of expropriation, Tunisia had paid £800,000 for agricultural equipment, livestock, crops. (*Keesing's* 20152)

Tunisian trade with France (million dollars)

	Exports	Imports
1962	61.3	113.4
1963	62.8	106.9
1964	66.0	109.9

Tunisian trade with France (*continued*)

	Exports	Imports
1965	37.3	96.5
1966	48.6	86.0
1967	41.9	82.9
1968	36.5	72.4
1969	44.1	86.7

Source: IMF.

Nationalization law is estimated to affect 670,000 acres under French ownership. (*Keesing's* 20152)

Calculated Economic Impact

	Annual cost to target country
Reduction in Tunisian exports to France; welfare loss estimated at 35 percent of loss in value of 1965–66 exports to France from average 1962–64 levels.	$7 million
Suspension of French bilateral aid to Tunisia; welfare loss valued at 90 percent of proposed transfers.	8 million
Offset	
Allowance for Tunisian net gain on expropriation of French holdings after partial payments (amortized over two years to correspond to period of reduced bilateral trade/aid).	($3 million)
Total	$12 million

Relative Magnitudes

Gross indicators of Tunisian economy	
Tunisian GNP (1964)	$827 million
Tunisian population (1966)	4.5 million
Annual effect of sanctions related to gross indicators	
Percentage of GNP	1.5
Per capita	$2.67

Gross indicators of Tunisian economy (continued)	
Tunisian trade with France as percentage of total trade	
Exports (1964)	51
Imports (1964)	44
Ratio of French GNP (1964: $88 billion) to Tunisian GNP (1964: $827 million)	106

AUTHORS' SUMMARY

Overall assessment	*Assigned scores*
☐ Policy result, scaled from 1 (failed) to 4 (success)	3
☐ Sanctions contribution, scaled from 1 (none) to 4 (significant)	3
☐ Success score (policy result *times* sanctions contribution), scaled from 1 (outright failure) to 16 (significant success)	9

Political and economic variables

☐ Companion policies: J (covert), Q (quasi-military), or R (regular military)	—
☐ International cooperation with sender, scaled from 1 (none) to 4 (significant)	1
☐ International assistance to target: A (if present)	—
☐ Sanctions period (years)	2
☐ Economic health and political stability of target, scaled from 1 (distressed) to 3 (strong)	2
☐ Presanction relations between sender and target, scaled from 1 (antagonistic) to 3 (cordial)	3
☐ Type of sanction: X (export), M (import), F (financial)	F, M
☐ Cost to sender, scaled from 1 (net gain) to 4 (major loss)	2

BIBLIOGRAPHY

International Monetary Fund. *Direction of Trade Statistics.* Various issues.
Keesing's Contemporary Archives. 1963–64, 1969–70.

Case 65–1 US v. Chile

(1965–66: Copper Price)

CHRONOLOGY OF KEY EVENTS

1964 President Eduardo Frei, with substantial backing from US companies and CIA, receives 56 percent of vote in national election. US supports Frei regime with $97 million in bilateral aid in 1965, $35 million IMF credits, debt rescheduling. (Berteau 175–76; US Senate Select Committee 14)

20 October 1965 Responding to upward price pressure caused by strong global demand for copper, Chilean Copper Department increases price 2¢/lb.—36¢ to 38¢. (Futures price for copper on New York Commodity Exchange is 60¢/lb.) (Berteau 178)

29 October 1965 US aluminum industry raises aluminum price 5¢/lb. Because aluminum often is substitute for copper, this allows comparable action by copper producers. US government regards increase as threat to general price stability. (Berteau 178)

1 November 1965 Copper Range Company, small US producer, raises its price to 38¢/lb.; increase is adopted by other small producers on 6 November, Anaconda on 8 November. (Berteau 178)

10 November 1965 Yielding to US government pressure, Alcoa, Reynolds announce aluminum price rollback. (Berteau 179)

11 November 1965 Rhodesian Unilateral Declaration of Independence (UDI) creates doubts about security of supply of Zambian copper, drives futures price higher. (Berteau 181)

13 November 1965 US State Department sends Ambassador W. Averell Harriman and Assistant Secretary of State Anthony Solomon on mission to achieve rollback of Chilean price to 36¢/lb., stiffen Chilean resistance to future price increases. Mission emphasizes threat of long-term substitution of aluminum for copper, adverse impact on US ability to give aid, US willingness to eliminate 1.7¢/lb. copper tariff as quid pro quo for Chilean concessions. (Berteau 180)

15–18 November 1965	In secret meeting with President Frei and senior officials in Santiago, Harriman and Solomon reach agreement that: Chile will ship 100,000 tons of copper to Anaconda at 36¢ per pound; Anaconda, Kennecott will adopt more conciliatory attitude in takeover negotiations; US Agency for International Development (AID) will extend to Chile $10 million for 40 years on favorable terms—10 years at 1 percent interest, 30 years at 2½ percent interest; Chile will be allowed to float $20 million bond issue in US market; US will suspend copper import duty. (Berteau 186–87)
17 November 1965	US Secretary of Defense Robert S. McNamara releases 200,000 tons of copper from stockpile, imposes controls on copper exports, proposes legislation to suspend import duty, requests New York Commodity Exchange to increase margin on copper futures contracts. (Berteau 182)
2 January 1966	African copper producers increase price to 42¢/lb. Chile seeks more compensation from US based on 6¢/lb. instead of 2¢/lb. price differential. US balks but Anaconda agrees to give Chile makeup payment of $3.5 million (approximately equal to Anaconda's saving from suspension of US import duty); Chile keeps price for exports to US at 36¢/lb. (Berteau 189–90)
25 January 1966	Copper arrangement made public in Chile, leads to initiation of impeachment proceedings against finance minister; President Frei is criticized severely. (Berteau 191)
14 February 1966	US AID extends program loan of $80 million to Chile; US Export–Import Bank extends loan of $23 million for purchase of Boeing 727s. (Berteau 187–88)
23 June 1966	US Congress passes two-year tariff suspension bill on copper amid complaints of "bad odor," and "rinky-dink" deals. (Berteau 192)
Mid-August 1966	Chile begins selling copper at London Metal Exchange price. Solomon opposes any effort to renew agreement with Chile; agreement lapses in 1967. (Berteau 192, 194)

GOALS OF SENDER COUNTRY

US State Department
Memorandum of 13 November 1965: " . . . an effort should be made to get Frei to agree: (a) to roll back copper price from 38¢ to 36¢ *contingent* on U.S. industry taking the lead and, (b) regardless of Frei's willingness to do a rollback, to agree to resist pressure . . . for additional price rises. Avoidance of additional price increases in view of the uncertain Zambian situation is even more important than the rollback." (Berteau 183)

Chairman of Council of Economic Advisers Gardner Ackley
In 8 November 1965 comment to President Lyndon B. Johnson: "We can't welcome a copper price increase in the middle of the aluminum crisis . . . it would be very desirable if Kennecott or Phelps Dodge could be persuaded to hold off on a price increase. . . ." (Berteau 179)

RESPONSE OF TARGET COUNTRY

Raul Saez (Saez is Frei's special negotiator on copper)
Chile would be more receptive to US request to roll back copper prices if US "encourag[ed] U.S. companies to accept [a] reasonable solution of remaining points of difference on [the] copper bill." He added that "it would be politically useful for President Frei to be able to announce not only an expansion program in copper production but also a really substantial program for the development of copper manufacturing in Chile." (Berteau 185)

ECONOMIC IMPACT

Observed Economic Statistics

Producer price of copper jumps from 31¢/lb. in early 1964 to 36¢/lb. in May 1965. At same time, futures prices are about 60¢ and 70¢/lb., respectively, on New York and London exchanges. (Berteau 174)

Copper accounts for about three-fourths of Chilean exports in 1964. (Berteau 174)

Subsidiaries of Kennecott, Anaconda mine 88 percent of Chilean copper during 1955–64. (Berteau 174)

"Anaconda relied most heavily upon imported copper, with 58 percent of its total production being imports from Chile." (Berteau 176)

Calculated Economic Impact

	Annual cost to target country
Reduction in Chilean copper export earnings from 6¢/lb. loss on shipments to US in 1966; welfare loss valued at 100 percent.	$12.0 million
Offsets	
Compensating US program loans at preferential rates; one-time benefit estimated at 80 percent of face value of loan ($10 million).	($8.0 million)
Compensating payment by Anaconda to Chile (approximately equivalent to Anaconda's tariff saving).	(3.5 million)
Total	$0.5 million

Relative Magnitudes

Gross indicators of Chilean economy	
Chilean GNP (1966)	$7.7 billion
Chilean population (1965)	8.5 million
Annual effect of sanctions related to gross indicators	
Percentage of GNP	0.01
Per capita	$0.06
Chilean trade with US as percentage of total trade	
Exports (1965)	43
Imports (1965)	31
Ratio of US GNP (1966: $756 billion) to Chilean GNP (1966: $7.7 billion)	98

ASSESSMENT

David Berteau
" . . . the Chilean copper deal had its desired effect. Anaconda announced a price rollback within 24 hours of the conclusion of the agreement with Chile, and the rest of the copper industry followed suit. . . . [T]he Johnson administration won a major victory in its price-stabilization campaign." (Berteau 189)

AUTHORS' SUMMARY

Overall assessment	Assigned scores
☐ Policy result, scaled from 1 (failed) to 4 (success)	3
☐ Sanctions contribution, scaled from 1 (none) to 4 (significant)	4
☐ Success score (policy result *times* sanctions contribution), scaled from 1 (outright failure) to 16 (significant success)	12

Political and economic variables

☐ Companion policies: J (covert), Q (quasi-military), or R (regular military)	—
☐ International cooperation with sender, scaled from 1 (none) to 4 (significant)	1
☐ International assistance to target: A (if present)	—
☐ Sanctions period (years)	1
☐ Economic health and political stability of target, scaled from 1 (distressed) to 3 (strong)	2
☐ Presanction relations between sender and target, scaled from 1 (antagonistic) to 3 (cordial)	2
☐ Type of sanction: X (export), M (import), F (financial)	F, M
☐ Cost to sender, scaled from 1 (net gain) to 4 (major loss)	2

BIBLIOGRAPHY

Berteau, David. 1982. "The Harriman-Solomon Mission and the 1966 Chilean Copper Agreement." In *Economic Coercion and U.S. Foreign Policy: Implications of Case Studies from the Johnson Administration*, ed. Sidney Weintraub. Boulder, Colo.: Westview Press.

US Congress. Senate Select Committee to Study Governmental Operations with Respect to Intelligence Activities. 1975. *Covert Action in Chile 1963–1973*. Staff Report. 94 Cong., 1 sess.

Case 65–2   US v. India

(1965–67: Agricultural Priorities)

CHRONOLOGY OF KEY EVENTS

1964 President Lyndon B. Johnson concludes that PL 480 food aid artificially depresses Indian farm prices, thereby discouraging agricultural production, leading to greater dependence by India on external food sources. (Castore 134)

31 June 1965 President Johnson terminates long-term PL 480 agreement as way of pressuring India to emphasize agricultural production; grain shipments suspended until short-term PL 480 agreement is reached 26 July 1965. (Castore 134)

August 1965 Pakistan invades Kashmir; US terminates military aid to both India, Pakistan. (Castore 134)

Fall 1965 Poor monsoon rains threaten India with famine; Indian press, certain US observers interpret US reluctance to sign long-term PL 480 agreement as tilt toward Pakistan; Secretary of State Dean Rusk cables Ambassador Chester Bowles otherwise. (Castore 134)

6 December 1965 Indian Agricultural Minister Chidambara Subramaniam succeeds in having a package of agricultural reforms—including "the import of new high-yielding varieties of seeds, improved price incentives to producers, and a concentration of expensive inputs in irrigated areas"—incorporated into upcoming five-year plan. (Paarlberg 294)

December 1965 US Department of Agriculture economist, Lester Brown, cables assessment that famine will strike India in 1966; Johnson approves emergency shipment of 1.5 million tons of wheat under Titles II and III of PL 480, but postpones long-term agreement. (Castore 137; Paarlberg 295)

January 1966 Tashkent Agreement ends Indo-Pakistan hostilities; Prime Minister Bahadur Shastri of India dies; succeeded by Indira Gandhi. (Castore 138)

March 1966 On visit to US, Gandhi requests $200 million from IMF, rescheduling of $125 million debt. US agrees to provide $385 million loans from Agency for International Development (AID), $50 million Eximbank loans in FY 1967. India agrees to liberalize import controls, attract foreign private investment to Indian fertilizer plants; accelerate family planning. (Castore 139)

May–June 1966   US resumes negotiations on three agricultural development projects. India devalues rupee from Rs 4.76 to Rs 7.5 per $1, requests $900 million of nonproject aid from World Bank; US agrees to provide $335 million of requested amount. (Castore 139–40)

Fall 1966   India faces another drought. According to AID Administrator William Gaud: "The Indian Government has clearly made agriculture its number one priority." Progress cited in fertilizer plants, fertilizer imports, agricultural development in irrigation and high-yielding species. (Castore 141–42)

February 1967   US signs long-term PL 480 agreement. (Castore 143)

GOALS OF SENDER COUNTRY

Carolyn Castore
"By refusing to sign a new long-term agreement covering grain shipments, the United States is apparently trying to force India to stop using American food shipments as . . . crutch and to stimulate greater efforts by India to increase her food production." (Castore 136)

Robert Paarlberg
"From the start. . . . Lyndon Johnson was inclined to manipulate food aid to India for purposes which went far beyond [Secretary of Agriculture] Orville Freeman's objective of prompting agricultural policy reforms within India. Even so, Freeman's objectives were at the heart of the 'short tether' exercise. . . . In return for US food aid, India would be asked to increase its acreage under irrigation, and increase its fertilizer production. . . . At least two additional economic policy conditions—a more vigorous Indian family planning policy, and a devaluation of the rupee—were later added to this original list of food power demands." (Paarlberg 292–93)

RESPONSE OF TARGET COUNTRY

Carolyn Castore
"Indian leaders and the Indian press at first believed that the economic pressure stemmed from U.S. support of Pakistan . . . [and] that President Johnson was reacting to Prime Minister Shastri's critical comments concerning American involvement in Vietnam." (Castore 131)

"By the beginning of 1967 the Indian government had complied in large part with U.S. formal objectives." (Castore 131)

Robert Paarlberg
". . . all the early suspicion in India, that Johnson was using food power to force a

change in India's foreign policy, nonetheless proved beneficial to Subramaniam. It focused political and press concern on foreign policy questions, and so it distracted those in the Indian opposition who might have otherwise noticed and objected to the link which had been forged between U.S. food aid shipments and Indian concessions on agricultural policy." (Paarlberg 297)

ECONOMIC IMPACT

Observed Economic Statistics

"India's dependence on concessional grain shipments from the U.S. had become critical even before 1965. But then came two years of severe drought, beginning in 1965–66, when Indian foodgrain production fell to only 72 million tons, a disastrous 19 percent below the harvest of the previous year. . . . The next year's foodgrain harvest was scarcely better, equaling only 76 million tons . . . It was in response to this Indian food emergency that PL 480 wheat imports from the U.S. were sharply increased, to 6.35 million tons in 1965, and then to a record 8.06 million tons in 1966. In 1967, with the effects of the drought still being felt, food aid imports from the U.S. remained at a substantial 5.96 million tons." (Paarlberg 286)

Wheat imports are only 8 percent to 10 percent of total foodgrain consumption but are 60 percent of total public foodgrain distribution. (Paarlberg 287)

"The same drought that had devastated India's foodgrain production has also cut into the production of cash export crops—such as cotton and jute." (Paarlberg 288)

At time of first monsoon failure in 1965, US provided 96 percent of India's concessional food aid. (Paarlberg 308)

Indian balance of payments (million dollars)

	1966–67	1967–68
Current account deficit	− 2,025	− 2,226
Financed by		
Food aid	607	556
Program aid	513	975
Project aid	660	695
IMF	187	—
Decrease in reserves	58	—

— Zero or negligible.
Source: Castore 145.

Calculated Economic Impact

	Annual cost to target country
Reduction in PL 480 shipments; welfare loss estimated at 10 percent of value of reduced food aid, calculated as 0.6	$41 million

	Annual cost to target country

million tons delayed for one month at $57/ton. (The threat
of a more permanent embargo was the principal sanction.)

Relative Magnitudes

Gross indicators of Indian economy

Indian GNP (1964)	$51 billion
Indian population (1965)	483 million

Annual effect of sanctions related to gross indicators
Percentage of GNP	negl.
Per capita	$0.08

Indian trade with US as percentage of total trade
Exports (1964)	18
Imports (1964)	30

Ratio of US GNP (1964: $688 billion) to Indian GNP (1964: $50.6 billion)	13

ASSESSMENT

Carolyn Castore
" . . . the use of pressure did achieve most of the formal U.S. objectives. The primary
reasons for success appear to be the following:

☐ U.S. aid was significant. Over 56 percent of all aid to India came from the United
States.

☐ The drought and ensuing famine made India vulnerable to U.S. pressure since it
increased Indian dependence on imported food. Other sources of cheap food were not
readily available, and because of the internal political situation, India was diffident
about asking for help from other nations." (Castore 146–47)

Robert Paarlberg
"The short tether experience does confirm that under select circumstances a substantial
short run food power advantage can be gained by an exporting country. But the short
tether experience also raises doubts about the extent and duration of such an advantage.
Lyndon Johnson was originally successful in his use of food power to persuade the Indian
government to adopt a variety of internal agricultural policy and economic policy reforms.
This initial success was made possible, however, by an extra-ordinary combination of
favorable circumstances. . . . Moreover, despite this combination of exceptionally favorable
circumstances, the food power advantage enjoyed by the U.S. was not enough to produce
total compliance with U.S. economic reform demands, and it certainly was not sufficient
to produce any visible gains for the U.S. in the diplomatic realm. . . . Under the best
possible circumstances, food power was therefore able to produce only a limited range
of advantages for the exporting country." (Paarlberg 377–78)

AUTHORS' SUMMARY

Overall assessment	Assigned scores
☐ Policy result, scaled from 1 (failed) to 4 (success)	4
☐ Sanctions contribution, scaled from 1 (none) to 4 (significant)	4
☐ Success score (policy result *times* sanctions contribution), scaled from 1 (outright failure) to 16 (significant success)	16

Political and economic variables

☐ Companion policies: J (covert), Q (quasi-military), or R (regular military)	—
☐ International cooperation with sender, scaled from 1 (none) to 4 (significant)	1
☐ International assistance to target: A (if present)	—
☐ Sanctions period (years)	2
☐ Economic health and political stability of target, scaled from 1 (distressed) to 3 (strong)	2
☐ Presanction relations between sender and target, scaled from 1 (antagonistic) to 3 (cordial)	2
☐ Type of sanction: X (export), M (import), F (financial)	F
☐ Cost to sender, scaled from 1 (net gain) to 4 (major loss)	1

BIBLIOGRAPHY

Castore, Carolyn. 1982. "The United States and India: The Use of Food to Apply Economic Pressure—1965–1967." In *Economic Coercion and U.S. Foreign Policy: Implications of Case Studies from the Johnson Administration*, ed. Sidney Weintraub. Boulder, Colo.: Westview Press.

Paarlberg, Robert L. 1984. *The Limits of Food Power: Lyndon Johnson's "Short Tether" Policy against India, 1965–67*. Paper presented at the American Political Science Association Convention, 30 August. Washington.

Case 65–3   UK and UN v. Rhodesia

(1965–79: Black Majority Rule)

CHRONOLOGY OF KEY EVENTS

1962–63   UN General Assembly affirms that South Rhodesia is a "non-self-governing territory," calls on UK to convene constitutional conference with full participation of all political parties to replace constitution of December 1961. Resolution also calls on UK "to take immediate steps to restore all rights to the non-European population. . . ." However, elections proceed in November 1962 under 1961 constitution, and United Federal Party government is replaced by "right-wing" Rhodesian Front Party of Ian Smith, which retains power until 1979. In 1963 UN Security Council votes on draft resolution calling on UK not to transfer sovereignty to South Rhodesia until "fully representative government had been established." UK vetoes resolution on ground that British acquiescence would prevent "orderly devolution" of power to Federation of Rhodesia and Nyasaland. (Lillich 391–92)

11 November   Government of Prime Minister Ian Smith issues Unilateral Declaration
1965   of Independence (UDI). (Renwick 25–26; Anglin 2)

November 1965   UK stops aid, freezes Rhodesian sterling assets in London, excludes Rhodesia from sterling area, Commonwealth preferences. (Renwick 27)

20 November   UN Security Council Resolution 217 calls on member states to:
1965   withhold recognition of Rhodesia; give no assistance to Smith government; break economic relations with Rhodesia; embargo petroleum exports. (Losman 94; Renwick 27; Anglin 11)

17 December 1965   UK bans tobacco, sugar purchases, most other imports from Rhodesia; embargoes shipment of oil, to take effect in January 1966. Oil companies build up stocks prior to effective date. Commonwealth Sanctions Committee established for monitoring purposes. (Losman 92; Doxey 1971, 102, 109)

February 1966   UK imposes almost total ban on exports, embargoes all but 5 percent

February 1966 *(continued)*	of imports; British navy blockades port of Beira against vessels with Rhodesia-bound oil. (Losman 99)
16 December 1966	UN Security Council Resolution 232 imposes mandatory, but selective, sanctions covering imports of Rhodesian asbestos, iron ore, chrome, pig iron, sugar, tobacco, copper, meat, hides and skins, leather goods; exports to Rhodesia of arms and equipment for their manufacture, aircraft, petroleum, motor vehicles. Implementation depends on enabling legislation by member states; furthermore, UN resolution applies only to new contracts. (Losman 94–95; Anglin 11)
29 May 1968	UN Security Council Resolution 253 imposes mandatory comprehensive sanctions calling for: complete ban on all imports from Rhodesia, all exports to Rhodesia (except medical supplies, humanitarian goods); ban on air transport; withdrawal of consular, trade representatives. Subsequent UN monitoring shows about 50 violations of sanctions annually. However, the few important cases "were initially brought to light through the detective work of investigative journalists." (Doxey 1971, 103–4; Anglin 11)
November 1971	Byrd amendment authorizes US purchases of strategic raw materials from Rhodesia. US imports $212 million of ferrochrome, other materials until law is repealed in 1977. (Strack 146–52)
1973	UN Security Council passes Resolution 333, which calls on member states to punish any of their citizens continuing to deal with clients in South Africa, Mozambique, Angola, Portuguese Guinea, and Namibia "after it had become known that such clients were shipping goods either to or from Rhodesia." (Lillich 402)
1976	UN Security Council attempts to tighten sanctions further by passing Resolution 388, which forbids insuring of "commodities exported from, imported to, or located within Rhodesia." (Lillich 403)
August–September *1976*	South African Prime Minister B. J. Vorster imposes severe economic sanctions on Rhodesia to compel Smith to accept formula of US Secretary of State Henry A. Kissinger for transition to majority rule in two years in return for the lifting of sanctions and $1 billion development fund. Proposed agreement is rejected by Rhodesian nationalist and other African leaders because it involves continued white control during transition. (Anglin 20; Good 171–72, 185)
1977	"Anglo-American Plan" calls for peaceful settlement with protection for white minority political, economic interests. (Weissman 133)
1978	Smith offers "Internal Settlement" plan supported by three major black leaders; proposal is rejected by Zimbabwe African People's Union (ZAPU) and Zimbabwe African Nationalist Union (ZANU); US Senate votes to lift sanctions, US House refuses. (Weissman 134)
Summer 1978	Case-Javits amendment (Senators Clifford Case, R–NJ, Jacob K. Javits, R–NY) allows President Jimmy Carter to lift sanctions if he

determines Rhodesia is negotiating in good faith and freely elected government has been installed. (Weissman 136)

January–April 1979   New constitution that presages controlled movement toward majority rule is accepted by white electorate; leads to April election that installs Bishop Abel Muzorewa as prime minister. (Renwick 54)

December 1979   With British mediation, Lancaster House agreement is signed between opposition front and white minority leaders; government accedes to black majority rule; sanctions are lifted. (Renwick 55)

GOALS OF SENDER COUNTRIES

27 October 1964
Perhaps anticipating UDI, Prime Minister Harold Wilson states six British objectives: guarantees of unimpeded progress toward majority rule, as contained in 1961 constitution; guarantees against amendment of constitution; immediate improvement of political status of Africans; progress toward cessation of racial discrimination; acceptance of proposed basis for independence by people of Rhodesia as a whole; no oppression of majority by minority, or vice versa. (Losman 92)

11 November 1965
Wilson takes ambiguous attitude toward UN sanctions for fear that leadership on Rhodesian question will pass to UN: "I think that the problem will be to avert excessive action by the United Nations. As for the economic sanctions, I think that it will be right for us to concentrate on trying to get others to follow our lead, rather than seeing them get too far ahead of us." (Anglin 5)

RESPONSE OF TARGET COUNTRY

1965
"In anticipation of sanctions, Rhodesian importers had tended to place larger than usual orders and to contract for longer than normal periods. . . . In this fashion enacting sanctions that exempted existing contracts delayed effective imposition of the embargo. . . ." (Losman 95)

26 April 1967
Statement by Roger Hawkins, Rhodesian minister of transport and power: ". . . whatever any particular government says, of course, is quite different to what their businessmen do and this is precisely how Rhodesia . . . is winning the war." (Anglin 26)

1965–75
"In the decade from 1965 to 1975 the Rhodesian economy was transformed from virtually total dependence on the importation of manufactured goods in exchange for raw materials to a remarkable degree of self-sufficiency in most areas except oil and industrial plant and machinery." (Renwick 85)

ATTITUDE OF OTHER COUNTRIES

Organization of African Unity
"On 5 December 1965, the Organisation of African Unity (OAU) met in Ghana to consider the Rhodesian crisis, and the OAU Council of Ministers called on Britain to take decisive action—including an oil embargo—to crush the rebellion, threatening to break off diplomatic relations with Britain if Smith was not toppled within ten days." (Bailey 122)

Tanzania
In April 1966, President Julius Nyerere warns of African military intervention, supported by USSR, Eastern Europe, or China, unless Smith government is toppled. (Nyerere 385)

Soviet Union
Proposes that any UN member that fails to participate in sanctions should itself be a target. Proposal is not accepted. (Doxey 1971, 91)

Germany, France, United Kingdom, United States
Trade with Rhodesia drops 45 percent to 70 percent in 1960s as a result of sanctions. Generally, sanctions apply only to new contracts. (Grieve 438; Losman 95)

Portugal, South Africa
Actively oppose sanctions, become major conduits for Rhodesian imports, exports. (Grieve 438)

LEGAL NOTES

UN Charter, Article 41
"The Security Council may decide what measures not involving the use of armed force are to be employed to give effect to its decisions, and may call upon the Members of the United Nations to apply such measures. These may include complete or partial interruption of economic relations, and of rail, sea, air, postal, telegraphic, radio and other means of communication, and the severance of diplomatic relations."

Note: UN Article 41 gives Security Council great flexibility in choice of means to pursue its ends, by contrast with automatic boycott prescribed by League of Nations Article 16. (Doxey 1971, 91)

UN Charter, Article 39
Provides that, if Security Council finds "threat to the peace," it can seek to alter status quo, not merely restore it. (Doxey 1971, 84)

ECONOMIC IMPACT

Observed Economic Statistics

"GDP grew on average in real terms at about 6 percent per annum between 1965 and 1974." (Renwick 57; also see Anglin 13–14)

"The value of Rhodesian exports had more than doubled between 1968 and 1974. From 1974–77 it progressed only from R$519 [million] to R$541 million—a significant decline in real terms." (Renwick 48)

"Import prices rose much faster than those of exports: the terms of trade in 1979 were over 40 percent worse for Rhodesia than in 1965." (Renwick 56)

In 1965, 5 percent of total population is white. During UDI period, 133,000 whites settle in Rhodesia, 121,000 abandon country. (Anglin 16)

"In response to UK financial measures, Rhodesia repudiated its debt obligations in London and to the World Bank, which were estimated at £108 million." (Losman 106)

Costs to UK of enforcing oil embargo: £6 million for airlift of oil to Zambia from December 1965 to June 1966; estimates of costs of blockade of Beira are in excess of £100 million. (Bailey 122)

Rhodesian trade with South Africa (million dollars)

	Exports	Imports
1966	60	110
1967	80	135
1968	80	150
1969	85	155
1970	95	180
1971	105	215
1972	130	182
1973	200	220
1974	250	230
1975	302	270

Source: Strack 117.

Calculated Economic Impact

	Annual cost to target country
(a) Immediate reduction in trade in 1966–67 from presanction levels; welfare loss estimated at 30 percent of reduced trade flows.	$68 million
(b) Increased costs resulting from trade diversion and higher transport costs; welfare loss estimated at 15 percent of value of average annual trade with South Africa ($332 million 1966–75).	50 million
(c) Decline in Rhodesia's terms of trade by average of 20 percent during sanctions period (1966–79); welfare loss estimated at 20 percent of average of total trade for 1966–75, excluding trade with South Africa, Zambia.	93 million

Calculated Economic Impact (*continued*)

	Annual cost to target country
Total: for 1966–67 (a + b + c)	$211 million
for 1968–79 (b + c)	$143 million
Average for 1966–79	$153 million
Offset	
Repudiation of approximately $300 million of external debt, amortized over 13 years.	($23 million)
Total	$130 million

Calculated Impact on Third Countries

	Annual cost to third country
Zambia	
In 1965–72, $100 million additional public expenditures; welfare loss estimated at 30 percent of expenditure. (Doxey 1971, 98)	$30 million
Mozambique	
In 1975–79, $110 million to $165 million loss of transit activity; welfare loss estimated at 50 percent of lost revenue. (Doxey 1971, 99)	$70 million

Relative Magnitudes

Gross indicators of Rhodesian economy	
Rhodesian GNP (1965)	$1.0 billion
Rhodesian population (1965)	4.5 million
Annual effect of sanctions related to gross indicators	
Percentage of GNP	13
Per capita	$28.89
Rhodesian trade with UN (less South Africa, Zambia, Mozambique) as percentage of total trade	
Exports (1965)	65
Imports (1965)	72

Ratio of OECD GNP (1965: $1,388 billion) to Rhodesian GNP (1965:   1,388
$1.0 billion)

ASSESSMENT

Harold Wilson, January 1966
Predicts fall of Smith government "within weeks, not months." (Anglin 1)

Minister of Commonwealth Affairs Ernest Bowden, 21 March 1967
"Given a little time—and it is not very much more than six weeks—I think you will be quite happy with the results of selective mandatory sanctions." (Grieve 435)

T. R. C. Curtin, April 1968
"Even over a long haul the success of sanctions is not assured." (Curtin 110)

Martin Bailey, 1979
"The story of the oil embargo shows the way in which the powerful international oil companies frustrated the attempt to crush the Smith regime by sanctions. This obviously had a profound effect on political developments in Rhodesia, and in Southern Africa as a whole." (Bailey 264)

Anonymous trader, 1969
Survey of experienced international traders in 1969 elicited this response: "I have worked 63 years in export/import and have never seen a boycott which was really effective! [For instance] the present boycott of Rhodesia is a farce." (Losman 98)

Margaret P. Doxey, 1972
"The implementation of sanctions against Rhodesia has been full of weaknesses: the Security Council Committee set up to supervise the program has emphasized in its report that it is virtually impossible to operate an effective control system, or to verify the true source and destination of goods suspected of being part of continuing Rhodesian trade. The experience of the UN in the Rhodesian case—which recalls that of the League in applying sanctions to Italy—will not have been lost on other members." (Doxey 1972, 544)

Economist, 1980
"It was Rhodesia's inability to raise long-term credit on the international capital market that put the biggest economic strain on its resources and this, together with the civil war, brought its recalcitrant politicians to the negotiating table." (*Economist* [London], 19 July 1980, 16)

Robin Renwick, 1981
"Sanctions against Rhodesia did exert some pressure for a negotiated solution, though the pressure was never irresistible and they did so at the considerable political cost of tending to consolidate rather than diminish white support for the regime. They had perverse effects on the Rhodesian economy, encouraging self-reliance and diversification. But their overall effect was to limit its expansion and in the long run to weaken the regime to which they were applied." (Renwick 89–90)

Douglas G. Anglin, 1983
"A significant part of the credit for whatever verbal concessions Smith was forced to voice must go to sanctions, but the major contributing factors were undoubtedly the economic impact of the war, the oil price hike, and Pretoria's penchant for flexing its economic muscle periodically as a reminder of its regional hegemony." (Anglin 18; Strack 146–64)

AUTHORS' SUMMARY

Overall assessment	Assigned scores
□ Policy result, scaled from 1 (failed) to 4 (success)	4
□ Sanctions contribution, scaled from 1 (none) to 4 (significant)	3
□ Success score (policy result *times* sanctions contribution), scaled from 1 (outright failure) to 16 (significant success)	12

Political and economic variables

□ Companion policies: J (covert), Q (quasi-military), or R (regular military)	Q
□ International cooperation with sender, scaled from 1 (none) to 4 (significant)	4
□ International assistance to target: A (if present)	A
□ Sanctions period (years)	14
□ Economic health and political stability of target, scaled from 1 (distressed) to 3 (strong)	2
□ Presanction relations between sender and target, scaled from 1 (antagonistic) to 3 (cordial)	3
□ Type of sanction: X (export), M (import), F (financial)	F, X, M
□ Cost to sender, scaled from 1 (net gain) to 4 (major loss)	3

Comments

Initially, economic sanctions imposed on Rhodesia had perverse effect of uniting white population behind government and of promoting self-reliance in the economy. Over long term, however, economic and moral weight of sanctions increased pressure on Smith government and, hence, contributed to negotiated settlement.

BIBLIOGRAPHY

Anglin, Douglas G. 1985. "United Nations Economic Sanctions Against Rhodesia and South Africa." In *The Utility of Economic Sanctions*, ed. David Leyton-Brown. London: Croom Helm. Forthcoming.
Bailey, Martin. 1979. *Oilgate: The Sanctions Scandal.* London: Hodder and Stoughton.
Curtin, T. R. C. 1968. "Rhodesian Economic Development under Sanctions and the 'Long Haul.'" 67 *African Affairs* (April): 100–110.
———. July 1969. "Total Sanctions and Economic Development in Rhodesia." 7 *Journal of Commonwealth Political Studies* (July): 126–31.

Curtin, T. R. C., and D. Murray. 1967. *Economic Sanctions and Rhodesia*, Research Monograph no. 12. London: Institute of Economic Affairs.

Doxey, Margaret P. 1971. *Economic Sanctions and International Enforcement*. London: Oxford University Press for Royal Institute of International Affairs.

———. 1972. "International Sanctions: A Framework for Analysis with Special Reference to the UN and South Africa." 26 *International Organization* (Summer): 527–50.

Galtung, Johan. 1967. "On the Effects of International Economic Sanctions: With Examples from the Case of Rhodesia." 19 *World Politics* (April): 378–416.

Good, Robert G. 1973. *UDI: The International Politics of the Rhodesian Rebellion*. Princeton, NJ: Princeton University Press.

Grieve, Muriel J. 1968. "Economic Sanctions: Theory and Practice." 3 *International Relations* (October): 431–43.

Kapungu, Leonard T. 1973. *The United Nations and Economic Sanctions against Rhodesia*. Lexington, Mass.: D. C. Heath and Co.

Kuyper, P. J. 1978. *The Implementation of International Sanctions: the Netherlands and Rhodesia*. Alphen aan der Rijn: Sijthoff & Noordhoff.

Lake, Anthony. 1973. *The 'Tar Baby' Option: American Policy Toward Southern Rhodesia*. New York: Columbia University Press.

Lillich, Robert, and Frank C. Newman. 1979. *International Human Rights: Problems of Law and Policy*. New York: Little, Brown & Co.

Losman, Donald L. 1979. *International Economic Sanctions: The Cases of Cuba, Israel, and Rhodesia*. Albuquerque: University of New Mexico Press.

McKinnell, R. T. 1969. "Sanctions and the Rhodesian Economy." 7 *Journal of Modern African Studies* 559–81.

Nyerere, Julius. 1966. "Rhodesia in the Context of Southern Africa." 44 *Foreign Affairs* (April): 373–86.

Porter, Richard C. 1978. "Economic Sanctions: The Theory and Evidence from Rhodesia." 3 *Journal of Peace Science* (Fall): 93–110.

Renwick, Robin. 1981. *Economic Sanctions*. Harvard Studies in International Affairs No. 45. Cambridge, Mass.: Harvard University Center for International Affairs.

Strack, Harry R. 1978. *Sanctions: The Case of Rhodesia*. New York: Syracuse University Press.

UN Security Council Exports Committee. UN Docs. S/8954, 30 December 1968; S/9252, 12 June 1969; S/9844, 15 June 1970; S/10299, 16 June 1971.

US General Accounting Office. 1977. *Report of the Comptroller General of the United States: Implementation of Economic Sanctions against Rhodesia*. 20 April. Washington.

Weissman Stephen R., and Johnnie Carson. 1981. "Economic Sanctions against Rhodesia." In *Congress, the Presidency, and American Foreign Policy*, ed. John Spanier and Joseph Nogee. New York: Pergamon Press.

Case 65–4   US v. Arab League

(1965–   : Antiboycott Measures)

CHRONOLOGY OF KEY EVENTS

Also see Case 46–1 Arab League v. Israel (1946–   :Palestine)

1965	US Under Secretary of State George Ball: "In our judgment [S. 948, an antiboycott amendment to the Export Control Act] could interfere seriously with the programs of economic denial that we are now conducting against several communist countries." (Lowenfeld 34)
30 June 1965	Amendment to Export Control Act of 1949 calls for US firms to report boycott requests to secretary of commerce "for such action as he may deem appropriate." (Lowenfeld 34)
30 December 1969	Congress approves Export Administration Act of 1969 that extends *inter alia* antiboycott provisions of Export Control Act. (Commerce Report 1977, 15)
1975	US secretary of commerce, in response to congressional pressure, modifies regulations to require reporting as to whether the exporter had complied with boycott request. Previously, exporter merely reported request. (Lowenfeld 36)
	President Gerald R. Ford, quoting President Washington, said the Ford administration would give "to bigotry no sanction." Subsequently, secretary of commerce issues new regulations prohibiting discrimination, as among US citizens, on basis of race, color, religion, sex, or national origin. (Lowenfeld 36–37; *Fed. Reg.* 54770)
January 1976	*US v. Bechtel Corp.* Civ. No. C–76–99 (N.D. Calif.) filed by US Justice Department, alleges antitrust violation by Bechtel on account of discrimination; settled by consent decree 10 January 1977. (*New York Times*, 17 January 1976, A5)
1976	Tax Reform Act of 1976 enacted with antiboycott provision (amendment by Senator Abraham Ribicoff, D–Conn.) providing that foreign tax credits, tax deferral on earnings of foreign subsidies, and Domestic

International Sales Corporation (DISC) benefits be denied to firms that comply with foreign boycott not sanctioned by US government. (Sec. 999, Internal Revenue Code). (*New York Times*, 17 September 1976, A1; 5 October 1976, A24).

22 *June 1977*   Amendments to Export Administration Act of 1977 (PL 95–52) prohibit compliance with most foreign boycott requirements—including those involving handling of letters of credit by US banks—and provide substantial penalties for violations. (Commerce Report 1977, 16)

1979   Export Administration Act of 1979 enacted with antiboycott provision. (Comerce Report 1980, 1)

GOALS OF SENDER COUNTRY

Howard Stanislawski
Antiboycott amendments attached to EAA passed on 22 June 1977, "implemented by detailed Department of Commerce regulations, prohibit compliance by US persons with secondary and tertiary boycott conditions, both discriminatory and restrictive trade in nature. A compulsory comprehensive reporting mechanism was established, requiring that all cases of boycott requests be reported to the Secretary of Commerce, together with information regarding the disposition of those requests, and that the information thus compiled would be available to the public. The EAA amendments of 1977 constitute the most extensive set of antiboycott provisions enacted in any jurisdiction in the world." (Stanislawski 19)

RESPONSE OF TARGET COUNTRIES

Howard Stanislawski
"The American-Arab relationship has grown dramatically since 1973, notwithstanding the enactment and implementation in 1976 and 1977 of rigorous antiboycott legislation by the Congress. . . . Substantial alterations in boycott clause terminology have been provided by Arab boycotting states so as to make compliance with the American law simpler and much less problematic." (Stanislawski 25–26)

ATTITUDE OF OTHER COUNTRIES

Canada
Donald Jamieson, minister of industry, trade and commerce, during debate on 21 October 1976, in House of Commons: "The government has clarified its position in relation to international boycotts and has strongly affirmed its opposition to discrimination and boycotts based on race, national or ethnic origin, or religion. Accordingly, the government will take measures to deny its support of facilities for various kinds of trade transactions in order to combat any discriminatory effects which such boycotts may have on Canadian firms and individuals." (Turck 714–15)

France
French pass antiboycott law in 1977, but its application is hamstrung by ministerial decree issued shortly thereafter that excludes government-guaranteed contracts in Middle East. "Practically, because of the ambiguity of the law and because of the Prime Minister's [Raymond Barre] decree, the law appears to have had little if any effect on French-Mideast trade." (Turck 726)

United Kingdom
"In Britain, the House of Lords conducted an extensive investigation of the Arab boycott but thereafter the British government did little or nothing, while professing its opposition to the boycott." (6 *Boycott Report*, January 1982: 1)

From letter from British Foreign Secretary Lord Carrington to British Arab Boycott Coordination Committee: "We firmly believe that it would be wrong to interfere with the commercial judgment of firms, and we leave it to individual firms to decide whether or not to comply with the boycott. We believe that the introduction of legislation on this matter could seriously damage British commercial and political interests. We see it as our first priority to help resolve the Arab-Israel conflict which gives rise to the boycott." (6 *Boycott Report*, March 1982: 9)

ECONOMIC IMPACT

Observed Economic Statistics

Tax benefits denied to US companies complying with boycott (thousand dollars)

	Foreign tax credit	*DISC benefits*	*Deferral*	*Total*
1976	57	25	200	282
1977	734	657	1,254	2,645
1978	5,298	472	5,559	11,329
1979	3,898	688	5,376	9,962

Source: US Treasury 4.

Calculated Economic Impact

	Annual cost to target country
Increased import costs estimated at 1977–79 average of forgone tax benefits of reporting companies under US antiboycott regulations.	$8 million

420   ECONOMIC SANCTIONS RECONSIDERED

Relative Magnitudes

Gross indicators of Arab League economies	
Arab League GNP (1965)	$22.1 billion
Arab League population (1965)	136.6 million
Annual effect of sanctions related to gross indicators	
Percentage of GNP	negl.
Per capita	$0.06
Arab League trade with US as percentage of total trade	
Exports (1965)	4
Imports (1965)	15
Ratio of US GNP (1965: $691.1 billion) to Arab League GNP (1965: $22.1 billion)	31

ASSESSMENT

Commerce Department official (anonymous)
Commenting on Export Administration Act: "Business on the whole has complied with the boycott. The law allows the boycott to go forward." (*New York Times*, 22 October 1981, D1)

Treasury Department lawyer (anonymous)
Commenting on Tax Reform Act of 1976: "There are probably many people out there in flagrant violation of the law, and they never get caught. A lot of people are simply ignorant of the law. I suspect there are people falling through the cracks. And a lot of people are just not filing." (*New York Times*, 22 October 1981, D1)

AUTHORS' SUMMARY

Overall assessment	Assigned scores
□ Policy result, scaled from 1 (failed) to 4 (success)	2
□ Sanctions contribution, scaled from 1 (none) to 4 (significant)	3
□ Success score (policy result *times* sanctions contribution), scaled from 1 (outright failure) to 16 (significant success)	6

Political and economic variables

□ Companion policies: J (covert), Q (quasi-military), or R (regular military)	—
□ International cooperation with sender, scaled from 1 (none) to 4 (significant)	2
□ International assistance to target: A (if present)	—
□ Sanctions period (years)	19+

Political and economic variables (continued)	Assigned scores
☐ Economic health and political stability of target, scaled from 1 (distressed) to 3 (strong)	3
☐ Presanction relations between sender and target, scaled from 1 (antagonistic) to 3 (cordial)	2
☐ Type of sanction: X (export), M (import), F (financial)	F, X
☐ Cost to sender, scaled from 1 (net gain) to 4 (major loss)	2

BIBLIOGRAPHY

Federal Register. 1975. V. 40, 54770.

Lowenfeld, Andreas F. 1977. "... 'Sauce for the Gander': The Arab Boycott and United States Political Trade Controls." 12 *Texas International Law Journal* 25–39.

Stanislawski, Howard. 1985. "The Impact of the Arab Economic Boycott of Israel on the United States and Canada." In *The Utility of Economic Sanctions,* ed. David Leyton-Brown. London: Croom Helm. Forthcoming.

Turck, Nancy. 1978. "A Comparative Study of Non-United States Responses to the Arab Boycott." 8 *Georgia Journal of International and Comparative Law* 3: 711–39.

US Department of Commerce. 1977. *Export Administration Report.* 116th Report on US Export Controls to the President and the Congress, April–September. Washington.

———. 1980. *Export Administration, Annual Report FY 1980.* Washington.

US Department of the Treasury. 1982. *The Operation and Effect of the International Boycott Provisions of the Internal Revenue Code,* 3d report, May. Washington.

Case 67–1   Nigeria v. Biafra

(1967–70: Civil War)

CHRONOLOGY OF KEY EVENTS

1 October 1960	Following independence, Federation of Nigeria is made up of five major regions—the East, North, West, South (Lagos), and Midwest. Eastern Ibo tribe dominates many top civil, military posts. (Nwankwo 1)
15–18 January 1966	Young military officers wipe out most of political, military leadership in coup attempt but are themselves quickly toppled. Countercoup is led by Major General Aguiyi Ironsi who, with assistance of Lieutenant Colonel Yakubu Gowon, rallies loyal troops to defeat plotters. Ironsi becomes head of new federal military government in Lagos, appoints military governors in four other regions who are directly responsible to him. Lieutenant Colonel C. Odumegwu Ojukwu is appointed in East. (St. Jorre 32–39)
29–31 July 1966	While Ironsi is on tour of country, another coup is initiated by group of Northern officers, and many Ibo officers, soldiers are killed. Gowon, from North, is chosen to become supreme commander. Coup "succeeded in every region but the East" where Ojukwu refuses to recognize Gowon as supreme commander. (St. Jorre 67–75)
9 August 1966	Because of continuing hostility between soldiers from northern and eastern regions, Gowon orders all troops back to regions of their origin. (St. Jorre 80)
September–October 1966	Conference in Lagos, held to determine future of Nigerian federation, is interrupted on 29 September by rioting in North that leads to massacre of thousands of Ibos and exodus of nearly a million Ibos to East. (St. Jorre 82–88)
4–5 January 1967	Military governors of each of regions in Nigeria meet with Gowan in Aburi, Ghana. Aburi agreement essentially converts Nigeria into confederation, with more autonomy for regions. (St. Jorre 95)
20 February 1967	Ojukwu announces that, unless Aburi agreements are fully implemented by 31 March, he will implement them unilaterally. "Most

20 February 1967 (continued)	people understood this to be notice of the East's impending secession." Gowon responds that he is prepared to use force to preserve unity of Nigeria. (St. Jorre 102)
March–April 1967	Ojukwu issues "survival edicts" by which East Nigeria takes over many federal functions. Under these edicts, East Nigeria collects and spends tax revenues; establishes law school, court of appeals; takes control of several central government-owned enterprises; directly markets its goods abroad, thereby retaining foreign exchange. In response, Lagos imposes "diplomatic, economic, and military blockade against the East." On 1 April, Lagos declares revenue edict (collecting and spending tax revenues) "illegal and unconstitutional." On 4 April, Nigerian Airways flights to East Nigeria are suspended. On 5 April, all foreign transactions with East are frozen. On 19 April, Nigerian Produce Marketing Company declares it illegal to deal with any other authority, orders ships bound for ports in the East to unload in Lagos. On 29 April, Lagos announces that savings bank deposits, savings stamps, certificates, bonds sold in East after 31 March no longer will be recognized by central government. (Nwankwo 236–38)
1 May 1967	Western region threatens to secede if East does so. (St. Jorre 108)
30 May 1967	Ojukwu proclaims independent Republic of Biafra. Western region does not follow suit. (Nwankwo 1; St. Jorre 122)
June–July 1967	Shell/British Petroleum agrees to "token" payment of £250,000 to Biafra to keep petroleum flowing but denies payment implies recognition of new state. Nigeria responds with total blockade of Biafran coast. Shortly thereafter, British government prohibits the payment. "The Biafrans were also running into trouble as a result of the federal blockade which, though far from total in the early days, was beginning to throttle the Biafran economy." (St. Jorre 140–41)
July 1967	Civil war breaks out. (St. Jorre 147)
25 July 1967	"[P]ursuing his strategy of strangulation, Gowon's forces capture Bonny island on the Biafran coast in the first seaborne assault of the war. This was a blow for Biafra for a number of reasons. It gave the Nigerians a toehold on the coastline; enabled them to enforce the blockade more effectively, especially against the oil for which Bonny was the only terminal (there were about three million barrels of crude oil in the tanks); and it brought them within 35 miles of Port Harcourt, Biafra's major port and most important commercial city." (St. Jorre 151)
Early 1968	Nigeria announces it will issue new currency, allowing only 19 days to complete switch. Biafra is caught by surprise and, though it undertakes "a panic operation of offloading Nigerian currency notes at rock-bottom prices to anyone who would take them," government still loses estimated £30 million. (St. Jorre 187)

After more than two years of war, Nigerian forces take last Biafran stronghold, Ojukwu flees country. (St. Jorre 397)

GOALS OF SENDER COUNTRY

Arthur A. Nwanko and Samuel U. Ifejika
Following declaration of blockade, Lieutenant Colonel Gowon's actions are characterized as being "intended to be punitive rather than to resolve the crisis." (Nwankwo 238)

John de St. Jorre
In summer 1967: "Gowon, sticking to his limited police action formula, was aiming at a swift-moving military operation, from carefully selected points and backed up by a tightening of the economic blockade to bring down 'Ojukwu and his rebel gang.'" (St. Jorre 151)

In late 1967-early 1968: "Reduced to its essentials, the federal government's minimal demand was a return to the fold: Biafra should give up its independence and accept the new 12-state structure dividing the Eastern region into three states, only one of which— the East-Central—would be primarily for the Ibos and under the control of an Ibo government." (St. Jorre 190)

RESPONSE OF TARGET COUNTRY

John de St. Jorre
"The Biafrans, aware that African recognition was the most effective passkey to outside involvement and help, called on the OAU [Organization of African Unity] to intervene and assiduously lobbied the summit meeting at Kinshasha in September 1967. But they were on shaky ground for the very existence of Biafra challenged two of the pillars on which the organisation had been built: noninterference in the internal affairs of a member state and a rigid respect for colonial boundaries." (St. Jorre 191)

ATTITUDE OF OTHER COUNTRIES

United States
Secretary of State Dean Rusk at beginning of war: "We regard Nigeria as part of Britain's sphere of influence." US imposes arms embargo on both sides. (St. Jorre 181)

United Kingdom
"Britain, while maintaining it was 'neutral,' continued its 'traditional' (small arms, armoured cars, etc.) and 'purely defensive' (antiaircraft guns) supplies to Nigeria but resisted federal pressure to sell aircraft, bombs, tanks, and heavy field guns." (St. Jorre 181)

Netherlands, Italy, France, Belgium
These countries ban arms sales to Nigeria in June 1968. (St. Jorre 209)

France
French government speaks of self-determination, allows French arms to be indirectly shipped to Biafra. "In fact, full recognition and open-ended support never materialised

but this limited move was sufficient to encourage the Biafrans to fight on, to provide the means for them to do so, and to ensure that countless thousands of them needlessly died. For French intervention decisively saved the Biafrans from defeat, decisively prolonged the war, and—equally decisively—fell short of enabling them to win it." (St. Jorre 211)

Soviet Union
"The decisive factor, which brought the Soviet Union down irrevocably on the federal side, seems to have been a combination of the refusal of the Americans and the British to supply the arms the Nigerians requested and its assessment of the likely outcome of the war at the end of July . . . Their early commitment consisting of a few old planes was not large; they were making useful foreign exchange out of it; there was no danger of annoying their other African allies (all of whom were technically on Nigeria's side, too), or the OAU; and the potential gain, a real foothold in Africa's most populous state, was enormous." (St. Jorre 183)

Czechoslovakia
Under orders from Moscow, Czech government provides "a variety of weapons," including jet fighters, to Nigerians except for brief lull in late spring of 1968 when Alexander Dubcek, Communist leader, bans arms sales to both sides. (St. Jorre 184)

People's Republic of China
"Peking first began supporting Biafra when it was clear that the Russians were backing Nigeria. This was undoubtedly the main incentive for Communist China's unwavering support for the Biafrans throughout the war. . . . But, again, the Biafrans were out of luck. Despite many stories about Chinese aid, 'instructors,' and arms flooding into Biafra from Dar-es-Salaam, there was never any evidence to show that Peking's backing went beyond a torrent of jargon over the airwaves." (St. Jorre 185)

Organization of African Unity
Resolution adopted at Kinshasha summit in September 1967 "reaffirmed respect for the 'sovereignty and territorial integrity of member states,' condemned secession, and accepted that the situation of the crisis was primarily the responsibility of the Nigerians themselves." (St. Jorre 191)

Algeria, Libya, Egypt, Sudan
"Arab support was invaluable to the Nigerians, both materially and diplomatically. . . . Egypt supplied pilots and technicians and Sudan and Libya, traditional users of British weaponry, sold Nigeria some of the equipment Britain refused to provide." (St. Jorre 219)

Tanzania, Gabon, Ivory Coast, Zambia
These countries recognize the Republic of Biafra in April, May 1968. (St. Jorre 193)

Portugal, South Africa, Rhodesia
"Biafra also had friends in southern Africa. . . . By helping to sustain a civil war in Africa's most populous and potentially strongest country, these three white-supremacist governments undermined African unity, weakened the African liberation movements' drive against themselves . . . and nourished their own propaganda message depicting black Africa's inherent and incurable instability." (St. Jorre 218)

ECONOMIC IMPACT

Observed Economic Statistics

Biafran population (1967): 15 million. (Nwankwo 236)

Nigerian federation 1965 financial data (million pounds sterling)

	Federal total	East Nigeria	East Nigerian percentage of total
Exports	263	99	38
Tax revenues	140.7	48.4	34

Source: Nwankwo 237.

When Nigeria changes its currency: "The Biafran government is reliably estimated to have lost £30 million altogether, and although it managed to put its own new currency efficiently and rapidly into circulation, the operation dealt a massive blow at the country's financial resources." (St. Jorre 187)

"[T]here was no doubt that the average person was suffering as a result of the phenomenal rise in prices and the shortages and hardships imposed by the blockade. Beef had risen from 3 to 60 shillings a pound, but was rarely obtainable; eggs, formerly 4 shillings a dozen went up to 38; a chicken which cost perhaps 15 shillings before the war rose to first £5, then £15, and just before the war ended was fetching £30. Dried fish—one of the main sources of protein for the population, had risen from 5 shillings a pound to 60, and, most dramatically of all, salt, formerly 1 penny a cup, was 20 shillings." (St. Jorre 225)

Inadvertent contribution of churches' relief efforts to Biafra's foreign exchange resources is estimated at £1.5 million to £8.5 million. (St. Jorre 250)

Calculated Economic Impact

	Annual cost to target country
Reduction in trade resulting from Nigerian blockade; welfare loss valued at 75 percent of lost trade (estimated at 90 percent of value of 1965 exports).	$160 million
Loss of monetary reserves from change in Nigerian currency; welfare loss valued at 100 percent of currency not exchanged or sold at a discount.	72 million
Offset	
Contributions from church relief efforts; welfare gain valued at 100 percent of estimated foreign exchange transfers.	($12 million)
Total	$220 million

Relative Magnitudes

Gross indicators of Biafran economy	
Biafran GDP† (1967)	$1,445 million
Biafran population (1967)	15 million
Annual effect of sanctions related to gross indicators	
Percentage of GDP	15.2
Per capita	$14.67
Biafran trade with Nigeria as percentage of total trade	
Exports (1967 est.)	50
Imports (1967 est.)	50
Ratio of Nigerian GDP excluding Biafra (1967: $4,130 million) to Biafran GDP (1967: $1,445 million)	3

† Assumes Biafran GDP is equal to 35 percent of national total (same percentage as East Nigerian contribution to total tax revenues in 1965).

ASSESSMENT

John de St. Jorre
"A federal spokesman admitted that the blockade itself would not bring Biafra down but said it was designed 'as a softening-up process to lower Eastern morale.' Feeling was running so high in the East that although prices rose, it was doubtful whether it achieved this. However, in the longer term it was one of the main causes of Biafra's defeat." (St. Jorre 141)

"[B]y simply declaring a blockade the federal government could, and did, scare off the bulk of the foreign shipping that operated in the area, whether it had a navy to enforce it or not. . . . Nevertheless, several ships did get through and Biafra managed to send out one or two valuable cargoes of palm oil before the war started." (St. Jorre 142)

"The biggest loophole was not the sea at all but along the Cameroon border. . . . African borders are notoriously difficult to control and there was a steady flow of smuggled goods, Biafran VIPs and charter flights until the fighting imposed its own deadly and far more effective blockade. Trade also continued spasmodically across the Niger throughout the war and played an important part in keeping Biafra going. However, as with the oil embargo, Nigeria itself suffered from the effects of the blockade, and coal—the Enugu mines were, of course, under Biafran control—had to be hurriedly shipped from West Germany and later Poland to keep the railways and thermal power stations running." (St. Jorre 142)

AUTHORS' SUMMARY

Overall assessment	Assigned scores
☐ Policy result, scaled from 1 (failed) to 4 (success)	4
☐ Sanctions contribution, scaled from 1 (none) to 4 (significant)	3

	Assigned scores
Overall assessment (continued)	
☐ Success score (policy result *times* sanctions contribution), scaled from 1 (outright failure) to 16 (significant success)	12
Political and economic variables	
☐ Companion policies: J (covert), Q (quasi-military), or R (regular military)	R
☐ International cooperation with sender, scaled from 1 (none) to 4 (significant)	1
☐ International assistance to target: A (if present)	—
☐ Sanctions period (years)	3
☐ Economic health and political stability of target, scaled from 1 (distressed) to 3 (strong)	1
☐ Presanction relations between sender and target, scaled from 1 (antagonistic) to 3 (cordial)	3
☐ Type of sanction: X (export), M (import), F (financial)	F, X, M
☐ Cost to sender, scaled from 1 (net gain) to 4 (major loss)	3

BIBLIOGRAPHY

De St. Jorre, John. 1972. *The Nigerian Civil War*. London: Hodder and Stoughton.
Nwankwo, Arthur Agwuncha, and Samuel Udochukwu Ifejika. 1969. *The Making of a Nation: Biafra*. London: C. Hurst and Co.

Case 68–1   US v. Peru

(1968: Purchase of French Jets)

CHRONOLOGY OF KEY EVENTS

Also see Case 68–2 US v. Peru (1968–74: Expropriation)

October 1967	Peru decides "to purchase 12 French Mirage supersonic jets for a price exceeding $20 million." (*New York Times*, 4 October 1967, A1)
13 December 1967	Congress approves a foreign aid bill, with the Conte-Long (Congressman Silvio Conte, R–Mass., and Senator Russell B. Long, D–La.) amendment requiring that economic aid to developing countries be reduced if country purchases "sophisticated weaponry." (*New York Times*, 14 December 1967, A1)
15 May 1968	As mandated by Conte-Long amendment, Johnson administration suspends development aid to Peru for current fiscal year because of its decision to purchase jets. Senator Long states that resumption of aid in fiscal year beginning on 1 July depends on size of Peruvian defense budget. (*New York Times*, 17 May 1968, A1)
23 May 1968	Administration officials deny that Conte-Long amendment has been invoked vis-à-vis Peru. Rather than being "cut off," they say, loans simply were not made during FY 1968. According to concerned diplomats, loans also were unlikely to be made in FY 1969 "unless the United States and Peru patch up their differences." In Peru, resolution is proposed to expropriate US mining concessions and other private investment, nationalize other American business holdings, cancel Peruvian debts to US, but is defeated as being too extreme. (*New York Times*, 24 May 1968, A7)
August 1968	Tentative settlement is reached between Peruvian government and US-owned International Petroleum Company on disposition of company's holdings in Peru. (*Keesing's* 23101)
October 1968	President Fernando Belaunde Terry is overthrown by military, new government renounces August agreement. Suspension of US aid is now dominated by concerns for expropriated property. (*Keesing's* 23101)

GOALS OF SENDER COUNTRY

Senator Russell B. Long
"A country is perfectly free to divert its own resources from economic development to defense, but not United States funds. Nor should United States funds rush in to fill the gap." (*New York Times*, 17 May 1968, A1)

New York Times
"American policy is seeking to discourage excessive military expenditures by underdeveloped Latin American nations on the ground that such expenditures waste money desperately needed to improve standards of living." (*New York Times*, 24 May 1968, A7)

"To have invoked the amendment, officials said, might have risked repercussions in Latin America, including demands for the withdrawal of United States aid missions. To avoid this, the funds were quietly withheld under the 'intent' of Congress. Later the news leaked to the press, through Congress." (*New York Times*, 24 May 1968, A7)

Text of Conte-Long amendment to Foreign Assistance Act of 1967
"The president is directed to withhold economic assistance in an amount equivalent to the amount spent by any underdeveloped country for the purchase of sophisticated weapons systems, such as missile systems and jet aircraft for military purposes from any country, unless the president determines that such purchases or acquisition of weapons systems is important to the national security of the United States and reports within 30 days each such determination to the Congress." (Kuczynski 159)

RESPONSE OF TARGET COUNTRY

President Fernando Belaunde Terry
(Paraphrased by *New York Times*): "It would be as foolish for the United States to try to [dictate policy to Peru] as it would be for Peru to suggest to the United States that the American expenditures in Vietnam could be better spent improving the lot of the Asian people or of the impoverished people of the United States itself." (*New York Times*, 24 May 1968, A7)

ECONOMIC IMPACT

Observed Economic Statistics
Agency for International Development (AID) allocation for Peru in FY 1968, $37 million, is canceled. Technical assistance, food programs valued at $10 million to $12 million continue. (*New York Times*, 17 May 1968, A1)

US aid to Peru (million dollars)

	AID	PL 480	Eximbank loans	Total economic†	Military
1965	7.4	6.5	13.0	36.1	11.5
1966	18.6	7.8	3.0	42.6	9.8
1967	22.7	2.4	5.7	33.0	5.0

US aid to Peru *(continued)*

	AID	PL 480	Eximbank loans	Total economic†	Military
1968	5.5	6.7	4.7	18.5	1.4
1969	4.0	7.8	10.8	21.9	0.6

† Includes aid programs not shown here.
Source: AID.

Calculated Economic Impact

	Annual cost to target country
Suspension of US economic aid to Peru in 1968; welfare loss estimated as 90 percent of reduced transfers.	$33 million

Relative Magnitudes

Gross indicators of Peruvian economy	
Peruvian GNP (1968)	$4.7 billion
Peruvian population (1968)	12.7 million
Annual effect of sanctions related to gross indicators	
Percentage of GNP	0.7
Per capita	$2.60
Peruvian trade with US as percentage of total trade	
Exports (1968)	11
Imports (1968)	8
Ratio of US GNP (1968: $873.4 billion) to Peruvian GNP (1968: $4.7 billion)	186

ASSESSMENT

Pedro-Pablo Kuczynski
"The Mirage purchase could not have come at a more difficult financial moment . . . and, paradoxically, may have led to President Belaunde's loss of power over the armed forces, who successfully insisted that he allow the purchase. The US State and Defense Departments also had an important role: by dilly-dallying in early 1967 with the Peruvian Air Force over the sale of F-5 [US] jets, . . . they caused a tide of national feeling among Peruvian officers, who felt themselves dependent on the existing old US equipment. . . . The various contradictory statements of the spokesmen from the various interested agencies in the US government appeared to confirm to many people the view that the US was not opposed to the purchase of warplanes at all, but to the purchase of non-US warplanes." (Kuczynski 158–59)

AUTHORS' SUMMARY

Overall assessment	Assigned scores
□ Policy result, scaled from 1 (failed) to 4 (success)	1
□ Sanctions contribution, scaled from 1 (none) to 4 (significant)	1
□ Success score (policy result *times* sanctions contribution), scaled from 1 (outright failure) to 16 (significant success)	1

Political and economic variables

□ Companion policies: J (covert), Q (quasi-military), or R (regular military)	—
□ International cooperation with sender, scaled from 1 (none) to 4 (significant)	1
□ International assistance to target: A (if present)	—
□ Sanctions period (years)	1
□ Economic health and political stability of target, scaled from 1 (distressed) to 3 (strong)	2
□ Presanction relations between sender and target, scaled from 1 (antagonistic) to 3 (cordial)	2
□ Type of sanction: X (export), M (import), F (financial)	F
□ Cost to sender, scaled from 1 (net gain) to 4 (major loss)	1

BIBLIOGRAPHY

Agency for International Development. *Overseas Loans and Grants*. Various issues.
Keesing's Contemporary Archives. 1967–68.
Kuczynski, Pedro-Pablo. 1977. *Peruvian Democracy under Economic Stress*. Princeton, NJ: Princeton University Press.

Case 68–2   US v. Peru
(1968–74: Expropriation)

CHRONOLOGY OF KEY EVENTS

Also see Case 68–1, US v. Peru (1968: Purchase of French Jets

July 1963   President Fernando Belaunde Terry, supported by armed forces, takes office in Peru, concentrates on settlement with International Petroleum Company (IPC), subsidiary of Standard Oil of New Jersey. In negotiations, Belaunde is "constantly reminded" by US of Hickenlooper amendment (Senator Bourke B. Hickenlooper, R–Iowa), which requires a termination of US aid to countries that do not make progress in settling expropriation disputes. (Olson 396–98)

July 1968   IPC, concerned that worse leader will follow Belaunde in 1969 elections, adopts more conciliatory tack in negotiations. (Olson 398)

22 August 1968   Belaunde reaches agreement with IPC on northern Peru oil fields, Peruvian tax claims against IPC. IPC yields its claim to subsoil rights; Peru yields its claims for past debt, taxes. (Olson 395–96)

13 September 1968   Chief Peruvian negotiator claims public version of IPC agreement does not contain key page listing IPC's debts to Peru. In October, military deposes Belaunde, using IPC agreement as pretext, expropriates Peruvian assets of IPC. (Olson 395)

1968–69   US aid to Peru is reduced; World Bank, Inter-American Development Bank (IDB) authorizations cut dramatically in 1969, 1970; International Monetary Fund (IMF) stand-by loan is canceled. (Olson 407)

7 April 1969   Two days before Hickenlooper amendment is scheduled to take effect, President Juan Velasco Alvarado invents administrative appeal process; US government then finds sufficient progress to avert imposition of Hickenlooper amendment. (Olson 409)

1969–70   Peru nationalizes W. R. Grace sugar estates, Cerro Corporation grazing lands, ITT telephone system, Chase Manhattan branch bank, other enterprises. (Olson 411)

| *9 August 1973* | US, Peru agree to negotiate on expropriation claims. (Gantz 392) |

19 February 1974   US, Peru sign compensation agreement for expropriated properties of US nationals; Peru pays $76 million to US to settle claims plus about $74 million directly to individual claimants. IPC receives less than market value for its claims, other companies receive approximately market value. (Gantz 392)

GOALS OF SENDER COUNTRY

David A. Gantz
"The IPC expropriation resulted in a further cooling of bilateral relations that had been strained sporadically by the IPC problem since the early 1960s. Bilateral economic assistance, except for humanitarian assistance following the earthquake of 1969, was virtually halted, consistent with the spirit, if not the letter, of United States law." (Gantz 391)

RESPONSE OF TARGET COUNTRY

David A. Gantz
"Whether because of the IPC dispute or as a result of the revolutionary government's general views on the role of foreign capital under the revolution and control of its natural resources, other major American firms such as Cerro Corporation and W. R. Grace Company began to experience serious problems with their operations in Peru." (Gantz 391)

Peruvian delegate to IDB
1969: "It may be that we ourselves are responsible for the fact that no new loans have been made to Peru, but is it not the case that certain of the principles [of the IDB concerning apolitical loan consideration] have been overlooked?" (Olson 407)

Richard Stuart Olson
In April 1969, President Velasco unfolds counterstrategy in response to threatened invocation of Hickenlooper amendment: he notes that IPC is Canadian firm, rhetorically asks origins of US involvement; distinguishes IPC from other foreign investment in Peru; threatens retaliation if Hickenlooper is invoked; appeals to other Latin American governments for moral support; welcomes Soviet trade delegation, thereby raising specter of "another Cuban threat"; extends military control over Peru. (Olson 409)

ECONOMIC IMPACT

Observed Economic Statistics

Aid to Peru (million dollars)

	US economic	US military	IBRD	IDB
1965	23.1	11.5	21.5	7.7
1966	39.6	9.8	42.1	39.0

Aid to Peru (*continued*)

	US economic	US military	IBRD	IDB
1967	27.3	5.0	10.0	19.0
1968	13.8	1.4	17.5	22.5
1969	13.1	0.6	—	—
1970	16.8	0.6	—	9.0

— Zero or negligible.
Source: AID.

Calculated Economic Impact

	Annual cost to target country
Reduction of about $25 million in US aid, from 1965–67 levels (about $45 million/year) to 1968–71 levels (about $20 million/year), evaluated at 100 percent of face amount.	$25 million
Reduction in World Bank authorizations in 1969, 1970 by about $20 million/year (from 1968 level of $20 million to 1969 and 1970 levels of zero), evaluated at 20 percent of face amount.	4 million
Reduction in IDB authorizations in 1969 to zero, against 1967–68 average level of about $21 million, evaluated at 20 percent of face amount.	4 million
Cancellation of IMF stand-by letter of credit of $75 million, evaluated at 10 percent of face amount.	7.5 million
Cancellation of European Consortium loan of $80 million, evaluated at 5 percent of face amount.	4 million
Outflow of capital, measured by errors, omissions in Peruvian balance of payments of $128 million in 1968, evaluated at 5 percent of face amount.	6.4 million

Offset

Allowance for Peruvian gain on acquisition of IPC assets, valued (by Peru) at $71 million against payment of $22 million compensation amortized over 3 years (corresponding to period of reduced bilateral aid).	($16.3 million)
Total	$34.6 million

Relative Magnitudes

Gross indicators of Peruvian economy	
Peruvian GNP (1968)	$4.7 billion
Peruvian population (1968)	12.7 million
Annual effect of sanctions related to gross indicators	
Percentage of GNP	0.7
Per capita	$2.72
Peruvian trade with US as percentage of total trade	
Exports	11
Imports	8
Ratio of US GNP (1968: $873.4 billion) to Peruvian GNP (1968: $4.7 billion)	186

ASSESSMENT

Senior US official
Speaking in April 1969, just after US decides not to impose Hickenlooper: "Maybe there was an element of brinksmanship in this whole situation . . . and, if so, we blinked." (Olson 410)

David A. Gantz
" . . . from a foreign policy point of view, a fiscally responsible, although not democratically elected, government with an obviously determined and sincere interest in bettering the lives of its people was, in effect, excluded from full participation in the United States bilateral assistance program; and the failure of IPC and the Peruvian government to reach a settlement adversely affected Peru's credit rating insofar as the international financial institutions, especially the World Bank and Inter-American Bank, were concerned." (Gantz 391)

AUTHORS' SUMMARY

Overall assessment	Assigned scores
☐ Policy result, scaled from 1 (failed) to 4 (success)	3
☐ Sanctions contribution, scaled from 1 (none) to 4 (significant)	4
☐ Success score (policy result *times* sanctions contribution), scaled from 1 (outright failure) to 16 (significant success)	12

Political and economic variables

☐ Companion policies: J (covert), Q (quasi-military), or R (regular military)	—
☐ International cooperation with sender, scaled from 1 (none) to 4 (significant)	1

Political and economic variables (continued)	Assigned scores
☐ International assistance to target: A (if present)	—
☐ Sanctions period (years)	6
☐ Economic health and political stability of target, scaled from 1 (distressed) to 3 (strong)	2
☐ Presanction relations between sender and target, scaled from 1 (antagonistic) to 3 (cordial)	2
☐ Type of sanction: X (export), M (import), F (financial)	F
☐ Cost to sender, scaled from 1 (net gain) to 4 (major loss)	1

BIBLIOGRAPHY

Agency for International Development. *Overseas Loans and Grants.* Various issues.

Gantz, David A. 1976. "The United States–Peruvian Claims Agreement of February 19, 1974." 10 *International Lawyer* (Summer): 389–99.

Goodwin, Richard N. "Letter from Peru." *New Yorker,* 17 May 1969, 41–44.

Kuczynski, Pedro-Pablo. 1977. *Peruvian Democracy under Economic Stress.* Princeton, NJ: Princeton University Press.

Olson, Richard Stuart. 1975. "Economic Coercion in International Disputes: The United States and Peru in the IPC Expropriation Dispute of 1968–71." 9 *Journal of Developing Areas* (April): 395–413.

Case 70–1 US v. Chile
(1970–73: Allende)

CHRONOLOGY OF KEY EVENTS

25 March 1970 and 27 June 1970 In two successive meetings, National Security Adviser Henry A. Kissinger, as chair of 40 Committee, which oversees CIA, authorizes that agency to spend up to $435,000 in opposition to election of Salvador Allende Gossens as president of Chile. Additional contributions of some $350,000 are made by ITT to Jorge Alessandri campaign, with CIA knowledge. Allende narrowly wins, forcing runoff election against Alessandri in congress. (Fagen 298; Hersh 37–39)

4 September 1970 Edward J. Gerrity, senior vice president of ITT, and William Broe, a senior CIA official, discuss program "aimed at inducing economic collapse" in Chile before October congressional runoff election, with view to averting election of Allende. However, there is no evidence of subsequent US business cooperation with contemplated program. (Sigmund, January 1974, 323–24; Hersh 38)

14 September 1970 After considering and rejecting support for military coup in Chile, Kissinger mounts campaign for Chilean congress to vote Jorge Alessandri into presidency, authorizes CIA to expend $250,000 in bribes to achieve this result. President Richard M. Nixon orders CIA Director Richard Helms to block Allende's election, continue exploring military coup (so-called Track II). (Fagen 297–98; Hersh 41–43)

24 October 1970 Allende wins congressional election. (Hersh 57)

9 November 1970 Nixon issues secret National Security Decision Memorandum 93 calling for: no new bilateral financial assistance to Chile; possible cancellation of existing bilateral financing; pressure on international financial institutions to limit credit to Chile; expressions of concern to private US businesses operating in Chile. US Secretary of the Treasury John B. Connally, who is reported "miffed when foreign nations expropriate US assets," takes lead in cutting off official credit to Chile. (Hersh 57; Petras 142)

| 1970 to mid-1972 | US banks reduce Chile's lines of short-term credit from $219 million to $32 million. (Farnsworth 132; Sigmund, January 1974, 332–33) |

1971   Through combination of price controls, wage gains for poorest groups, against background of underutilized capacity, Allende increases industrial production while inflation declines. However, Chile's external accounts are worsened by sharp drop in price of copper. (Sigmund, January 1974, 325)

1971 through 1973   New CIA director, William Colby: CIA was authorized to spend up to $8 million "in an effort to make it impossible for President Salvador Allende Gossens to govern." Among other activities, CIA financed prolonged truckers' strike October 1972–August 1973. (Fagen 298, 305; Sigmund, 1975, 375)

January 1971   Inter-American Development Bank (IDB) approves two new loans for Chile, $7 million for Catholic University, $4.6 million for Universidad Austral. No other loans are made during Allende regime, even though Chile offers various proposals. Between December 1970, December 1972, IDB disburses $54 million from existing loans. (Sigmund, January 1974, 327)

August 1971   US Export–Import Bank (Eximbank) defers $21 million loan for purchase of Boeing jets pending resolution of looming compensation dispute between Chile, copper companies. (Sigmund, January 1974, 330)

September 1971   Chile nationalizes Kennecott, Anaconda properties, designates $774 million as prior "excess profits" to be offset against compensation to be paid, sum that exceeds proposed compensation. On 13 October 1971, US Secretary of State William P. Rogers warns that proposed expropriation could jeopardize private capital, foreign aid to Chile. (Fagen 307–8; Farnsworth 135; Petras 140)

September–October 1971   World Bank refuses new development loans to Chile, citing both absence of "reasonable progress" toward compensation of copper companies, Chile's doubtful creditworthiness. Between 1 July 1970 and 30 June 1973, World Bank disburses $46 million from existing loans. (Sigmund, January 1974, 328–29)

October 1971   ITT submits Chile White Paper to US State Department calling for seven-point program of overt economic sanctions, limiting trade, curtailing disbursements for approved projects. William R. Merriman, ITT official, calls upon US to impose "economic squeeze" on Chile so that ensuing "economic chaos" will convince armed forces "to step in and restore order." Proposal is given cool reception by Secretary of State Rogers. (Sigmund, January 1974, 331–32; Farnsworth 135)

Kennecott brings litigation in France, other West European countries to seize copper shipped from Chile; lawsuits slow down Chilean exports. (Farnsworth 137)

November 1971	Chile declares moratorium on payment of foreign debt. (Sigmund, Fall 1974, 145)
December 1971	International Monetary Fund lends Chile $39.5 million in 1971, $42.8 million in 1972 to offset drop in copper price. (Sigmund, January 1974, 239)
19 January 1972	US policy statement on expropriation hammered out between State and Treasury, announced by Nixon: When a country expropriates US property without compensation, US "will not extend new bilateral economic benefits," will "withhold its support from loans under consideration in multilateral development banks. . . ." However, US loans to Chilean military will not be affected by general US policy against bilateral assistance. (Fagen 308; Petras 155; Sigmund, January 1974, 330–31, 334–35)
January 1972	Chile reaches refinancing agreement with private banks, calling for "symbolic payment" of 5 percent in 1972, 1973, more thereafter. (Sigmund, January 1974, 335)
February 1972	Eximbank suspends loan guarantees, citing Chile's moratorium on foreign debt. (Sigmund, Fall 1974, 146)
Early 1972	US Congress enacts González amendment (Congressman Henry B. González, D–Tex.) instructing US to vote against multilateral development bank (MDB) loans to countries that expropriate US companies without compensation. (Sigmund, January 1974, 326)
April 1972	Chile reaches agreement with Paris Club creditors (except US) for rescheduling debts to foreign governments. Chile also agrees to accept "the principles of payment of a just compensation for all nationalizations in conformity with Chilean and international law." However, Allende rejects attempt by US Ambassador Edward M. Korry to work out long-term, low-interest compensation for copper companies. (Sigmund, January 1974, 335–36; Farnsworth 135; Sigmund, 1975, 376)
11 September 1973	Allende is assassinated in military coup. "There is no evidence that the CIA played a direct role in the Allende coup, nor is there evidence that the Nixon administration was involved—through third parties— in Allende's death." (Farnsworth 140; Hersh 58)
18 September 1973	IDB grants Chile $65 million loan for hydroelectric project. In April 1974, IDB extends $22 million loan to state bank; soon thereafter $75 million credit for construction of hydroelectric plant, $422 million for agricultural development. (Farnsworth 140–41; Sigmund, January 1974, 327)
September– November 1973	US Department of Agriculture grants $52 million credit to buy wheat, corn. (Farnsworth 140)
January– February 1974	Chile agrees to compensate copper companies; Paris Club then reaches rescheduling arrangement with Chile. (Farnsworth 140)

March 1974 National Foreign Trade Council estimates official lending to Chile reaches $470 million, US bank credits reach pre-Allende levels of about $250 million. (Farnsworth 140)

GOALS OF SENDER COUNTRY

National Security Adviser Henry A. Kissinger
Commenting on 27 June 1970 on prospect of an Allende election victory in September: "I don't see why we need to stand by and watch a country go Communist due to the irresponsibility of its people." (Hersh 37)

Commenting on prospect of Allende victory in October congressional runoff election: "So I do not think we should delude ourselves that an Allende takeover in Chile would not present massive problems for us, and for democratic forces and for pro-US forces in Latin America, and indeed to the whole Western Hemisphere." (Hersh 40)

National Security Decision Memorandum 93
"Policy toward Chile," 9 November 1970, states that Nixon administration will undertake "vigorous efforts . . . to assure that other governments in Latin America understand fully that the United States opposes consolidation of a Communist state in Chile hostile to the interests of the United States and other hemisphere nations. . . ." (Hersh 57)

RESPONSE OF TARGET COUNTRY

November 1972
Chile reports it has obtained $250 million in short-term credits from Western Europe, other hard-currency countries; $103 million short-term from USSR; $446 million long-term from USSR, China, Eastern Europe; $70 million short-term from Latin America. (Sigmund, January 1974, 336)

December 1972
President Allende, speaking at UN, accuses US of imposing "invisible financial and economic blockade" against Chile. (Sigmund, January 1974, 322)

ECONOMIC IMPACT

Observed Economic Statistics

On 30 August 1973, short-term credits available to Allende government are $574 million, compared to $310 million at his election. (Sigmund, January 1974, 337)

Between 1970–1973, Chile increases money supply by 1,000 percent; 52 percent of national budget is financed by newly printed money; inflation rate is 323 percent July 1972–July 1973. (Sigmund, January 1974, 338–39)

Chilean imports rise from $1 billion in 1970 to $1.6 billion in 1973; most of increase is food, imports of which rise from $173 million to $683 million. (Sigmund, Fall 1974, 147)

Chilean foreign debt increases from $2.5 billion to $3.5 billion December 1970–September 1973, mostly from Western Europe, Latin America. Chile also runs down foreign exchange reserves of $343 million. (Sigmund, Fall 1974, 147)

Calculated Economic Impact

	Annual cost to target country
Reduction in short-term credits (mostly from US) to Chile; welfare loss estimated at 10 percent of volume of credits.	$9 million
Reduction in IBRD, IDB loan authorizations; welfare loss estimated at 25 percent of loans approved right after fall of Allende.	97 million
Chaos induced in Chilean economy by truckers' strike, estimated at 0.5 percent of GNP.	53 million
Deferral of Eximbank loan; welfare loss estimated at 20 percent of value of loan.	4 million
Total	$163 million

Relative Magnitudes

Gross indicators of Chilean economy	
Chilean GNP (1971)	$10.6 billion
Chilean population (1971)	9.5 million
Annual effect of sanctions related to gross indicators	
Percentage of GNP	1.5
Per capita	$17.16
Chilean trade with US as percentage of total trade	
Exports (1971)	10
Imports (1971)	23
Ratio of US GNP (1971: $1,078 billion) to Chilean GNP (1971: $10.6 billion)	102

ASSESSMENT

Emmanuel de Kadt, University of Sussex
"Whatever the importance of the US-inspired quasi-blockade and of the obstructiveness of Chilean private enterprise, very few observers disagree that [the Unidad Populár's] management of the economy was disastrous. . . ." (Sigmund, Fall 1974, 152)

Paul E. Sigmund
"What this [program of sanctions] adds up to is a slowdown, amounting in practice to no action on new loan requests from the multilateral banks but continued substantial lending from the pipeline; two large loans from the IMF; a mutual agreement by AID and the Allende government not to ask for or suggest new AID loans but continued pipeline loans, technical assistance, and Food for Peace; a highly publicized postponement

of a loan by the Eximbank in 1971 and termination of its guarantees in 1972; and a gradual diminution of credits by US private banks—although $35 million was still outstanding in 1973." (Sigmund, Fall 1974, 146)

"The basic causes of Allende's overthrow lie elsewhere, however." Namely: runaway inflation; intensification of class struggle; Allende's circumvention of the law; Allende's complicity in stockpiling arms by leftists. (Sigmund, January 1974, 338–39)

AUTHORS' SUMMARY

Overall assessment	Assigned scores
□ Policy result, scaled from 1 (failed) to 4 (success)	4
□ Sanctions contribution, scaled from 1 (none) to 4 (significant)	3
□ Success score (policy result *times* sanctions contribution), scaled from 1 (outright failure) to 16 (significant success)	12

Political and economic variables

□ Companion policies: J (covert), Q (quasi-military), or R (regular military)	J
□ International cooperation with sender, scaled from 1 (none) to 4 (significant)	1
□ International assistance to target: A (if present)	—
□ Sanctions period (years)	3
□ Economic health and political stability of target, scaled from 1 (distressed) to 3 (strong)	1
□ Presanction relations between sender and target, scaled from 1 (antagonistic) to 3 (cordial)	2
□ Type of sanction: X (export), M (import), F (financial)	F
□ Cost to sender, scaled from 1 (net gain) to 4 (major loss)	1

BIBLIOGRAPHY

Fagen, Richard R. 1975. "The United States and Chile: Roots and Branches." 53 *Foreign Affairs* (January): 297–313.

Farnsworth, Elizabeth. 1974. "Chile: What Was the US Role?—More than Admitted." 16 *Foreign Policy* (Fall): 127–41.

Hersh, Seymour. 1982. "The Price of Power: Kissinger, Nixon, and Chile." *The Atlantic* (December): 31–58.

Petras, James F., and Robert LaPorte, Jr. 1972. "Can We Do Business with Radical Nationalists?—Chile: No." 7 *Foreign Policy* (Summer): 132–58.

Sigmund, Paul E. 1974. "The 'Invisible Blockade' and the Overthrow of Allende." 52 *Foreign Affairs* (January): 322–40.

———. 1974. "Chile: What Was the US Role?—Less than Charged." 16 *Foreign Policy* (Fall): 142–56.

———. 1975. "Correspondence." 53 *Foreign Affairs* (January): 375–77.

Case 71–1   US v. India and Pakistan

(1971: Bangladesh)

CHRONOLOGY OF KEY EVENTS

December 1970– *early 1971*	Free elections are held in Pakistan in December 1970 after 12 years of military rule. Pakistan People's party, led by former Foreign Minister Zulfikar Ali Bhutto, wins 85 of 144 seats in West Pakistan while Awami League party, led by Sheikh Mujibar Rahman, wins 167 of 169 seats in East Pakistan. The two major parties split on issue of economic, political autonomy for the East. Bhutto, followers refuse to attend opening session of National Assembly, fearing it will be dominated by Awami League representatives. In February, President Agha Mohammed Yahya Kahn postpones opening of Assembly indefinitely, returns full political control to army. (Lillich 485)
March 1971	Early March is marked by strikes, sporadic violence in East Pakistan. On 23 March, Sheikh Mujibar Rahman declares emancipation for Bangladesh. He, other Bengali nationalist leaders are arrested; troops from West Pakistan are flown in on 25 March to restore order. This precipitates civil war that lasts through end of year, leaving estimated 1 million to 3 million Bengalis dead, causing 10 million to flee to India. Reports of civilian deaths prompt US to suspend new military assistance to Pakistan. However, export licenses continue to be issued; already authorized aid shipments go forward into November. (Lillich 486; Jackson 49; Hochman 106)
Early May 1971	Pakistan unilaterally declares six-month moratorium on debt repayments to World Bank aid-Pakistan consortium. US Senate Foreign Affairs Subcommittee holds hearings on aid to Pakistan, on 7 May votes to end arms sales to Pakistan. Bipartisan group of senators calls upon Secretary of State William P. Rogers to suspend all aid until Pakistan allows Red Cross to institute relief measures for famine victims in East Pakistan. (Jackson 49)
17 May 1971	Pakistan informs UN Secretary General U Thant it will accept UN aid in East Pakistan so long as it is coordinated locally. On 21 May, US government spokesman announces that, contrary to reports, economic assistance to Pakistan will not be terminated. (Jackson 50)

21 June 1971	World Bank's aid consortium for Pakistan adjourns without agreeing on continued development aid other than humanitarian relief assistance. (Jackson 62)
Mid-July 1971	US announces economic, technological assistance will be withheld "only till a fresh list of development projects [is] submitted 'taking into account the present situation' in East Pakistan." However, previous request for $188 million in aid to Pakistan will be pursued, humanitarian relief to East Pakistan will be increased. On 15 July, House Foreign Affairs Committee votes 17 to 6 to suspend economic aid to Pakistan "until the situation had returned to normal in the East." However, full Congress never adopts resolution to suspend economic aid. (Jackson 63–64)
15 July 1971	President Richard M. Nixon reveals National Security Adviser Henry A. Kissinger, with assistance of Pakistani officials, has secretly visited People's Republic of China. (Jackson 71)
9 August 1971	India, Soviet Union sign 20-year Treaty of Peace, Friendship and Cooperation. (Jackson 71)
8 November 1971	Administration announces that, with agreement of Pakistani government, "remaining licenses for the export of American arms to Pakistan were being suspended." Licenses were for $3.6 million in military equipment. (Jackson 93; Hochman 110)
Late 1971	Flow of East Pakistani refugees into India continues, clashes along Indo-Pakistani border intensify. On 24 November, Indian Prime Minister Indira Gandhi reveals Indian troops have crossed border on three occasions in "self-defense." On 28 November, Indian Defense Minister Jagjwan Ram announces his country has adopted policy of "hot pursuit" along border. (*Facts on File* 221; Lillich 487)
1 December 1971	US suspends arms shipments to India (including $2 million in ammunition and "related production equipment") because of India's refusal to withdraw forces from Pakistan border. (Jackson 105)
3 December 1971	Pakistan launches "preemptive" air strike against India's airfields. In response, India sends troops across both East, West Pakistani borders. US revokes all remaining licenses for military sales to India. (Lillich 487; Jackson 125)
4 December 1971	At US request, UN Security Council considers resolution calling for cessation of hostilities in East Pakistan, which is vetoed by USSR. On 7 December, General Assembly in 104 to 11 vote calls for immediate cease-fire. (Burke 212)
6 December 1971	India officially recognizes provisional government of Bangladesh. US, calling India "main aggressor" in war, suspends $87.6 million in development loans to that country. On 8 December, administration announces that no provision should be made in US Agency for International Development (AID) 1972 budget for India. (Jackson 125, 127; Hochman 105)

7 December 1971	Kissinger calls press conference to combat perception that administration is "anti-India." He points out that $35 million in military assistance to Pakistan was suspended in March, though $5 million in spare parts already in pipeline did get through. He adds that no new development loans have been extended to Pakistan since March. (Jackson 209–11)
10 December 1971	US dispatches naval task force, including aircraft carrier *Enterprise*, from South China Sea to Bay of Bengal. On 15 December, US officials say task force may be used to evacuate West Pakistani troops from East Pakistan after cease-fire is arranged. (Jackson 139)
December 1971– April 1972	On 17 December 1971, cease-fire is declared between Pakistan, India. US naval task force withdraws from Indian Ocean in January. On 4 April 1972, US recognizes independent state of Bangladesh. (Jackson 145; Blechman 179)

GOALS OF SENDER COUNTRY

S. M. Burke
"During the crisis the efforts of the United States were directed toward persuading the parties to arrive at a peaceful settlement. Though Nixon's critics made much of the American 'tilt' in favor of Pakistan, in fact the United States was not insensitive to the reality that 'a lasting political solution of the problem could be found only on the basis of some form of autonomy for East Pakistan . . . and made clear to all parties' that she favored such a solution." (Burke 211)

Joan Hochman
"[The] 'tilt' [toward Pakistan] policy, while reflecting overwhelming presidential concern with the China initiative, was also a response to counterbalance what was perceived as an attempt by the Soviets to increase their influence and political leverage on the subcontinent." Congress, US public are more sympathetic toward India while administration favors Pakistan. (Hochman 107)

"According to State and AID officials, the United States was maximizing its political influence by not suspending aid toward Pakistan and by suspending aid toward India because Pakistan was a friend and India was an 'aggressor.'" (Hochman 110)

"The suspension of economic assistance to India was a manifestation of United States disapproval of Indian military and political activity on the subcontinent; it did not represent a significant cutback in the existing levels of assistance to the nation." (Hochman 105)

Klaus Knorr
US State Department spokesman on suspension of development loans in December: "The United States is not making a short-term contribution to the Indian economy to make it easier for the Indian government to sustain its military effort." (Knorr 138)

"The motivation of the American Government is not clear from the available records. But it is hard to believe that the action did not result from a sheer and petulant desire to punish and rebuke New Delhi." (Knorr 138)

Barry M. Blechman, Stephen S. Kaplan
"One is forced to conclude that Nixon and Kissinger were attempting to signal the possibility of more severe economic and military sanctions if India continued its military offensive, rather than actually trying to cripple the Indian economic base." (Blechman 187)

RESPONSE OF TARGET COUNTRIES

Joan Hochman
"A history of continued political tension between India and Pakistan since partition, . . . West Pakistani military activities in the East, and the burden of caring for 10 million Bengali refugees made Indian involvement in the Pakistani dispute predictable." (Hochman 106)

Klaus Knorr
"The Indian government lashed out scornfully against the notion that the receipt of American aid would make her subservient to Washington's dictates." (Knorr 138)

Barry M. Blechman, Stephen S. Kaplan
"Pakistani president Yayha Kahn remained convinced throughout 1971 that his role as liaison between them ensured that Peking and Washington would bail him out of any international problem into which he stumbled." (Blechman 208)

ATTITUDE OF OTHER COUNTRIES

World Bank Aid-Pakistan Consortium
"This decision to terminate World Bank development aid [to Pakistan] was influenced by the strenuous diplomatic efforts which India had made since April. . . . But probably even more important was the highly critical oral report made by Mr. Peter Cargill, the head of the ten-man team of World Bank officials which had been established in May to study economic prospects in both West and East Pakistan on behalf of the Bank. . . . The report concluded that administrative and commercial and industrial life had virtually come to a halt. Renewed international development assistance 'would serve little purpose now.'" In next few weeks, Britain, Sweden, Netherlands, West Germany also suspended bilateral economic assistance pending "firm evidence of progress towards a political solution in the East wing." (Jackson 62–63)

Soviet Union
"In July, as the Western powers moved one by one to suspend economic assistance to Pakistan, Russian aid [to India] continued." (Jackson 70)

"The USSR was nudged from neutrality in the dispute during the summer of 1971 by Pakistan's active cultivation of Chinese support against India and by Nixon's dramatic breakthrough in relations with China." (Blechman 197)

China
"The primary Chinese interests engaged by the Indo-Pakistani war were the desire to deny any major expansion of Soviet power in Southern Asia and the need to preserve Pakistan as a viable buffer and a partial counterbalance to India's growing power. . . . During 1971 China provided Pakistan with extensive diplomatic, economic, and military

assistance in its growing dispute with India but, like the USSR, China remained wary of making any firm military commitment to its subcontinent client over the war issue." (Blechman 203)

ECONOMIC IMPACT

Observed Economic Statistics

The $87.6 million loan to India, which US suspended in December, accounts for 39 percent of all development loans allocated to India in FY 1971 by AID. Not suspended are $30 million in project aid for specific purposes, $105 million to support India's commodity import program, $235 million in PL 480 food aid. Amount suspended as portion of total aid, therefore, is "marginal." With respect to multilateral assistance, US abstains from voting on proposed loans to India during December, January instead of actively opposing them. (Hochman 105)

"Washington found it as difficult to stop aid to India as it had been to stop aid to Pakistan, and for many of the same legal and economic reasons. In light of India's protest against arms to Pakistan, it is interesting that when the $87.6 million economic assistance cut was made, Washington also cancelled $11.5 million in military sales licenses to India, which was about three times the amount then outstanding in licenses for Pakistan." (Wilcox 52)

US aid to India and Pakistan (million dollars)

	Economic		Military	
Fiscal year	India	Pakistan	India	Pakistan
1969	477.5	111.4	0.1	0.1
1970	449.7	209.8	0.1	0.2
1971	444.5	107.9	0.1	0.2
1972	113.5	165.1	—	0.1
1973	81.7	177.9	—	0.3

— Zero or negligible.
Source: AID.

Calculated Economic Impact

	Annual cost to target country
Suspension of US economic aid to India; welfare loss valued at 90 percent of reduced transfers.	$79 million
Suspension of US military sales to India; welfare loss valued at 40 percent of reduced sales.	5 million

Calculated Economic Impact (*continued*)

	Annual cost to target country
Suspension of US military assistance to Pakistan; welfare loss valued at 90 percent of reduced transfers.	32 million
Suspension of US military sales to Pakistan; welfare loss valued at 40 percent of reduced sales.	1 million
Total	$117 million
Of which:	
India	$84 million
Pakistan	$33 million

Relative Magnitudes

Gross indicators of Indian economy	
Indian GNP (1971)	$57.7 billion
Indian population (1971)	551 million
Annual effect of sanctions related to gross indicators	
Percentage of GNP	0.1
Per capita	$0.15
Indian trade with US as percentage of total trade	
Exports (1971)	17
Imports (1971)	23
Ratio of US GNP (1971: $1,078 billion) to Indian GNP (1971: $57.7 billion)	19

Gross indicators of Pakistani economy	
Pakistani GNP (1971)	$10.5 billion
Pakistani population (1971)	117 million
Annual effect of sanctions related to gross indicators	
Percentage of GNP	0.3
Per capita	$0.28
Pakistani trade with US as percentage of total trade	
Exports (1971)	10
Imports (1971)	25
Ratio of US GNP (1971: $1,078 billion) to Pakistani GNP (1971: $10.5 billion)	103

ASSESSMENT

Joan Hochman
"While the benefits of the suspension are debatable, the costs, some of which were unanticipated, were significant. In the sense that the cutoff was one symbolic gesture of the tilt towards Pakistan whose objective was to send a 'political signal' to the Indians, it is clear that the Indians 'got the message.' How United States' interests were furthered by the sending of the message, however, is not clear. It took almost 14 months after the initial cutoff to unsuspend the $87.6 million in the AID pipeline that had been blocked in the Indian accounts but not allocated to other nations. The tilt jeopardized the entire US political relationship with India . . . and made reestablishing relations a difficult, painstaking and yet uncompleted process. While the decision can be considered 'effective' in the limited sense that the United States' objective of informing the Indians of the country's opposition to Indian support of the Bengalis was achieved, the costs were great and the validity of this objective can be called into question by the fact that aid was not resumed once the war was over." (Hochman 114)

Wayne Wilcox
"In fact, short of military intervention, which was logistically difficult and politically absurd, there was very little that the United States could do to stop India from its actions. A UN resolution, sure to be vetoed by the USSR, could indicate official displeasure. New AID projects could be stopped. Private statements could be issued. But there was no way to favorably influence the course of major events in the subcontinent, and that presumably was the object of American policy. Mrs. Gandhi had won." (Wilcox 52)

AUTHORS' SUMMARY

Overall assessment	*Assigned scores*
☐ Policy result, scaled from 1 (failed) to 4 (success)	2
☐ Sanctions contribution, scaled from 1 (none) to 4 (significant)	1
☐ Success score (policy result *times* sanctions contribution), scaled from 1 (outright failure) to 16 (significant success)	2

Political and economic variables

☐ Companion policies: J (covert), Q (quasi-military), or R (regular military)	Q
☐ International cooperation with sender, scaled from 1 (none) to 4 (significant)	1
☐ International assistance to target: A (if present)	—
☐ Sanctions period (years)	1
☐ Economic health and political stability of target, scaled from 1 (distressed) to 3 (strong)	2
☐ Presanction relations between sender and target, scaled from 1 (antagonistic) to 3 (cordial)	2
☐ Type of sanction: X (export), M (import), F (financial)	F, X
☐ Cost to sender, scaled from 1 (net gain) to 4 (major loss)	1

BIBLIOGRAPHY

Agency for International Development. *Overseas Loans and Grants.* Various issues.
Blechman, Barry M., and Stephen S. Kaplan. 1978. *Force without War: U.S. Armed Forces as a Political Instrument.* Washington: Brookings Institution.
Burke, S. M. 1974. *Mainsprings of Indian and Pakistani Foreign Policies.* Minneapolis: University of Minnesota Press.
Choudhury, G. W. 1975. *India, Pakistan, Bangladesh, and the Major Powers.* New York: Free Press.
Facts on File. 1971.
Hochman, Joan. 1975. "The Suspension of Economic Assistance to India." In vol. 3, *Appendices: Commission on the Organization of the Government for the Conduct of Foreign Policy.* Washington: GPO.
Jackson, Robert. 1975. *South Asian Crisis: India-Pakistan-Bangladesh.* International Institute for Strategic Studies. Studies in International Security, no. 17. London: Chatto and Windus.
Knorr, Klaus. 1975. *The Power of Nations: The Political Economy of International Relations.* New York: Basic Books.
Lillich, Richard B., and Frank C. Newman. 1979. *International Human Rights: Problems of Law and Policy.* Boston: Little, Brown & Co.
Wilcox, Wayne. 1973. *The Emergence of Bangladesh.* Foreign Affairs Study, no. 7. Washington: American Enterprise Institute.

Summary S–1   US v. Countries Supporting International Terrorism
(1972–   : Overview)

CHRONOLOGY OF KEY EVENTS

1972 Israeli athletes are massacred at 1972 Olympics; President Richard M. Nixon forms Cabinet Committee to Combat Terrorism, introduces Draft Convention in UN. (Flores 535–36)

15 February 1973 US, Cuba reach accord calling for: extradition or prosecution of hijackers; ban on island raids by Cuban exiles in US. (Flores 536)

March 1973 US Ambassador to Sudan Cleo Noel, Deputy Chief of Mission George Moore are kidnapped and murdered by Black September terrorists in Khartoum. (Flores 536)

October 1977 Senator Abraham Ribicoff (D–Conn.) introduces "Omnibus Antiterrorism Act of 1977" requiring president to publish list of countries aiding international terrorism, permitting Congress to add countries to the list, mandating termination of commercial air service with listed countries, refusing entry to US of aliens who have traveled to or through designated countries. Administration of President Jimmy Carter strenuously opposes Omnibus Act because it would limit presidential discretion, also objects to similar mandatory bills introduced in 1978 and 1979. (Flores 544–58)

11 September 1979 Congresswoman Millicent Fenwick (R–NJ) introduces an amendment requiring administration to notify Congress of proposed exports to country that has "repeatedly provided support for acts of international terrorism" if exports would significantly contribute to country's "military potential" or would "enhance the ability of such country to support acts of international terrorism." Congressional support for amendment is prompted by US State Department approval, in 1979, of sale of three Boeing 747s and two Boeing 727s to Libya and, in 1978, four L-100 cargo aircraft to Syria. On 29 September 1979, Congress enacts Export Administration Act of 1979, including Fenwick antiterrorist amendment. (Flores 563–64)

1980 State Department lists Libya, Syria, Iraq, South Yemen as states that have "repeatedly provided support for acts of international terrorism." (Flores 570)

26 February 1982	State Department deletes Iraq, adds Cuba to list of terrorist-supporting nations. (*Facts on File* 162)

23 January 1984	State Department adds Iran to list of nations accused of supporting terrorism after alleging that it was involved in October 1983 bombing of US Marine base in Beirut, Lebanon. Officials say, however, that action will not affect US oil imports from Iran, which were resumed in 1982, and amounted to about 500 million barrels in 1983. (*Washington Post*, 24 January 1984, A8; *Wall Street Journal*, 23 January 1984, 8)

LEGAL NOTES

1937
League of Nations Convention on Terrorism is ratified only by India. (Flores 532–33)

1972
US introduces in UN, Draft Convention for the Prevention and Punishment of Certain Acts of International Terrorism. UN members are unable to agree on distinction between acts of "peoples struggling for their liberation" and "international terrorism." (Flores 533)

1974
Congress enacts Antihijacking Act of 1974 (49 U.S.C. 1514–15), empowering US secretary of transportation to revoke or limit commercial air travel with countries that do not maintain adequate airline security. (Flores 539)

June 1976
Congress amends Foreign Assistance Act of 1961 (22 U.S.C. 2371(a)) to terminate aid to any country that aids or abets international terrorism, with presidential national security waiver. (Flores 539)

1977
In Export Administration Act Amendments of 1977 (50 U.S.C. 2402(8)), Congress provides presidential mandate to use export controls "to encourage other countries to take immediate steps" to discourage international terrorism. (Flores 543)

1979
In Export Administration Act of 1979, Congress includes Fenwick amendment, requiring administration to notify Congress of proposed exports to country that has "repeatedly provided support for acts of international terrorism." (Flores 563–64)

BIBLIOGRAPHY

Bienen, Henry, and Robert Gilpin. 1979. "Evaluation of the Use of Economic Sanctions to Promote Foreign Policy Objectives." Boeing Corp., unpublished, 2 April.
Facts on File. 1982.
Flores, David A. 1981. "Export Controls and the US Effort to Combat International Terrorism." 13 *Law and Policy in International Business* 521–90.
Mickolus, Edward F. 1976. *Annotated Bibliography on Transnational and International Terrorism.* Washington: Central Intelligence Agency.
Wolfgang, Marvin E., ed. 1982. "International Terrorism." 463 *Annals of the American Academy of Political and Social Science* (September): Special issue.

Case 72–1   UK and US v. Uganda

(1972–79: Idi Amin)

CHRONOLOGY OF KEY EVENTS

25 January 1971   Major General Idi Amin Dada ousts President Milton Obote, becomes president of Uganda. (Jorgensen 256)

August 1971   Amin expels 49,000 Asians from Uganda; much of their "abandoned" property is distributed to Amin's supporters. (Jorgensen 288)

1971–78   Military expenditures expand from 10 percent to 40 percent of state budget; Ugandan production of wide range of goods drops sharply, on average to only 30 percent of capacity; cost of living of low-income workers increases 530 percent between 1971–77; smuggling, corruption grow rampant. Many prominent Ugandans are murdered or "disappear"; estimated total deaths by violence range up to 500,000; Jorgensen estimates deaths at hands of state agents at 12,000 to 30,000. (Jorgensen 274, 296–300, 309–15; Department of State 291)

1972   UK suspends most of its aid to Uganda following expulsion of Asians. (Jorgensen 317)

1973–74   Uganda nationalizes most British firms, with exception of Shell-BP, private banks; Uganda seizes assets of Asians with British passports. (Jorgensen 317)

1973   US closes embassy in Uganda following Amin's two "totally unacceptable" telegrams to President Richard M. Nixon concerning Watergate and US role in Vietnam, and because of concerns about safety of US personnel there. (Jorgensen 317; *Keesing's* 26062; Fredman 1151)

7 June 1976   Palestinian hijackers, with collaboration of Amin, force Air France plane to Entebbe; Israeli commandos free 100 hostages, event that underscores Amin's military weakness. (Jorgensen 316)

1976   UK breaks diplomatic relations with Uganda following murder of Dora Bloch, British subject, in aftermath of Entebbe raid. (Jorgensen 317)

January 1977	East African Community collapses; East African Airways service is suspended; Uganda becomes totally dependent on Kenya for ocean access. (Jorgensen 318–19)
February 1978	US Deputy Assistant Secretary of State for African Affairs William C. Harrop tells House subcommittee that without international support US boycott of Uganda will fail. (Miller 120)
July 1978	Three US oil companies (Caltex, Exxon, Mobil)—suppliers of 40 percent of Ugandan petroleum—cut shipments by 35 percent after Uganda falls behind on payments. (Miller 123)
	British Foreign Minister David Owen tells US Congressman Stephen J. Solarz (D–NY) that Britain would seriously consider imposing embargo if US took lead. (Miller 124)
10 October 1978	President Jimmy Carter signs legislation, initiated by Congress, calling for total trade ban against Uganda. (Miller 118)
October 1978	US oil companies suspend all shipments to Uganda. (Miller 123)
27 October 1978	Uganda occupies Kagera Salient on Tanzanian border. USSR, principal supplier of military aid to Uganda, refuses Amin's pleas for support in dispute with Tanzania. (Jorgensen 317, 319)
December 1978	Tanzanian President Julius K. Nyerere hints to Ugandan exile groups that Tanzania counterattack would not be limited to Kagera Salient; exiles support Tanzanian incursion. (Jorgensen 319–20)
January 1979	Tanzania counterattacks with tacit US, West European support. Paul Bomani, Tanzanian ambassador to US: "The US boycott was a definite factor in our counterattack . . . we sensed that public opinion would not be violently opposed to Tanzania's measures." (Miller 125)
March 1979	UK suspends shipment of luxury goods for Ugandan military. (Miller 124)
25 March 1979	Amin flees from Kampala, Uganda, to Libya. (*Facts on File* 257)
11 April 1979	About 5,000 Tanzanian troops, 3,000 Ugandan exiles occupy Kampala; provisional government, led by Yusufu K. Lule, is formed. (*Facts on File* 257)

GOALS OF SENDER COUNTRIES

Authors' view
Initial UK goal is to retaliate for expulsion of Asians, nationalization of British property; following murder of Dora Bloch and other atrocities, UK acquiesces, in 1978, in US congressional efforts to destabilize Amin.

Judith Miller
" . . . Congress, over the staunch opposition of [the] administration, legislated mandatory economic sanctions against a nonbelligerent state to protest . . . the consistent pattern of gross violations of human rights." (Miller 120)

"The boycott was to a large extent the work of Congress, and in particular Congressman Donald J. Pease [D–Ohio], who . . . openly acknowledged that it was a boycott designed not to reform Amin but to destroy him." (Miller 120)

RESPONSE OF TARGET COUNTRY

Judith Miller
In late October 1978, Ugandan forces attack Tanzania. "Amin may have provoked a crisis with Tanzania to demonstrate to his own people and to the world that he was still a strong and influential leader, despite the action taken by the United States." (Miller 125)

ATTITUDE OF OTHER COUNTRIES

European Community
On 18 December 1978, David Owen of UK reports "no sign of general support within the Community for the institution of a trade embargo." However, Shell Oil, British Petroleum "were not making up any shortfall in the normal level of supplies to Uganda resulting from the suspension of deliveries by the US companies." (Miller 124)

Tanzania
President Nyerere orders military intervention in Uganda. "[T]he embargo's imposition 'might have been a factor in persuading Nyerere that the time was propitious for intervention in Uganda.'" (Miller 125)

ECONOMIC IMPACT

Observed Economic Statistics

Coffee prices, production, trade (Miller 121–22):

☐ World coffee prices drop from $3.33/lb. in April 1977 to $1.31/lb. in February 1979.
☐ October 1977 to September 1978: Uganda produces 2.2 million bags of coffee (60 kilograms each), exports 1.9 million.
☐ October 1978 to September 1979: Uganda produces 2.0 million bags, exports 2.2 million.
☐ During 1977, US imports about $246 million of Ugandan coffee (equal to 33 percent of Ugandan coffee exports but only 6 percent of US coffee imports). In May–June 1978, US imports total 9.1 million pounds worth $13.2 million. Imports plunge during July–August to 1.4 million pounds or $1.8 million, become negligible soon thereafter.
☐ "Soon after the boycott was imposed, it became practically impossible to obtain spare parts for American-manufactured products. This shortage affected a wide variety of sectors of the Ugandan economy, including road construction, agriculture, and services."

US and UK trade with Uganda, 1977–79 (million dollars)

| | Exports | | Imports | |
	US	UK	US	UK
1977	14	37	254	58
1978	3	60	85	67
1979	1	40	85	41

Source: IMF.

Calculated Economic Impact

	Annual cost to target country
Decline in US exports to Uganda; welfare loss estimated at 60 percent of reduced trade.	$7 million
Decline in US imports from Uganda (mostly coffee); welfare loss estimated at 10 percent of reduced trade (other markets are found for lost US sales).	17 million
Decline in total trade with UK in 1979; welfare loss estimated at 40 percent of reduced trade from 1977–78 average.	12 million
Total	$36 million

Relative Magnitudes

Gross indicators of Ugandan economy	
Ugandan GNP (1971)	$1.4 billion
Ugandan population (1972)	10.5 million
Annual effect of sanctions related to gross indicators	
Percentage of GNP	2.6
Per capita	$3.44
Ugandan trade with US and UK as percentage of total trade	
Exports (1972)	33
Imports (1972)	11
Ratio of combined US and UK GNP (1971: $1,204 billion) to Ugandan GNP (1971: $1.4 billion)	860

ASSESSMENT

US Deputy Assistant Secretary of State for African Affairs William C. Harrop
Trade ban "had far more psychological and political impact than we had anticipated." (Miller 126)

Judith Miller

"Nevertheless there is considerable evidence that while the coffee boycott failed, the American sanctions proved devastating to the Ugandan economy and that they helped set in motion the events that led to the fall of the regime. In that respect, the US boycott can appropriately be called a success." (Miller 119)

"The oil shortage was an important factor in Amin's downfall. But sensitive about advocating oil embargoes and concerned about the jurisdictional question, neither the House nor the Senate committees that considered the boycott legislation ever called an oil company spokesman to testify about what impact a petroleum suspension would have. 'Of all the instruments of policy, an oil boycott was one we didn't want to fool around with,' said one official." (Miller 123–24)

AUTHORS' SUMMARY

Overall assessment	Assigned scores
□ Policy result, scaled from 1 (failed) to 4 (success)	4
□ Sanctions contribution, scaled from 1 (none) to 4 (significant)	3
□ Success score (policy result *times* sanctions contribution), scaled from 1 (outright failure) to 16 (significant success)	12

Political and economic variables

□ Companion policies: J (covert), Q (quasi-military), or R (regular military)	—
□ International cooperation with sender, scaled from 1 (none) to 4 (significant)	2
□ International assistance to target: A (if present)	—
□ Sanctions period (years)	7
□ Economic health and political stability of target, scaled from 1 (distressed) to 3 (strong)	1
□ Presanction relations between sender and target, scaled from 1 (antagonistic) to 3 (cordial)	2
□ Type of sanction: X (export), M (import), F (financial)	F, X, M
□ Cost to sender, scaled from 1 (net gain) to 4 (major loss)	2

Comments

In this case, as in several others, military pressure (here, by a third country, Tanzania) was decisive factor in successful outcome. Nevertheless, economic sanctions imposed by US, UK adversely affected Ugandan economy, helped undermine residual domestic support for Amin, created an atmosphere conducive to Tanzanian military operations, ultimately promoting Amin's downfall.

BIBLIOGRAPHY

Facts on File. 1979.
Fredman, Steven J. 1979. "Comment: US Trade Sanctions against Uganda: Legality under International Law." 11 *Law and Policy in International Business* 1149-91.

International Monetary Fund. 1981. *Direction of Trade Statistics.*

Jorgensen, Jan Jelmert. 1981. *Uganda: A Modern History*, New York: St. Martin's Press.

Keesing's Contemporary Archives. 1973.

Miller, Judith. 1980. "When Sanctions Worked." 39 *Foreign Policy* (Summer): 118–29.

US Department of State. 1982. *Country Reports on Human Rights Practices for 1981*. Report submitted to US House of Representatives, Committee on Foreign Affairs, and Senate Committee on Foreign Relations. 97 Cong., 2 sess. February. Washington.

Summary S–2   US v. Countries Violating Human Rights

(1973–   : Overview)

CHRONOLOGY OF KEY EVENTS

10 December 1948   By resolution of General Assembly, UN issues its Universal Declaration of Human Rights. While US does not ratify Declaration, it subsequently does ratify five UN, five OAS human rights treaties; it does not ratify some 20 other treaties on human rights. (CRS 50–51)

13 December 1973   US Congress enacts section 32 of Foreign Assistance Act of 1973 (87 Stat. 733) stating: "It is the sense of the Congress that the President should deny any . . . military assistance to the government of any foreign country which practices the internment or imprisonment of that country's citizens for political purposes." (Cohen 250)

1974–81   Country-specific riders are attached to military aid bills denying or reducing assistance on human rights grounds for one or more fiscal years to: South Korea (1975); Chile (1975 and indefinitely thereafter); Uruguay (1977, 1978); Philippines (1977); Brazil (1978); El Salvador (1978); Guatemala (1978, 1981); Nicaragua (1978); Paraguay (1978); Ethiopia (1978); Argentina (1978 forward); Zaire (1980, 1981). (Cohen 246–56)

December 1974   Following more than year of hearings critical of administration, US Congress, at instigation of Congressman Donald Fraser (D–Minn.) passes section 502B of the Foreign Assistance Act of 1974 (sec. 46, 88 Stat. 1815) that states: "It is the sense of the Congress that, except in extraordinary circumstances, the President shall substantially reduce or terminate security assistance to any government which engages in a consistent pattern of gross violations of internationally recognized human rights. . . ." Foreign Assistance Act defines gross violations as "including torture or cruel, inhuman or degrading treatment or punishment; prolonged detention without charges; or other flagrant denials of the right to life, liberty, and the security of the person." (Cohen 251)

May 1976   Frustrated by administration's refusal to deny military assistance or arms sales on human rights grounds, Congress deletes "sense of the Congress" language, makes section 502B legally binding. President

461

May 1976 (continued)	Gerald R. Ford vetoes new legislation. Compromise language is then agreed upon stating that the section 502B standard is "the policy of the United States." (Cohen 252–53)
3 June 1976	Congress creates Commission on Security and Cooperation in Europe (PL 94–304) to monitor actions of signatories to Final Act of the Conference on Security and Cooperation in Europe (Helsinki accords). (CRS 55)
1976	US Congress authorizes and directs Executive Directors of Inter-American Development Bank and African Development Fund to vote against loans to countries that violate human rights. "In the face of congressional action, administration policies on international human rights underwent significant changes in the 1973–76 period." (CRS 55)
20 October 1976	Secretary of State Henry A. Kissinger declares "quiet diplomacy" is more effective than "public crusade" in achieving human rights. (CRS 56; Kissinger 97)
Early 1977	Declaring new approach, President Jimmy Carter in inaugural address claims "Our commitment to human rights must be absolute. . . ." Symbolizing new approach, Carter writes to Soviet dissident, Andrei Sakharov, and receives Soviet exile Vladimir Bukovsky. (*Department of State Bulletin*, February 1977, 121; CRS 57)
1977	Congress creates position of Assistant Secretary of State for Human Rights (sec. 9, 91 Stat. 846); amends Export–Import Bank Act of 1945 to require that Eximbank consult with secretary of state as to observance of human rights in borrowing nations; places similar restrictions on agricultural export credits (PL 95–88). (CRS 60; Cohen 253)
March 1977	State Department submits human rights reports on 82 countries, in compliance with section 502B of Foreign Assistance Act of 1961, as amended. In protest against report and US aid reductions, five nations renounce US military aid: El Salvador, Argentina, Brazil, Guatemala, Uruguay. (CRS 57)
17 March 1977	Carter calls for strengthening UN Human Rights Commission: "All the signatories of the UN Charter have pledged themselves to observe and respect basic human rights. Thus no member of the United Nations can claim that mistreatment of its citizens is solely its own business. Equally, no member can avoid responsibilities to review and to speak when torture or unwarranted deprivation occurs in any part of the world." (CRS 57; *Department of State Bulletin*, April 1977, 332)
October 1977	"The quiet diplomatic approach in advocating improvements in human rights situations in other countries appears to be the recent administration course. . . . In contrast to his March 1977 speech, President Carter's October 4, 1977, speech at the United Nations did not mention the topic of human rights at all." (CRS 58)

October 1978	Congress amends section 502B to delete "the policy of the United States" language and make section binding (22 U.S.C. 2304(a)(2)). (Cohen 254)

1978   Congress, in Foreign Assistance and Related Programs Appropriations Act of 1978 (PL 95–148), prohibits *direct* US aid for Uganda, Vietnam, Cambodia, Laos, Angola, Mozambique, Cuba. Compromise is reached after Robert S. McNamara, World Bank president, says (August 1977) that bank will not accept US funds with restrictions against expenditure in named countries and Carter promises (October 1977) to instruct US representatives to vote against loans to these countries. (CRS 59)

1977–81   Carter administration resists making findings that particular countries are "gross violators" of human rights; instead it withholds security assistance on case-by-case basis without explicit finding of gross violation. Nevertheless, implied list of section 502B countries develops from case-by-case administration decisions. In Latin America: Argentina, Bolivia, El Salvador, Guatemala, Haiti, Nicaragua, Paraguay, Uruguay; in East Asia: Philippines, South Korea; in Middle East: Iran; in Africa: Zaire. However, "extraordinary circumstances" prolong security assistance to Philippines, South Korea, Iran, Zaire, also keep Indonesia off implied list. (Cohen 264–65, 269–70)

7 December 1978   Carter asserts "Human rights is the soul of our foreign policy." Cohen: "Yet a careful examination of actual decisions under section 502B leads to a very different conclusion: that the Carter administration exhibited a remarkable degree of tentativeness and caution, so that its pursuit of human rights goals was anything but 'single-minded.'" (Cohen 264)

1981   US Ambassador to UN Jeane Kirkpatrick, as an academic, distinguishes between "authoritarian" right-wing governments and "totalitarian" Communist regimes: former are more amenable to democratic liberalization than latter, thus should receive more sympathetic treatment from US. This analysis becomes cornerstone of human rights program during administration of President Ronald Reagan. (*Newsweek*, 14 February 1983, 55)

Senate rejects nomination of Ernest Lefever (exponent of Kirkpatrick analysis) as Assistant Secretary for Human Rights and Humanitarian Affairs; administration leaves post vacant for year before naming Elliott Abrams. (*Facts on File* 392, 809)

8 July 1981   Reagan administration policy directive on conventional arms sales drops Carter administration linkage with human rights. (Labrie 15–18)

1981–83   Reagan administration focuses on human rights abuses in USSR, other "totalitarian" states; threatens to revoke most-favored-nation (MFN) treatment for Romania; publicly praises Philippine President Ferdinand E. Marcos, South Korean President Chun Doo Hwan for adherence to democracy, freedom; reverses Carter administration

1981–83	policy of opposing multilateral aid to Chile, Argentina, Paraguay,
(continued)	Uruguay on human rights grounds; seeks to restore military aid to
	Argentina, Guatemala; certifies that El Salvador is making progress
	on human rights.

Meanwhile, administration carries out quiet diplomatic efforts. Assistant Secretary Abrams: "We don't sermonize. We tell them that 'the kind of relationship you'd like to have and we'd like to have, can't be attained unless there is a substantial improvement in your human rights record.'" (Tonelson 57–58; *Newsweek*, 14 February 1983, 55)

| 31 November | Reagan vetoes legislation tying continuation of aid to progress on |
| 1983 | human rights. (*Washington Post*, 1 December 1983, A1) |

BIBLIOGRAPHY

Cohen, Stephen B. 1982. "Conditioning US Security Assistance on Human Rights Practices." 76 *American Journal of International Law* (April): 246–79.
Congressional Research Service (CRS), Library of Congress. 1977. *The Status of Human Rights in Selected Countries and the US Response.* Prepared for Subcommittee on International Organizations of the House Committee on International Relations. 95 Cong., 1 sess., 25 July. Washington.
Facts on File. 1981.
Kirkpatrick, Jeane. 1979. "Dictatorship and Double Standards." 68 *Commentary* (November): 34–45.
Kissinger, Henry. 1977. "Continuity and Change in American Foreign Policy." 15 *Society* 97–103.
Labrie, Roger P., John G. Hutchins, and Edwin W. A. Paura. 1982. *US Arms Sales Policy: Background and Issues.* Washington: American Enterprise Institute.
Lefever, Ernest W. 1978. "The Trivialization of Human Rights." *Policy Review* (Winter): 11–26.
Lillich, Richard B. 1980. *US Legislation Relating Human Rights to US Foreign Policy.* Washington: International Human Rights Law Group.
Tonelson, Alan. 1982–83. "Human Rights: The Bias We Need." 49 *Foreign Policy* (Winter): 52–74.
US Congress. House Committee on Foreign Affairs, Subcommittee on International Organizations. *Hearings on International Protection of Human Rights.* 93 Cong., 1 sess., 1973; Subcommittee Report, *Human Rights in the World Community: A Call for U.S. Leadership.* 93 Cong., 2 sess., 1974.
————. House Committee on International Relations, Subcommittee on International Organizations. 1977. *Hearings on Human Rights and United States Foreign Policy: A Review of the Administration's Record.* 95 Cong., 1 sess., 23 October.
————. Joint Economic Committee. 1981. *Hearings on The Ottawa Summit and US International Economic Policy.* July 14, 16, pp. 22–58.

Case 73–1   Arab League v. US and Netherlands

(1973–74: October War)

CHRONOLOGY OF KEY EVENTS

Summer 1967   Arab League Central Boycott Office (CBO) proposes general embargo on trade with US, Britain, France in retaliation against their support of Israel in Six Day War. By August 1967, embargo is abandoned as ineffective. (Doxey 24)

1972   Saudi Arabia warns US that oil weapon will be used if US continues to give Israel military support. (Doxey 24)

6 October 1973   Egypt attacks Sinai; Syria joins Egypt in war against Israel. (Doxey 25)

16 October 1973   "The Gulf Six unilaterally raise the posted price of Saudi marker crude from $3.01 to $5.12 per barrel." (Vernon 283)

17 October 1973   In emergency meeting of oil ministers of Abu Dhabi, Algeria, Bahrain, Egypt, Iraq, Kuwait, Libya, Qatar, Saudi Arabia, and Syria, Arab League decides: to cut oil production by 5 percent per month from September 1973 level until Israeli forces are evacuated from territory occupied in 1967 war, legitimate rights of Palestinians are restored; to embargo oil to unfriendly countries; to maintain supplies to friendly countries. (Doxey 25)

19–28 October 1973   Following President Richard M. Nixon's request to Congress 19 October to appropriate $2.2 billion in military aid for Israel in current fiscal year, Arab oil-exporting nations embargo oil shipments to US. In subsequent days, Netherlands is included in embargo for its support of Israel. "The trend towards escalation [in the use of the 'oil weapon'] was soon to be reversed, partly in view of the less biased attitudes which gradually developed in Western Europe and Japan, and partly because of the relative success of the efforts for reaching a peaceful settlement in the area." (Shihata 594–95)

24 October 1973   Cease-fire is reached on Suez, Syrian fronts. (Doxey 25)

4–5 November 1973	OPEC oil ministers decide general 25 percent production cut from September 1973 levels is necessary to enforce embargo on US, Netherlands, plus further cut of 5 percent per month. (Doxey 28)
28 November 1973	Arab countries decide 5 percent cut in production scheduled for December will not be applied against European Community (EC). (Vernon 284)
26–28 November 1973	Arab Summit conference resolves to continue use of oil weapon; establishes committee to distinguish between "friendly," "neutral," "supporting enemy" countries. Following this classification, Japan, Philippines are exempted from supply cuts; Portugal, Rhodesia, South Africa, plus US, Netherlands, are subject to total embargo. (Doxey 25–26)
8 December 1973	Arab states hold out prospect of lifting embargo on US, contingent on Israeli withdrawal from Jerusalem, occupied territories. (Doxey 26)
24–25 December 1973	Arab oil ministers meeting in Kuwait decide to cancel 5 percent production cut scheduled for January, instead vote to increase production from 75 percent to 85 percent of September level. (Shihata 596; Vernon 284)
18 March 1974	All Arab states except Libya, Iraq lift embargo against US. (Doxey 26)
July 1974	Embargo against Netherlands lifted. (Doxey 26)

GOALS OF SENDER COUNTRIES

Arab League
From resolution passed by Arab countries (Saudi Arabia, Kuwait, Libya, Algeria, Abu Dhabi, Egypt, Syria, Bahrain, Qatar; Iraq attended but did not sign resolution) meeting in Kuwait:

"*Decided* that each Arab oil exporting country immediately cuts its oil production by a recurrent monthly rate of no less than 5 percent to be initially counted on the virtual production of September, and henceforth on the last production figure until such a time as the international community compels Israel to relinquish our occupied territories or until the production of every individual country reaches a point where its economy does not permit of any further reduction without detriment to its national and Arab obligations.

"Nevertheless, the countries that support the Arabs actively and effectively or that take important measures against Israel to compel its withdrawal shall not be prejudiced by this production cut and shall continue to receive the same oil supplies that they used to receive prior to the reduction. Though the cut will be uniform in respect of every individual oil exporting country, the decrease in the supplies provided to the various consuming countries may well be aggravated proportionately with their support to and cooperation with the Israeli enemy.

"The Participants also recommend to the countries party to this resolution that the United States be subjected to the most severe cut proportionately with the quantities of crude

oil, oil derivatives, and hydrocarbons that it imports from every exporting country."
(Shihata 593–94)

J. J. Paust, A. P. Blaustein
"The stated objectives of the initiators were couched for the most part in terms of an overall effort to regain 'occupied territory.' But other objectives were also articulated by Arab spokesmen:

"(1) To force an overall settlement on Israel on terms satisfactory to the Arabs through the coercion of Israel itself or through the use of force to make others pay more attention to Arab claims and demands;
"(2) To seek a continued embargo against any country supporting Israel in any manner, with each country classified as either friendly to the Arabs, neutral, or supporting Israel;
"(3) To force other states to sever diplomatic and trade relations with Israel;
"(4) To compel other states to extend economic aid to the Arabs;
"(5) To compel other states to extend military aid to the Arabs." (Paust 1974, 427)

I. F. Shihata
"Other wild objectives propagated by the Western press and quoted in Paust and Blaustein (1974), never figured in the original cutback decision or in subsequent official Arab joint statements." (Shihata 594)

International Institute for Strategic Studies
"By resorting to the oil weapon the OAPEC members hoped to affect the outcome of the Arab-Israeli conflict. Their other objective, distinct from the first, was to obtain higher prices for oil, and in this they had the support of non-Arab oil producers." (115 *Adelphi Paper* 32)

George Lenczowski
"While the price crisis partly overlapped the boycott crisis, it differed from the latter in two respects: first, the reasons for raising prices were primarily economic, as opposed to the political reasons for the boycott; secondly, it was OPEC as a whole rather than the Arab oil-producing group that initiated the price increases." (Lenczowski 68)

RESPONSE OF TARGET COUNTRIES

October 1973–July 1974
Sanctions are widely evaded through three means: some Arab countries do not cut production according to target, in particular Libya, Iraq; oil from various sources, but particularly Libya, Iraq, Abu Dhabi, reaches US through Caribbean; major oil companies soften impact of embargo by internal, secret reallocation of supplies. (Doxey 26)

October–November 1973
US Secretary of State Henry A. Kissinger labels embargo blackmail, discusses possible use of force. US Congress studies feasibility of food embargo, US military occupation of Middle Eastern oil fields. Congress states that complete OPEC oil embargo could be endured by US but "serious oil embargoes would shatter Western Europe and Japan. . . ." (Doxey 27)

November 1974
Industrial oil-consuming nations form International Energy Agency (IEA), with mandate to work out energy-sharing arrangements in event of future embargoes. (Doxey 27)

Fall 1976
President Gerald R. Ford and nominee Jimmy Carter declare they will not tolerate future oil embargoes. (Doxey 28)

ATTITUDE OF OTHER COUNTRIES

North Atlantic Treaty Organization
In October 1973, all NATO countries except Portugal refuse to cooperate in US airlift to Israel. (Doxey 27)

Japan
"Japan's reaction to the crisis . . . was at first complacent, then pessimistic, and finally fatalistic. When the war broke out, few Japanese realized that their country was about to face an oil embargo which she had successfully escaped during the 1967 six-day war by remaining politically neutral. . . . On 22 November, 35 days after the embargo was announced, Japan abandoned her neutralism for a pro-Arab stance, even at the risk of antagonizing the pro-Israeli United States. Civilian oil consumption was curtailed and some military exercises halted." (115 *Adelphi Paper* 25)

In November–December 1973, Takeo Miki, deputy prime minister of Japan, visits eight Arab states; offers Egypt 25-year loan of $140 million for improvement of Suez Canal, other projects. Japan is later exempted from boycott. (Doxey 25–26)

European Community
On 8 December 1973, responding to shift in EC position, Arab oil ministers place EC (other than Netherlands) in exempt category. (Doxey 26)

Italy, West Germany
On 18 March 1974, Arab League classifies Italy, West Germany as "friendly" countries. (Doxey 26)

Third World
"One would expect the poor members of the Third World to be resentful towards their oil-rich *confréres*. Yet to date no developing country has criticized the oil producers for hurting them. . . . The action taken by OPEC appeared to many Third World countries as redressing the economic injustice inflicted for over a century by the raw-material consuming West on the raw-material producing East. So far the developing countries have abstained from taking sides in this confrontation, and for that they have been materially rewarded by OPEC. . . . The sketchy data available at present indicate that the total flow of assistance from OPEC to developing countries amounted to $8.6 billion during January–September 1974—a tenth of their surplus unabsorbed oil revenues." (115 *Adelphi Paper* 33–34)

ECONOMIC IMPACT

Observed Economic Statistics
Posted price of Arabian light crude rises from $2.59/barrel (bbl.) in January 1973 to $5.12/bbl. in October, $11.65/bbl. in January 1974. (Darmstadter 26)

"Production of crude oil in the ten countries attending the meeting averaged in September 1973 around 19.5 million barrels a day. A 5 to 10 percent cut meant a reduction of between 1 and 2 million, or roughly from 3 to 6 percent of the volume of oil exports then moving in world trade." (Shihata 594)

US oil imports from Arab countries average 1.8 million–1.9 million barrels a day before embargo—28 percent of total US oil imports, 10 percent of consumption. Dutch preembargo imports of Arab oil average 1.5 million barrels a day, 71 percent of all oil imports. (Shihata 595)

Oil imports (by quarter; million dollars)

	1973:3	1973:4	1974:1
US	584.2	588.3	473.9
Netherlands	193.0	212.5	180.8
Total	777.2	800.8	645.7

Source: Petroleum Economist (1974), 98, 424; Survey of Current Business, December 1974, S-35.

US imports of crude oil, petroleum products fall from 6.6 million barrels per day in November (before embargo effects are felt) to 5.1 million barrels per day in January. Projected average for 1974 first quarter is 7.8 million barrels per day. Shortfall against first quarter projection is 11 percent to 14 percent. Imports from Saudi Arabia decline from 18 million barrels in November, to 7 million in December, to 1 million in January, to 0.5 million in February. Embargo against Netherlands causes "a serious problem only for a short period in December." (Maull 6–7)

"Comparison of the Dutch oil deficit during the third quarter of 1973 with that of other EEC countries and the United States shows that the shortfall was indeed spread fairly evenly, and definitely not in accordance with Arab categorizations of friendly, neutral, and hostile. Deficits ranged from 9 percent (Netherlands) to 25 percent (Denmark), with the United States, Germany, France, and Italy in the 11–14 percent range." (Maull 7)

Calculated Economic Impact

	Annual cost to target country
Increase in cost of oil imports; welfare cost estimated at 75 percent of increased oil bill resulting from price hikes in late 1973.	$5,697 million

Relative Magnitudes

Gross indicators of US and Dutch economies	
US and Dutch GNP (1973)	$1,367 billion
US and Dutch population (1973)	223 million
Annual effect of sanctions related to gross indicators	
Percentage of GNP	0.4
Per capita	$25.55

US and Dutch trade with OAPEC as percentage of total trade
Exports (1973)   2
Imports (1973)   3

Ratio of OAPEC GNP (1973: $58.3 billion) to US and Dutch GNP
(1973: $1,367 billion)   .04

ASSESSMENT

International Institute for Strategic Studies
"On the level of economic sanctions, the Arab oil embargo was the first effective instance of these at the highest political level since the Industrial Revolution." (115 *Adelphi Paper* v)

Margaret P. Doxey
"One has to conclude that among oil consumers discretion was the guiding principle and conciliation rather than aggravation the primary response. In other words, economic pressure worked." (Doxey 28)

Fuad Itayim, editor and publisher of Middle East Economic Review
"[The embargo's] main accomplishments can be stated as follows: (1) The Arab oil embargo was probably the major cause of the change towards a more realistic American policy in the Middle East, represented by the administration's current initiative to promote a peace settlement. . . . (2) During and after the October War, there was considerable movement on the part of the EEC countries and Japan towards a closer identification with the Arab interpretation of UN Security Council Resolution 242. . . . (3) Largely as a result of the war and the growing weight of the Arab world, some thirty African countries have severed diplomatic relations with Israel . . . (4) These policy shifts towards the Arab position have greatly aggravated Israel's political isolation, and are having an effect on Israeli morale and bargaining power." (115 *Adelphi Paper* 4)

Hans Maull
"However, even though the Arab oil producers managed to build up economic pressure, they were not totally successful. The embargo did not work properly for two reasons: firstly, some Arab oil evidently 'leaked' to the United States despite the embargo, and, secondly, the international oil distribution system was managed in such a way as to spread the damage fairly evenly, by diverting Arab oil from embargoed ports and replacing it with non-Arab oil." (Maull 6)

"To sum up, it is certainly true that the use of the oil weapon caused a change in the Middle East policies of the main consumer countries, but this change did not constitute a total reversal of previous policies and, at least in the case of the United States, stopped well short of complete acceptance of Arab objectives. The fact that the oil weapon was sheathed again before any of the stated Arab objectives had been achieved underlines that its success was not unqualified." (Maull 10)

Roy Licklider
"However, the fact that the oil weapon did not achieve its stated goals need not mean it was a total failure. In fact it was probably useful in improving the Arabs' negotiating

position and at least in the short run, may have strengthened the domestic position of the actor governments; either or both of these may have been the 'real' goal all along.'' (Licklider 21)

Wall Street Journal
''The influential organization of Arab Petroleum Exporting Countries said in the October issue of its monthly publication, OAPEC, that 'the answer to the question of whether the embargo accomplished its goal is no'. . . . The group said that the purpose of imposing the oil embargo a decade ago was 'simply to help bring about a complete Israeli withdrawal from an Arab territory occupied in 1967 and to help restore the legitimate rights of the Palestinian people. That action achieved neither.'

''The Arab oil exporters acknowledged that the embargo drew the world's attention to their cause. 'The sudden perceived shortage of fuel brought home to a wide segment of the American public the fact that the Middle East is more than just Israel,' the editorial said. But the political move failed to gain any long-lasting attention to the Arab cause, it said. . . .

''Recourse to an oil embargo is not always the only or even the strongest option open to the Arab nation in its continuing struggle against Zionist invasion and occupation. Oil is a powerful component to a whole array of factors that could be drawn upon if a comprehensive marshalling of resources is deemed necessary whether to deflect a perceived danger, to defend a right, or to regain a nation's usurped territory. . . .'' (*Wall Street Journal*, 20 October 1983, 34)

AUTHORS' SUMMARY

Overall assessment	Assigned scores
☐ Policy result, scaled from 1 (failed) to 4 (success)	3
☐ Sanctions contribution, scaled from 1 (none) to 4 (significant)	3
☐ Success score (policy result *times* sanctions contribution), scaled from 1 (outright failure) to 16 (significant success)	9

Political and economic variables

☐ Companion policies: J (covert), Q (quasi-military), or R (regular military)	—
☐ International cooperation with sender, scaled from 1 (none) to 4 (significant)	3
☐ International assistance to target: A (if present)	A
☐ Sanctions period (years)	1
☐ Economic health and political stability of target, scaled from 1 (distressed) to 3 (strong)	3
☐ Presanction relations between sender and target, scaled from 1 (antagonistic) to 3 (cordial)	2
☐ Type of sanction: X (export), M (import), F (financial)	X
☐ Cost to sender, scaled from 1 (net gain) to 4 (major loss)	1

Comments

Oil embargo did not force Israel to give up occupied territories or persuade US to alter its pro-Israeli stance; thus, it did not contribute to two Arab goals. It played modest role in inducing pro-Arab shift in Japanese, West European foreign policies and it supported OPEC oil price increases. From Arab perspective, therefore, sanctions made modest contribution to outcome that, on balance, was positive.

BIBLIOGRAPHY

Congressional Research Service (CRS), Library of Congress. 1973. *Data and Analysis Concerning the Possibility of a US Food Embargo as a Response to the Present Arab Oil Embargo.* Prepared for House Committee on Foreign Affairs. Washington.

――――. 1975. *Oil Fields as Military Objectives: A Feasibility Study.* Prepared for House Committee on International Relations. Washington.

Darmstadter, Joel, and Hans Landsberg. 1975. "The Economic Background." *Daedalus* (Fall): 15–38.

Doxey, Margaret P. 1980. *Economic Sanctions and International Enforcement.* 2d ed. New York: Oxford University Press for Royal Institute of International Affairs.

Lenczowski, George. 1975. "The Oil-Producing Countries." *Daedalus* (Fall): 59–72.

Licklider, Roy. 1985. "The Arab Oil Weapon of 1973–1974." In *The Utility of Economic Sanctions,* ed. David Leyton-Brown. London: Croom Helm. Forthcoming.

Maull, Hans. 1975. "Oil and Influence: The Oil Weapon Examined." *Adelphi Paper* no. 117. London: International Institute for Strategic Studies.

Paust, J. J., and A. P. Blaustein. 1974. "The Arab Oil Weapon—A Threat to International Peace." 68 *American Journal of International Law* 410–39.

――――. 1977. *The Arab Oil Weapon.* Dobbs Ferry, NY: Oceana.

Shihata, I. F. 1974. "Destination Embargo of Arab Oil." 68 *American Journal of International Law* 591–627.

"The Middle East and the International System; Part II. Security and the Energy Crisis." 1975. *Adelphi Paper* no. 115. London: International Institute for Strategic Studies.

Vernon, Raymond, ed. 1975. "The Oil Crisis: In Perspective." *Daedalus* (Fall): Special issue.

Case 73–2   US v. South Korea

(1973–77: Human Rights)

CHRONOLOGY OF KEY EVENTS

1963   "President [John F.] Kennedy told [President Park Chung Hee]— without massive publicity—that failure to hold democratic elections would jeopardize US aid to Korea. This threat was used to the full, and it worked. Elections were held, and for nearly a decade the ROK [Republic of Korea] enjoyed an essentially democratic system." (Buss 131)

17 October 1972   In response to military buildup in North Korea and internal political challenge from dissident Kim Dae Jung, President Park proclaims martial law, suspends part of constitution, dissolves National Assembly, closes universities. (CRS 31; Scalapino 17)

August 1973   Kim Dae Jung is kidnapped in Tokyo by Korean Central Intelligence Agency (CIA), is released only after foreign intervention. Incident sparks protests in South Korea; government responds by further restricting political freedom through series of emergency decrees. (Scalapino 17)

1973   US Congress enacts section 26 of Foreign Assistance Act of 1973 (PL 93–559) limiting military assistance to South Korea "until the President submits a report to Congress . . . stating that the Government of South Korea is making substantial progress in the observance of internationally recognized human rights." (CRS 31)

August 1974   US State Department publicly disapproves of political arrests, trials by Park government. (CRS 31)

November 1974   President Ford stops in South Korea on way to Vladivostok for arms talks with Soviets. ". . . Ford's visit helped solidify Park's leadership and in effect condoned his continuous violations of human rights in South Korea." (Lee 92)

December 1974   Congress votes to reduce military assistance to South Korea by $20 million. (Lee 92)

March 1976	Group of Korean liberals deliberately violates Park's emergency decrees, gathers at Myong Dong cathedral to call for restoration of democratic constitution. All those involved, including Kim Dae Jung, are arrested, convicted under August 1973 decrees. This incident becomes a major issue in the US presidential campaign. (Scalapino 18–20)
1976	US Congress enacts section 412 of International Security Assistance and Arms Control Act (PL 94–329), requesting president to convey congressional concern over erosion of civil liberties by South Korean government. (CRS 31)
1977	President Jimmy Carter, while critical of South Korean human rights performance, resists linkage of human rights with security assistance. (Buss 134–35)
June 1979	President Carter visits Seoul, meets with South Korean political dissidents, emphasizes importance of human rights in joint communiqué despite objections of President Park. "Yet the Carter-Park summitry did not improve the conditions of human rights in South Korea." (Lee 93)
26 October 1979	President Park is assassinated by Korean CIA. He eventually is succeeded, in August 1980, by General Chun Doo Hwan. President Carter rejects congressional suggestions that US Export–Import Bank loans to Korea be suspended. (Buss 15–23, 136)
January 1981	President Ronald Reagan invites President Chun to Washington. "The issue of human rights was conspicuously absent in the Reagan-Chon [Chun] summit discussions and their joint communique. . . . Hence, the Reagan Administration . . . effectively removed human rights from the diplomatic agenda between Washington and Seoul." (Lee 94)

GOALS OF SENDER COUNTRY

Congressman Donald Fraser (D–Minn.)
In July 1974, Fraser called Korea "a 'police state' practicing executions, torture, and arbitrary arrests and detentions. He suggested that 'because the South Korean Government is increasingly oppressive and pays little heed to internationally recognized human rights for the Korean people, the military assistance to South Korea should be reduced or eliminated.'" (Lee 90)

Philip C. Habib, assistant secretary of state for East Asian and Pacific affairs
Testifying before International Relations Committee of House of Representatives in Summer 1975: "Since our policies toward individual countries represent a mix of interests, objectives, and relationships, we know that neglect of human rights may well adversely affect the achievement of other important objectives." (Buss 132–33)

Robert A. Scalapino
"After Carter's election, American policy began to follow two tracks. On the one hand, private talks between American officials and the Korean government on the subject of human rights continued, with the former urging a liberalization of policies both to improve the general climate of relations and to avert Congressional punishment. . . . On the other hand, the American government continued to assert publicly that the maintenance of its commitments to Korea, being vital to the stability of northeast Asia, and particularly to Japan, was strongly in the national interest of the United States, and required some modification of the priorities placed upon human rights." (Scalapino 20)

RESPONSE OF TARGET COUNTRY

Robert A. Scalapino
"As long as the American presence, both in Korea and in Asia, seemed assured, Pak [Park] could be persuaded to experiment with political liberalization, though it fitted neither his personality nor his sense of Korea's needs. . . . [However] in a troubled international environment and with South-North relations taking a new turn, political stability became the chief desiderata for the Republic of Korea government. It was precisely these two factors that Pak was to cite in declaring martial law in the fall of 1972." (Scalapino 15–16)

ECONOMIC IMPACT

Observed Economic Statistics

US aid to Korea (million dollars)

Fiscal year	Economic		Military
	PL 480	*Total*	
1970	104.1	140.7	353.1
1971	107.4	169.9	677.9
1972	211.7	252.2	745.4
1973	159.4	188.5	384.4
1974	7.2	37.1	168.5
1975	14.4	36.7	144.6
1976	117.1	124.7	188.6
TQ†	13.3	13.8	135.6
1977	75.1	77.4	155.0
1978	56.3	58.6	276.9

† Transitional quarter (1 July to 30 September 1976): beginning of US fiscal year changed from June to October.
Source: AID.

Calculated Economic Impact

	Annual cost to target country
Decline in US economic aid (mostly PL 480) to South Korea; welfare loss estimated at 80 percent of reduced transfers.	$97 million
Decline in US military assistance; welfare loss estimated at 70 percent of reduced transfers.	236 million
Total	$333 million

Relative Magnitudes

Gross indicators of South Korean economy	
South Korean GNP (1974)	$18.3 billion
South Korean population (1974)	34.7 million
Annual effect of sanctions related to gross indicators	
Percentage of GNP	1.8
Per capita	$9.60
South Korean trade with US as percentage of total trade	
Exports (1974)	35
Imports (1974)	23
Ratio of US GNP (1974: $1,434 billion) to South Korean GNP (1974: $18.3 billion)	78

ASSESSMENT

Chae-Jin Lee, Hideo Sato
"The forceful argument that the continued violation of human rights would erode U.S. military protection of South Korea led to President Park's grudging promise to effect a gradual release of political prisoners, but he presented all kinds of excuses not to implement his promise to a satisfactory extent. At times the Carter Administration used the instruments of indirect economic sanctions (such as abstention in international financial institutions' decisions for South Korea's loan applications), but they were less than effective in influencing Park's domestic policies. More significantly, the Carter Administration [did not cut foreign aid to] South Korea. . . . President Carter chose not to take this extreme step, because it contained a risk of undermining political stability in South Korea and upsetting the military balance in the Korean peninsula as well as Northeast Asia." (Lee 93)

Robert A. Scalapino
"Undoubtedly, these pressures [1973–77] had some influence, especially those coming via official channels. The ROK government urgently wanted an improvement in overall

American-Korean relations, and at a later point, specifically hoped for a visit from President Carter in connection with his 1979 Asian trip. Thus, most liberal Korean critics were given suspended sentences or released from prison well before their sentences had run their full course. . . . Among the 4,000 prisoners released, 106 were reported to be violators of emergency decrees like [Kim Dae Jung]." (Scalapino 21)

AUTHORS' SUMMARY

Overall assessment	Assigned scores
□ Policy result, scaled from 1 (failed) to 4 (success)	2
□ Sanctions contribution, scaled from 1 (none) to 4 (significant)	2
□ Success score (policy result *times* sanctions contribution), scaled from 1 (outright failure) to 16 (significant success)	4

Political and economic variables

□ Companion policies: J (covert), Q (quasi-military), or R (regular military)	—
□ International cooperation with sender, scaled from 1 (none) to 4 (significant)	1
□ International assistance to target: A (if present)	—
□ Sanctions period (years)	4
□ Economic health and political stability of target, scaled from 1 (distressed) to 3 (strong)	2
□ Presanction relations between sender and target, scaled from 1 (antagonistic) to 3 (cordial)	3
□ Type of sanction: X (export), M (import), F (financial)	F
□ Cost to sender, scaled from 1 (net gain) to 4 (major loss)	1

Comments

Sanctions were forced by Congress with little administration support and seem to have had little effect in South Korea. General amnesty declared after Carter had substituted public criticism for manipulation of assistance, seems to have been prompted more by political, diplomatic concerns than fear of sanctions.

BIBLIOGRAPHY

Agency for International Development. *Overseas Loans and Grants*. Various issues.
Buss, Claude A. 1982. *The United States and the Republic of Korea: Background for Policy*. Stanford, Calif.: Hoover Institution Press.
Congressional Research Service (CRS), Library of Congress. 1977. *The Status of Human Rights in Selected Countries and the US Response*. Prepared for Subcommittee on International Organizations of the House Committee on International Relations. 95 Cong., 1 sess., 25 July. Washington.

Lee, Chae-Jin, and Hideo Sato. 1982. *U.S. Policy toward Japan and Korea: A Changing Influence Relationship.* New York: Praeger.

Scalapino, Robert A. 1979. *The United States and Korea: Looking Ahead.* The Washington Papers 69. Washington: Georgetown University Center for Strategic and International Studies.

US Department of State. 1982. *Country Reports on Human Rights Practices for 1981.* Report submitted to US House of Representatives, Committee on Foreign Affairs, and Senate Committee on Foreign Relations. 97 Cong., 2 sess., February. Washington.

Case 73–3   US v. Chile

(1973– : Human Rights)

CHRONOLOGY OF KEY EVENTS

11 September 1973	President Salvador Allende Gossens is assassinated (see Case 70–1 US v. Chile [1970–73: Allende]). General Augusto Pinochet Ugarte becomes president, dissolves legislature, censors press, suspends constitution. Pinochet regime is soon charged with widespread violations of human rights. (CRS 8)
12–17 October 1973	Organization of American States (OAS) Inter-American Commission on Human Rights visits Chile. Subsequent commission reports in 1974, 1976, 1977 indicate violations of human rights. (OAS, cited in Lillich 311–13)
17 December 1973	US Congress mandates president, in section 35 of Foreign Assistance Act of 1973 (PL 93–189) to: request Chile to protect human rights; support UN, Red Cross assistance to political refugees; support voluntary agencies in providing emergency relief; request Inter-American Commission on Human Rights to investigate events in Chile. (CRS 8)
1 March 1974	Chairman of UN Human Rights Commission calls for end to human rights violations, expresses concern for lives of particular individuals. On 17 May 1974, UN Economic and Social Council (ECOSOC) passes resolution condemning human rights violations by Chile. (UN cited in Lillich 293–96)
April 1974	US congressional subcommittee, at invitation of General Pinochet, sends study mission to Chile. In July 1974, mission reports "torture and illegal detention continue to be systematically employed by the Chilean Government." (CRS 9)
September 1974	US Secretary of State Henry A. Kissinger rebukes US ambassador to Chile, David Popper, for linking human rights to discussion of military aid. (CRS 9)
6 November 1974	UN General Assembly adopts resolution condemning human rights violations by Chile; calls for Committee of Inquiry. On 27 February

6 November 1974 (continued)	1975, UN Human Rights Commission forms Ad Hoc Working Group; Chile offers, withdraws invitation to Working Group to visit Chile in July 1975. (CRS 10)
December 1974	US Congress, in section 25 of Foreign Assistance Act of 1974 (PL 93–559), prohibits military assistance to Chile for fiscal year 1975, limits economic assistance to $25 million. President Gerald R. Ford states that cutting off military assistance is not effective means of promoting human rights in Chile. (CRS 9)
19 May 1975	US supports OAS General Assembly resolution calling on Inter-American Commission on Human Rights to continue investigation. In November 1975, US supports UN General Assembly resolution condemning human rights violations in Chile. (CRS 10)
1975	US Congress enacts section 320 of International Development and Food Assistance Act of 1975 (PL 94–161) that further restricts economic assistance to Chile. (CRS 10)
May 1976	Pinochet gives US Treasury Secretary William E. Simon assurances that human rights conditions will be improved; Simon asks Congress to continue economic aid. (CRS 11)
1976	US Congress enacts section 406 of International Security Assistance and Arms Export Act of 1976–77 (PL 94–329), which terminates military assistance to Chile, puts $27.5 million limit on economic assistance in FY 1977, specifies human rights improvements that will lead to additional aid. (CRS 10)
September 1976	Orlando Letelier, "a former ambassador and Minister of State under Allende who was living in exile in Washington, D.C.," is assassinated there by carbomb. His colleague, Ronnie Moffitt, is killed as well. Letelier's friends and associates accuse Chilean Embassy of complicity. (Merrill 178–79)
November 1976	Chile releases 300 political prisoners; rate of political detentions drops to nearly zero. (CRS 11)
February 1977	UN Human Rights Commission charges that "rate of disappearance has considerably increased." (CRS 11)
1979–80	US imposes diplomatic, economic sanctions against Chile following Pinochet refusal to extradite two military officers implicated in Letelier assassination. Sanctions include 10 percent–15 percent reduction in personnel at US Embassy in Santiago, "the termination of all foreign military sales to Chile (including those in the pipeline); the removal of the small US military mission in Chile; and a ban on US Export-Import Bank (Eximbank) financing or Overseas Private Investment Corporation guarantees in Chile." (Merrill 179)
February 1981	Administration of President Ronald Reagan lifts ban on Eximbank financing for Chile, reverses Carter policy of opposing multilateral

development loans. (Merrill 180; *New York Times*, 20 November 1984, D15)

October 1981 At Reagan's request, US Congress authorizes resumption of military aid to Chile when president can certify that Chile has made "significant progress in complying with internationally recognized principles of human rights" and that "the government of Chile is not aiding or abetting international terrorism and has taken appropriate steps to cooperate to bring to justice by all legal means available in the United States or Chile those indicted by a United States grand jury in connection with the murders of Orlando Letelier and coworker Ronnie Moffitt." (*Washington Post*, 23 October 1981, A1; Merrill 180)

October 1982 Following internal review, US Secretary of State George P. Shultz declines to certify that Chile has made "significant progress in complying with internationally recognized principles of human rights." (*Washington Post*, 22 October 1982, A20)

November– Tensions between US, Chile increase as Reagan administration
December 1983 continues to press for negotiated settlement between Pinochet government, opposition. Chilean government is particularly disturbed by lifting of ban on military sales to neighboring Argentina, following inauguration of civilian government there. Similar certification is not planned for Chile. (*Washington Post*, 24 November 1983, A38; 9 December 1983, A1)

6 November 1984 Pinochet imposes state of siege; US ponders action on pending loans to Chile from Inter-American Development Bank (IDB). (*New York Times*, 20 November 1984)

2 February 1985 Following extension of state of siege, US abstains on IDB loan vote for $130 million. "The U.S. decision came after congressional pressure to oppose multilateral aid to the Pinochet government because of its poor human rights record." (*Washington Post*, 8 February 1985, A24)

GOALS OF SENDER COUNTRY

Secretary of State Henry A. Kissinger
8 June 1976: "The condition of human rights has impaired our relationship with Chile and will continue to do so." (CRS 11)

Andrea T. Merrill
"The election of Jimmy Carter to the United States presidency increased the strains, as the new administration condemned Chile's human rights record in international organizations, officially received opposition figures like [former President Eduardo] Frei [Montalvo, Coldoniro] Almeyda, [a former official under Allende] and pressured the Chilean regime to improve its human rights record." (Merrill 177)

Following Chilean government's refusal to extradite two officers implicated in Letelier case: "The State Department . . . issued a statement in which it described the conduct of the government of Chile in the case as 'deplorable . . . in particular its refusal to conduct a full and fair investigation of this crime.'" (Merrill 179)

RESPONSE OF TARGET COUNTRY

Andrea T. Merrill
"The Chilean government has been highly sensitive to [UN] criticism [about its human rights situation], and it became an article of faith among regime supporters that foreign criticism of Chile was the result of a well-orchestrated, worldwide Communist campaign to discredit Chile. Criticism from non-Communist sources was attributed to the effectiveness of Communist propaganda in infecting even Chile's natural allies." (Merrill 177)

Shortly after coming to power, military regime tried to improve relations with US "by negotiating compensation for properties nationalized under the previous regime and liberalizing foreign investment rules. . . ." (Merrill 178)

As regards sanctions imposed following Letelier assassination, "Chile's minister of foreign affairs accused the US of adopting 'old-fashioned imperialistic methods.'" (Merrill 179)

ATTITUDE OF OTHER COUNTRIES

United Nations
"The United Nations General Assembly voted yearly between 1974 and 1980—by overwhelming margins that ranged from 96 to 14 in 1977 to 93 to 6 in 1979—to condemn the human rights situation in Chile." (Merrill 177)

ECONOMIC IMPACT

Observed Economic Statistics

US aid to Chile (million dollars)

Fiscal year	Economic[†]	Military
1973	3.8	15.0
1974	9.8	15.9
1975	33.1	0.7
1976 + TQ[††]	21.5	0
1977	1.7	0

† Excluding Food for Peace program.
†† Transitional quarter: beginning of US fiscal year changed from June to October.
Source: AID.

Between 1974 and 1978, loans to Chile from US, international agencies fell from $330 million to $38 million but "loans from private sources (primarily US-based banks) grew from virtually nothing to nearly $1 billion in 1978 and some US $4 billion in 1981." (Merrill 177)

Calculated Economic Impact

	Annual cost to target country
Reduction in US military aid to Chile; welfare loss estimated at 90 percent of reduced transfers.	$15 million
Reduction in US economic aid to Chile; welfare loss estimated at 100 percent of reduced transfers.	21 million
Total	$36 million

Relative Magnitudes

Gross indicators of Chilean economy	
Chilean GNP (1975)	$8.3 billion
Chilean population (1975)	10.2 million
Annual effect of sanctions related to gross indicators	
Percentage of GNP	0.4
Per capita	$3.53
Chilean trade with US as percentage of total trade	
Exports (1975)	9
Imports (1975)	27
Ratio of US GNP (1975: $1,549.2 billion) to Chilean GNP (1975: $8.3 billion)	187

ASSESSMENT

US State Department
"In the period 1973–77, the regime undertook to curb dissent through a series of repressive measures. These included mass arrests, torture, exile and the disappearance of hundreds of persons. . . . The human rights situation in Chile has improved significantly since 1977. No confirmed 'disappearances' have occurred since October of that year and, although there continue to be sworn statements reporting the use of force in some interrogations, treatment of prisoners and general police procedures have improved. However, arrests and expulsions for nonviolent political activities continued to occur in 1981." (US State Department 369)

Washington Post
Chile's Human Rights Commission says in 1982 annual report that "repression has reached the highest level since 1977." US government concludes in its 1982 human rights reports to Congress that "the pace of improvement has slowed in the past few

years," and administration reportedly has "all but abandoned plans to certify Chile to Congress this year." (*Washington Post*, 24 March 1983, A21)

AUTHORS' SUMMARY

Overall assessment	Assigned scores
☐ Policy result, scaled from 1 (failed) to 4 (success)	2
☐ Sanctions contribution, scaled from 1 (none) to 4 (significant)	3
☐ Success score (policy result *times* sanctions contribution), scaled from 1 (outright failure) to 16 (significant success)	6

Political and economic variables

☐ Companion policies: J (covert), Q (quasi-military), or R (regular military)	—
☐ International cooperation with sender, scaled from 1 (none) to 4 (significant)	1
☐ International assistance to target: A (if present)	—
☐ Sanctions period (years)	11+
☐ Economic health and political stability of target, scaled from 1 (distressed) to 3 (strong)	1
☐ Presanction relations between sender and target, scaled from 1 (antagonistic) to 3 (cordial)	2
☐ Type of sanction: X (export), M (import), F (financial)	F
☐ Cost to sender, scaled from 1 (net gain) to 4 (major loss)	1

BIBLIOGRAPHY

Agency for International Development. *Overseas Loans and Grants*. Various issues.

Congressional Research Service (CRS), Library of Congress. 1977. *The Status of Human Rights in Selected Countries and the U.S. Response*. Prepared for Subcommittee on International Organizations of the House Committee on International Relations. 95 Cong., 1 sess., 25 July. Washington.

Lillich, Richard B., and Frank C. Newman. 1979. *International Human Rights: Problems of Law and Policy*. Boston: Little, Brown & Co.

Merrill, Andrea T. 1982. *Chile: A Country Study*. Washington: Headquarters, Department of the Army.

Organization of American States (OAS). 1977. *Third Report on the Situation of Human Rights in Chile*. Inter-American Commission on Human Rights. OEA/Ser. L/VII.40, doc. 10.

United Nations. 1974. *Report of the Commission on Human Rights*. 30 sess., 56 UN ECOSOC Supp. (no. 5), 56 UN Doc. (E5464, E/CN.4/1154).

US Department of State. 1982. *Country Reports on Human Rights Practices for 1981*. Report submitted to US House of Representatives, Committee on Foreign Affairs, and Senate Committee on Foreign Relations. 97 Cong., 2 sess., February. Washington.

Summary S–3   US and Canada v. Countries Pursuing Nuclear Option

(1974–   : Overview)

CHRONOLOGY OF KEY EVENTS

1949–64	During this period, USSR (1949), UK (1952), France (1960), China (1964) acquire nuclear weapons. (Yager 2)
December 1953	In dramatic reversal of previous US policy of nuclear secrecy and technology denial to foreign countries, President Dwight D. Eisenhower outlines his "Atoms for Peace" proposal before the UN. Policy seeks to encourage peaceful use of nuclear energy. (Potter 264)
1953–55	Under "Atoms for Peace" program, US negotiates "Agreements for Cooperation Concerning the Civil Uses of Atomic Energy" with 22 countries. Such agreements are prerequisite for most nuclear exports from US. (GAO 1980, 4)
July 1957	International Atomic Energy Agency (IAEA) is established in Vienna as autonomous UN organization. (Potter 264)
1968–70	Treaty on the Non-Proliferation of Nuclear Weapons (nuclear Non-Proliferation Treaty [NPT]) is negotiated in July 1968, enters into force in March 1970. Signatories agree to subject their nonmilitary nuclear facilities to IAEA safeguards; nonnuclear countries commit not to acquire nuclear weapons. All agree to share nuclear technology for peaceful purposes. (Potter 264; Yager 2)
1974	US Atomic Energy Commission (AEC) suspends signing of new contracts for enrichment services. "The reason given by the AEC for its cessation of fuel export commitments was that projected commercial demands for enriched uranium were outstripping the capacity of its three enrichment plants." (Potter 18)
May 1974	India explodes what it claims is peaceful nuclear device. Canada responds by suspending, eventually terminating nuclear assistance to India. (Potter 264)
June 1974	Zangger Committee (named after its chairman, Claude Zangger, Swiss energy expert), consisting of representatives from Australia, Austria,

June 1974 (continued)	Belgium, Canada, Czechoslovakia, Denmark, Finland, West Germany, East Germany, Ireland, Italy, Japan, Luxembourg, Netherlands, Norway, Poland, Sweden, Switzerland, UK, US, USSR draws up list of nuclear technology and equipment, export of which will trigger safeguards. Enrichment, reprocessing technologies are of particular concern. (Potter 264; *Washington Post*, 3 January 1983, A5)
1975	US suspends enriched uranium supplies to South Africa because of its efforts to develop indigenous enrichment capacity. (Bissell 108)
1976	Senators Stuart Symington (D–Mo.), John H. Glenn (D–Ohio), obtain passage of amendments to Foreign Assistance Act of 1961 (22 U.S.C. 2429) that require suspension of economic, military assistance to countries either buying or selling facilities for enrichment or reprocessing facilities that are not signatories to NPT or have not accepted full-scope safeguards. (GAO 1980, 8)
January 1976	Subgroup of Zangger Committee, known as Nuclear Suppliers' Group (NSG) or "London Club," secretly adopts "Guidelines for Nuclear Transfer" that are more restrictive than Zangger trigger list. Third World nations accuse London Club members of "forming a cartel designed to perpetuate their lead in nuclear technology." (Potter 265; *Washington Post*, 3 January 1983, A5)
	South Korea announces it will not go ahead with plans to purchase nuclear reprocessing plant from France. Pressure from US, Canada is reported principal reason. (*New York Times*, 30 January 1976, A1)
December 1976	Canada announces it is terminating nuclear assistance to Pakistan because of Pakistan's unwillingness to apply more stringent safeguards or to forego reprocessing. Canada also announces it is dissatisfied with efforts of Zangger Committee and NSG, is unilaterally adopting stricter nuclear export policy. (*Washington Post*, 4 January 1977, A9; Government of Canada 10)
January 1977	Canada suspends uranium shipments to European Community, Japan pending negotiations to bring their safeguards arrangements into line with Canada's new policy. (Government of Canada 14)
March 1978	US Congress passes Nuclear Non-Proliferation Act (NNPA) that, like Canadian policy, makes approval of nuclear exports dependent on buyer's acceptance of full-scope safeguards and veto rights over retransfer or reprocessing of US-supplied fuel. NNPA also requires renegotiation of bilateral cooperation agreements to incorporate new restrictions. Countries most affected are Brazil, Argentina, India. Brazil, India receive fuel shipments during 18-month grace period but are cut off from US supply after September 1980. (Yager 416–17)
April 1979	US cuts off economic, military aid to Pakistan after it is revealed that Pakistan is pursuing enrichment capability. Administration of President Jimmy Carter offers to renew aid after Soviet invasion of

Afghanistan in December 1979 but Pakistan rejects offer as inadequate. (*New York Times*, 7 April 1979, A1; *New York Times* 14, 16 January 1980, A1)

June 1981   Israel attacks French-supplied nuclear reactor nearing completion in Iraq, claiming it will be used to manufacture nuclear weapons. (Potter 265)

July 1981   President Ronald Reagan makes first major statement on nonproliferation policy, stresses importance of reestablishing US as "reliable supplier." (Reagan)

January 1983   US is reported secretly negotiating with other members of Zangger Committee to develop stricter, more detailed trigger list so as to bring other suppliers' policies more into line with those of US. (*Washington Post*, 3 January 1983, A5)

October 1983   General Accounting Office study reveals Reagan administration has approved 57 licenses for export of controlled dual-use technologies to South Africa, India, Argentina, Israel, despite their unwillingness either to adhere to NPT or to accept full-scope safeguards. Following release of report, House of Representatives accepts amendment to Export Administration Act that closes loopholes in NNPA that permitted these sales. (*Washington Post*, 16 October 1983, A6)

April 1984   British journal on defense affairs claims that Iran is close to achieving a nuclear weapons capability. US State Department expresses doubt that Iran has necessary equipment but announces that, even though the shah's government had signed the NPT, the US will not permit transfer of US-origin nuclear materials or technology. US also encourages other countries "not to engage in nuclear cooperation with Iran." (*New York Times*, 26 April 1984, A3)

July 1984   Western members of London Club meet secretly for first time in seven years to discuss tightening restrictions on nuclear exports to countries which have not signed NPT. General agreement on need for full-scope safeguards is achieved but specifics for implementing it not worked out. US State Department spokesman, Alan Romberg, says Western suppliers agreed not to invite Eastern bloc members until they had reached tentative agreement among themselves. Several participants, led by France, react angrily to US publication of meeting saying they had agreed to take part only if it were kept secret. (*Washington Post*, 17 July 1984, A3; *Wall Street Journal*, 30 November 1984, 34)

November 1984   US pressures Belgium not to accept $1 billion contract to advise and assist Soviet Union in construction of two nuclear reactors in Libya. Other West European countries agree not to take Belgium's place. As NPT signatory, Libyan nuclear program is subject to IAEA safeguards. Unwillingness of US and others to cooperate reveals lack of trust in NPT/IAEA safeguards, as does US attitude toward Iran. (*New York Times*, 21 November 1984, A3)

1984   A proposed Sino-American nuclear cooperation agreement is held up by congressional opposition sparked by reports that China, which has not signed the NPT, has assisted Pakistan in its attempts to build a nuclear weapon. (*Wall Street Journal*, 26 September 1984, 36)

GOALS AND ASSESSMENTS

United States

William C. Potter
"Most supporters of stringent export controls acknowledge that the ability of the United States to influence proliferation developments unilaterally through export policy is limited. They also recognize the fallacy of viewing the proliferation danger as a simple function of the availability of nuclear technology. They are convinced, however, that what the United States does can have an important demonstrative effect. What is essential, they contend, is not to view U.S. export policy in isolation, but rather as part of a broad nonproliferation strategy which includes self-restraint in domestic nuclear development, the promotion of more effective international safeguards, creation of nonproliferation incentives through guarantees of fuel supply, reduction of security or prestige motives to acquire nuclear weapons, and development of an international consensus on how to manage the nuclear fuel cycle and inhibit weapons proliferation. These initiatives, it generally is acknowledged, may at times cause friction among states with different energy requirements and security concerns and will not guarantee the containment of nuclear weapons proliferation. Supporters hope, however, that prudent restraints on the transfer of sensitive technologies and material can play an important role as part of a long-term nonproliferation strategy whose immediate objective is to buy time for the development of more effective safeguards and more proliferation-resistant technology." (Potter 24)

"The effectiveness of sanctions depends on the nature of the incentives for the Nth country to go nuclear, the political and economic vulnerability of the proliferator, and the degree of support from the international community for specific sanctions. The nature of the Nth country's proliferation motives are critical since some, such as perceived threats to national survival, may not be susceptible to influence by any form of sanction but might be reduced by security guarantees. Some domestic political and international prestige pressures to proliferate, moreover, might actually be intensified rather than reduced by the imposition of sanctions which would produce a nationalist reaction. While unilateral action by a great power may work well in selected cases where overwhelming leverage can be exerted (e.g., US success in inducing South Korea to rescind its order for a French reprocessing plant), unilateral sanctions against other Nth countries are apt to be futile. For countries such as Brazil, Argentina, and South Africa, for example, even multilateral sanctions involving both superpowers probably could only raise the cost but not prevent the implementation of a decision to produce nuclear weapons." (Potter 208)

Ambassador Gerard C. Smith
On the effect of the US defense of Israel on the credibility of the US nonproliferation effort: "We know that Israel is producing plutonium for weapons, but that doesn't affect the level of economic aid to Israel and this discrimination isn't lost on other countries. I think some of them feel if we were really serious about nonproliferation we would do something serious about the Israel program." (*Wall Street Journal*, 30 November 1984, 34)

Bohdan Denysk, deputy assistant secretary of commerce for export administration
In hearings before Congress, 2 December 1982: "While actively working to reduce the risks of proliferation, the Administration is also desirous of establishing the United States as a reliable supplier of equipment for peaceful nuclear uses under appropriate and adequate safeguards. . . . The President believes that [such] a policy is essential to U.S. non-proliferation goals for, if we are not an active partner, other countries will tend to go their own ways. This would reduce our influence and, thus, our effectiveness in gaining the support we need to pursue our non-proliferation objectives." (US House 156-7)

Authors' comments
Exports of nuclear fuel and most nuclear technologies are still forbidden by NNPA but Reagan administration has been more willing than Carter administration to sell non-sensitive dual-use technologies, and has been more accommodating in allowing target countries to find alternative suppliers despite contractual obligations with US companies. In cases involving Argentina, Brazil, South Africa, and India, Reagan administration has proffered carrots in an effort to regain some influence over local nuclear programs. Congress has become increasingly critical of what is seen as an exploitation of loopholes in contravention of congressional intent. Senator William Proxmire (D–Wis.) introduced a bill in January 1985 (S. 1147) which seeks to close these loopholes.

Canada
"Canada's nonproliferation and safeguards policy has two objectives: to promote the emergence of a more effective and comprehensive international nonproliferation regime; and to assure the Canadian people and the international community that Canadian nuclear exports will not be used for any nuclear explosive purpose. By emphasizing the key role of the NPT, by promoting reliance upon and improvements in the IAEA safeguards system, by treating nuclear weapon and nonnuclear weapon states alike regarding Canadian nuclear exports, by working for new approaches covering the sensitive phases (e.g., reprocessing) of the nuclear fuel cycle, Canada's policy promotes attainment of the first objective. The latter objective is served through the network of bilateral nuclear agreements that Canada has put into place with its nuclear partners. Those agreements provide assurance that Canada's nuclear exports are used solely for legitimate, peaceful, nuclear energy production purposes." (Government of Canada 21)

BIBLIOGRAPHY

Bissell, Richard E. 1982. *South Africa and the United States: The Erosion of an Influence Relationship*. New York: Praeger.
Government of Canada, Department of External Affairs. 1982. *Canada's Nuclear Non-Proliferation Policy*. Canadian Foreign Policy Texts no. 82/2.
Jones, Rodney. 1984. *Proliferation of Small Nuclear Forces*. Report for Defense Nuclear Agency. Washington: Georgetown University Center for Strategic and International Studies.
Jones, Rodney, Joseph Pilat, Cesare Merlini, and William C. Potter, eds. *The Nuclear Suppliers and Nonproliferation: Dilemmas and Policy Choices*. Lexington, Mass.: Lexington Books, forthcoming.
Poneman, Daniel. 1982. *Nuclear Power in the Developing World*. London: George Allen & Unwin.

Potter, William C. 1982. *Nuclear Power and Nonproliferation*. Cambridge, Mass.: Oelgeschlager, Gunn, & Hain.

Reagan, Ronald. 1981. "Nuclear Nonproliferation." US Department of State, *Current Policy* no. 303, 16 July. Washington.

US Congress. House Foreign Affairs Committee, Subcommittee on International Economic Policy and Trade. 1983. *Hearings on Controls on Exports to South Africa*. 97 Cong., 2 sess., 9 February and 2 December 1982.

———. Office of Technology Assessment. 1977. *The Role of Sanctions in Non-Proliferation Strategy*.

US General Accounting Office. 1980. *Evaluation of Selected Features of U.S. Nuclear Non-Proliferation Law and Policy*. Washington.

———. 1983. *Controlling Exports of Dual-Use, Nuclear-Related Equipment*. GAO/NSIAD–83–28. Washington.

Yager, Joseph A., ed. 1980. *Nonproliferation and U.S. Foreign Policy*. Washington: Brookings Institution.

Case 74–1   US v. Turkey

(1974–78: Cyprus)

CHRONOLOGY OF KEY EVENTS

June 1964   President Lyndon B. Johnson warns Turkish Prime Minister Ismet Inonu that Turkey is not permitted to use US military equipment against Cyprus. (Karaosmanoglu 158)

15 July 1974   With collaboration from Greek military government, coup overthrows government of Archbishop Makarios in Cyprus. (Legg 108–9)

20 July 1974   Turkish troops invade northern part of Cyprus, justifying intervention under 1960 treaty with Cyprus. (Legg 108–9)

22 July 1974   Cease-fire reached between Greek, Turkish troops on Cyprus. Greek military government collapses next day; former Prime Minister Constantine Karamanlis heads new civilian government. (Legg 108–9)

8 August 1974   President Richard M. Nixon resigns. (Legg 108–9)

14 August 1974   Turks occupy nearly 40 percent of Cyprus. Congressman John D. Brademas (D–Ind.) proposes ban on military assistance to Turkey. (Legg 108–9)

September–October 1974   US Congress decisively votes to cut off military aid to Turkey. President Gerald R. Ford vetoes two cut-off bills, but ultimately consents to postponing aid cut-off until 10 December 1974. (Legg 108–9)

31 December 1974   Ford signs military, economic assistance bill that defers aid cut-off until 5 February 1975. (Legg 108–9)

February 1975   Immediately before cut-off date, Defense Department announces plan to sell $230 million of tank equipment to Turkey. (Legg 120)

5 February 1975   US Secretary of State Henry A. Kissinger tries to broker concessions from Turkey for congressional relaxation of embargo; Congress refuses to play. Embargo on military aid to Turkey goes into effect. (Legg 108–9; 120)

May 1975   US Senate votes to resume all military aid to Turkey after American military activity there had been limited by Turkish government. (Legg 121)

August 1975   US House votes to permit sale to Turkey of military goods already contracted for under aid program plus new outright purchases, but continues prohibition on new military grants. (Legg 121)

Early 1976   Ford administration unveils new US-Turkey joint defense program calling for $1 billion in grants over four years, reopening of 26 US bases; simultaneously discusses bases with Greece. (Legg 121)

September 1976   Ford administration announces plan to sell $125 million in military equipment to Turkey; because of embargo on use of credit under Foreign Military Sales program, encourages Turkey to buy direct from military suppliers. (Legg 122)

January 1977   Administration of President Jimmy Carter abandons attempt to enact bases agreement; instead, obtains legislation imposing $175 million ceiling on FY 1978 arms sales to Turkey. (Legg 122)

2 April 1978   Carter, reversing previous position, makes repeal of military aid restrictions "highest foreign policy" priority. (Legg 108–9, 122)

July–August 1978   Congress repeals military aid restrictions. (Legg 123)

27 September 1978   Pursuant to legislation, Carter certifies Turkey is acting in good faith to resolve Cyprus question; Turkey agrees to reopen four bases used for intelligence operations; president lifts restrictions on arms aid to Turkey. (Legg 123)

GOALS OF SENDER COUNTRY

Fall of 1974
Pro-Greek members of Congress introduce, finally win passage of, legislation limiting US military assistance to Turkey as means of persuading Turkey to reach agreement on Cyprus. Contemplated agreement would entail some withdrawal of Turkish troops from occupied territory. (Legg 119–20)

RESPONSE OF TARGET COUNTRY

February–March 1975
Turkey limits US military activity; many of 26 US bases in Turkey are closed. (Legg 121)

1976
Under Turkish prodding, Ford administration proposes new joint defense agreement coupled with $1 billion in grants. (Legg 121)

1977
Turkish government pressures Carter administration to win congressional approval of new bases agreement; opens contacts with USSR, Arab countries; circulates rumors of possible withdrawal from NATO; requests departure of US troops. (Legg 122)

Late 1978
Following repeal of embargo, Turkey allows US to reopen four intelligence bases. (Legg 123)

ATTITUDE OF OTHER COUNTRIES

Western Europe
Throughout embargo, Turkey obtains military goods from Italy, Federal Republic of Germany, NATO maintenance and supply agency. (Legg 123)

ECONOMIC IMPACT

Observed Economic Statistics

Turkish military budget increases in constant dollars from $1,270 million (1974) to $1,640 million (1975) to $2,230 million (1976). (Legg 131)

Turkish arms imports (million dollars)

1974	232	1977	140
1975	238	1978	220
1976	291		

Source: ACDA.

US military aid to Turkey (million dollars)

1970	181.6	1974	190.8
1971	214.4	1975	109.1
1972	223.2	1976–77	250.0
1973	245.1	1978	175.4

Source: Legg 131.

Calculated Economic Impact

	Annual cost to target country
Reduction in US military aid from FY 1975–78; welfare loss estimated at 90 percent of reduced transfers from earlier aid levels.	$69 million
Increased cost of non-US military purchases to cover reduction in sales of US military equipment; welfare loss estimated at 10 percent of reduced trade 1975–78.	8 million
Total	$77 million

Relative Magnitudes

Gross indicators of Turkish economy	
Turkish GNP (1975)	$37.1 billion
Turkish population (1975)	40.0 million
Annual effect of sanctions related to gross indicators	
Percentage of GNP	0.2
Per capita	$1.92
Turkish trade with US as percentage of total trade	
Exports (1975)	11
Imports (1975)	13
Ratio of US GNP (1975: $1,549.2 billion) to Turkish GNP (1975: $37.1 billion)	42

ASSESSMENT

Keith Legg
"Clearly, the embargo had not induced Turkish concessions on Cyprus, nor had it facilitated direct Greek-Turkish dialogue on other outstanding issues. From the first, spokesmen for the executive branch maintained that the embargo would not be effective in pushing the Turks toward concessions on Cyprus. This was eventually viewed, especially by pro-Greek congressmen, as a self-fulfilling prophecy." (Legg 121, 123)

"The real effect of the embargo . . . was to prevent an alteration of the balance of forces in the Aegean Sea." (Legg 124)

Ali S. Karaosmanoglu
"The embargo also did great harm to Turkey's armed forces. Turkey's arms imports dropped steeply, and by the late 1970s it was unable to import the minimum of its arms needs. The Turkish armed forces are today still in an equipment crisis, with much weaponry out of date or deteriorating." (Karaosmanoglu 158)

AUTHORS' SUMMARY

Overall assessment	Assigned scores
□ Policy result, scaled from 1 (failed) to 4 (success)	1
□ Sanctions contribution, scaled from 1 (none) to 4 (significant)	1
□ Success score (policy result *times* sanctions contribution), scaled from 1 (outright failure) to 16 (significant success)	1

Political and economic variables

□ Companion policies: J (covert), Q (quasi-military), or R (regular military)

Political and economic variables (continued)	Assigned scores
□ International cooperation with sender, scaled from 1 (none) to 4 (significant)	1
□ International assistance to target: A (if present)	—
□ Sanctions period (years)	4
□ Economic health and political stability of target, scaled from 1 (distressed) to 3 (strong)	2
□ Presanction relations between sender and target, scaled from 1 (antagonistic) to 3 (cordial)	3
□ Type of sanction: X (export), M (import), F (financial)	F
□ Cost to sender, scaled from 1 (net gain) to 4 (major loss)	1

BIBLIOGRAPHY

Arms Control and Disarmament Agency. 1980. *World Military Expenditures and Arms Transfers 1970–79*.

Congressional Research Service (CRS), Library of Congress. 1975. *Greece and Turkey: Some Military Implications Related to NATO and the Middle East*. 94 Cong., 2 sess., 28 February. Washington.

———. 1981. "Congressional-Executive Relations and the Turkish Arms Embargo." Published as House Foreign Affairs Committee Print, Congress and Foreign Policy Series, no. 3. 97 Cong., 1 sess., June. Washington.

Deering, Christopher J. 1980. "The Turkish Arms Embargo: Arms Transfers, European Security, and Domestic Politics." Paper presented at the International Studies Association, March. Los Angeles.

Karaosmanoglu, Ali S. 1983. "Turkey's Security and the Middle East." 62 *Foreign Affairs* (Fall): 157–75.

Legg, Keith R. 1981. "Congress as Trojan Horse? The Turkish Embargo Problem, 1974–1978." In *Congress, The Presidency and American Foreign Policy*, ed. John Spanier and Joseph Nogee. New York: Pergamon Press.

US Congress. Senate Committee on Armed Services. 1978. *Hearings on The Military Aspects of Banning Arms Aid to Turkey*. 95 Cong., 2 sess., June 25.

———. Senate Committee on Foreign Relations. 1976. *Hearings on United States–Turkish Defense Cooperation Agreement*. 95 Cong., 2 sess., September 15.

Wilson, Andrew. 1979. *The Aegean Dispute*. Adelphi Paper no. 155. London: International Institute for Strategic Studies.

Case 74–2 Canada v. India

(1974–76: Nuclear Explosion)

CHRONOLOGY OF KEY EVENTS

18 May 1974 India explodes underground nuclear device, claiming peaceful purposes. (*New York Times*, 19 May 1974, A1)

22 May 1974 Canadian External Affairs Minister Mitchell Sharp announces suspension of nuclear cooperation with India; says suspension of all other nonfood aid is under consideration. "What concerns us about this matter is that the Indians, notwithstanding their great economic difficulties, should have devoted tens of hundreds of millions of dollars to the creation of a nuclear device for a nuclear explosion." Canada calls on other nations to assess "the broad international implications" of India's explosion. (*Asian Recorder* 12035; *Canadian News Facts* 1207)

August 1974– Meetings in Ottawa, New Delhi lead to Canadian admission that
January 1975 Canadian-Indian nuclear agreement had not been broken technically, but Canadians insist spirit of agreement had been violated. No understanding is reached on resumption of nuclear cooperation. (*New York Times*, 3 August 1974, A4; *Canadian News Facts* 1323)

18 May 1976 After further negotiations, Canadian External Affairs Minister Allan McEachen announces permanent suspension of nuclear cooperation with India: "We are involved in giving food and agricultural aid to India and this is likely to continue. But the nuclear side of our relationship is finished. India's detonation of a nuclear explosive device in 1974 made it evident that Canada and India have taken profoundly different views of what should be encompassed in the peaceful application of nuclear energy by nonnuclear weapon states. . . . [The Canadian government] has decided that it would agree to make new nuclear shipments only on an undertaking by India that Canadian supplies, whether of technology, nuclear equipment or materials, whether past or future shall not be used for the manufacture of a nuclear device. . . . In the present case, this undertaking would require that all nuclear facilities in India using Canadian technology would be safeguarded. . . . The decision reached by the Government relating to this aspect of our relations is not intended to preclude the pursuit of other elements of mutual interest in our overall links with India. . . ." (*Asian Recorder* 13225)

GOALS OF SENDER COUNTRY

Authors' note
Sanctions were partially punitive in nature. Canadians felt used by Indians, were genuinely concerned about spread of nuclear weapons, wanted to strengthen safeguards on Canadian-supplied fuel and equipment to prevent future nuclear explosions, whether or not for peaceful purposes.

Summary of Canada's nonproliferation policy:
"A. Nuclear cooperation will be authorized only for those nonnuclear weapon states that have made a general commitment to nonproliferation by either having ratified the NPT or having taken an equivalent binding step and that have thereby accepted IAEA [International Atomic Energy Agency] safeguards on the full scope of their nuclear activities (such IAEA safeguards are hence known as NPT-type full-scope safeguards).

"B. Nuclear exports can go forward only to those states (both nonnuclear and nuclear weapon states) which have undertaken to accept in a formal agreement a number of additional requirements designed to minimize the proliferation risk associated with Canadian nuclear exports. These requirements are:

 i) an assurance that Canadian-supplied nuclear items (nuclear material, heavy water, nuclear equipment and technology) will not be used in connection with the production of nuclear explosive devices;
 ii) a provision for fallback safeguards in the event that a situation arises where the IAEA is unable to continue to perform its safeguards functions;
 iii) a control over the retransfer of Canadian-supplied nuclear items;
 iv) a control over the reprocessing of Canadian-origin spent fuel, subsequent storage of the separated plutonium and enrichment beyond 20 percent U-235 of Canadian-origin uranium;
 v) an assurance that adequate physical protection measures will be applied." (Government of Canada 10–11)

RESPONSE OF TARGET COUNTRY

18–25 May 1974
India asserts that explosive device was "peaceful nuclear explosion" (PNE). Statement by Prime Minister Indira Gandhi: "Is it the contention that it is all right for the rich to use nuclear energy for destructive purposes but not right for a poor country to find out whether it can be used for construction?" (*New York Times*, 26 May 1974, A15; *Asian Recorder* 12033)

28 May 1974
Indian newspapers criticize Canadian decision to suspend aid. Indian government seeks to assure Canada that PNE had been developed solely from indigenous materials, that no agreement had been broken. (*New York Times*, 23 May 1974, A6)

20 May 1976

Statement by Indian External Affairs Minister H. B. Chawan: "The Government of India cannot but regret Canada's decision to terminate nuclear cooperation. . . . It was also explained to the Canadian side at the highest level that in conducting the Peaceful Nuclear Experiment which India had every right to do as PNE is an internationally recognized concept, we had not violated any provision of any agreement with Canada, a fact which was subsequently recognized by the Canadian Government. . . . It is regrettable that after three long months of almost continuous dialogue the Canadian Government has now decided to turn its back on the negotiated settlement and its contractual obligations." (*Asian Recorder* 13224)

ATTITUDE OF OTHER COUNTRIES

General reaction

No other nation joins Canada in sanctions, although Japan reduces aid to India for 1974. US, USSR do not denounce so-called "peaceful nuclear experiment." (*Asian Recorder* 12035)

Japan

Japanese Foreign Minister Masayoshi Ohira: "The Government can only express regret [for the test] because we have been, and still are, against any nuclear test by any nation for any reason. We also express our hope that it does not jeopardize the climate of détente on the Indian subcontinent." (*Asian Recorder* 12035)

United States

US announces its arms sales policy toward Pakistan, India would not be altered because of test. (*Asian Recorder* 12035)

Soviet Union

Tass, Soviet news agency, reports Indian PNE incident without comment. (*Asian Recorder* 12035)

Yugoslavia

Purportedly speaking for nonaligned nations, Yugoslavia congratulates India on demonstration of technological prowess, accepts India's PNE rationale. (*Asian Recorder* 12035)

ECONOMIC IMPACT

Observed Economic Statistics

All nuclear fuel, equipment, spare parts for India's CIRUS research reactor, RAPP I and II power reactors were supplied by Canada before sanctions. After sanctions, no further shipments are made. RAPP II had not been completed when sanctions were imposed. Indians had indigenous capability to complete facility but there was long delay in doing so. (*New York Times*, 19 May 1976, A8)

Nuclear aid from Canada to India amounts to $96.5 million from initiation in 1956 to suspension in 1974. With suspension, Canada also decides not to refinance $8.5 million loan, for short time suspends $127 million in additional nonfood aid. (*New York Times*, 23 May 1974, A1)

Calculated Economic Impact

	Annual cost to target country
Delay in completion of RAPP II; welfare loss estimated at 25 percent of capital outlays for plant in 1977.	$27 million
Suspension of nuclear assistance from Canada; welfare loss estimated at 75 percent of reduced transfers.	4 million
Suspension of $8.5 million Canadian agricultural loan; welfare loss estimated at 25 percent of value of loan.	2 million
Total	$33 million

Relative Magnitudes

Gross indicators of Indian economy	
Indian GNP (1974)	$86 billion
Indian population (1974)	588 million
Annual effect of sanctions related to gross indicators	
Percentage of GNP	negl.
Per capita	$.06
Indian trade with Canada as percentage of total trade	
Exports (1974)	1
Imports (1974)	3
Ratio of Canadian GNP (1974: $151 billion) to Indian GNP (1974: $86 billion)	2

ASSESSMENT

Ravindra Tomar
Because of Canadian sanctions, commissioning of Indian nuclear power plant RAPP II is delayed by three years (from early 1975 to 1978). (Tomar 525)

Canadian government
"After Canada suspended nuclear cooperation with India in 1974, it tried over the next two years to secure upgraded nonproliferation arrangements for Canadian-supplied nuclear items and facilities in India, but its efforts proved unsuccessful. As a result, Canada announced in May 1976 that it was terminating its nuclear relationship with India. The two RAPP reactors continue to be subject to IAEA safeguards. The CIRUS reactor continues to operate free of IAEA safeguards." (Government of Canada 15)

Overall assessment	Assigned scores
□ Policy result, scaled from 1 (failed) to 4 (success)	2
□ Sanctions contribution, scaled from 1 (none) to 4 (significant)	2
□ Success score (policy result *times* sanctions contribution), scaled from 1 (outright failure) to 16 (significant success)	4

Political and economic variables

□ Companion policies: J (covert), Q (quasi-military), or R (regular military)	—
□ International cooperation with sender, scaled from 1 (none) to 4 (significant)	2
□ International assistance to target: A (if present)	—
□ Sanctions period (years)	2
□ Economic health and political stability of target, scaled from 1 (distressed) to 3 (strong)	3
□ Presanction relations between sender and target, scaled from 1 (antagonistic) to 3 (cordial)	2
□ Type of sanction: X (export), M (import), F (financial)	F, X
□ Cost to sender, scaled from 1 (net gain) to 4 (major loss)	2

BIBLIOGRAPHY

Asian Recorder. 4–10 June 1974, 12033, 12035; 24–30 June 1976, 13224, 13225.

Canadian News Facts. 16–31 May 1974, 1207; 1–15 January 1975, 1323; 1–15 March 1976, 1541.

Government of Canada, Department of External Affairs. 1982. *Canada's Nuclear Non-Proliferation Policy.* Canadian Foreign Policy Texts no. 82/2.

Kapur, Ashok. 1976. *India's Nuclear Option: Atomic Diplomacy & Decisionmaking.* New York: Praeger.

Poneman, Daniel. 1982. *Nuclear Power in the Developing World.* London: George Allen & Unwin.

Tomar, Ravindra. 1980. "The Indian Nuclear Power Program: Myths and Mirages." 20 *Asian Survey* (May): 517–31.

Case 74–3 Canada v. Pakistan

(1974–76: Nuclear Safeguards)

CHRONOLOGY OF KEY EVENTS

Also see Case 74–2 Canada v. India (1974–76: Nuclear Explosion) and Case 79–2 US v. Pakistan (1979–80: Nuclear Safeguards)

November 1974	Canada refuses to negotiate new fuel contract for Pakistan's KANUPP reactor until safeguards agreement to preclude peaceful nuclear explosions (PNEs) is negotiated (India's PNE had taken place in May 1974). Pakistan refuses, Canada bans shipment of spare parts for KANUPP, delays shipment of fabrication facility already negotiated. (Ebinger 12)
March 1976	Pakistan signs agreement with France for sale of reprocessing plant. (Tahir-Kheli 90)
4 December 1976	Following negotiations in Ottawa between Prime Ministers Zulfikar Ali Bhutto and Pierre Trudeau in February 1976, Canada presents Pakistan with ultimatum in form of three options: □ If Pakistan cancels reprocessing agreement with France, renegotiates its safeguards agreement, Canada would agree to supply fuel, services for Pakistan's nuclear program for 10 years (subject to renewal at end of period) and would ship fuel fabrication plant as agreed. □ If Pakistan goes ahead with French reprocessing plant but agrees to renegotiate safeguards, Canada would provide nuclear fuel, services for five years, but only if Pakistan allows Canada veto rights over disposition of spent fuel from KANUPP, whether or not reprocessed. Under this option, fabrication facility would not be shipped. □ If Pakistan refuses to cancel reprocessing deal or allow Canada veto over KANUPP's spent fuel, but renegotiates safeguards agreement, Canada would continue nuclear cooperation for two years. Pakistan refuses to accept any of three options. (Ebinger 13)
22 December 1976	Canada announces termination of nuclear cooperation with Pakistan. Pakistan shuts down KANUPP reactor in 1977 for lack of fuel, spare parts. (*Washington Post*, 4 January 1977, A9)

1977   Canada enacts law requiring full-scope safeguards on all exports of
nuclear materials, equipment, or technology. (Government of Canada
10–11)

GOALS OF SENDER COUNTRY

Late 1974
Canada becomes concerned that safeguards agreement with Pakistan will not prevent
nuclear explosion such as India had demonstrated earlier that year. Initial goal is to
renegotiate safeguards agreement to preclude possible PNE. (Ebinger 12–13)

Early 1976
Either cancellation of French reprocessing plant, or Canadian veto over use of spent fuel
from Canadian-supplied reactor at Karachi, become goals of equal importance to
renegotiation of safeguards agreement. (Ebinger 12–13)

RESPONSE OF TARGET COUNTRY

25 February 1976
At end of summit in Ottawa, Bhutto states that Pakistan would consider "adequate
safeguards" on Canadian-supplied KANUPP reactor but rejects Canada's attempt to apply
them to non-Canadian facility. (*New York Times*, 26 February 1976, A1)

January 1977
Minister of Defense and Foreign Affairs Aziz Ahmed of Pakistan, responding to Canada's
termination of nuclear cooperation: "No third country has any right to demand that
Pakistan should abandon the reprocessing plant. . . . It [Canada] demanded that we
accept some totally unreasonable conditions as the price for Canada's continuing
cooperation with us while pleading helplessness to get India to accept similar conditions."
Canada's conditions "were so unreasonable and one-sided that Pakistan could not but
reject them. Canada has no right to make any of these demands in the first place."
(*Washington Post*, 4 January 1977, A9)

Late 1970s
"In early 1979, surreptitious Pakistani efforts to buy the components for a centrifugal
enrichment facility came to light. Dummy companies were set up to buy the necessary
parts in the United States, Canada, Great Britain, and Switzerland, sometimes on the
pretext that these sophisticated electrical converters and the like were required for textile
production." (Poneman 56)

ATTITUDE OF OTHER COUNTRIES

United States
Administration of President Jimmy Carter pressures France not to provide entire reprocessing plant to Pakistan; closely monitors, and blocks, Pakistan's worldwide efforts to
obtain key components of enrichment, reprocessing plants. (Spector interview)

ECONOMIC IMPACT

Observed Economic Statistics

KANUPP plant, with rating of 125 megawatts (MWe), is completed in December 1972. A second reactor, with rating of 600 MWe, "has been deferred repeatedly." (Poneman 51)

In 1974, Canada offers Pakistan a $1.7 million interest-free loan to finance foreign exchange component of Rs 35 million ($3.5 million) fuel fabrication plant to be supplied by Canada. Plant is never shipped. Before 1975, Canada supplied all of Pakistan's imports of nuclear fuel, spare parts for KANUPP reactor; following sanctions, Canada supplies nothing. (*Asian Recorder* 11877, 12107)

"Some estimates indicate that KANUPP operated at a miserable load factor of 15.6 percent of capacity from 1976 to 1980, and only 5.5 percent in the latter half of that period." (Poneman 55)

Calculated Economic Impact

	Annual cost to target country
Suspension of Canadian fuel, spare parts for KANUPP reactor; welfare loss estimated at 70 percent of value of decreased output.	$11 million
Cancellation of shipment of Canadian fuel fabrication plant to be financed through $1.7 million interest-free loan; welfare loss estimated at 60 percent of plant's value.	2 million
Total	$13 million

Relative Magnitudes

Gross indicators of Pakistani economy	
Pakistani GNP (1976)	$13.6 billion
Pakistani population (1976)	72.4 million
Annual effect of sanctions related to gross indicators	
Percentage of GNP	0.1
Per capita	$0.18
Pakistani trade with Canada as percentage of total trade	
Exports (1976)	1
Imports (1976)	2
Ratio of Canadian GNP (1976: $194 billion) to Pakistani GNP (1976: $13.6 billion)	14

ASSESSMENT

Authors' note
Canada did not achieve its goal of strengthening safeguards agreement applied to KANUPP. However, within year after sanctions were implemented, reactor was shut down and in 1978 French contract for reprocessing plant was cancelled. Responding to US, Canadian concerns, France offered to sell Pakistan coprocessing, rather than reprocessing, plant. Coprocessing plant would produce material unsuitable for nuclear weapons. Pakistan rejected new terms.

AUTHORS' SUMMARY

Overall assessment	Assigned scores
☐ Policy result, scaled from 1 (failed) to 4 (success)	2
☐ Sanctions contribution, scaled from 1 (none) to 4 (significant)	2
☐ Success score (policy result *times* sanctions contribution), scaled from 1 (outright failure) to 16 (significant success)	4

Political and economic variables

☐ Companion policies: J (covert), Q (quasi-military), or R (regular military)	—
☐ International cooperation with sender, scaled from 1 (none) to 4 (significant)	2
☐ International assistance to target: A (if present)	—
☐ Sanctions period (years)	2
☐ Economic health and political stability of target, scaled from 1 (distressed) to 3 (strong)	2
☐ Presanction relations between sender and target, scaled from 1 (antagonistic) to 3 (cordial)	2
☐ Type of sanction: X (export), M (import), F (financial)	X
☐ Cost to sender, scaled from 1 (net gain) to 4 (major loss)	2

BIBLIOGRAPHY

Asian Recorder. 26 February–4 March 1976, 11877; 16–22 July 1976, 12107.
Ebinger, Charles K. 1979. "US Nuclear Nonproliferation Policy: The Pakistan Controversy." 3 *Fletcher Forum* 1–22.
Government of Canada, Department of External Affairs. 1982. *Canada's Nuclear Nonproliferation Policy.* Canadian Foreign Policy Texts no. 82/2.
Poneman, Daniel. 1982. *Nuclear Power in the Developing World.* London: George Allen & Unwin.
Spector, Leonard. Minority Staff, US Senate, Governmental Affairs Committee, Subcommittee on Energy, Nuclear Proliferation, and Government Processes. Interview with authors, 24 January 1983.
Tahir-Kheli, Shirin. 1982. *The United States and Pakistan: Evolution of an Influence Relationship.* New York: Praeger.

Case 75–1   US and Canada v. South Korea

(1975–76: Forego Nuclear Reprocessing)

CHRONOLOGY OF KEY EVENTS

1974   South Korea sounds out France on possible purchase of nuclear reprocessing plant. South Korea simultaneously negotiates purchase of heavy-water reactor from Canada. (*New York Times*, 30 January 1976, A1)

March 1975   South Korean National Assembly ratifies Non-Proliferation Treaty (NPT) that government had signed in 1968. Shortly thereafter (May 28) government reaches agreement with Canada for $300 million loan to finance purchase of 600 megawatt reactor. At about same time, bill requesting approval of $315 million Eximbank loan to Korea is submitted to US Congress. (*Keesing's* 27275)

June 1975   South Korea publicly discloses intention of buying reprocessing plant from France. US, Canada pressure South Korea not to go forward; US threatens to block South Korea's purchase of reactors for peaceful purposes; both US, Canada tighten financing terms of nuclear transactions with South Korea. (*New York Times*, 30 January 1976, A1)

29 January 1976   Myron Kratzer, acting assistant secretary of state for oceans, environment and scientific affairs, announces South Korea has cancelled plans to purchase reprocessing plant: "The South Korean Government reached the decision that the cancellation of its plans was in its own interest." (*New York Times*, 30 January 1976, A1)

1 February 1976   Unofficial South Korean comment: "The United States made the strongest possible representations to the Korean and French governments." (*New York Times*, 1 February 1976, A1)

GOALS OF SENDER COUNTRIES

Franklin B. Weinstein, Fuji Kamiya
"According to one US government analyst, in 1975 the Koreans were 'running all over the world picking up material and equipment' for a nuclear-weapons program. The

reprocessing plant, in his words, was 'practically the last thing on the list of things they needed. . . .' To stop the Korean effort, the . . . administration [of President Gerald R. Ford] threatened, in effect, to bring South Korea's civilian nuclear-power program to a halt by blocking the sale of reactors ordered from Westinghouse and by persuading Canada to suspend negotiations for a similar sale." (Weinstein 113)

RESPONSE OF TARGET COUNTRY

President Park Chung Hee
In an interview with *Washington Post* 12 June 1975: "If the United States withdraws their nuclear umbrella, we shall have to develop our own nuclear capacity to defend ourselves." (*Keesing's* 27275)

ECONOMIC IMPACT

Calculated Economic Impact
None, since economic sanctions did not go beyond threat stage.

Relative Magnitudes

Gross indicators of South Korean economy	
South Korean GNP (1974)	$18.1 billion
South Korean population (1974)	34.7 million
Annual effect of sanctions related to gross indicators	
Percentage of GNP	nil
Per capita	nil
South Korean trade with US, Canada as percentage of total trade	
Exports (1974)	38
Imports (1974)	26
Ratio of US, Canadian GNP (1974: $1,585 billion) to South Korean GNP (1974: $18.3 billion)	87

ASSESSMENT

Albert Wohlstetter
"The effectiveness of the levers at our disposal can be illustrated by the extreme sensitivity in various programs in the nonweapon states of the Third World (where the impending spread is now most threatening) to simple alterations in the terms of financing. Korea, for example, has drastically cut back its nuclear program in response to a slight hardening in Canadian and American financial terms. And the effectiveness of our political and military levers is illustrated by the cancellation of the Korean reprocessing plant." (Wohlstetter 168)

Franklin B. Weinstein and Fuji Kamiya

" . . . South Korea was seriously considering [the development of nuclear weapons] in 1975, until the United States acted to prevent the sale by France of reprocessing facilities to South Korea." (Weinstein 113)

"Furthermore, the South Koreans have given no indication of a revived interest in reprocessing facilities, although they have expressed an interest in participating in joint reprocessing projects under international auspices." (Weinstein 114)

AUTHORS' SUMMARY

Overall assessment	Assigned scores
□ Policy result, scaled from 1 (failed) to 4 (success)	4
□ Sanctions contribution, scaled from 1 (none) to 4 (significant)	4
□ Success score (policy result *times* sanctions contribution), scaled from 1 (outright failure) to 16 (significant success)	16

Political and economic variables

□ Companion policies: J (covert), Q (quasi-military), or R (regular military)	—
□ International cooperation with sender, scaled from 1 (none) to 4 (significant)	2
□ International assistance to target: A (if present)	—
□ Sanctions period (years)	1
□ Economic health and political stability of target, scaled from 1 (distressed) to 3 (strong)	3
□ Presanction relations between sender and target, scaled from 1 (antagonistic) to 3 (cordial)	3
□ Type of sanction: X (export), M (import), F (financial)	—
□ Cost to sender, scaled from 1 (net gain) to 4 (major loss)	2

BIBLIOGRAPHY

Keesing's Contemporary Archives. 1975.

Weinstein, Franklin B., and Fuji Kamiya, eds. 1980. *The Security of Korea: U.S. and Japanese Perspectives on the 1980s.* Boulder, Colo.: Westview Press.

Wohlstetter, Albert. 1976/1977. "Spreading the Bomb Without Quite Breaking the Rules." 25 *Foreign Policy* (Winter): 88–96, 145–79.

Case 75–2   US v. USSR

(1975–   : Emigration)

CHRONOLOGY OF KEY EVENTS

22–29 May 1972   Richard M. Nixon becomes first American president to visit USSR. "Soon after the summit, Governor Nelson Rockefeller ([of New York]—who was not in Moscow but who was a confidant of [National Security Adviser Henry A.] Kissinger's—reported that Nixon and the Soviet leadership had a 'meeting of minds' and there was an understanding that the 1972 outflow of [Jewish] emigrants would reach 35,000. . . . [A]pproximately 32,000 Jews emigrated in 1972." Concurrently, joint US-USSR trade commission is created as first step toward better trade relations. In July 1972, US, USSR conclude three-year $750 million grain deal. (Stern 15, 18; Sobel 138)

3 August 1972   USSR imposes tax on "educated emigrants," that effectively restricts many Jewish emigrants. (Stern 18)

4 October 1972   Senator Henry M. Jackson (D–Wash.) introduces amendment prohibiting extension of most-favored-nation (MFN) status to nations with centrally planned economies that restrict emigration. Six days later, Congressman Charles Vanik (D–Ohio) introduces similar amendment in US House of Representatives. (Stern 18, 54)

18 October 1972   US, USSR initial comprehensive trade agreement in which US promises to seek MFN status for USSR exports, USSR promises to pay $722 million to US to settle World War II Lend-Lease debt. Nixon authorizes Export–Import Bank credit for USSR. That same day, Moscow grants exemptions from emigration tax (about $195,000) to 19 Soviet families destined for Israel. (Sobel 142; Stern 44)

15 March 1973   Jackson attaches his amendment to Trade Reform Act, indicating USSR waiver of tax will not satisfy requirements of amendment. (Stern 67)

20 March 1973   Eximbank signs its first agreement with USSR, for $101.2 million in direct loans, same amount in guarantees for purchase of US industrial equipment. (Stern 68)

| 17 June 1973 | Senator Adlai E. Stevenson III (D–Ill.) introduces amendment that would limit credit to USSR to $300 million and would require congressional review of all transactions of more than $50 million. (Stern 118) |

26 September 1973   House Ways and Means Committee approves Trade Reform Act with Vanik amendment attached. (Sobel 155)

October 1973   October War in Middle East strengthens support for Jackson-Vanik amendment, forces Nixon to ask Congress to delay consideration of MFN for USSR. (Sobel 160)

November 1973   US State Department reveals that number of Jewish emigrants from USSR already has reached 32,000 during 1973. (Stern 101)

5 June 1974   Henry A. Kissinger reports on Soviet "concessions" to Senate amendment sponsors: "[Foreign Minister Andrei] Gromyko had suggested to Kissinger that 45,000 emigrants a year might be an agreeable number, and he had indicated that Soviet authorities would state that harassment was inconsistent with Soviet law." (Stern 114)

9 August 1974   Nixon resigns as president; Gerald R. Ford assumes office. (Sobel 171)

18 October 1974   Jackson, Kissinger exchange letters at White House that supposedly settle controversy over Jewish emigration from USSR. Kissinger offers assurances that flow of emigrants will improve in exchange for inclusion of presidential waiver in amendment. In press conference following White House ceremony, Jackson singles out controversial number of 60,000 emigrants as benchmark against which USSR behavior will be measured. (Stern 166)

26 October 1974   Gromyko sends Kissinger letter denying USSR has given assurances of 60,000 emigrants, as Jackson had claimed a week earlier. Kissinger does not reveal receipt of letter. (Stern 169)

December 1974   Kissinger, testifying before Senate Finance Committee, is deliberately vague about assurances from USSR: ". . . if I were to assert here that a formal agreement on emigration exists between our governments, that statement would immediately be repudiated by the Soviet government. . . ." (Stern 174)

18 December 1974   USSR releases text of October letter to Kissinger but Congress, calling Soviet protestations merely "face-saving," gives final approval to Trade Act of 1974 and Export–Import Bank Act, with Jackson-Vanik, Stevenson amendments attached. (Stern 183, 185)

4–5 January 1975   President Ford signs Trade Act of 1974, Export–Import Bank Act. Negotiations now must be initiated with USSR concerning assurances necessary for waiver, length of trade agreement. Original trade agreement was to have lasted three years but Congress restricts presidential waiver to only 18 months. (Stern 187)

10–13 January 1975	USSR indicates it cannot accept added restrictions, thus will not implement 1972 trade agreement. Ford decides not to exercise waiver authority necessary to bring trade agreement into force. (Stern 190–91)
1984	For the first time since 1970, Jewish emigration drops to below 1,000 (896) according to American Jewish officials. (*New York Times*, 4 January 1985, A4)

GOALS OF SENDER COUNTRY

US Congress

14 September 1972, Senator Jacob K. Javits (R–NY)
"A determined group of legislators can block trade relations with the Soviet Union for several years unless 'justice' is granted to Soviet Jews over the exit tax imposed by the USSR." (Sobel 142)

27 September 1972, Senator Henry M. Jackson (D–Wash.)
"The principal and immediate cause of concern is the imposition by the Soviet Union of a head tax. . . ." Stern, however, claims "Jackson's amendment had a dual diplomatic aim: to liberalize Soviet emigration policy and to retard the development of trade and détente between the two superpowers." (Stern 18, 21)

15 January 1975
Following USSR repudiation of trade agreement, Jackson blames Moscow: "The compromise of October 18, which was freely entered into by all concerned, appears to have lost its appeal to the Soviets only when it became apparent that the Congress would not approve government credits for multibillion dollar development programs in the Soviet Union." (Sobel 181)

Administration

Summer 1972
At same time Jackson is trying to link Jewish emigration to trade, Kissinger is attempting to link settlement of war in Vietnam with trade. "Two days before Kissinger embarked on his four-day trip [10–13 September] to Moscow . . . the VC [Viet Cong] issued a new proposal. The USSR later informed Kissinger that that was the Vietnam peace breakthrough for which he'd been waiting for three years. The VC would accept a cease-fire without prior removal of South Vietnamese President Nguyen Van Thieu. All indications were that Kissinger was advancing by linking the USSR's desire for MFN and credits and America's desire to end the Vietnam war." (Stern 29)

10 April 1973
Nixon: "I do not believe a policy of denying MFN treatment to Soviet exports is a proper or even an effective way of dealing with this problem [emigration]." (Stern 69)

That same day, Jackson amendment is reintroduced, this time attached to comprehensive trade bill. Kissinger responds by indicating that, "If the president asked my opinion today I'd recommend a veto. We cannot accept the principle that our entire foreign policy—or even an essential component of that policy such as normalization of our trade relations—

should be made dependent on the transformation of the Soviet domestic structure." (Sobel 162)

26 September 1973
Kissinger's response to House passage of Vanik amendment: "If MFN is blocked, then the most serious questions have to be raised about the degree to which other countries, in this case the Soviet Union, can rely on a complex negotiation, on the performance of the United States over a period of time, on its commitments." (Sobel 155)

4 January 1975
After signing Trade Act of 1974 with emigration amendment attached, Ford says: "I must express my reservations about the wisdom of legislative language that can only be seen as objectionable and discriminatory by other sovereign states." (Stern 188)

14 January 1975
Kissinger commenting on decision not to bring US-USSR trade agreement into force: "The Administration regrets that turn of events. It has regarded and continues to regard an orderly and mutually beneficial trade relationship with the Soviet Union as an important element in the overall improvement of relations." (*Facts on File* 14)

RESPONSE OF TARGET COUNTRY

June 1973
While in Washington, Leonid Brezhnev, Soviet Communist chief, tries to persuade selected members of Congress, leaders in American Jewish community that trade will be beneficial to US and Jackson amendment is unnecessary since free emigration already exists in Soviet Union. (Stern 83)

17 June 1974
While USSR seems willing to make concessions for Jackson's sake, Lev Tolgunov, editor of *Izvestia*, states that USSR "could not agree to any publicly announced quota for emigration." (Stern 112, 130–31)

25–26 October 1974
Following trip to Moscow, Kissinger "explained that Brezhnev had been 'livid' over Jackson's claims [at the time the compromise letters were signed]. Reportedly, Brezhnev 'reacted violently to the manner' of Jackson's White House announcement." Soviets seemingly are more upset by public nature of compromise than by its substance. (Stern 168)

16 December 1974
"Tass is authorized to state that leading circles in the Soviet Union flatly reject as unacceptable any attempts . . . to interfere in internal affairs that are entirely the concern of the Soviet state and no one else." (Stern 180)

3 January 1975
Ambassador Anatoly Dobrynin tells *Washington Post* reporter Murrey Marder that "the United States was told on December 18 that if the conditions for freer emigration of Soviet Jews, known as the Jackson amendment, are enacted into law and enforced, the Kremlin would consider the 1972 accord invalid, and each portion (including repayment of Lend-Lease) would be up for reexamination on a piece-by-piece basis." (Stern 187)

December 1976
Brezhnev: "Those who believe that discrimination in economic relations can influence our policy or arrest our economic development are deeply mistaken. The Soviet Union has never made itself dependent in these matters on the benevolence of Western partners." (Knorr 106)

ECONOMIC IMPACT

Observed Economic Statistics

Soviet trade with US (million dollars)

	Exports[†]	Imports[†]
1972	7.96	45.57
1973		
Quarter 1	15.47	103.40
Quarter 2	13.39	127.93
Quarter 3	16.80	92.72
Quarter 4	26.14	72.76
1974		
Quarter 1	33.06	55.12
Quarter 2	29.67	50.39
Quarter 3	25.58	33.04
Quarter 4	28.42	66.04
1975		
Quarter 1	26.33	92.11
Quarter 2	18.84	82.39
Quarter 3	18.10	140.18

† Figures are monthly averages.
Source: OECD.

US imports from USSR (million dollars)

1975	280	1979	873
1976	239	1980	453
1977	422	1981	347
1978	540	1982	228

Source: OTA; IMF.

Average rate of duty on dutiable imports from nonmarket economies is 24 percent compared to 8.6 percent for those having MFN status. (US Senate, 1975, 34)

Over 14-month period from late 1972 to early 1974, USSR receives $567 million in Eximbank credits. (US Senate, 1975, 60)

At time trade agreement is signed in October 1972, both sides expect total US-USSR trade during three-year duration of pact will reach $1.5 billion—triple rate of 1969–71 period. In fact, according to Soviet weekly *Economic Gazette* (10 April), even without agreement, Soviet trade with West rises 40 percent in 1973 and for first time Western countries account for more than 25 percent of total Soviet trade. US trade with USSR doubles in 1973 and US has $1 billion surplus using Soviet exchange rates. However, "The dreams of a Soviet-American trade boom died after Congress in 1974 linked trade to the issue of emigration for Soviet Jews and other minorities. However, trade with West Germany and other Western countries, including Japan, has been increasing sharply ever since." (*Washington Post*, 24 July 1982, A1; Sobel 142, 162)

" . . . Soviet economic health improved dramatically between the fall of 1972 when Jackson first introduced his amendment and the early months of 1974 when there had been a recovery thanks to, among other things, a quadrupling in the price of Soviet oil as well as increased earnings for other Soviet exports, which helped gain for them hard currency and a better balance of payments and as a corollary, less need for American trade concessions and less vulnerability to leverage applied by Jackson." (Stern 140)

Calculated Economic Impact

	Annual cost to target country
Reduction in Eximbank loans, guarantees; welfare loss estimated at 10 percent of face value of funds credited from late 1972 to early 1974.	$49 million
Denial of MFN tariff treatment to USSR; welfare loss estimated at 100 percent of tariff increase on exports to the United States (assuming increase of 15 percentage points over all exports).	63 million
Total	$112 million

Relative Magnitudes

Gross indicators of USSR economy	
USSR GNP (1975)	$890 billion
USSR population (1975)	254 million
Annual effect of sanctions related to gross indicators	
Percentage of GNP	negl.
Per capita	$0.44

Gross indicators of USSR economy (continued)

USSR trade with US as percentage of total trade
Exports (1975)   1
Imports (1975)   6

Ratio of US GNP (1975: $1,537 billion) to USSR GNP (1974: $890
billion)   2

Emigration from USSR	
1948–67	Total of 6,000 "elderly pensioners" allowed to leave. (Stern 4)
Six Day War (1967)–Fall 1968	None (Stern 4)
Fall 1968–70	A few hundred (Stern 4)
1971–73	Average of 2,500 per month: 32,122 in 1972; 34,805 in 1973. (Stern 4, 218)
1974:1	Drops 25 to 30 percent compared with same period of previous year. By midyear emigration falls by 40 percent compared with 1973. (Stern 121, 141)
All of 1974	20,000 (Stern 218)
1975–76	14,000 each year (lowest annual rate since 1971). (Stern 198)
1977	16,737 (Stern 215)
1978	28,864
1979	51,320
1980	21,471
1981	9,447
1982	2,688
1983	1,315
1984	896

Source: Spectre interview; *New York Times*, 4 January 1985, A4.

ASSESSMENT

Paula Stern
"The contrast between Kissinger's linkage on Vietnam and Jackson's on emigration is instructive. The demands Kissinger made on the Soviet Union were relatively marginal—cooperation with American efforts to negotiate a peace agreement with the Soviets' ally, North Vietnam. America's quid pro quo was kept so secret that Kissinger even denied ever trying to achieve Soviet cooperation for American trade. . . .

"The Jackson attempt to link trade and emigration was anything but small and discreet. His desired change in Soviet behavior arguably touched the fundamental basis of the regime. It was big, political, and noisy. It dragged out over two and one-half years, thereby affecting the Soviet regime at times when it was not so needy of American trade concessions. By the fall of 1973, the multiplying prices of oil and gold—important Soviet commodities—gave the Soviet Union a $3 billion a year windfall. The harvest in the year the Soviet Union rejected Jackson's demands was the second best in history. Jackson used trade overtly and as a weapon, a stick, not as a carrot. . . .

"The possibilities that Jackson would abandon his amendment and that the Nixon administration's pledge to grant credits and MFN would be fulfilled seemed to gain Soviet cooperation on the emigration question. . . . The Soviet leadership seemed willing to cooperate in this small way in the spring of 1973, and again in the fall of 1974, when it came close to making an accommodation on more fundamental emigration policy, in hopes that Jackson would—in 1973—abandon his amendment and then—in 1974—compromise his amendment, and they would receive the trade benefits. Both times, the Soviet leaders seemed to have been operating as if in an incentive system—that is, if they cooperated, they would be rewarded. . . .

"The Soviet Union's apparent willingness to accommodate even Jackson's broader demands indicates that Jackson's linkage might have worked had he settled for small gains early and quietly. . . ."
(Stern 201–2)

Secretary of State Henry Kissinger, 3 December 1974
"It is difficult, of course, to know the precise causes for changes in emigration rates. We know that during the period of improving relations and quiet representations, emigrations rose from 400 in 1968 to about 33,500 in 1973. We believe that increase, as well as recent favorable actions on longstanding hardship cases, was due at least in part to what we had done privately and unobtrusively.

"We are not convinced that these methods led to the suspension of the emigration tax in 1973. We can only speculate whether the decline of about 40 percent in 1974 was the result of decisions by potential applicants or whether it was also affected by the administration's inability to live up to the terms of the trade agreement we had negotiated with the Soviet Union in 1972." (US Senate, 1975, 52)

AUTHORS' SUMMARY

Overall assessment	Assigned scores
☐ Policy result, scaled from 1 (failed) to 4 (success)	2
☐ Sanctions contribution, scaled from 1 (none) to 4 (significant)	2
☐ Success score (policy result *times* sanctions contribution), scaled from 1 (outright failure) to 16 (significant success)	4

Political and economic variables

☐ Companion policies: J (covert), Q (quasi-military), or R (regular military)	—
☐ International cooperation with sender, scaled from 1 (none) to 4 (significant)	1

Political and economic variables *(continued)*	Assigned scores
☐ International assistance to target: A (if present)	—
☐ Sanctions period (years)	9+
☐ Economic health and political stability of target, scaled from 1 (distressed) to 3 (strong)	3
☐ Presanction relations between sender and target, scaled from 1 (antagonistic) to 3 (cordial)	1
☐ Type of sanction: X (export), M (import), F (financial)	F, M
☐ Cost to sender, scaled from 1 (net gain) to 4 (major loss)	2

Comments

Jewish emigration from USSR did increase in period 1972–74 when Jackson-Vanik amendment was under consideration. Thus, congressional concern perhaps played a role in contributing to positive result. When amendment actually became law, however, sanction became explicit, Soviets abrogated trade agreement, emigration dropped abruptly.

BIBLIOGRAPHY

Beasley, Michael W., Thomas F. Johnson, and Judith A. Mather. 1976. "An Interim Analysis of the Effects of the Jackson-Vanik Amendment on Trade and Human Rights." 8 *Law and Policy in International Business* 193–221.

Facts on File. 1975.

International Monetary Fund. *Direction of Trade Statistics.* Various issues.

Knorr, Klaus. 1977. "International Economic Leverage and Its Uses." In *Economic Issues and National Security*, ed. Klaus Knorr and Frank N. Traeger. Lawrence, Kan.: Regents Press.

Organization for Economic Cooperation and Development. *Statistics on Foreign Trade: Monthly Bulletin.* Various issues.

Sobel, Lester A., ed. 1975. *Kissinger and Détente.* New York: Facts on File, Inc.

Spectre, George. International Council of B'nai B'rith. Interview with authors, June 1983.

Stern, Paula. 1979. *Water's Edge: Domestic Politics and the Making of American Foreign Policy.* Westport, Conn.: Greenwood Press.

US Congress. Office of Technology Assessment. 1979. *Technology and East-West Trade.*

———. 1983. *Technology and East-West Trade: An Update.*

US Congress. Senate Committee on Finance. 1974. *The Trade Reform Act of 1974.* 93 Cong., 2 sess.

———. 1975. *Hearings on Emigration Amendment to the Trade Reform Act of 1974.* 93 Cong., 2 sess., 3 December 1974.

Case 75–3   US v. Eastern Europe
(1975–   : Emigration)

CHRONOLOGY OF KEY EVENTS

Also see Case 75–2 US v. USSR (1975–   :Emigration)

4 October 1972	Senator Henry M. Jackson (D–Wash.) introduces amendment to prohibit extension of most-favored-nation (MFN) status to nations with centrally planned economies that restrict emigration. Six days later, Congressman Charles Vanik (D–Ohio) introduces similar amendment in House. (Stern 18, 54)
17 June 1973	Senator Adlai E. Stevenson III (D–Ill.) introduces amendment to limit credit to centrally planned economies to $300 million over four years, require congressional review for all transactions of more than $50 million. (Stern 118)
18 December 1974	Congress gives final approval to Trade Act of 1974, Export–Import Bank Act, with Jackson-Vanik and Stevenson amendments attached. (Stern 183, 185)
4–5 January 1975	President Gerald R. Ford signs both pieces of legislation. Negotiations must now be initiated with Soviet bloc countries concerning assurances necessary for waiver, length of each trade agreement. (Stern 187)
10–13 January 1975	USSR indicates it cannot accept Jackson-Vanik restrictions, thus will not implement trade agreement providing for extension of MFN privileges. Ford decides not to exercise waiver authority necessary to bring trade agreement into force. (Stern 190–91)
April 1975	Ford waives requirement of Jackson-Vanik amendment (section 402), US and Romania conclude trade agreement that includes MFN status for Romania. (Beasley 201)
July 1975	House and Senate committees favorably report out concurrent resolution approving Romanian waiver. Both houses approve measure later that month. (Beasley 207–8)

1978   President Jimmy Carter waives section 402 so Hungary may receive MFN status. Congress approves. (Beasley 201, 207–8)

1979   Carter waives section 402 so China may receive MFN status. Congress approves. (Law Group 11)

3 March 1983   President Ronald Reagan threatens to revoke Romania's MFN status unless it rescinds "education tax" on emigrants (similar tax had been imposed by USSR in August 1973). (*Washington Post*, 3 March 1983, A17)

19 May 1983   Romania decides to lift emigration tax so as not to lose MFN status. (*New York Times*, 19 May 1983, A3)

GOALS OF SENDER COUNTRY

Michael W. Beasley, Thomas F. Johnson, Judith A. Mather
"Congress imposed several conditions on the authority of the President to extend nondiscriminatory [MFN] treatment. Section 402 [of the Trade Act of 1974] provides that no nonmarket country is eligible to receive MFN treatment, receive US government credits, credit guarantees, or investment guarantees, or conclude a US commercial agreement if the President determines that such country:

(1) denies its citizens the right or opportunity to emigrate;
(2) imposes more than a nominal tax on emigration or on the visas or other documents required for emigration, for any purpose or cause whatever; or
(3) imposes more than a nominal tax, levy, fine, fee or other charge on any citizen as a consequence of the desire of such citizen to emigrate to the country of his choice. . . .

"Title IV also contains an important waiver provision allowing the President to waive by executive order the freedom of emigration requirements with respect to any country, if he reports to Congress that he has determined that such waiver will substantially promote the objectives of free emigration, and that he has received assurances that the emigration practices of that country will eventually lead to free emigration." (Beasley 195)

"The conclusion to be drawn from these factors [Romania's accession to GATT, membership in World Bank and IMF, high volume of trade with Western countries, refusal to endorse the Soviet rejection of US-USSR Trade Agreement] was that it was in the United States' best political interest to support Romania's independence of action through a trade agreement." (Beasley 205)

RESPONSE OF TARGET COUNTRIES

Early 1983: "Not long ago, Romanian President Nicolae Ceausescu was rebutting foreign criticisms on the basis that emigration is a domestic matter and asserting that, since the emigrants acquired education and professional skills from the Romanian state, it was both 'moral and correct' that they should refund those costs when they left the country." (*Christian Science Monitor*, 8 June 1983, 7)

May 1983: "'The situation is 'sticky in that it involves a major retreat by Ceausescu,' [State Department Counselor Edward J.] Derwinski said. He added, though, that the Romanians now understand that they will lose their MFN status if they retain the tax and that Foreign Minister Stefan Andrei, who was here [Washington] for talks last week, 'was looking for ways to crawl off the limb as gracefully as possible.'" (*Washington Post*, 26 May 1983, A24)

ECONOMIC IMPACT

Observed Economic Statistics

US imports from Eastern Europe (million dollars)

	Bulgaria	Czechoslovakia	GDR	Hungary	Romania
1974	9	51	15	79	139
1975	21	38	12	38	147
1976	28	40	15	53	218
1977	19	41	18	50	254
1978	20	65	38	74	376
1979	37	56	37	122	358
1980	27	72	49	118	341
1981	34	67	48	129	560
1982	28	62	54	133	348

Source: OTA; IMF.

At time of enactment of agreement, about 25 percent of Romania's exports to US are eligible for lower tariff rates under MFN, "and it is expected that trade will expand in types of goods not imported because of high duty rates." (Beasley 210)

If, by 30 June 1983, Romania had not rescinded education tax, it could have lost Generalized System of Preferences (GSP) benefits as well as access to Eximbank, Commodity Credit Corporation (CCC) credits. (*Journal of Commerce*, 9 March 1983, 23B)

Loss of MFN privileges was expected to make 75 of Romania's top 80 exports to US "significantly less competitive" and force 29 of those out of market completely. (*Journal of Commerce*, 9 March 1983, 23B)

If Romania's MFN status had been revoked because of emigration tax, it would have been at cost of about $200 million in 1984, in lost exports to the US. (*New York Times*, 19 May 1983, A3)

Calculated Economic Impact

	Annual cost to target country
Additional US import duties charged on exports from Bulgaria, Czechoslovakia and East Germany as a result of non-MFN status; welfare loss estimated at 15 percent of average annual imports (assumes average duty of 24 percent instead of MFN average rate of 9 percent).	$17 million
Additional US import duties charged on exports from Hungary from 1975–78; welfare loss valued at 30 percent of lost trade (estimated as difference in average annual exports in 1979–82 from pre-MFN period, 1975–78).	22 million
Total	$39 million

Relative Magnitudes

Gross indicators of East European[†] economies	
East European GNP	$283.3 billion
East European population (1975)	72.1 million
Annual effect of sanctions related to gross indicators	
Percentage of GNP	negl.
Per capita	$0.54
East European trade with US as percentage of total trade	
Exports (1975)	1
Imports (1975)	1
Ratio of US GNP (1975: $1,549 billion) to East European GNP (1975: $283 billion)	5

† Bulgaria, Czechoslovakia, German Democratic Republic, Hungary, Romania.

Emigration from Eastern Europe

Hungary
Emigration from Hungary remains at relatively low level, but more because of lack of demand than harassment. (Spectre interview)

Romania
During visit to Washington 11 June 1975, President Nicolae Ceausescu reportedly tells President Ford that of 400,000 Jews formerly in Romania, 300,000 already have emigrated. In 1974, some 300 exit permits a month are issued. (*Keesing's* 27309)

"The Romanians . . . conceded [in talks with US] that the numbers of Jewish emigrants had declined in recent years but denied that any large-scale restrictions were in force." (*Keesing's* 32096)

Romanian emigration

1975	2,372	1980	1,043
1976	1,982	1981	1,042
1977	1,547	1982	1,513
1978	1,141	January–May 1983	458
1979	991		

Source: Spectre interview.

ASSESSMENT

William Korey
"In 1982, President Reagan decided to utilize the certification procedure to warn Romania that its 'normalized' status could be in jeopardy if its emigration procedures were not improved and if Jewish emigration to Israel did not increase substantially. The tough position, perhaps not surprisingly, produced a positive consequence—a 50 percent increase during 1982 in the Jewish immigration rate." (Korey 15)

New York Times
Summer 1983: "State Department officials said that the Rumanians yielded on the emigration tax not only because they did not want to erode their billion-dollar a year trade with the United States but also because they enjoyed being alone, with Hungary, of the Soviet bloc, in receiving the most-favored-nation treatment." (*New York Times*, 4 June 1983, 24)

"In approving the most-favored-nation treatment for Hungary, Mr. Reagan said: 'Hungary continues to take a positive and constructive approach to emigration matters and there are no outstanding problems.' . . . He said that China 'continued its open emigration policy throughout the past year.' . . . 'The limiting factor on Chinese emigration remains less official constraint than the limited ability or willingness of this and other countries to receive large numbers of potential Chinese immigrants,' Mr. Reagan said." (*New York Times*, 4 June 1983, 24)

Authors' note
Poland, Yugoslavia already had been granted MFN status before passage of 1974 Trade Act, are exempt from its provisions.

AUTHORS' SUMMARY

	Assigned
Overall assessment	*scores*
☐ Policy result, scaled from 1 (failed) to 4 (success)	3
☐ Sanctions contribution, scaled from 1 (none) to 4 (significant)	4
☐ Success score (policy result *times* sanctions contribution), scaled from 1 (outright failure) to 16 (significant success)	12

Political and economic variables

☐ Companion policies: J (covert), Q (quasi-military), or R (regular military)	—

Political and economic variables (continued)	Assigned scores
□ International cooperation with sender, scaled from 1 (none) to 4 (significant)	1
□ International assistance to target: A (if present)	—
□ Sanctions period (years)	9+
□ Economic health and political stability of target, scaled from 1 (distressed) to 3 (strong)	3
□ Presanction relations between sender and target, scaled from 1 (antagonistic) to 3 (cordial)	1
□ Type of sanction: X (export), M (import), F (financial)	F, M
□ Cost to sender, scaled from 1 (net gain) to 4 (major loss)	1

Comments

Although East Germany, Czechoslovakia, Bulgaria refused to comply, MFN lever was used successfully in inducing Hungary, Romania to extend assurances on freer emigration. Thus, Jackson-Vanik amendment was a significant factor in positive outcome on more liberal emigration practices in Eastern Europe.

BIBLIOGRAPHY

Beasley, Michael W., Thomas F. Johnson, and Judith A. Mather. 1976. "An Interim Analysis of the Effects of the Jackson-Vanik Amendment on Trade and Human Rights." 8 *Law and Policy in International Business* 193–221.

International Human Rights Law Group. 1982. *U.S. Legislation Relating Human Rights to U.S. Foreign Policy.* 3d ed. Washington: IHRLG.

International Monetary Fund. *Direction of Trade Statistics.* Various issues.

Keesing's Contemporary Archives. 1975, 1983.

Knorr, Klaus. 1977. "International Economic Leverage and Its Uses." In *Economic Issues and National Security,* ed. Klaus Knorr and Frank N. Traeger. Lawrence, Kan.: Regents Press.

Korey, William. 1983. *World Reports: Analyses of Critical Issues Confronting the Jewish World.* Washington: International Council of B'nai B'rith.

Sobel, Lester A., ed. 1975. *Kissinger and Détente.* New York: Facts on-File, Inc.

Spectre, George. International Council of B'nai B'rith. Interview with authors, June 1983.

Stern, Paula. 1979. *Water's Edge: Domestic Politics and the Making of American Foreign Policy.* Westport, Conn.: Greenwood Press.

US Congress. Office of Technology Assessment. 1983. *Technology and East-West Trade: An Update.*

———. Senate Committee on Finance. 1975. *Hearings on Emigration Amendment to the Trade Reform Act of 1974.* 93 Cong., 2 sess., 3 December 1974.

Case 75–4   US v. South Africa
(1975–82 : Nuclear Safeguards)

CHRONOLOGY OF KEY EVENTS

1954   US, UK, Canada invite South Africa (along with Belgium, Australia, Portugal) to join in formation, under auspices of UN, of International Atomic Energy Agency (IAEA), which begins operation in 1957. This qualifies South Africa as permanent member of IAEA Board of Governors. (Hearings 43)

1957   US signs Agreement for Cooperation with South Africa providing for sale, fueling of Safari-I research reactor which uses high-enriched uranium (HEU). Agreement also provides for supplying low-enriched uranium (LEU) to Koeberg I and II commercial power reactors (French-supplied). Safeguards agreement with IAEA is signed in 1967, Agreement for Cooperation with US is extended for additional 30 years at its expiration in 1977. (Hearings 43)

Early 1970s   South Africa announces secret new uranium enrichment process. This process becomes basis for South Africa's contention that to sign Non-Proliferation Treaty (NPT, adopted by UN General Assembly 12 June 1968) and to accept "full-scope" IAEA safeguards might jeopardize its control, commercial exploitation of its enrichment process. (Bissell 108, 115)

1975   US Congressional Black Caucus forces temporary halt in fuel shipments for Safari-I because of racial discrimination in South Africa. President Gerald R. Ford later extends ban when South Africa announces plans to develop its indigenous uranium enrichment capability for commercial export purposes. (Bissell 108)

17 June 1977   Nigeria proposes Egypt as replacement for South Africa on IAEA Board, primarily in retaliation for South Africa's apartheid policy. Move is opposed by most Western developed nations, including US, but carries in September 1977 meeting. (*Times* [London], 18 June 1977, 4; Bissell 114)

June 1977   Joseph S. Nye, Jr., President Jimmy Carter's chief nonproliferation adviser: "We approached the South African government in April at the time

June 1977 (continued)	of the question of their membership on the IAEA Board and indicated that we believe their membership in the Non-Proliferation Treaty would be essential to their ability to maintain their Board seat." (Hearings 57)
6 August 1977	Carter learns from Leonid Brezhnev, Soviet leader, that Soviet satellite has discovered apparent preparations for nuclear test in Kalahari Desert of South Africa. UK, FRG, France are notified. US asks South Africa for explanation and commitment that no such test will be conducted. US threatens to terminate uranium supplies to Koeberg, hints it might alter its opposition to UN economic sanctions unless accommodation is reached. South Africa denies test is planned, saying preparations are for military airfield, but refuses to make future commitments. (Bissell 110–12)
23 August 1977	Carter holds press conference, announces South Africa has promised that "no nuclear explosive test will be taken . . . now or in the future." (Washington Post, 28 August 1977, A1)
1977	Carter makes it clear that, in order to receive HEU ordered for Safari-I, South Africa must sign NPT. As counter conditions, South Africa insists on: resumption of HEU deliveries for Safari-I; assured supply of LEU for Koeberg I, II; assured licenses for nonsensitive technology for enrichment plant; US help in regaining its seat on IAEA Board. US considers these demands prohibitive. (Betts 398)
July–November 1978	US informs South Africa that its 1975 order for HEU will not be filled and that $1 million will be returned. (FBIS E2; New York Times, 13 November 1978, IV2)
September 1979	Suspicious "flash" is detected by satellite in South Atlantic. There is speculation it might have been nuclear explosive test, conducted by South Africa, possibly in collusion with Israel, but no definitive evidence is found. (New York Times, 26 October 1979, A1; Bissell 112–13)
5 December 1979	Forty-nine nonaligned, East bloc, and developing countries outvote 24 Western industrial nations, including US, to bar South Africa from participation in 1979 IAEA general conference. (New York Times, 6 December 1979, A14)
April 1982	Reagan administration approves export of powerful computer to South African organization which conducts military research for state-owned arms manufacturer. Critics fear computer could be used to design nuclear weapons. (Washington Post, 8 August 1982, A1; Wall Street Journal, 28 November 1984, 34)
September 1983	US General Accounting Office (GAO) report reveals that from 1 July 1981 to 30 June 1982, South Africa was the third largest recipient of US nuclear exports. Reagan administration approved seven nuclear-related exports in that year while Department of Energy approved "a total of 13 licenses for nuclear transfers to South Africa"

for the year through June 1983. (*Congressional Record-Senate*, 3 January 1985, S-261)

<table>
<tr><td>*September–*
October 1983</td><td>Westinghouse Electric applies for US approval for 10-year, $50 million contract to provide technical, training, maintenance services for South Africa's two atomic power plants. Reagan administration approves license despite congressional opposition. (*Washington Post* 20 September 1983, D7; *Congressional Record-Senate*, 3 January 1985, S-261)</td></tr>
</table>

GOALS OF SENDER COUNTRY

Richard E. Bissell
"The need to obtain South Africa's signature to the NPT, which would involve adherence to the safeguards of the International Atomic Energy Agency (IAEA), has been a major priority of the United States." (Bissell 104)

"In the 1977 environment, then, a whole host of US concerns was converging on South Africa, with the ongoing nuclear programs in the civilian field becoming a weak tactic for dealing with the South Africans. The US wanted majority rule for the blacks in South Africa, adherence to the NPT, and termination of any development of nuclear weapons." (Bissell 105)

RESPONSE OF TARGET COUNTRY

1975
Following President Ford's extension of congressionally imposed temporary ban on shipments of HEU for South Africa's Safari-I research reactor, South Africa accuses US of economic blackmail. (Bissell 115)

16 June 1977
Kurt von Schinding, South Africa's representative to IAEA Board, responding to Nigerian action: ". . . the group of states which has resolved to take action aimed at depriving South Africa of its rightful position on the Board was not, needless to say, interested in upholding the statute of the agency; it was not interested in the reputation of the Board for impartiality and integrity; it had only one goal—the pursuit of a narrow, political vendetta, regardless of the consequences. That was a ruthless political action in which all considerations of law and facts were being brushed aside, a completely illegal action based on internal domestic considerations which were of no more concern to the Board than were the domestic policies of the state which initiated the action." (Cervenka 8)

August–October 1977
South Africa denies any present intention of conducting nuclear explosive test. In October press appearance, however, Prime Minister B. J. Vorster says: "I am not aware of any promise I gave to President Carter [never to conduct nuclear explosive test]. I repeated a statement which I have made very often, that as far as South Africa is concerned, we are only interested in peaceful development of nuclear facilities." (Bissell 109, 111)

5 December 1979
South African delegate J. W. de Villiers denounces IAEA expulsion resolution "as patently

illegal, blatantly unconstitutional, politically motivated," further charges that it "will sow the seeds of destruction" for IAEA. (*New York Times*, 6 December 1979, A14)

ATTITUDE OF OTHER COUNTRIES

European Community, Canada, Japan, together with United States
Vote against 1977 Nigerian-initiated proposal to remove South Africa from IAEA Board, saying it would further weaken any influence agency had on South Africa's nuclear program, might jeopardize safeguards being applied. (*Times*, 18 June 1977, 4D)

18 African, Asian, Latin American, East European countries
Support Nigerian initiative to replace South Africa with Egypt as representative for Africa on IAEA Board of Governors. (*Times*, 18 June 1977, 4D)

Nigeria, Egypt, Pakistan
Nigeria, sponsor of 1979 resolution to temporarily oust South Africa from IAEA, opposes South Africa's participation on racial grounds. Ahmen Osman of Egypt says South Africa should be barred "because 'its nuclear ambitions' were contrary to both African aspirations and the principles of the Agency." Responding to arguments by agency's director, Sigvard Eklund, and head of US delegation, Gerard Smith, that expulsion of South Africa would "undermine nonproliferation efforts," jeopardize any possibility that it might sign NPT, Pakistan's Abdul Satter charges that acceptance of that line of reasoning "would amount to acquiescence in blackmail." (*New York Times*, 6 December 1979, A14)

Soviet Union
Brezhnev's message to Carter in August 1977 indicates his belief that failure to stop alleged South African test "would have the most serious and far-reaching aftermaths for international peace and security." (*Washington Post*, 28 August 1977, A1)

France, Germany
"The U.S. position has not been aided by several of its allies, including France and Germany, that have not been as assiduous in seeking adherence to the NPT, and thus nuclear policy toward South Africa has increased tensions with European allies." (Bissell 104)

In August 1977 Kalahari test crisis, "French sources made it plain to reporters that there might be no limit on the consequences on its part [if the alleged test were not abandoned], from termination of the nuclear reactor contracts to a full break in diplomatic and trade relations." (Bissell 111)

LEGAL NOTES

IAEA membership
South Africa contends its removal from IAEA Board of Governors is illegal because that agency's statute requires that regional representatives have most advanced nuclear technology in region. South Africa's nuclear program was and still is far more advanced and sophisticated than Egypt's. (*Times*, 18 June 1977, 4D)

US nuclear cooperation
Agreement for Cooperation between US, South Africa was extended in 1977 until 2007, has not been abrogated. US Nuclear Non-Proliferation Act (NNPA) forbids export of

nuclear materials or technology to South Africa unless that country accepts full-scope safeguards. However, as long as agreement remains in effect, cooperation still is possible if South Africa changes its policy about safeguards or US president waives full-scope requirement. (Bissell 107)

ECONOMIC IMPACT

Observed Economic Statistics

South Africa
Turns to Europe for fuel for Koeberg I and II reactors but has not found alternate supplier for HEU for Safari-I, which has been operating at just one-eighth capacity. This has adversely affected isotope production, Atomic Energy Board's research program. (FBIS E2)

United States
Based on applications submitted to NRC but never issued, US nuclear industry lost sales of about $134 million by not being permitted to supply fuel to Koeberg reactors. Figure may be overstated, however, as one US company, Edlow Inc., is widely suspected of having indirectly sold one fuel load to South Africa by routing it through Europe; these allegations have never been proved. (*Pending Report*; Moore interview)

Calculated Economic Impact

	Annual cost to target country
Decline in output of Safari-I reactor caused by HEU shortage; welfare loss estimated at 70 percent of value of underutilized capacity.	$2 million

Relative Magnitudes

Gross indicators of South African economy	
South African GNP (1975)	$35.9 billion
South African population (1975)	25.5 million
Annual effect of sanctions related to gross indicators	
Percentage of GNP	negl.
Per capita	$0.08
South African trade with US as percentage of total trade	
Exports (1975)	7
Imports (1975)	17
Ratio of US GNP (1975: $1,549 billion) to South African GNP (1975: $35.9 billion)	43

ASSESSMENT

Richard E. Bissell
"The United States faced two major problems in trying to influence South Africa positively: (1) In a commercial sense, South Africa and the United States were as competitive as the United States is with its allies in the industrial world. U.S. actions were frequently interpreted in terms of commercial advantage, causing the South Africans to reject U.S. advances. (2) With the military isolation of South Africa in the late 1970s, an increasing proportion of its elite argued for the contingency creation of a nuclear laager.*" (Bissell 117)

"Perceiving the importance of the NPT, however, the South Africans have steadily raised the 'price' to the United States for adherence, to a level unacceptable to overall U.S. policies." (Bissell 104)

National Security Adviser Zbigniew Brzezinski
In off-the-record comment following August 1977 Kalahari Desert "test crisis": "In the absence of outside pressures . . . South Africa might have gone on to detonate a bomb there within a matter of weeks, assuming that the explosive material was in hand and that it chose to move full speed ahead." (Bissell 110)

Wall Street Journal
"The Reagan administration . . . has quietly eased rules on nuclear cooperation with South Africa. . . . [T]his is part of the Reagan administration's policy of cajoling South Africa into making some concessions on nuclear matters. But so far the policy hasn't worked. South Africa has assured the US that it won't sell uranium or sensitive technology to any country without approval from the [IAEA]. But talks on making South Africa itself a signatory to the [NPT] remain stalemated over the country's refusal to allow international inspections of its enrichment facilities." (*Wall Street Journal*, 28 November 1984, 34)

* Laager refers to defensive encampments used by Dutch settlers fighting the British in the Boer War, similar to "circling the wagons" in American West.

AUTHORS' SUMMARY

Overall assessment	Assigned scores
☐ Policy result, scaled from 1 (failed) to 4 (success)	2
☐ Sanctions contribution, scaled from 1 (none) to 4 (significant)	2
☐ Success score (policy result *times* sanctions contribution), scaled from 1 (outright failure) to 16 (significant success)	4

Political and economic variables

☐ Companion policies: J (covert), Q (quasi-military), or R (regular military)	—
☐ International cooperation with sender, scaled from 1 (none) to 4 (significant)	2

Political and economic variables (continued)	Assigned scores
☐ International assistance to target: A (if present)	—
☐ Sanctions period (years)	7
☐ Economic health and political stability of target, scaled from 1 (distressed) to 3 (strong)	3
☐ Presanction relations between sender and target, scaled from 1 (antagonistic) to 3 (cordial)	2
☐ Type of sanction: X (export), M (import), F (financial)	X
☐ Cost to sender, scaled from 1 (net gain) to 4 (major loss)	2

Comments

Although restrictions on exports of fuel and sensitive nuclear technologies remain in place, the administration has placed greater emphasis on "carrots," granting licenses for "non-sensitive" nuclear-related exports that approach "gray area" of shipments banned by NNPA, in lieu of more restrictive sanctions. Policy has become cooperative instead of confrontational since licensing decisions of 1982.

BIBLIOGRAPHY

Betts, Richard K. 1980. "A Diplomatic Bomb? South Africa's Nuclear Potential" and "Preventing the Development of South African Nuclear Weapons." In *Nonproliferation and U.S. Foreign Policy*, ed. Joseph A. Yager. Washington: Brookings Institution.

Bissell, Richard E. 1982. *South Africa and the United States: The Erosion of an Influence Relationship*. New York: Praeger.

Cervenka, Zdenek, and Barbara Rogers. 1978. *The Nuclear Axis: Secret Collaboration between West Germany and South Africa*. New York: New York Times Books.

Foreign Broadcasting Information Service. 1978. "Daily Report: Sub-Saharan Africa." 6 July, E2.

Moore, Neil. Senior Licensing Officer, Exports/Imports, Office of International Programs, Nuclear Regulatory Commission. Interviews with authors, August–September 1982.

US Congress. House Committee on International Relations, Subcommittee on Africa. 1978. *Hearings on United States South African Relations: Nuclear Cooperation*. 95 Cong., 1 sess., 30 June 1977, 12 July 1977.

US Nuclear Regulatory Commission, Office of International Programs, Exports/Imports. 1982. *Pending Export Applications Report*. June. Washington.

Case 75–5   US v. Kampuchea
(1975–79: Aftermath of Vietnam War)

CHRONOLOGY OF KEY EVENTS

1963–69 Prince Norodom Sihanouk renounces US aid, tries to balance between right and left internally, and between the US, North Vietnam, China externally. (Shawcross 397–98)

18 March 1970 Sihanouk is deposed by General Lon Nol, who is more amenable to US objectives. (Shawcross 398)

30 April 1970 President Richard M. Nixon announces US, South Vietnamese forces have crossed into Cambodian territory in attempt to destroy National Liberation Front (NLF) bases there. Nixon also announces resumption of aid to Cambodia. (Shawcross 161, 398)

27 January 1973 Article 20 of Paris Agreement "ending the war in Vietnam" calls for withdrawal of all foreign troops from Cambodia. (Shawcross 400)

12 April 1975 US evacuates embassy in Phnom Penh. (Shawcross 401)

17 April 1975 Phnom Penh falls to National United Front of Kampuchea composed of nationalist elements under Prince Sihanouk and communist Khmer Rouge, which declares Democratic Republic of Kampuchea. Almost the entire populations of Phnom Penh, other major cities, are forcibly evacuated in "back to the land" movement. US refuses to recognize new government. (Zasloff 123; Shawcross 401)

8 May 1975 Leaders of new Democratic Kampuchea emphasize Maoist self-reliance, reject all external assistance, even trade. "In April 1975, Cambodia was almost completely cut off from the outside world, and for three years it hardly opened its frontiers, except for Chinese technicians and advisers." This position is later modified to accept assistance extended without conditions. (Shawcross 368, 374; *Keesing's* 27470)

16 May 1975 President Gerald R. Ford imposes total trade embargo on Kampuchea, freezes $9 million in Kampuchean assets in US. (Zasloff 17)

4 April 1976	Prince Sihanouk resigns as head of state, is replaced by Khieu Samphan of Khmer Rouge. New cabinet is headed by Pol Pot. First official estimates from Thailand indicate nearly 10,000 Kampuchean refugees have fled to Thailand, but other estimates put number at 30,000 to 50,000. Reports of widespread executions of former officials, supporters of previous regime circulate. (*Keesing's* 27757–58)
June 1976	US Congress attaches amendment to Foreign Assistance Act barring aid to Kampuchea. (Zasloff 26)
Summer/Fall 1977	Estimates of number of deaths in Kampuchea from executions, starvation, malnutrition, overwork since 1975 range from half-million to 1.2 million. (*Keesing's* 28805; Shawcross 381)
31 December 1977	Phnom Penh suspends relations with Hanoi. The next year is marked by intermittent border fighting between Kampuchea, Vietnam. (Shawcross 401)
December 1978– January 1979	Vietnamese troops invade Kampuchea, rout Khmer forces, install new government in Phnom Penh. US finds common cause with China in removal of Vietnamese forces from Kampuchea. Also see Case 78–7 China v. Vietnam (1978–79: Regional Influence). (Shawcross 402)

GOALS OF SENDER COUNTRY

President Richard M. Nixon
In spring 1970, following US invasion of Cambodia: "The aid we will provide will be limited to the purpose of enabling Cambodia to defend its neutrality and not for the purpose of making it an active belligerent on one side or another." (Shawcross 161)

National Security Adviser Henry A. Kissinger
Summer 1970: "The President is determined to keep an anti-Communist government alive in Phnom Penh." (Shawcross 161)

Authors' note
When Phnom Penh fell, American objectives were frustrated, Kampuchea no longer sought assistance. Subsequently, question of economic relations with Kampuchea was tied, first, to human rights and, later, to removal of Vietnamese forces.

US State Department
Following installation of Heng Samrin regime in Phnom Penh by Vietnamese in 1979, US diplomatically supports Khmer resistance coalition composed of Prince Sihanouk, former Prime Minister Son Sann, and Pol Pot's Khmer Rouge. US denies, however, that it provides assistance to or has any contact with Pol Pot. (*Department of State Bulletin,* November 1983, 36)

RESPONSE OF TARGET COUNTRY

Joseph J. Zasloff, MacAlister Brown
"Despite the desperate needs at the end of the war, no outside assistance was sought or

received from international organizations. The economy has been devoted overwhelmingly to 'cooperative agriculture' and previously existing light industries serving the agricultural sector have been gradually restored to production." (Zasloff 144)

Prince Norodom Sihanouk
In 1975, when asked whether Cambodia, like Vietnam, would demand reparations from US for war damages, the prince replied: "We will never do so. Our blood is not to be commercialized. The United States will have to pay for its crimes in the pages of history." (Shawcross 379)

ATTITUDE OF OTHER COUNTRIES

China
"China had been the Cambodian Communists' only reasonably consistent supporter throughout the 1970–75 war, and when it ended only China was allowed real access to the country." (Shawcross 387)

Vietnam
"The Vietnamese claimed that China encouraged Khmer Rouge harassment along the border and that Peking's purpose was to 'provoke a disease that was not fatal to us, but would keep us always sick.' Vietnam's fear of encirclement by China and Cambodia matched Chinese fears of encirclement by the USSR and a pro-Soviet Vietnam." Vietnamese policy culminated in invasion of Kampuchea in early 1979, brief border clash with China later that year. (Shawcross 387)

ECONOMIC IMPACT

Observed Economic Statistics

Cambodian exports, in 1969, principally rice, rubber, corn: $90 million. By end of 1970, exports declined to zero. (Shawcross 220–21)

US aid to Cambodia (1971–75): $217 million in economic aid; $503 million in military aid; $1.8 billion in military matériel, training. (Zasloff 143; Shawcross 319)

Results of 1970–75 war, US aid: "The initial grants were to help Cambodia import commodities that had previously been financed by its exports. . . . The rubber plantations in the east of the country were burned down, bombed or occupied by the Communists; thousands of hectares of paddy field had been abandoned, and those still being harvested . . . were required for domestic consumption. Within a few months the country's economic independence was destroyed." (Shawcross 221)

By fall 1973, "the economy was in ruin. Inflation ran at about 250 percent a year, industrial and agricultural production was permanently declining, exports were almost nonexistent. The government and the population it controlled were now on American welfare—about 95 percent of all income came from the United States. . . ." (Shawcross 349)

By spring 1975, "There was little or no food to be had by anybody—refugee, civilian or soldier. Malnutrition became rampant, especially in Phnom Penh, and spread to all classes of the Khmer society." (Shawcross 349)

"Cambodia has accepted only the most meager foreign assistance since the war. A few hundred Chinese technicians have helped restore some industry and communications—the PRC was for a time the only country whose aid Cambodia accepted. Additional aid is now [1977–78] being received from North Korea, Yugoslavia, and Romania." (Zasloff 144)

Calculated Economic Impact

	Annual cost to target country
Freeze of Kampuchean assets in the US; welfare loss valued at 100 percent (amortized over three years).	$3 million
Reduction in US economic aid to Kampuchea; welfare loss estimated at 90 percent of lost transfers from average levels in 1971–75.	39 million
Total	$42 million

Relative Magnitudes

Gross indicators of Kampuchean economy	
Kampuchean GNP (1975)	$614 million
Kampuchean population (1975)	6.7 million
Annual effect of sanctions related to gross indicators	
Percentage of GNP	6.8
Per capita	$6.27
Kampuchean trade with US as percentage of total trade	
Exports (1975)	nil
Imports (1975)	nil
Ratio of US GNP (1975: $1,549 billion) to Kampuchean GNP ($614 million)	2,523

ASSESSMENT

Authors' view
US sanctions severed economic ties with regime that was determined to cut relations with US. Economic pressure did nothing to deter human rights abuses or otherwise influence policies of Sihanouk or Pol Pot regimes. Loss of US aid did, however, contribute to deterioration of Kampuchean economy, and thus, in limited sense, prepared path for Vietnamese takeover in 1979.

AUTHORS' SUMMARY

Overall assessment	Assigned scores
□ Policy result, scaled from 1 (failed) to 4 (success)	1
□ Sanctions contribution, scaled from 1 (none) to 4 (significant)	1
□ Success score (policy result *times* sanctions contribution), scaled from 1 (outright failure) to 16 (significant success)	1

Political and economic variables

□ Companion policies: J (covert), Q (quasi-military), or R (regular military)	—
□ International cooperation with sender, scaled from 1 (none) to 4 (significant)	1
□ International assistance to target: A (if present)	—
□ Sanctions period (years)	4
□ Economic health and political stability of target, scaled from 1 (distressed) to 3 (strong)	1
□ Presanction relations between sender and target, scaled from 1 (antagonistic) to 3 (cordial)	2
□ Type of sanction: X (export), M (import), F (financial)	F, X, M
□ Cost to sender, scaled from 1 (net gain) to 4 (major loss)	1

BIBLIOGRAPHY

Keesing's Contemporary Archives. 1975, 1976, 1978.

Shawcross, William. 1979. *Sideshow: Kissinger, Nixon and the Destruction of Cambodia*. New York: Simon & Schuster.

Zasloff, Joseph J., and MacAlister Brown. 1978. *Communist Indochina and U.S. Foreign Policy: Postwar Realities*. Westview Special Studies in International Relations. Boulder, Colo.: Westview Press.

Case 76–1   US v. Uruguay

(1976–81: Human Rights)

CHRONOLOGY OF KEY EVENTS

1968–72   Tupamaro urban guerrillas launch series of political kidnappings; victims include foreign diplomats. Dan Mitrione, US police adviser, is killed in August 1970. In response, government of Uruguay vigorously attacks first, Tupamaros, later, Communists; suspends constitutional powers, increasingly succumbs to military influence. (CRS 63–64)

June 1973   Amnesty International charges torture has become "a common method of interrogation." (CRS 64)

17 December 1973   US Congress, in response to events in Uruguay, enacts section 32 of Foreign Assistance Act of 1973 (PL 93–189), prohibiting police training by US government employees in foreign countries. (CRS 67)

30 December 1974   US Congress enacts Foreign Assistance Act of 1974 (PL 93–559) prohibiting all US government-sponsored training of foreign police officers in US or abroad. Act also recommends termination or suspension of aid to country that grossly violates internationally recognized human rights. (CRS 67)

1975–76   Congress passes series of measures that prohibit US economic, military aid, as well as US support of Inter-American Development Bank (IDB) assistance to any country "which engages in a consistent pattern of gross violations of internationally recognized human rights." (CRS 67)

February 1976   Amnesty International charges 22 persons have died as result of torture, and that Uruguay holds 5,000 to 6,000 political prisoners. (CRS 65)

June 1976   US State Department: "It is in our national interest to maintain good relations with Uruguay, in part because of the influence that Uruguay—in spite of its size—exerts in hemispheric and world affairs. Uruguay has been consistently friendly toward the United States." (CRS 66)

July–August 1976	US State Department concedes human rights violations are occurring in Uruguay, denies there is "consistent pattern of gross violation," maintains US diplomatic representations have prompted improvements by Uruguay. (CRS 68)
1 October 1976	US Congress accepts Koch amendment to Foreign Assistance and Related Programs Appropriations bill denying $3 million military aid to Uruguay in fiscal 1977, despite US State Department opposition. (CRS 67–68)
October 1976	Uruguay denounces military aid cut-off. (CRS 69)
21 December 1976	Uruguay reduces penalties for subversive crimes, releases some political prisoners. (CRS 69)
24 February 1977	US Secretary of State Cyrus Vance requests no new military aid, reduces economic aid to nominal $25,000 for Uruguay for fiscal 1978 because of human rights abuses. (CRS 69; *Keesing's* 28343)
March 1977	Uruguay rejects economic aid from US following reduction; says US actions are "an inadmissible intrusion into Uruguayan domestic affairs." Argentina takes similar action on same day. (CRS 69; *Facts on File* 142; *Keesing's* 29146)
July 1977	Congress freezes sale of police equipment to Uruguay, other countries. (*Keesing's* 29146)
1978	Relations between US, Uruguay improve slightly following visit to Uruguay by delegation of American Bar Association (ABA). Uruguayan junta publishes ABA recommendations along with reply that implicitly admits past abuses, promises to undertake to fulfill recommendations. (*Keesing's* 29146)
October 1979	Organization of American States (OAS) adopts resolution condemning human rights violations in Uruguay, Chile, Paraguay. However, in 1980, US allows Uruguay to purchase small military items on case-by-case basis, some on credit. (*Keesing's* 30139, 30278)
1 July 1981	Administration of President Ronald Reagan reverses policy of President Jimmy Carter, decides to vote for "international credit" to Uruguay citing State Department report that human rights situation there has improved. (*Facts on File* 553)
23 July 1981	Amnesty International disputes State Department report, asserts that human rights abuses in Uruguay have increased. (*Facts on File* 553)
25 November 1984	Military permits elections, although banning participation of two of three principal opposition leaders. Julio Sanguinetti of the centrist Colorado Party is elected as president, takes office on 1 March 1985 but must govern under military constitution for first year. (*Economist* [London], 1 December 1984, 50)

GOALS OF SENDER COUNTRY

Keesing's
US bans military aid to Uruguay "on the grounds that its government systematically violated human rights." (*Keesing's* 23217)

State Department report on Uruguay, submitted to Congress March 1977, finds "'no independent corroboration' of government claims to have taken disciplinary actions against authorities accused of arbitrary killing and torture; it added that the armed forces dominate the government, and that military courts tried cases of terrorism and subversion." (*Keesing's* 28344)

RESPONSE OF TARGET COUNTRY

Keesing's
Following US denial of military aid, "Institutional Act No. 5 was passed . . . recognizing the right of Uruguayan citizens to the protection of the state as a guarantee of human rights. The act also stated that subversion and terrorism had become commonplace in democratic states, representing a threat to individual and human rights which were traditionally protected only from attacks by the state, and that for this reason the state was forced to apply norms and methods to protect its people against individuals and organizations which undermined these rights in pursuit of their aims." (*Keesing's* 28217)

ECONOMIC IMPACT

Observed Economic Statistics

US aid to Uruguay (million dollars)

	Economic	*Military*
1972	10.1	6.8
1973	8.3	3.1
1974	0.9	5.5
1975	12.9	9.2
1976 + TQ†	0.7	3.7
1977	0.6	—
1978	0.2	—
1979	0.2	—
1980	—	—
1981	0.1	—
1982	0.8	—

— Zero or negligible.
† Transitional quarter: beginning of US fiscal year changed from June to October.
Source: AID.

Calculated Economic Impact

	Annual cost to target country
Reduction in US economic aid from average levels of 1972–76; welfare loss valued at 80 percent of reduced transfers.	$5 million
Reduction in US military aid from average levels of 1972–76; welfare loss valued at 90 percent of reduced transfers.	5 million
Total	$10 million

Relative Magnitudes

Gross indicators of Uruguayan economy	
Uruguayan GNP (1976)	$3.8 billion
Uruguayan population (1976)	2.8 million
Annual effect of sanctions related to gross indicators	
Percentage of GNP	0.3
Per capita	$3.57
Uruguayan trade with US as percentage of total trade	
Exports (1976)	11
Imports (1976)	9
Ratio of US GNP (1976: $1,718 billion) to Uruguayan GNP (1976: $3.8 billion)	452

ASSESSMENT

US State Department
"Antiterrorist activities during 1971–73, conducted with little regard for individual rights, resulted in the virtual elimination of the Tupamaros. Further security arrests in 1975–77 concentrated on Communists and Far-Left activists. The period from 1976 to 1979 was marked by the de facto suspension of the political rights of political leaders, restrictions on the freedom of expression and loss of an independent judiciary.

"In each year since 1978 there have been fewer violations of individual rights. . . .

"Following internal measures taken in 1979 to curb the use of torture, credible reports of physical brutality have continued to decline. . . .

"Since 1978 there have been no reported disappearances. . . ." (*Country Reports*)

AUTHORS' SUMMARY

Overall assessment	Assigned scores
☐ Policy result, scaled from 1 (failed) to 4 (success)	3
☐ Sanctions contribution, scaled from 1 (none) to 4 (significant)	2
☐ Success score (policy result *times* sanctions contribution), scaled from 1 (outright failure) to 16 (significant success)	6

Political and economic variables

☐ Companion policies: J (covert), Q (quasi-military), or R (regular military)	—
☐ International cooperation with sender, scaled from 1 (none) to 4 (significant)	1
☐ International assistance to target: A (if present)	—
☐ Sanctions period (years)	5
☐ Economic health and political stability of target, scaled from 1 (distressed) to 3 (strong)	2
☐ Presanction relations between sender and target, scaled from 1 (antagonistic) to 3 (cordial)	2
☐ Type of sanction: X (export), M (import), F (financial)	F, X
☐ Cost to sender, scaled from 1 (net gain) to 4 (major loss)	1

BIBLIOGRAPHY

Agency for International Development. *Overseas Loans and Grants.* Various issues.

Congressional Research Service (CRS), Library of Congress. 1977. *The Status of Human Rights in Selected Countries and the US Response.* Prepared for Subcommittee on International Organizations of the House Committee on International Relations. 95 Cong., 1 sess., 25 July. Washington.

Facts on File. 1977, 1981.

Keesing's Contemporary Archives. 1969–70, 1977, 1978, 1980.

US Department of State. 1982. *Country Reports on Human Rights Practices for 1981.* Report submitted to US House of Representatives, Committee on Foreign Affairs, and Senate Committee on Foreign Relations. 97 Cong., 2 sess., February. Washington.

Case 76–2   US v. Taiwan

(1976–77: Nuclear Reprocessing)

CHRONOLOGY OF KEY EVENTS

29 August 1976   "Knowledgeable" officials from US Arms Control and Disarmament Agency (ACDA) and Energy Research and Development Agency (ERDA) reveal existence of CIA reports asserting that Taiwan is secretly reprocessing spent fuel, possibly to make weapons-grade material. Spent fuel came either from Canadian-supplied reactor (which had been loosely safeguarded since Canada broke relations with Taiwan in 1970) or was purchased abroad (possibly from South Africa). ACDA officials reveal US has been stalling license application for two power reactors for Taiwan since January 1976, and a fuel shipment is being held up in order to "send a signal" to Taiwan to stop reprocessing. (*Washington Post*, 29 August 1976, A1)

5 September 1976   Taiwan asserts that reports reflect confusion over activities of "hot cell facility" in Taiwan. Taiwanese Prime Minister Chiang Ching-Kuo later pledges not to acquire reprocessing facilities. (*New York Times*, 5 September 1976, A5; 23 September 1976, A5)

Early 1977   Hot cell facility at Taiwan's Institute for Nuclear Energy Research is dismantled prior to visit of US inspection team, but team questions links between Nuclear Institute and Chungshen Institute for Science and Technology, military research entity. Findings of visit are not revealed but 40 megawatt research reactor is shut down, not restarted until mid-1978. (Yager 80)

GOALS OF SENDER COUNTRY

31 August 1976

Officials of administration of President Gerald R. Ford report that disclosure of intelligence reports is intended "as a warning to the Taipei Government" and that "the Ford Administration has repeatedly warned Taiwan not to reprocess uranium into plutonium over the last year." ACDA official is quoted as saying: "I don't like Taiwan reprocessing secretly or openly, large or small." (*New York Times*, 31 August 1976, A6; *Washington Post*, 29 August 1976, A1)

RESPONSE OF TARGET COUNTRY

31 August 1976
Victor Cheng, secretary general of Taiwan's Atomic Energy Council, denies secret reprocessing of spent fuel for possible weapons use; reaffirms Taiwan's adherence to Non-Proliferation Treaty (NPT). He says Taiwan does not have operational reprocessing facility but points out existence of small-scale research facility that potentially could have annual capacity of 15 grams of plutonium. (*New York Times*, 31 August 1976, A6)

5 September 1976
Cheng asserts that US reports reflect confusion over hot cell facility that was to have gone into operation in April, but has been delayed since US has not yet approved use of US-supplied fuel in it. Cheng also states that there is no other facility for reprocessing in Taiwan and hot cell "was designed purely for research, to study the fuel cycle." (US officials privately say hot cell facility is not source of present concern.) (*Washington Post*, 29 August 1976, A1; *New York Times*, 5 September 1976, A5)

17 September 1976
From diplomatic note to US from Taiwan: "The Government of the Republic of China has no intention whatsoever to develop nuclear weapons or a nuclear explosive device; or to engage in any activities related to reprocessing purposes." (*New York Times*, 23 September 1976, A5)

ECONOMIC IMPACT

Observed Economic Statistics

Nuclear exports to Taiwan were not cut off but export licenses were deliberately delayed. Affected licenses involved: two power reactors (boiling water type) with capacity of 604 megawatts each; one license for small amount of low-enriched uranium (LEU) for research reactor at Tsinghua University. Money involved probably was about $3 million to $5 million (authors' estimate). (*Washington Post*, 29 August 1976, A1; *New York Times*, 5 September 1976, 5)

Calculated Economic Impact

	Annual cost to target country
Delay in licensing nuclear fuel shipments to Taiwan, resulting in reduced output from nuclear power plants; welfare loss estimated at 10 percent of value of annual production.	$16 million
Delay in license for research reactor at Tsinghua University; welfare loss estimated at 30 percent of value of reduced shipments.	1 million
Total	$17 million

Relative Magnitudes

Gross indicators of Taiwanese economy	
Taiwanese GNP (1976)	$17.2 billion
Taiwanese population (1976)	16.8 million

Annual effect of sanctions related to gross indicators
Percentage of GNP	0.1
Per capita	$1.01

Taiwan trade with US as percentage of total trade
Exports (1976)	41
Imports (1976)	22

Ratio of US GNP (1976: $1,718 billion) to Taiwanese GNP (1976: $17.2 billion)	100

ASSESSMENT

Assistant Secretary of State Arthur Hummel, Jr.
". . . we are, in a practical sense, Taiwan's only source of reactors and enriched uranium fuel for its nuclear power program. This reduces the problems of coordination with other suppliers and increases Taiwan's dependence on a cooperative US attitude in order to maintain its nuclear power program." (*Department of State Bulletin*, 11 October 1976, 454)

AUTHORS' SUMMARY

Overall assessment	*Assigned scores*
☐ Policy result, scaled from 1 (failed) to 4 (success)	4
☐ Sanctions contribution, scaled from 1 (none) to 4 (significant)	4
☐ Success score (policy result *times* sanctions contribution), scaled from 1 (outright failure) to 16 (significant success)	16

Political and economic variables

☐ Companion policies: J (covert), Q (quasi-military), or R (regular military)	—
☐ International cooperation with sender, scaled from 1 (none) to 4 (significant)	1
☐ International assistance to target: A (if present)	—
☐ Sanctions period (years)	1
☐ Economic health and political stability of target, scaled from 1 (distressed) to 3 (strong)	3
☐ Presanction relations between sender and target, scaled from 1 (antagonistic) to 3 (cordial)	3
☐ Type of sanction: X (export), M (import), F (financial)	X
☐ Cost to sender, scaled from 1 (net gain) to 4 (major loss)	2

BIBLIOGRAPHY

Yager, Joseph A., ed. 1980. *Nonproliferation and U.S. Foreign Policy*. Washington: Brookings Institution.

Case 76–3   US v. Ethiopia

(1976–   : Expropriation; Human Rights)

CHRONOLOGY OF KEY EVENTS

1953–76	US leases Kagnew Communications Center, at its peak manned by 4,000 American military personnel, for satellite tracking, monitoring Soviet missile tests. During this period, US provides $606 million in military, economic aid to Ethiopia. (Nelson 259)
12 September 1974	Emperor Haile Selassie dethroned; Provisional Military Administrative Council (PMAC) assumes control. (Nelson 50)
23 November 1974	General Aman, chairman of PMAC, numerous other leaders killed in power struggle; General Teferi becomes chairman. (Nelson 51)
January– February 1975	PMAC nationalizes all banks, 72 industrial and commercial firms; however, wholesale, retail, import-export trade remain in private hands. (Nelson 52)
March–July 1975	PMAC nationalizes all rural land, limits holdings to 10 hectares per family. Subsequently, PMAC nationalizes all urban land, apartments. (Nelson 51)
Early 1976	US refuses to supply $60 million in ammunition to support Eritrean campaigns, disagrees with Ethiopia over Foreign Military Sales (FMS) credit terms. (Nelson 221)
May 1976	Lieutenant Colonel Mengistu, member of ruling council, opens military procurement talks with USSR, signs equipment agreement in December 1977; USSR endorses PMAC approach to Eritrean battle. (Nelson 55, 221)
August 1976	US Assistant Secretary of State for African Affairs William Schaufele describes PMAC as "unstable, prone to violations of human rights, incapable of managing Ethiopia's deteriorating economy, and beset by insurgencies and incipient insurgencies." (Nelson 221)
31 December 1976	Ethiopia refuses to make future repayments on 1974, 1975 FMS agreements. (Nelson 222)

3 February 1977	Lieutenant Colonel Mengistu kills his chief rival, General Teferi, other associates, assumes power, inaugurates Red Terror. Later in 1977, Amnesty International declares that, since 1974, "there has developed a consistent pattern of widespread gross human rights violations." Subsequent estimates place death toll from Red Terror of 1977–78 at 30,000. (Nelson 54–55, 286)
February 1977	Secretary of State Cyrus Vance testifies that US will terminate all military grants to Ethiopia because of gross, persistent human rights violations but recommends that $10 million in military credits, $13.9 million in military assistance be continued. Vance's statement is seen in Ethiopia as direct attack on Mengistu. US further informs Ethiopia that Kagnew Communications Center will be closed by 30 September 1977. (Nelson 222, 261; *Facts on File* 142)
23 April 1977	Ethiopia closes US military mission, four other US offices in Ethiopia. (*Facts on File* 327)
6 May 1977	Ethiopia signs treaty of cooperation and friendship with USSR. (*Facts on File* 390)
July 1977	US House of Representatives omits Ethiopia from foreign military aid bill, thereby denying military credits as well as grants. President Jimmy Carter signs bill 1 November 1977. (*Facts on File* 815, 834)
14 January 1978	Ethiopia threatens to break relations with US for giving verbal support to Somalia. However, in February 1978 agreement is reached on a new US Ambassador to Ethiopia, Frederic L. Chapin, and on shipment of trucks and parts already paid for by Ethiopia. (Nelson 224)
February–March 1978	Ethiopia, assisted by Cuban, South Yemen, East German, Soviet military personnel, wages successful Ogaden counteroffensive against Somalia; Somalia withdraws all troops from Ogaden on 9 March 1978, but continues guerrilla tactics. (Nelson 224)
July 1978	US Ambassador Chapin offers economic assistance to Ethiopia provided progress could be made on compensation for expropriated US property. No progress is made, and its absence subsequently triggers economic sanctions under US law. (Nelson 224)
February 1979	Brooke amendment, which allows termination of aid to countries in default of required payments for more than a year, is invoked because of Ethiopian default on FMS debts; all new economic assistance projects are terminated. (Nelson 222)
July 1979	Hickenlooper amendment, which bars aid to countries expropriating US property, is invoked, US bilateral aid is phased out; however, humanitarian aid of $31.5 million is continued in FY 1979. González amendment, allowing Hickenlooper amendment to be applied to loan requests is invoked; US votes against loans to Ethiopia in multilateral development banks (MDBs). (Nelson 224–25)

1979   US withdraws Generalized System of Preferences (GSP) privileges from Ethiopia. (Nelson 225)

July 1980   Ethiopia demands recall of US Ambassador Chapin. (*Facts on File* 661)

Fall 1984   As drought in Ethiopia worsens and publicity increases, Western countries pledge over 300,000 tons of food aid. US is "by far the largest donor" but continues to be prohibited by the Hickenlooper amendment from engaging in "food-for-work" or other programs which might be construed as developmental. (*Washington Post*, 31 December 1984, A1)

GOALS OF SENDER COUNTRY

Harold D. Nelson, Irving Kaplan
"The United States government [in 1976] was particularly concerned about human rights and Ethiopia's failure to compensate American citizens and corporations for property seized since 1975. The United States abstained in several votes in international lending organizations to demonstrate the concern." (Nelson 221)

RESPONSE OF TARGET COUNTRY

April 1977
Upon closing four US agencies, government of Ethiopia states: "The existence of an American Military Assistance Advisory Group is useless at a time when the American government takes every opportunity to create hatred against revolutionary Ethiopia by depicting her as a country in which human rights are violated." (Nelson 222)

April–May 1977
Ethiopia abrogates 1953 Mutual Defense Assistance Agreement; US withholds $75 million of military equipment for which Ethiopia already has paid $12 million; Ethiopia expels US military attachés, cuts US Embassy staff by half. Ethiopia turns to USSR, allies for military assistance. (Nelson 223, 260–63)

ATTITUDE OF OTHER COUNTRIES

Soviet Union
In December 1976, Mengistu leads PMAC delegation to Moscow; signs arms agreement for $385 million. (Nelson 260)

Over period 1977–80, USSR provides massive military assistance, totaling about $1 billion by mid-1980; cumulative debt related to military purchases from USSR reaches $1.7 billion, payable over 10 years at 2 percent interest; plus $300 million for common use items (trucks, cranes). USSR, Ethiopia sign 20-year treaty of friendship and cooperation; USSR gains access to Eritrean ports for Indian Ocean, Red Sea operations. In 1980, 1,000 Soviet military personnel are reported in Ethiopia. (Nelson 262–63)

Cuba
In May 1977, Cuba sends small contingent of military advisers to Ethiopia; by Spring 1978, number reaches 17,000, is at 13,000–15,000 in 1980. (Nelson 262)

United Kingdom
In March 1978, Foreign Minister David Owen tells Ethiopian ambassador that Soviet, Cuban presence in Ethiopia threatens world peace. (Nelson 226)

West Germany
In 1978, Ethiopia asks West German ambassador to leave following FRG extension of aid to Somalia. (Nelson 226)

China
Mengistu includes China among "thirteen reactionary countries" that had "directly or indirectly launched a concerted assault against us." (Nelson 228)

East Germany
Ethiopia, GDR sign military aid agreement; about 400 East German military advisers are provided. (Nelson 263)

ECONOMIC IMPACT

Observed Economic Statistics

US economic aid to Ethiopia: $15.9 million in 1979 (of which $12.6 million is PL 480); $15 million in 1980 (all PL 480); $5 million in 1981 (all PL 480). (AID)

Calculated Economic Impact

	Annual cost to target country
Suspension of US military assistance; welfare loss estimated at 90 percent of reduced transfers.	$57 million
Suspension of US economic aid (excluding PL 480); welfare loss estimated at 90 percent of reduced transfers.	3 million
Suspension of tariff preferences for Ethiopian exports to US; welfare loss estimated at 10 percent of value of US imports from Ethiopia.	10 million
Offsets	
USSR military aid 1977–80; welfare gain estimated at 80 percent of transfers.	($200 million)
Concessional loans from USSR for military purchases; welfare gain estimated at 60 percent of interest subsidy on loans.	(30 million)
Total (gain)	($160 million)

Relative Magnitudes

Gross indicators of Ethiopian economy	
Ethiopian GNP (1976)	$2.9 billion
Ethiopian population (1976)	28.2 million
Annual effect of sanctions related to gross indicators	
Percentage of GNP (gain)	(5.5)
Per capita (gain)	($5.67)
Ethiopian trade with US as percentage of total trade	
Exports (1976)	33
Imports (1976)	10
Ratio of US GNP (1976: $1,718 billion) to Ethiopian GNP (1976: $2.9 billion)	592

AUTHORS' SUMMARY

Overall assessment	Assigned scores
☐ Policy result, scaled from 1 (failed) to 4 (success)	1
☐ Sanctions contribution, scaled from 1 (none) to 4 (significant)	1
☐ Success score (policy result *times* sanctions contribution), scaled from 1 (outright failure) to 16 (significant success)	1

Political and economic variables

☐ Companion policies: J (covert), Q (quasi-military), or R (regular military)	—
☐ International cooperation with sender, scaled from 1 (none) to 4 (significant)	2
☐ International assistance to target: A (if present)	A
☐ Sanctions period (years)	8+
☐ Economic health and political stability of target, scaled from 1 (distressed) to 3 (strong)	1
☐ Presanction relations between sender and target, scaled from 1 (antagonistic) to 3 (cordial)	2
☐ Type of sanction: X (export), M (import), F (financial)	F, M
☐ Cost to sender, scaled from 1 (net gain) to 4 (major loss)	1

Comments

Soviet bloc aid to Ethiopia more than offset the economic impact of US sanctions. Thus, sanctions did little to promote American goals.

BIBLIOGRAPHY

Agency for International Development. *Overseas Loans and Grants.* Various issues.
Facts on File. 1977, 1980.
Nelson, Harold D., and Irving Kaplan, eds. 1981. *Ethiopia: A Country Study.* American
University Area Handbook Series. Washington: GPO.

Case 77–1   US v. Paraguay
(1977–81: Human Rights)

CHRONOLOGY OF KEY EVENTS

1954   President Alfredo Stroessner, Colorado party gain power through coup d'état; Stroessner continues tradition, established in 1929, of imposing "state of siege" that permits suspension of constitutional guarantees. (CRS 37)

March 1974   Inter-American Human Rights Commission hears charges that government of Paraguay is committing acts of genocide against Ache Indians. In August 1975, commission report concludes government is not engaged in campaign against the Ache but that private citizens may have committed abuses. (CRS 42)

December 1974   Stroessner inaugurates wave of repression following discovery of assassination plot against him. Two hundred persons are arrested immediately; others, many of whom are alleged Communists, are arrested in December 1975; members of alleged guerrilla networks are arrested in March–May 1976. International League for Human Rights alleges that arrests in all three episodes total 500 to 1,500 persons. US State Department estimates 400 are held as political prisoners. (CRS 39–40)

December 1975   Paraguayan government halts Project Marandu, devoted to protecting interests of Ache Indians; arrests, tortures director, senior staff. In February 1976, US Assistant Secretary of State Robert J. McCloskey asserts that Project Marandu is "an exclusive Paraguayan responsibility." (CRS 41–43)

12 June 1976   Paraguayan Catholic Church asserts government is responsible for "the revival of the practice of torture." (CRS 40)

1977   Congress eliminates military aid to Paraguay. (Cohen 255)

January–   Paraguay releases some political prisoners. (CRS 43)
February 1977

17 August 1977   Terence Todman, US assistant secretary of state for inter-American affairs, comments on visit to Paraguay that he is pleased with progress in human rights there. However, relations cool next year following arrest of opposition leader who spoke out in US and at OAS meeting about human rights violations in Paraguay, and called on US to cut off economic aid. (*Keesing's* 28763, 29255; *Facts on File* 559)

1978–79   US vetoes or abstains on human rights grounds in votes on seven loans for Paraguay from multilateral development banks. Most of $141.6 million of loans are for highway projects. "[W]hile no loans were formally denied because of opposition from the United States, the Carter administration policy served to deter loan applications by Latin America's most repressive governments." (Schoultz 297, 299)

1 July 1981   Administration of President Ronald Reagan reverses policy of former President Jimmy Carter, decides to vote for international credit to Paraguay, citing State Department report that human rights situation there has improved. (*Facts on File* 553)

23 July 1981   Amnesty International disputes State Department report, asserts that human rights abuses have increased in Paraguay. (*Facts on File* 553)

GOALS OF SENDER COUNTRY

Assistant Secretary of State Terence Todman
In August 1977 reporting on trip to Paraguay (as well as Chile, Argentina, Uruguay): "They are coming to realize that they have to move toward greater liberalization of their regimes and provide more opportunities to participate in the governmental process." (*New York Times*, 26 August 1977, A9)

RESPONSE OF TARGET COUNTRY

President Alfredo Stroessner
During Todman's visit to Paraguay in August 1977, Stroessner insists that "individual rights were respected and that 'peace and tranquility' had prevailed during his 23 years in power." (*New York Times*, 18 August 1977, A14)

ECONOMIC IMPACT

Observed Economic Statistics

US aid to Paraguay (million dollars)

	Economic	Military
1972	4.9	2.6
1973	7.3	1.9
1974	5.8	2.4
1975	8.0	1.6

US aid to Paraguay *(continued)*

	Economic	Military
1976 + TQ†	6.8	3.3
1977	3.2	0.7
1978	3.5	0.6
1979	10.3	—
1980	3.6	—
1981	6.2	—
1982	3.8	—

— Zero or negligible.
† Transitional quarter: beginning of US fiscal year changed from June to October.
Source: AID.

Calculated Economic Impact

	Annual cost to target country
Reduction in US military aid; welfare loss estimated at 90 percent of average transfers from 1972–76.	$2 million

Relative Magnitudes

Gross indicators of Paraguayan economy	
Paraguayan GNP (1977)	$2 billion
Paraguayan population (1977)	2.8 million
Annual effect of sanctions related to gross indicators	
Percentage of GNP	0.1
Per capita	$0.71
Paraguayan trade with US as percentage of total trade	
Exports (1977)	14
Imports (1977)	12
Ratio of US GNP (1977: $1,918 billion) to Paraguayan GNP (1977: $2 billion)	959

ASSESSMENT

Congressional Research Service
"Human rights activists in Paraguay credit Carter's human rights policy for any softening on political prisoners by the Government." (CRS 43)

AUTHORS' SUMMARY

Overall assessment	Assigned scores
☐ Policy result, scaled from 1 (failed) to 4 (success)	2
☐ Sanctions contribution, scaled from 1 (none) to 4 (significant)	3
☐ Success score (policy result *times* sanctions contribution), scaled from 1 (outright failure) to 16 (significant success)	6

Political and economic variables

☐ Companion policies: J (covert), Q (quasi-military), or R (regular military)	—
☐ International cooperation with sender, scaled from 1 (none) to 4 (significant)	1
☐ International assistance to target: A (if present)	—
☐ Sanctions period (years)	4
☐ Economic health and political stability of target, scaled from 1 (distressed) to 3 (strong)	3
☐ Presanction relations between sender and target, scaled from 1 (antagonistic) to 3 (cordial)	2
☐ Type of sanction: X (export), M (import), F (financial)	F
☐ Cost to sender, scaled from 1 (net gain) to 4 (major loss)	1

BIBLIOGRAPHY

Agency for International Development. *Overseas Loans and Grants.* Various issues.

Congressional Research Service (CRS), Library of Congress. 1977. *The Status of Human Rights in Selected Countries and the US Response.* Prepared for Subcommittee on International Organizations of the House Committee on International Relations. 95 Cong., 1 sess. Washington.

Facts on File. 1977, 1981.

Keesing's Contemporary Archives. 1978.

Schoultz, Lars. 1981. *Human Rights and United States Policy Toward Latin America.* Princeton, NJ: Princeton University Press.

Case 77–2 US v. Guatemala

(1977– : Human Rights)

CHRONOLOGY OF KEY EVENTS

1977	In response to perceived violations of human rights, President Jimmy Carter blocks World Bank and Inter-American Development Bank (IDB) loans to Guatemala. (*New York Times*, 10 October 1982, 17)
March 1977	Guatemala rejects US military aid following publication by State Department of reports criticizing human rights violations in many Latin American countries. No military aid is authorized for Guatemala in subsequent years. (*Keesing's* 28343)
1978	Human rights situation in Guatemala leads Carter to ban further sale of military equipment through Pentagon's foreign military sales program, even though Guatemala had already rejected future US military assistance. (*New York Times*, 8 January 1983, A1)
June 1979	Carter designates Frank Ortiz as ambassador to Guatemala. Ortiz is removed 11 months later because he is perceived to be too close to government of President Fernando Romeo Lucas García, which was installed in 1978. (Anderson 46)
1980	Amnesty International reports 2,000 persons a year are being killed, by both right and left, in Guatemala. Jesuits there charge "that the level of repression was as high as it had ever been in the history of the country." Carter bans all military sales to Guatemala. (Anderson 35, 46; *New York Times*, 8 January 1983, A1)
23 March 1982	General Efraín Rios Montt becomes president of Guatemala. (*Keesing's* 31607)
8 October 1982	Amnesty International charges Guatemalan forces have "massacred more than 2,600 Indians and peasants since General Rios Montt came to power." (*New York Times*, 10 October 1982, A17)
10 October 1982	Administration of President Ronald Reagan finds "a commitment to positive change and new opportunity in Guatemala" and "improvements in the human rights situation." As result, six World Bank and

IDB loans, totaling $170 million, are unblocked. (*New York Times*, 10 October 1982, A17)

7 *January 1983*   Reagan administration lifts embargo on arms sales to Guatemala, citing "significant steps" to end human rights abuses. This would permit Guatemala to purchase $6.3 million of spare parts, other equipment for its air force. Congressman Michael Barnes (D–Md.) characterizes decision as "most unfortunate." (*New York Times*, 8 January 1983, A1)

March 1983   Reagan administration recalls its Ambassador to Guatemala, Frederic L. Chapin, defers $10 million in economic aid following murder by member of Guatemala's armed forces of a Guatemalan linguist working on project for the US Agency for International Development (AID). (*New York Times*, 11 September 1983, A1)

7 *March 1983*   Pope John Paul II calls for end to "flagrant injustices" in Guatemala. (*Washington Post*, 8 March 1983, A1)

18 *May 1983*   Excessive brutalities are reported by Guatemalan refugees in Mexico. For example: "They killed my wife with a bullet between the eyes while she was nursing our baby. Then they killed the baby." (*Wall Street Journal*, 18 May 1983, 1)

August 1983   Brigadier General Oscar Mejia Victores ousts Rios Montt, possibly with US knowledge, acquiescence. (*New York Times*, 13 August 1983, A3)

Early November 1983   Second Guatemalan AID-supported linguist dies in suspicious circumstances; another disappears. On 12 November, US Congress votes down resolution that would have authorized $13.5 million in economic aid to Guatemala. (*Washington Post*, 11 November 1983, A22; 28 November 1983, A1)

29 *November 1983*   Reagan administration officials reveal that previously approved sale of spare helicopter parts is being delayed because of "resurgence of human rights violations in Guatemala." (*Washington Post*, 29 November 1983, A2)

1 *July 1984*   Guatemala holds elections for constituent assembly that will draft constitution and electoral law for voting on civilian president in 1985. Reagan administration hails elections as sign that Mejia intends to keep his promise to restore democracy. In addition, administration officials hope elections will improve chances for congressional approval of $10 million aid request for Guatemala for 1985. (*Washington Post*, 2 July 1984, A13)

4 *February 1985*   Reagan budget for FY 1986 includes $35.3 million in military assistance for Guatemala. Administration justifies request by pointing out that military regime has promised elections which could result in civilian government by 1 October. Senator Christopher J. Dodd (D–Conn.) calls request "exorbitant, excessive and not justified by

GOALS OF SENDER COUNTRY

Thomas P. Anderson
"With the number of political killings reaching 20 a day by mid-July 1980, the Carter Administration, with the situation in El Salvador and Nicaragua also in mind, had decided that supporting the Lucas government was not in the best interest of the United States. . . . George Landau, the former ambassador to Chile who had raised a storm over human rights violations in that country and over Chile's failure to prosecute the murderers of [Orlando] Letelier [in US], was to be given [Ortiz's] post. This was clearly designed to raise the hackles of the Guatemalan government, and did so." (Anderson 46)

State Department spokesman John Hughes
January 1983: "While we want to see further progress in Guatemala in promoting respect for human rights, President Rios Montt has taken significant steps in this area. Progress has been made." (*New York Times*, 8 January 1983, A1)

RESPONSE OF TARGET COUNTRY

Richard E. Feinberg
"It was in response to the human rights policy in general, more than in opposition to any bilateral slight, that the governments of Guatemala and El Salvador rejected U.S. security assistance in 1977." (Feinberg 61)

Thomas P. Anderson
Following change in ambassadors: "President Lucas publicly announced that he hoped for a Reagan victory in the November 1980 presidential election and refused to accept Landau's appointment. When Reagan did indeed win, there was general rejoicing among Lucas' circle, and an assumption that military aid would be restored." (Anderson 46)

ECONOMIC IMPACT

Observed Economic Statistics

US aid to Guatemala (million dollars)

	Economic	Military
1972	16.6	2.2
1973	12.0	4.0
1974	4.7	2.4
1975	14.1	2.9
1976 + TQ†	47.9	2.2
1977	20.8	0.5
1978	10.6	—

US aid to Guatemala (*continued*)

	Economic	Military
1979	24.7	—
1980	13.0	—
1981	19.0	—
1982	15.5	—

— Zero or negligible.
† Transitional quarter: beginning of US fiscal year changed from June to October.
Source: AID.

"One important source of political stability in Guatemala has been the surprising resilience of the economy, occurring despite the political turmoil and massive capital flight. The debt situation was the best of any Latin American state. The real growth rate of the economy was 4.5 percent in 1979 and 3.5 percent in 1980. . . ." (Anderson 56)

"Despite the capital flight, there was still some private investment in 1980 . . . toward the end of the year. The government was increasingly able to obtain loans from such agencies as the Inter-American Development Bank, one instance being a $51 million loan for a hospital-building program." (Anderson 57)

After US military aid cut-off in 1977, Israel reportedly provides $90 million cumulative military assistance as of March 1982. (*Keesing's* 31604)

Calculated Economic Impact

	Annual cost to target country
Suspension of US military aid ($2.6 million), and blocking of multilateral development loans (estimated at $34 million/year) to Guatemala; welfare loss estimated at 80 percent of the value of the reduced transfers.	$29 million
Reduction in US economic aid; welfare loss estimated at 90 percent of value of reduced transfers.	8 million
Offset	
Increase in military aid from Israel; welfare gain valued at 90 percent of transfers.	($16 million)
Total	$21 million

Relative Magnitudes

Gross indicators of Guatemalan economy	
Guatemalan GNP (1977)	$5.4 billion
Guatemalan population (1977)	6.63 million

Annual effect of sanctions related to gross indicators

Percentage of GNP	0.4
Per capita	$3.17

Guatemalan trade with US as percentage of total trade

Exports (1977)	37
Imports (1977)	36

Ratio of US GNP (1977: $1,918 billion) to Guatemalan GNP (1977: $5.4 billion)	355

ASSESSMENT

State Department 1979 report on human rights
". . . the overall level of both political violence and human rights violations remained lower than during the decade prior to 1976. . . ." However, it cites continuing grim statistics: "Deaths which appeared to have political overtones averaged about twenty each month;. . . anticriminal 'death squad' killings . . . average about forty per month." (Schoultz 352–53)

Richard E. Feinberg
"Many [in the Guatemalan government and military] blamed the turmoil in Nicaragua and El Salvador on 'destabilizing' U.S. human rights policies. With a firm hold on the reins of government, a strong balance of payments, and access to alternative sources of weaponry, the Guatemalan government felt no need to sacrifice its perceived security interests to appease the United States." (Feinberg 64)

AUTHORS' SUMMARY

Overall assessment	Assigned scores
☐ Policy result, scaled from 1 (failed) to 4 (success)	2
☐ Sanctions contribution, scaled from 1 (none) to 4 (significant)	2
☐ Success score (policy result *times* sanctions contribution), scaled from 1 (outright failure) to 16 (significant success)	4

Political and economic variables

☐ Companion policies: J (covert), Q (quasi-military), or R (regular military)	—
☐ International cooperation with sender, scaled from 1 (none) to 4 (significant)	1
☐ International assistance to target: A (if present)	A
☐ Sanctions period (years)	7 +
☐ Economic health and political stability of target, scaled from 1 (distressed) to 3 (strong)	2

Political and economic variables (continued)	*Assigned scores*
☐ Presanction relations between sender and target, scaled from 1 (antagonistic) to 3 (cordial)	2
☐ Type of sanction: X (export), M (import), F (financial)	F
☐ Cost to sender, scaled from 1 (net gain) to 4 (major loss)	1

BIBLIOGRAPHY

Agency for International Development. *Overseas Loans and Grants.* Various issues.

Anderson, Thomas P. 1982. *Politics in Central America.* New York: Praeger.

Feinberg, Richard E., ed. 1982. *Central America: International Dimensions of the Crisis.* New York: Holmes & Meier.

Keesing's Contemporary Archives. 1977, 1982.

Schoultz, Lars. 1981. *Human Rights and United States Policy Toward Latin America.* Princeton, NJ: Princeton University Press.

Case 77–3   US v. Argentina

(1977–83: Human Rights)

CHRONOLOGY OF KEY EVENTS

February 1977   Administration of President Jimmy Carter announces reductions in aid to Argentina, Uruguay, Ethiopia because of human rights considerations. Argentine share is pared from $36 million to $15 million for military aid in FY 1978. Argentina rejects all military aid from US with strings attached. (Lillich 853; *Keesing's* 28343)

July 1977   US Export–Import Bank refuses to authorize $270 million loan to Argentina after consultation with State Department "until the administration reported an improvement in the human rights situation in Argentina." Loan was to be for purchase of electrical equipment from Allis-Chalmers for hydroelectric project on Parcina River. US freezes sale of police equipment to Argentina. (*Keesing's* 29146; Lillich 853)

29 September 1978   Defense Department suspends consideration of 212 pending license requests for $100 million in US military equipment, citing human rights reasons. In preceding months, however, exceptions had been made for $120 million in military sales to Argentina. (Lillich 857–62)

November 1978   Carter administration, reportedly on president's personal orders, reverses itself on Eximbank loan to Argentina for electrical equipment. "Human rights activists here, who keep track of arrests, releases of prisoners, disappearances, and judicial moves to protect detained persons, say that there has been a limited improvement in recent months." (Lillich 863)

1979   Amnesty International, despite release of many of those detained, still could find "no significant improvement in human rights." (Schoultz 348)

September 1981   US Senate votes to repeal 1978 ban on arms sales, aid to Argentina pending presidential certification that human rights have improved. (*Washington Post*, 23 October 1981, A1)

Following election of Raúl Alfonsín, State Department announces that President Ronald Reagan, to mark inauguration of first civilian government in Argentina in nearly decade, will certify to Congress that human rights situation in Argentina has improved. Certification will make Argentina eligible for renewed military assistance but officials stressed requests would be reviewed on case-by-case basis. (*Washington Post*, 9 December 1983, A1)

GOALS OF SENDER COUNTRY

Keesing's
State Department report on human rights in Argentina concludes that "'the rights of life, liberty and security of person are violated regularly by terrorists at both ends of the political spectrum' but that right-wing violence was carried out by squads 'operating with apparent immunity.'" (*Keesing's* 28344)

Washington Post
"US military ties with Argentina were broken . . . after charges that the Argentine military was responsible for the murder or disappearance of thousands of suspected leftists. Congress then specified that aid could not be resumed unless the president certified that Argentina was making human-rights improvements, including accounting for those who had disappeared." (*Washington Post*, 9 December 1983, A34)

RESPONSE OF TARGET COUNTRY

February 1977
Following reduction in aid "[T]he Argentinian Foreign Ministry condemned the US move on February 28, accusing the United States of interfering in the country's internal affairs, 'ignorance of Argentinian reality' and trying to set itself up as an 'international court of justice.'" (*Keesing's* 28343)

ECONOMIC IMPACT

Observed Economic Statistics

US aid to Argentina (million dollars)

	Economic	*Military*
1972	—	20.6
1973	—	12.1
1974	—	23.0
1975	0.1	30.1
1976 + TQ†	—	34.4
1977	0.1	0.7
1978	—	—

US aid to Argentina (*continued*)

	Economic	Military
1979	0.1	—
1980	—	—
1981	—	—

— Zero or negligible.
† Transitional quarter: beginning of US fiscal year changed from June to October.
Source: AID.

Calculated Economic Impact

	Annual cost to target country
Reduction in military aid from US; welfare loss valued at 90 percent of reduced transfers.	$22 million
Suspension of Eximbank loan for electrical equipment for 16 months; welfare loss estimated at 10 percent of face value of loan.	20 million
Reduction in imports of US military equipment; welfare loss estimated at 20 percent of trade.	20 million
Total	$62 million

Relative Magnitudes

Gross indicators of Argentine economy	
Argentine GNP (1977)	$49.9 billion
Argentine population (1977)	26.06 million
Annual effect of sanctions related to gross indicators	
Percentage of GNP	0.1
Per capita	$2.38
Argentine trade with US as percentage of total trade	
Exports (1977)	7
Imports (1977)	19
Ratio of US GNP (1977: $1,918 billion) to Argentine GNP (1977: $49.9 billion)	38

AUTHORS' SUMMARY

Overall assessment	Assigned scores
☐ Policy result, scaled from 1 (failed) to 4 (success)	3
☐ Sanctions contribution, scaled from 1 (none) to 4 (significant)	2
☐ Success score (policy result *times* sanctions contribution), scaled from 1 (outright failure) to 16 (significant success)	6

Political and economic variables

☐ Companion policies: J (covert), Q (quasi-military), or R (regular military)	—
☐ International cooperation with sender, scaled from 1 (none) to 4 (significant)	1
☐ International assistance to target: A (if present)	—
☐ Sanctions period (years)	6
☐ Economic health and political stability of target, scaled from 1 (distressed) to 3 (strong)	2
☐ Presanction relations between sender and target, scaled from 1 (antagonistic) to 3 (cordial)	2
☐ Type of sanction: X (export), M (import), F (financial)	F, X
☐ Cost to sender, scaled from 1 (net gain) to 4 (major loss)	2

Comments

Human rights in Argentina improved somewhat in later years of military rule and significantly since election of Alfonsín. US sanctions, however, seem to have played little role in the improvement.

BIBLIOGRAPHY

Agency for International Development. *Overseas Loans and Grants*. Various issues.

Lillich, Richard B., and Frank C. Newman. 1979. *International Human Rights: Problems of Law and Policy*. Boston: Little, Brown & Co.

Schoultz, Lars. 1981. *Human Rights and United States Policy Toward Latin America*. Princeton, NJ: Princeton University Press.

US Department of State. 1982. *Country Reports on Human Rights Practices for 1981*. Report submitted to US House of Representatives, Committee on Foreign Affairs, and Senate Committee on Foreign Relations. 97 Cong., 2 sess., February. Washington.

Case 77–4   Canada v. Japan and EC

(1977–78: Nuclear Safeguards)

CHRONOLOGY OF KEY EVENTS

22 December 1976   Canada announces that, as "London Club" of nuclear fuel and technology suppliers has been unable to agree on more restrictive nuclear exports policy, it is unilaterally "intensify[ing] its nuclear exports and safeguards policy." (*Keesing's* 28303)

1 January 1977   Canada suspends uranium shipments to Japan, European Community (EC) pending renegotiation of safeguards arrangements there, particularly as regards reprocessing. (*Keesing's* 28596; Pringsheim 24; Goverment of Canada 14)

11–12 July 1977   After meeting with Canadian Prime Minister Pierre Trudeau, German Chancellor Helmut Schmidt announces that Canadian government has accepted idea of "interim arrangement for the supply of nuclear fuel to the EC." (*Keesing's* 28596)

16 January 1978   EC, Canada negotiate three-year agreement on supply of uranium, safeguards. First deliveries are arranged for 2,500 tons and 500 tons for UK, Germany respectively. (*Keesing's* 28962)

Japan, Canada also conclude bilateral safeguards agreement; uranium shipments proceed. (Pringsheim 24; Government of Canada 14)

10 August 1979   Japanese atomic energy commission decides not to import CANDU (Canadian-built natural uranium) reactor system, choosing instead US light water reactor systems and Japanese advanced thermal reactor, fueled by mixture of uranium and plutonium. (Pringsheim 24)

September 1980   Canada, Japan ratify bilateral safeguards agreement. (Government of Canada 14)

GOALS OF SENDER COUNTRY

Canadian News Facts
Because Japan has ratified Non-Proliferation Treaty (NPT), its nuclear program already is under comprehensive International Atomic Energy Agency (IAEA) safeguards program. However, Canada wants veto rights over retransfer or reprocessing of Canadian-supplied nuclear technology or materials.

"Canada suspended uranium shipments to the EEC January 1, 1977, because the Community had not accepted Canadian safeguards against using nuclear material for explosive purposes."

In addition to full-scope safeguards, Canada also wanted assurances that Canadian-supplied fuel would not be used in France's military nuclear program, and that France would accept safeguards on civilian power program. France was major obstacle in reaching agreement because it is not NPT signatory. (*Canadian News Facts* 1878, 1893–94, 1999)

ECONOMIC IMPACT

Observed Economic Statistics

Canada supplies approximately 31 percent of Japan's needs for uranium, costing $250 million per year. Prior to embargo, Canada had supplied 70 percent. Uranium is shipped to US, then enriched and re-exported to Japan. (Pringsheim 22; *Keesing's* 28962)

Of EC members, UK and FRG are reported most dependent on Canadian fuel supplies, with FRG importing 1,500 tons/year, 40 percent of its requirements. (*Keesing's* 28596)

Prior to embargo, Canada had supplied about one-third of Community's annual requirement of 9,000 tons of uranium. (*Keesing's* 28962)

Calculated Economic Impact

	Annual cost to target country
Suspension of Canadian shipments of uranium to Japan; welfare loss valued at 30 percent of trade.	$75 million
Suspension of Canadian shipments of uranium to EC; welfare loss valued at 30 percent of trade.	$40 million

Relative Magnitudes

Gross indicators of Japanese economy	
Japanese GNP (1977)	$687 billion
Japanese population (1977)	114 million

Annual effect of sanctions related to gross indicators	
Percentage of GNP	negl.
Per capita	$0.66
Japanese trade with Canada as percentage of total trade	
Exports (1977)	2
Imports (1977)	4
Ratio of Canadian GNP (1977: $196 billion) to Japanese GNP (1977: $687 billion)	0.3

Gross indicators of EC economy	
EC GNP (1977)	$1,604 billion
EC population (1977)	259 million
Annual effect of sanctions related to gross indicators	
Percentage of GNP	negl.
Per capita	$0.15
EC trade with Canada as percentage of total trade	
Exports (1977)	1
Imports (1977)	1
Ratio of Canadian GNP (1977: $196 billion) to EC GNP ($1,604 billion)	0.1

ASSESSMENT

Klaus H. Pringsheim
"There are additional considerations working against the Canadian system (CANDU), not the least of which is the fact that Canada severely bruised Japanese trust of Canada as a stable supplier of Japan's nuclear industry when the Canadian Government in 1977 suddenly imposed an embargo on uranium shipments to Japan, after India had used plutonium in its nuclear explosion experiment. Canada then imposed a new regime of safeguards which she forced Japan to accept before uranium shipments were resumed in January of 1978." (Pringsheim 24)

AUTHORS' SUMMARY

Overall assessment	*Assigned scores*
☐ Policy result, scaled from 1 (failed) to 4 (success)	3
☐ Sanctions contribution, scaled from 1 (none) to 4 (significant)	3
☐ Success score (policy result *times* sanctions contribution), scaled from 1 (outright failure) to 16 (significant success)	9

Political and economic variables	Assigned scores
□ Companion policies: J (covert), Q (quasi-military), or R (regular military)	—
□ International cooperation with sender, scaled from 1 (none) to 4 (significant)	1
□ International assistance to target: A (if present)	—
□ Sanctions period (years)	1
□ Economic health and political stability of target, scaled from 1 (distressed) to 3 (strong)	3
□ Presanction relations between sender and target, scaled from 1 (antagonistic) to 3 (cordial)	3
□ Type of sanction: X (export), M (import), F (financial)	X
□ Cost to sender, scaled from 1 (net gain) to 4 (major loss)	2

BIBLIOGRAPHY

Government of Canada, Department of External Affairs. 1982. *Canada's Nuclear Nonproliferation Policy.* Canadian Foreign Policy Texts no. 82/2.
Pringsheim, Klaus H. 1981. "Major Functions of the Canada-Japan Relationship." Working Paper Series, Canada and the Pacific: Agenda for the Eighties. University of Toronto and York University, Center on Modern East Asia, 5 May.

Case 77–5   US v. Nicaragua

(1977–79: Somoza)

CHRONOLOGY OF KEY EVENTS

15 June 1977   Administration of President Jimmy Carter announces that, because of human rights violations, it is withholding $2.5 million in military credits for Nicaragua in 1977. In July, US suspends sale of police equipment intended for national guard of General Anastasio Somoza Debayle. Later that summer, Congress authorizes military aid; administration decides to sign military assistance agreement with Nicaragua but suspends $12 million in economic aid because human rights situation has not improved. (*Keesing's* 28625, 28762)

January 1978   Pedro Joaquín Chamorro Cardenal, publisher of *La Prensa*, is shot down in Managua street following exposé about Somoza-owned operation. His death unites opposition against Somoza; general strike is called, which provokes violence, repression by national guard. These events revive flagging Sandinista rebels, prompt US to reduce military aid in February. (Anderson 157; *Keesing's* 29021)

May 1978   Economic assistance to Nicaragua is resumed under congressional pressure. (*Keesing's* 29373)

September 1978   Carter administration again suspends military aid and sales. Following month *Financial Times* (London) reports that Carter "had finally decided that Somoza must go." (Schoultz 266, 330; *Facts on File* 839)

Fall 1978   Civil war intensifies; Carter sends representatives to Nicaragua to mediate. Somoza informally rejects proposed plebiscite, backed by US. Carter tries to pressure Somoza into accepting plebiscite by persuading International Monetary Fund (IMF) to postpone approval of a $65.7 million loan desperately needed by Somoza to service external debts of $1 billion coming due that year. (Anderson 160; *Latin America Political Report*, 10 November 1978, 350)

15 January 1979   Somoza formally rejects plebiscite proposal; in February, Carter administration announces it is ending all military aid to Nicaragua, freezing $10.5 million in economic assistance appropriated for 1979, although much in pipeline has been disbursed already. (Anderson 160; *Keesing's* 29805)

14 May 1979   US tolerates IMF approval of previously postponed loan, and half the money is delivered in June "just in time for Somoza to take it into exile." (Anderson 160; *Keesing's* 29805)

19 July 1979   Sandinistas overthrow Somoza. (Anderson 162)

Fall 1979   In attempt to gain influence with Sandinista government, US unfreezes economic aid and supplies $8 million in emergency economic assistance. Also see Case 81–1 US v. Nicaragua (1981–   : El Salvador War). (Anderson 168)

GOALS OF SENDER COUNTRY

Lars Schoultz
"At first [the State Department's Human Rights Bureau] viewed the threat of aid reductions as a tool to force decreases in recipients' levels of political repression. . . . By 1978 . . . [they] began to speak of aid reductions as a tool not to reduce repression but to dissociate the United States from repressive regimes." (Schoultz 205)

Richard E. Feinberg
"By alternatively applying pressures and offering positive inducements, the administration sought to improve President Somoza's respect for civil liberties. The administration did not, however, appear to question the legitimacy of the regime itself. . . . The popular insurrection of September 1978 convinced the United States that a more urgent and deeper U.S. engagement was required. The administration had concluded that Somoza's removal was a sine qua non for avoiding a deepening spiral of radicalization and violence that would consume moderate and centrist elements and present the Sandinista Liberation Front (FSLN) with the opportunity to seize power." (Feinberg 66)

Facts on File
"The Carter Administration did not specifically support the anti-Somoza drive, but its neutrality—a departure from normal US support of the Somoza family—was a boon to the opposition in itself." (*Facts on File* 91)

RESPONSE OF TARGET COUNTRY

Thomas P. Anderson
"[D]espite whatever signals were being sent by the Executive Branch, Somoza had powerful friends in Congress. . . . Delegations of conservative Congressmen from the United States continued to make fact-finding tours of the embattled country . . . to find that Somoza was our only hope against a Communist takeover." (Anderson 160)

Richard E. Feinberg
"Somoza had used the [American] mediation to splinter the opposition, buy time and rearm his National Guard. . . . When the mediation team finally left in frustration, Somoza felt strong enough to resist at least mild U.S. steps." (Feinberg 66)

ECONOMIC IMPACT

Observed Economic Statistics

US aid to Nicaragua (million dollars)

	Economic	Military
1972	4.7	1.0
1973	26.8	3.0
1974	15.5	2.1
1975	42.2	4.3
1976 + TQ†	20.2	3.8
1977	3.3	3.1
1978	14.0	0.4
1979	18.5	—

— Zero or negligible.
† Transitional quarter: beginning of US fiscal year changed from June to October.
Source: AID.

Calculated Economic Impact

	Annual cost to target country
Delay in IMF loan; welfare loss valued at 15 percent of face amount of loan.	$10 million
Suspension of US military aid; welfare loss valued at 90 percent of average aid levels FY 1975–77.	3 million
Reduction in US economic aid; welfare loss at 75 percent of decline from average aid levels of FY 1975–77.	9 million
Total	$22 million

Relative Magnitudes

Gross indicators of Nicaraguan economy	
Nicaraguan GNP (1977)	$2.1 billion
Nicaraguan population (1977)	2.32 million
Annual effect of sanctions related to gross indicators	
Percentage of GNP	1.0
Per capita	$9.48

Nicaraguan trade with US as percentage of total trade
Exports (1977)   24
Imports (1977)   29

Ratio of US GNP (1977: $1,918 billion) to Nicaraguan GNP (1977:
$2.1 billion)   913

ASSESSMENT

Lars Schoultz
"[In] Nicaragua . . . there was a rising tide of public opposition to existing repressive regimes that *coincided* with the renewed emphasis upon human rights. . . . I believe the human rights policy of the United States helped to create this opposition." (Schoultz 363)

Richard E. Feinberg
"The administration would have confronted powerful domestic opposition had it attempted more biting pressures (for example, working alone or in the OAS to curtail official and commercial credits and arms supplies, and/or to sever diplomatic relations). Whether Somoza would have bowed to concerted U.S. pressures will forever remain a hypothetical question.

"Ironically, it was the pressure of conservatives, both within and outside, which inhibited the administration from acting to preempt a Sandinista military victory." (Feinberg 67)

AUTHORS' SUMMARY

Overall assessment	*Assigned scores*
□ Policy result, scaled from 1 (failed) to 4 (success)	4
□ Sanctions contribution, scaled from 1 (none) to 4 (significant)	3
□ Success score (policy result *times* sanctions contribution), scaled from 1 (outright failure) to 16 (significant success)	12

Political and economic variables

□ Companion policies: J (covert), Q (quasi-military), or R (regular military)	—
□ International cooperation with sender, scaled from 1 (none) to 4 (significant)	1
□ International assistance to target: A (if present)	—
□ Sanctions period (years)	2
□ Economic health and political stability of target, scaled from 1 (distressed) to 3 (strong)	1
□ Presanction relations between sender and target, scaled from 1 (antagonistic) to 3 (cordial)	3
□ Type of sanction: X (export), M (import), F (financial)	F, X
□ Cost to sender, scaled from 1 (net gain) to 4 (major loss)	1

Comments

Withdrawal of economic, military assistance, while explicitly tied to human rights violations, clearly conveyed the message that US was ceasing support for Somoza regime. Even more important than economic pressure caused by Carter's policy was its political impact in strengthening opposition, thereby contributing to Somoza's downfall.

BIBLIOGRAPHY

Agency for International Development. *Overseas Loans and Grants.* Various issues.

Anderson, Thomas P. 1982. *Politics in Central America.* New York: Praeger.

Facts on File. 1978, 1979.

Feinberg, Richard E., ed. 1982. *Central America: International Dimensions of the Crisis.* New York: Holmes & Meier.

Keesing's Contemporary Archives. 1977, 1978, 1979.

Schoultz, Lars. 1981. *Human Rights and United States Policy Toward Latin America.* Princeton, NJ: Princeton University Press.

US Department of State. 1982. *Country Reports on Human Rights Practices for 1981.* Report submitted to US House of Representatives, Committee on Foreign Affairs, and Senate Committee on Foreign Relations. 97 Cong., 2 sess., February. Washington.

Case 77–6   US v. El Salvador

(1977–81: Human Rights)

CHRONOLOGY OF KEY EVENTS

Early 1977 El Salvador (along with Brazil, Argentina, Guatemala) rejects US military assistance following congressional criticism of human rights record. Aid already authorized continues to be delivered but no new aid is authorized for two years. Economic assistance is reduced from approximately $20 million to $10 million. (LeoGrande 1089)

Summer 1977 US vetoes $90 million Inter-American Development Bank (IDB) loan to El Salvador following threats by right-wing death squad to murder all Jesuits in country because of their alleged promotion of Communism. Approval of loan is granted in October when threatened massacre does not occur, after some temporary easing of official repression, slowdown in death squad activity. (LeoGrande 1090)

Late 1978–early 1979 "[A] series of human rights reports from Amnesty International, the International Commission of Jurists, the Organization of American States, and the U.S. Department of State unanimously condemned the Romero government for its systematic torture, murder, and persecution of political dissidents." (LeoGrande 1091)

November 1979 US ships El Salvador "a limited amount of riot control equipment along with six US advisers to teach them how to use it." This occurs one month after overthrow of General Carlos Humberto Romero by group of younger Army officers. "The coup was hailed even in some conservative circles and welcomed by the U.S. embassy as a move toward stability." (LeoGrande 1097; Anderson 75)

November– December 1979 "While the left refused to accept the [new] junta, the army and security forces seemed determined to ignore it, returning very soon to their old policies of making people disappear and attacking villages suspected of harboring radicals." (Anderson 78)

January 1980 Junta falls because of inability to control military. It is replaced by group composed of many of same people; however, new regime drops insistence on civilian control of military. (Anderson 80)

Early Spring 1980	US provides $6 million in military aid, $50 million in economic assistance to El Salvador. In March, Robert White, human rights activist, replaces Frank Devine as US ambassador in San Salvador. American assistance is continued, although "the general level of violence had become appalling. Amnesty International estimated that 2,000 persons were killed between January and April." On 24 March Archbishop Oscar Arnulfo Romero y Galdames, who had urged President Jimmy Carter to suspend aid to government, is assassinated. (LeoGrande 1097; Anderson 84–86)
May 1980	Rightist forces under Major Roberto D'Aubuisson again attempt coup but fail, D'Aubuisson is arrested. His supporters respond by surrounding the US Embassy, making White virtual prisoner 9–12 May until they are dispersed by State Department "security agents" and Marines. (Anderson 87)
Fall 1980	President Jimmy Carter suspends all military aid to El Salvador following allegations of involvement by El Salvadoran national guard in slayings of four American churchwomen and pending investigation of its suspected complicity. (*Washington Post*, 20 July 1983, A1)
January 1981	Three days before leaving office, Carter authorizes $5 million in emergency military assistance for El Salvador in response to a major guerrilla offensive. (*Washington Post*, 20 July 1983, A1)
1981	Congress passes legislation making aid to El Salvador contingent on improved human rights. Certification of progress by president is required every six months. Certifications are made routinely, aid continues despite protests from human rights groups, some congressmen. (*New York Times*, 22 January 1983, A1)
29 October 1982	US Ambassador Deane Hinton criticizes human rights abuses of death squads in El Salvador before American Chamber of Commerce. Speech had not been authorized by State Department and, within months, Hinton is replaced by Thomas R. Pickering. (*Washington Post*, 26 November 1983, A1)
18 July 1983	President Ronald Reagan appoints bipartisan commission headed by Henry A. Kissinger to investigate situation in Central America, propose long-term strategy for US policy in region. (*New York Times*, 19 July 1983, A1)
Fall 1983	Reagan administration increases diplomatic pressure on El Salvador to rein in death squads. Over two-month period, Kissinger, Under Secretary of Defense Fred Iklé, Ambassador Pickering publicly warn Salvadoran government officials about necessity of improving human rights situation if aid is to be continued. (*Washington Post*, 13 October 1983, A1; 26 November 1983, A1)
31 November 1983	Reagan vetoes legislation tying continuation of aid to progress on human rights. (*Washington Post*, 1 December 1983, A1)

January 1984	Kissinger Commission reports that growing influence of Soviet Union, Cuba in Central America threatens US security, recommends increasing both military, economic aid. Report also recommends linking that aid to progress in human rights, even though Kissinger dissents from linkage approach. (*Newsweek*, 23 January 1984, 28–31)
6 May 1984	Moderate Christian Democrat José Napoleon Duarte defeats right-wing candidate Roberto D' Aubuisson for presidency. Reagan administration hopes Duarte's election and his pledge to bring death squads under control will make US Congress more amenable to continued military aid for El Salvador. (*Economist* [London], 12 May 1984, 19)

GOALS OF SENDER COUNTRY

William LeoGrande, Carla Anne Robbins
"Military assistance to El Salvador was interrupted when Congress began introducing human rights concerns into the allocation of U.S. foreign assistance. . . . El Salvador first attracted high-level attention in the Carter Administration in June 1977, when one of the right-wing death squads . . . accused the Salvadorean Catholic Church of promoting communism, and threatened to kill all the Jesuits in the country. . . . Under pressure from U.S. church groups and members of Congress, the Carter administration launched an intensive campaign to convince General Romero that El Salvador's relations with the United States depended upon preventing the prospective massacre." (LeoGrande 1089–90)

"Since the October [1979] coup, the policy of the United States has been to support the government of El Salvador in its attempts to carry out significant social reform and forge a viable political center. . . . The proximate objectives of the United States since October have been to encourage El Salvador's rulers to implement their promised reforms, to protect them from a rightist coup, and avert an open civil war." (LeoGrande 1097)

RESPONSE OF TARGET COUNTRY

William LeoGrande, Carla Anne Robbins
Fall 1979: "Romero responded [to American pressures] with promises of reform, including a pledge that the 1980 congressional elections would be internationally supervised to ensure fairness. But he was adamant in his refusal to reschedule the presidential election which was not due until 1982. . . . Even the moderates refused to confer with the government on its proposed reforms until the violence of the security forces was ended. Romero would not or could not end it." (LeoGrande 1092)

Richard E. Feinberg
"It was in response to the human rights policy in general, more than in opposition to any bilateral slight, that the governments of Guatemala and El Salvador rejected U.S. security assistance in 1977." (Feinberg 61)

ATTITUDE OF OTHER COUNTRIES

Federal Republic of Germany
Government of Chancellor Helmut Schmidt suspends economic and technical assistance

to El Salvador in 1979 because of human rights violations there. Two years later, West Germany recalls its ambassador from San Salvador for "security reasons." "The decision was widely regarded as a sign of displeasure over the death squad activities." Following election of Duarte as president in spring 1984, Chancellor Helmut Kohl invites Duarte to visit, names new ambassador, pledges $18 million in aid to El Salvador. "West German officials said the Bonn government decided to resume development aid to El Salvador because murders of civilians carried out by right-wing death squads have lessened since Duarte's election in May." (*Washington Post*, 18 July 1984, A1)

ECONOMIC IMPACT

Observed Economic Statistics

"The gross domestic product fell 3.5 percent in 1979. During the course of the year, 20 factories closed, laying off 12,000 workers, and a massive flight of capital took place. The country was also suffering from a severe balance of payments problem, especially within the Central American Common Market. Economics Minister Hinds and Finance Minister Ernesto Arbizu found that these problems were practically insoluble." (Anderson 77)

US aid to El Salvador (million dollars)

	Economic	Military
1976 + TQ†	7.3	1.1
1977	6.8	—
1978	10.9	—
1979	11.4	—
1980	58.3	5.9
1981	114.0	35.5
1982	182.2	82.0

— Zero or negligible.
† Transitional quarter: beginning of US fiscal year changed from June to October.
Source: AID.

Calculated Economic Impact

	Annual cost to target country
Reduction in planned US economic aid from about $20 million per year to $10 million; welfare loss valued at 90 percent of lost transfers.	$9 million
Several months' delay in approval of $90 million IDB loan to El Salvador; welfare loss estimated at 3 percent of value of loan (equal to 1 percent per month interest charge).	3 million

Calculated Economic Impact (*continued*)

	Annual cost to target country
Suspension of US military aid; welfare loss estimated at 90 percent of lost transfers.	1 million
Total	$13 million

Relative Magnitudes

Gross indicators of Salvadoran economy	
Salvadoran GNP (1977)	$2.8 billion
Salvadoran population (1977)	4.3 million
Annual effect of sanctions related to gross indicators	
Percentage of GNP	0.5
Per capita	$3.02
Salvadoran trade with US as percentage of total trade	
Exports (1977)	33
Imports (1977)	30
Ratio of US GNP (1977: $1,918 billion) to Salvadoran GNP (1977: $2.8 billion)	685

ASSESSMENT

William LeoGrande, Carla Anne Robbins
As of 1980: "[P]olitical violence has thrown the Salvadorean economy into such a crisis that economic assistance is virtually indispensable. Consequently, Washington's threat to withdraw aid has already been successfully used to induce the government to expropriate the large landed estates and to deter the right from expropriating the government." (LeoGrande 1100)

Piero Gleijeses
"Confronted by a credible U.S. threat [to cut off economic assistance as well as military aid], and fully cognizant of their own military weakness, the Salvadoran officers would not react with suicidal pride and defy the 'Yanquis.' Rather, two deeply rooted and mutually supporting impulses would prevail: personal opportunism and the desire to save the military institution. Both require not defiance, but acquiescence to U.S. will." (Gleijeses 1057)

AUTHORS' SUMMARY

Overall assessment	Assigned scores
☐ Policy result, scaled from 1 (failed) to 4 (success)	2
☐ Sanctions contribution, scaled from 1 (none) to 4 (significant)	3
☐ Success score (policy result *times* sanctions contribution), scaled from 1 (outright failure) to 16 (significant success)	6

Political and economic variables

☐ Companion policies: J (covert), Q (quasi-military), or R (regular military)	—
☐ International cooperation with sender, scaled from 1 (none) to 4 (significant)	1
☐ International assistance to target: A (if present)	—
☐ Sanctions period (years)	4
☐ Economic health and political stability of target, scaled from 1 (distressed) to 3 (strong)	1
☐ Presanction relations between sender and target, scaled from 1 (antagonistic) to 3 (cordial)·	2
☐ Type of sanction: X (export), M (import), F (financial)	F
☐ Cost to sender, scaled from 1 (net gain) to 4 (major loss)	1

BIBLIOGRAPHY

Agency for International Development. *Overseas Loans and Grants*. Various issues.
Anderson, Thomas P. 1982. *Politics in Central America*. New York: Praeger.
Feinberg, Richard E., ed. 1982. *Central America: International Dimensions of the Crisis*. New York: Holmes & Meier.
Gleijeses, Piero. 1983. "The Case for Power Sharing in El Salvador." 61 *Foreign Affairs* (Summer): 1048–63.
LeoGrande, William, and Carla Anne Robbins. 1980. "Oligarchs and Officers: The Crisis in El Salvador." 58 *Foreign Affairs* (Summer): 1084–1103.

Case 77–7   US v. Brazil

(1977–84: Human Rights)

CHRONOLOGY OF KEY EVENTS

1975–76   Repression is eased after General Ernesto Geisel becomes president with intention of "redemocratizing" country after 10 years of harsh military rule. (Wesson 92)

1976–early 1977   International Security Assistance Act requires US State Department "to submit to Congress a report on all 82 countries receiving military or security assistance." Prior to submission, State Department sends Brazilian government copy of report "as a courtesy." (Wesson 94)

24 February 1977   US Secretary of State Cyrus Vance informs members of Senate Foreign Appropriations Subcommittee that administration of President Jimmy Carter has decided to reduce economic, military aid to Argentina, Uruguay, Ethiopia because of human rights abuses. (*Keesing's* 28343)

5 March 1977   After studying State Department report on human rights, Brazil decides to reject future military aid, days later abrogates (effective 1978) 1952 military aid agreement with US. (*Keesing's* 28343)

12 March 1977   State Department's *Country Reports on Human Rights Practices*, including the one on Brazil, are submitted to Senate Committee on Foreign Relations. (Wesson 94)

September 1977   ". . . the Brazilians completed the erasure of old military agreements by terminating the US naval mission and the US-Brazil joint military commission, left over from World War II." (Wesson 95)

March 1978   Carter visits Brazil, takes "a conciliatory position. . . . The Carter visit was generally seen as putting an end to the asperity that marked the first year of the new administration." (Wesson 95–96)

6 February 1984   Administration of President Ronald Reagan resumes military ties with Brazil, agreeing to provide advanced weapons technology to Brazil's large arms industry. Traditional military aid is not sought by Brazil. (*New York Times*, 7 February 1984, A3)

GOALS OF SENDER COUNTRY

Robert Wesson

"The application of the human rights policy to Brazil . . . was rather incidental. . . . There is no evidence that Carter intended in advance to make a great issue of human rights, but they were brought to center stage by repressive measures taken by the Soviet and Czechoslovak governments about the time Carter entered office. . . . If condemnation of Soviet maltreatment of intellectuals was not to be merely anti-Soviet or anti-Communist politics, it had to be applied to friends and allies such as Brazil, as well as nonfriends. In fact, it seemed to many that the policy in fact penalized pro-American governments much more than anti-American, since the sanctions behind it were denial of assistance and loans, which anti-American governments would not be likely to get in any case." (Wesson 93)

RESPONSE OF TARGET COUNTRY

Robert Wesson

"It is possible that the government was less infuriated by a relatively mild statement of well-known facts than it was glad to break formal ties which the Armed Forces had been considering terminating for a year or more in any case. The reaction was conditioned, moreover, by irritation at American pressure in the nuclear question—the report was presented to the Brazilian government at the very time [Deputy Secretary of State] Warren Christopher came to argue the nuclear case. Some Brazilian military men contended that Carter was using the campaign for human rights as a means for forcing modification of the nuclear power program." (Wesson 94)

ECONOMIC IMPACT

Observed Economic Statistics

US aid to Brazil (million dollars)

	Economic	Military	Eximbank loans
1974	17.2	52.7	325.7
1975	14.7	65.4	256.5
1976 + TQ†	6.0	44.8	116.9
1977	4.3	0.1	47.3
1978	2.1	—	104.7
1979	2.1	—	212.6

— Zero or negligible.
† Transitional quarter: beginning of US fiscal year changed from June to October.
Source: AID.

Calculated Economic Impact

	Annual cost to target country
Reduction in US military, economic aid to Brazil; welfare loss valued at 70 percent of reduced transfers from annual average levels in 1974–75.	$52 million
Reduction in Eximbank loans in 1977–78; welfare loss estimated at 20 percent of reduced loans from 1974–75 levels.	42 million
Total	$94 million

Relative Magnitudes

Gross indicators of Brazilian economy	
Brazilian GNP (1977)	$164 billion
Brazilian population (1977)	112.2 million
Annual effect of sanctions related to gross indicators	
Percentage of GNP	0.1
Per capita	$0.84
Brazilian trade with US as percentage of total trade	
Exports (1977)	17
Imports (1977)	20
Ratio of US GNP (1977: $1,918 billion) to Brazilian GNP (1977: $164 billion)	12

ASSESSMENT

Robert Wesson

"It has never been officially admitted, of course, that Carter policies had the slightest influence on Brazilian performance. They were hardly decisive, because improvement began with the beginning of the Geisel administration and was marked . . . from the end of 1975. But the respect for human rights gradually improved through 1977, despite some reversal of the process of liberalization in April, and the cause continued through 1978 and 1979. . . . It seems probable that the official human rights policy—although less important than the pressures of public opinion and private organizations in the United States and Europe—contributed to an improvement in civil and political freedoms in Brazil. . . . The means employed have been primarily informational, but the U.S. Congress tried to give the policy teeth by linking foreign aid and commercial or financial advantages to human rights performance. . . . But such measures as holding up Eximbank loans have not proved very effective and have been largely given up." (Wesson 98)

"The pressure for better observance of human rights was also resented as intrusive but it was more successful [than US nuclear nonproliferation policy] because of the legitimacy of its purpose and because it corresponded to the aspirations of very many Brazilians." (Wesson 67)

AUTHORS' SUMMARY

Overall assessment	Assigned scores
☐ Policy result, scaled from 1 (failed) to 4 (success)	3
☐ Sanctions contribution, scaled from 1 (none) to 4 (significant)	3
☐ Success score (policy result *times* sanctions contribution), scaled from 1 (outright failure) to 16 (significant success)	9

Political and economic variables

☐ Companion policies: J (covert), Q (quasi-military), or R (regular military)	—
☐ International cooperation with sender, scaled from 1 (none) to 4 (significant)	1
☐ International assistance to target: A (if present)	—
☐ Sanctions period (years)	7
☐ Economic health and political stability of target, scaled from 1 (distressed) to 3 (strong)	2
☐ Presanction relations between sender and target, scaled from 1 (antagonistic) to 3 (cordial)	2
☐ Type of sanction: X (export), M (import), F (financial)	F
☐ Cost to sender, scaled from 1 (net gain) to 4 (major loss)	1

BIBLIOGRAPHY

Agency for International Development. *Overseas Loans and Grants.* Various issues.
Keesing's Contemporary Archives. 1977.
Wesson, Robert. 1981. *The United States and Brazil: Limits of Influence.* New York: Praeger.

Case 78–1 China v. Albania
(1978–83: Rhetoric)

CHRONOLOGY OF KEY EVENTS

July 1977   Editorial in official newspaper of Albanian Communist party indirectly criticizes "the basic policy orientation of China" by attacking "the Maoist thesis of the division of the world into three groups of countries—superpowers, developed countries and developing countries." In Peking, officials announce that differences of opinion between friendly states are "quite natural," no change in relations with Albania is expected. (*Keesing's* 28546)

Fall–Winter 1977   September visit of Yugoslav President Tito to China is harshly attacked by Albania. "Notwithstanding strained interparty relations between the two countries, Chinese aid to Albania seemed to continue much as before, with two Chinese delegations visiting Albania during October 1977 to discuss scientific and technical cooperation." (*Keesing's* 28809)

11 July 1978   China terminates economic aid, recalls its specialists, expels Albanian students in China. As result 104 Albanian students leave China, 513 Chinese experts return from Albania. (*Keesing's* 29276–77)

Spring 1983   Chinese trade delegation visits Albania amid speculation that China fears renewed Soviet influence in Albania after 74-year-old Communist leader Enver Hoxha dies. (*Wall Street Journal*, 18 May 1983, 38; *Economist* [London], 23 April 1983, 48; *Washington Post*, 2 June 1983, A23)

4 October 1983   China, Albania sign trade and payments protocol. (*New York Times*, 23 October 1983, 12)

GOALS OF SENDER COUNTRY

Keesing's
"A statement, issued [by China] two days after the termination of aid, explains the reasons: 'All the facts show that the Albanian leadership has decided to pursue the anti-China course, deliberately abandoned the agreements signed between the two sides providing Chinese aid to Albania, slandered and tried to fabricate trumped-up charges

against Chinese experts and sabotaged the economic and military cooperation between China and Albania in a planned and systematic way, making it impossible for our aid work to go on.'" (*Keesing's* 29277)

Economist
"In spite of the sweet talk the Chinese have been getting from Moscow recently, they do not want to see Russia extend its influence in any part of the world, including the Balkans, where they can see that Russia may want to exploit Rumania's and Jugoslavia's present economic and political difficulties, and where it is already trying to woo an already isolated Albania back into the Soviet sphere." (*Economist*, 23 April 1983, 48)

RESPONSE OF TARGET COUNTRY

Keesing's
Albanian officials denounce China's termination of aid as "unilateral and arbitrary" and intended to "damage the economy of socialist Albania. . . . The official Albanian statement added that 'pressure and blackmail' would 'never force the Albanian people to give up its just Marxist-Leninist attitude or to deviate from the struggle against imperialism and revisionism of all colors.'" (*Keesing's* 29276–77)

ATTITUDE OF OTHER COUNTRIES

Yugoslavia
". . . The Yugoslav leaders, frightened about the effects of a post-Hoxha upheaval of the fragile geopolitical patchwork of the region and, without Tito [who had died in 1980], feeling evermore under pressure from Moscow, are reportedly relieved by Hoxha's recent decision to resume ties with China. They hope the Chinese will be a hedge against future Balkan instability." (*Washington Post*, 2 June 1983, A23)

ECONOMIC IMPACT

Observed Economic Statistics

Press reports quote estimates that some $5 billion in aid has been extended by China to Albania between 1960 and break in 1978. (*Wall Street Journal*, 18 May 1983, 38; *Economist*, 23 April 1983, 48; *Washington Post*, 2 June 1983, A23) (Authors' note: We believe this figure is too high.)

Chinese interest-free credits to Albania total $316 million 1961–69, $180 million 1970–75. More than half of Albania's trade is with China "and over 2,000 Chinese development experts had enabled Albania to set up some 30 new industrial undertakings, equipped mainly with Chinese-made machines." (*Keesing's* 28824)

Michael Ellman estimates that, through 1974, Chinese aid financed more than a third of Albania's imports. From 1975 to the rupture in 1978, Albania had a trade surplus with China and shortly thereafter appears to have achieved an overall balance of payments equilibrium. (Ellman 336)

Albanian trade with China: 1975, $180 million; 1976, $135 million; 1978, $75 million; 1979, $20 million. (Ellman 338)

"Although for many years Albania was dependent on foreign aid, she is no longer so. The country has become self-supporting." (Ellman 340)

Albanian trade with Western countries, 1974–80† (million dollars)

	Exports	Imports
1974	92	72
1975	95	83
1976	62	69
1977	82	105
1978	97	83
1979	137	176
1980	192	221

† Figures are derived from reports of Western countries.
Source: IMF.

CIA estimates total Albanian exports, imports in 1978 at $151 million and $173 million, respectively. (ACDA)

Calculated Economic Impact

	Annual cost to target country
Cut-off of Chinese economic aid from average annual levels of 1970–75; welfare loss estimated at 90 percent of lost transfers.	$27 million
Reduction in trade with China; welfare loss estimated at 15 percent of reduction in trade (in light of increased trade with West) in 1978–79 as compared to 1975–76 average.	16 million
Total	$43 million

Relative Magnitudes

Gross indicators of Albanian economy	
Albanian GNP (1976)	$1.3 billion
Albanian population (1978)	2.6 million
Annual effect of sanctions related to gross indicators	
Percentage of GNP	3.3
Per capita	$16.54
Albanian trade with China as percentage of total trade	
Exports (est. 1975–76)	34
Imports (est. 1975–76)	34
Ratio of Chinese GNP (1976: $324 billion) to Albanian GNP (1976: $1.3 billion)	249

ASSESSMENT

Wall Street Journal
"Clearly the [Albanian Communist] party realizes that development is impossible without outside help, and it has started a policy of gradually improving economic relations with a select number of small and medium-sized countries in the West. . . . And yet, diplomats note, these changes in foreign trade haven't been accompanied by similar changes in Albanian foreign policy. . . . In the case of the new agreement with China, 'I think it is strictly trade, and nothing else will come from it while Hoxha is alive,' says Radio Free Europe's Mr. [Louis] Zanga." (*Wall Street Journal*, 18 May 1983, 38)

Michael Ellman
"First, although the break with China caused a decline in Albania's total foreign trade, this was temporary and Albania was able to replace China by other trading partners. Secondly, after the break with China, the West became Albania's main trading partner. Thirdly, Albania has not become dependent on the West and has a significant trade with Eastern Europe." (Ellman 338)

AUTHORS' SUMMARY

Overall assessment	Assigned scores
□ Policy result, scaled from 1 (failed) to 4 (success)	1
□ Sanctions contribution, scaled from 1 (none) to 4 (significant)	1
□ Success score (policy result *times* sanctions contribution), scaled from 1 (outright failure) to 16 (significant success)	1

Political and economic variables

□ Companion policies: J (covert), Q (quasi-military), or R (regular military)	—
□ International cooperation with sender, scaled from 1 (none) to 4 (significant)	1
□ International assistance to target: A (if present)	—
□ Sanctions period (years)	5
□ Economic health and political stability of target, scaled from 1 (distressed) to 3 (strong)	3
□ Presanction relations between sender and target, scaled from 1 (antagonistic) to 3 (cordial)	3
□ Type of sanction: X (export), M (import), F (financial)	F, X, M
□ Cost to sender, scaled from 1 (net gain) to 4 (major loss)	2

BIBLIOGRAPHY

Arms Control and Disarmament Agency. *World Military Expenditures and Arms Transfers, 1970–79.* Various issues.
Ellman, Michael. 1984. "Albania's Economy Today and Tomorrow." 7 *World Economy* (September): 333–40.
International Monetary Fund. 1981. *Direction of Trade Statistics.*
Keesing's Contemporary Archives. 1977, 1978.

Case 78–2   US v. Brazil
(1978–81: Nuclear Safeguards)

CHRONOLOGY OF KEY EVENTS

1967   Brazil agrees to buy two nuclear power reactors from Westinghouse. Fuel for reactors is to be mined in Brazil, enriched in US. (Wesson 77)

1968   Brazil refuses to sign Non-Proliferation Treaty (NPT). (Wesson 78)

1974   Several events intensify Brazil's desire to have entire nuclear fuel cycle under its own control: oil prices quadruple, posing serious problem for Brazil, which is dependent on imported oil; India's "peaceful" nuclear explosion "gave Brazil a feeling of lagging and spread the idea that nuclear explosives might be useful"; US Atomic Energy Commission informs several countries, including Brazil, that because of supply constraints it may not be able to deliver enriched uranium as promised. (Wesson 78)

June 1975   Brazil announces $10 billion contract with West Germany that will provide Brazil with "self-contained nuclear power industry." Deal provides eight reactors, fuel fabrication, reprocessing, enrichment facilities. Safeguards more stringent than those imposed by International Atomic Energy Agency or NPT are required as part of contract. (Courtney 244; Wesson 79)

January 1977   President Jimmy Carter, immediately upon inauguration, takes more forceful stance on nonproliferation, including increasing pressure on Germany "to pull back from commitments to supply nuclear technology to Brazil." (Wesson 80)

November 1977   Carter administration recommends approval of shipment of 54 tons of low-enriched uranium to Brazil. Officials state this should not be construed as lessening of opposition to Brazil's contract with Germany. (*New York Times*, 17 November 1977, A12)

10 March 1978   Carter signs Nuclear Non-Proliferation Act (NNPA). Most countries with which US has nuclear dealings already are under full-scope safeguards. Those that are not—Brazil, Argentina, India, South

10 March 1978 (continued)	Africa—refuse to accept comprehensive safeguards, generally turn to other suppliers. (Clausen 1; *Washington Post,* 11 March 1978, A2; authors' summary)
24 August 1979	Brazil applies to US for shipment of 1,726 kg. of 3.45 percent uranium fuel for Angra Dos Reis I. Application was still pending in 1984. (*Pending Report*)
3 December 1979	Brazil applies for shipment of 16,242 kg. of 3.35 percent material for Brazil's Angra I reactor, also still pending in 1984. (*Pending Report*)
October 1981	Administration of President Ronald Reagan waives cancellation charge of $3 million on contract for low-enriched uranium, thereby allowing Brazil to turn to alternative fuel supplier (in this case France) without penalty. (Spector, Moore interviews)
6 February 1984	US Secretary of State George P. Shultz, Foreign Minister Ramiro Elisio Saraiva Güerreiro of Brazil sign agreement settling "past differences over the supply of fuel for Brazil's nuclear power station." Agreement includes formal cancellation of financial penalty waived in 1981, provides for US to "repair defective fuel elements supplied before the dispute erupted." (*New York Times,* 7 February 1984, A3)

GOALS OF SENDER COUNTRY

1975
Before and after announcement of German-Brazilian deal: "The chief concern of the State Department was to meet congressional criticism of dereliction in not pressing the Germans on the issue; the administration had to equivocate slightly, claiming to have evinced opposition without having made loud noises. It is to be noted that the question was raised not with the Brazilian buyers but with the German sellers, presumably because it was felt that the United States had leverage with the Germans dependent on NATO and American security forces." (Wesson 80)

Fall 1977
". . . the Administration had tried a little carrot-and-stick diplomacy by recommending the furnishing to Brazil of 54 tons of low-enriched uranium, followed by a warning that future uranium deliveries would be questionable if Brazil proceeded to acquire reprocessing facilities. The Brazilians do not appear to have been impressed." (Wesson 81)

RESPONSE OF TARGET COUNTRY

Robert Wesson
Visiting Brasilia in March 1977, Deputy Secretary of State Warren Christopher "is said to have presented the government with a version of the accord as the administration would like it to be. But his discussions ended after only one day when the Brazilians flatly rejected the suggestion that enrichment be done in the United States or under international or multinational control." (Wesson 81)

"The Brazilian reaction to the US attack on the nuclear program was the more negative because it [the attack] came late and seemed a capricious change of the new administration. But to reject US interference was a matter of basic pride, an assertion of economic and political independence. . . . For Brazil, nuclear development, without conditions imposed from without, was integral to technological maturity and symbolic of modernity; the United States seemed to wish to divide the nations into those entitled to enjoy enrichment and reprocessing facilities, and those unworthy—the industrialized and powerful on one side, the poor and weak on the other. To yield would be to sacrifice both development and security and to admit permanent inferiority." (Wesson 82–83)

ATTITUDE OF OTHER COUNTRIES

Federal Republic of Germany
"In response to widespread criticism of the deal's dangers, West Germany obtained Brazil's reluctant agreement to a framework for international inspection that goes far beyond the safeguards required by the International Atomic Energy Agency (IAEA) to detect any diversion of nuclear equipment or materials for weapons production." Federal Republic of Germany did not, however, require that Brazil sign NPT or accept full-scope safeguards covering future nuclear technology imports or indigenous developments. (Gall 158)

ECONOMIC IMPACT

Observed Economic Statistics

In 1979, Brazil applies for US shipments of 3 percent low-enriched uranium, totaling 17,968 kilograms worth an estimated $13.5 million. (*Pending Report*)

US Department of Energy waives $3 million cancellation charged when Brazil turned to alternative supplier. (Spector, Moore interviews)

Calculated Economic Impact

	Annual cost to target country
Suspension of US shipments of low-enriched uranium; welfare loss valued at 40 percent of trade.	$5 million

Relative Magnitudes

Gross indicators of Brazilian economy	
Brazilian GNP (1978)	$201.2 billion
Brazilian population (1978)	112.9 million
Annual effect of sanctions related to gross indicators	
Percentage of GNP	negl.
Per capita	$0.04

Gross indicators of Brazilian economy (continued)

Brazilian trade with US as percentage of total trade
Exports (1978)   23
Imports (1978)   21

Ratio of US GNP (1978: $2,164 billion) to Brazilian GNP (1978:
$201.2 billion)   11

ASSESSMENT

Robert Wesson

"It thus appeared that efforts to use American influence to restrict the nuclear development of Brazil and other countries were costly in good-will and ineffective. It would have been unfortunate if Germany had yielded to the pleas to withdraw from its engagement; Brazil would only have been infuriated and the more determined to secure nuclear technology elsewhere. In any event, the United States appeared as a poor friend and unreliable partner, opposing the progress of a faithful ally; Brazil saw itself as treated as untrustworthy and inferior like the rest of the Third World." (Wesson 88)

"In the nuclear issue, the Carter administration was more exercised, but it failed to assess its lack of leverage and to perceive that it would become a point of honor for Brazil, to a lesser extent for West Germany, not to be coerced. Washington also failed to anticipate that Brazil and Germany would take a cynical view of its motives. The effect was negative, increased determination of Brazil to proceed; only after the United States backed away and dropped the subject could Brazilian opposition to the program take shape." (Wesson 167)

AUTHORS' SUMMARY

Overall assessment	Assigned scores
□ Policy result, scaled from 1 (failed) to 4 (success)	2
□ Sanctions contribution, scaled from 1 (none) to 4 (significant)	2
□ Success score (policy result *times* sanctions contribution), scaled from 1 (outright failure) to 16 (significant success)	4

Political and economic variables

□ Companion policies: J (covert), Q (quasi-military), or R (regular military)	—
□ International cooperation with sender, scaled from 1 (none) to 4 (significant)	1
□ International assistance to target: A (if present)	—
□ Sanctions period (years)	3
□ Economic health and political stability of target, scaled from 1 (distressed) to 3 (strong)	2

	Assigned scores
Political and economic variables (continued)	
☐ Presanction relations between sender and target, scaled from 1 (antagonistic) to 3 (cordial)	2
☐ Type of sanction: X (export), M (import), F (financial)	X
☐ Cost to sender, scaled from 1 (net gain) to 4 (major loss)	2

BIBLIOGRAPHY

Clausen, Peter. 1982. "The Reagan Nonproliferation Policy." 12 *Arms Control Today* (December): 1.

Congressional Research Service (CRS), Library of Congress. 1980. *Nuclear Proliferation Factbook.* Prepared for US Senate, Committee on Governmental Affairs, Subcommittee on Energy, Nuclear Proliferation, and Federal Services, and House Committee on Foreign Affairs, Subcommittee on International Economic Policy and Trade. 96 Cong., 2 sess., September. Washington.

Courtney, William H. 1980. "Brazil and Argentina: Nuclear Choices for Friendly Rivals." In *Nonproliferation and U.S. Foreign Policy*, ed. Joseph A. Yager. Washington: Brookings Institution.

Gall, Norman. 1976. "Atoms for Brazil, Dangers for All." *Foreign Policy* (Summer): 155–201.

Moore, Neil. Senior Licensing Officer, Exports/Imports Office of International Programs, Nuclear Regulatory Commission. Interviews with authors, August–September 1982, and January 1983.

Reagan, Ronald. 1981. "Nuclear Nonproliferation." US Department of State, *Current Policy* no. 303, 16 July. Washington.

Science. 1982. "India-US Wrangle over Nuclear Fuel Ended." (13 August): 614–16.

Spector, Leonard. US Senate Committee on Governmental Affairs, Subcommittee on Energy, Nuclear Proliferation and Government Processes. Interview with authors, 24 January 1983.

US Nuclear Regulatory Commisssion, Office of International Programs, Exports/Imports. 1982. *Pending Export Applications Report.* June. Washington.

Wesson, Robert. 1981. *The United States and Brazil: Limits of Influence.* New York: Praeger.

Case 78–3   US v. Argentina

(1978–82: Nuclear Safeguards)

CHRONOLOGY OF KEY EVENTS

1960s "To avoid dependence on enriched uranium . . . Argentina rejected US-built nuclear power plants and turned to West Germany and Canada, which supplied it with heavy-water reactors using uranium that Argentina can supply itself." US continues to supply enriched uranium for Argentina's research reactors. (*Washington Post*, 31 August 1982, A14)

1974 Argentina's first nuclear power reactor goes into operation. (Potter 191, n. 153)

9 March 1978 President Jimmy Carter signs Nuclear Non-Proliferation Act (NNPA). (Yager 30)

12 April 1979 Argentina applies to US for 12 kilograms of 90 percent fuel for research reactor. Application was still pending in mid-1984. (*Pending Report*)

7 September 1979 Argentina applies for 50 kilograms of 20 percent fuel for RA-6 (research reactor); application still pending in mid-1984. (*Pending Report*)

19 July 1982 Administration of President Ronald Reagan authorizes sale of process control system for use in Swiss-supplied heavy-water plant in Argentina. "Since [Argentina's] power reactors are fueled with natural uranium—which is plentiful in Argentina—and do not require the enriched uranium used by nuclear power plants in the United States, completion of the heavy-water production plant will significantly reduce Argentina's dependence on foreign suppliers." (*Washington Post*, 19 July 1982, A1)

May 1983 Argentina's second nuclear power plant is inaugurated. By mid-1983, "Argentina expects to meet about 7 percent of its overall electricity needs from nuclear energy. . . ." (*Journal of Commerce*, 13 May 1983, 11A)

| *2 August 1983* | US approves sale of 143 tons of German-owned heavy water to Argentina; approval of $100 million transaction is required because heavy water was produced in US. (*Washington Post*, 18 August 1983, A1) |

| *18 November 1983* | Rear Admiral Carlos Castro Madero, president of Argentina's National Atomic Energy Commission, announces that nation has developed capacity to enrich uranium. Plant, under construction five years, is expected to be fully operational in 1985. Argentine President-elect Raúl Alfonsín issues statement asserting intentions of maintaining "tight control over all our nuclear policy . . . to limit this development to strictly peaceful uses." Energy Secretary Conrado Storani, however, reaffirms Argentina's opposition to nuclear Non-Proliferation Treaty (NPT), Treaty of Tlateloco, which would ban nuclear weapons in South America. (*Washington Post*, 19 November 1983, A21; *New York Times*, 19 November 1983, A1; *Wall Street Journal*, 21 November 1983, 29) |

| *9 December 1983* | US government officials reveal estimates that Argentina will be able to produce four small atomic weapons per year from uranium enrichment plant after it becomes fully operational. Argentine officials, however, indicate willingness to drop their long-held opposition to international safeguards, perhaps even ratify Treaty of Tlateloco if US assistance is received in settling Malvinas/Falklands issue with UK. According to unnamed Argentine official, "What impedes US in the nuclear field is the question of the Malvinas. With the Malvinas question unresolved, we don't have freedom of action on anything else. It distorts all our foreign policies." (*Washington Post*, 9 December 1983, A25, A28) |

GOALS OF SENDER COUNTRY

Washington Post
"The Carter administration resisted nuclear sales to Argentina. It pressured West Germany and Canada not to sell Argentina a heavy-water nuclear plant unless that country agreed to place all its facilities under international safeguards." (*Washington Post*, 18 August 1983, A1)

In May 1982, after approving sale of computer system to Switzerland for use in heavy-water production plant for Argentina: "The Reagan administration has repeatedly emphasized that it felt the Carter administration policies were too rigid, and has contended that the United States can only exercise influence on other countries' nuclear programs by reestablishing America's position as a leading nuclear exporter." (*Washington Post*, 19 July 1982, A1)

"[Deputy Assistant Secretary of State James B.] Devine said that while the Reagan administration thinks nuclear-supplier countries should require that buyers place all their nuclear facilities under international safeguards 'as a condition of receiving significant new supplies, I don't think we consider this transaction [for the sale of heavy water] a significant new supply.'" (*Washington Post*, 18 August 1983, A1)

RESPONSE OF TARGET COUNTRY

1960s

Since 1960s, Argentina had sought to build independent nuclear program. When US withheld nuclear materials, Argentina turned to other suppliers—FRG, USSR—for heavy water, enriched uranium to run its power and research reactors, respectively. Argentina then contracts with Switzerland for heavy-water plant to be completed in mid-1980s.

November 1983

Announcing development of uranium enrichment capability, Admiral Castro Madero, president of Argentine National Atomic Energy Commission, "said the top-secret project, which has cost $62.5 million, was started in 1978 after the Carter administration refused to sell Argentina enriched uranium for its research reactors. 'The great power's policy of not providing technology to developing countries has proved unsuccessful.'" (*Wall Street Journal*, 21 November 1983, 29; *Washington Post*, 19 November 1983, A21; *Washington Post*, 31 August 1982, A14)

26 November 1983

To avoid nuclear safeguards, "the Argentines have been striving to create a wholly indigenous nuclear fuel cycle, involving purchases from abroad and therefore no inspection." Argentina already possesses indigenous uranium reserves, fuel fabrication facility; has conducted extensive research in reprocessing area with pilot facility scheduled for completion in 1986. (*Economist* [London], 26 November 1983, 32)

December 1983

Admiral Castro Madero: Argentina has "absolutely" no intention of producing highly enriched uranium from which nuclear bomb could be made. (*Wall Street Journal*, 5 December 1983, 33)

ATTITUDE OF OTHER COUNTRIES

Canada

As requested, Argentina provides "non-explosive use commitment," with regard to all nuclear materials and technology supplied by Canada following India's PNE in May 1974. Argentina refuses, however, to sign NPT or accept full-scope safeguards as required by Canada's strict new policy implemented in January 1977. "Canada continues to fulfill its obligations under the December 1973 contract between Atomic Energy of Canada Ltd. and Comisión Nacional de Energía Atómica de Argentina but Argentina has been advised that no further nuclear cooperation can take place until Argentina fully meets Canada's non-proliferation policy requirements." (Government of Canada 16)

Switzerland

Swiss company, Sulter Brothers, contracts with Argentina to supply heavy-water production plant. Plant, under construction at Arroyitos, expected to come on line in 1985–86. (*Washington Post*, 19 July 1982, A1; *Journal of Commerce*, 13 May 1983, 11A)

West Germany

With US approval, Germany in 1983 provides Argentina with 143 tons of US-produced heavy water, valued at $100 million. (*Washington Post*, 18 August 1983, A1)

Soviet Union
After NNPA is adopted in US, Argentina reportedly receives unspecified quantities of enriched uranium, at least one shipment of 11 tons of heavy water from USSR. (*Washington Post*, 18 August 1983, A1; 31 August 1982, A14)

ECONOMIC IMPACT

Observed Economic Statistics

In 1979, Argentina applies for 12.03 kilograms of 90 percent high-enriched uranium (worth $430,000), 50.125 kilograms of 19.9 percent low-enriched uranium (worth $37,400) (authors' estimates). Both applications are held up and were still pending in mid-1984. (*Pending Report*)

Between 1976 and 1983, Argentina spends $4.1 billion on nuclear program, approximately 1 percent of GNP. (*Wall Street Journal*, 5 December 1983, 33)

Calculated Economic Impact

	Annual cost to target country
Suspension of US shipments of nuclear fuel; welfare loss valued at 40 percent of trade.	$0.2 million

Relative Magnitudes

Gross indicators of Argentine economy	
Argentine GNP (1978)	$64.3 billion
Argentine population (1978)	26.9 million
Annual effect of sanctions related to gross indicators	
Percentage of GNP	negl.
Per capita	negl.
Argentine trade with United States as percentage of total trade	
Exports (1978)	9
Imports (1978)	19
Ratio of US GNP (1978: $2,164 billion) to Argentine GNP (1978: $64.3 billion)	34

ASSESSMENT

Wall Street Journal
" . . . the fact that Argentina is producing enriched uranium on a pilot scale puts it just a step away from becoming the first Latin American country able to make an atomic

bomb. And if the Argentines did decide secretly to become a nuclear power, there is little that the U.S. or other nuclear powers could do to stop them.

"Despite heavy pressure, especially from Washington, Argentina refuses to sign the Nuclear Nonproliferation Treaty. As a result, all the critical facilities in its production chain that could lead to a bomb are outside the safeguard surveillance mechanisms of the United Nations' International Atomic Energy Agency." (*Wall Street Journal*, 21 November 1983, 29)

Washington Post
" . . . Argentina is also counting on the United States and Western Europe to continue the present rather slack enforcement of their own [NPT] commitments. If Argentina can get the equipment and materials it wants from the Northern Hemisphere without signing the nonproliferation treaty, why should it sign?" (*Washington Post*, 1 December 1983, A22)

Wall Street Journal
"Argentina's costly nuclear power program is drawing sharp criticism—from Argentines, from neighboring Latin American nations and from international regulators who worry that Argentina could sell nuclear technology to other Third World countries without taking adequate safety precautions." (*Wall Street Journal*, 5 December 1983, 33)

AUTHORS' SUMMARY

Overall assessment	*Assigned scores*
☐ Policy result, scaled from 1 (failed) to 4 (success)	2
☐ Sanctions contribution, scaled from 1 (none) to 4 (significant)	2
☐ Success score (policy result *times* sanctions contribution), scaled from 1 (outright failure) to 16 (significant success)	4

Political and economic variables

☐ Companion policies: J (covert), Q (quasi-military), or R (regular military)	—
☐ International cooperation with sender, scaled from 1 (none) to 4 (significant)	2
☐ International assistance to target: A (if present)	—
☐ Sanctions period (years)	4
☐ Economic health and political stability of target, scaled from 1 (distressed) to 3 (strong)	2
☐ Presanction relations between sender and target, scaled from 1 (antagonistic) to 3 (cordial)	2
☐ Type of sanction: X (export), M (import), F (financial)	X
☐ Cost to sender, scaled from 1 (net gain) to 4 (major loss)	2

BIBLIOGRAPHY

Congressional Research Service (CRS), Library of Congress. 1980. *Nuclear Proliferation Factbook.* Prepared for Senate Committee on Governmental Affairs, Subcommittee on Energy, Nuclear Proliferation, and Federal Services, and House Committee on Foreign Affairs, Subcommittee on International Economic Policy and Trade. 96 Cong., 2 sess., September.

Government of Canada, Department of External Affairs. 1982. *Canada's Nuclear Non-Proliferation Policy.* Canadian Foreign Policy Texts no. 82/2.

Potter, William C. 1982. *Nuclear Power and Nonproliferation.* Cambridge, Mass.: Oelgeschlager, Gunn & Hain.

Reagan, Ronald. 1981. "Nuclear Nonproliferation." US Department of State, *Current Policy* no. 303, 16 July. Washington.

Science. 1982. "India-US Wrangle over Nuclear Fuel Ended." 217 (13 August): 614–16.

US Nuclear Regulatory Commission, Office of International Programs, Exports/Imports. 1982. *Pending Export Applications Report.* June. Washington.

Yager, Joseph A., ed. 1980. *Nonproliferation and U.S. Foreign Policy.* Washington: Brookings Institution.

Case 78–4   US v. India

(1978–82: Nuclear Safeguards)

CHRONOLOGY OF KEY EVENTS

1963   US, India sign 30-year pact for fuel supplies for Tarapur Atomic Power Station (TAPS), providing *inter alia* that spent fuel from these reactors may be reprocessed only with US approval. India later disputes this interpretation when fuel shipments for TAPS are restricted under 1978 Nuclear Non-Proliferation Act. (Yager 331–34; *New York Times*, 15 July 1983, A22)

1974   India conducts a "peaceful nuclear explosion." (See Case 74–2 Canada v. India [1974–76: Nuclear Explosion]).

10 March 1978   Congress passes Nuclear Non-Proliferation Act (NNPA), which establishes new criteria for nuclear exports, including strict limitations on export of highly enriched (more than 20 percent content) uranium, requirement that recipient countries accept full-scope safeguards on all facilities in nuclear program. (NNPA codifies policies that had begun to emerge during administration of President Gerald R. Ford.) All Agreements for Cooperation not incorporating these criteria must be renegotiated. Two-year grace period is permitted during which exports can go forward while negotiations take place. Among countries that do not have full-scope safeguards and with which US has agreements for cooperation are Brazil, Argentina, India, South Africa. (Moore interview; *Keesing's* 29025)

1978–80   Two uranium shipments are approved for India, one by President Jimmy Carter after tie vote by Nuclear Regulatory Commission (NRC), other on 3 to 2 vote by NRC. (Moore interview; Yager 332–34)

10 March 1980   Deadline for renegotiation of Agreements for Cooperation passes. India refuses to accept full-scope safeguards, blaming what it calls nuclear oligopoly aspects of US policy. (Moore interview; *Keesing's* 30435)

August–September 1980   Presidential waiver allowing fuel shipment of 38 tons of uranium for TAPS after NNPA deadline is upheld in Congress by one vote.

Carter maintains that denial of fuel would be interpreted by India as a unilateral abrogation of US-India Agreement for Cooperation, thereby releasing India from its obligations, including those for partial safeguards, US approval of reprocessing. (Moore interview; *New York Times*, 10 July 1983, 7; *Keesing's* 30435)

25 September 1980   India applies for second shipment of 19,858 kilograms of 2.7 percent fuel for TAPS; application remains pending as of 1984. (*Pending Report*)

29 July 1982   US, India preliminarily resolve dispute over fuel for TAPS. Agreement allows France to supply fuel for TAPS in return for Indian agreement to maintain safeguards on facility. (*Science* 614)

25 November 1982   Agreement signed by France, India for supply of low-enriched uranium for TAPS under US-India Agreement for Cooperation. As finally agreed, safeguards will continue to apply only on TAPS facility; "pursuit" and "perpetuity" provisions of guidelines will not be invoked (former requires safeguards on any facility in which the fuel or its byproducts are used, latter requires safeguards to continue beyond 1993 termination date of agreement). (*Washington Post*, 27 November 1982, A21)

21 February 1983   India begins reprocessing spent fuel from Canadian-supplied reactors at Rajasthan into fuel-grade plutonium at TAPS. (*New York Times*, 21 February 1983, A4)

May 1983   Indian officials accuse US of "reneging on a promise" made previous year after conclusion of fuel agreement to begin shipping spare parts for TAPS. *Economist* speculates that cutback in operations at TAPS, perhaps by as much as 50 percent, may be caused by safety hazards created by lack of spare parts rather than the lack of fuel: even though first shipment of French fuel has arrived, India has announced that part of TAPS will be shut down. (*Washington Post*, 13 May 1983, A21; *Economist* [London], 21 May 1983, 62)

30 June 1983   On visit to India, US Secretary of State George P. Shultz announces that US, concerned about possible radiation hazards, may supply safety-related spare parts to India if they cannot be obtained elsewhere. (*Washington Post*, 1 July 1983, A1; 26 July 1983, A18)

4 August 1983   Resolutions introduced in both houses of Congress oppose export of spare parts to India unless "stronger nuclear nonproliferation guarantees" are obtained. (*Washington Post*, 5 August 1983, A8)

2 November 1983   India reaches agreement with West German company to supply spare parts for TAPS reactors. (*Washington Post*, 2 November 1983, A19)

GOALS OF SENDER COUNTRY

US Atomic Energy Act of 1954
As amended by NNPA 1978, sec. 123 (2) and sec. 128 (a)(1) and (2): "(a)(1) As a

condition of continued United States export of source material, special nuclear material, production or utilization facilities, and any sensitive nuclear technology to non-nuclear-weapon states, no such export shall be made unless IAEA [International Atomic Energy Agency] safeguards are maintained with respect to all peaceful nuclear activities, in, under the jurisdiction of, or carried out under the control of such state at the time of the export. (2) The President shall seek to achieve adherence to the foregoing criterion by recipient non-nuclear-weapon states."

President Ronald Reagan
On 16 July 1981, Reagan modifies strict denial approach of Carter administration, emphasizes importance of US's being "reliable supplier" in order to maintain leverage over potential nuclear weapon states: "In the final analysis, the success of our efforts [to prevent proliferation] depends on our ability to improve regional and global stability and reduce those motivations that can drive countries toward nuclear explosives. . . . We must reestablish this nation as a predictable and reliable partner for peaceful nuclear cooperation under adequate safeguards. This is essential to our nonproliferation goals. If we are not such a partner, other countries will tend to go their own ways and our influence will diminish." (Reagan)

RESPONSE OF TARGET COUNTRY

April 1977
Indian Prime Minister Morarji R. Desai: ". . . informed the Indian parliament that he had told the US that any delay in the supply of enriched fuel would hurt the operation of the Tarapur Power Station and thus hurt the energy supply in Western India, and that delays contravened the obligations of the US under the intergovernmental contract on fuel supply (which mandated US shipments for Tarapur for 30 years). He also hinted that India might 'improve' fuel (perhaps a mixed oxide) for Tarapur if faced with a cutoff. Scientists subsequently worked hard to develop such a substitute. . . . The Indian stand was . . . to threaten to take possession of spent fuel if the US voided the 1963 cooperation agreement and to establish that it would not be bound to feed the Tarapur reactors with only American fuel as the 1963 agreement specified." (Yager 331, 333)

ATTITUDE OF OTHER COUNTRIES

Soviet Union
USSR supplies heavy water for CANDU (Canadian-supplied) reactor at Kota to offset suspension of supplies from Canada. (Yager 98, 109)

In May 1983, USSR offers to set up nuclear power plant in India with two 440-megawatt reactors. (*Washington Post*, 13 May 1983, A21)

Canada
Suspends nuclear cooperation with India after 1974 test explosion. (Yager 97)

France
Agrees to step in as alternative fuel supplier at request of US after suspending negotiations because of Indian intransigence on safeguards issue. Eventually, France agrees to provide uranium without more stringent safeguards it had hoped to attain. (*Washington Post*, 27 November 1982, A21)

ECONOMIC IMPACT

Observed Economic Statistics

India applies for two shipments of 2.7 percent low-enriched uranium, totaling 29,718 kgs. worth $29.8 million (authors' estimate). (*Pending Report*)

". . . the Uranium Corporation of India stockpiled a 10-year fuel supply [of natural uranium for its CANDU reactors] in the late 1970s." (Yager 329)

"The Tarapur reactors are of the light-water variety, and the others are heavy-water reactors. Cumulative generating capacity in megawatts (electric) projected in 1978 for 1985 is 1,660." (Yager 96)

Calculated Economic Impact

	Annual cost to target country
Suspension of shipment of nuclear fuel to India; welfare loss estimated at 40 percent of value.	$12 million

Relative Magnitudes

Gross indicators of Indian economy	
Indian GNP (1978)	$118.7 billion
Indian population (1978)	638.4 million
Annual effect of sanctions related to gross indicators	
Percentage of GNP	negl.
Per capita	$0.02
Indian trade with US as percentage of total trade	
Exports (1978)	13
Imports (1978)	12
Ratio of US GNP (1978: $2,164 billion) to Indian GNP (1978: $118.7 billion)	18

ASSESSMENT

Economist
"India is paying a heavy price for the 'peaceful' nuclear explosion it staged in 1974. That increased the international pressure for India to accept full-scope safeguards. Instead of accepting them, India has decided to go it alone in nuclear power, using reactors which could be fueled by natural uranium mined in India and thus avoiding dependence on the imported enriched uranium needed by reactors of the Tarapur type.

"The bid for self-sufficiency has proved to be a disaster financially and only a limited success technically." (*Economist*, 21 May 1983, 62)

Robert F. Goheen, former US ambassador to India
"There is not a chance in a million that U.S. denial of replacement parts for the Tarapur reactors will make India toe our line." (*New York Times*, 18 November 1983, A34)

AUTHORS' SUMMARY

Overall assessment	Assigned scores
□ Policy result, scaled from 1 (failed) to 4 (success)	2
□ Sanctions contribution, scaled from 1 (none) to 4 (significant)	2
□ Success score (policy result *times* sanctions contribution), scaled from 1 (outright failure) to 16 (significant success)	4

Political and economic variables

□ Companion policies: J (covert), Q (quasi-military), or R (regular military)	—
□ International cooperation with sender, scaled from 1 (none) to 4 (significant)	2
□ International assistance to target: A (if present)	—
□ Sanctions period (years)	4
□ Economic health and political stability of target, scaled from 1 (distressed) to 3 (strong)	3
□ Presanction relations between sender and target, scaled from 1 (antagonistic) to 3 (cordial)	2
□ Type of sanction: X (export), M (import), F (financial)	X
□ Cost to sender, scaled from 1 (net gain) to 4 (major loss)	2

BIBLIOGRAPHY

Congressional Research Service (CRS), Library of Congress, 1980. *Nuclear Proliferation Factbook*. Prepared for US Senate Committee on Governmental Affairs, Subcommittee on Energy, Nuclear Proliferation, and Federal Services, and House Committee on Foreign Affairs, Subcommittee on International Economic Policy and Trade. 96 Cong., 2 sess., September. Washington.

Keesing's Contemporary Archives. 1978, 1980.

Moore, Neil. Senior Licensing Officer, Exports/Imports Office of International Programs, Nuclear Regulatory Commission. Interviews with authors, August, September 1982, January 1983.

Reagan, Ronald. 1981. "Nuclear Nonproliferation." US Department of State, *Current Policy* no. 303, 16 July. Washington.

Science. 1982. "India-US Wrangle over Nuclear Fuel Ended." 217 (13 August): 614–16.

US Nuclear Regulatory Commission, Office of International Programs, Exports/Imports. 1982. *Pending Export Applications Report*. June. Washington.

Yager, Joseph A., ed. 1980. *Nonproliferation and U.S. Foreign Policy*. Washington: Brookings Institution.

Case 78–5   US v. USSR

(1978–80: Dissident Trials)

CHRONOLOGY OF KEY EVENTS

Spring 1977–
Summer 1978
Soviet dissidents Aleksandr Ginzburg, Anatoly B. Shcharansky are arrested, charged with high treason, "anti-Soviet agitation." Trial is set for 10 July 1978. (*Keesing's* 29229; *New York Times*, 8 July 1978, A1)

8 July 1978
US Secretary of State Cyrus Vance condemns trial, cancels planned visit to USSR by scientific, environmental protection delegation. Meeting scheduled for August between Vance and USSR Foreign Minister Andrei Gromyko to discuss strategic arms limitation is not cancelled. (*Keesing's* 29230)

12 July 1978
President Jimmy Carter denies Shcharansky was ever spy for CIA, says US will "let the Soviets know of our displeasure and also work toward the minimization of any punishment meted out to Mr. Shcharansky." (*Keesing's* 29230)

14–15 July 1978
Ginzburg, Shcharansky are found guilty. Ginzburg is sentenced to eight years in labor camp, followed by three years in exile; Shcharansky to 13 years in prison and labor camps. (*New York Times*, 14 July 1978, A1; 15 July 1978, A1)

18 July 1978
White House officials cancel sale of Sperry Univac computer to Tass, announce that all US exports of oil technology will require validated licenses, thus giving Department of Commerce (DOC) case-by-case review, veto power. (Oil technology sales had been restricted until 1972, when Nixon administration permitted exports to USSR except in cases of potential military application.) (*New York Times*, 19 July 1978, A1)

5 April 1979
DOC approves export license for modified version of Sperry-Univac computer canceled previously. However, USSR reportedly already had arranged to buy similar computer from French manufacturer. (*Facts on File* 287)

27 April 1979
Ginzburg, four other Soviet dissidents are exchanged in New York for two Soviet citizens convicted in US of espionage. Shcharansky remains in prison. (*Keesing's* 29725)

11 January 1980 As part of sanctions against USSR for invasion of Afghanistan, DOC suspends all outstanding validated licenses and new applications for sale of oil, gas field technology and goods to USSR pending policy review. (Up to January 1980, all license applications for shipments of oil equipment to USSR under 1978 regulations had been granted.) Policy review is completed in March. New guidelines include "a presumption against granting applications for the export of technology for manufacturing oil and gas exploration and production equipment, but a presumption in favor of granting applications to export the equipment itself." See Case 80–1 US v. USSR (1980–81: Afghanistan). (Moyer 34–36)

GOALS OF SENDER COUNTRY

President Jimmy Carter
14 July 1978: "Our sympathies and our support remain with Mr. Shcharansky, Orlov, and with Ginzburg and others. Obviously, we have no mechanism nor any desire to interfere in the internal affairs of the Soviet Union. But the arousing of public condemnation around the world for the violation of these principles of human freedom is a legitimate role for me as a leader and for the people of our country." (Carter 1282)

RESPONSE OF TARGET COUNTRY

Izvestia
Soviet newspaper reports "pressure in trade or other areas was not in the interest of the United States and would lead to a 'path of confrontation.'" (*New York Times*, 20 July 1978, A4)

ATTITUDE OF OTHER COUNTRIES

Coordinating Committee for Multilateral Export Controls
Lawrence Brady, former senior Commerce Department official responsible for export controls: ". . . in the instance of the Sperry Univac computer, the United States requested its COCOM partners to cooperate in the denial of a large computer for national security reasons and because of the internment of Soviet dissident Anatoly Shcharansky; the Japanese cooperated with us, but the French refused to go along. The French did not take us seriously, and when we suddenly granted Sperry Univac a license a few months later, their reasoning was proven to be essentially correct. The Japanese, who had passed up a contract in order to heed our request, felt betrayed." (Subcommittee on Investigations 62)

ECONOMIC IMPACT

Observed Economic Statistics

January 1977–July 1978, USSR buys more than $540 million of oil-related equipment from US firms. US Department of Energy estimates USSR will be seeking $1 billion worth over next three years. (*New York Times*, 19 July 1978, A1)

Calculated Economic Impact

	Annual cost to target country
Increased cost to USSR of imports of oil, gas field technology, equipment; welfare loss valued at 15 percent of actual and planned purchases 1977–80 (assumes loss caused by delays in shipment of about $342 million per year, added cost of substitutes).	$51 million

Relative Magnitudes

Gross indicators of USSR economy	
USSR GNP (1979)	$1,375 billion
USSR population (1978)	262 million
Annual effect of sanctions related to gross indicators	
Percentage of GNP	negl.
Per capita	$0.19
USSR trade with US as percentage of total trade	
Exports (1978)	1
Imports (1978)	5
Ratio of US GNP (1979: $2,418 billion) to USSR GNP (1979: $1,375 billion)	2

ASSESSMENT

Lawrence Brady
"Because these suspensions were often so short-lived, however, it became difficult to take them seriously, or to transmit our seriousness to our COCOM partners." (Subcommittee on Investigations 62)

Carl Gersham
"The Carter administration quickly backed off and approved all 74 of the applications submitted for the export of oil technology to the Soviet Union." (Gersham 7)

AUTHORS' SUMMARY

Overall assessment	Assigned scores
☐ Policy result, scaled from 1 (failed) to 4 (success)	1
☐ Sanctions contribution, scaled from 1 (none) to 4 (significant)	1
☐ Success score (policy result *times* sanctions contribution), scaled from 1 (outright failure) to 16 (significant success)	1

Political and economic variables	Assigned scores
☐ Companion policies: J (covert), Q (quasi-military), or R (regular military)	—
☐ International cooperation with sender, scaled from 1 (none) to 4 (significant)	2
☐ International assistance to target: A (if present)	—
☐ Sanctions period (years)	2
☐ Economic health and political stability of target, scaled from 1 (distressed) to 3 (strong)	3
☐ Presanction relations between sender and target, scaled from 1 (antagonistic) to 3 (cordial)	1
☐ Type of sanction: X (export), M (import), F (financial)	X
☐ Cost to sender, scaled from 1 (net gain) to 4 (major loss)	2

BIBLIOGRAPHY

Carter, Jimmy. 1978. *Public Papers of the Presidents of the United States*, vol. 2. Washington. *Facts on File.* 1979.

Gersham, Carl. 1979. "Selling Them the Rope—Business and the Soviets." *Commentary* (April). Reprinted in *Hearings on Transfer of Technology to the Soviet Bloc,* US Senate Subcommittee on Investigations. 96 Cong., 1 sess., 20 February 1980.

Keesing's Contemporary Archives. 1978, 1979.

Moyer, Homer E., Jr., and Linda A. Mabry. 1983. "Export Controls as Instruments of Foreign Policy: The History, Legal Issues, and Policy Lessons of Three Recent Cases." 15 *Law and Policy in International Business* 1–171.

US Congress. Senate Committee on Banking, Housing, and Urban Affairs, Subcommittee on International Finance. 1980. *Hearings on U.S. Embargo of Food and Technology to the Soviet Union.* 96 Cong., 2 sess., 22 January, 24 March.

———. Senate Committee on Governmental Affairs, Subcommittee on Investigations. 1980. *Transfer of Technology to the Soviet Bloc.* 96 Cong., 2 sess., 20 February.

Case 78–6 Arab League v. Egypt

(1978–83: Peace Treaty with Israel)

CHRONOLOGY OF KEY EVENTS

17 September   Israel, Egypt sign Camp David accords laying out framework for
1978   conclusion of peace treaty. (*Keesing's* 29941)

24 September   Arab League members (except Morocco, Sudan, Oman) release
1978   communiqué in which they pledge "(i) to establish a unified political
and military command to resist President [Anwar] Sadat's policies,
(ii) to seek closer relations with the Soviet Union to counter U.S.
influence in the Middle East, (iii) to institute a complete economic
boycott of Egypt and to sever all remaining political and cultural
links with that country and (iv) to seek the removal of the Arab
League headquarters from Cairo to another Arab capital." Arab states
discuss ways to tighten embargo against Egypt at Baghdad conference
in late October. (*Keesing's* 29659–60)

26 March 1979   Israel, Egypt sign peace treaty in Washington, ratify it following
month, formally ending state of war between the two states. (*Keesing's*
29941)

11 April 1979   US Secretary of State Cyrus Vance testifies before Senate Foreign
Relations Committee that administration plans to extend $4.8 billion
in additional financial assistance to Egypt, Israel over next three
years as cement for peace treaty. Including existing assistance, $4
billion will go to Israel, $1.8 billion to Egypt. Larger amount allocated
to Israel compensates for its withdrawal from Sinai. (*Keesing's* 29950)

27–31 March   Arab League meets in Baghdad to discuss implementation of retal-
1979   iatory measures decided in November 1978. Iraq, Syria, PLO walk
out in protest against perceived attempts by moderates, led by Saudi
Arabia, to "water down" implementation of November decisions.
Compromise agreement entails economic boycott of Egypt but does
not require withdrawal of funds from Egyptian banks or establishment
of exchange controls. Embargo on oil supplies is applied against
Egypt but not against US and other supporters of peace treaty.
(*Keesing's* 29951)

| 10 October 1981 | Arab leaders boycott funeral of slain Egyptian leader Sadat. (*New York Times*, 11 October 1981, A1) |

| 25 April 1982 | Israel completes withdrawal from Sinai. (*New York Times*, 31 October 1982, A16) |

| 7–8 June 1983 | Speculation increases on rapprochement between Egypt, other Arab states. Moroccan Foreign Minister Mohammed Boucetta refers to visit to Egypt as "initial step of Egypt's reconciliation with the Arab world." (*New York Times*, 8 June 1982, A5) |

| 22 December 1983 | On visit to Amman, Egyptian Trade Minister Mustafa Saeed announces that Jordan has agreed to end trade sanctions against Egypt. Decision coincides with public reconciliation between President Hosni Mubarak of Egypt and PLO leader Yasser Arafat in Cairo 22 December. (*New York Times*, 23 December 1983, A1, A8) |

| Late December 1983 | Egyptian trade delegation goes to Saudi Arabia to discuss reopening trade ties, then plans to visit United Arab Emirates. (*Wall Street Journal*, 29 December 1983, 16) |

| January 1984 | Islamic Conference votes to readmit Egypt. Move is thought to be preliminary step toward Egypt's readmission into Arab League at conference later in year. (*New York Times*, 20 January 1984, A1) |

| 25 September 1984 | Jordan announces its resumption of diplomatic ties with Egypt, is the first Arab country to do so. (*New York Times*, 26 September 1984, A1) |

GOALS OF SENDER COUNTRIES

October 1978
From communiqué issued at end of Baghdad conference: "The conference decided to call on the Egyptian Government to abrogate these agreements and not to sign any reconciliation treaty with the enemy. The conference hoped that Egypt would return to the fold of joint Arab action and not act unilaterally in the affairs of the Arab-Zionist conflict." (*Keesing's* 29660)

March 1979
Following signing of peace treaty in March, Arab League members accuse Egypt of having "deviated from the Arab ranks and . . . chosen, in collusion with the United States, to stand by the side of the Zionist enemy," of having "relinquished its Pan-Arab duty of liberating the occupied Arab territories, particularly Jerusalem, and of restoring the Palestinian Arab peoples' inalienable national rights. . . ." (*Keesing's* 29951)

RESPONSE OF TARGET COUNTRY

Late 1977
Following Arab condemnation of Sadat's visit to Israel in November 1977, Egypt breaks diplomatic relations with Syria, Algeria, Libya, South Yemen, Iraq. (*Keesing's* 29659)

September 1978
Sadat, in report to Parliament following signing of Camp David agreements: "While acknowledging that the Arab claim to East Jerusalem and the issue of the ultimate sovereignty of the West Bank and Gaza had not yet been resolved, he urged Jordan and Syria to take advantage of the framework for discussions established at Camp David to negotiate with Israel. He added that other Arab states should 'share in these steps' and not allow the Arab world to slide into 'frustration or collapse.'" (*Keesing's* 29664)

September 1982
Egyptian Foreign Minister Kamal Hassan Ali: "We welcome any resumption of relations with the Arab world, but we are not in a hurry. We have our contacts with most of them." (*New York Times*, 31 October 1982, A16)

December 1983
Egyptian Trade Minister Mustafa Saeed: "We are urging the Jordanians and the Palestinians to go for negotiations because through this, they will be able, with the Arab world united behind them, to achieve what we did in Sinai." (*New York Times*, 23 December 1983, A8)

ECONOMIC IMPACT

Observed Economic Statistics

Egyptian trade with Arab League[†] (million dollars)

	Exports	Imports
1977	162.0	133.3
1978	161.8	164.4
1979	106.7	81.2
1980	83.2	91.1
1981	117.7	109.6

† Algeria, Bahrain, Iran, Iraq, Jordan, Kuwait, Lebanon, Libya, Qatar, Saudi Arabia, Syria, and United Arab Emirates.
Source: IMF.

Egyptian trade with Israel (million dollars)

	Exports	Imports
1979	—	—
1980	182.3	1.0
1981	549.3	9.8

— Zero or negligible.
Source: IMF.

US aid to Egypt (million dollars)

	Economic	Military
1976	464.3	—
TQ†	552.5	—
1977	907.7	—
1978	943.0	0.2
1979	1,088.1	1,500.4
1980	1,166.4	0.8
1981	1,130.4	550.8
1982	1,064.9	902.4

— Zero or negligible.
† Transitional quarter (1 July to 30 September 1976): beginning of US fiscal year changed from June to October.
Source: IMF.

Egyptian officials say that despite the Arab boycott of Egypt, Arab investment in Egypt increased from 16 percent to 23 percent of total investment in 1982. (*New York Times,* 26 September 1984, A1)

Calculated Economic Impact

	Annual cost to target country
Decline in trade with Arab League countries; welfare loss estimated at 30 percent of reduction of average total trade with Arab League 1979–81 from presanction levels (average 1977–78).	$34 million
Offset	
Increased Egyptian trade with Israel; welfare gain estimated at 30 percent of average trade in 1980–81.	($111 million)
Total (gain)	($77 million)

Relative Magnitudes

Gross indicators of Egyptian economy	
Egyptian GNP	$19 billion
Egyptian population	41 million
Annual effect of sanctions related to gross indicators	
Percentage of GNP (gain)	(0.4)
Per capita (gain)	($1.88)

Egyptian trade with Arab League as percentage of total trade

Exports (1978)	6
Imports (1978)	2

Ratio of Arab League GNP[†] (1979: $300 billion) to Egyptian GNP (1979: $19 billion)   16

[†] Based on Algeria, Iran, Iraq, Kuwait, Libya, Qatar, Saudi Arabia, Syria.

ASSESSMENT

Margaret P. Doxey
"Arab League boycotts of Egypt since the Israeli-Egyptian peace treaty was signed in 1979 are reported to have caused internal economic difficulties, but Egypt has looked to the West and particularly to the United States for help and has no doubt received it." (Doxey 152)

Wall Street Journal
"Some Arab nations have taken a more conciliatory attitude toward Egypt in recent months, in part due to the continued war between Iran and Iraq in the Persian Gulf. Jordan's renewal of trade relations with Egypt, for instance, reflects Jordan's eagerness to find new markets to make up for the decline in its trade with Iraq." (*Wall Street Journal*, 29 December 1983, 16)

AUTHORS' SUMMARY

Overall assessment	*Assigned scores*
☐ Policy result, scaled from 1 (failed) to 4 (success)	1
☐ Sanctions contribution, scaled from 1 (none) to 4 (significant)	1
☐ Success score (policy result *times* sanctions contribution), scaled from 1 (outright failure) to 16 (significant success)	1

Political and economic variables

☐ Companion policies: J (covert), Q (quasi-military), or R (regular military)	—
☐ International cooperation with sender, scaled from 1 (none) to 4 (significant)	3
☐ International assistance to target: A (if present)	A
☐ Sanctions period (years)	5
☐ Economic health and political stability of target, scaled from 1 (distressed) to 3 (strong)	2
☐ Presanction relations between sender and target, scaled from 1 (antagonistic) to 3 (cordial)	3
☐ Type of sanction: X (export), M (import), F (financial)	F, X, M
☐ Cost to sender, scaled from 1 (net gain) to 4 (major loss)	3

BIBLIOGRAPHY

Agency for International Development. *Overseas Loans and Grants*. Various issues.
Doxey, Margaret P. 1982. "The Application of International Sanctions." In *National Economic Security: Perceptions, Threats, and Policies*, ed. Frans A. M. Alting von Geusau and Jacques Pelkmans. Tilburg, The Netherlands: John F. Kennedy Institute.
Keesing's Contemporary Archives. 1979.

Case 78–7 China v. Vietnam

(1978–79: Regional Influence)

CHRONOLOGY OF KEY EVENTS

Early 1973   China agrees to provide North Vietnam with aid at 1973 level for five years. (Pike 5)

30 April 1975   Saigon falls to North Vietnamese forces. Chinese grants and military aid are terminated. (*Keesing's* 27496; Pike 5)

6–16 May 1975   Australia, Japan, UK, Denmark recognize Provisional Revolutionary Government of South Vietnam. (*Keesing's* 27496)

2 July 1976   National Assembly representing North and South declares reunification of country under name of Socialist Republic of Vietnam (SRV). (*Keesing's* 27917)

31 December 1977   Following intermittent, increasingly intense fighting along Kampuchean-Vietnamese border, Kampuchean Foreign Ministry announces government's intention to break diplomatic relations with Vietnam until all Vietnamese forces are withdrawn from Kampuchean territory. Announcement includes request for Vietnamese Embassy personnel to leave by 7 January, at which time air service between the two countries is to be suspended. (*Keesing's* 29274)

10 January 1978   Vietnam and China sign new aid agreement. (Pike 4)

February–March 1978   Increasingly serious incidents occur on Sino-Vietnamese border. (Pike 4)

April–May 1978   Chinese aid to Hanoi is reduced by half. (Pike 5)

June 1978   Council for Mutual Economic Assistance (COMECON) unanimously approves Vietnamese membership. On 19 June, China closes four Vietnamese consulates. (Duiker 44; Pike 5)

July 1978   China cuts off all aid to Vietnam, orders home all Chinese technical assistants there. (Pike 5)

December 1978–	Kampuchea alleges invasion of its territory by Vietnamese in late
January 1979	December. On 6 January, Vietnamese Foreign Ministry labels report "odious slander." On 8 January, "People's Revolutionary Council," composed of pro-Vietnamese members, is established as provisional government in Phnom Penh. (*Keesing's* 29614–15)
17 February 1979	China invades Vietnam but with very limited objectives, primary one being "exploding the myth of the invincibility of the 'Asian Cuba.'" Chinese forces are withdrawn in March; peace negotiations begin in April. (Duiker 55–57)

GOALS OF SENDER COUNTRY

Douglas Pike
"The Cambodia-Vietnam war was seen as an effort by Vietnam to establish regional hegemony. Vietnam's increasing intimacy with the USSR smacked of collusion, a conspiracy by Moscow and Vietnam as a surrogate force, to shut China out of Southeast Asia. Overseas Chinese in Vietnam were being mistreated. . . . Hanoi was behind certain anti-Chinese moves by Laos. Finally, the Vietnamese were behaving in an ideologically improper manner." (Pike 5)

Congressional Research Service
"China's precise motives for changing its approach toward Vietnam are still far from clear. It does seem clear that the overall Chinese objective in the region remained the development of a favorable balance of influence that would reduce or preclude the expansion of Soviet power and the power of countries seen by China as Soviet surrogates. . . . It is probably more than coincidence that the new more forceful approach toward Vietnam was closely associated with Vice Premier Deng Xiaoping, whose influence grew tremendously in Chinese leadership councils during 1978. Deng was especially outspoken in his criticism of Vietnam and of Vietnamese-Soviet relations during conversations with Western visitors to China in mid-1978. . . . The new Chinese attitude toward Vietnam also coincided with a generally more assertive Chinese foreign policy against suspected Soviet expansion abroad. . . ." (CRS 43)

RESPONSE OF TARGET COUNTRY

William J. Duiker
"The end of the war thus appears to have marked a significant shift in Vietnamese foreign policy from nonalignment in the Sino-Soviet dispute and towards a clear preference for Moscow. . . . The Party leadership may well have decided that a policy of 'lean to one side' was justified if it served to persuade Moscow to finance Hanoi's ambitious plans for socialist reconstruction, yet there were probably deeper underlying issues at work as well. . . . Territorial disagreements, carefully hidden during the war, were beginning to emerge into open view. Beneath it all lay a primordial distrust of China which transcended the ties of ideology and practical interest and must have festered under the surface during a generation of outward intimacy." (Duiker 23)

Following Chinese criticism of Vietnam's entry into CMEA (COMECON) in summer 1978: "Hanoi defended its actions by saying that it had been necessitated by Peking's cancellation of several projects in May. In the words of SRV Secretary of State Nguyen Co Thach: 'Without the cutting off of aid this would not have been necessary. We entered COMECON only to find assistance.''' (Duiker 44)

ATTITUDE OF OTHER COUNTRIES

Soviet Union
"Moscow's generous support and active encouragement of closer Soviet-Vietnamese relations provided Hanoi with a way to deal with Pol Pot and with China." (CRS 46)

United States
" . . . cautious efforts by the SRV to revitalize the negotiations with the United States (by suggesting that Hanoi might be willing to drop its demand for reconstruction assistance as a precondition for diplomatic ties) had so far elicited little response from Washington. The Carter Administration, beset with foreign policy problems of its own, now seemed in no hurry to seek a rapprochement with Vietnam." (Duiker 45)

"The invasion [of Kampuchea], coupled with the Sino-Vietnamese War, wrote at least a temporary halt to American interest in improving relations with Hanoi. The United States did not wish to jeopardize prospects for a rapprochement with Peking at a time when a breakthrough was imminent. To put it bluntly, the Carter Administration felt that it had little to gain in normalizing ties with Vietnam. It had a good deal to lose." Also see Case 75–5 US v. Kampuchea (1975–79: Aftermath of Vietnam War). (Duiker 54)

COMECON
"Vietnam did gain some economic advantage in joining COMECON. The socialist group agreed to take over certain abandoned Chinese aid projects, and granted Vietnam a preferential exchange rate which in effect was a subsidy for Vietnam's foreign trade." (Pike 7)

Japan, Denmark
On 10–23 January 1979, Japan announces it is freezing aid to Vietnam that had been extended with "the understanding that Vietnam would settle the conflict with Cambodia peacefully. . . ." Aid, offered in December 1978 for year beginning 1 April 1979, would have amounted to $195 million in grant aid, $487.5 million in commodity loans, 150,000 tons of rice. Denmark also cancels (£10 million) aid program. (*Keesing's* 29473, 29616)

United Kingdom
On 3 July 1979, Prime Minister Margaret Thatcher informs Parliament that British aid to Vietnam will be discontinued "so long as the present circumstances continue." She rejects, however, "a proposal to cancel an agreement to build three cargo ships for Vietnam." (*Keesing's* 30080)

European Community
On 4 July 1979, European Commission decides to cancel its food aid program for Vietnam, divert aid to UN high commissioner for refugees (UNHCR] "for the use of Indochinese refugees." Measure is opposed by Denmark, Netherlands, France; France because it has "the appearance of a measure of reprisals." European Commissioner Claude Cheysson, however, states that "the agreement between Vietnam and the UNHCR on the departure of refugees should be effectively applied, and said if Vietnam's response was positive the Community would resume its food aid to Vietnam." (*Keesing's* 30080)

On 24 July 1979, European Community's Council of (Foreign) Ministers agrees "to increase their aid to the Indochinese refugees and to continue the suspension of aid to Vietnam." Council votes to consider resumption of aid after report by UN Secretary General Kurt Waldheim on Vietnamese compliance with emigration program that was negotiated in May 1979. (*Keesing's* 30082)

Federal Republic of Germany
On 6 July 1979, FRG announces it is canceling its planned development aid to Vietnam, instead, will donate it "to the care of the refugees." (*Keesing's* 30080)

France
On 23 December 1981, agreement is signed in Paris between France, Vietnam under which France will provide $40 million in concessional credit. Foreign Minister Cheysson denies action signifies "any relaxation in French insistence that Vietnamese troops should be withdrawn from Kampuchea. . . ." (*Keesing's* 31593)

Australia
Government suspends economic aid, cultural exchanges with Vietnam.

In March 1983, Australian Labor party (ALP) defeats ruling Liberal-National party coalition in general election. New government is sworn in 11 March with Labor leader Robert Hawke as prime minister. ALP had earlier committed itself to resuming aid to Vietnam if elected. (*Keesing's* 29616, 32126–27; *Economist* [London], 21 May 1983, 62)

On 22 November 1983, at conclusion of two-day trip to Thailand, Prime Minister Hawke announces that differences of opinion between his government and Association of Southeast Asian Nations (ASEAN) members over aid to Vietnam have been resolved. Hawke says ASEAN countries, while fearing Australian policies will encourage Vietnam to stay in Cambodia, have decided not to object to Australia's intention of extending $500,000 in emergency relief aid to Hanoi. Hawke says no decision has been made on resumption of development aid to Vietnam but reiterates belief that "keeping Vietnam politically and economically isolated" will only increase reliance on Soviet Union. (*Washington Post*, 23 November 1983, A15)

Association of Southeast Asian Nations
"ASEAN's strategy includes applying political, diplomatic and economic pressures on Vietnam to persuade Hanoi that a political settlement is in its own interests." (*Department of State Bulletin*, November 1983, 37)

ECONOMIC IMPACT

Observed Economic Statistics

French aid to Vietnam (1973–78): $50 million. (Pike 18)

"The amount of [Chinese] aid varied from year to year, depending in part on the amount of political pressure that China wanted to apply on North Vietnam." (Pike 15)

Chinese aid to North Vietnam is cut by 20 percent in 1969, 50 percent in 1970 to show displeasure with Vietnamese negotiations with US. Conversely, in 1971–72, amount is increased to induce Vietnamese acquiescence in normalization. (Pike 15)

Estimates of Chinese aid to Vietnam 1958–78 vary from $10 billion to $18 billion. Until 1975 it had been primarily military in nature. In 1976, aid reportedly totaled $330 million but was considerably reduced in following two years. Aid from the USSR has been estimated at about $500 million per year in recent years. (*Keesing's* 29471)

Original estimate of planned Chinese aid to Vietnam (1976–80) is $1.9 billion. It is estimated that $800 million is delivered before 1978 termination. (Pike 15)

"Hanoi's only support comes from the USSR and Soviet allies. The Soviet Union provides Vietnam with military and economic aid exceeding $1 billion annually. This aid supports Vietnam's war effort in Kampuchea and keeps the Vietnamese economy functioning at a minimal level but is insufficient to allow Hanoi to reconstruct and develop the country." (*Department of State Bulletin*, November 1983, 37)

Vietnamese trade with USSR and Eastern Europe (million dollars)

	Exports	Imports
1975	3.0	9.5
1976	3.4	6.9
1977	5.1	8.9
1978	9.5	64.9
1979	10.4	71.3
1980	16.6	145.0
1981	10.6	89.9

Source: UN.

"[The Vietnamese economy in December 1978] is now in a condition of considerable malaise. . . . The serious economic situation was admitted and discussed with some candor by Premier Pham Van Dong . . . [who] said the economic troubles were due to the halt in Chinese aid and to recent flooding which destroyed much of the rice crop." (Pike 15)

"As far as shipment of food is concerned, Vietnam's aid dependency has passed at least for the moment from substantial to extreme. The plain fact is that without extensive input of food for the next year or so, Vietnam will starve." (Pike 16)

"Vietnam now is being carried economically by the Communist world, chiefly by the USSR, and all indications are that this situation will continue." (Pike 17)

Calculated Economic Impact

	Annual cost to target country
Reduction in Chinese aid to Vietnam; welfare loss estimated at 90 percent of value of reduced transfers.	$330 million

Calculated Economic Impact (*continued*)

	Annual cost to target country
Offset	
Increased aid from COMECON to compensate for withdrawal of Chinese aid; welfare gain valued at 90 percent of transfers (estimated as 30 percent of increased imports from COMECON countries).	($76 million)
Total	$254 million

Relative Magnitudes

Gross indicators of Vietnamese economy	
Vietnamese GNP (1976)	$7.2 billion
Vietnamese population (1976)	48.8 million
Annual effect of sanctions related to gross indicators	
Percentage of GNP	3.5
Per capita	$5.20
Vietnamese trade with China as percentage of total trade	
Exports (1978)	22
Imports (1978)	2
Ratio of Chinese GNP (1976: $293 billion) to Vietnamese GNP (1976: $7.2 billion)	41

ASSESSMENT

Authors' comments
COMECON aid to Vietnam only partially offset Chinese sanctions which imposed a relatively high cost. Nevertheless, Vietnamese troops remain in Kampuchea and there has been little improvement in Sino-Vietnamese relations.

AUTHORS' SUMMARY

Overall assessment	Assigned scores
☐ Policy result, scaled from 1 (failed) to 4 (success)	1
☐ Sanctions contribution, scaled from 1 (none) to 4 (significant)	1
☐ Success score (policy result *times* sanctions contribution), scaled from 1 (outright failure) to 16 (significant success)	1

Political and economic variables	Assigned scores
☐ Companion policies: J (covert), Q (quasi-military), or R (regular military)	R
☐ International cooperation with sender, scaled from 1 (none) to 4 (significant)	3
☐ International assistance to target: A (if present)	A
☐ Sanctions period (years)	1
☐ Economic health and political stability of target, scaled from 1 (distressed) to 3 (strong)	2
☐ Presanction relations between sender and target, scaled from 1 (antagonistic) to 3 (cordial)	3
☐ Type of sanction: X (export), M (import), F (financial)	F
☐ Cost to sender, scaled from 1 (net gain) to 4 (major loss)	1

BIBLIOGRAPHY

Congressional Research Service (CRS), Library of Congress. 1982. *Vietnam's Future Policies and Role in Southeast Asia.* Prepared for Senate Committee on Foreign Relations. 97 Cong., 2 sess. Washington.

Duiker, William J. 1980. *Vietnam Since the Fall of Saigon.* Center for International Studies Southeast Asia Series no. 56. Athens: Ohio University.

Keesing's Contemporary Archives. 1975, 1976, 1978, 1979, 1980, 1982, 1983.

Pike, Douglas. 1979. *Vietnam's Foreign Relations 1975–78.* Prepared for House Committee on Foreign Affairs, Subcommittee on Asian and Pacific Affairs. 96 Cong., 1 sess. Washington.

United Nations. *Statistical Yearbook for Asia and the Pacific.* Various issues.

Case 78–8   US v. Libya
(1978–   : Qaddafi)

CHRONOLOGY OF KEY EVENTS

Also see Summary S–1 US v. Countries Supporting International Terrorism (1972– : Overview)

1978	US bans military equipment sales to Libya in retaliation for Libyan support of terrorist groups. (*New York Times*, 21 January 1982, A1)
2 March 1979	Deputy Assistant Secretary of State Morris Draper informs Congress that State Department, after having received assurances that they would be used only for national airline, has approved sale of three Boeing 747 planes, two 727 planes to Libya. (*New York Times*, 3 March 1979, A5)
29 September 1979	Revised Export Administration Act, with Fenwick amendment (Congresswoman Millicent Fenwick, R–NJ) on terrorism attached, is enacted. In accordance with amendment, State Department names Libya, Syria, Iraq, and South Yemen as countries which, because of support for terrorism, may not receive certain US exports; export of some other goods contingent upon congressional approval. (Flores 564, 570)
May 1981	US closes Libyan diplomatic mission. (*New York Times*, 7 May 1981, A1)
August 1981	US jets down two Libyan aircraft over Gulf of Sidra. (*New York Times*, 20 August 1981, A1)
28 October 1981	US imposes controls on exports of small aircraft, helicopters, aircraft parts, avionics to Libya to "limit Libyan capacity to support military adventures in neighboring countries." (GAO 4)
November 1981	Exxon abandons Libyan operations. (*Wall Street Journal*, 11 December 1981, 3)
6 December 1981	US defense attaché murdered in Paris; some observers suspect Libyan involvement. (Schott 16; Flores 582)

7 December 1981	President Ronald Reagan claims US has evidence that President Muammar al-Qaddafi has sent assassination teams to murder top US officials. (*Washington Post*, 11 December 1981, A28)

| 11 December 1981 | Reagan administration calls on Americans residing in Libya (primarily 1,500 technicians) to leave "as soon as possible," citing "the danger which the Libyan regime poses to American citizens." US passports declared invalid for travel in Libya. (*Washington Post*, 11 December 1981, A1; *Wall Street Journal*, 11 December 1981, 3) |

| 12 December 1981 | US oil firms agree to withdraw US personnel from Libya but announce they will be replaced with other foreign technicians. (*Washington Post*, 12 December 1981, A1) |

| 21 January 1982 | Libya is reported to have rebuilt 400 heavy duty trucks (sold to Libya by Oshkosh Trucks) to carry tanks and for other military purposes, despite written guarantees in February 1978 that vehicles would be used solely for agricultural purposes. (*New York Times*, 21 January 1982, A1) |

| 10 March 1982 | Reagan embargoes crude oil imports from Libya, invoking section 232 of Trade Expansion Act of 1962, drawing on same national security finding made in case of Iranian oil. Presidential Proclamation 49072 states: "Libyan policy and action supported by revenues from the sale of oil imported into the United States are inimical to United States national security." In addition, US restricts exports of sophisticated oil, gas equipment and technology but does not impose retroactive controls or embargo export of items that are available abroad. (Schott 18, 39; *Wall Street Journal*, 9 November 1982, 39) |

| 9 November 1982 | US State Department warns oil companies (notably Charter Oil, Coastal Corp.) against selling refined products derived from Libyan crude in US. (*Wall Street Journal*, 9 November 1982, 39) |

| December 1982 | US bars Boeing sale of 12 commercial jets to Libyan Arab Airlines for $600 million. (*New York Times*, 26 August 1983, A24) |

| August 1983 | Libya sends troops into Chad in hope of overthrowing government of Hissen Habre. France, US support Habre. Reagan administration is divided over export license application for shipment of $40 million marine mooring system to Libya. (*New York Times*, 19 August 1983, A1, A6; 26 August 1983, A24) |

| 5 December 1983 | Reagan reportedly considers "State Department proposal to block exports of any US-made product that would contribute substantially to the development of Libya's economy." Proposed policy, arising out of Libyan request to purchase irrigation and oil-refining equipment, would effectively block "almost all major exports to Libya." Other elements of administration continue opposition to restrictive approach on exports to Libya. (*Wall Street Journal*, 5 December 1983, 3; *New York Times*, 16 December 1983, A18) |

GOALS OF SENDER COUNTRY

December 1981
Administration official states Libya has stirred up trouble in at least 20 other nations; has supported terrorist groups in Arab countries, Italy, Ireland; has committed assorted anti-US acts. (*Wall Street Journal*, 11 December 1981, 3)

December 1981
Administration officials emphasize that anti-Qaddafi strategy is not response to assassination reports. Instead, they say strategy is linked "to a presidential decision, taken months ago, to devote major US efforts to the task of weakening the Qadhafi regime." On 11 December, Deputy Secretary of State William P. Clark states that administration has acted in response to Qaddafi's "well-known efforts over the course of many years to undermine US interests and those of our friends, as well as Libya's support for international terrorism." Anti-Qaddafi strategy involves many potential options, including oil embargo, other trade restrictions, military contingency plans. Other options require prior departure of US residents, lest they become hostages. (*Wall Street Journal*, 11 December 1981, 3, 31; *Washington Post*, 11 December 1981, A28)

November 1982
CIA mounts opposition to Libyan occupation of Chad; assists Libyan exiles. CIA Director William Casey says these activities might lead to "ultimate" removal of Qaddafi. (*Newsweek*, 8 November 1982, 55)

August 1983
Anonymous administration official: "American policy is for Libya to get out of Chad. . . . The Libyans should not be in Chad. We have to show the Libyans they cannot win in Chad. . . . " (*New York Times*, 19 August 1983, A6)

RESPONSE OF TARGET COUNTRY

11 December 1981
Libyan Oil Minister Abdessalem Mohammed Zagaar labels Reagan administration measures "an act of aggression," calls upon OPEC for assistance; OPEC rejects proposal for joint action. (*Washington Post*, 11 December 1981, A1; 12 December 1981, A1)

19 August 1983
Establishing friendly government in Chad is viewed by Western diplomats as part of Qaddafi's grander plan of unifying sub-Saharan Moslem Africa under Libyan banner. (*New York Times*, 19 August 1983, A6)

ATTITUDE OF OTHER COUNTRIES

West Germany, France
On 12 December 1981, West German Foreign Minister Hans-Dietrich Genscher, French Foreign Minister Claude Cheysson, among other Europeans, urge Secretary of State Alexander M. Haig, Jr., to treat Libya in a more friendly fashion. According to one French diplomat, Haig in appeal for NATO support against Libya only "convinced himself." (*Washington Post*, 11 December 1981, A25; 12 December 1981, A18)

"But although France has also reacted with concern to Libyan moves in Africa, it has refused in part for economic reasons to treat Colonel Qaddafi as a pariah. It buys oil from Libya and argues that it is important to keep lines of communication open with the Libyans. In addition to this specific difference, President François Mitterrand of France has sought to distance his policy toward Chad from Washington's. But American officials in the White House, Pentagon and State Department all said today that American and French policy has been closely coordinated." (*New York Times*, 19 August 1983, A6)

Organization of Petroleum Exporting Countries
On 12 December 1981, ministers reject Libyan appeal for "joint action" against US. (*Washington Post*, 12 December 1982, A1)

ECONOMIC IMPACT

Observed Economic Statistics

US sales of small aircraft, helicopters, aircraft parts, avionics to Libya in 1980 total $7.58 million. (GAO 19)

Mobil announces termination of Libyan operations—100,000 barrels (bbls.)/day in 1980; 30,000–40,000 bbls./day in late 1982. (*Washington Post*, 26 February 1982, A1; *New York Times*, 5 January 1983, D6)

US oil imports pre-March 1982 are approximately 150,000 bbls./day (because of recession, down from 700,000 bbls./day in 1981). (Schott 18)

US oil company assets in Libya, at end of 1981, are valued at $600 million. (Schott 16)

US trade with Libya (million dollars)

	Exports	Imports
1980	509	7,395
1981	803	5,476
1982	301	533

Source: IMF.

Potential impact of December 1983 proposed change in policy toward exports to Libya is estimated at $150 million a year. (*Wall Street Journal*, 5 December 1983, 3)

Calculated Economic Impact

	Annual cost to target country
Cut-off of US imports of 150,000 bbls./day of Libyan oil; with no reduction in overall Libyan exports,† cut-off forces Libya to discount price by estimated 10 percent (or $3.70/ bbl.)—of which 5 percent is attributable to market forces, 5 percent to sanctions.	$101 million

	Annual cost to target country
Reduction in nonoil US-Libyan trade as result of export/import controls; welfare loss estimated at 30 percent of face value of trade (including welfare cost of blocked US exports of sensitive oil, gas field technology).	10 million
Withdrawal of US citizens from Libya; estimated 10 percent increase in estimated $75,000 annual salary to hire non-US oil field workers to replace about 750 US employees who leave.	6 million
Suspension of sale of Boeing jets to Libya; welfare loss estimated at 10 percent of value of trade.	60 million

Offset

Sale of Exxon assets in Libya for less than book value ($121 million v. $95 million settlement), valued at 100 percent.	($26 million)
Total	$151 million

† During this period Libya sends crude to European refineries for processing, charges price tied to output of product (which yields substantially less than official price of Libyan crude). During 1982, Libya substantially increases crude sales (from 0.9 million bbls./day to 1.7 million bbls./day) through this subterranean method of discounting price of crude oil.

Relative Magnitudes

Gross indicators of Libyan economy	
Libyan GNP (1978)	$18.3 billion
Libyan population (1978)	2.7 million
Annual effect of sanctions related to gross indicators	
Percentage of GNP	0.8
Per capita	$55.93
Libyan trade with US as percentage of total trade	
Exports (1980)	34
Imports (1980)	6
Ratio of US GNP (1978: $2,164 billion) to Libyan GNP (1978: $18.3 billion)	118

ASSESSMENT

Wall Street Journal
Administration official projects "a modest near-term effect" on Libya resulting from sanctions. (*Wall Street Journal*, 11 December 1981, 3)

Washington Post
Anonymous Arab editor: "To you in the United States [Qaddafi] may be a villain, but to many Arabs, the more he is attacked, the more he comes out a hero, a man who can stand up to a superpower." (*Washington Post*, 9 December 1981, A11)

Jeffrey J. Schott
"It is safe to say that the world oil glut and the consequent fall in oil prices have hurt the Libyans more than the US trade sanctions. Any subsequent moderation in Qaddafi's policies was probably attributable more to financial constraints imposed by the market than by the United States." (Schott 18)

"The Exxon pullout probably would have occurred even without the political pressures that built up during 1981." (Schott 39)

AUTHORS' SUMMARY

Overall assessment	Assigned scores
□ Policy result, scaled from 1 (failed) to 4 (success)	2
□ Sanctions contribution, scaled from 1 (none) to 4 (significant)	2
□ Success score (policy result *times* sanctions contribution), scaled from 1 (outright failure) to 16 (significant success)	4

Political and economic variables	
□ Companion policies: J (covert), Q (quasi-military), or R (regular military)	Q, J
□ International cooperation with sender, scaled from 1 (none) to 4 (significant)	1
□ International assistance to target: A (if present)	—
□ Sanctions period (years)	6+
□ Economic health and political stability of target, scaled from 1 (distressed) to 3 (strong)	3
□ Presanction relations between sender and target, scaled from 1 (antagonistic) to 3 (cordial)	1
□ Type of sanction: X (export), M (import), F (financial)	X, M
□ Cost to sender, scaled from 1 (net gain) to 4 (major loss)	3

BIBLIOGRAPHY

Bienen, Henry, and Robert Gilpin. 1979. "Evaluation of the Use of Economic Sanctions to Promote Foreign Policy Objectives." Boeing Corp., unpublished, 2 April.

Flores, David A. 1981. "Export Controls and the US Effort to Combat International Terrorism." 13 *Law and Policy in International Business* 521–90.

Schott, Jeffrey J. 1982. "Trade Sanctions and US Foreign Policy." Carnegie Endowment for International Peace, unpublished, 14 September.

US General Accounting Office. 1983. *Administration Knowledge of Economic Costs of Foreign Policy Export Controls*. Report to Senator Charles H. Percy. 2 September. Washington.

Case 79–1 US v. Iran

(1979–81: Hostages)

CHRONOLOGY OF KEY EVENTS

16 January 1979   Shah Reza Mohammad Pahlavi flees Iran for Egypt; Ayatollah Ruhollah Khomeini, religious leader, announces from exile in Paris he will appoint provisional government to rule Iran. (CRS 12)

1 February 1979   Khomeini returns to Tehran; on 11 February, Prime Minister Shahpour Bakhtiar is succeeded by Mehdi Bazargan, Khomeini supporter. (CRS 12, 14–15)

14 February 1979   US Embassy is attacked, overrun; about 100 hostages are taken but released few hours later when Khomeini supporters disperse militants. (Rubin 369)

9 March 1979   *Middle East Economic Digest* reports large US oil companies, with US government support, have agreed to boycott Iranian oil on world market. (CRS 19)

22 October 1979   Shah arrives unannounced in New York City for medical treatment. On 3 November, Iranian Foreign Minister Ibrahim Yazdi formally protests US decision to admit shah. (CRS 34–35)

4 November 1979   Demonstrators overrun US Embassy in Tehran, taking approximately 100 hostages, about 60 of whom are Americans. Demonstrators demand US extradite shah. (CRS 35)

5 November 1979   Iran abrogates 1959 Cooperation Treaty with US, 1921 Friendship Treaty with USSR. Khomeini condones embassy takeover. (CRS 36)

6 November 1979   President Jimmy Carter sends Ramsey Clark, former attorney general, William Miller, Senate Intelligence Committee staff chief, to Iran to negotiate hostage release; Khomeini refuses to meet them. (CRS 36)

8 November 1979   US halts shipment of military spare parts to Iran. (CRS 38)

10 November 1979   Carter orders 50,000 Iranian students in US to report to immigration office with view to deporting those in violation of their visas. On 27

December 1979, US appeals court allows deportation of Iranian students found in violation. (CRS 38, 71)

12 November 1979	Invoking section 232 of Trade Expansion Act of 1962, and finding national emergency, Carter embargoes oil imports from Iran. Iran responds with oil export embargo against US. (CRS 38)
13 November 1979	US House of Representatives votes 379 to 0 to prohibit foreign aid, military assistance to Iran. (CRS 38)
14 November 1979	Invoking International Emergency Economic Powers Act, Carter freezes Iranian deposits in US banks and foreign subsidiaries, following announcement indicating that Iran might withdraw those assets. Tehran press announces closing of Iranian airspace, territorial waters to US aircraft, shipping. (CRS 39)
18 November 1979	Iran releases black and most women hostages. (CRS 40)
23 November 1979	Foreign Minister Abol Hassan Bani Sadr repudiates Iran's foreign debt. Iran estimates it at $15 billion, *Washington Post* at "closer to $7 billion." (CRS 42)
4 December 1979	UN Security Council resolution calls for release of hostages, peaceful settlement of US-Iranian differences, participation by Secretary General Kurt Waldheim in resolving dispute. (CRS 50)
15 December 1979	International Court of Justice orders release of hostages, restoration of US property. (CRS 61)
26 December 1979	USSR occupies Afghanistan. (*New York Times*, 27 December 1979, 1)
29 December 1979	US proposes in UN Security Council that Secretary General Waldheim return to Tehran for another attempt at mediation; US also proposes economic sanctions if agreement can not be reached within one to two weeks. (CRS 73)
12 January 1980	Half an hour before a scheduled UN vote on sanctions, Iran submits written three-part proposal for releasing hostages. Vote is postponed to clarify details of proposal, which seems to involve UN investigation into "crimes" of the shah, UN endorsement of Iran's extradition request to Panama, return of shah's assets to Iran. (CRS 83)
13 January 1980	Iran fails to clarify its proposal; USSR vetoes US proposal for economic sanctions. US reiterates its determination to apply unilateral economic sanctions, seek allied support. (CRS 84)
29 January 1980	Six Americans are smuggled out of Iran by Canadian Embassy officials. (Rubin 375)
7 February 1980	US State Department announces additional economic sanctions will be held in abeyance while diplomatic negotiations at UN continue. (CRS 101)

| 7 April 1980 | Carter escalates program of economic sanctions: breaks diplomatic relations with Iran; imposes export embargo (excluding food, medicine); orders inventory of $8 billion in frozen assets and inventory of US financial claims against Iran to be paid out of those assets; cancels all Iranian entry visas; closes Iranian Embassy, five consulates, orders departure of all 35 remaining diplomats, 209 military students. Carter threatens to take "other actions" if hostages are not released promptly. (CRS 148) |

| 17 April 1980 | Carter announces further economic measures. He prohibits all financial transactions between US citizens and those of Iran; imposes import embargo; bans travel to Iran except for journalists; releases, for US purchase, impounded military equipment intended for use in Iran; requests Congress to pass legislation to permit use of frozen assets for claims, reparations. (CRS 158) |

| 25–27 April 1980 | Carter launches unsuccessful military attempt to rescue hostages; Secretary of State Cyrus Vance resigns; shah dies in Egypt. (CRS 168, 250) |

| 22 September 1980 | Iran-Iraq border dispute intensifies into full-scale war. (CRS 301) |

| 2–20 November 1980 | Iranian parliament (Majlis) issues conditions for release of hostages: US to pledge not to interfere in Iranian affairs in future; US to release frozen assets; US to lift economic sanctions; US to return shah's wealth to Iran. Carter responds that the conditions "appear to offer a positive basis" for resolution of crisis. On 10 November secret negotiations, led by Deputy Secretary of State Warren Christopher, commence in Algeria. On 20 November, Secretary of State Edmund S. Muskie says US has accepted conditions "in principle." (CRS 367, 391) |

| 29 November 1980 | Militants at US Embassy in Tehran transfer responsibility for hostages to government. (CRS 398–99) |

| 19 January 1981 | Algeria announces commitments agreed to by US and Iran pertaining to release of hostages: declaration of noninterference in Iran by US; establishment of escrow account in Bank of England for transfer of frozen assets; agreement for settlement of claims; revocation of sanctions; release of hostages; blocking of transfer of shah's wealth, giving government of Iran access to US courts to sue for its return; prohibition on prosecution by hostages or their families of claims against Iran for seizure of embassy. (*New York Times*, 20 January 1981, 1; Carswell 254) |

| 20 January 1981 | Ronald Reagan is inaugurated as president; hostages are released in exchange for partial transfer of Iranian assets; on 18 February 1981, Reagan administration decides not to renounce accords. (Malawer 485) |

| 2 July 1981 | US Supreme Court in *Dames & Moore v. Regan* (453 US 654, 1981) upholds accords by denying right of US firm to make claims against |

Iranian assets except in context of arbitration agreement. (Malawer 477)

18 August 1981   US transfers Iranian funds to escrow account in The Hague, as authorized by accords. (Malawer 485)

April 1983   "Business contacts and commercial agreements between the United States and Iran, interrupted four years ago when Ayatollah Ruhollah Khomeini came to power, are slowly, haltingly resuming." (*Washington Post*, 10 April 1983, F1)

GOALS OF SENDER COUNTRY

14 November 1979
"Although it was not universally understood, from the beginning the blocking had a dual purpose, the release of the hostages and the protection of the property claims of US individuals and corporations against Iran. The President's report to the Congress on [this day] explicitly stated those objectives." (Carswell 249)

28 November 1979
President Carter: "For the last 24 days our nation's concern has been focused on our fellow Americans being held hostage in Iran. We have welcomed some of them home to their families and their friends. But we will not rest nor deviate from our efforts until all have been freed from their imprisonment and their abuse. We hold the Government of Iran fully responsible for the well-being and the safe return of every single person." (Alexander 481)

22 January 1980
Carter says US is ready to help Iran meet Soviet threat from Afghanistan, establish new relationship following release of hostages. (CRS 90)

5 April 1980
White House press secretary Jody Powell states president's intent of applying political and economic sanctions if hostages are not transferred to government custody. (CRS 146)

20 October 1980
Carter says that if Iran will free hostages, the US will release frozen assets, lift economic sanctions, seek normal relations with Iran. (CRS 347)

RESPONSE OF TARGET COUNTRY

5 November 1979
Khomeini speaking immediately after embassy takeover: " . . . if they do not give up the criminals [the shah and Shahpour Bakhtiar, former prime minister, exiled in France] . . . then we shall do whatever is necessary. . . ." (CRS 36)

28 December 1979
Iranian Foreign Minister Sadegh Ghotzbadeh warns that increasing US economic pressure will result in quick trial of hostages. On 14 January 1980, Ghotzbadeh says Iran could hold hostages "more or less forever." (CRS 72, 84)

11 January 1980
Iranian Oil Minister Ali Akbar Moinfar says Iran will cut oil shipments to any nation supporting economic sanctions against Iran. He says Iran ships 1 million barrels per day to Western Europe, Japan. (CRS 82, 86)

15 February 1980
Director of Iran's central bank says US must release $6 billion in assets frozen by Carter in November 1979 before hostages will be freed. (CRS 106)

4 April 1980
Conservative clerical forces in Iran oppose any concessions to US, threaten total oil embargo—with help of Saudi Arabia, Bahrain, Kuwait, Iraq—against West Europe, US if sanctions are imposed. (CRS 146)

8 April 1980
Iranian leaders almost welcome imposition of general economic sanctions, generally agreeing they will help rid Iran of American influence. Khomeini says sanctions are "good omen" because they signal US recognition of permanent loss of influence in Iran; students at embassy are pleased because sanctions will stop diplomatic efforts to have hostages released; Bani Sadr (now president) says Iran can handle effects of sanctions, says they allow Iran to "break free" of US; Revolutionary Council also "welcomes" action. Iran threatens again to halt oil shipments to any other nation supporting sanctions. (CRS 149)

19 April 1980
Iran imposes oil embargo against Portugal. (CRS 160)

24 April 1980
Foreign Minister Ghotzbadeh says it is "regrettable" that Europe has joined US sanctions but that Iran would never surrender to "force" and "pressure." (CRS 164)

13–14 June 1980
Bani Sadr says economic situation is worsening, and inflation, economic blockade, in conjunction with people's fears, could create "sick economy." Ghotzbadeh claims sanctions are not affecting Iran. (CRS 207, 208)

3 August 1980
Bani Sadr says US economic sanctions have increased cost of Iran's imports by 20 percent to 25 percent, that Iran needs spare parts denied by sanctions, concedes that sanctions are hurting Iran. (CRS 256)

1 September 1980
Ettelaat (newspaper in Iran) says Majlis should take up hostage question as soon as possible because economic sanctions are causing "severe pressure" on Iran. (CRS 280)

2 September 1980
Iranian Oil Minister Moinfar says sanctions have failed, attributes drop in oil production to deliberate decision to conserve resources rather than lack of spare parts or foreign technicians. (CRS 281)

7 October 1980
Mansur Farhang, former Iranian representative to UN, currently aide to Bani Sadr, says it no longer is in Iran's interest to hold hostages. (CRS 327)

13 October 1980
New Iranian Prime Minister Mohammed Ali Rajai states it is in Iran's interest to solve hostage crisis but that US, for political reasons of its own, does not want it resolved. (CRS 336)

LEGAL NOTES

US International Emergency Economic Powers Act of 1977, Sec. 203(a)(1)
"At the times and to the extent specified in section 202, the President may, under such regulations as he may prescribe by means of instructions, licenses, or otherwise—

(A) investigate, regulate, or prohibit—
 (i) any transactions in foreign exchange
 (ii) transfers of credit or payments between, by, through, or to any banking institution to the extent that such transfers or payments involve any interest of any foreign country or a national thereof
(iii) the importing or exporting of currency or securities; and

(B) investigate, regulate, direct and compel, nullify, void, prevent or prohibit, any acquisition, holding, withholding, use, transfer, withdrawal, transportation, importation or exportation of, or dealing in, or exercising any right, power, or privilege with respect to, or transactions involving, any property in which any foreign country or a national thereof has any interest; by any person, or with respect to any property, subject to the jurisdiction of the United States."

ATTITUDE OF OTHER COUNTRIES

Mexico
On 4 December 1979, President José Lopez Portillo says US decision to freeze assets is "hasty," causes international monetary problem. (CRS 51)

Japan
On 14 December 1979, limits purchases of Iranian oil to 602,000 barrels per day, level prior to hostage takeover. Foreign Minister Saburo Okita says Japan has been forced to buy Iranian oil on spot market because of cutbacks in shipments by major US companies. (CRS 61)

On 18 January 1980, Japan announces willingness to cooperate with sanctions with exception of Japan/Iranian petrochemical project at Bandar Khomeini. (CRS 87)

On 22 April 1980, Japan says it will go along with sanctions supported by EC; Japanese cabinet announces sanctions will become effective 2 June 1980. (CRS 87, 115)

Austria
30 December 1979: Tehran Radio reports Austrian Ambassador to Iran as saying his country will not cooperate with US economic sanctions against Iran. (CRS 74)

Soviet Union
9 January 1980: Tass says USSR "will not allow the US to impose a decision to apply economic sanctions against Iran." (CRS 81)

On 22 April 1980, USSR signs new trade agreement with Iran that, according to Iranian finance minister, is expected to offset US sanctions. (CRS 163)

Australia
On 15 January 1980, in response to US request, Australia reviews trade relations with Iran. (CRS 85)

On 19 February 1980, it sells 450,000 tons of wheat to Iran for delivery in March, July 1980. (CRS 108)

On 21 April 1980, Australia bans all trade with Iran except for food, medicine. (CRS 162)

On 20 May 1980, Australia cancels all contracts, including those signed before 4 November 1979. (CRS 189)

China
30 January 1980: Tehran Radio announces China has agreed to maintain normal economic, commercial relations with Iran, not cooperate with economic sanctions. (CRS 96)

Poland
On 6 May 1980, signs trade protocol with Iran. (CRS 176)

European Community, and other West European countries
On 17 January 1980, Chancellor Helmut Schmidt announces German support for sanctions against Iran. (CRS 87)

On 17 April 1980, Portugal bans all trade with Iran—first US ally to do so. (CRS 158)

On 22 April 1980, EC foreign ministers agree to reduce diplomatic representation in Iran, suspend arms sale, require visas for Iranian travel in Europe, discourage purchase of Iranian oil at prices above OPEC standard of $32.50/bbl. (Iran is asking $35.50/bbl.). Export embargo is threatened if "decisive progress" is not made by May 17. (CRS 163)

Sweden says it will not impose sanctions. Denmark, Britain, Norway recall ambassadors from Iran. (CRS 163)

On 28 April 1980, following military rescue attempt, EC heads of state reaffirm solidarity with US, commitment to sanctions. (CRS 170)

On 13 May 1980, UK House of Commons passes enabling legislation for economic sanctions; Danish Parliament votes to apply sanctions. (CRS 183)

On 18 May 1980, EC issues communiqué stating that, on 22 May 1980, all contracts concluded with Iran since 4 November 1979 will be suspended. (CRS 187)

On 19 May 1980, Britain decides against retroactive action on contracts concluded since 4 November 1979; instead bans all new contracts after 22 May 1980. Other EC countries express dismay at Britain's action. (CRS 188)

On 21 May 1980, West German, French, Italian cabinets approve, take necessary legal steps for implementation of EC sanctions. (CRS 190)

Canada
On 23 May 1980, Canada bans exports to Iran, discourages citizens from travel there. (CRS 191)

ECONOMIC IMPACT

Observed Economic Statistics

Iranian trade (million dollars)

	Exports		Imports	
	US	OECD	US	OECD
1978	2,880	18,636	3,684	15,432
1979	2,784	15,084	1,020	5,885
1980	336	10,560	24	7,716
1981	63	6,996	300	8,088

Source: OECD.

Iranian assets subject to US freeze and their disposition (billion dollars)

Assets held outside US of which:	5.6
Claims representing Western loans to Iran	3.7
Escrow account for unresolved claims (nonsyndicated loans of US banks, about $130 million of contested interest)	1.4
Cash returned to Iran	0.5
Assets in US of which:	6.4
Holdings in nonbank US companies, on deposit in US commercial banks	3.6
Deposits with NY Federal Reserve Bank, returned to Iran	2.4
On deposit at US Treasury against orders for US defense equipment	0.4
Total	12.0

Source: Carswell 256; Malawer 479.

Calculated Economic Impact

	Annual cost to *target country*
Reduction of Iranian imports from US during 1980–81 by annual average of $858 million from 1979 level; welfare loss calculated at 30 percent of face value of trade.	$257 million

Calculated Economic Impact (*continued*)

	Annual cost to target country
Reduction in Iranian exports to OECD area during 1980–81 by annual average of $6.3 billion from 1979 level; welfare loss calculated at 30 percent of face value of trade.	1,892 million
Estimated annual loss resulting from freeze of about $12 billion of Iranian assets, at 10 percent of face value.	1,200 million
Total	$3,349 million

Relative Magnitudes

Gross indicators of Iranian economy	
Iranian GNP (1979)	$87.4 billion
Iranian population (1979)	37.0 million
Annual effect of sanctions related to gross indicators	
Percentage of GNP	3.8
Per capita	$90.51
Iranian trade with US as percentage of total trade	
Exports (1979)	14
Imports (1979)	12
Ratio of US GNP (1979: $2,418 billion) to Iranian GNP (1979: $87.4 billion)	28

ASSESSMENT

Robert A. Carswell
"Assessing the effect of the trade sanctions is difficult, particularly since the results of economic mismanagement in Iran can easily be confused with problems arising from externally caused shortages . . . even though the sanctions largely prevented direct resupply of these critical areas (many units of the armed forces and key installations in the gas and oil sector), Iran apparently was able, by paying exorbitant prices through middlemen, to meet its most critical needs. . . . Hence, the best that can be said now is that the sanctions undoubtedly caused Iran difficulties but probably not insuperable ones." (Carswell 254)

"In sum, the financial sanctions employed against Iran over the hostage issue were effective because of special circumstances that differentiated the situation sharply from other cases where economic sanctions had historically been attempted. And the freeze of Iranian assets not only created negotiating complications but involved both short and long-term costs that cannot yet be fully assessed, as well as risks of a major change in banking practice that could seriously affect the status of the dollar as the world's principal reserve currency. Finally, it must again be emphasized that the degree of leverage the sanctions exerted . . . depended on a high degree of cooperation by other countries." (Carswell 264)

Economist
"The Europeans, for example, imposed sanctions on Iran mainly to show their solidarity with the United States, rather than in the hope that they would help free the hostages." (*Economist* [London], 2 October 1982, 102)

AUTHORS' SUMMARY

Overall assessment	Assigned scores
☐ Policy result, scaled from 1 (failed) to 4 (success)	4
☐ Sanctions contribution, scaled from 1 (none) to 4 (significant)	3
☐ Success score (policy result *times* sanctions contribution), scaled from 1 (outright failure) to 16 (significant success)	12

Political and economic variables

☐ Companion policies: J (covert), Q (quasi-military), or R (regular military)	Q
☐ International cooperation with sender, scaled from 1 (none) to 4 (significant)	3
☐ International assistance to target: A (if present)	—
☐ Sanctions period (years)	2
☐ Economic health and political stability of target, scaled from 1 (distressed) to 3 (strong)	1
☐ Presanction relations between sender and target, scaled from 1 (antagonistic) to 3 (cordial)	3
☐ Type of sanction: X (export), M (import), F (financial)	F, X, M,
☐ Cost to sender, scaled from 1 (net gain) to 4 (major loss)	3

Comments

US objective was specific: safe return of hostages. While progress was painstakingly slow, desired result was achieved, although at very high economic, political cost. Sanctions, in particular financial controls, made modest contribution to outcome by increasing cost of traded goods in Iranian economy and, more importantly, by freezing substantial share of Iran's financial reserves held in US banks.

BIBLIOGRAPHY

Alexander, Yonan, and Allan Nanes, eds. 1980. *The United States and Iran: A Documentary History*. Frederick, Md.: University Publications of America.
Carswell, Robert. 1981–82. "Economic Sanctions and the Iran Experience." 60 *Foreign Affairs* (Winter): 247–65.
Congressional Research Service (CRS), Library of Congress. 1981. *The Iran Hostage Crisis: A Chronology of Daily Developments*. Prepared for House Committee on Foreign Affairs. 97 Cong., 1 sess. March. Washington.
Malawer, Stuart S. 1981–82. "Rewarding Terrorism: The US-Iranian Hostage Accords." 6 *International Security Review* (Winter): 477–96.
Organization for Economic Cooperation and Development. *Statistics on Foreign Trade, Monthly Bulletin*. Various issues.
Rubin, Barry. 1980. *Paved with Good Intentions*. New York: Oxford University Press.

Case 79–2 US v. Pakistan

(1979–80: Nuclear Safeguards)

CHRONOLOGY OF KEY EVENTS

18 March 1976   Pakistan signs agreement with France for purchase of nuclear fuel reprocessing plant. (Tahir-Kheli 90)

August 1976   US Secretary of State Henry A. Kissinger tries to convince Prime Minister Zulfikar Ali Bhutto to withdraw from reprocessing agreement. He offers to sell Pakistan 100 A-7 jet fighters (sale later rejected by administration of President Jimmy Carter) for canceling deal, warns Bhutto to negotiate with "understanding Republican Administration" rather than wait for Carter who will "make a horrible example of you." Meanwhile, administration of President Gerald R. Ford quietly urges France to cancel agreement. (Tahir-Kheli 124, 126)

5 July 1977   General Mohammed Zia ul-Haq deposes Prime Minister Bhutto. (Tahir-Kheli 93)

1977   France delays transferring blueprints to Pakistan, raises costs, pressures Pakistan to shift from reprocessing to coprocessing technology. Pakistan, however, refuses to cancel or modify agreement. (Tahir-Kheli 128–29)

24 August 1978   After France refuses to go through with reprocessing plant sale as originally negotiated, Pakistan pronounces it officially dead. (Tahir-Kheli 130)

6 April 1979   Evidence of Pakistani construction of enrichment plant, detected by European intelligence sources in late 1978, is confirmed by CIA. (Evidence includes identification of Pakistani spy who obtained lists of enrichment plant components from UK, Netherlands, Germany.) US suggests International Atomic Energy Agency (IAEA) safeguards as alternative to sanctions but Pakistan refuses to acknowledge existence of plant. On 6 April 1979, US discontinues all military, economic aid, amounting to $80 million–$85 million. US reaches understanding with France not to ship reprocessing plant to Pakistan;

US blocks Pakistan's attempts to buy components of reprocessing or enrichment plants elsewhere. (*New York Times*, 7 April 1979, A1; Spector interview)

17 April 1979   Changing tactics in hopes of avoiding Pakistan/India nuclear arms race, President Carter offers fighter planes, nuclear power development assistance if Pakistan will restrict nuclear weapons program. (*New York Times*, 17 April 1979, A3)

January 1980   Following Soviet invasion of Afghanistan, Carter offers to resume aid at level of $400 million, divided evenly between economic, military. Pakistan rejects offer as inadequate. (*New York Times*, 14 January 1980, A1)

15 June 1981   State Department announces agreement on $3.2 billion aid package over six years at $400 million per year for military purchases, $100 million per year in economic aid, including at least 15 F-16s. (*New York Times*, 16 June 1981, A1)

15 September 1981   Pakistan formally accepts aid package after adjustment to provide equal amounts of economic, military aid within same total; F-16 sale increased to 40. (*New York Times*, 16 September 1981, A1)

September– December 1981   House Foreign Affairs Committee initiates hearings aimed at lifting ban on aid to Pakistan; Congress approves 1982 foreign assistance authorization that includes aid to Pakistan. (*New York Times*, 15 December 1981, A29)

16 April 1982   President Ronald Reagan asks Congress to appropriate $275 million to begin implementation of aid program to Pakistan. (*New York Times*, 16 April 1982, A6)

January 1983   IAEA official reports "Pakistan is building, or has completed, another nuclear plant, not under IAEA inspection, theoretically capable of reprocessing spent nuclear fuel into weapons-grade plutonium." Agreement is reached, however, to increase IAEA surveillance over power station. (*Financial Times* [London], 13 January 1983, 4)

16 July 1984   Federal grand jury indicts three "Pakistani nationals for trying to ship parts for nuclear weapons to Pakistan. . . . " Officials in Pakistan deny the men are employed by Pakistani government and reiterate commitment to peaceful uses of nuclear energy. (*Washington Post*, 17 July 1984, A3; *New York Times*, 16 July 1984, A1)

12 September 1984   Reagan sends personal letter to President Zia warning him that US-Pakistani security assistance relationship is endangered by apparent nuclear-weapons development program. Senator Alan Cranston (D– Calif.) and unnamed Arms Control and Disarmament Agency officials lobby for stronger action. (*Wall Street Journal*, 25 October 1984, 37)

GOALS OF SENDER COUNTRY

Howard B. Schaffer, country director for India, Nepal, and Sri Lanka affairs, US State Department
1 December 1979: "Our ability to provide Pakistan with the support we would wish to give it has been restricted by Pakistan's nuclear activities. Our legislation mandates a cutoff of most development and military assistance to countries which import certain sensitive nuclear equipment, material, and technology, including equipment used for uranium enrichment. The fact that Pakistan has been developing a uranium enrichment program which is inconsistent with its power generation or research needs has caused us deep concern. We have cut off further economic development assistance, valued at about $40 million annually, as well as terminated our modest military training program. This action, as I have said, was required by US law. We have expressed our concern to the Pakistanis about their nuclear activities and have urged them not to move forward to develop a nuclear explosives capability. We believe that the development of such a capability would aggravate rather than relieve their security concerns and could be a major source of instability in the South Asian region." (*Department of State Bulletin*, February 1980, 63)

President Jimmy Carter
State of the Union message, 21 January 1980: "A high priority for us in the region is to manage our nuclear concerns with India and Pakistan in ways that are compatible with our global and regional priorities. The changed security situation in South Asia arising from the Soviet invasion of Afghanistan calls for legislative action to allow renewed assistance to Pakistan. But this in no way diminishes our commitment to prevent nuclear weapons proliferation, in Pakistan or elsewhere." (*Department of State Bulletin*, February 1980, special section, p. L)

RESPONSE OF TARGET COUNTRY

1977
Refusing to relent to French pressure to either modify or cancel reprocessing agreement, Pakistan undertakes a media blitz concentrating on peaceful nature of nuclear program. (Tahir-Kheli 130)

9 April 1979
Pakistan Ministry of Foreign Affairs attributes US ban to influence of "Zionist circles" that it says fear that development of atomic bomb in this Islamic country would be used by "Moslem world" to menace Israel. Official labels ban "discriminatory" and "incomprehensible," concedes that while amount of aid involved is small ($80 million per year) "any diminution would be felt." (*New York Times*, 9 April 1979, 1)

17 April 1979
"Pakistan denies that it is seeking nuclear weapons, but in private, Pakistani officials say their government is determined to keep its nuclear option open." (*New York Times*, 17 April 1979, A3)

Summer 1979
President Zia declares "Pakistan would never compromise on its sovereignty. Our economic aid has been affected but we have absorbed its impact and the entire nation supports the government's stand because it is united on this issue . . . we shall eat crumbs [but] not

allow our national interest to be compromised in any manner whatsoever." (Tahir-Kheli 135)

22 July 1979
Khalid Ali, press counselor at Pakistan Embassy in US: ". . . Pakistan is prepared to make a joint declaration with India and other states in South Asia to renounce the acquisition or manufacture of nuclear weapons. Pakistan is ready to proceed with the establishment of a nuclear-free zone in South Asia. Pakistan would also be prepared to accept international inspection of all nuclear facilities in the South Asian region, or if India prefers, a system of bilateral inspection on a reciprocal basis." (*New York Times*, 22 July 1979, IV 18)

23 September 1979
President Zia: "Pakistan is not making a bomb, Pakistan is not in a position to make a bomb and has no intention of making a bomb. . . . Pakistan is close to it, if we have not already acquired the technology of making enriched uranium. . . . We need enriched uranium to run the lightweight reactors of modern technology." (*New York Times*, 23 September 1979, A14)

ATTITUDE OF OTHER COUNTRIES

World Bank, Germany, Japan
In May 1979, World Bank and International Development Association (IDA) announce approval of loans totaling $79 million to Pakistan, Bangladesh, Philippines. In June 1980, US responds to pressure from Japan, FRG, allows rescheduling of Pakistan's $5.1 billion debt held by consortium of advanced countries. (*New York Times*, 1 June 1979, IV 18)

Middle East, Northern Africa
In early April 1979, Saudi Arabia, other unnamed Gulf states increase financial aid to Pakistan to offset US cut-off. Saudi Arabia agrees to contribute $40 million together with unspecified amounts from other Gulf states. (FBIS 53)

China
US intelligence sources say China has provided Pakistan with sensitive nuclear weapon design information; Pakistan's nuclear program since mid-1970s has been "clearly aimed at developing nuclear weapons." They believe US efforts have delayed but not diverted drive for atomic bomb. "By confirming for Pakistan that a particular weapon design could work, the Chinese may have made it possible for Pakistan to proceed with its effort to build atomic bombs without staging an early nuclear test that would bring a cutoff of American military aid." (*Washington Post*, 28 January 1983, A1)

LEGAL NOTES

Symington amendment to Foreign Assistance Act of 1961 in International Security Assistance Act of 1977
"Sec. 669. Nuclear Enrichment Transfers. (a) Except as provided in subsection (b), no funds to be authorized by this Act or the Arms Export Control Act may be used for the purpose of providing economic assistance, providing military or security supporting

assistance or granting military education or training, or extending military credits or making guarantees, to any country which, on or after the date of enactment of the International Security Assistance Act of 1977, delivers nuclear enrichment equipment, materials, or technology to any other country, or receives such equipment, materials, or technology from any other country, unless before such delivery,

"(1) the supplying country and receiving country have reached agreement to place all such equipment, materials, or technology upon delivery, under multilateral auspices and management when available; and

"(2) the recipient country has entered into an agreement with the International Atomic Energy Agency to place all such equipment, materials, technology, and all nuclear fuel and facilities in such country under the safeguards system of such Agency.

"(b) The President may waive this requirement if he determines that:

"(1) the termination of such assistance would have a serious adverse effect on vital United States interests; and (2) he has received reliable assurances that the country in question will not acquire or develop nuclear weapons or assist other nations in doing so." (CRS 31)

ECONOMIC IMPACT

Observed Economic Statistics

Pakistani economic indicators

	Merchandise exports (million dollars)	Merchandise imports (million dollars)	External debt (billion dollars)	Inflation rate (percentage)
1976	1,167	2,192	6.1	6.7
1977	1,121	2,487	6.9	9.2
1978	1,397	3,221	7.7	6.3
1979	1,948	4,289	8.4	8.6
1980	2,569	5,445	9.5	10.5
1981	2,730	5,660	9.7	12.1

Source: IMF.

Calculated Economic Impact

	Annual cost to target country
Reduction in US military, economic aid ($82.5 million) in 1979; welfare loss estimated at 90 percent of reduced transfers.	$74 million

	Annual cost to target country
Offset	
Increased aid from Saudi Arabia, other Gulf countries; welfare gain valued at 100 percent of transfers.	($40 million)
Total	$34 million

Relative Magnitudes

Gross indicators of Pakistani economy	
Pakistani GNP (1979)	$21.3 billion
Pakistani population (1979)	79.8 million
Annual effect of sanctions related to gross indicators	
Percentage of GNP	0.2
Per capita	$0.43
Pakistani trade with US as percentage of total trade	
Exports (1979)	6
Imports (1979)	13
Ratio of US GNP (1979: $2,418 billion) to Pakistani GNP (1979: $21.3 billion)	114

ASSESSMENT

US State Department
April 1979: Department of State officials say they doubt aid cut-off would restrain Pakistanis' nuclear ambitions; some suggest it could move them closer to building bomb. "As a result, the officials said, the administration had decided to couple the aid cutoff with offers of sales of arms and technical help for the small Pakistani program to produce nuclear power. The purpose of the offers, they said, is to induce the government into talks on placing all its nuclear facilities under international safeguards which are designed to deter weapons production. . . . Although a senior State Department official said the cutoff would convince Pakistan and other would-be nuclear powers 'that we mean business in our nuclear nonproliferation policy,' numerous officials insisted that in halting over $80 million in economic assistance, the administration lost the little leverage it had on Pakistan's nuclear plans." (*New York Times*, 17 April 1979, A3)

" 'So far the net result of all our actions has been simply for the Pakistanis to dig in their heels,' a State Department official observed." (*New York Times*, 24 August 1979, A4)

New York Times
"In interviews the previous week, administration officials conceded that the aid cutoff had had no success in getting Zia to renounce the nuclear option and accept full-scope safeguards." (*New York Times*, 12 August 1979, A1)

Central Intelligence Agency
January 1982: Agency estimates that Pakistan will have capability to detonate device within three years but probably would choose not to do so, at least in part because of ". . . President Muhammed Zia ul-Haq's unwillingness to jeopardize the Reagan administration's six-year $3.2 billion military and economic aid program." (*New York Times*, 24 January 1982, A6)

Shirin Tahir-Kheli
"At the very least, the pressure applied by the Carter Administration on Pakistan hardened the latter's attitude and pushed the issue within the rhetoric of intense nationalism." (Tahir-Kheli 127)

Ashok Kapur
"Instead of probing the subnational units of behavior and change, US public antiproliferation diplomacy had the effect of inducing Pakistan to take a public response against bowing to foreign pressure. It is arguable that discussing the issue publicly in terms of proliferation is actually to invite proliferation." (Kapur 510)

Wall Street Journal
". . . US intelligence reports suggest that Pakistan hasn't modified its program the way the Reagan administration had hoped. The Pakistanis have continued work on a centrifuge facility at Kahuta . . . that can enrich uranium to weapons-grade material. The Pakistanis are also continuing to purchase other items that could be used to make a nuclear bomb." (*Wall Street Journal*, 25 October 1984, 37)

AUTHORS' SUMMARY

Overall assessment	Assigned scores
☐ Policy result, scaled from 1 (failed) to 4 (success)	2
☐ Sanctions contribution, scaled from 1 (none) to 4 (significant)	2
☐ Success score (policy result *times* sanctions contribution), scaled from 1 (outright failure) to 16 (significant success)	4

Political and economic variables

☐ Companion policies: J (covert), Q (quasi-military), or R (regular military)	—
☐ International cooperation with sender, scaled from 1 (none) to 4 (significant)	2
☐ International assistance to target: A (if present)	A
☐ Sanctions period (years)	1
☐ Economic health and political stability of target, scaled from 1 (distressed) to 3 (strong)	2
☐ Presanction relations between sender and target, scaled from 1 (antagonistic) to 3 (cordial)	2
☐ Type of sanction: X (export), M (import), F (financial)	F
☐ Cost to sender, scaled from 1 (net gain) to 4 (major loss)	1

BIBLIOGRAPHY

Congressional Research Service (CRS), Library of Congress. 1980. *Nuclear Proliferation Factbook*. Prepared for Subcommittee on Energy, Nuclear Proliferation and Federal Services of the Senate Committee on Governmental Operations, and the Subcommittee on International Economic Policy and Trade of the House Committee on Foreign Affairs. 96 Cong., 2 sess., Summer. Washington.

Foreign Broadcasting Information Service. 1979. "Daily Report: the Middle East and Northern Africa." 13 April, S3.

International Monetary Fund. 1980. *International Financial Statistics Yearbook*.

Kapur, Ashok. 1980. "A Nuclearizing Pakistan: Some Hypotheses." 20 *Asian Survey* (May): 495–516.

Spector, Leonard. US Senate Governmental Affairs Committee, Subcommittee on Energy, Nuclear Proliferation and Government Processes. Interview with authors, 24 January 1983.

Tahir-Kheli, Shirin. 1982. *The United States and Pakistan: Evolution of an Influence Relationship*. New York: Praeger.

Yager, Joseph A., ed. 1980. *Nonproliferation and U.S. Foreign Policy*. Washington: Brookings Institution.

Case 79–3   Arab League v. Canada

(1979: Proposed Embassy Move)

CHRONOLOGY OF KEY EVENTS

4 June 1979   Joseph Clark is sworn in as Canada's prime minister. On 5 June, he reiterates campaign promise to move Canadian Embassy in Israel from Tel Aviv, where most foreign embassies are located, to Jerusalem, which, since taking of old city in 1967 war, the Israelis consider to be their national capital. (*Facts on File* 424)

7 June 1979   Arab ambassadors meet with Canadian Foreign Minister Flora MacDonald to warn her of consequences of projected embassy move, including possible trade boycott. (*Facts on File* 467)

14 June 1979   Clark announces he is considering fact-finding commission to investigate potential consequences of embassy move. (*Facts on File* 467)

18 June 1979   Arab Monetary Fund suspends dealings with Canadian financial institutions. (Takach 55)

23 June 1979   "Responding to intense pressure from Arabs, businessmen, and Western allies," Prime Minister Clark postpones embassy move for at least a year, appoints Robert Stanfield to undertake "a comprehensive study of Canada's Middle East relations." (*Facts on File* 502)

27 June 1979   Iraq threatens Canada with oil embargo, including indirect export of oil to Canada through third countries, if Canada proceeds with embassy move. (*Facts on File* 502)

29 June 1979   In unpublicized ministerial meeting, Arab League decides to halt economic activity in Canada for one year, threatens total embargo if embassy move takes place. (*Facts on File* 502)

September 1979   "Pakistan introduced on behalf of the Arab participants a resolution at the Conference of the Nonaligned States in Havana condemning any country which moved its embassy in Israel from Tel Aviv to Jerusalem." (Takach 55)

29 October 1979   Clark, following return of Special Envoy Stanfield from Middle East, officially cancels plans to move Canadian Embassy to Jerusalem. (*Facts on File* 833)

April 1980   Iraqi Oil Minister Tayen Abdul Karim, admits "that an embargo had been in place [against Canada] since the middle of June 1979." (Takach 57)

GOALS OF SENDER COUNTRIES

Authors' comments
The Arab states have never conceded that the old city of Jerusalem will not be returned to Jordan. Arab opposition to Israel's adoption of Jerusalem as its capital has deterred all but a few countries from moving their embassies there from Tel Aviv.

RESPONSE OF TARGET COUNTRY

George Takach
"While Arab sanctions were unimportant in themselves, their significance was not lost on Ottawa's foreign policy bureaucracy. In each case, ITC [Industry, Trade and Commerce] and External Affairs officials argued the 'straw in the wind effect'; that is, these mini-sanctions were perceived to be only the tip of the iceberg, as it were, of bigger things to come." (Takach 57)

ATTITUDE OF OTHER COUNTRIES

Western Allies
If the Arab League had imposed an oil embargo against it, ". . . Canada would have had little success in attempting to draw on the International Energy Agency for assistance because the Jerusalem affair was solely of Canada's doing and Ottawa received precious little in the way of sympathy from other western capitals." (Takach 61)

ECONOMIC IMPACT

Observed Economic Statistics

Arab Monetary Fund (AMF) had invested $17.2 million in Canada but that "was believed to have been withdrawn at the end of 1978. Consequently, apart from contributing to a modest decline in the value of the Canadian dollar (from US cents 85.52 to 85.02), the AMF announcement was not all that damaging in and of itself." (Takach 56)

"The net effect of the Iraqi oil embargo was that Petrofina, the only Canadian oil company heavily dependent on Iraqi supplies, had to procure crude from other sources, mainly Iran, at a higher price (US $23.50 a barrel vs. $21.96) and absorb the extra cost." (Takach 57)

Result of Arab League decision in late June to cease economic activity in Canada for one year was cancellation of some $3.9 million in contracts, mostly for planned lumber sale worth $3.6 million. (Takach 57)

In 1979, Arab crude accounted for 30 percent of Canadian imports, 14 percent of total Canadian supply, or 250,000 barrels a day out of total Canadian demand of 1.8 million barrels a day. (Takach 60)

Canadian trade with Arab League (million dollars)

	Exports	Imports
1977	505	1,313
1978	571	1,295
1979	551	1,464
1980	790	2,483

Source: IMF.

Calculated Economic Impact

	Annual cost to target country
Reduction in Arab League projects in Canada; welfare loss estimated at 30 percent of value of trade.	$1 million
Decline in Canadian exports to Arab League countries; welfare loss estimated at 30 percent of cut in trade from 1978 level.	6 million
Total	$7 million

Relative Magnitudes

Gross indicators of Canadian economy	
Canadian GNP (1979)	$223 billion
Canadian population (1979)	23.7 million
Annual effect of sanctions related to gross indicators	
Percentage of GNP	negl.
Per capita	$0.30
Canadian trade with Arab League as percentage of total trade	
Exports (1979)	1
Imports (1979)	3
Ratio of Arab League† GNP (1979: $270 billion) to Canadian GNP (1979: $223 billion)	1

† Iraq, Iran, Kuwait, Libya, United Arab Emirates, Saudi Arabia, Syria, Qatar.

ASSESSMENT

George Takach
"Canada's economic relationship with the Arab world, based as it is upon a rather inelastic demand for petroleum and investment capital and a desire to acquire a larger share of the lucrative Arab market, is extremely vulnerable. . . . As one ITC official put it, 'the Arabs could cut us off tomorrow both in terms of imports and exports, and not so much as feel a tickle in the nose.'" (Takach 63)

Washington Post
"Clark . . . quietly shelved the project after an uproar in Arab capitals. Saudi Arabia, however, is reliably reported to have insisted that the 40-year-old Conservative prime minister announce his reversal publicly. . . . In insisting that Clark renege on his campaign promise, the Saudis were indirectly supported by many Canadian businessmen who saw their Middle East contracts endangered at a time of economic slowdown in Canada." (*Washington Post*, 30 October 1979, A1)

AUTHORS' SUMMARY

Overall assessment	Assigned scores
□ Policy result, scaled from 1 (failed) to 4 (success)	4
□ Sanctions contribution, scaled from 1 (none) to 4 (significant)	3
□ Success score (policy result *times* sanctions contribution), scaled from 1 (outright failure) to 16 (significant success)	12

Political and economic variables

□ Companion policies: J (covert), Q (quasi-military), or R (regular military)	—
□ International cooperation with sender, scaled from 1 (none) to 4 (significant)	3
□ International assistance to target: A (if present)	—
□ Sanctions period (years)	1
□ Economic health and political stability of target, scaled from 1 (distressed) to 3 (strong)	3
□ Presanction relations between sender and target, scaled from 1 (antagonistic) to 3 (cordial)	2
□ Type of sanction: X (export), M (import), F (financial)	F, X, M
□ Cost to sender, scaled from 1 (net gain) to 4 (major loss)	2

BIBLIOGRAPHY

Facts on File. 1979.
International Monetary Fund. *Direction of Trade Statistics.* Various issues.
Takach, George. 1980. "Clark and the Jerusalem Embassy Affair: Initiative and Restraint in Canadian Foreign Policy." Unpublished. Carleton University, Ottawa, Ontario, Canada.

Case 79–4   US v. Bolivia

(1979–82: Democracy; Human Rights; Drug Traffic)

CHRONOLOGY OF KEY EVENTS

July–August 1979   Presidential elections are held in Bolivia but no candidate receives absolute majority required by law. National Congress appoints Walter Guevara Arce to fill presidency until new elections can be held in 1980. (*Keesing's* 30137)

1 November 1979   Colonel Alberto Natusch Busch overthrows Guevara, declares state of seige, imposes curfews, press censorship. (*Keesing's* 30137)

2 November 1979   US condemns coup, announces it is suspending military, economic assistance for 1980 fiscal year. (*Keesing's* 30137)

16–18 November 1979   US promises to resume aid to Bolivia following Natusch resignation, installation of Sra. Lidia Gueiler Tejada, president of lower house, as interim president. (*Keesing's* 30138)

12 January 1980   President Gueiler announces elections will be held 29 June 1980. (*Keesing's* 30139)

29 June 1980   Dr. Hernán Siles Zuazo wins plurality of votes for president (38.7 percent) but not required absolute majority; Congress is mandated to choose president from among top three contenders. (*Keesing's* 30585)

17 July 1980   Before Congress convenes, military seizes power, installs a junta headed by General Luís García Meza. Junta announces that it has taken over "because of economic disintegration and leftist subversion" and is "canceling the election results, dissolving Congress, and imposing a curfew and martial law." (*Keesing's* 30585)

18 July 1980   US withdraws ambassador, suspends all aid to Bolivia. On 25 July, US military training mission is withdrawn. In August all cooperation with Bolivia on narcotics control is terminated "because of 'numerous and continuing allegations' about involvement of the military in the drug trade. . . ." (*Keesing's* 30586)

28 September 1980	Junta issues decree declaring itself "the supreme governing body" for at least three years. (*Keesing's* 30585)

8 April 1981	Bolivian government announces it will "renew participation in the [Andean] Group's economic activities" after having reiterated its intention to withdraw as late as 18 December 1980 because of interference by Andean nations in Bolivia's human rights policies. (*Keesing's* 31022)

4 August 1981	General García Meza resigns as president, cedes power to other junta members. A month later, another junta member, General Celso Torrelio Villa assumes presidency. General Torrelio attempts to deter drug trafficking, normalize international relations; however, he maintains strict curfew, other restrictions. (*Keesing's* 31125; *New York Times*, 24 September 1981, A13)

August 1981	Administration of President Ronald Reagan decides against resuming aid to Bolivia because of its continuing lack of cooperation with US Drug Enforcement Agency. (*New York Times*, 2 September 1981, A26)

October 1981	Following promises by General Torrelio and successor, General Guido Vildoso, to restore democracy, combat illegal drug trafficking more extensively, US recognizes Bolivian regime, sends new ambassador, Edwin G. Corr, to La Paz. (*Keesing's* 31946)

May 1982	Paramilitary group in Bolivia threatens to kill Ambassador Corr unless he leaves country within three weeks. Group accuses Corr of insulting military by linking some upper echelon officers with cocaine trade. Corr remains in La Paz. (*New York Times*, 22 May 1982, A3)

October 1982	Civilian government under Dr. Siles Zuazo is finally installed after military junta agrees to withdraw from government. US subsequently resumes economic assistance. (*Keesing's* 31942)

January 1984	US ambassador to Bolivia is recalled to Washington for consultations. Other US officials learn from top Bolivian officials that US support for government may be reduced unless greater progress is achieved in controlling drug traffic. (*Washington Post*, 18 January 1984, A1; 23 January 1984, A1)

30 June 1984	Siles Zuazo is kidnapped for brief time as part of abortive coup attempt by rightist military leaders. Bolivian officials speculate that coup failure will solidify Bolivian democracy, discourage future coup attempts. US strongly condemns attempt. (*New York Times*, 2 July 1984, A3; *Washington Post*, 2 July 1984, A15)

GOALS OF SENDER COUNTRY

2 November 1979
"The State Department [said] that relations with Bolivia were being reexamined in the

light of the interruption of the constitutional process set in motion by President Guevara."
(*Keesing's* 30137)

23 July 1980
The State Department issues statement "deploring the disruption of the democratic process
and the reports of 'widespread, even savage' violations of human rights." State Department
later terminates assistance on narcotics control, saying allegations of military involvement
in drug traffic "call into question the degree of cooperation which may be expected from
this Bolivian regime in the control of drug traffic." (*Keesing's* 30586)

Fall 1981
"Reagan Administration officials had said before the latest change of Bolivian governments
that restoration of aid and an ambassador depended on Bolivian actions to fight the drug
traffic, not promises, which had been heard before." (*New York Times*, 24 September
1981, A13)

October 1982
Following installation of civilian government: "[US officials] said that among the concerns
that could influence the total amount [of aid if resumed] will be the new government's
policies toward drug trafficking, international economic problems and the Bolivian
Communist party." (*New York Times*, 11 October 1982, A3)

RESPONSE OF TARGET COUNTRY

Keesing's
"Sr. Guevara, who went into hiding with most of his government, said that he intended
to organize a clandestine government in opposition to Colonel Natusch, and he sent
telegrams to the presidents of Colombia, Ecuador, Peru and Venezuela [Bolivia's partners
in the Andean group], as well as to President [Jimmy] Carter and the United Nations,
calling for support for maintaining his government in power." (*Keesing's* 30137)

Following request from Andean Group to Organization of American States (OAS) to send
commission to Bolivia to investigate human rights abuses: "Captain Sosa, the Bolivian
Energy Minister, subsequently said on September 2 that Bolivia would withdraw from
the Andean Group because it had interfered in the affairs of a member state and that it
would join a 'Southern Cone pact'. . . ." (*Keesing's* 30586)

New York Times
Fall 1981: "Bolivian military leaders and government officials say the economic pressure
and diplomatic isolation of their country by the Reagan administration were a major
stimulus behind the military infighting that forced the resignation of General Luís García
Meza as President August 4 and the departure September 4 of the junta that succeeded
him . . . General Celso Torrelio said shortly after taking over as president September 4
that 'the normalization of relations is the immediate priority task of his government. He
also promised a crackdown on drug trafficking, moves to improve the economy and
elections in three years." (*New York Times*, 24 September 1981, A13)

ATTITUDE OF OTHER COUNTRIES

Venezuela/Andean Group
Along with US, Venezuelan government cuts off aid to short-lived Natusch government. After establishment of military junta in July 1980, Venezuela, other members of Andean Group (Ecuador, Peru, Colombia) condemn "interruption of the democratic process in Bolivia." (*Keesing's* 30586)

Argentina
Following rumors of Argentine complicity in coup, Argentine government is first to recognize new regime under General García Meza. In August, Argentina offers "food and financial assistance to Bolivia, stating that if Dr. Siles Zuazo had taken power 'ideas contrary to our way of life and the permanence here of a military government' would have placed Argentina at risk." (*Keesing's* 30586)

ECONOMIC IMPACT

Observed Economic Statistics

Aid appropriated for Bolivia in FY 1980: military, $6 million; economic, $50 million. Of latter, $28.5 million in food aid would not have been affected by termination of other assistance. (*Keesing's* 30137)

"One of the main concerns of each administration in the period 1980–82 was the rapidly deteriorating economic situation in the country. By 1982 the Bolivian external debt had reached $3,800 million and the debt service falling due in the course of that year was estimated at up to 80 percent of the anticipated total income from legal exports. [The value of legal exports was expected to be about $900 million as against proceeds from illegal narcotics exports worth in excess of $1,000 million.] The rate of inflation which was stated officially to have been 32 percent in 1981, was expected to be well over 200 percent (and some sources estimated 400 percent) in 1982." (*Keesing's* 31945)

In January 1984, "The economic situation is chaotic even by the exaggerated standards of South America's poorest country. The treasury is effectively empty and inflation for last year was estimated at 300 percent. Crippled by poor management, poor international conditions, and natural disasters, economic production has dropped by at least 20 percent since 1981." (*Washington Post*, 18 January 1984, A1)

US aid to Bolivia (million dollars)

	Economic	PL 480	Military	Multi-lateral aid[†]
1976	—	—	—	115.6
1977	45.6	6.7	3.1	132.0
1978	53.2	16.5	0.8	165.0
1979	51.1	19.0	6.7	158.7
1980	30.1	24.8	0.3	90.3

	Economic	PL 480	Military	Multi-lateral aid[†]
1981	12.8	9.5	—	8.2
1982	19.7	16.4	—	99.9

— Zero or negligible.
† IBRD.
Source: AID.

"The World Bank has indefinitely delayed almost all the new projects it had planned for this year while the International Monetary Fund has all year been putting off a Bolivian request for an emergency stand-by loan." (*New York Times*, 24 September 1981, A13)

"Diplomats say that United States pressure has been critical in the decisions by the international agencies . . . the actions have been justified by the instability in the country." (*New York Times*, 24 September 1981, A13)

US diplomats say amount of "budgeted economic aid withheld since 1980 is $125 million." (*New York Times*, 24 September 1981, A13)

In 1980–81, Argentina reportedly provides $250 million in economic assistance to Bolivia. (*New York Times*, 24 September 1981, A13)

Calculated Economic Impact

	Annual cost to target country
Reduction in US economic aid to Bolivia; welfare loss valued at 90 percent of reduced transfers.	$26 million
Suspension of US military aid to Bolivia; welfare loss valued at 90 percent of lost transfers.	6 million
Reduction in World Bank loans to Bolivia; welfare loss estimated at 40 percent of value of deferred loans.	41 million
Offset	
Argentine economic assistance; welfare gain at 20 percent of reported assistance (probably loans) spread over two years.	($25 million)
Total	$48 million

Relative Magnitudes

Gross indicators of Bolivian economy	
Bolivian GNP (1979)	$4.3 billion
Bolivian population (1979)	5.5 million

Gross indicators of Bolivian economy (continued)

Annual effect of sanctions related to gross indicators	
Percentage of GNP	1.7
Per capita	$8.73
Bolivian trade with US as percentage of total trade	
Exports (1979)	27
Imports (1979)	17
Ratio of US GNP (1979: $2,418 billion) to Bolivian GNP (1979: $4.3 billion)	562

ASSESSMENT

Keesing's
"Colonel Natusch's withdrawal from office had been accelerated by mounting economic difficulties compounded by the effects of the general strike, the cessation of US and Venezuelan aid, and a strong run on the peso." (*Keesing's* 30139)

"The removal of General García Meza in September 1981 and his replacement by General Torrelio did not appear to effect any significant improvement in the human rights situation in Bolivia . . . At the beginning of March 1982, church leaders issued a report on political prisoners, specifically mentioning 80 currently in jail in La Paz who had recently been tortured, and declaring that 'the statistical balance of repression shows that, far from having entered a period of social peace, the population overall lives subjected to the constant threat of arrest and torture." (*Keesing's* 31945)

State Department Country Reports
February 1981: "Bolivia's military regime, which seized power last July, 'ended the progress that had been made in restoring constitutional democracy and destroyed the favorable human rights climate' that developed after an earlier military regime left power in 1977. . . . " (*New York Times*, 10 February 1981, A10)

New York Times
"A virtual blockade of international economic aid led by the Reagan Administration is held responsible in large part for the fall of two Bolivian governments in one month." (*New York Times*, 24 September 1981, A13)

AUTHORS' SUMMARY

Overall assessment	*Assigned scores*
☐ Policy result, scaled from 1 (failed) to 4 (success)	2
☐ Sanctions contribution, scaled from 1 (none) to 4 (significant)	3
☐ Success score (policy result *times* sanctions contribution), scaled from 1 (outright failure) to 16 (significant success)	6

Political and economic variables	Assigned scores
☐ Companion policies: J (covert), Q (quasi-military), or R (regular military)	—
☐ International cooperation with sender, scaled from 1 (none) to 4 (significant)	2
☐ International assistance to target: A (if present)	A
☐ Sanctions period (years)	3
☐ Economic health and political stability of target, scaled from 1 (distressed) to 3 (strong)	1
☐ Presanction relations between sender and target, scaled from 1 (antagonistic) to 3 (cordial)	2
☐ Type of sanction: X (export), M (import), F (financial)	F
☐ Cost to sender, scaled from 1 (net gain) to 4 (major loss)	1

BIBLIOGRAPHY

Agency for International Development. *Overseas Loans and Grants*. Various issues.
Keesing's Contemporary Archives. 1980, 1981, 1983.

Case 80–1 US v. USSR

(1980–81: Afghanistan)

CHRONOLOGY OF KEY EVENTS

20 October 1975   US, USSR sign bilateral framework agreement on supply of grain, leaving tonnages to be negotiated periodically. (Schnittker 1)

3 October 1979   Administration of President Jimmy Carter approves export of 8 million metric tons (mmt) of grain to USSR. (CRS 2)

26 December 1979   Soviet troops enter Afghanistan, stage coup in which President Hafizullah Amin is killed, establish Babrak Karmal (Afghanistan's ambassador to Czechoslovakia) as president. (Falkenheim 1)

4 January 1980   Carter announces actions against USSR. He stops licenses of high technology, strategic goods exports to USSR pending review of licensing procedures; embargoes grain exports of 17 mmt that exceed 8 mmt already committed under 1975 agreement; curtails USSR fishing rights in US 200-mile zone from 435,000 metric tons to 75,000 metric tons in 1980, zero after that; hints at later Olympic boycott; defers cultural-scientific exchanges; delays opening of consular facilities in Kiev, New York; restricts Aeroflot service; requests Senate to defer consideration of SALT II; pledges military, other assistance to Pakistan, possibly other countries in area. CIA provides covert assistance to Afghan rebels. (CRS 20–26; Falkenheim 38; *Washington Post*, 28 July 1984, A1)

5 January 1980   Secretary of Agriculture Bob Bergland announces steps to reduce impact of embargo on US farmers: incentives for adding grain to farmer-owned grain reserve; additional purchases by Commodity Credit Corporation (CCC) of up to 4 mmt; paid acreage diversion program in 1980 if supply and demand conditions warrant; additional export promotion funding for CCC; incentives for production of gasohol. (CRS 26)

11 January 1980   Department of Commerce (DOC) begins review of high technology exports, suspends issuance of new licenses pending completion of review, suspends previously issued validated licenses for goods not

11 January 1980 *(continued)*	yet shipped, announces denial of 8 licenses for goods that could be put to military use (such as seismic data processing equipment), revokes license for export of spare parts for Kama River truck plant (trucks from plant were used in Afghanistan). (CRS 65; Falkenheim 3)
14 January 1980	UN General Assembly resolution adopted by vote of 104 to 8 (29 abstentions) calls for withdrawal of all foreign troops from Afghanistan; does not name USSR. (UN 3)
18 January 1980	Carter restricts 1980 imports of Soviet ammonia, expected to rise from 0.7 mmt to 1.5 mmt, to 1 million short tons, citing potential "market disruption." (CRS 59)
20 January 1980	Carter proposes summer 1980 Olympics be postponed or transferred from Moscow unless Soviet troops leave Afghanistan in one month. International Olympic Committee opposes moving games. (Falkenheim 3–4)
25 January 1980	In State of the Union address, Carter warns USSR that US will react with force if Soviets approach Persian Gulf, offers to resume US military assistance to Pakistan, authorizes sale of military-related technology to China, proposes draft registration. (*Facts on File* 42)
5 February 1980	DOC announces exports of phosphate rock, concentrates of phosphoric acids, concentrates of phosphatic fertilizer to USSR will require validated rather than general licenses; no applications for validated licenses will be considered pending interagency review. On 25 February 1980, Secretary of Commerce Philip M. Klutznick announces ban on exports of phosphates for fertilizer will continue indefinitely. (CRS 53)
20 February 1980	Carter announces US boycott of summer Olympic games to be held in Moscow 19 July—3 August. On 28 March 1980, administration embargoes all exports intended for Olympics except medical supplies. On 12 April 1980, US Olympic Committee votes to boycott Olympics. (CRS 79, 86)
18 March 1980	DOC announces that completed review of high technology export licensing procedures points to more restrictive guidelines: "[it] looks like [the new controls] will cover anything that is remotely of possible military or strategic use." Restrictive criteria are applied to: computers, software, high technology defense goods, technology for manufacture of oil and gas equipment, with revised Commodity Control List (CCL) taking effect 25 June 1980. US also adopts "no exceptions policy" vis-à-vis Coordinating Committee for Multilateral Export Controls (COCOM), a significant departure since US had requested more exceptions than all other members since mid-1970s. (CRS 66)
20 March 1980	International Trade Commission holds that imports from USSR of ammonia do not cause "market disruption," thereby nullifying Carter's retaliatory quota. (CRS 65)

26 September 1980	US Senate votes to block funds for grain embargo. However, similar measure is defeated in House in July. (*New York Times*, 27 September 1980, A29)
21 January 1981	Ronald Reagan is inaugurated as president.
24 April 1981	Announcing that "the United States . . . remains opposed to the Soviet occupation of Afghanistan and other aggressive acts around the world and will react strongly to acts of aggression wherever they take place," Reagan lifts Carter grain embargo and restrictions on all other agricultural commodities, including fertilizer phosphates. As result, USSR is committed, under old agreement, to purchase 6 mmt to 8 mmt of grain a year. (*Weekly Compilation of Presidential Documents*, 27 April 1981; *New York Times*, 25 April 1981, A1; 18 May 1983, D1)
October 1982	Reagan offers to raise limit on USSR purchases for 1982–83 crop year to 23 mmt but Moscow ignores offer. (*New York Times*, 21 October 1982, A1; 26 March 1983, D1)
May 1983	In effort to improve image as "reliable supplier," US gives Saudi Arabia unilateral no-embargo pledge on farm exports. (*Washington Post*, 10 May 1983, D7)
August 1983	US, USSR enter five-year agreement providing for purchases of 9 mmt to 12 mmt annually. As concession to USSR, US agrees not to impose export controls for foreign policy purposes nor to use short-supply "escape clause." (*New York Times*, 2 August 1983, D1)
25 July 1984	State Department announces Reagan has approved lifting of ban on Soviet fishing in US waters. Soviets will be allowed "to catch 50,000 tons of fish off Alaska and western coast" of US." 'They still have to accept it,' an official said, but added that the response is expected to be positive since Moscow has been seeking reinstatement of its fishing rights." (*Washington Post*, 26 July 1984, A1)
27 July 1984	Congressional sources reveal that the House Appropriations Committee has approved $50 million in new assistance for Afghan rebels as requested by President Reagan. If approved by whole House and Senate this would bring total funding for rebels this year to $85 million. Aid to resistance has averaged $30 million to $35 million since invasion. (*Washington Post*, 28 July 1984, A1; *Wall Street Journal*, 27 July 1984, 1)

GOALS OF SENDER COUNTRY

President Jimmy Carter
Address to nation 4 January 1980: "We must recognize the strategic importance of Afghanistan to stability and peace. A Soviet-occupied Afghanistan threatens both Iran and Pakistan and is a stepping stone to possible control over much of the world's oil supplies." (CRS 20)

Briefing for members of Congress, 8 January 1980: "In my judgment our own nation's security was directly threatened. There is no doubt that the Soviet move into Afghanistan, if done without adverse consequences, would have resulted in the temptation to move again and again until they reached warm water ports or until they acquired control over a major portion of the world's oil supplies." Carter admits he did not expect sanctions to cause USSR to withdraw from Afghanistan, says the sanctions were intended primarily "to make the Soviets pay a price for aggression" and to deter the USSR from further aggression. (CRS 20)

January 1980: ". . . the exports being curtailed by this action make a significant contribution to the military potential of the Soviet Union that is detrimental to the national security of the United States." (*Weekly Compilation of Presidential Documents*, 28 January 1980, 185).

Under Secretary of State Richard N. Cooper
20 August 1980: "It is, of course, obvious that any interference with trade would involve costs for the exporting country as well as for the importing country. But under the circumstances it was inappropriate to maintain business as usual." (Cooper 46)

Congressional Research Service
April 1981: "The United States acted to inflict economic costs on the Soviet Union in order to reduce the prospects [for the USSR-sponsored regime in Kabul] and to deter Soviet leaders from using the Afghanistan invasion as a prototype for other such extensions of power by inflicting 'punishment.'" (CRS 19)

"The political message of the largely economic sanctions was probably as effective as political-military action and far less risky. . . . Initial statements on the invasion of Afghanistan by President Carter and other members of the administration strongly implied that the administration viewed the Soviets' motivations as expansionistic. Concern that the invasion, if not reacted to, might serve as a pattern for future Third World ventures led the Carter administration to impose the economic sanctions announced on January 4 and elaborated during the months that followed." (CRS 19)

"Like the other sanctions, the grain embargo was not expected to induce a Soviet withdrawal but was intended to inflict damage on the Soviet feed and grain-livestock complex. While administration officials did not specify how much damage they intended to inflict, the president did state that the intent was not to starve Soviet citizens, but to deny them a planned improvement in their diet." (CRS 38)

"Although [the Carter administration] recognized that ready foreign availability reduced the effectiveness [of high tech controls]. . . without this control the United States would not have as many means of communicating its views to the USSR." (CRS 78)

Peggy L. Falkenheim
"The popular impression is that the sanctions were invoked to persuade the Soviet Union to withdraw its troops from Afghanistan. However, it seems doubtful that this interpretation accurately reflects Carter's main objective. . . . He imposed the sanctions because he felt that forcing Moscow to pay a price for its intervention would deter it from future acts of aggression. . . . Although Carter did not feel that the primary purpose of the sanctions was to get the Soviet troops out of Afghanistan, he felt that the sanctions should remain in effect until the troops were withdrawn. . . ." (Falkenheim 10)

"Although foreign policy considerations may have provided the main impetus for the sanctions, domestic political pressure was also important. In the United States, the invasion of Afghanistan occurred at the beginning of the primary campaign for the 1980 presidential election. Carter's popularity was low, and public opinion polls revealed a lack of confidence in his leadership abilities. . . ." (Falkenheim 11)

"The post-Afghanistan sanctions provided a pretext for the American government to take steps which had been advocated for other reasons. For a number of years before the invasion there had been growing pressure within the US government to impose tighter restrictions on high technology exports to the Soviet Union." (Falkenheim 11)

RESPONSE OF TARGET COUNTRY

Robert L. Paarlberg
Head of Soviet grain purchasing agency went to Buenos Aires, negotiated "an agreement whereby Argentina would supply the Soviet Union, over the next five years, with at least 20 million tons of corn and grain sorghum, and with 2.5 million tons of soybeans." Russians reportedly offered to pay up to 25 percent above US prices to obtain immediate shipments. (Paarlberg 153)

Tass
"Even if one cannot rule out the possibility that a tear may roll, unbidden, from the wistful eye of a ruminating cow in Russia as a result of Washington's grain decision, the Soviet people will not shed tears. . . . The fact is that the Soviet Union today is not the poor czarist Russia where a piece of bread was frequently a coveted dream for the masses. Today, the USSR is a mighty industrial power with a developed agriculture." (*New York Times*, 10 January 1980, 18)

Shaheen Ayubi et al.
"Given the political interest of the Soviet leadership in promoting self-reliance and downplaying the significance of sanctions, as well as the plain fact that they did find replacements for most imports of grain outside the United States, the grain embargo became almost a nonevent in Soviet thinking." (Ayubi 30)

V. Malkevich
"It would be useful to recall, as well, that no one has yet succeeded in influencing the home or foreign policy of the USSR by means of economic blackmail, discrimination, or *diktat*. If it ever had any effect, moreover, it has been simply the opposite of the one counted on: tension between countries always forces each of them to harden its position." (Malkevich 15)

ATTITUDE OF OTHER COUNTRIES

Grain Embargo

Coordinated action by Canada, EC, Australia, Argentina
Conference of grain exporting nations on 12 January 1980 approves following statement: "There is general agreement among the export representatives here that their governments would not directly or indirectly replace the grain that would have been shipped to the Soviet Union prior to the actions announced by President Carter." In later interpretations, officials of Canada, Australia, EC say statement "was viewed as a commitment not to allow sales to the USSR to exceed 'normal' or 'traditional' levels." (CRS 7)

Subsequently, export levels of sales exceed "normal" levels for previous several years. (CRS 43)

Thus "during the last months of 1980 Allied support for the continuation of restrictions on grain sales to the Soviet Union appeared to be crumbling." (CRS 47)

Argentina

Saying it has no legal means to control activities of its private traders, Argentina refuses to "participate in economic sanctions" or to "control its sales by destination." Preembargo Argentine grain shipments to USSR average 1.5 mmt; sales for 1979–80 reach 7.6 mmt. In July 1980 Argentina signs pact with USSR guaranteeing 4.5 mmt annually for five years. (CRS 37; Falkenheim 6)

Brazil

Increases grain sales to USSR in 1979–80; in 1981, signs five-year agreement for exchange of Soviet oil for Brazilian soybeans, soya oil, corn. (Falkenheim 6)

Canada

Unlike President Carter, Prime Minister Joseph Clark sees sanctions as means of persuading USSR to leave Afghanistan: "We are expecting that our actions and, more particularly, the actions of a number of countries acting together may persuade the Soviet Union to withdraw from Afghanistan. That is the point of the exercise." (*Globe and Mail* [Toronto], 12 January 1980, 1)

In November 1980, Prime Minister Pierre Elliott Trudeau lifts partial embargo imposed by former Prime Minister Clark. Partial embargo had limited grain sales to 3.8 mmt during 1979–80 crop year (already higher than sales during three previous years). Timing of Trudeau's decision seemingly is influenced by US-China grain agreement of October 1980, which erodes "traditional" Canadian market, Ronald Reagan's election as US president on campaign pledge to lift grain embargo. In December 1980, Canada agrees to sell 4.7 mmt the next year, removes all quantitative restrictions on future sales to the USSR. In May 1981, Canada signs five-year agreement with USSR providing up to 5 mmt annually. (CRS 47; Falkenheim 6–7)

Australia

Australia agrees to limit 1980–81 sales to 1979–80 level of 4.2 mmt (a record) but seeks early talks with Reagan administration on lifting embargo. (CRS 48)

European Community

France seeks to end sanctions on ground that other countries are violating them but EC agrees to limit 1980–81 sales to previous year's level of 1.7 mmt. (CRS 48)

Olympic Boycott *(CRS 79–93)*

United Kingdom

On 22 January 1980, Prime Minister Margaret Thatcher requests British Olympic Committee (BOC) not to participate in games; in early March Parliament endorses this position; however, on 25 March 1980, BOC votes to attend.

Canada

On 26 January 1980, Prime Minister Clark supports boycott, position endorsed by Canadian Olympic Committee.

Australia, New Zealand, Italy
These governments take position similar to US, Canada but, like Britain, their Olympic committees vote to attend. (Falkenheim 9)

China, Zaire, Saudi Arabia, Egypt, Israel, Germany (FRG), Japan, Norway, Monaco, Liechtenstein
Olympic committees, at the urging of their governments, vote not to attend.

High Tech Exports

Western Europe
Beginning in spring 1980, West Germany, other European nations actively explore USSR-Europe gas pipeline project. See Case 81–3 US v. USSR (1981–82: Poland).

France
In 1980, Armco (US), Nippon Steel (Japan) are denied permission to use American technology in building steel plant at Novolipetsk; Creusot-Loire (France) then signs contract to build cold rolling mill at same site. (*New York Times*, 15 October 1980, A1)

Japan
In spring 1980, Tokyo successfully persuades Washington to exempt joint Sakhalin oil, gas development project with Soviet Union from sanctions. (Falkenheim 9)

LEGAL NOTES

US Export Administration Act of 1979
"Sec. 3(2)—It is the policy of the United States to use export controls only after full consideration of the impact on the economy of the United States and only to the extent necessary. . . . (B) to restrict the export of goods and technology where necessary to further significantly the foreign policy of the United States or to fulfill its international obligations. . . .

"Sec. 6(a) Authority—(1) In order to carry out the policy set forth in paragraph (2), (3), (7) or (8) of Section 3 of this Act, the President may prohibit or curtail the exportation of any goods, technology, or other information subject to the jurisdiction of the United States or exported by any person subject to the jurisdiction of the United States, to the extent necessary to further significantly the foreign policy of the United States or to fulfill its international obligations."

ECONOMIC IMPACT

Observed Economic Statistics

US exports to USSR (billion dollars)

	Total	*Agriculture*
1979	3.6	3.0
1980	1.5	1.2
1981	2.4	1.7

Source: Schnittker 4.

USSR grain imports (July–June year; million metric tons)

	1979–80	1980–81	1981–82
US	15.2	8.0	11.0
Argentina	5.1	11.2	12.0
Canada	3.4	6.9	8.5
Australia	4.0	2.9	2.5
EC	0.9	1.1	2.5
Others	1.8	3.9	3.0
Misc. grains (all sources)	0.6	0.5	0.5
Total	31.0	34.5	40.0

Source: Schnittker 10.

Effect on meat production: USDA estimate of 15.1 mmt produced in 1980 is 600,000 tons below planned goal, 2.6 percent lower than 1979; this would imply per capita consumption of 57 kilograms vs. 58 kilograms in 1979. USDA estimates milk production 4 percent lower in 1980 than 1979, in part because of bad weather. (CRS 38; Falkenheim 12)

For year beginning January 1980, US exports of high tech goods to USSR fall 52 percent vs. same period in 1979; that is, from $155 million to $74 million. Over same period, total US exports to USSR decline 67 percent. (CRS 76)

Calculated Economic Impact

	Annual cost to target country
Embargo on US grain shipments to USSR, in excess of 8 mmt committed by 1975 grain pact:	$89 million
☐ reduction in total Soviet grain of 2.5 mmt from levels projected prior to embargo; welfare loss estimated at 30 percent of trade.	
☐ additional transshipment costs for grain purchased to compensate for blocked US shipments	23 million
☐ additional cost of 4.5 mmt of corn, grain sorghum bought from Argentina at 25 percent premium.	99 million
Reduction of 600,000 metric tons in Soviet meat production; welfare loss estimated at 10 percent of value of reduced output, $1,500 per metric ton.	90 million
Ban on US high technology exports; welfare loss estimated at 30 percent of $80 milion reduction in trade.	24 million

	Annual cost to target country
Ban on US shipments of 1 mmt of superphosphoric acid (SPA); welfare loss estimated at 50 percent of $400 million projected sales value (US accounts for 90 percent of world production of SPA).	200 million
Total	$525 million

Relative Magnitudes

Gross indicators of USSR economy	
USSR GNP (1979)	$1,375 billion
USSR population (1979)	263 million
Annual effect of sanctions related to gross indicators	
Percentage of GNP	0.04
Per capita	$2.00
USSR trade with US as percentage of total USSR trade	
Exports (1979)	1
Imports (1979)	6
Ratio of US GNP (1979: $2,418 billion) to USSR GNP (1979: $1,375 billion)	2

ASSESSMENT

Robert L. Paarlberg
Fall 1980: "However slim its chances of success, the grain embargo must have appeared, last January, as more attractive than the alternative. The alternative was to continue with plans, which had been made the previous October, to sell in 1980 an all-time record 25 million tons of US grain to the Soviet Union. For reasons unrelated to domestic food prices, these sales would have proved at least as embarrassing to the President [Carter], this year, as his ineffectual embargo. Without an embargo of some kind, the President would have found himself presiding over the largest 'Russian grain deal' on record, much larger than Richard Nixon's still remembered sale to the Russians in 1972, the so-called Great Grain Robbery. To important allies abroad, this would have been an inappropriate token of the administration's new policy toward the Soviet Union, so soon after Afghanistan. Likewise, to his political audience at home, these sales would have raised large doubts, at the time, about the President's capacity to make hard decisions. Politically, the only thing worse than announcing a grain embargo two weeks before the Iowa caucuses would have been *not* to announce such an embargo. The President's entire foreign policy would have appeared hostage, in a moment of crisis, to a few Iowa corn growers." (Paarlberg 160)

President Ronald Reagan
30 July 1982: "In the spring of 1981, I lifted the grain embargo imposed by the previous administration because it was not having the desired effect of seriously penalizing the USSR for its brutal invasion and occupation of Afghanistan. . . . [Increased sales by other suppliers] substantially undercut the tremendous sacrifices of our farmers, and I vowed at the time not to impose a grain embargo unilaterally unless it was part of a general cutoff of trade between the US and the Soviet Union. . . . Grain sales have little impact on Soviet military-industrial capability. They absorb hard currency earnings and feed the people of the Soviet Union who are suffering most from the disastrous economic policies of the Soviet Government." (*Department of State Bulletin*, October 1982, 40–41)

Congressional Research Service
"The policy of economic punishment was neither clearly successful in the short run nor likely to become effective in the long run." (CRS 6)

Peggy L. Falkenheim
"The sanctions would have been considered a failure by those who expected them to bring about a withdrawal of Soviet troops from Afghanistan. They would also have disappointed those whose primary aim was to inflict punishment on the Soviet Union in order to deter it from future agression. . . . Even if support for the sanctions had been greater, it is unlikely that they would have been effective. . . ." (Falkenheim 12, 13)

Washington Post
In course of renegotiating grain agreement in 1983, Acting Under Secretary of Agriculture Alan Tracy, speaking in Moscow, "blamed the Carter administration's grain embargo for 'long-term damage to our trade' with Moscow." Principal suppliers to USSR now are Argentina, Canada. US share of Soviet grain import market drops from 74 percent year before embargo to 19 percent in 1982–83. (*Washington Post*, 26 March 1983, A1; *Journal of Commerce*, 7 March 1983, 3A; *US Export Weekly*, 3 January 1984, 495)

AUTHORS' SUMMARY

Overall assessment	Assigned scores
☐ Policy result, scaled from 1 (failed) to 4 (success)	1
☐ Sanctions contribution, scaled from 1 (none) to 4 (significant)	1
☐ Success score (policy result *times* sanctions contribution), scaled from 1 (outright failure) to 16 (significant success)	1

Political and economic variables

☐ Companion policies: J (covert), Q (quasi-military), or R (regular military)	J
☐ International cooperation with sender, scaled from 1 (none) to 4 (significant)	3
☐ International assistance to target: A (if present)	—
☐ Sanctions period (years)	1
☐ Economic health and political stability of target, scaled from 1 (distressed) to 3 (strong)	3

Political and economic variables (continued)	*Assigned scores*
☐ Presanction relations between sender and target, scaled from 1 (antagonistic) to 3 (cordial)	1
☐ Type of sanction: X (export), M (import), F (financial)	X
☐ Cost to sender, scaled from 1 (net gain) to 4 (major loss)	3

Comments

Grain embargo had no impact on Soviet intervention in Afghanistan. Nor did it perceptibly weaken Soviet military apparatus. It is unknown what effect, if any, economic sanctions had on Soviet calculations with respect to adventures in other parts of world.

BIBLIOGRAPHY

Ayubi, Shaheen, Richard E. Bissell, Nana Amu-Brafih Korsah, and Laurie A. Lerner. 1982. *Economic Sanctions in U.S. Foreign Policy.* Philadelphia Policy Papers. Philadelphia: Foreign Policy Research Institute.

Brougher, Jack. 1980. "U.S.-U.S.S.R. Trade After Afghanistan." *Business America* (April 7): 3–7.

Congressional Research Service (CRS), Library of Congress. 1981. *An Assessment of the Afghanistan Sanctions: Implications for Trade and Diplomacy in the 1980s.* Prepared for House Committee on Foreign Affairs. 97 Cong., 1 sess. Washington.

Cooper, Richard N. 1980. "Export Restrictions in the USSR." Statement before the Senate Committee on Banking, Housing and Urban Affairs. 96 Cong., 2 sess., 20 August. Reprinted in 80 *Department of State Bulletin* 2043, October 1980.

———. 1985. "Trade Policy and Foreign Policy." Paper presented to the Conference on US Trade Policies in a Changing World Economy. University of Michigan, 28–29 March.

Facts on File. 1980.

Falkenheim, Peggy L. 1985. "Post Afghanistan Sanctions." In *The Utility of Economic Sanctions,* ed. David Leyton-Brown. London: Croom Helm. Forthcoming.

Malkevich, V. 1981. *East-West Economic Cooperation and Technological Exchange.* Moscow: Academy of Sciences.

Paarlberg, Robert L. 1980. "Lessons of the Grain Embargo." 59 *Foreign Affairs* (Fall): 144–62.

Schnittker Associates. 1982. *Effects of the 1980 and 1981 Limitations on Grain Exports to the USSR on Business Activity, Jobs, Government Costs, and Farmers.* Report prepared for National Corn Growers Association, 12 February.

United Nations. 1980. "Resolutions and Decisions Adopted by the General Assembly at its Sixth Emergency Special Session: 10–14 January 1980." Press release GA/6172, 21 January.

Case 80–2 US v. Iraq
(1980–82: Terrorism)

CHRONOLOGY OF KEY EVENTS

Also see Summary S–1 US v. Countries Supporting International Terrorism (1972–   : Overview)

July 1979   Congress passes Fenwick amendment (Congresswoman Millicent Fenwick, R–NJ) to Export Administration Act requiring notification of "the appropriate Congressional committees before any license is approved for the export of goods or technology valued at more than $7 million to any country supporting terrorism." (Flores 567)

29 December 1979   Administration of President Jimmy Carter cites Iraq, along with Syria, Libya, and South Yemen as countries that support terrorism. (*New York Times*, 6 August 1980, A5)

23 January 1980   US Commerce Department approves license for General Electric to export eight engine cores, valued at $11.4 million, to Italy, for use in manufacture of four frigates destined for Iraq. Fenwick protests that license violates spirit of Fenwick amendment. (Flores 572–73)

6 February 1980   Commerce Department, responding to congressional pressure, reverses itself, suspends export license for eight turbine engine cores. (*New York Times*, 7 February 1980, D2)

April 1980   Secretary of State Cyrus Vance, National Security Adviser Zbigniew Brzezinski recommend allowing sale of engine cores as means of improving ties with Iraq. (*New York Times*, 10 April 1980, A16)

7 April 1980   Arab Liberation Front (ALF), supported by Iraq, attacks Israeli kibbutz, killing three. Congressional criticism of Iraqi frigate decision escalates sharply; deal is placed under review again. (Flores 573–74; *New York Times*, 10 April 1980, A16)

14 May 1980   Members of House Subcommittee on Middle East accuse administration of breaking the law by not notifying Congress of its decision in January to approve engine sale to Iraq via Italy. Assistant Secretary of State Deane R. Hinton acknowledges mistake but says adminis-

tration did not break law because engines were not on list of items restricted from sale to terrorist-supporting nations. (*New York Times*, 15 May 1980, A16)

Early August 1980 State Department decides not to block engine deal; on 5 July announces administration is considering sale of five Boeing commercial jets to Iraq. (*New York Times*, 6 August 1980, A5)

29 August 1980 State Department, responding to congressional pressure, disapproves $208 million sale of commercial jets to Iraq. (Flores 575; *New York Times*, 30 August 1980, A2)

25 September 1980 Claiming need to demonstrate neutrality in Iran-Iraq war, Carter administration suspends export of six remaining turbine engine cores, two having been shipped already. "'In the middle of a conflict, when we proclaim our neutrality, we don't want stories saying that we are supplying either side, however indirectly,' a US official said." This decision comes after Senator Richard Stone (D–Fla.) threatens to attach amendment opposing sale to upcoming foreign aid bill "'because of Iraq's 'support for international terrorism.'" (*New York Times*, 26 September 1980, A7)

25 December 1980 Congressman Benjamin S. Rosenthal (D–NY) releases censored version of General Accounting Office (GAO) report that criticizes handling of Iraqi frigate deal. Report blames "bureaucratic bungling" for approval of deal. "Although the export license is technically still valid, the General Electric Company, which makes the engines, has voluntarily complied with a State Department request [made in September] not to ship them." (*New York Times*, 26 December 1980, A23)

1 March 1982 US lifts export restraints against Iraq imposed on antiterrorist grounds; considers sale of Boeing aircraft. Deputy Assistant Secretary of State Ernest Johnson defends decision to Congress, saying US intelligence has shown Iraq to have reduced its support of terrorism. (*Washington Post*, 19 March 1982, A27; American Israel Public Affairs Committee 1)

13 May 1982 House Foreign Affairs Committee votes to restore Iraq to list of terrorist-supporting nations. (*Washington Post*, 14 May 1982, A2)

8 September 1982 Commerce Department issues license for export of six small jets, four with military applications, to Iraq. Congressman Jonathan B. Bingham (D–NY) strongly opposes sale. (*Washington Post*, 14 September 1982, A12)

November 1982 Abu Nidal, widely known Palestinian terrorist who admitted his involvement in shooting of Israeli Ambassador Shlomo Argov in London, is admitted to Iraq. (*Washington Post*, 9 November 1982, A1)

October 1983 State Department announces it will not return Iraq to list of nations supporting terrorism despite congressional pressure to do so. "State Department spokesman Alan Romberg [says] US has no evidence that Iraq has supported international terrorism since publicly renouncing it a little more than a year ago." Romberg adds that Abu Nidal and his followers are not allowed freedom of movement in Iraq but are restricted by government there. (*Washington Post*, 8 October 1983, A25)

GOALS OF SENDER COUNTRY

April 1980
Combination of factors—hostage crisis in Iran, Soviet invasion of Afghanistan, Iraq-Iran war, "a widening schism between Iraq and the Soviet Union"—make American officials anxious to develop closer association with Iraq. "[Secretary of State Cyrus] Vance, with the backing of Zbigniew Brzezinski, President Carter's national security adviser, decided to allow the sale [of the turbine engines] to signal interest in building a new relationship with Iraq." However, deal again was "under review" after 7 April ALF attack on Israeli kibbutz. (*New York Times*, 10 April 1980, A16)

August 1980
"[State] Department informed the Commerce Department that it 'cannot recommend' issuance of export licenses for the [five Boeing] aircraft in view of recent terrorist incidents which appear to have Iraqi involvement or support, and the clear sentiment of Congress with respect to international terrorism." (*Facts on File* 662)

October 1983
State Department officials, defending decision not to restore Iraq to list of terrorist-supporting nations, "said that the US wants to foster Iraq's independence, keep it from the Soviet orbit and maintain lucrative trade links. . . . They added that it also wishes to encourage what it perceives as increasing moderation in recent years in Iraq's attitude toward the Arab-Israeli conflict." (*Washington Post*, 8 October 1983, A25)

RESPONSE OF TARGET COUNTRY

September 1980
Following disapproval of Boeing plane sale: "[Ath-Thawrah, Baghdad newspaper] adds that this measure is part of the Zionist, US and Persian quarters' frenzied campaign against Iraq's principled stands and firm confrontation of imperialist machinations and plots to liquidate the Palestinian issue. Ath-Thawrah also notes that Iraq will not succumb to pressure and blackmail. It will continue to remain the vanguard of pan-Arab struggle and faithful to this struggle's principles and mission, until all the pan-Arab objectives are achieved." (FBIS)

ATTITUDE OF OTHER COUNTRIES

Israel
In June 1981, Israel bombs Iraqi nuclear reactor scheduled to go critical very shortly. Israel claims reactor would be used to manufacture nuclear weapons for use against it. (Potter 265)

In March 1982, "the [Israeli] intelligence chief [Gen. Yehoshua Seguy] said Iraq supported a 'May 15' terror group that had carried out a string of bombings at El Al [Israeli airline] offices in Europe, the bombing last August of Israel's embassy in Vienna and Israel's diplomatic mission in Athens, and the time-bombing of a passenger ship bound for Israel last December 20. . . . Iraq, he said, trains terrorists from all around the world, and the effort is supported by the Ba'ath Party." (Potter 265; Associated Press, 2 March 1982, as quoted by American Israel Public Affairs Committee 2)

ECONOMIC IMPACT

Observed Economic Statistics

Iraqi trade with US (million dollars)

	Imports from US	Total imports	US percentage of total
1979	486	7,006	6.9
1980	797	13,642	5.8
1981	1,005	19,040	5.3
1982	931	19,936	4.7

Source: IMF.

Calculated Economic Impact

	Annual cost to target country
Reduction in US exports of engine cores, commercial jets; welfare loss estimated at 10 percent of face value of trade (given availability of alternate suppliers).	$22 million

Relative Magnitudes

Gross indicators of Iraqi economy

Iraqi GNP (1979)	$35.2 billion
Iraqi population (1979)	12.9 million

Annual effect of sanctions related to gross indicators
| Percentage of GNP | 0.1 |
| Per capita | $1.71 |

Iraqi trade with US as percentage of total trade
| Exports (1979) | 3 |
| Imports (1979) | 7 |

Ratio of US GNP (1979: $2,418 billion) to Iraqi GNP (1979: $35.2 billion) — 69

ASSESSMENT

David Flores
"It seems unlikely that the denial of exports to the four terrorist-supporting countries named by the Department of State will greatly influence them to halt their support of terrorism. Products comparable to the US exports, at least in the case of commercial aircraft, can usually be obtained from sources other than the United States." (Flores 589)

AUTHORS' SUMMARY

Overall assessment	*Assigned scores*
☐ Policy result, scaled from 1 (failed) to 4 (success)	2
☐ Sanctions contribution, scaled from 1 (none) to 4 (significant)	2
☐ Success score (policy result *times* sanctions contribution), scaled from 1 (outright failure) to 16 (significant success)	4

Political and economic variables

☐ Companion policies: J (covert), Q (quasi-military), or R (regular military)	—
☐ International cooperation with sender, scaled from 1 (none) to 4 (significant)	1
☐ International assistance to target: A (if present)	—
☐ Sanctions period (years)	2
☐ Economic health and political stability of target, scaled from 1 (distressed) to 3 (strong)	2
☐ Presanction relations between sender and target, scaled from 1 (antagonistic) to 3 (cordial)	2
☐ Type of sanction: X (export), M (import), F (financial)	X
☐ Cost to sender, scaled from 1 (net gain) to 4 (major loss)	2

BIBLIOGRAPHY

American Israel Public Affairs Committee. 1982. "Iraq and International Terrorism." 16 March. Washington.

Facts on File. 1980.

Flores, David A. 1981. "Export Controls and the US Effort to Combat International Terrorism." 13 *Law and Policy in International Business* 521–90.

Foreign Broadcasting Information Service. 1981. "Daily Report: Middle East and North Africa." 3 September, E1.

General Accounting Office. 1980. *Licensing for Export of Turbine Engine Cores to Italy for Use in Iraqi Frigates.* Washington.

International Monetary Fund. 1982. *Direction of Trade Statistics.*

Potter, William C. 1982. *Nuclear Power and Nonproliferation.* Cambridge, Mass.: Oelgeschlager, Gunn & Hain.

Case 81–1   US v. Nicaragua

(1981–   : El Salvador War)

CHRONOLOGY OF KEY EVENTS

Also see Case 77–5 US v. Nicaragua (1977–79: Somoza)

19 July 1979	Sandinistas, with moral and economic support from US, oust General Anastasio Somoza-Debayle as president. (*Wall Street Journal*, 11 November 1982, 1)
Fall 1979	President Jimmy Carter unfreezes $10.5 million in economic assistance, extends $8.8 million in emergency assistance to Nicaragua, submits $75 million aid package to Congress. "For many reasons, there were endless and unfortunate delays, until the Nicaraguans began to feel that the money was being politically held over their heads." (Anderson 168)
17 October 1980	US, Nicaragua finally sign $75 million aid agreement but only after Carter provides assurances to Congress that Sandinistas are not aiding leftist insurgents in El Salvador. Congress stipulates money "could be recalled at any time, with immediate payment made in full, including interest, if the United States determined that Nicaragua was indeed engaging in subversion abroad." (Anderson 168, 190)
22 January 1981	President Ronald Reagan freezes: aid approved previous year (of which only $15 million had not been transferred); $9.6 million wheat sale; Food for Peace aid. On 1 April 1981, Reagan suspends aid indefinitely because of Sandinistas' support of leftist guerrillas in El Salvador. Cancellation of wheat sale reportedly results in flour shortage, rationing in Nicaragua. Sandinista leadership warns US actions amount to "economic aggression." (*Keesing's* 30975; Anderson 190)
August 1981	US Assistant Secretary of State Thomas O. Enders visits Managua, promises US aid and noninterference if Sandinistas terminate support of El Salvadoran leftists. (*Newsweek*, 8 November 1982, 48)
December 1981	Reagan administration authorizes $20 million for CIA plan to create

December 1981 (continued)	500-man paramilitary force of Nicaraguan rebels in Honduras to cut off Nicaraguan arms and other supplies to El Salvador, indirectly to destabilize Sandinista regime. In companion action, Argentina agrees to train additional 1,000 men. (*Newsweek*, 8 November 1982, 43, 48)
Late 1981	US vetoes Nicaraguan request for $30 million credit from special operations fund of Inter-American Development Bank (IDB) for fisheries project. (*Washington Post*, 1 July 1983, A1)
April 1982	US Ambassador to Honduras John Negroponte establishes contact with exiled Somoza supporters (Somocistas) living in Honduras; directs 50 CIA personnel, related operatives in Honduras; coordinates military operations with Honduran army. US provides Honduran military with $187 million in 1981–82, proposes $78 million for 1983. (*Newsweek*, 8 November 1982, 43–48; *New York Times*, 4 December 1982, A1; *Washington Post*, 19 January 1983, A10)
Summer–Fall 1982	Reagan expresses "great interest" in Mexican-Venezuelan proposal to restore Nicaragua-Honduras peace; supports "fully verifiable regional agreement" to ban arms imports, foreign military advisers in Central America. Honduras, however, declines to enter talks, preferring to follow Declaration of San Jose, regional peace plan signed by US, six Caribbean countries. (*Wall Street Journal*, 11 November 1982, 24; *Newsweek*, 8 November 1982, 48)
December 1982	US Congress passes amendment, offered by Congressman Edward P. Boland (D–Mass.), prohibiting US from providing "military equipment, military training, or advice or support for military activities for the purposes of overthrowing the government of Nicaragua or provoking a military exchange between Nicaragua and Honduras." Purpose of amendment is to block CIA plans to train a paramilitary force of 500 commandos to strike at economic targets in Nicaragua. Senator Daniel Patrick Moynihan (D–NY): "[it is] difficult to draw the line between harassment activities and a deliberate attempt to destabilize or overthrow a government." (*Washington Post*, 1 January 1983, A10)
March 1983	Under Secretary of Defense Fred C. Iklé testifies before Congress that USSR has provided $440 million in aid to Nicaragua since Sandinistas took power. Iklé expresses irritation that nearly four times that much, some $1.6 billion, has come from non-Soviet sources, most of them "misguided" European governments. (*Washington Post*, 5 April 1983, A1)
7 April 1983	Leaked National Security Council document on US policy in Central America calls for "increasing the pressure on Nicaragua and Cuba to increase for them the costs of intervention." (*New York Times*, 7 April 1983, A16)
Spring 1983	CIA informs Congress that $20 million previously authorized for operation in Honduras is not sufficient, will use another $11 million

from its fund for covert operations (which do not require congressional approval). Congress becomes increasingly concerned that administration is violating Boland amendment, despite presidential assurances. (*New York Times*, 15 April 1983, A1; *Wall Street Journal*, 15 April 1983, 2; *Newsweek*, 11 April 1983, 50)

3 May 1983   House Select Committee on Intelligence votes to cut off all funds in support of covert activity in Nicaragua. Reagan labels vote "partisan" and "irresponsible." Committee's initiative is opposed by Senate, ultimately abandoned by House. (*New York Times*, 7 May 1983, A1; *Wall Street Journal*, 5 May 1983, 3; *Washington Post*, 19 November 1983, A21)

9 May 1983   US officials reveal Reagan administration will redistribute most of Nicaragua's sugar quota among "Central American nations friendly to US." Honduras would receive largest share; El Salvador, Costa Rica also would benefit; total sugar exports from these countries to US would increase by about $14 million. Subsequently Nicaragua contests action in GATT. (*Washington Post*, 10 May 1983, A1; *New York Times*, 11 May 1983, A12; *Journal of Commerce*, 14 March 1984, 9A)

14 May 1983   Senate Intelligence Committee approves $19 million increase in funds for covert operations in Nicaragua but asserts its authority to approve or disapprove special operations after 1 October 1983. (*New York Times*, 18 May 1983, A8)

27 May 1983   US State, Defense Departments release White Paper that links Cuba, Nicaragua in efforts to destabilize the governments of El Salvador, Honduras, Costa Rica. (*New York Times*, 28 May 1983, A3)

7 June 1983   US closes all six Nicaraguan consulates around country, expels 21 consular officials in retaliation for ouster of 3 US diplomats from Managua. (*New York Times*, 8 June 1983, A1)

29 June 1983   US vetoes Nicaraguan request for extension of time to complete $18 million rural road financed by IDB loan granted in 1976. By voting against extension, US essentially deprives Nicaragua of remaining $2.2 million that was unspent because of flooding in project area. (*Economist* [London], 9 July 1983, 19)

30 June 1983   US Treasury official announces US will vote against World Bank and IDB loans to Nicaragua until Sandinistas "revitalize the private sector," "improve the efficiency of the public sector." US has power to block loans from IDB's special operations fund but cannot unilaterally block regular loans from World Bank or IDB. In 1982 Nicaragua obtains loans of $16 million, $34 million, respectively from those two institutions. (*Washington Post*, 1 July 1983, A1)

July 1983   Reagan announces appointment of special bipartisan commission, chaired by Henry A. Kissinger, to suggest long-term US strategy toward Central America. In subsequent days Reagan announces plans

July 1983 (continued)	for large-scale military exercises involving air, land, sea forces to be held in and off coast of Honduras. Meanwhile, Nicaragua backs off earlier insistence on holding bilateral talks with US and Honduras, indicates willingness to discuss regional problems in regional forum. (*New York Times*, 22 July 1983, A1; *Washington Post*, 26 July 1983, A1)
4 August 1983	US, Nicaraguan officials announce cancellation of $7.5 million loan for rural education appropriated in 1978 but never disbursed. US spokesman in Managuan Embassy, Gilbert Callaway, says Nicaragua never submitted plan showing how money would be spent and, "On top of that, Nicaragua never fulfilled certain [unspecified] requirements necessary for the disbursement of the loan." "Education Minister Carlos Tunnerman called the decision 'one more proof of the political and economic blockade imposed on Nicaragua by the United States.'" (*Washington Post*, 5 August 1983, A16)
21 October 1983	Sandinistas propose security accords with US prior to House vote (227 to 194) to cut off covert assistance to Nicaraguan rebels. (*Washington Post*, 21 October 1983, A1)
18 November 1983	House yields to Senate; Congress provides $24 million in covert funds for anti-Sandinista rebels, amount estimated to last through June 1984. CIA concludes, however, that US-backed "contra" forces of 10,000 to 20,000 guerrillas cannot achieve victory over Sandinista government. Curtin Winsor, Jr., US ambassador to Costa Rica, remarks, "An invasion of Nicaragua is not impossible." (*Washington Post*, 19 November 1983, A21; 25 November 1983, A1)
Early 1984	Nicaragua's main port at Corinto, two other ports are mined, allegedly with direct CIA assistance. Attacks by air, small boats also are carried out by anti-Sandinista rebels against ships in Corinto's harbor. French government offers to help Nicaragua clear ports if "one or several friendly European powers" will cooperate. "[T]he attacks on the ports have the potential to devastate Nicaragua's foreign trade." (*Washington Post*, 2 April 1984, A1; 6 April 1984, A1)
13 March 1984	GATT Council unanimously adopts report charging US with violation of GATT obligations in cutting Nicaragua's quota for US sugar imports. Acting deputy US trade representative in Geneva, Warren Lavorel, says US did not oppose panel report, would be willing to open talks with Nicaragua. However, US officials refuse to comply with GATT ruling, noting that "in order for the United States to solve the problem of Nicaraguan sugar quotas, the larger political issues between the United States and Nicaragua had to be addressed." (*Journal of Commerce*, 14 March 1984, 9A; *Wall Street Journal*, 9 March 1984, 35; *New York Times*, 14 March 1984, D1)
April 1984	US informs International Court of Justice it will not accept court's jurisdiction over Nicaraguan suit filed against US role in mining of Nicaragua's harbors. "State Department officials acknowledged that it was the first time since the United States joined the World Court

in 1946 that it had taken such an action to block resolution of a specific dispute." (*New York Times*, 10 April 1984, A1)

25 June 1984   Following two House votes opposing additional aid to Nicaraguan rebels, Senate votes 88 to 1 to delete $21 million for contras from emergency spending bill which also includes funds for domestic programs. Administration had requested additional funds reportedly because CIA had only $100,000 of the $24 million originally appropriated left. Administration officials and Senate Republican leaders vow to revive aid issue later this year, House Speaker Thomas P. (Tip) O'Neill, Jr., (D–Mass.) said the aid request was "dead." Further, he said, "The Senate's action should bring to a close US support for the war in Nicaragua." (*New York Times*, 26 June 1984, A1; 27 June 1984, A1)

4 November 1984   Nicaragua holds elections, junta leader Daniel Ortega is elected president. US labels elections "a sham" because major opposition parties did not participate. (*Washington Post*, 12 January 1985, A11)

December 1984   Senator David F. Durenberger (R–Minn.), new chairman of Senate Intelligence Committee, makes known his opposition to renewal of covert aid to contras; proposes that administration find ways to apply overt and legal pressure on Sandinistas. (*Washington Post*, 12 January 1985, A11)

GOALS OF SENDER COUNTRY

Newsweek
Following Reagan's authorization in December 1981 of $20 million for CIA operations on Honduran-Nicaraguan border, anonymous source states: "The focus was on action which would interdict the flow of arms to guerrillas in the friendly countries. Nowhere does [the scope paper] talk about overthrow." Another senior official adds ". . . there are secondary and tertiary consequences which you can't control. . . ." (*Newsweek*, 8 November 1982, 44–45)

"While US officials maintain that the primary objective of the operation remains cutting off the supply routes, they also hope that a threatened Sandinista government will bring itself down by further repressing its internal opposition, thereby strengthening the determination of moderate forces to resist." (*Newsweek*, 8 November 1982, 48)

US Department of State
By December 1982, senior State Department officials are telling "members of Congress and reporters in background briefings that the administration's primary goal was to isolate and pressure the Sandinista government until it becomes more democratic and gives up some control to more moderate political forces in the country." (*Washington Post*, 1 January 1983, A1)

Secretary of State George P. Shultz, congressional testimony on 22 March 1983: " . . . we are working to persuade the Sandinistas that they should come to the bargaining table ready to come to terms with their own society and their neighbors." (*Department of State Bulletin*, April 1983, 37)

In September 1983, Shultz broadens US objectives to encompass halt to all Sandinista support of revolution in Central America, in addition to stopping arms shipments from Nicaragua to leftist guerillas in El Salvador. (*Washington Post*, 21 September 1983, A29)

Thomas O. Enders, assistant secretary of state for inter-American affairs
"Since the Somoza government collapsed and the Sandinistas came to power, US policy in Nicaragua has focused on attempting to convince Nicaragua to:
—renounce support for insurgency in neighboring countries;
—abandon its pursuit of dominant military power in Central America; and
—come to terms with its own society through the creation of democratic institutions."
(Enders 1)

James W. Conrow, director of US Treasury office on multilateral development banks
Explaining US policy on multilateral development assistance to Nicaragua: "When they show progress, we would support them. . . . [T]he economic problems in Nicaragua now are so widespread that I can't see any loan that we would support until there are some fundamental changes in their policy." (*Washington Post*, 1 July 1983, A1)

Washington Post
". . . many members of the congressional oversight committees reportedly have become convinced that the administration is willing to end its secret war against Nicaragua as soon as the Sandinistas give concrete and verifiable assurances that they will no longer give aid, command and control and logistical support to the Salvadoran guerrilla movement." (*Washington Post*, 25 November 1983, A38)

New York Times
In April 1984, allegations of CIA involvement in mining of Nicaragua's ports renew debate over Reagan administration's objectives in Central America. "In an effort to contain the uproar, President Reagan sent the Senate a carefully drafted letter last week asserting that his objectives were to get Nicaragua to 'cease to involve itself in the internal or external affairs of its neighbors' and to draw the Sandinistas into 'meaningful negotiations' for a Central American peace settlement. On other occasions, the president has said that one objective is to stop arms flowing from Nicaragua to leftist guerrillas in El Salvador. In his letter, he denied his administration was trying to overthrow or disrupt the Sandinista Government." (*New York Times*, 11 April 1984, A1)

RESPONSE OF TARGET COUNTRY

August 1981
Sandinistas ignore offer of US aid in exchange for pledge of nonintervention in El Salvador. (*Newsweek*, 8 November 1982, 48)

December 1981
Nicaraguan Foreign Minister Miguel D'Escoto denies his country supports El Salvador leftists. (*Newsweek*, 8 November 1982, 48)

August 1982
Nicaraguan Ambassador to US, Francisco Fiallo Navarro, says virtual state of war exists between Honduras, Nicaragua. (*Newsweek*, 8 November 1982, 48)

November 1982
Daniel Ortega, head of Sandinista junta, states: "The United States has fixed December for a move against the Sandinista revolution." Nicaraguan Defense Ministry alleges that US supports 3,500 Nicaraguan exiles in Honduras who make hit-and-run attacks under protection of Honduran army. (*Wall Street Journal*, 11 November 1982, 1; *New York Times*, 4 December 1982, A7)

Spring 1983
Nicaragua twice takes case before UN Security Council, accusing US of waging war against it. First debate ends without resolution or vote but majority of delegates are sympathetic to Nicaraguan position. In May, resolution submitted to Security Council is so innocuous that both US, Nicaragua support it. (*Washington Post*, 10 May 1983, A14; *New York Times*, 20 May 1983, A3)

5 April 1983
Spokesman for Nicaraguan Embassy in Washington, in response to proposed sugar quota reduction, calls it "economic attack" intended to "kill the Nicaraguan revolution." On 11 May 1983, quota reduction is criticized by Orlando Solorzano, acting foreign trade minister, as "a hard blow . . . taken for purely political reasons, which goes against all principles of international trade." Nicaragua files GATT complaint against quotas; it is upheld in March 1984. (*Washington Post*, 5 April 1983, A11; *Financial Times* [London], 12 May 1983, 45; *Journal of Commerce*, 14 March 1984, 9A)

July 1983
Nicaraguan Planning Minister, Henry Ruiz, in response to question about whether US economic pressure would force Nicaragua to follow Cuban example: "Cuba was isolated. They had to survive. If the same pressure is applied to us, we have to survive. We're not going to commit suicide. If they push us, there will have to be alterations in the plan, but I'd prefer a market that is close to us, a close place to buy and sell, I would prefer normality." (*Washington Post*, 1 July 1983, A1)

September 1983
Nicaragua announces it will pay all external debt (some $3.3 billion), compensate foreign owners of nationalized mines. Agreement reached to pay Amax, parent of one of the nationalized mining companies, for $8.8 million claim. (*Journal of Commerce*, 30 September 1983, 3A)

24 October 1983
Nicaragua cuts fuel rations 10 percent to 30 percent in response to shortages caused by rebel attacks. (*New York Times*, 25 October 1983, A5)

April 1984
Nicaragua files suit in International Court of Justice claiming US has participated in mining of harbors in violation of international law. (*New York Times*, 10 April 1984, A1)

ATTITUDE OF OTHER COUNTRIES

Cuba
In 1981–82, Cuba supplies 4,000 civilian specialists and 2,000 military advisers to Nicaragua; acts as channel for military equipment from USSR. (*Newsweek*, 8 November 1982, 49)

Soviet Union
In October 1982, Nicaraguan Interior Minister Tomas Borge asks USSR for financial assistance, receives $100 million credit for agricultural equipment (Nicaragua already has abundance of unused farm equipment). (*Wall Street Journal*, 11 November 1982, 24)

Argentina
"[T]he reliance on Argentina [as a main conduit for initial CIA aid] drew the United States indirectly into support of paramilitary units that seek to overthrow the Sandinistas and include former supporters of General Somoza." (*New York Times*, 4 December 1982, A7)

Following US support of Britain in Falklands war in spring 1982, Argentina withdraws its miltary advisers from Honduras. (*New York Times*, 4 December 1982, A1)

Mexico, Venezuela, Panama, Colombia
Form "Contadora Group" that attempts to mediate regional conflict with encouragement of UN Security Council. (*New York Times*, 20 May 1983, A3)

UN Conference on Trade and Development
"It was in large part the American measures against Nicaragua that impelled [UNCTAD] in Belgrade last weekend to denounce, with some anger, intimidation of poor countries by rich." Eighty-one UNCTAD delegates, most from developing countries, vote for motion that "denounced coercive economic measures applied for political reasons"; 18 delegates, most from industrialized states, vote against resolution, seven abstain. (*Economist*, 9 July 1983, 20; *Washington Post*, 3 July 1983, A25)

United Nations
On 19 May 1982, UN Security Council (15 to 0) adopts resolution asking Contadora Group to renew settlement efforts. (*New York Times*, 20 May 1983, A3)

Western Europe
France, Spain, West Germany, Netherlands, Sweden extend lines of credit to Nicaragua for purchases of machinery, other goods despite opposition from US. (*New York Times*, 26 September 1983, A10; *Journal of Commerce*, 30 September 1983, 3A)

In August 1983, Federal Republic of Germany weighs proposal to end economic aid to Nicaragua. (*Washington Post*, 10 August 1983, A16)

Algeria, Iran, France
Purchase Nicaraguan sugar previously sold to US. (*Journal of Commerce*, 30 September 1983, 3A)

Central America
Costa Rica, El Salvador, Guatemala, Honduras quietly refuse to join US economic boycott of Nicaragua. (*New York Times*, 26 September 1983, A10)

ECONOMIC IMPACT

Observed Economic Statistics
Nicaragua incurs additional $800 million in debt July 1979–July 1982 for social welfare programs; by end of 1982, external debt reaches $2.5 billion. Doubts are expressed about

country's ability to pay $40 million in interest due in December 1982 on debt of about $970 million. (*Wall Street Journal*, 11 November 1982, 1)

In mid-1983 Nicaraguan Central Bank estimates civil war has cost economy $58 million in damages, lost production. Defense expenditures account for 40 percent of $1.4 billion national budget. A year later, junta leader Daniel Ortega estimates that "direct war losses" over the previous four years total $237 million. He notes that this does not include the loss in potential production. (*Wall Street Journal*, 31 May 1983, 1; 2 October 1984, 34)

Economic activity declines by 5 percent in 1982. (*Wall Street Journal*, 11 November 1982, 1, 24)

"Export earnings [in 1983] of $400 million were dwarfed by an import bill roughly twice as large." (*Times* [London], 6 March 1984, 8)

US aid to Nicaragua (million dollars)

	Economic	PL 480
1977	9.8	0.4
1978	14.6	0.1
1979	18.5	7.0
1980	38.7	18.0
1981	59.9	1.2

Source: AID.

From 1979–82, Nicaragua receives $125 million in military equipment, supplies from USSR, $121 million in economic assistance from US. (Enders 1, 10)

In August 1979, after Somoza's fall, IMF approves $35.9 million loan, basically "a revamped version of the loan originally promised to Somoza." IDB extends $88.5 million loan, nearly $2 million in grants. (Anderson 168)

Following Reagan administration suspension of aid to Nicaragua, cancellation of wheat sale, USSR agrees to deliver 20,000 tons of wheat beginning in May 1981; Bulgaria promises another 10,000 tons. Libya signs agreement for $100 million grant for development of mixed agricultural enterprise, Cuba pledges $64 million in aid for 1981. Nicaragua is said to receive about $500 million in aid annually in recent years, including assistance from OPEC ($10 million), loan from Libya ($100 million), aid from various West European countries. (*Keesing's* 30975; *New York Times*, 13 August 1983, A3)

In 1982, Nicaragua earns $15.6 million from sugar sales to US—only 3 percent of country's total exports. Sanctions, which take effect in October 1983, reduce Nicaragua's sugar quota from 58,800 short tons to 6,000 short tons. (*New York Times*, 6 April 1983, D9; Bureau of National Affairs, *US Import Weekly*, 11 May 1983, 202)

In June 1983, Nicaragua fails to make repayment of $45 million owed to foreign commercial banks, first such delay. (*Washington Post*, 1 July 1983, A1)

In August 1983, Mexico makes further oil shipments contingent on Nicaraguan commitment to pay Venezuela $20 million, Mexico some $300 million; Venezuela already had suspended shipments in June. (*Wall Street Journal*, 8 June 1983, 30; *New York Times*, 13 August 1983, D3)

Nicaragua suggests US sanctions have cost $354 million in 1983. (Authors' note: We regard this figure as much too high.) Estimates indicate $18 million loss from lower sugar quota, $112.5 million in multilateral loans that US has blocked since 1980. (*Journal of Commerce*, 5 August 1983, 23B)

Nicaraguan GNP declines by 2 percent in 1982, in contrast with drops of 3 percent to 7 percent in Guatemala, El Salvador, Costa Rica. (*New York Times*, 13 August 1983, A3)

Calculated Economic Impact

	Annual cost to target country
Suspension of US economic aid in 1981; welfare loss valued at 90 percent of average aid levels FY 1979–81.	$35 million
Reduction of 90 percent in US sugar import quota for Nicaragua; welfare loss valued at 40 percent of value of 1981 trade.	6 million
Suspension of US wheat sale and PL 480 food aid; welfare loss valued at 40 percent of trade and aid.	9 million
Reduction in concessional loans from IDB 1981–83 because of US vetoes; welfare loss estimated as 75 percent of value of loans ($32.2 million) lost during three-year period.	8 million
Offsets	
Increase in official grants, loans from USSR, Cuba, Libya; welfare gain valued at 70 percent of transfers. (Note: No estimate is made for possibly offsetting European assistance.)	($106 million)
Increased shipments of 30,000 tons of grain from USSR, Bulgaria, valued at 40 percent.	(2 million)
Total (gain)	($50 million)

Relative Magnitudes

Gross indicators of Nicaraguan economy	
Nicaraguan GNP (1979)	$1.4 billion
Nicaraguan population (1980)	2.7 million
Annual effect of sanctions related to gross indicators	
Percentage of GNP (gain)	(3.6)
Per capita (gain)	($18.52)

Nicaraguan trade with US as percentage of total trade
Exports (1980)   35
Imports (1980)   34

Ratio of US GNP (1979: $2,418 billion) to Nicaraguan GNP (1979:
$1.4 billion)   1727

ASSESSMENT

Thomas P. Anderson
"As relations worsened on the American continent, Nicaragua appeared to be turning more and more toward contacts with Cuba and the Soviet bloc. . . . If the United States and Nicaragua did not manage to patch up their quarrel over the loan and the Salvadoran civil war, it was quite likely that Nicaragua would continue turning toward Havana." (Anderson 189, 192)

Wall Street Journal
"President Reagan's economic reprisals have aggravated a sickly economy that has Nicaraguans grumbling about having to wait in lines for scarce gasoline and to carry ration cards for many staples. . . . But while the Reagan administration has succeeded in putting Nicaragua in a pressure cooker, its policies haven't succeeded in forcing the nation into ending support for revolutionaries in El Salvador or reversing the military buildup that alarms its neighbors. . . . [Sanctions] may only be producing a more radical regime. Already the Nicaraguan government has nationalized distribution of many basic foods, and officials explain the step was necessary to ensure equitable distribution of goods during a national emergency." (*Wall Street Journal*, 31 May 1983, 1)

AUTHORS' SUMMARY

Overall assessment	*Assigned scores*
☐ Policy result, scaled from 1 (failed) to 4 (success)	2
☐ Sanctions contribution, scaled from 1 (none) to 4 (significant)	2
☐ Success score (policy result *times* sanctions contribution), scaled from 1 (outright failure) to 16 (significant success)	4

Political and economic variables

☐ Companion policies: J (covert), Q (quasi-military), or R (regular military)	Q, J
☐ International cooperation with sender, scaled from 1 (none) to 4 (significant)	1
☐ International assistance to target: A (if present)	A
☐ Sanctions period (years)	3 +
☐ Economic health and political stability of target, scaled from 1 (distressed) to 3 (strong)	2

Political and economic variables (continued)	Assigned scores
☐ Presanction relations between sender and target, scaled from 1 (antagonistic) to 3 (cordial)	2
☐ Type of sanction: X (export), M (import), F (financial)	F, M
☐ Cost to sender, scaled from 1 (net gain) to 4 (major loss)	2

BIBLIOGRAPHY

Agency for International Development. *Overseas Loans and Grants*. Various issues.
Anderson, Thomas P. 1982. *Politics in Central America*. New York: Praeger.
Keesing's Contemporary Archives. 1981.
US Senate. Committee on Foreign Relations, Subcommittee on Inter-American Affairs. 1983. *US Policy toward Nicaragua and Central America*. Statement by Assistant Secretary of State Thomas O. Enders. 98 Cong., 1 sess., 12 April.

Case 81–2 US v. Poland

(1981–84: Martial Law)

CHRONOLOGY OF KEY EVENTS

Also see Case 81–3 US v. USSR (1981–82: Poland)

September 1981	Poland's Solidarity trade union holds national convention; leader Lech Walesa is criticized as too moderate. (Simes 52)
October 1981	General Wojciech Jaruzelski replaces Stanislaw Kania as prime minister. (Simes 52)
2 December 1981	Military crushes cadet strike at firefighters' academy. (Simes 52)
13 December 1981	Martial law declared in Poland. Solidarity leaders, including Walesa, subsequently arrested. (*New York Times*, 14 December 1981, A1)
23 December 1981	President Ronald Reagan announces sanctions against Poland: ends US Export–Import Bank credit insurance; suspends Polish airline (LOT) landing rights; suspends Polish fishing rights in US waters; requests allies to restrict high tech sales to Poland. Reagan says that if authorities will ease repression, US will help rebuild Polish economy. Poland suspends principal, interest payments on debt to foreign governments. (*Wall Street Journal*, 24 December 1981, 1; *Washington Post*, 24 December 1981, A1; *Financial Times* [London], 2 March 1983, 1)
29 December 1981	US extends sanctions to USSR. (*Washington Post*, 30 December 1981, A1)
January–February 1982	US government pays $71 million guaranteed loan rather than declare Poland in default. House of Representatives rejects proposal that would force administration to declare Poland in default. (*New York Times*, 3 February 1982, A1; *Washington Post*, 10 February 1982, A18)
Early July 1982	Western bankers, Polish officials meet on debt rescheduling. Poland faces $7 billion in principal, $3 billion in interest payments due in

Early July 1982 *(continued)*	1982, with prospect of no new credits, few hard currency exports. Western governments, led by US, refuse to discuss rescheduling. On 14 September 1982, Western banks agree Poland may postpone payment of two-thirds of $1.1 billion interest payments due. Meanwhile, US blocks Polish application to join International Monetary Fund (IMF). (*Financial Times*, 9 July 1982, 18; *New York Times*, 15 September 1982, D1; *Washington Post*, 22 May 1983, A13; 30 September 1983, A30)
8 October 1982	Polish parliament outlaws Solidarity. (*New York Times*, 9 October 1982, A1)
9 October 1982	Reagan announces suspension of Poland's MFN status, received 22 years earlier, citing Poland's failure to increase imports by 7 percent/ year as promised upon accession to GATT. Reagan later submits proposal to Congress for approval. (*New York Times*, 10 October 1982, A1; *Congressional Quarterly*, 16 October 1982, 2693)
Mid-November *1982*	Lech Walesa is freed. (*New York Times*, 15 November 1982, A1)
Late November– *early December* *1982*	Rumors circulate that Jaruzelski will lift martial law on first anniversary of imposition. Reagan says that if regime takes "genuine liberalizing actions," US will respond accordingly. (*Washington Post*, 11 December 1982, A1)
30 December 1982	Jaruzelski suspends some martial law regulations but replaces many of them with new, harsher laws. Western governments accordingly refuse to reschedule debt. West German bank official remarks: "There is a perception among Western governments that Poland has institutionalized martial law. The Poles will have to do something to change this perception before we will get much help from governments." (*Wall Street Journal*, 30 December 1982, 9)
10 January 1983	"Although the internment of political dissidents was formally ended December 30 with the suspension of the basic provisions of martial law, the authorities are still arresting underground Solidarity activists." (*New York Times*, 10 January 1983, A1)
21 January 1983	Poland attempts to change terms of membership in GATT in order to undermine legal arguments offered by US in revocation of MFN status in October 1982. Poland explores possibility of replacing its 7 percent/year import growth commitment with cap on tariffs, as most other GATT participants have done. (*Wall Street Journal*, 21 January 1983, 26)
May 1983	US Assistant Secretary of State Richard Burt explores with US allies in Europe possible ways to lift sanctions gradually, with each step conditioned on reciprocal steps by Polish government. (*Washington Post*, 22 May 1983, A13)
June 1983	Pope John Paul II visits Poland, admonishes leadership, sees Walesa. (*Washington Post*, 24 June 1983, A1)

21 July 1983	Poland ends 19 months of martial law, proclaims partial amnesty for political prisoners. In response, Reagan comments, "We're going to go by deeds, not words." US State Department spokesman elaborates: "In particular we will be focusing on whether the vast majority of political prisoners are being released." (*Washington Post*, 22 July 1983, A1)
29 July 1983	US agrees with Western allies to resume talks with Poland on rescheduling foreign debt. (*Washington Post*, 30 July 1983, A1)
18 August 1983	Poland reaches agreement with several international banks to reschedule 1983 commercial debt service of $1.5 billion principal, $1.1 billion interest. Terms provide five-year grace period on principal, new trade credits for 65 percent of 1983 interest due ($715 million). (*Wall Street Journal*, 19 August 1983, 1)
3 November 1983	In response to "very modest improvement in the human rights situation" in Poland, Reagan administration relaxes restrictions on Polish fishing in US waters (no practical effect until 1984), indicates willingness to discuss debt rescheduling. Poland denounces these "two limited steps" as "merely of an illusory nature." US ban on Polish airline, restrictions on high tech sales, freeze on new credits, denial of MFN status, veto on IMF membership all remain in place. (*New York Times*, 4 November 1983, A3)
5 December 1983	Walesa calls for end to Western sanctions because of pain economic crisis is causing Polish people. He repeats plea for reconciliation between government and people in Nobel Peace Prize acceptance speech delivered for him by colleague in Oslo. (*Washington Post*, 12 December 1983, A21)
20 January 1984	Reagan administration, in response to appeal from Walesa, lifts ban against Polish fishermen, allows chartered flights to US by Polish airline LOT. Administration spokesmen cite both Walesa appeal and "positive developments" in Poland as reasons for actions. (*New York Times*, 20 January 1984, A1; *Washington Post*, 20 January 1984, A16; *Wall Street Journal*, 20 January 1984, 8)
21 July 1984	Polish parliament approves amnesty for almost all prisoners, including 652 political prisoners. US State Department calls it a "positive move." On 25 July, administration officials indicate willingness to lift remaining minor sanctions; stiffer sanctions to remain in effect until implementation of amnesty studied. Polish spokesman Jerzy Urban criticizes reported steps as "comical" and "not serious." Reportedly, Polish leaders are most interested in having US veto on Polish membership in IMF withdrawn. (*Wall Street Journal*, 20 July 1984, 25; 23 July 1984, 21; 24 July 1984, 38; *Financial Times*, 24 July 1984, 14; *Washington Post*, 25 July 1984, A22; *New York Times*, 25 July 1984, A11)
3 August 1984	Reagan lifts ban on regular flights to US by Polish national airline and scientific and cultural exchanges, pledges to lift other sanctions

<table>
<tr><td>3 August 1984
(continued)</td><td>if there is "further significant movement toward national reconciliation." In particular, Reagan says he will "withdraw the US objection" to Poland's application for membership in IMF upon "complete and reasonable" implementation of amnesty decree. "Complete" is defined as meaning release of all 652 political prisoners including 11 top Solidarity and KOR (Workers' Defense Committee) leaders. So far 518 have been freed but many of most prominent remain in jail. "'Reasonable' was said to mean that there would not be rearrests or other steps that would undercut the sincerity of the amnesty." Poland identifies sanctions lifted as "less significant" ones and calls for unconditional lifting of all those remaining. (Washington Post, 4 August 1984, A1)</td></tr>
<tr><td>December 1984</td><td>Final two jailed Solidarity activists are released. US lifts objection to Polish re-entry into IMF. (New York Times, 15 December 1984, A1)</td></tr>
<tr><td>January 1985</td><td>Following approval of Poland's economic and financial plans, 17 Western governments agree to reschedule $10.5 billion of Poland's debt. US officials estimate that $1.4 billion is owed to the US. (Wall Street Journal, 17 January 1985, 31)</td></tr>
</table>

GOALS OF SENDER COUNTRY

23 December 1981

Reagan declares in Christmas address: "I want to state emphatically tonight that, if the outrages in Poland do not cease, we cannot and will not conduct 'business as usual' with the perpetrators and those who aid and abet them.

"Make no mistake: their crime will cost them dearly in their future dealings with America and free peoples everywhere.

"I have urged [Jaruzelski] to free those in arbitrary detention, to lift martial law, and to restore the internationally recognized rights of the Polish people to free speech and association." (*Washington Post*, 24 December 1981, A1)

9 October 1982

Following ban on Solidarity, Reagan declares: "There can only be one path out of the current morass in Poland and that is for the military regime to stand up to its own statements of principle, even in the face of severe outside pressure from the Soviet Union, to lift martial law, release Lech Walesa and his colleagues now languishing in prison, and begin again the search for social peace through the arduous but real process of dialogue and reconciliation with the church and Solidarity." (*New York Times*, 10 October 1982, A16)

24 June 1983

Holding out possibility of step-by-step reconciliation, Reagan states: "We are currently consulting with our allies on the Polish question . . . if the Polish government takes meaningful liberalizing measures, we are prepared to take equally significant and concrete steps of our own." (*Washington Post*, 24 June 1983, A11)

2 November 1983
Upon announcing willingness to reopen negotiations on Polish debt and to discuss fishing arrangements, White House spokesman, Larry Speakes says, "Reagan's actions are aimed at 'inducing the Polish government to begin a path of national reconciliation and restore free trade unions. Very serious problems still remain. The Polish government continues to defy the wishes of the majority of the Polish people.'" (*Washington Post*, 3 November 1983, A27)

22 July 1984
State Department calls amnesty announcement a "positive move," but indicates "that it wants Warsaw to take additional actions." Administration official suggests that, "The White House also will have to consider the domestic political consequences of any decision regarding sanctions in light of the significant number of Polish-American voters and President Reagan's hard-line conservative constituency." (*Wall Street Journal*, 23 July 1984, 21)

3 August 1984
"A State Department official [unnamed at his request] said the opening of a 'genuine dialogue' with the Polish labor movement would be required for lifting of . . . broader sanctions [such as restoration of official credits and MFN status]. He added that the United States is not asking that the banned union, Solidarity, be reinstated. . . . [W]e face a real opportunity in Eastern Europe, including Poland, to open a new chapter at a time when there is 'an inability on the Soviet part to meet the economic needs' there and 'considerable tension' in Soviet–East European relations." (*Washington Post*, 4 August 1984, A1)

RESPONSE OF TARGET COUNTRY

January 1982
Zbigniew Karcz, head of finance ministry foreign department, speaking on Polish debt, suspension of rescheduling negotiations: "I am waiting for the normal situation with Western countries to be restored. Every week we wait is lost. It is not a secret that Poland will suffer most. I have said this many times during the talks in Paris. But Western countries will suffer also." (*New York Times*, 28 January 1982, D3)

3 February 1982
Polish government spokesman Urban: "We are not hiding the fact that sanctions hit us in a touchy spot." He and Agriculture Minister Jerzy Wojtecki declare planned reorientation of national priorities would make Poland self-sufficient in agriculture, ending dependency on imported US corn for poultry industry. "Polish officials suggested today that the US sanctions were helping to strangle the livestock industry here and starve the country." (*Washington Post*, 4 February 1982, A1)

Early June 1982
Leading members of Polish chamber of foreign trade say Reagan administration should make "realistic reassessment" of sanctions policy. They claim neither country gains by sanctions and they should be rescinded. (*Journal of Commerce*, 11 June 1982, 1A)

July 1982

"It is true that [sanctions] pressure was a factor behind General Jaruzelski's moves in early May to free some internees and partially to relax the curfew. But this liberalisation came to a dead halt when it became clear that the Polish people did not feel grateful but merely freer to express their feelings in street protests." (*Financial Times*, 9 July 1982, 18)

Fall 1982

"Mr. Kaczurba [Poland's permanent representative to GATT] says Poland's exporters have been 'having a hard time with the problem' of no longer receiving most-favored-nation treatment from the US. . . ." (*Wall Street Journal*, 21 January 1983, 26)

June 1983

Vice Premier Janusz Obodowski proposes that Western banks accept eight-year moratorium on principal and interest due on $25 billion debt. (*Washington Post*, 15 June 1983, A21)

12 July 1983

Polish government spokesman Urban states: "At an appropriate moment Poland will present the United States with a bill of the losses suffered by Poland as a result of the unilateral severance of [the 1970 bilateral economic] agreement, and we will demand an appropriate compensation at a proper time." In June 1983 Vice Premier Obodowski states that Western sanctions, particularly those imposed by US, have cost Poland $6 billion, not counting "rather considerable indirect losses." (*Washington Post*, 13 July 1983, A14)

July 1983

After lifting martial law, General Jaruzelski states: "There are still governments that cherish illusions toward Poland. Recently they have tried the stick-and-carrot approach. It is ridiculous now. The stick proved too short and the carrot not fresh enough. . . . We are ready to normalize mutual relations, but any conditions are out of the question." (*New York Times*, 22 July 1983, A1)

21 July 1984

In speech to parliament, Jaruzelski "alluded to the period of Solidarity as one of chaos and warned his political opponents that 'anarchy' would never again reign in Poland. . . . [He] spoke disparagingly of the 'imperialist' US and its 'superpower arrogance.' But he left open a window for improved political and economic relations with Washington and the West, saying: 'Poland doesn't want to be an isolated island.'" (*Wall Street Journal*, 23 July 1984, 21)

24 July 1984

Following reports of planned US response to amnesty, Urban calls American demands "dishonest" and accuses Reagan administration of repeatedly "chang[ing] the conditions for ending the sanctions, ignoring developments here [in Poland] and aiming to weaken Poland's place in the world as part of a general anticommunist policy. . . . 'The dishonesty of the demands [is] becoming increasingly clear. The demands are being multiplied and modified and are increasingly unrelated to the situation in Poland. The United States knows that we will not change our political system in answer to its demands, so it doesn't really expect its demands to be fulfilled.'" (*Washington Post*, 25 July 1984, A22)

ATTITUDE OF OTHER COUNTRIES

North Atlantic Treaty Organization
On 11 January 1982, NATO Foreign Ministers meet in Brussels, condemn violation of human rights in Poland, call for Jaruzelski to take steps outlined by Reagan as conditions for lifting sanctions; also decide to suspend future commercial credits except for food; delay negotiations on rescheduling Poland's debt to NATO governments; study possible long-term sanctions. (*Washington Post*, 12 January 1982, A1)

European Community
Communiqué from Foreign Ministers' meeting, 4 January 1982: "Other measures will be considered as the situation in Poland develops, in particular measures concerning credit and economic assistance to Poland, and measures concerning the Communities' commercial policy with regard to the USSR. In addition, the 10 will examine the question of further aid to Poland." (*Wall Street Journal*, 5 January 1982, 2)

On 11 October 1982, reacting to Reagan's suspension of Poland's MFN status: "Irritation was reported from several European capitals yesterday that President Ronald Reagan had once again taken unilateral action without prior consultation with US allies." (*Financial Times*, 12 October 1982, 3)

Federal Republic of Germany
On 5 January 1982, Chancellor Helmut Schmidt of West Germany, meeting with Reagan, "gave some support to the American moves in the Polish crisis but held out little hope that he would follow the US in imposing economic sanctions against the Soviet Union." (*Wall Street Journal*, 6 January 1982, 1)

Senior West German politician, commenting in September 1983: "The American approach to Poland still emphasizes punishment. Our approach is broader. We are neighbors. We must show the Polish people that we care for them but must also do what we can to prevent the awful day when Soviet tanks move in." (*Washington Post*, 30 September 1983, A30)

United Kingdom
In late February 1982, Prime Minister Margaret Thatcher announces movements of Polish and Soviet diplomats will be restricted, no new financial credits granted to Poland. British official states: "They are not really sanctions as such but a signal to the Polish and Soviet authorities of Allied disapproval. We believe this is just as strong a signal as the US measures." (*Washington Post*, 16 February 1982, A1)

Japan
Bans new government-sponsored credits, suspends negotiations on rescheduling debt; imposes travel restrictions on Polish diplomats. Chief Cabinet Secretary Kiichi Miyazawa says actions are taken because "unity and cooperation among Western countries are of utmost importance in coping with the Polish question." (*Washington Post*, 23 February 1982, A13)

Belgium
Suspends negotiations on rescheduling of Polish debt and scientific and technical accords with Poland. (*Washington Post*, 23 February 1982, A13)

Soviet Union
On 6 January 1982, USSR extends $3.4 billion credit to Poland to cover part of 1981

trade deficit, anticipated 1982 deficit; continues to supply Poles with Soviet energy, raw materials. (*Washington Post*, 7 January 1982, A1)

In late October 1982, Western sources predict Soviet shipments of goods, raw materials to Poland will reach record levels in 1982—18 percent higher than 1981. Wharton Econometrics report, however, says USSR has reduced aid, exports to Poland (latter by some 10 percent vs. 1981). (*Journal of Commerce*, 28 October 1982, 1A; *Wall Street Journal*, 9 November 1982, 39)

July 1984; "President Konstantin Chernenko seems to have carried on his predecessor's policy of allowing Poland some political as well as economic leeway in sorting out its problems. His despatch of Mr. Nikolai Tikhonov, the Soviet Prime Minister, to the amnesty ceremony said as much." (*Financial Times*, 24 July 1984, 14)

ECONOMIC IMPACT

Observed Economic Statistics

Credit freeze
Total Polish external debt, end-1981: $29 billion, of which about $7.4 billion in loans from US, West European, Japanese banks are not guaranteed by Western governments; another $8.5 billion in bank loans are guaranteed by Western governments. Of unguaranteed loans, about $1.2 billion is owed to US banks. In 1982 Poland owes $10 billion in current interest, principal payments to Western banks, governments. (*Washington Post*, 15 January 1982, A1; *New York Times*, 15 January 1982, D1)

"According to Wharton Econometric Forecasting Associates, for every dollar decline in Poland's bank loans [through default], its debt to governments increases by about 90 cents." (*Washington Post*, 30 September 1983, A30)

In early 1982, US denies Poland $740 million credit for purchase of US corn. Chicken is 10 percent of each person's average 5.5 pounds meat/month; poultry industry depends heavily on imported feed corn. As of February 1982, Poland is short 3 million to 3.5 million tons of grain, which could lead to loss of 350,000 tons of poultry. However, Western analysts estimate that about one-third of Polish grain shortfall reflects refusal of Polish farmers to sell to government. (*Washington Post*, 4 February 1982, A1)

In early 1982, default debate rages in Western circles. Arguments in favor of declaring Poland in default on loans:

☐ "Would put the financial burden of the Polish economy where it belongs, on the Soviet Union's shoulders";
☐ Resulting drain on Soviet resources would force USSR to reduce military spending, foreign adventurism;
☐ Default would punish Polish martial law government.

Arguments against default declaration:

☐ US taxpayers would have to pick up $2.4 billion tab—$1.9 billion in government guaranteed credits, $500 million in tax write-off claims by commercial banks.
☐ Ripple effects of default would cause major lending crisis in Third World; some developing countries might also be forced to default as result.

□ US would lose all influence over events in Poland.

□ Default would force Poland deeper into Soviet orbit, discourage future liberalization. (*Wall Street Journal*, 26 February 1982, 34)

MFN revocation

"While there are varying estimates of how much the US action is costing financially ailing Poland, Mr. Kaczurba said, 'It definitely goes into tens of millions of dollars a year, if it's going to last that long, for direct loss and potential losses.'" (*Wall Street Journal*, 21 January 1983, 26)

About two-thirds of Polish imports into US are manufactured goods that now will be subject to higher tariffs. Current tariffs on textile imports (19 percent of Polish exports to US) range from 5 percent to 40 percent; non-MFN rates are 10 percent to 60 percent. (*New York Times*, 10 October 1982, A1)

Polish trade (million dollars)

	Exports (fob)			Imports (fob)		
	1981	*1982*	*1981–82 percentage change*	*1981*	*1982*	*1981–82 percentage change*
US	329	220	− 33	879	142	− 84
FRG	1,097	959	− 13	903	736	− 18
France	288	306	+ 6	614	431	− 30
UK	396	400	+ 1	419	331	− 21
Total non-Socialist countries	5,446	5,183	− 5	5,959	4,020	− 33

Source: Vanous.

In 1982, Polish exports to USSR grow almost 30 percent over 1981 levels; imports fall more that 1 percent, mostly because of drop in machinery imports. "Net *real* inflow of resources to the Polish economy from the Soviet Union (in terms of 1981 prices) declined from 1,653 million rubles to a mere 270 million rubles." (Vanous 1)

Poland passes 1983 budget that will mean $3 billion increase in overall Western debt, reflecting plans for new short-term credits, rescheduling of the entire $4 billion in principal due in 1983, postponement of repayment of more than $2 billion in interest. (*Wall Street Journal*, 30 December 1982, 9)

Poland estimates the cost of sanctions as $12 billion to $13 billion, "a figure based largely on the impact on its economy of the cut off in Western government trade and food credits, but clearly much inflated by a failure to recognise that most of this credit would have dried up for 'economic' not 'political' reasons, anyway." (*Financial Times*, 24 July 1984, 14)

Calculated Economic Impact

	Annual cost to target country
Reduction in trade with US; welfare loss calculated at 40 percent of reduced trade flows.	$338 million
Increase in US import duties on Polish manufactured exports; welfare loss reflects estimated average 20 percent ad valorem tariff increase on two-thirds of total 1982 Polish exports to US.	29 million
Suspension of Commodity Credit Corporation (CCC) and Eximbank direct credits and guarantees; welfare loss estimated at 10 percent of value of credit line affected.	77 million
Offsets	
Interest paid by US government on Poland's CCC loans; welfare gain estimated at 40 percent of deferred payments.	($28 million)
Credits from USSR to cover 1981–82 trade deficits; welfare gain estimated at 5 percent of total transfers.	(170 million)
Total	$246 million

Relative Magnitudes

Gross indicators of Polish economy	
Polish GNP (1981)	$178 billion
Polish population (1981)	36 million
Annual effect of sanctions related to gross indicators	
Percentage of GNP	0.1
Per capita	$6.83
Polish trade with US as percentage of total trade	
Exports (1981)	3
Imports (1981)	5
Ratio of US GNP (1981: $2,938 billion) to Polish GNP (1981: $178 billion)	17

ASSESSMENT

Journal of Commerce
"The effectiveness of the sanctions depended largely on Comecon [Council for Mutual Economic Assistance] coming to the aid of one of its member states. US policy-makers expected that the Soviet Union, along with the other Eastern bloc nations, would be forced to stretch already limited resources to bail out the crippled Polish economy. These added economic burdens would, in turn, yield political advantages for the United States vis-à-vis the Soviet bloc. . . . Neither the Soviet Union nor the other Comecon countries are subsidizing the Polish economy. In fact, during the last 10 months, Polish exports to the Comecon countries have exceeded imports and its trade deficit with the Soviet Union has substantially decreased. . . . As is evident by these measures [intended to contain the economic crisis to Poland] the American sanctions have merely served to hasten the reintegration of the Polish economy into the Soviet system." (*Journal of Commerce*, 6 December 1982, 1A)

Dimitri K. Simes
"The marginal sanctions adopted by Reagan hardly suffice to influence Polish and Soviet policy concerning an interest as vital as the survival of communism in Poland." (Simes 63)

"Washington's casual use of marginal sanctions, which the West Europeans did not support and never were expected to support, succeeded only in communicating America's sense of frustration and impotence." (Simes 64)

New York Times
"Were the sanctions a mistake in the first place? Probably not. Even if they could not much influence events in Poland, both American and Polish outrage required some expression. But the sanctions could have been better designed. . . . The debt could have become a political weapon only if assigned to governments and manipulated by them in political bargains with Poland and the ultimate Polish power, the Soviet Union." (*New York Times*, 23 July 1983, A22)

Economist
July 1984: "After martial law, the west set three conditions for lifting the economic sanctions it then imposed. The release of those jailed for supporting Solidarity meets the second of them. The first, the lifting of martial law, happened a year ago. This third condition—the reopening of a dialogue between the Polish government and the Polish people—is as far off as ever." (*Economist* [London], 28 July 1984, 10)

Wall Street Journal
"Polish official sources and Western diplomats believe [Jaruzelski] was willing to take the bold action of freeing 652 political prisoners largely due to his desperate need for western capital to restructure and revive the economy . . . Those in the US who have supported the sanctions are gloating that their policy is directly responsible for Poland's amnesty program. However, others argue that the policy has only distanced Poland from the West, and that domestic considerations ruled Warsaw's decision." (*Wall Street Journal*, 24 July 1984, 38)

"The Reagan administration's decision [to lift some sanctions], although pegged to Polish liberalization moves, reflects a US acknowledgement that American sanctions haven't significantly altered Polish policies or forced the Polish government to allow a revival of the Solidarity trade union. Instead, both the Polish amnesty program and the Reagan administration's response signal a recognition that the Polish turbulence of the late 1970s and early 1980s has largely passed." (*Wall Street Journal*, 3 August 1984, 2)

Jan Vanous, Wharton Econometric Forecasting Associates
"I can't imagine the Soviets put them up to this (amnesty). You can interpret this that the Poles didn't get what they were hoping to get from Moscow. Hence, the only hope they have is money from the West." (*Wall Street Journal*, 24 July 1984, 38)

Solidarity
Communiqué of July 29, released by Solidarity leaders Wladislaw Frasyniuk (freed by amnesty) and Zbigniew Bujak (still underground): "'Polish society, Solidarity militants, the Roman Catholic Church and the West' had pressured the country's Communist government into declaring [the] amnesty. . . . 'This measure, which could have marked an important step in Polish life, is aimed at serving the current interests of power.'"

"Solidarity in an illegal radio broadcast Monday [23 July] said that the government amnesty was a sham aimed at improving the country's international image." (*International Herald Tribune* [Paris], 1 August 1984, 1)

Andrzei Gwiazda, prominent Solidarity activist freed by amnesty
"It remains absolutely impossible for the government to gain any credibility from society. The rulers have pressing economic problems which they think they can cure with dollars from the West [in return] for the amnesty. But really nothing has changed. They have not made any political concessions and society cannot accept anything less than real political concessions." (*New York Times*, 5 August 1984, IV 5)

Lech Walesa
Solidarity leader calls amnesty a positive move while reiterating need for trade union pluralism. He later welcomes Reagan administration's partial lifting of sanctions: "As a Pole I am happy." (*Wall Street Journal*, 23 July 1984, 21; *Washington Post*, 4 August 1984, A1)

AUTHORS' SUMMARY

Overall assessment	Assigned scores
□ Policy result, scaled from 1 (failed) to 4 (success)	3
□ Sanctions contribution, scaled from 1 (none) to 4 (significant)	2
□ Success score (policy result *times* sanctions contribution), scaled from 1 (outright failure) to 16 (significant success)	6

Political and economic variables

□ Companion policies: J (covert), Q (quasi-military), or R (regular military)	—
□ International cooperation with sender, scaled from 1 (none) to 4 (significant)	3
□ International assistance to target: A (if present)	A
□ Sanctions period (years)	3

Political and economic variables (continued)	Assigned scores
☐ Economic health and political stability of target, scaled from 1 (distressed) to 3 (strong)	1
☐ Presanction relations between sender and target, scaled from 1 (antagonistic) to 3 (cordial)	2
☐ Type of sanction: X (export), M (import), F (financial)	F, X, M
☐ Cost to sender, scaled from 1 (net gain) to 4 (major loss)	2

Comments

While domestic economic and political factors were undoubtedly uppermost in General Jaruzelski's mind at all times, the Western sanctions seem to have been a concern as well. Polish claims of the adverse impact of sanctions on their economy are undoubtedly exaggerated and, at least in part, an excuse for inept political and economic management in Poland. Nonetheless, the angry reaction by Polish spokesmen, both in November 1983 and July–August 1984, to the limited steps taken by the Reagan administration in response to liberalizing measures in Poland indicates that lifting the sanctions was one objective of Polish policy. Thus, the sanctions seem to have made a limited contribution to a somewhat positive outcome.

BIBLIOGRAPHY

Simes, Dimitri K. 1982. "Clash over Poland." 46 *Foreign Policy* (Spring): 49–66.
Vanous, Jan. 1983. "Polish Foreign Trade Performance in 1982." Washington: Wharton Econometric Forecasting Associates, April 29.
Woolcock, Stephen. 1982. *Western Policies on East-West Trade.* Chatham House Papers, no. 15. London: Royal Institute of International Affairs.

Case 81–3   US v. USSR

(1981–82: Poland)

CHRONOLOGY OF KEY EVENTS

Also see Case 81–2 US v. Poland (1981–84: Martial Law)

12 December 1980	NATO ministers issue communiqué warning Soviets that: "Any intervention [in Poland] would fundamentally alter the entire situation. The Allies would be compelled to react in the manner which the gravity of this development would require." (Marantz 1)
24 April 1981	President Ronald Reagan lifts grain embargo imposed by President Jimmy Carter in retaliation for USSR invasion of Afghanistan. (*New York Times*, 25 April 1981, A1)
Late July 1981	At Ottawa summit, Reagan presses European and Japanese leaders for tighter restrictions by Coordinating Committee for Multilateral Export Controls (COCOM). He also urges reconsideration of Yamal pipeline deal in which Western European firms provide pipeline equipment in return for gas deliveries later. Europeans agree to review COCOM but refuse to drop pipeline. (*Journal of Commerce*, 21 January 1982, 2A)
24 July 1981	USSR, Germany conclude outline agreement for financing pipeline. (*Business Week*, 10 August 1981, 36)
1 October 1981	US extends existing grain agreement for one year, will allow USSR to buy up to 15 million metric tons (mmt) above 8 mmt allowed without consultation under old agreement. (*New York Times*, 2 October 1981, A1)
6 October 1981	Italy announces signing of agreement in principle to buy USSR natural gas, first firm commitment by West European country. (*New York Times*, 19 October 1981, D8)
20 November 1981	FRG, USSR sign agreement for delivery of gas, clearing way for pipeline to go forward. (*Washington Post*, 21 November 1981, A1)

13 December 1981	Martial law is declared in Poland; USSR rushes to nail down contracts for pipeline equipment. (*Washington Post*, 14 December 1981, A1)
23 December 1981	Reagan's Christmas address to nation announces sanctions against Poland. (*Washington Post*, 24 December 1981, A1)
29 December 1981	US sanctions imposed on USSR for role in declaration of martial law in Poland are characterized by US Secretary of State Alexander M. Haig, Jr., as "interim step that hardly exhausts the list of potential actions." Actions taken include: suspension of Aeroflot flights; suspension of export licenses for high tech items including oil, gas equipment; closing of Soviet Purchasing Commission office in New York; suspension of negotiations on new long-term grain agreement; suspension of new maritime agreement; allowing technical exchange agreements to lapse—energy, space in May, science, technology in July. (*Washington Post*, 30 December 1981, A1)
11 January 1982	NATO Council condemns Soviet interference in Poland, agrees to: restrictions on activities of Soviet, Polish diplomats; reduction of scientific and technical exchanges with USSR. (*Department of State Bulletin*, February 1982, 19)
Early January 1982	US refuses to grant export licenses to General Electric to ship $175 million worth of components for gas compressor turbines to be built for pipeline by Nuovo Pignone of Italy, AEG Telefunken of West Germany, John Brown Engineers, Ltd., of Great Britain. (*New York Times*, 11 January 1982, A1)
23 January 1982	France concludes 25-year contract with USSR for 280 billion cubic feet of gas per year, one-third of France's gas imports. (*Washington Post*, 24 January 1982, A1)
28 January 1982	Italy reaches tentative agreement with USSR on price, volume of gas shipments. (*Wall Street Journal*, 29 January 1982, 33)
Early June 1982	Participants at Versailles economic summit discuss subsidized export credits to USSR. Reagan pressures Western Europe to charge market interest rates on such credits. Final summit communiqué calls for "prudent and diversified economic approach to the Soviet bloc and to take into account a need for 'commercial prudence' in limiting export credits to the Soviet Union and its allies." However, "conflicting statements from US and European officials in the week following the summit indicated that the communiqué did not reflect a consensus on the subject of export credits." (Moyer 81)
18 June 1982	Reportedly in response to reluctance of West European allies, particularly France, to limit export credits to Soviet bloc, US extends ban on sale of oil, gas equipment to foreign subsidiaries of US companies and foreign companies producing equipment under US license, effective 22 June 1982. (*Washington Post*, 19 June 1982, A1)
Late June 1982	"European governments promptly denounced the extraterritorial extension of U.S. regulation as violative of their sovereignty, contrary

Late June 1982 *(continued)*	to international law, inconsistent with the understandings purportedly reached at the Versailles Summit, and insensitive to their commercial interests." (Moyer 81–82)
22 July 1982	France orders French companies to honor their contracts and supply equipment for pipeline despite Reagan's ban. (*Washington Post*, 23 July 1982, A1)
	OECD officials announce agreement on new arrangement for export credits. Included is reclassification of USSR, other East European countries from intermediate to "relatively rich" category, which increases minimum allowable rate for USSR from 10.5 percent to a range of 12.15 percent to 12.40 percent. (*Keesing's* 31639)
25 July 1982	Italy announces "signed agreements will be honored" but stops short of ordering its companies to fulfill contracts associated with pipeline. (*Wall Street Journal*, 26 July 1982, 21)
26 July 1982	Belgium postpones signing of contract with USSR for gas. (*Financial Times* [London], 27 July 1982, 4)
28 July 1982	UK announces it will not order British companies to defy US sanctions but that British government will defend firms from US retaliation if they choose to go ahead with pipeline deals. (*Washington Post*, 29 July 1982, A30)
30 July 1982	Reagan announces one-year extension of grain agreement with USSR but refuses to negotiate new long-term agreement because the Soviet Union "should not be afforded the additional security of a new long-term grain agreement as long as repression continues in Poland." (*Department of State Bulletin*, October 1982, 40–41)
2 August 1982	UK reverses policy, orders British companies to fulfill contracts for pipeline equipment. Trade Secretary Lord Cockfield invokes Protection of Trading Interests Act in issuing the order. In preelection speech to National Corn Growers Association, Reagan says Russians can buy as much grain as they want if they pay cash. (*Washington Post*, 3 August 1982, A4, A11)
11 August 1982	House Foreign Affairs Committee votes 22 to 12 to rescind administration's pipeline sanctions. (*Washington Post*, 12 August 1982, A1)
23 August 1982	France orders Dresser-France to deliver 21 pipeline booster compressors already on order. Dresser Industries orders its French subsidiary to comply with French order, files suit in US federal court to block implementation of US penalties for violating sanctions. (*Wall Street Journal*, 26 August 1982, 4; *New York Times*, 24 August 1982, D1)
25 August 1982	Germany informs its firms that US sanctions are illegal under international law, violate German sovereignty. (*Washington Post*, 26 August 1982, A1)

26 August 1982	Three compressors leave French port of Le Havre bound for USSR. US bans Dresser-France, Creusot-Loire from importing any US goods, services, or technology until further notice. (*Financial Times*, 27 August 1982, 14)
27 August 1982	Senior administration officials say sanctions could be lifted "if other means could be found to keep equivalent economic pressure on Moscow." Goal still is said to be end to repression in Poland; desired means are said to include: limiting expor: credits; tightening technology transfer controls; withholding exports of other oil, gas technology and equipment; canceling second strand of gas pipeline. (*New York Times*, 28 August 1982, A1)
1 September 1982	US Treasury Secretary Donald T. Regan announces sanctions on French firms will be lessened to restrict only imports of US oil, gas equipment. (*New York Times*, 2 September 1982, A1)
6 September 1982	US imposes sanctions on Nuovo Pignone of Italy for shipping three pipeline turbines with US parts to USSR. (*Wall Street Journal*, 7 September 1982, 3)
10 September 1982	US imposes sanctions against British firm, John Brown Engineers, Ltd. (*Wall Street Journal*, 10 September 1982, 5)
16 September 1982	European nations say it is US responsibility to resolve dispute caused by its unilateral action. (*Financial Times*, 16 September 1982, 3)
5 October 1982	US imposes sanctions against AEG-Kanis and Mannesmann of Germany for shipping two turbines for pipeline to USSR. AEG-Kanis announces it was not certain it would fulfill rest of its contract for pipeline turbines. (*Washington Post*, 6 October 1982, A20; 7 October 1982, A37)
15 October 1982	Reagan says USSR can buy up to 23 mmt of grain in 1982, guarantees contract sanctity if orders are placed before November 30; USSR does not oblige. (*Weekly Compilation of Presidential Documents*, 18 October 1982; *Financial Times*, 20 October 1982, 19)
16 October 1982	Administration officials announce they have provided British, French, Italian, West German officials with draft proposal that could lead to lifting of sanctions. (*New York Times*, 17 October 1982, A1)
18 October 1982	Reagan publicly states willingness to consider lifting sanctions. (*Wall Street Journal*, 19 October 1982, 3)
11 November 1982	Leonid Brezhnev, Soviet president and Communist party general secretary, dies. (*New York Times*, 12 November 1982, A1)
13 November 1982	Reagan announces lifting of sanctions, saying US, West European allies have reached "substantial agreement" on overall economic strategy with East. France immediately announces it is not party to agreement. Reagan's announcement pertains only to restrictions on sales of oil, gas equipment, does not affect curbs on airlines or other

13 November 1982 (continued)	sanctions imposed on Poland, Russia for martial law in Poland. Main elements of agreement are as follows: not to engage in trade agreements that "contribute to the military or strategic advantage of the USSR," particularly high tech goods and oil, gas equipment; not to give preferential aid; not to sign new gas agreements pending completion of energy alternative study by allies; to strengthen COCOM controls; to monitor financial relations with view to harmonizing credit policies. (*Congressional Quarterly,* 20 November 1982, 2883; *Department of State Bulletin,* January 1983, 28)

In practice, new policy means that validated export licenses will be required only for oil, gas exploration, production equipment, no longer for oil and gas transmission and refining equipment exported by domestic US companies and their overseas subsidiaries. In addition, all enforcement actions against these subsidiaries are dropped. (*New York Times,* 14 November 1982, A1; Moyer 83–85) |
6 January 1983	USSR announces completion of 2,000-mile trunk gas pipeline linking Siberia with Ukraine, expects completion of Siberian–West European pipeline by end of 1983. (*Journal of Commerce,* 6 January 1983, 1A)
11 January 1983	Reagan announces he will sign legislation "that substantially restricts the power of the president to limit grain sales abroad as an instrument of foreign policy." Under new legislation, restrictions will not affect "agricultural exports covered by contracts calling for delivery within 270 days of an embargo announcement." However, president still will have authority to restrict foreign grain sales in declared national emergencies. (*New York Times,* 12 January 1983, A1)
22 April 1983	Reagan lifts ban on negotiations for a long-term grain agreement with Soviet Union; stated reason is "to reaffirm our reliability as a supplier of grain" to USSR. In July 1982, president had said ban would continue "until the Soviet Union indicates that it is prepared to permit the process of reconciliation in Poland to go forward and demonstrates this desire with deeds and not just words." On 22 April 1983, Mark Palmer, acting assistant secretary of state for European affairs, states, "It's not linked to the situation in Poland. We continue to be deeply concerned about developments in Poland." US Trade Representative William Brock adds that ban on negotiations "simply had no validity as a tool in that capacity anymore . . . we believe this sanction has made its political point." (*New York Times,* 23 April 1983, A1)
8 May 1983	US and Europe, negotiating in context of International Energy Agency (IEA), agree on pledge to avoid "undue dependence" by Europe on Soviet energy. Agreement falls short of European commitment to abandon planned second strand of USSR-European gas pipeline. (*Wall Street Journal,* 9 May 1983, 37; *Washington Post,* 10 May 1983, A12)
20 August 1983	Following policy battle between Defense Secretary Caspar W. Weinberger on one side and Commerce Secretary Malcolm Baldrige and

Secretary of State George P. Shultz on other, Reagan lifts export controls on sale of Caterpillar Tractor pipelayers to USSR. Controls had been imposed in July 1978 by Carter in response to jailing of dissidents Anatoly B. Shcharansky and Aleksandr Ginzburg, and continued by Reagan as part of pipeline embargo. While Commerce Department had approved licenses for sale of 200 pipelayers costing $90 million, USSR diverted its orders to Komatsu of Japan as long as vestigial US export controls remained in place. Lifting all controls is said to represent "a major policy shift by the administration because pipelayers have become the touchstone of East-West trade policy." (*New York Times*, 21 August 1983, A1; *Washington Post*, 20 August 1983, A1)

25 August 1983   US, USSR sign five-year grain agreement, raising minimum annual Soviet purchases from 6 mmt to 9 mmt and containing a "no-export-control" clause. (*Washington Post*, 26 August 1983, A19)

January 1984   Fire reportedly destroys imported electronic equipment at pumping station at Urengoy, largest of 41 such stations on pipeline. Western sources estimate damage could delay Urengoy commissioning six months or more. Soviet sources had claimed pipeline had been completed months ahead of schedule despite sanctions and that gas shipments to France through it had begun. One Western diplomatic source expressed skepticism that pipeline would be completed before 1985 or even 1986. (*New York Times*, 11 January 1984, A1)

GOALS OF SENDER COUNTRY

29 December 1981
Reagan: "The repression in Poland continues and President Brezhnev has responded in a manner which makes it clear the Soviet Union does not understand the seriousness of our concern and its obligations under the Helsinki Final Act and the UN Charter.

"By our actions we expect to put powerful doubts in the minds of the Soviet and Polish leaders about this continued repression. . . . The whole purpose of our actions is to speak for those who have been silenced and to help those who have been rendered helpless."

Secretary of State Haig: Sanctions are needed because "we just could not go on doing business as usual while freedom is being trampled in Poland." He lists US goals as: lifting of martial law in Poland, freeing of Solidarity leaders, opening of dialogue with Solidarity. (*Washington Post*, 30 December 1981, A1)

31 January 1982
"One month after President Reagan announced economic sanctions against the Soviet Union for its 'heavy and direct responsibility for the repression in Poland' the administration is studying new steps that could delay if not block the completion of the largest single East-West project: the $25 billion natural gas pipeline from Western Siberia to Europe." (*Washington Post*, 31 January 1982, A1)

10 February 1982
It is believed that delaying or blocking pipeline could significantly affect Soviet economy,

which needs revenues from gas sales to replace hard currency lost from declines in oil exports as reserves are depleted. Pipeline also has raised concern because of potential leverage it could provide USSR over Western Europe if Soviet Union threatened to cut off gas supplies, or did so. (*New York Times,* 10 February 1982, D1)

18 June 1982
Reagan, announcing extension of pipeline sanctions to US subsidiaries and licensees abroad: "The objective of the United States in imposing the sanctions has been and continues to be to advance reconciliation in Poland. Since December 30, 1981, little has changed concerning the situation in Poland; there has been no movement that would enable us to undertake positive reciprocal measures." (*Washington Post,* 19 June 1982, A1)

23 July 1982
Assistant Secretary of Commerce for Trade Administration Lawrence J. Brady: "There is little question that if the West exercises its collective will to enforce these sanctions, the entire Soviet bloc will find itself in very difficult straits throughout the rest of the decade." (*Washington Post,* 24 July 1982, A1)

30 July 1982
Under Secretary of State James L. Buckley: "Above all, we seek an end to the repression of the Polish people. The sanctions imposed against the sale of oil and gas equipment increase the internal costs to the Soviet Union of the project and cause an additional strain on already thinly stretched Soviet resources." (*Department of State Bulletin,* September 1982, 38)

September 1982
US Trade Representative Brock: "We cannot continue to provide subsidized export credits to the Soviets which they can then use to strengthen their military capacity, further threaten us—because it forces us to respond, and it costs everybody in any number of ways." (*US News & World Report,* 13 September 1982, 27–29)

21 September 1982
Secretary of Defense Weinberger: "In recent weeks the evidence has been mounting that the Soviet Union may be using slave labor" to build pipeline. Weinberger concedes "the evidence is not conclusive" but is "profoundly troubling." He also reiterates administration's other fears: ". . . it is a little hard to see how trade of this kind, that has such an obvious military advantage in providing this much [hard currency earnings] most of which would go into military spending, can do anything but increase the danger to all of us." (*Washington Post,* 22 September 1982, A14)

27 September 1982
Secretary of State Shultz, in New York for opening of UN General Assembly, meets with French, West German representatives but avoids discussion of pipeline sanctions because of divisiveness of issue.

The previous week, "a senior administration official, speaking with reporters on background, [had] warned that unless the allies agree on measures even tougher than the US strategy on the pipeline, President Reagan intends to keep pursuing his current strategy." (*Washington Post,* 28 September 1982, A20)

13 November 1982
Reagan's radio address announcing lifting of sanctions: "The understanding we and our partners have reached and the actions we are taking reflect our mutual determination to overcome differences and strengthen our cohesion. I believe this new agreement is a victory for all the allies. It puts in place a much-needed policy in the economic area to complement our policies in the security area." (*New York Times*, 14 November 1982, A1)

RESPONSE OF TARGET COUNTRY

19 November 1981
Vladimir Filanovsky, chief of oil and gas industry department of USSR state planning committee: "The USSR has never used its gas supplies as a lever to pressure its partners, nor is it going to. Also, it has always honored scrupulously its commitments." (*Journal of Commerce*, 20 November 1981, 1A)

30 December 1981
Tass: "The Soviet Union is a great power which has never allowed and will never allow anyone to speak to it in the language of blackmail and diktat. . . . [President Reagan is trying] to hurl the world back to the dark times of the cold war." (*Washington Post*, 31 December 1981, A1)

Mid-July 1982
From Soviet journal *Liturnaya Gazeta*: "The master of the White House wanted to disrupt or slow down the construction of the gas pipeline but he achieved quite an opposite effect: the embargo only piqued the pride of the Soviet people and worked up the workers' enthusiasm. In this sense, Reagan's embargo has boomeranged against him." (*New York Times*, 20 July 1982, D1)

14 November 1982
Tass: The sanctions have failed. "By means of those measures, Washington unsuccessfully tried to frustrate the construction of the Siberian–Western European gas pipeline." (*Washington Post*, 15 November 1982, A15)

16 November 1982
USSR Minister of Foreign Trade Nikolai Patolichev says US-Soviet trade would increase only after Soviets had "regained complete confidence that agreements will not be broken. It is necessary for the US to renounce once and for all the doctrine of using trade as a weapon against our country." (*Financial Times*, 17 November 1982, 1)

Spring 1983
"In order to speed the completion of the export line the Ministry of Gas and Oil Construction seems likely to opt for its own Soviet built compressors rather than wait for the delivery of all the import compressor units ordered from Western European manufacturers." (*Financial Times*, 5 April 1983, 14)

ATTITUDE OF OTHER COUNTRIES

North Atlantic Treaty Organization and European Community
30 December 1981: In meetings of EC officials in London and NATO ambassadors in Brussels, Allies are reluctant to follow US lead; "agreed only to continue consultations at a special meeting of their foreign ministers in Brussels Monday." (*Washington Post*, 31 December 1981, A1)

NATO Council Declaration
11 January 1982: "Recognizing that each of the Allies will act in accordance with its own situation and laws, they will examine measures which could involve arrangements regarding imports from the Soviet Union, maritime agreements, air service agreements, the size of Soviet commercial representation and the conditions surrounding export credits." (*Department of State Bulletin*, February 1982, 20)

NATO
January 1982: Allies pledge not to "undermine" US-imposed sanctions but do not commit themselves to taking any specific trade actions. Compliance is uncertain as FRG goes ahead with sale of turbines for pipeline to USSR despite US ban on US components. (*Washington Post*, 15 January 1982, A1; Moyer 80)

European Community
12 August 1982: EC issues formal protest against pipeline sanctions, saying they violate both international, American law. Protest note also states: "The recent US measures provide the Soviets with a strong inducement to enlarge their own manufacturing capacity and to accelerate their own turbine and compressor developments, thus becoming independent of Western sources." (*Washington Post*, 13 August 1982, A12)

September 1982: "The Europeans have opposed the US tactics as interference in their internal affairs, as a contributor to unemployment at a time when their economies are in recession, and as an ineffective and potentially dangerous way to deal with Moscow." (*Washington Post*, 28 September 1982, A20)

NATO and EC
November 1982: Sources say November agreement entails little in way of new commitments by Allies, "with one apparent exception, an undertaking not to sign or approve new contracts for the purchase of Soviet natural gas while a series of studies are under way. The agreement covers areas where attempts have been made for years to coordinate Western policy." These sources say Europeans made no concessions and elements announced by Reagan "represented studies rather than concessions to harder trade policies with the Soviet Union." Oil glut, they say, makes new gas contracts with Soviets a dead letter in any event. (*New York Times*, 14 November 1982, A1)

"All European sources concur that the 'substantial agreement' is so vague that 'it doesn't mean anything,' in the words of one German official, but most of the Europeans accepted it as a means for Reagan to get off a hook that was causing trouble at home as well as abroad." (*Journal of Commerce*, 29 December 1982, 1A)

Italy
29 December 1981: Prime Minister Giovanni Spadolini of Italy says his country is reconsidering participation in the Soviet gas pipeline deal. (*New York Times*, 30 December 1981, A6)

7 July 1982: Spadolini announces that Italy will fulfill its commitment to provide turbines (produced under GE license) for pipeline despite US embargo. (*New York Times*, 8 July 1982, A1)

West Germany
29 December 1981: "Although the West Germans have not ruled out the theoretical possibility of participating in sanctions—they seemed relieved that the Reagan adminis-

tration's first package of measures involving the Polish military regime was essentially mild—their attitude in the past about the use of such pressures has been both negative and contradictory." (*New York Times*, 30 December 1981, A6)

9 July 1982: Chancellor Helmut Schmidt: "We will stick to the agreements our firms made with the Soviet Union and so will France and Britain. . . . This will create some irritation in our relations with the United States but that will have to be overcome." (*Washington Post*, 10 July 1982, A24)

29 July 1982: Minister of Economics Otto Graf Lambsdorff: "The West Europeans are in agreement: the application of the principle of extraterritoriality in US government decisions is unacceptable to us. It violates our sovereignty. Therefore, we have to reject it . . . we have no differences of opinion on the events in Poland. The declaration of NATO in January 1982 was unanimous. But we do doubt that embargoes are an adequate answer. In my opinion, this applies to both the pipeline and the grain!" (*Washington Post*, 28 July 1982, A21)

Horst Kerlen, vice president of AEG-Kanis: "There is a doubt, a lack of trust, a feeling against the United States, that is the worst thing to come out of this affair. We have to be very cautious now about any new contracts that would bind us so totally to the United States." (*Journal of Commerce*, 29 December 1982, 1A)

United Kingdom
30 June 1982: Britain's Trade Ministry "issued an order under the Protection of Trading Interests Act of 1980, asserting that the US move was damaging to British trading interests. This enables Britain to take whatever legal steps are available to overturn the embargo." (*Washington Post*, 1 July 1982, A1)

14 November 1982: UK Foreign Secretary Francis Pym: "We now have a broad measure of agreement to guide the West's economic approach to the East. More work remains to be done but a good start has been made." (*Washington Post*, 14 November 1982, A9)

France
4 July 1982: "French President François Mitterrand, who feels he was duped by Reagan at the Versailles Summit into believing that such an extension of the pipeline equipment ban—already in force for American firms—would not take place, said publicly last week that Reagan had exhibited 'a grave lack of solidarity with his allies.'" (*Washington Post*, 4 July 1982, F1)

13 November 1982: Mitterrand says sanctions had been directed against Allies rather than USSR and no concessions would be connected to their removal. France, however, is expected to accede to agreement later. (*New York Times*, 14 November 1982, A1)

14 November 1982: "It was the joining of the East-West trade agreement and the lifting of the sanctions in the same public announcement that left the French 'very disappointed, very surprised,' the sources said." (*Washington Post*, 15 November 1982, A15)

"True, after dinner at the Quai d'Orsay, Mr. Shultz and French Foreign Minister Claude Cheysson, both dressed in dinner jackets, sipping drinks, and speaking English—a sign, I suppose of the Frenchman's extraordinary willingness to please—jointly briefed a few reporters. That hardly amounted to a joint statement, much less a formal agreement. . . .

". . . all future efforts to broaden the studies into a general economic strategy will be met by the French with at best delaying tactics—and at worst, with open opposition." (*New York Times*, 4 January 1983, A19)

LEGAL NOTES

West German minister of economics
"The West Europeans are in agreement: the application of the principle of extraterritoriality in US government decisions is unacceptable to us. It violates our sovereignty. Therefore, we have to reject it. This is the unanimous position in Bonn, London, Paris and Rome—despite the content and clauses in civil law contracts between European and US companies. Such private agreements, the concrete content of which still would have to be examined carefully, cannot and must not alter the legal basis of international relations between states. Above all, they must not retroactively block execution of contracts that were concluded between the European companies and the Soviet Union long before the events in Poland." (Senate, Trowbridge 10)

Duane D. Morse and Joan S. Powers
"The novel question raised but not resolved in the pipeline controversy is whether the Act [EAA] authorizes the president to impose new restrictions on foreign use of commodities or technical data that have *previously* been exported from the United States and punish foreign nationals who refuse to observe these new restrictions. . . .

"The pipeline controversy marked the first time wholly foreign nationals faced the denial of export privileges for reexporting previously exported commodities or foreign-produced products of previously exported technical data to newly forbidden destinations. . . .

"Recognizing . . . the possibility that trade restrictions may prompt international resentment and retaliatory measures against the United States, Congress has confined the president's delegated power to apply export control restrictions to persons or property 'subject to the jurisdiction of the United States.' The pipeline controversy illustrates quite clearly the dangers of ignoring that limitation. Once goods and technical data have left U.S. shores and reached foreign hands, the United States must relinquish jurisdiction to regulate, at least absent a direct threat to our national security. That international and domestic furor that surrounded the United States' largely unsuccessful attempt to impede construction of the Soviet pipeline provides an important lesson as to the limits of U.S. regulatory power." (Morse 545, 553, 567)

ECONOMIC IMPACT

Observed Economic Statistics

Initial press reports indicate pipeline will be installed at expected capital cost of $10 billion to $15 billion; that total USSR hard currency earnings in 1981 from oil and gas were $17 billion; earnings from new gas flow could be as much as $6.5 billion. (*Washington Post*, 21 November 1981, A1; Hewett 15–18)

However, primarily because of estimates of declining demand and, secondarily, warnings from US about dependence on Soviet energy, project is scaled back. Under agreements as signed, Soviets are committed to gradually increasing existing gas exports, if demanded by buyers, up to approximately 60 billion cubic meters (BCM) annually. USSR currently is delivering 27 BCM of gas to Europe. "The FRG has signed a contract for 10.5 BCM, with an additional 0.7 BCM for West Berlin; France for 8 BCM; Austria for 1.5 BCM, with an option on an additional 1 BCM; and Switzerland for 0.36 BCM. There is a strong indication that Italy will eventually sign for 8 BCM; Belgium, the Netherlands, Spain and Greece may be interested in small volumes at some later date." (Stern 22; also see *The German Tribune* [Hamburg], 8 May 1983, 6)

Contract for new USSR gas has floor price, rising at 3 percent per year in real terms, to reach $5.70 per million BTUs in 1990 (1981 dollars), plus base price indexed to oil prices. (*Wall Street Journal*, 15 March 1983, 26)

". . . only some 21 BCM have thus far been firmly contracted. . . . At a level of 21 BCM, Soviet hard currency earnings from Urengoy sales will amount to $3.8 billion per year in 1982 dollars, considerably less than the often quoted sum of $10 billion per year." (Stern 23; also see *New York Times*, 29 July 1983, D1)

"A total of 45,000 people now work on the 7.5 billion roubles (£6.8 billion) export line. So far they have laid over three-quarters of the 4,500km pipeline. The export line is but one of six being laid along the 'energy corridor' from Urengoi. Some 25 billion roubles (£22.7 billion) is being invested during the 1980–85 period on these pipelines which total 20,000 kilometres in length." (*Financial Times*, 5 April 1983, 14)

Imports account for about 30 percent of pipelaying machinery used on export line. Another $3.5 billion has been spent on imported pipe, turbines, ancillary equipment. (*Financial Times*, 5 April 1983, 14)

Under Secretary of State James Buckley: "US firms have lost at least $800 million worth of potential business with the Soviet Union. . . ." Press report cites US, West European, Japanese sources as saying US lost at least $1 billion in contracts related to pipeline. (*Department of State Bulletin*, September 1982, 38; *Journal of Commerce*, 16 September 1982, 1A)

Washington Post estimates loss to US companies, subsidiaries from sanctions at $2.2 billion. Under Secretary of Commerce Lionel H. Olmer says that $2.2 billion estimate covers three-year period, feels most of it could be recouped. (*Washington Post*, 14 November 1982, A1; *New York Times*, 15 November 1982, A10)

Wharton Econometrics estimates that, by importing 1 mmt of grain at cost of $160 million, USSR can free sufficient resources to produce 2.8 mmt of oil, worth $700 million on world market. (*Financial Times*, 20 October 1982, 19)

State Department estimates Soviets lost $122 million in exports of furs, diamonds, caviar, salmon, other products to EC because of their ban on imports of 56 Soviet products. (House, Wallis 10)

Calculated Economic Impact

	Annual cost to target country
Delay in construction of pipeline; welfare loss estimated at 15 percent of value of reduced gas production (assumes either deferred export earnings or diversion of domestic gas supplies to export sales).	$190 million
Increased construction cost of pipeline caused by unavailability of US equipment and technology; welfare loss	200 million

	Annual cost to target country
estimated at 25 percent of value of canceled US purchases ($800 million).	
Suspension of export licenses for oil, gas field equipment, high technology exports; welfare loss estimated at 60 percent of reduced US exports ($150 million).	90 million
Total	$480 million

Relative Magnitudes

Gross indicators of USSR economy	
USSR GNP (1981)	$1,587 billion
USSR population (1981)	268 million
Annual effect of sanctions related to gross indicators	
Percentage of GNP	negl.
Per capita	$1.79
USSR trade with US as percentage of total trade	
Exports (1981)	0.3
Imports (1981)	3
Ratio of US GNP (1981: $2,958 billion) to USSR GNP (1981: $1,587 billion)	2

ASSESSMENT

Homer E. Moyer, Jr., and Linda A. Mabry
"The effects of the pipeline controls on the Soviet Union appear to have been negligible. Even advocates of the controls admitted that the sanctions would only cause approximately a two-year delay in the completion of the project. This projection assumed, of course, that the controls would remain in place. . . . The pipeline controls, in fact, remained in place only five months, and were generally disregarded by foreign subsidiaries of US companies under contract to supply pipeline equipment to the Soviets. As a result, it appears that the sanctions neither thwarted nor appreciably delayed construction of the Yamal pipeline." (Moyer 88–89)

" . . . it is not too harsh to characterize the pipeline controls as perhaps the least effective and most costly controls in U.S. history." (Moyer 91)

Congressional Quarterly
"Reagan initially imposed the sanctions in December 1981 as a protest against Soviet pressure on the Communist government of Poland, which had imposed martial law and imprisoned leaders of the independent Solidarity trade union. But as it became increasingly

clear that the sanctions were having no effect on Soviet behavior, Reagan shifted their focus to disrupting construction of a 2,600-mile natural gas pipeline from Siberia to Western Europe." (*Congressional Quarterly*, 20 November 1982, 2882)

"The reaction from US allies was less than enthusiastic. Although praising Reagan's decision to lift the sanctions, allied leaders made it clear that they had agreed only to study future limits on trade with the Soviet Union and had not committed themselves in advance to take specific actions." (*Congressional Quarterly*, 20 November 1982, 2883–84)

Paul Marantz
"Moscow was informed that should its troops be sent into Poland, the West would respond with a broad range of economic sanctions. Although little is known about Kremlin decision-making during the Polish crisis, it may well be that Soviet concern about the effect of an invasion on East-West economic relations was one of the factors that caused the Soviet leadership to temporize for so long and ultimately to choose a more indirect and less provocative means of crushing Solidarity." (Marantz 1)

"If anything Moscow was probably sorry to see US Secretary of State George Shultz succeed in negotiating a face-saving compromise that enabled the United States to abandon its ill-fated attempt to stop the pipeline. From the Soviet perspective, the minor economic inconvenience caused by having to shift to European suppliers was far outweighed by the political benefits resulting from the deep cleavage in the Western alliance that was provoked by American attempts to limit the activities of European companies." (Marantz 1)

". . . perhaps we should be thankful that the attempt to apply sanctions against Poland and the Soviet Union was anemic and half-hearted. Had Western nations moved more forcefully, in all likelihood they would have done more damage to their own economies and alliance structure, without in any way loosening the cruel repression that has been inflicted upon the Polish people." (Marantz 25)

"The unwillingness of the Europeans to impose stronger sanctions meant that the Soviet Union was made to pay only a minor economic penalty for its actions in Poland, a penalty which indeed was insufficient to alter Soviet conduct." (Marantz 9)

". . . rather than limit their exports which would directly affect employment in their own industries, they [the Europeans] curtailed imports from the Soviet Union. . . . The truly significant commodities such as oil, natural gas, and raw materials were never even considered for restrictions, and as a result, it was estimated that the measures adopted would affect no more than 1.5 percent of the $10 billion in goods that the nations of the EEC import annually from the Soviet Union." (Marantz 12)

Journal of Commerce
"While the measures may have slowed pipeline progress somewhat, they did not stop the project. They did cost American companies hundreds of millions of dollars. They also showed the world that the United States does not fully respect contracts and is prone to the use of trade sanctions as foreign policy weapons." (*Journal of Commerce*, 9 May 1983, 4A)

Gordon Crovitz
"President Reagan did not adequately emphasize the credits and hard currency issues and instead cited the Soviet role in Poland's martial law as the reason for the sanctions. Although in the end the sanctions were lifted without any firm agreement on future trade, it is doubtful that there would even now be any debate about East-West trade if

the United States had not applied its temporary sanctions against the pipeline." (Crovitz 407)

Richard Pipes, former Soviet expert on National Security Council
"It is an open secret that the Reagan Administration is not of one mind on the issue of trade with the Communist bloc. . . . One school of thought, strongly represented in the Departments of Commerce and State, regards embargoes on energy equipment as not only futile but also counterproductive. . . . The other school, forcefully championed by the Department of Defense, views all commerce with the Communist bloc in the context of 'Grand Strategy.' It wishes to deny the Soviet Union the opportunity to earn additional hard currency from energy exports on the grounds that such money would be used to bolster Soviet military capabilities and to make Western Europe dependent on Soviet good-will. Rather than give up on embargoes as unenforceable, we should agree with our Allies on a coordinated policy of economic containment. . . . The Soviet Union is one giant war machine. . . . Thus, Western energy assistance helps the USSR to build up its military and to avoid shifts in budgetary allocations that now favor the military. . . ." (*New York Times*, 21 August 1983, F2)

Under Secretary of State for Economic Affairs Allen W. Wallis
"[T]he Soviets completed the pipelaying phase of this project last year [1983], installed a small number of compressor sets, and have transported relatively small amounts of gas over the line. . . . However, we should recall that the Soviets originally planned to complete the project, including both laying the pipe and installing all associated compressor stations, by 1984. We now estimate that this task will not be finished until 1986. We believe that much of this delay can be attributed to our sanctions. Moreover, in evaluating the effectiveness of our sanctions, it is impossible for us to ascertain to what extent the Soviets have been forced to divert resources from other priority projects simply to meet this delayed target for pipeline completion." (House, Wallis 6)

AUTHORS' SUMMARY

Overall assessment	Assigned scores
□ Policy result, scaled from 1 (failed) to 4 (success)	1
□ Sanctions contribution, scaled from 1 (none) to 4 (significant)	1
□ Success score (policy result *times* sanctions contribution), scaled from 1 (outright failure) to 16 (significant success)	1

Political and economic variables

□ Companion policies: J (covert), Q (quasi-military), or R (regular military)	—
□ International cooperation with sender, scaled from 1 (none) to 4 (significant)	2
□ International assistance to target: A (if present)	—
□ Sanctions period (years)	1
□ Economic health and political stability of target, scaled from 1 (distressed) to 3 (strong)	3

	Assigned scores
Political and economic variables (continued)	
☐ Presanction relations between sender and target, scaled from 1 (antagonistic) to 3 (cordial)	1
☐ Type of sanction: X (export), M (import), F (financial)	X
☐ Cost to sender, scaled from 1 (net gain) to 4 (major loss)	3

BIBLIOGRAPHY

Crovitz, Gordon. 1982. "The Soviet Gas Pipeline: A Bad Idea Made Worse." 5 *World Economy* (December): 407–13.

Drabek, Zdenek. 1983. "The Impact of Technological Differences on East-West Trade." 119 *Weltwirtschaftliches Archiv.* 630–48.

Hewett, Edward A. 1982. "The Pipeline Connection: Issues for the Alliance." *The Brookings Review* (Fall): 15–20.

Marantz, Paul. 1985. "Economic Sanctions in the Polish Crisis." In *The Utility of Economic Sanctions*, ed. David Leyton-Brown. London: Croom Helm. Forthcoming.

Morse, Duane D., and Joan S. Powers. 1983. "U.S. Export Controls & Foreign Entities: The Unanswered Questions of Pipeline Diplomacy." 23 *Virginia Journal of International Law* 537–67.

Moyer, Homer E., Jr., and Linda A. Mabry. 1983. "Export Controls as Instruments of Foreign Policy: The History, Legal Issues, and Policy Lessons of Three Recent Cases." 15 *Law and Policy in International Business* 1–171.

Stern, Jonathan P. 1982. "Specters and Pipe Dreams." 48 *Foreign Policy* (Fall): 21–36.

US Congress. House Committee on Foreign Affairs, Subcommittee on Europe and the Middle East. 1984. *Hearings on East-West Economic Issues: Sanctions Policy and the Formulation of International Economic Policy.* Statement by Under Secretary of State for Economic Affairs Allen W. Wallis. 98 Cong., 2 sess., 29 March.

———. Senate Committee on Foreign Relations, Subcommittee on International Economic Policy. 1982. *Hearings on Economic Relations with the Soviet Union.* 97 Cong., 2 sess., July 30, August 12–13.

———. 1982. Statement by Alexander B. Trowbridge, president, National Association of Manufacturers. August 13.

Case 81–4   EC v. Turkey
(1981–82: Restore Democracy)

CHRONOLOGY OF KEY EVENTS

September 1980   Group of generals seizes power in Turkey, suspends democratic institutions and processes in effort to restore order. (*Keesing's* 31285)

January 1981   West German Finance Minister Hans Matthofer refuses to coordinate OECD loan package for Turkey because of suspension of civil rights accompanying military takeover. (*Keesing's* 31287; *Times* [London], 15 January 1981, 17)

7 May 1981   Representatives of 17 OECD member countries agree on $940 million package of assistance to Turkey, with US offering $350 million, FRG $200 million, "a figure substantially lower than previous West German offers." It also is reported "that increasing pressure was being exerted by a number of West German politicians for general reductions in aid to Turkey, in view of the NSC's [Turkish National Security Council, composed of generals involved in coup] reluctance to commit itself to a timetable for a return to parliamentary democracy." (*Keesing's* 31287)

12 September 1981   European Trade Union Confederation urges European Community (EC) to "suspend all trade and assistance agreements with Turkey in protest at the suspension of Turkish trade union rights." (*Keesing's* 31287)

16 October 1981   Turkish NSC dissolves all political parties. Move is sharply criticized in Europe; EC announces intention to delay implementation of aid program. (*Keesing's* 31287)

Early November 1981   Following sentencing of former Turkish Prime Minister Bulent Ecevit to four-month prison sentence, Turkish ambassador to EC is warned of European concern about political developments in country, possibility that £290 million in aid, loans may be jeopardized. (*Times*, 5 November 1981, 10)

Mid-November 1981   Following visit to Turkey, West German Foreign Minister Hans-Dietrich Genscher reveals FRG will withhold $200 million in aid it had pledged to Turkey in May. (*Keesing's* 31287)

December 1981	European Council decides to advise European Commission not to approve £290 million aid package to Turkey. (*Times*, 5 December 1981, 4)
January 1982	European parliament votes to end links with Turkish parliamentarians as protest against actions of military regime in Ankara. Resolution calls for suspension of joint EC-Turkey Committee "until such time as the Turkish National Assembly has been freely elected in a secret ballot by direct universal suffrage and has taken office. . . ." (*Times*, 23 January 1982, 4)
30 March 1982	Foreign Minister Ilter Turkmen announces Turkey's intention of applying for full membership in EC despite freezing of grants and loans. (*Facts on File* 257)
7 November 1982	Turkish electorate overwhelmingly approves new constitution drawn up by NSC. "Temporary articles" provide for General Kenan Evran, head of NSC, to be president of the republic for seven years. Critics of regime claim that constitution, only alternative to continuing martial law, leaves room for human rights abuses, media censorship, excessive presidential powers. (*Keesing's* 32089–90)
1 December 1982	Foreign Minister Genscher reports to German cabinet on recent visit to Turkey and, asserting his belief that "the military regime will soon take steps towards restoration of democracy," convinces cabinet to resume aid to Turkey. Restoration of democratic processes had been "condition of a resumption of aid when it agreed in June to contribute [$119 million] towards a Western emergency aid package for Turkey. Another [$56 million] was also set aside this year for bilateral development aid projects." (*Times*, 2 December 1982, 6)
April 1983	NSC legalizes formation of political parties, announces parliamentary elections will be held November 6. Former political leaders are warned that their participation would endanger this schedule. (*Keesing's* 32287–88)
May 1983	Five new parties are formed; largest is disbanded by NSC 11 days after inception. In same month, however, European Commission of Human Rights announces it will "challenge the record of Turkey's military government the following October." (*Keesing's* 32287; *Times*, 7 May 1981, 5C)

GOALS OF SENDER COUNTRIES

November–December 1981
"The Commission has been particularly concerned about the democratic evolution inside Turkey in view of its application to become a full member of the Community. It continued to negotiate the aid package in the hope that democracy would be developing in parallel. . . . The sentence on Mr. Ecevit, despite the warnings, has crushed this hope, at least for the time being, and has led the Commission to recommend blocking the aid." (*Times*, 5 December 1981, 4)

Spring 1982
"Mr. Leo Tindeman's [President, EC Council of Ministers] had (in accordance with his mandate) impressed on the Turkish government the serious concern of the [EC] Ten with regard to human rights in Turkey, and had emphasized the need for that country to return as soon as possible to a democratic regime, which presupposes, in particular, the release of those arrested for their views or for trade union activities and the ending of martial law." (*Keesing's* 31644)

RESPONSE OF TARGET COUNTRY

Fall 1981
"General Evren repeatedly claimed during this period, however, that Turkey would not be hurried by foreign opinion into a premature move towards parliamentary democracy. . . ." (*Keesing's* 31287)

December 1981
Spokesman at Turkish Embassy to EC calls Commission recommendation on blocking aid "an attempt to interfere in domestic Turkish politics," adds, "such pressure has never succeeded in the past, so I don't see why it should now." (*Times*, 5 December 1981, 4)

ATTITUDE OF OTHER COUNTRIES

United States
US Defense Secretary Caspar W. Weinberger visits Turkey in December 1981, praises military regime for having "lived up to our great expectations . . . we admire the way in which the order and law have been restored in Turkey." Weinberger promises expanded military cooperation, aid. US officials reportedly urge concessions to repair breach with Europe. As one official notes, "The last thing the US wants is to have a Turkey isolated from Western Europe." (*Facts on File* 996)

ECONOMIC IMPACT

Observed Economic Statistics

"Under the EEC aid agreement Turkey is entitled to receive some $140 million (about £70 million) a year during the current five-year period." (*Times*, 26 November 1981, 9)

Times characterizes £290 million package of loans, aid as being "too small to have any significant financial impact on the Turkish economy. . . ." (*Times*, 5 December 1981, 4A)

In 1980, West German officials take lead in negotiating $1.2 billion OECD aid package. In January 1981, Turkish Deputy Prime Minister Turgut Ozal travels to FRG hoping to get $1.5 billion from OECD, including "expected contribution" from Saudi Arabia, not a member of organization. In September 1981, West German government signs agreement extending to Turkey $60 million in bilateral aid, contributing $216 million to OECD package for Turkey. (*Times*, 16 September 1981, 18)

West Germany's approval in December 1982 of its contribution to $1 billion OECD package for Turkey allows transfer of aid to occur. (*Times*, 20 November 1982, 5; 2 December 1982, 6)

US and EC aid to Turkey (million dollars)

	US Economic	US Military	EC
1979	69.7	180.3	—
1980	198.1	208.3	46.0
1981	201.0	252.8	135.0
1982	301.0	403.0	49.0

— Zero or negligible.
Source: AID.

During Weinberger's December 1981 visit to Turkey, "American officials noted that US aid, although forthcoming, would not be so ample as to make up for a loss of European assistance." (*Facts on File* 996)

Calculated Economic Impact

	Annual cost to target country
Suspension of EC grants, loans to Turkey from December 1981; welfare loss estimated at 90 percent of aid (£70 million), 20 percent of face value of loans (£220 million).	$203 million
Suspension of $276 million in bilateral assistance from FRG (its share of OECD consortium aid) November 1981– December 1982; welfare loss estimated at 90 percent of aid ($60 million), 20 percent of face value of loans ($216 million).	97 million
Total	$300 million

Relative Magnitudes

Gross indicators of Turkish economy	
Turkish GNP (1981)	$59 billion
Turkish population (1981)	46.4 million
Annual effect of sanctions related to gross indicators	
Percentage of GNP	0.5
Per capita	$6.47
Turkish trade with EC as percentage of total trade	
Exports (1981)	50
Imports (1981)	18
Ratio of EC GNP (1981: $2,335 billion) to Turkish GNP (1981: $59 billion)	40

ASSESSMENT

Nicholas S. Ludington and James W. Spain
"[West European] attacks, particularly the comparison to Poland, infuriate Turkey's generals. . . . They contend that many forms of democracy exist and that each country must find its own suitable system. In the words of one leading general: 'If the Western Europeans can accept only a carbon copy of their own system, we may have to reexamine our relationship with them.'" (Ludington 151)

AUTHORS' SUMMARY

Overall assessment	*Assigned scores*
☐ Policy result, scaled from 1 (failed) to 4 (success)	2
☐ Sanctions contribution, scaled from 1 (none) to 4 (significant)	3
☐ Success score (policy result *times* sanctions contribution), scaled from 1 (outright failure) to 16 (significant success)	6

Political and economic variables

☐ Companion policies: J (covert), Q (quasi-military), or R (regular military)	—
☐ International cooperation with sender, scaled from 1 (none) to 4 (significant)	2
☐ International assistance to target: A (if present)	—
☐ Sanctions period (years)	1
☐ Economic health and political stability of target, scaled from 1 (distressed) to 3 (strong)	2
☐ Presanction relations between sender and target, scaled from 1 (antagonistic) to 3 (cordial)	3
☐ Type of sanction: X (export), M (import), F (financial)	F
☐ Cost to sender, scaled from 1 (net gain) to 4 (major loss)	1

BIBLIOGRAPHY

Agency for International Development. *Overseas Loans and Grants*. Various issues.
Facts on File. 1981, 1983.
Keesing's Contemporary Archives. 1982, 1983.
Ludington, Nicholas S., and James W. Spain. 1983. "Dateline Turkey: The Case for Patience." 50 *Foreign Policy* (Spring): 150–68.

Case 82–1   UK v. Argentina

(1982: Falkland Islands)

CHRONOLOGY OF KEY EVENTS

2 April 1982   President Leopoldo Galtieri dispatches 4,000 Argentine troops to occupy Falkland Islands. (*New York Times*, 3 April 1982, A1)

3 April 1982   UK sends naval force to recapture Falklands; imposes financial sanctions on Argentina: Argentine assets in UK (about $1 billion) are frozen, but freeze does not apply to overseas branches of UK banks, and assets may be used in personal hardship cases; British banks may not extend new loans to Argentina; UK banks may continue to act as agents for syndicated Argentine loans; no new official export credits will be extended (official export credit agency, Export Credit Guarantees Department [ECGD], covers 60 percent of UK's $411 million exports to Argentina in 1980). (*New York Times*, 4 April 1982, A1; *Bank of England* regulations, 13 April 1982, 9; *Financial Times* [London], 14 April 1982, 4; *Economist* [London], 10 April 1982, 36)

6 April 1982   UK bans imports from Argentina (1980 total imports, $271 million). (UK Department of Trade press notice, 6 April 1982)

April 1982   Argentina retaliates with economic measures: freezes British assets in Argentina (about $4 billion); suspends principal and interest payments on $5.8 billion debt to British banks (but makes payment to escrow account in New York). (Daoudi 150; Pearce 15)

   UN Security Council Resolution 502 calls for cessation of hostilities, Argentine withdrawal; contrary to Argentine expectations, USSR does not cast veto. (Parsons 170–72)

14 June 1982   Argentine troops at Port Stanley surrender to British forces; Renaldo Bignone succeeds Galtieri as president. (*New York Times*, 15 June 1982, A1; 18 June 1982, A1; 23 June 1982, A18)

12 July 1982   Argentina recognizes "de facto cessation of hostilities"; UK returns 593 prisoners but maintains trade, financial sanctions. (*Washington Post*, 13 July 1982, A1)

| August 1982 | Argentina admits arrears of $2.3 billion on 1982 debt payments. (*Journal of Commerce*, 27 August 1982, 1A) |

9 September 1982   Under US pressure, UK backs down from insistence that unfreezing of financial assets be accompanied by general normalization of relations. (*Financial Times*, 9 September 1982, 1)

14 September 1982   Responding to US and private bank pressure, UK and Argentina lift mutual financial sanctions relating to bank debts, credits; Argentina resumes payments on British loans; mutual trade sanctions remain in place. (*Financial Times*, 14 September 1982, 1; 20 September 1982, 6)

10 August 1983   Under pressure from private bankers, Argentina lifts freeze on profit remittances imposed on British companies. Normalized economic relations with UK are seen as precondition for British participation in renegotiation of $39 billion of Argentine external debt. (*Washington Post*, 11 August 1983, D17; *Journal of Commerce*, 18 August 1983, 6A)

GOALS OF SENDER COUNTRY

M. S. Daoudi and M. S. Dajani

"From the beginning, Britain made it clear that its aims were limited to getting Argentina off the Falklands and restoring the British administration there. Consequently, the main aim of the sanctions in the initial stage was to gain time and increase nonmilitary pressure on Argentina in the hope of forestalling hostilities in the South Atlantic. Following the start of armed hostilities, sanctions were maintained to intensify pressure on the weak Argentine economy. However, at no time was there any illusion in Britain that the sanctions in themselves would force Argentina to withdraw its military forces. Therefore, in terms of their limited objective, it can be maintained that sanctions were by and large effective." (Daoudi 157)

RESPONSE OF TARGET COUNTRY

13 April 1982
Argentina bans imports from EC. (*Times* [London], 14 April 1982, 6)

May 1982
Economics Minister Roberto Alemann: "The Community is mistaken if it thinks it can persuade the president or the military junta . . . we are prepared to hold out as many months as necessary until our sovereignty is recognized." (*Financial Times*, 20 May 1982, 4)

May 1982
Argentina warns West Germany its position "may be irreparably harmed" if it continues to impose trade embargo beyond 17 May. (Financial Times, *Latin American Markets*, 10 May 1982, 5)

Foreign Minister Nicanor Costa Mendez to US Secretary of State Alexander M. Haig, Jr.: "[The] Argentine people will never forget that in a critical hour of their history . . . the US sided with an aggressor." Unloading of US ships in Buenos Aires is temporarily boycotted. However, Argentina dismisses US sanctions as "innocuous." (Financial Times, Latin American Markets, 10 May 1982, 3; Financial Times, 13 July 1982, 14)

June 1982
Economics Minister Alemann: "For the time being the sanctions have caused some damage, but not very much. We lost $21 million a month, half of that for meat, when the British suspended all shipments, even ones that were contracted for—contrary to all the rules of international commerce. But the other countries are not preventing the sale of contracted goods. We are looking for other markets. . . ." Accounts of widespread evasion, avoidance are published. (*Washington Post*, 6 June 1982, A1)

September 1982
"President Renaldo Bignone and Sr. Jorge Wehbe, the Economy Minister, are understood to be broadly in favor of lifting the sanctions on purely technical and financial grounds. Sr. Wehbe, in particular, is believed to have been convinced, during his recent trip to the IMF/World Bank meeting in Toronto, that a solution to Argentina's foreign debt problem hinged on an early normalisation of financial relations with Britain." (*Financial Times*, 15 September 1982, 1)

"Anti-American demonstrations have disappeared, and almost all the American businessmen and diplomats who left during the fighting have since returned." (*New York Times*, 27 September 1982, A9)

ATTITUDE OF OTHER COUNTRIES

Europe
On 10 April 1982, France, Belgium, West Germany, Netherlands ban arms sales to Argentina. On 13 April, Norway bans imports. (*Financial Times*, 10 April 1982, 9; *Times*, 13 April 1982, 2)

European Community
On 14 April 1982, EC imposes one-month import ban on Argentine goods contracted after April 17, invoking both Article 113 (collective measures) and Article 224 (national measures) of Treaty of Rome. Goods in transit are excluded from ban, as are preexisting long-term contracts on beef, grain, other goods. (1980 EC imports from Argentina: $2.2 billion; 1980 EC exports to Argentina: $3.0 billion.) On 24 May 1982, EC, excepting Italy and Ireland, extends import ban indefinitely.

In retaliation, Argentina bans all imports from EC.

On 20 June 1982, EC lifts trade embargo. On 27 September 1982, West Germany lifts arms embargo; delivers four frigates to Argentina over mild UK objections. (*Financial Times*, 27 September 1982, 3; *Times*, 14–15 April 1982, 6; *Washington Post*, 25 May 1982, A11; 10 September 1982, A18; 27 September 1982, A3; Daoudi 151–52)

Commonwealth nations and colonies
On 17 April 1982, New Zealand bans trade with Argentina; Canada bans imports, cancels export credits; Hong Kong bans imports with exception of goods for transshipment, for

example, to China; Australia bans imports. (*Times*, 13 April 1982, 9; *Washington Post*, 6 June 1982, A1; Daoudi 151)

United States

On 30 April 1982, US imposes total embargo on arms sales to Argentina (about $5.9 million; US Foreign Assistance Act of 1978 already had stopped new arms contracts on ground of human rights violations but preexisting contracts still were being fulfilled). US suspends disbursements on Eximbank loans (about $700 million in pipeline, principally Yacyreta hydroelectric power plant); suspends Eximbank guarantees; cancels Commodity Credit Corporation credit of $2 million. These actions are labeled "largely symbolic." Rumors suggest possible total trade embargo and assets freeze, plus time-consuming delays on World Bank, Inter-American Development Bank (IDB) loans. (Argentine debt to US banks, $9.2 billion; US direct investment in Argentina, $2.5 billion.) (*Washington Post*, 1 May 1982, D8; *Financial Times*, 1 May 1982, 1; Financial Times, *Latin American Markets*, 10 May 1982, 2)

On 12 July 1982, months after cessation of hostilities, US lifts economic sanctions but maintains arms embargo. On 29 September 1982, US ends ban on export of military goods supplied under contracts signed before 1978 human rights ban. In March 1983, US proposal to resume normal arms sales to Argentina meets British opposition. (*Washington Post*, 8 March 1983, A14; *Financial Times*, 29 September 1982, 6; Daoudi 152–53)

Spain, Brazil, Venezuela

Spain draws parallel between Falklands, Gibraltar; abstains from Council of Europe condemnation of Argentina; criticizes Britain for raiding Port Stanley. Brazil supports UN Resolution 502 requiring Argentine withdrawal but criticizes EC boycott, British attack; continues sale of military patrol planes. Venezuela staunchly supports Argentina—increases trade, provides some financial assistance—remembering loss of Essequibo territory through British intervention in 1905. (Financial Times, *Latin American Markets*, 10 May 1982, 5–6; *Journal of Commerce*, 28 May 1982, 1A; Daoudi 154)

LEGAL NOTES

General Agreement on Tariffs and Trade

Argentina contends, in GATT, that suspension of imports by UK, EC, Australia, Canada was not justified by GATT Article XXI (Security Exceptions to the General Agreement). "Following lengthy discussion by the Council, the chairman noted that there were widely differing views as to whether the trade measures in question violated GATT obligations, whether the measures were based on inherent or natural rights, whether justification, notification and/or approval were necessary, whether this was a North/South issue, and whether the matter under consideration was purely political and not within the competence of GATT. He suggested, and the Council so decided, that the matter should be kept on the agenda." (GATT 73)

ECONOMIC IMPACT

Observed Economic Statistics

Pre-April 1982: Argentine debt to Britain, $5.4 billion; short-term deposits $1 billion. Argentina withdraws $500 million in deposits in UK a few days before financial sanctions are imposed. Total Argentine external debt: $32 billion. (*Financial Times*, 8 September 1982, 16; *Journal of Commerce*, 16 June 1982, 1A; Daoudi 156)

Argentine freeze has limited impact because bulk of outstanding British loans to Argentina are syndicated; non-British banks were obligated to share Argentine repayments with British banks on pro rata basis. "In this way, the British banks received about 75 percent of the money due to them from Argentina during the freeze." (Daoudi 156)

"The start of military operations, together with the economic sanctions, put severe stress on the fragile Argentine economy, obliging the government on 5 May to declare a collection of measures intended to help finance the war and shore up the economy during the crisis. Among those economic measures were: (i) devaluation of the peso by 14.3 per cent against the US dollar, and the imposition of a special war tax of 1,000 pesos for each dollar exchanged, imposed on top of the existing 10 per cent tax on dollar transactions; (ii) increasing the tax rebate for manufacturers who exported goods; (iii) reducing from 90 per cent to 80 per cent the amount of government guarantees for bank deposits; (iv) increasing petrol prices by 30 per cent and imposing additional taxes on cigarettes and liquor." (Daoudi 150)

May–June 1982: Argentina attempts to sell 4 million metric tons (mmt) to 5 mmt of coarse grains to USSR but Moscow is slow to place new orders. (*Latin America Commodities Report*, 7 May 1982; 21 May 1982; 4 June 1982; Daoudi 156)

May–December 1982: Argentina devalues peso from 12,000 per $1.00 to 54,000 per $1.00. (IMF)

Argentine trade (million dollars)

	Exports	Imports	Merchandise trade balance
January–August 1981	6,870	6,630	240
January–August 1982	5,740	3,550	2,190

Source: Journal of Commerce, 29 September 1982, 23B.

Argentina may have avoided part of London financial squeeze by triangular banking as well as triangular trade relationships. Placements in US market by Ecuador, Venezuela (possible conduits for Argentine funds) jumped to almost $3 billion in April 1982 after averaging only $211 million over previous three months, as shown in following table:

Oil exporter placements in US banks, money market balances, and portfolio security holdings, 1982 (million dollars)

	Ecuador and Venezuela	Indonesia	Africa	Middle East[†]	Total
January	234	591	−300	1,432	1,957
February	34	12	−213	1,388	1,221
March	698	−114	−492	1,750	1,842
April	2,949	−290	506	645	3,810

[†] Excludes holdings of Saudi Arabian trust account with US Treasury.
Source: US Treasury *Bulletin* and *International Capital Movements*.

Calculated Economic Impact

	Annual cost to target country
Decline in exports, estimated at annual rate of $1.7 billion, with a welfare loss estimated at 15 percent of decline in trade.	$255 million
Decline in imports, estimated at annual rate of $4.6 billion, with a welfare cost estimated at 15 percent of decline in trade.	690 million
Suspension by US of military sales; welfare loss estimated at 20 percent of affected trade.	1 million
Increased cost of debt service for $12.7 billion due in second half of 1982, estimated at additional 0.5 percent risk premium.	63 million
Freezing of $1 billion of Argentine assets in UK banks from April to September 1982, estimated at 5 percent of initial assets.	50 million
Offsets	
Freezing of $4 billion of British assets in Argentina; welfare gain valued at 10 percent of estimated liquid assets (authors' estimate: liquid assets are 20 percent of total assets).	($80 million)
Suspension of principal, interest payments on $5.8 billion debt to British banks (these payments were made to escrow account in New York); welfare gain valued at 10 percent of share of payments actually withheld.	(19 million)
Total	$960 million

Relative Magnitudes

Gross indicators of Argentine economy	
Argentine GDP (1980)	$153 billion
Argentine population (1981)	28.1 million
Annual effect of sanctions related to gross indicators	
Percentage of GDP	0.6
Per capita	$34.16

Gross indicators of Argentine economy (continued)

Argentine trade with UK as percentage of total trade	
Exports (1980)	5
Imports (1980)	4
Ratio of UK GDP (1980: $525 billion) to Argentine GDP (1980: $153 billion)	3

ASSESSMENT

Lawrence Freedman

"The political and economic pressures faced by Buenos Aires were severe but resistable, given the domestic popularity of the government's positions . . . time was on Argentina's side. If Britain failed to get quick results, then its military operation would become difficult to sustain and it would be forced to retreat. By then the immediate fuss would have passed over. The international community would soon come to terms with the new situation and economic sanctions would fall into disrepair.

"The British assessment was not that different. There was little confidence in economic sanctions as a means of solving the dispute, although an arms embargo would be helpful if fighting began in earnest. The international support for Britain's stance was gratifying and probably important in terms of maintaining domestic support, but could not be decisive in solving the dispute." (Freedman 201)

M. S. Daoudi and M. S. Dajani

"There is no doubt that the multilateral sanctions imposed by Britain, the European Community and the United States had a considerable collective effect on the strained Argentinian economy." (Daoudi 155)

"Although the sanctions against Argentina came as a unique response to a unique event, the lessons to be drawn from this particular episode are instructive because they illustrate a more general law. Sanctions against Argentina were effective not solely because of the great power differential between the two groups of adversaries, but also because from the beginning no high expectations were placed upon them." (Daoudi 158)

Anthony Parsons

"In conclusion I venture to suggest that the reputation of Britain in the United Nations has been greatly enhanced by our handling of the Falklands crisis. Not only our allies and partners, but our adversaries too, could witness the unswerving determination with which we pursued all three aspects of our policy, diplomatic, military and economic. And I like to believe that many nonaligned countries may have felt reassured to know that Britain is still both capable and willing to act firmly when important national interests and internationally accepted principles are at stake." (Parsons 178)

AUTHORS' SUMMARY

Overall assessment	*Assigned scores*
□ Policy result, scaled from 1 (failed) to 4 (success)	4
□ Sanctions contribution, scaled from 1 (none) to 4 (significant)	3

Overall assessment (continued)	Assigned scores
☐ Success score (policy result *times* sanctions contribution), scaled from 1 (outright failure) to 16 (significant success)	12

Political and economic variables

☐ Companion policies: J (covert), Q (quasi-military), or R (regular military)	R
☐ International cooperation with sender, scaled from 1 (none) to 4 (significant)	3
☐ International assistance to target: A (if present)	—
☐ Sanctions period (years)	1
☐ Economic health and political stability of target, scaled from 1 (distressed) to 3 (strong)	1
☐ Presanction relations between sender and target, scaled from 1 (antagonistic) to 3 (cordial)	2
☐ Type of sanction: X (export), M (import), F (financial)	F, X, M
☐ Cost to sender, scaled from 1 (net gain) to 4 (major loss)	2

Comments

Military measures obviously were the decisive factor in UK's victory. But economic sanctions, particularly assets freeze, played modest role in UK's success because they impeded Argentine government's ability to sustain its military efforts.

BIBLIOGRAPHY

Daoudi, M. S., and M. S. Dajani. 1983. "Sanctions: The Falklands Episode." 39 *The World Today* (April): 150–60.

Freedman, Lawrence. 1982. "The War of the Falkland Islands: 1982." 61 *Foreign Affairs* (Fall): 196–210.

General Agreement on Tariffs and Trade (GATT). 1983. *GATT Activities in 1982*. April. Geneva.

Henderson, Nicholas. 1983. "America and the Falklands." *The Economist* (12 November): 31–42.

International Monetary Fund. 1983. *International Financial Statistics Yearbook*.

Pearce, Joan. 1982. "Economic Measures." In *The Falkland Islands Dispute: International Dimensions*. London: Royal Institute of International Affairs.

Parsons, Anthony. 1983. "The Falklands Crisis in the United Nations, 31 March–14 June 1982." 59 *International Affairs* (Spring): 169–78.

US Treasury. *Monthly Bulletin*. Various issues.

————. *International Capital Movements*. Periodic reports.

Case 82–2   Netherlands and US v. Suriname

(1982–   : Human Rights; Cuban-USSR Influence)

CHRONOLOGY OF KEY EVENTS

1975	Netherlands grants independence to Suriname. (*Wall Street Journal*, 26 January 1983, 20)
25 February 1980	Military, under leadership of Lieutenant Colonel Desi Bouterse stages coup, overthrows Prime Minister Henck Arron, installs Dr. Henck Chin-A-Sen as president. (*Wall Street Journal*, 26 January 1983, 1, 20; *Washington Post*, 26 December 1982, A33)
Spring 1980	Bouterse visits Castro in Havana; unconfirmed reports say they sign friendship treaty. (*Business Week*, 25 April 1983, 45)
January 1982	Bouterse overthrows President Chin-A-Sen, becomes military ruler. (*Wall Street Journal*, 26 January 1983, 20)
June 1982	Cuba, Suriname reportedly sign "umbrella" agreement on economic, cultural cooperation; no specific agreements are reported. (Lypyshym interview)
August–September 1982	USSR, Cuba open embassies in Suriname, sending key figures as diplomats; up to 400 Cubans are rumored to be in country. (*Wall Street Journal*, 26 January 1983, 20)
8 December 1982	Bouterse's "people's militia" brutally kills 15 leading civilian opponents. Expressions of "horror" are voiced by European Parliament, US State Department, AFL-CIO, other groups. (*Wall Street Journal*, 26 January 1983, 1; *Washington Post*, 26 December 1982, A33; *New York Times*, 27 January 1983, A14)
December 1982	Netherlands suspends implementation of 10–15 year $1.5 billion aid program, thereby withholding assistance of $110 million in 1983. US withholds $1.5 million of planned aid. (*Wall Street Journal*, 26 January 1983, 1, 20)
Early 1983	Covert CIA plan to overthrow Bouterse reportedly is dropped at insistence of House Intelligence Committee. CIA plan was said to be

Early 1983 (continued)	aimed at preventing Suriname from becoming base for USSR, Cuba to spread their influence in South America. (*Wall Street Journal*, 3 June 1983, 20; *New York Times*, 30 November 1983, A7)
October 1983	Inter-American Commission on Human Rights, organ of Organization of American States, finds "serious violations of important human rights" in Suriname, urges government "to radically correct its conduct." (*Washington Post*, 13 October 1983, A28)
October– November 1983	Following US invasion of Grenada, Bouterse expels "80 Cuban advisers and 25 embassy personnel, saying he feared they might support a left-wing coup against him." (*New York Times*, 30 November 1983, A7)
December 1983	Bauxite, aluminum workers strike over proposed tax increases; strike spreads to banks, schools, transit systems, power plants in Paramaribo. Bouterse regains control only after agreeing to program of gradual democratization. New coalition cabinet takes office in February 1984, with labor, business leaders joining Bouterse, military. (*Washington Post*, 13 March 1984, A1)
7 December 1984	"Suriname's Cabinet, apparently seeking restoration of $90 million in annual development money from the Netherlands, approve[s] a proposal . . . to create a national assembly." (*New York Times*, 9 December 1984, A15)

GOALS OF SENDER COUNTRIES

Business Week
"Dutch Prime Minister Ruud F. M. Lubbers acknowledged at the time of the aid cutoff that the regime in Paramaribo might turn to the Cubans and Soviets. But, he indicated, the Netherlands' policy of withholding aid from repressive regimes gave The Hague no alternative." (*Business Week*, 25 April 1983, 46)

Authors' view
Principal goal of US was to diminish Cuban, Soviet influence in Suriname.

Washington Post
"Dutch and U.S. officials have indicated their aid will not be renewed until the government takes concrete steps toward democracy and provides guarantees on human rights." (*Washington Post*, 13 March 1984, A1)

RESPONSE OF TARGET COUNTRY

February–March 1983
Colonel Bouterse arrests his No. 2 aide, Major Roy Horb, suspected of pro-American influence, on charges of plotting; Horb "commits suicide" in prison; Bouterse forms new government. (*Financial Times* [London], 22 April 1983, 4; *New York Times*, 30 November 1983, A7)

March 1983
Following concerted effort to replace suspended Dutch aid, Bouterse signs friendship treaty with Qadaffi of Libya. (*Business Week*, 25 April 1983, 45)

October 1983
According to anonymous diplomats: "The diplomatic game here [Paramaribo] is that the Brazilian Embassy watches the Cuban Embassy and the Cuban Embassy watches the Brazilian Embassy and Bouterse is happy because he's getting money from both of them." (*Washington Post*, 13 October 1983, A28)

"The current trend is that Suriname is trying to patch up with the United States. We are seeing a pragmatic policy change. [The Reagan administration] is not unreceptive." (*Washington Post*, 13 October 1983, A28)

26 October 1983
Suriname expels Cuban ambassador, suspends cultural, educational agreements; on October 30 orders more than 100 Cubans to leave. Bouterse "had been planning to reduce cooperation with Cuba but the United States-led invasion of Grenada hastened his plans." (*Washington Post*, 27 October 1983, A16; *New York Times*, 31 October 1983, A10)

February 1984
"The new coalition cabinet . . . hopes to win an International Monetary Fund loan of up to $100 million within the next few months. Officials say they then need to restore Dutch and U.S. aid by next year." (*Washington Post*, 13 March 1984, A1)

ATTITUDE OF OTHER COUNTRIES

Brazil
Pro-Communist government, influenced by USSR, Cuba, is regarded as potential security risk that Brazil "would never tolerate." (*Business Week*, 25 April 1983, 46)

In effort to diminish Cuban, Soviet influence (and partly in response to US initiatives), Brazil extends aid package including: military training for officers; military equipment; technical assistance on mineral surveys, palm oil extraction, similar projects; trade and sea connections; $15 million export credits; satellite transmission of Brazilian football matches instead of Cuban basketball games. Brazil warns Suriname not to allow Cuban or Soviet use of Suriname as operating base. (*New York Times*, 12 June 1983, 3; *Washington Post*, 13 October 1983, A28)

ECONOMIC IMPACT

Observed Economic Statistics
"Suriname's economy has long been kept afloat by aid from the Netherlands. As the former colonial power, Holland felt compelled to support the new state, and since 1975 a total of $630 million has been transferred—by far the largest element in the Surinamese budget. Another $670 million has been promised under a 10-year deal." (*Financial Times*, 4 May 1983, 4)

Dutch aid represents about 25 percent of annual government budget in Suriname. (*New York Times*, 12 June 1983, A3)

"The value of [Suriname's] bauxite, alumina and aluminum exports, responsible for 80 percent of foreign earnings, slid by more than 10 percent after 1980." (*Washington Post*, 13 March 1984, A1)

In 1983, Suriname runs budget deficit of $195 million, or more than 15 percent of GNP. "Supplies of foreign exchange . . . were all but exhausted." (*Washington Post*, 13 March 1984, A1)

Calculated Economic Impact

	Annual cost to target country
Suspension of aid from Netherlands, US; welfare loss estimated at 90 percent of reduced transfers.	$100 million
Offsets	
Increased aid flows from Cuba, USSR.	n.a., but small
Increased aid from Brazil; export credits valued at 40 percent of face value ($15 million); other assistance estimated at roughly $10 million.	($16 million)
Total	$84 million

n.a. Not available.

Relative Magnitudes

Gross indicators of Surinamese economy	
Surinamese GNP (1980)	$1,026 million
Surinamese population (1981)	395,000
Annual effect of sanctions related to gross indicators	
Percentage of GNP	8.2
Per capita	$212.66
Surinamese trade with Netherlands, US as percentage of total trade	
Exports (1980)	34
Imports (1980)	40
Ratio of Dutch and US GNP (1980: $2,632 billion) to Surinamese GNP (1980: $1.026 billion)	2,565

ASSESSMENT

Washington Post
"Though government authorities say they will allow some nongovernment media to reopen in May, strict controls on public expression continue. A weeknight curfew is still in effect in Paramaribo, and civilian politicians do not dare organize public meetings or speak out publicly yet.

"'Bouterse is still the dominant power of Suriname,' said a diplomat . . . 'He will not allow the moderates to go too far.'" (*Washington Post*, 13 March 1984, A1)

AUTHORS' SUMMARY

Overall assessment	Assigned scores
□ Policy result, scaled from 1 (failed) to 4 (success)	3
□ Sanctions contribution, scaled from 1 (none) to 4 (significant)	3
□ Success score (policy result *times* sanctions contribution), scaled from 1 (outright failure) to 16 (significant success)	9

Political and economic variables

□ Companion policies: J (covert), Q (quasi-military), or R (regular military)	J
□ International cooperation with sender, scaled from 1 (none) to 4 (significant)	2
□ International assistance to target: A (if present)	A
□ Sanctions period (years)	2 +
□ Economic health and political stability of target, scaled from 1 (distressed) to 3 (strong)	1
□ Presanction relations between sender and target, scaled from 1 (antagonistic) to 3 (cordial)	3
□ Type of sanction: X (export), M (import), F (financial)	F
□ Cost to sender, scaled from 1 (net gain) to 4 (major loss)	1

BIBLIOGRAPHY

Lypyshym, Susan. Department of State, Caribbean Affairs. Interview with authors, 8 April 1983.

Case 82–3 South Africa v. Lesotho

(1982–83: Expel Dissident Refugees)

CHRONOLOGY OF KEY EVENTS

December 1982   South African military raids Maseru, capital of Lesotho, in search of members of African National Congress who seek to overthrow South African government. "Since then, South Africa has imposed increasing economic pressures." (*Washington Post*, 12 August 1983, A1)

May 1983   South Africa responds to two "insurgent bombings" by slowing traffic into and out of Lesotho for "security checks." "The resulting long lines caused shortages of essential supplies in Lesotho. . . . " (*Washington Post*, 12 August 1983, A1)

3 June 1983   Lesothan Foreign Minister Evaristus R. Sekhonyana, South African Foreign Minister R. F. (Pik) Botha issue "a statement in which both governments agreed that neither should support elements involved in subversion against the other." South Africa then ends border slowdown. (*Washington Post*, 12 August 1983, A1)

Mid-July 1983   South Africa resumes stopping Lesothans crossing border, claiming Lesotho has not lived up to commitments of June declaration. (*Washington Post*, 12 August 1983, A1)

11 August 1983   Sekhonyana accuses South Africa of embargoing shipment of arms from US, UK to Lesotho. Arms are needed, he says "to counter an increasingly threatening insurgency against the government . . . Sekhonyana said that this 'strangulation' had forced his government to seek another meeting with South Africa, held yesterday in Pretoria." Sekhonyana adds that, because of South African pressure, Lesotho has informed UN that it intends to expel as many as 3,000 South African refugees unless South Africa can be persuaded to drop its demands. (*Washington Post*, 12 August 1983, A1)

8 September 1983   Twenty-two South African refugees volunteer to leave Lesotho for other African countries so "partial border blockade" imposed by South Africa may be lifted. "Informed source" says 200 more refugees may leave in near future, but this is not confirmed by government. (*Washington Post*, 9 September 1983, A14)

GOALS OF SENDER COUNTRY

Washington Post
"The Pretoria government has been trying to force out the refugees, charging they are really insurgents of the banned African National Congress which is trying to overthrow white minority rule in South Africa. . . .

"South Africa says the Congress uses the black-ruled country as a launch pad for guerrilla attacks. . . ." (*Washington Post*, 9 September 1983, A14)

New York Times
After Lesotho acceded, in part, to South African demands on refugee dissidents, Sekhonyana asserts: "What South Africa is really after is to anoint us as the high priest who will preside over the baptism of its illegitimate offspring, the Bantustans." South Africa denies this analysis, maintaining that sole purpose of sanctions is to prevent Lesotho from acting as "recruiting station" for African National Congress. (*New York Times*, 30 September 1983, A2)

RESPONSE OF TARGET COUNTRY

Foreign Minister Sekhonyana
August 1983: "But unless some kind of pressure can be brought to bear on South Africa there is nothing we can do. We will have to comply with the demands. Lesotho has no options." (*Washington Post*, 12 August 1983, A1)

ECONOMIC IMPACT

Observed Economic Statistics

"Lesotho is totally dependent on South Africa for all of its imports and exports, for supplies of fresh produce and for the employment of more than half its breadwinners as migrant workers in South Africa's mines and industries." (*Washington Post*, 12 August 1983, A1)

Border checks that slowed traffic between Lesotho, South Africa "struck at the heart of the Lesotho economy by blocking the flow of migrant workers." (*Washington Post*, 12 August 1983, A1)

Lesothan trade (million dollars)

	Exports	*Imports*
1978	33	223
1979	46	309
1980	60	403
1981	51	436

Source: IMF.

Calculated Economic Impact

	Annual cost to target country
Disruption of Lesothan trade for two months caused by South African border measures; welfare loss estimated at 5 percent of average value of Lesothan trade during the period 1978–81.	$19 million

Relative Magnitudes

Gross indicators of Lesothan economy	
Lesothan GNP (1979)	$527 million
Lesothan population (1981)	1.4 million
Annual effect of sanctions related to gross indicators	
Percentage of GNP	3.6
Per capita	$13.57
Lesothan trade with South Africa as percentage of total trade (including transshipments)	
Exports	est. 100
Imports	est. 100
Ratio of South African GNP (1979: $54.3 billion) to Lesothan GNP (1979: $527 million)	103

ASSESSMENT

Washington Post

Lesotho's ambassador to US asks rhetorically "whether the Lesotho decision [to dispel South African refugees] was a victory for South African pressure." (*Washington Post*, 9 September 1983, A14)

Following September announcement that 22 South African refugees were to be evacuated from Lesotho, "South African Foreign Minister R. F. (Pik) Botha declined to say whether the border restrictions would be lifted, but described the steps being taken by Lesotho as 'constructive.'" (*Washington Post*, 9 September 1983, A14)

"'We are almost a kidney in the body of South Africa,' said Lesotho Foreign Minister Evaristus R. Sekhonyana, who conceded that Pretoria could economically strangle this kingdom in less than a week if it chose to." (*Washington Post*, 27 November 1983, A31)

AUTHORS' SUMMARY

Overall assessment	Assigned scores
□ Policy result, scaled from 1 (failed) to 4 (success)	4
□ Sanctions contribution, scaled from 1 (none) to 4 (significant)	4
□ Success score (policy result *times* sanctions contribution), scaled from 1 (outright failure) to 16 (significant success)	16

Political and economic variables

□ Companion policies: J (covert), Q (quasi-military), or R (regular military)	Q
□ International cooperation with sender, scaled from 1 (none) to 4 (significant)	1
□ International assistance to target: A (if present)	—
□ Sanctions period (years)	1
□ Economic health and political stability of target, scaled from 1 (distressed) to 3 (strong)	2
□ Presanction relations between sender and target, scaled from 1 (antagonistic) to 3 (cordial)	3
□ Type of sanction: X (export), M (import), F (financial)	X, M
□ Cost to sender, scaled from 1 (net gain) to 4 (major loss)	2

BIBLIOGRAPHY

International Monetary Fund. *International Financial Statistics Yearbook.* Various issues.

Case 83–1 Australia v. France

(1983– : Nuclear Weapons Testing)

CHRONOLOGY OF KEY EVENTS

August 1981 "Queensland Mines of Australia contracts with Eléctricité de France ... to deliver 2,600 tons of uranium between 1982 and 1988." 900 tons are shipped over the next two years. (*Journal of Commerce*, 29 October 1984, 11A)

26 May 1983 France explodes 70-kiloton nuclear device on Mururoa atoll. Australian Foreign Minister Bill Hayden delivers strong protest to French Chargé d'Affaires Hervé Ladsous. (*Times* [London], 27 May 1983, 6; *New York Times*, 27 May 1983, A5)

9 June 1983 Australian Prime Minister Robert J. L. Hawke informs French President François Mitterrand that no further shipments of uranium will be made to France as long as nuclear weapons testing continues on Mururoa atoll. However, under existing contract, no further shipments are scheduled until October 1984. (*Times*, 10 June 1983, 28)

21 June 1983 French Special Envoy Regis Debray proposes to Hayden that Australia send scientific observers to "monitor" French tests on Mururoa. Hawke says he will put proposal to cabinet but notes Australian objection to testing is not just environmental but involves opposition to "nuclear programme itself." He also reaffirms "suspension of uranium exports to France in retaliation for the nuclear test." (*Times*, 22 June 1983, 4; 23 June 1983, 8)

30 June 1983 French government officials refuse to comment on report from New Zealand that France tested 50-kiloton nuclear device on Mururoa atoll previous day. (*Times*, 1 July 1983, 5)

5 July 1983 French commission of inquiry report asserts nuclear testing in South Pacific does not pose dangerous radioactive threat to environment. (*Times*, 6 July 1983, 6)

13 July 1983 Australia indicates willingness to participate in French-proposed scientific monitoring program if it is endorsed by countries of South

Pacific Forum scheduled to meet in Canberra following month. (*Times*, 14 July 1983, 7)

28–29 August 1983	South Pacific Forum "reaffirmed the total opposition of member states to the French underground nuclear testing programme at Mururoa Atoll in French Polynesia but failed to reach a common position in response to a French invitation for Forum members to send scientific observers to inspect the Mururoa site." (*Keesing's* 32571)
15 November 1983	French Foreign Minister Claude Cheysson affirms at a press conference that France will continue nuclear testing in South Pacific despite objections of countries in the region because, he says, "his government was convinced that the nuclear deterrent was the best arm for peace." (*Times*, 16 November 1983, 7)
July 1984	Ruling Australian Labor Party (ALP) confirms government uranium policy, including ban on shipments to France. Foreign Minister Hayden expresses concern that ban may damage Australia's reputation as reliable supplier, also fears France may retaliate in other areas of trade. (*Science*, 3 August 1984, 484; *Journal of Commerce*, 23 July 1984, 3A)
27 August 1984	14 Pacific states call for the region to be declared a nuclear-free zone. (*Washington Post*, 29 August 1984, A22)
October 1984	Australian government purchases remaining eight shipments (1,700 tons) of uranium destined for France from Queensland Mines. The government announces that it will stockpile uranium until France changes its policy on testing in South Pacific, or until another customer is found, in which case company has option to repurchase any or all of stockpile. (*Journal of Commerce*, 29 October 1984, 11A)

GOALS OF SENDER COUNTRY

Foreign Minister Bill Hayden
Following French nuclear weapons test: "We can make life uncomfortable for the French. If they're determined to test these things then let them test the damned things in the Atlantic, Mediterranean, or mainland France. Let them keep them out of our backyard." (*Times*, 27 May 1983, 6)

Times
Although no uranium shipments are scheduled until late 1984, Prime Minster Hawke makes clear that ". . . in the meantime, the Australian government would be using the threat of the embargo to bring pressure to bear on the French in negotiations to stop nuclear testing in the South Pacific. . . . The continuation of French nuclear tests was the only issue which acted as a barrier to the strengthening of relations between the two countries, Mr. Hawke said. But on that issue there could be no compromise." (*Times*, 10 June 1983, 28)

RESPONSE OF TARGET COUNTRY

Special Envoy Regis Debray
"[He] said that the suspension of uranium exports was considered 'unfriendly' by France."
(*Times*, 23 June 1983, 8)

Defense Minister Charles Hernu
Hernu "strongly" criticizes Hawke's reaffirmation of the uranium ban in July 1984, "complain[s] that it represents 'interference' in the country's internal affairs." (*Science*, 3 August 1984, 484)

ECONOMIC IMPACT

Observed Economic Statistics

Value of uranium shipped from Australia to France was $300 million in 1982. France depends on Australia for one-third of its uranium needs. (*Science*, 3 August 1984, 484)

Calculated Economic Impact

Negligible impact, since no uranium shipments were scheduled by contract until October 1984.

Relative Magnitudes

Gross indicators of French economy	
French GNP (1981)	$511 billion
French population (1982)	54 million
Annual effect of sanctions related to gross indicators	
Percentage of GNP	negl.
Per capita	negl.
French trade with Australia as percentage of total trade	
Exports (1982)	negl.
Imports (1982)	negl.
Ratio of Australian GNP (1981: $158 billion) to French GNP (1981: $511 billion)	0.3

ASSESSMENT

Journal of Commerce
July 1984: "There is no immediate prospect that France will abandon its South Pacific testing program. And there is every indication that the Australian government will pursue the ALP national conference recommendation [to continue ban on uranium exports to France]." (*Journal of Commerce*, 23 July 1984, 3A)

AUTHORS' SUMMARY

Overall assessment	*Assigned scores*
□ Policy result, scaled from 1 (failed) to 4 (success)	2
□ Sanctions contribution, scaled from 1 (none) to 4 (significant)	1
□ Success score (policy result *times* sanctions contribution), scaled from 1 (outright failure) to 16 (significant success)	2

Political and economic variables

□ Companion policies: J (covert), Q (quasi-military), or R (regular military)	—
□ International cooperation with sender, scaled from 1 (none) to 4 (significant)	1
□ International assistance to target: A (if present)	—
□ Sanctions period (years)	1 +
□ Economic health and political stability of target, scaled from 1 (distressed) to 3 (strong)	3
□ Presanction relations between sender and target, scaled from 1 (antagonistic) to 3 (cordial)	3
□ Type of sanction: X (export), M (import), F (financial)	X
□ Cost to sender, scaled from 1 (net gain) to 4 (major loss)	2

BIBLIOGRAPHY

Keesing's Contemporary Archives. 1983.

Case 83–2   US v. USSR

(1983: Korean Airline Flight 007)

CHRONOLOGY OF KEY EVENTS

30 August 1983   Korean Airline (KAL) flight 007, traveling from New York to Seoul with 269 passengers, crew members, disappears from radar screens between Anchorage, Alaska, and Tokyo. When plane does not arrive in Seoul as scheduled, it is reported initially as having landed safely in Soviet territory on Sakhalin Island. (*Washington Post*, 1 September 1983, A1)

1 September 1983   US Secretary of State George P. Shultz, in special press conference, accuses Soviets of having shot down airliner after it strayed off course and into Soviet airspace over sensitive military facilities. Official statement in Tass acknowledges only that Soviet fighter planes attempted to guide intruder plane out of its airspace but contends airliner did not respond, instead flew on toward Sea of Japan. Message to Shultz from USSR Foreign Minister Andrei Gromyko echoes Tass statement; it is rejected as inadequate by State Department spokesmen. (*Washington Post*, 2 September 1983, A1; *New York Times*, 2 September 1983, A1)

2 September 1983   UN Security Council, at request of US, Korea, opens debate on shooting. USSR admits only that its fighters fired warning shots and plane flew out of its airspace. Soviets contend plane was on deliberate spying mission sent by US, was flying without navigation lights, did not respond to signals. Shultz accuses Soviet Union of covering up truth. President Ronald Reagan questions "what can be the scope of legitimate mutual discourse with a state whose values permit such atrocities." Nevertheless, aides indicate arms control negotiations, grain sales, Shultz's meeting with Gromyko in Madrid next week all will go forward while US will call on allies to halt all air traffic to and from USSR for at least 60 to 90 days. (Flights by Aeroflot, Soviet state airline, to US have been suspended since December 1981 as part of sanctions against USSR inspired by Polish situation.) South Korean Foreign Minister Lee Bum Suk calls for apology and full financial compensation. (*New York Times*, 3 September 1983, A1)

| 5 | 5 September 1983 | Reagan appears on national television to denounce Soviet actions, demand full explanation, apology, reparations for families of victims. Specific US sanctions are announced, including cancellation of negotiations on cultural exchange agreement, opening of new US consulate in Kiev, transportation agreement. These are considered mild but Reagan "indicates that he is relying instead on international retaliation." (*Washington Post*, 6 September 1983, A1) |

| 6 | 6 September 1983 | USSR admits shooting down KAL flight 007 but continues to maintain it was on spying mission, asserts it was fired upon only after refusing signals to land and taking evasive action. US spokesmen reject statement as inadequate since Soviets neither apologize nor accept responsibility for incident. (*Wall Street Journal*, 7 September 1983, 3) |

| 7 | 8 September 1983 | Reagan closes two remaining Aeroflot ticket offices in US, expels three Aeroflot officials, asks Civil Aeronautics Board to restrict Aeroflot's sales of tickets in US for connecting flights elsewhere. In Madrid, Shultz cuts short meeting with Gromyko when latter refuses to offer "adequate" explanation or apology for KAL tragedy. (*Wall Street Journal*, 9 September 1983, 2) |

| 8 | 12 September 1983 | West Germany, Spain, Japan, UK impose two-week ban on flights to and from Soviet Union. Other NATO members, except for France, Greece, Turkey, are expected to join boycott. Commercial pilots in Italy, Netherlands, Norway, Denmark, Finland, Sweden, Spain announce they will join two-month ban on flights to USSR recommended by International Federation of Airline Pilots Associations (IFAPA). (*Washington Post*, 13 September 1983, A15) |

| 9 | 14–15 September 1983 | US House of Representatives and Senate unanimously approve resolution denouncing Soviet actions against Korean airliner. On 15 September, New York and New Jersey Port Authority bars Aeroflot planes carrying Soviet envoys to UN from landing at Kennedy, Newark airports. US officials say Gromyko must land at military airfield; USSR announces that, for first time since 1957, he will not be at UN General Assembly session. Other Soviet envoys arrive in New York on commercial flights from third countries. (*Washington Post*, 15 September 1983, A1; *Wall Street Journal*, 16 September 1983, 1; 19 September 1983, 1) |

| 20 | 28 September 1983 | Government-imposed two-week ban on Moscow air travel ends. For first time since downing of Korean airliner, Soviet leader Yuri Andropov comments publicly, calls incident "sophisticated provocation" by US intelligence agencies. (*Wall Street Journal*, 29 September 1983, 1; *Times* [London], 1 October 1983, 1) |

| 21 | 30 September 1983 | IFAPA announces it will end its ban on flights to Soviet Union on 30 October. Reason given is that lessening of tensions is necessary so International Civil Aeronautics Organization can find solution to prevent similar tragedies in future. (*Times*, 1 October 1983, 1) |

| 6 October 1983 | Intelligence experts say final review of evidence indicates Soviet pilot probably did not know he was firing on commercial airliner. In response to press questions, Les Janka, deputy White House press secretary, says, "We don't talk about intelligence or intelligence reporting." (*New York Times*, 7 October 1983, A1) |

GOALS OF SENDER COUNTRY

President Reagan
In speech to nation 5 September 1983: "It would be easy to think in terms of vengeance, but that is not a proper answer. We want justice and action to see that this never happens again . . . There is something I've always believed in but which now seems more important than ever. The Congress will be facing key national security issues when it returns from recess. There has been a legitimate difference of opinion I know, but I urge the members of that distinguished body to ponder long and hard the Soviets' aggression as they consider the security and safety of our people. . . ." (*Washington Post*, 6 September 1983, A4)

"Condemning Moscow for what he called the 'Korean Airline Massacre,' President Reagan last night shunned any tough retaliatory measures and instead used the incident to urge new support for his big defense buildup." (*Wall Street Journal*, 6 September 1983, 3)

Wall Street Journal
"What the president is hoping is that US allies will take similar actions against Aeroflot. If they do, the impact on the Soviet airline could be significant, US officials maintain." (*Wall Street Journal*, 9 September 1983, 2)

RESPONSE OF TARGET COUNTRY

Soviet television commentator
5 September 1983: "Our anti-air attack defense forces fulfilled their duty in defense of the motherland. The human sorrow, which we deeply share, is not our fault. I do not know who thought of this provocation but he either reckoned that the plane would carry out serious reconnaissance, or that what has happened would happen, and from this human misfortune he could build a wave of anti-Soviet hysteria." (*Washington Post*, 6 September 1983, A1)

Soviet Foreign Minister Gromyko
Before Conference on Security and Cooperation in Europe, 7 September 1983: "Soviet territory, the borders of the Soviet Union, are sacred. No matter who resorts to provocations, he should know that he will bear the full brunt of responsibility for it." (*Wall Street Journal*, 8 September 1983, 3)

On 14 September 1983, Aeroflot announces it no longer will accept tickets issued by American carriers. "A spokeswoman for the state-owned airline said the action was in response to similar measures taken by US airlines. . . ." (*Washington Post*, 15 September 1983, A18)

Tour executive, US-USSR Travel Report
"[T]o compensate for decreased airlift by NATO airlines, [Aeroflot] has put on extra flights to Finland, Austria, Marseilles, France, Yugoslavia, and East European capitals." (Hansen-Sturm, report update)

ATTITUDE OF OTHER COUNTRIES

Canada
On 5 September, Canada announces suspension of Soviet commercial landing rights for 60 days. (*Washington Post*, 6 September, 1983, A7)

France
French officials announce postponement of visit by Gromyko that was to have begun 5 September. (*Washington Post*, 6 September 1983, A7)

United Kingdom
British Airways halts flights to Moscow for 60 days effective 8 September. Shortly thereafter, British government announces two-week ban on Aeroflot flights into UK. (*Wall Street Journal*, 9 September 1983, 2; *New York Times*, 11 September 1983, A16)

Japan
Prime Minister Yasuhiro Nakasone strongly condemns Soviet actions but Japan takes only mild steps against USSR: bans chartered Aeroflot flights to Japan and government officials' flying on Aeroflot but not regularly scheduled Aeroflot flights. Japan laters joins most of NATO countries in two-week ban on Aeroflot flights. (*New York Times*, 11 September 1983, A14; *Washington Post*, 13 September 1983, A15)

NATO countries (except France, Greece, Turkey)
Governments of these countries impose two-week ban on air travel to and from Soviet Union. (*Washington Post*, 13 September 1983, A15)

ECONOMIC IMPACT

Observed Economic Statistics

"The comparative economic cost to the USSR from recent US unilateral travel controls is minimal. . . . The US government controls have actually increased Soviet share and power in the US-USSR bilateral travel market at the expense of US firms." (Hansen-Sturm, telex, 3)

"US-USSR travel has been little affected one week after the imposition of US-USSR air transportation sanctions." (Hansen-Sturm, report update)

Calculated Economic Impact

Negligible, since lost airline revenues were small, sanctions of very limited duration.

Relative Magnitudes

Gross indicators of USSR economy	
USSR GNP (1981)	$1,587 billion
USSR population (1981)	268 million
Annual effect of sanctions related to gross indicators	
Percentage of GNP	negl.
Per capita	negl.
USSR trade with US as percentage of total trade	
Exports (1981)	0.3
Imports (1981)	3.0
Ratio of US GNP (1981: $2,958 billion) to USSR GNP ($1,587 billion)	2

ASSESSMENT

Wall Street Journal
"Administration officials couldn't say what economic effect the sanctions against Aeroflot would have on the Soviets. Presidential spokesman Larry Speakes contended they would have an effect on Aeroflot's prestige and, to some extent, on its foreign exchange revenues." (*Wall Street Journal*, 9 September 1983, 2)

Cord D. Hansen-Sturm
Representative of tourist industry: "The new CAB-enforced sanctions will cause only minor additional Soviet foreign exchange losses and will not punish the Soviets." (Hansen-Sturm, telex)

AUTHORS' SUMMARY

Overall assessment	*Assigned scores*
☐ Policy result, scaled from 1 (failed) to 4 (success)	1
☐ Sanctions contribution, scaled from 1 (none) to 4 (significant)	1
☐ Success score (policy result *times* sanctions contribution), scaled from 1 (outright failure) to 16 (significant success)	1

Political and economic variables

☐ Companion policies: J (covert), Q (quasi-military), or R (regular military)	—
☐ International cooperation with sender, scaled from 1 (none) to 4 (significant)	4
☐ International assistance to target: A (if present)	—
☐ Sanctions period (years)	1

	Assigned scores
Political and economic variables (continued)	
☐ Economic health and political stability of target, scaled from 1 (distressed) to 3 (strong)	3
☐ Presanction relations between sender and target, scaled from 1 (antagonistic) to 3 (cordial)	1
☐ Type of sanction: X (export), M (import), F (financial)	M
☐ Cost to sender, scaled from 1 (net gain) to 4 (major loss)	2

BIBLIOGRAPHY

Hansen-Sturm, Cord D. 1983. Telex to US Civil Aeronautics Board, 12 September.
———. 1983. US-USSR Travel Report of US Tour Operators Coordinating Committee, 16 September; update 20 September.

Case 83–3 US v. Zimbabwe

(1983–84: UN Voting Record; Matabeleland)

CHRONOLOGY OF KEY EVENTS

1981   Director M. Peter McPherson of US Agency for International Development (AID), while visiting Zimbabwe, pledges $225 million in development aid over three years to help rebuild war-torn economy, foster democracy. (*Washington Post*, 5 January 1984, A22)

September 1983   In September, Zimbabwe abstains on US-sponsored UN Security Council resolution condemning Soviet Union for downing Korean airlines jet. (*Washington Post*, 5 January 1984, A22; *New York Times*, 28 December 1983, A23)

13 September 1983   After meeting with Prime Minister Robert G. Mugabe in Washington, President Ronald Reagan comments, "We didn't always agree, but have all gained from hearing your views, Mr. Prime Minister." Principal areas of disagreement are over linkage of withdrawal of Cuban troops from Angola and independence for Namibia, US policy toward South Africa, Zimbabwe's abstention from UN Security Council vote on Korean jetliner. (*New York Times*, 14 September 1983, A6)

October– November 1983   In October, Zimbabwe cosponsors UN resolution condemning US invasion of Grenada. In November, US is further irritated by absence of Zimbabwean officials at memorial service for French and Americans killed in Beirut and by Mugabe's efforts to forestall recognition of Israel by other African nations. (*Washington Post*, 5 January 1984, A22; *New York Times*, 28 December 1983, A23)

19 December 1983   Reagan administration cuts aid to Zimbabwe for FY 1984 from $75 million to $40 million claiming a lack of funds. Congressman William H. Gray (D–Pa.) calls this "tragic mistake," contends "there was enough money to do $75 million for Zimbabwe if they had wanted to." (*Washington Post*, 20 December 1983, A1)

4 February 1984   "The Mugabe government impose[s] . . . [24-hour] curfew restrictions on Matabeleland . . . following reports of increased activity by dissidents it contends are armed and supplied by South Africa." (*Washington Post*, 11 April 1984, A26)

March 1984   US government blocks emergency shipment of 30,000 tons of American corn worth $10 million until Zimbabwe provides assurances corn "would be distributed equitably among needy residents, including those in Matabeleland." (*Washington Post*, 11 April 1984, A26)

10 April 1984   Zimbabwe's State Security Minister Emmerson Munangagwa announces that, because of "decline in dissident activity in Matabeleland, the curfew would be enforced only on a dusk-to-dawn basis, that stores would be able to resume normal operating hours, and that full and regular food shipments would be resumed." On same day, US, Zimbabwe sign transfer agreement authorizing shipment of American corn. (*Washington Post*, 11 April 1984, A26)

GOALS OF SENDER COUNTRY

Washington Post
AID officials attribute reduction to "congressional cuts in the overall foreign aid appropriation. . . . But State Department sources said privately that Zimbabwe's recent votes against US positions at the United Nations 'played a big part in the decision.'" (*Washington Post*, 20 December 1983, A1)

Seymour Maxwell Finger
"As part of the 'get-tough' campaign, Washington has been computerizing individual Third World country votes in order to take them into account when considering aid requests. . . . Zimbabwe, the recipient of the largest US aid program in sub-Saharan Africa, votes with the United States less often than Libya." (Finger 442)

Frank J. Donatelli, assistant administrator for Africa, AID
"The US provides nearly $1 billion annually in foreign assistance to Africa's sub-Saharan countries. Yet the highest level of support for the US positions in the UN of any African country is 31 percent. . . . However, the Congress has directed us to consider a country's UN record when allocating assistance funds. . . . It is only one in a host of factors involved in allocating assistance to a particular country. . . . We value our relationship with Zimbabwe. We take pride in our efforts to promote economic growth and multiracial democracy in that country. And we look forward to a close relationship with Zimbabwe in the days to come." (*New York Times*, 16 January 1984, A14)

Washington Post
April 1984: US attaches conditions to emergency food shipment that "stipulate that US aid workers have the right to monitor food shipments to ensure the government is adequately supplying Matabeleland and grant the United States the option of recalling the food and turning it over to nongovernmental aid organizations if it determines the pledge has been violated." (*Washington Post*, 11 April 1984, A26)

RESPONSE OF TARGET COUNTRY

Prime Minister Mugabe
"Mugabe . . . referred to the [Korean] airplane incident as 'a horrible tragedy' but said that Zimbabwe had consulted seven nations in Africa [which it represents on the Security Council] on how to vote and all recommended abstaining." (*New York Times*, 14 September 1983, A4)

"Rejecting suggestions that he refuse all U.S. assistance, Mugabe declared: 'Whatever aid comes to us, provided it has no strings, we will accept.'" (*US News & World Report*, 16 January 1984, 32)

Washington Post
"Zimbabwean officials had informed the U.S. embassy last week that they considered the conditions [on food shipment] an unacceptable form of political pressure. But Prime Minister Robert Mugabe reportedly reversed the government's position late last week following strong urging by Agriculture Minister Denis Norman . . . [who argued] that the corn shipment was vital to help Zimbabwe avoid significant food shortages during the next two months until its own corn is ready for market." (*Washington Post*, 11 April 1984, A26)

ECONOMIC IMPACT

Observed Economic Statistics

Zimbabwe "is struggling to bind the wounds of a seven-year war for independence and faces the worst drought in a century. . . . There is . . . a possibility that the cut in American economic aid will hasten the prospect of starvation in some areas of Zimbabwe." (*New York Times*, 28 December 1983, A23)

"In terms of per capita GNP, Zimbabwe is one of the wealthier in sub-Saharan Africa, ranking even with oil-rich Nigeria. . . . No reductions are planned for ongoing programs in Zimbabwe dealing with food production, agricultural training, education or family planning." (*New York Times*, 16 January 1984, A14)

At formation of independent state of Zimbabwe in April 1980, UK pledges $165 million (over three years); UN, $140 million; US pledges $15 million in 1980, $25 million–$30 million in 1981; Nigeria, $17 million in economic aid to help rebuild Zimbabwean economy, resettle refugees. (Senate, Baker 16)

Calculated Economic Impact

	Annual cost to target country
Reduction in US economic aid to Zimbabwe; welfare loss valued at 90 percent of reduced transfers.	$31 million

Relative Magnitudes

Gross indicators of Zimbabwean economy	
Zimbabwean GNP (1981)	$6.4 billion
Zimbabwean population (1981)	7.6 million
Annual effect of sanctions related to gross indicators	
Percentage of GNP	0.5
Per capita	$4.08
Zimbabwean trade with US as percentage of total trade	
Exports (1982)	6
Imports (1982)	8
Ratio of US GNP (1981: $2,958 billion) to Zimbabwean GNP (1981: $6.4 billion)	462

ASSESSMENT

Sanford J. Ungar, senior associate, Carnegie Endowment for International Peace
"This cut—while it makes some American officials feel good—may well fuel instability in Zimbabwe. It will strengthen South Africa's position in the region and will certainly bolster the doctrinaire, anti-American elements in the Mugabe government who are pushing for more orthodox Marxism and a pro-Soviet stance." (*New York Times*, 28 December 1983, A23)

AUTHORS' SUMMARY

Overall assessment	Assigned scores
□ Policy result, scaled from 1 (failed) to 4 (success)	2
□ Sanctions contribution, scaled from 1 (none) to 4 (significant)	2
□ Success score (policy result *times* sanctions contribution), scaled from 1 (outright failure) to 16 (significant success)	4

Political and economic variables

□ Companion policies: J (covert), Q (quasi-military), or R (regular military)	—
□ International cooperation with sender, scaled from 1 (none) to 4 (significant)	1
□ International assistance to target: A (if present)	—
□ Sanctions period (years)	1
□ Economic health and political stability of target, scaled from 1 (distressed) to 3 (strong)	2
□ Presanction relations between sender and target, scaled from 1 (antagonistic) to 3 (cordial)	2
□ Type of sanction: X (export), M (import), F (financial)	F
□ Cost to sender, scaled from 1 (net gain) to 4 (major loss)	1

BIBLIOGRAPHY

Finger, Seymour Maxwell. 1983–84. "Jeane Kirkpatrick at the United Nations." 62 *Foreign Affairs* (Winter): 436–57.

US Congress, Senate Committee on Foreign Relations. 1980. *The Birth of Zimbabwe: A Turning Point for South Africa.* Report by Pauline H. Baker. 96 Cong., 2 sess., May.

Case 83–4   US and OECS v. Grenada

(1983: Restore Democracy; Human Rights)

CHRONOLOGY OF KEY EVENTS

13 March 1979   Maurice Bishop deposes Prime Minister Eric Gairy, establishes Marxist dictatorship. Bishop's requests for economic assistance from US are met coolly; "Cuba moves into the breach." (*Washington Post*, 27 February 1983, A1; 26 October 1983, A17)

16 April 1979   Grenada, Cuba establish diplomatic relations. Bishop charges US "had applied pressure on his government not to have a close relationship with Cuba." State Department says it "has told Grenada it would view with concern any move by Grenada to establish close military ties with Cuba." (*New York Times*, 17 April 1979, A5)

1981   President Ronald Reagan, concerned about growing Soviet influence in Western hemisphere and Cuban-assisted construction of airport in Grenada capable of handling military aircraft, authorizes CIA to plan covert operation aimed at destabilizing Bishop's government. Plan is shelved following its rejection by Senate Intelligence Committee in July. Operation is described as aiming at causing "economic difficulty for Grenada in hopes of undermining the political control of . . . Bishop." (*Washington Post*, 27 February 1983, A1)

28 July 1982   Bishop announces he has signed economic assistance agreement with USSR Premier Nikolai A. Tikhonov, intended to reduce Grenadan dependence on West. Under agreement, USSR grants Grenada $1.4 million for purchase of steel, flour, other essentials, extends 10-year credit of $7.7 million for purchase of equipment. (*New York Times*, 29 July 1982, A5)

November 1982   At meeting of Caribbean community, Bishop rejects pressure from neighboring countries to hold free elections, "accused other members of the organization of trying to isolate his country." (*New York Times*, 18 November 1982, A5)

June 1983   Bishop visits Washington seeking to improve relations, "establish some sort of a dialogue." He asserts, however, that CIA is trying to overthrow his government, accuses Reagan administration of "po-

| *June 1983* | litical interference that he said was preventing Grenada from receiving |
| *(continued)* | any loans from the World Bank or the International Monetary Fund." |

June 1983
(continued)
litical interference that he said was preventing Grenada from receiving any loans from the World Bank or the International Monetary Fund." Bishop does not meet with Reagan, as desired, but does see National Security Adviser William P. Clark and Deputy Secretary of State Kenneth W. Dam. (*New York Times*, 10 June 1983, A8)

August 1983
IMF approves a $14.1 million loan to Grenada over US objections. (*New York Times*, 27 August 1983, 36)

12–14 October 1983
Radical faction of Bishop's New Jewel Movement under leadership of Deputy Prime Minister Bernard Coard and General Hudson Austin overthrows Bishop, places him under house arrest. (*Washington Post*, 15 October 1983, A11)

19–20 October 1983
Bishop is rescued by crowd of supporters but is killed, along with several of closest advisers, by the Coard/Austin group. Austin immediately establishes 24-hour, shoot-on-sight curfew. Members of Caribbean Common Market (CARICOM) express revulsion at bloodshed; they "scheduled an emergency foreign ministers' meeting for Saturday, to consider proposals for economic and political sanctions against the island's Marxist-oriented military leadership." (*Washington Post*, 21 October 1983, A1)

22 October 1983
Leaders of Eastern Caribbean states meet in Trinidad "to consider sanctions against the new military government in Grenada that would range from a trade embargo to endorsement of possible US intervention." Grenada (not present) is suspended from Caribbean Economic Community. Members agree "to halt all supplies of currency to Grenada. . . . [and] to isolate Grenada by cutting all sea and air links." Reports circulate that "two U.S. Navy task forces, totalling 21 ships with 800 marines, have been diverted toward the island." Grenadan leaders express belief island "is in real danger of attack." (*Washington Post*, 23 October 1983, A1; *Journal of Commerce*, 27 October 1983, 23B)

25 October 1983
US marines, with small contingents from nations of Organization of Eastern Caribbean States (OECS), invade Grenada. Reagan cites threat to American lives as chief reason. Over weekend, members of OECS had publicly announced economic, diplomatic sanctions against Grenada while privately requesting US to intervene militarily. (*Washington Post*, *New York Times*, 26 October 1983, A1)

2 November 1983
Secretary of Defense Caspar W. Weinberger announces all hostilities have ceased, troops will begin to be withdrawn immediately. (*US News & World Report*, 14 November 1983, 22)

November 1983
Reagan allocates $3.5 million in economic aid to rebuild Grenada. AID Director M. Peter McPherson says no AID funds have gone to Grenada for past two years because "we felt uncomfortable with what was going on there politically." (*Washington Post*, 3 November 1983, A28–29)

GOALS OF SENDER COUNTRIES

Barbadian Prime Minister Tom Adams
Following coup and Bishop's murder: "I was horrified at these brutal and vicious murders, the most vicious act to disfigure the West Indies since the days of slavery. It will be very difficult indeed to see what future the regime that is stained by this record of murder can have in an association of peaceful and peace-loving CARICOM states. I, for one, will not be able to sit down at a table with these disgusting murderers." (*Washington Post*, 21 October 1983, A1)

US Pentagon official
22 October: ". . . [A]lthough many administration officials would like to see a friendlier government in Grenada, they are unlikely to seize this opportunity to install one. . . . It's one thing to feel that way, but it's another thing in this day and age to send in the marines. Reagan is just now overcoming a reputation of being trigger happy in the international field." (*Washington Post*, 23 October 1983, A1)

President Ronald Reagan
"President Reagan's decision to invade Grenada was driven by a long held view that the tiny island's 8,000 foot airport runway could be of significant military value to the Soviet Union and Cuba, plus more immediate fears that Americans might be taken hostage if he failed to act. . . ." (*Washington Post*, 26 October 1983, A1)

Prime Minister Eugenia Charles of Dominica
"It is not a matter of an invasion. It's a matter of preventing this thing [Marxist revolution] from spreading to all the islands." (*Washington Post*, 26 October 1983, A1)

RESPONSE OF TARGET COUNTRY

Prime Minister Maurice Bishop
Responding to question about why US would consider Grenada threat to its security: "The real reason has to do with the fact that we are determined to build our own path, refusing to accept dictation from anyone. Although we are small, we have the right to build our own future." (*New York Times*, 10 June 1983, A8)

Washington Post
Following murder of Bishop, imposition of 24-hour curfew: "Radio Free Grenada has said that all foreigners are safe in the 133-square-mile nation. . . . The Grenadan radio has accused the United States of creating unnecessary concern about the safety of the nearly 1,000 Americans there. It said the Americans are safe and have not been harmed in any way." (*Washington Post*, 23 October 1983, A1)

Grenadan Ambassador Dessima Williams
In letter to Organization of American States, March 1983: "To say that this modest airport represents a threat to the United States is not only provocative but utterly fatuous." (*Washington Post*, 26 March 1983, A14)

ATTITUDE OF OTHER COUNTRIES

Cuba

Since Bishop took power in 1979, Cuba had provided $10 million in aid, several hundred workers and technical advisers to assist in construction of Grenada's airport. At time of invasion, many Cubans on island resisted marine operation. (*Washington Post*, 25 October 1983, A1, A6)

Nicaragua

Nicaraguan officials condemn invasion, saying it was intended to intimidate Nicaragua, was prelude to US invasion of their own country. (*Washington Post*, 25 October 1983, A6)

United Kingdom

Prime Minister Margaret Thatcher says she had expressed doubts to Reagan about invasion, had refused to endorse it. One reason for misgivings was that British government had approved airport in Grenada, guaranteed $9.75 million of funds required. (*Washington Post*, 26 October 1983, A9; 31 October 1983, A20)

Soviet Union

"US aggression against Grenada is a challenge to the entire world community. All responsibility for the consequences of this criminal act rests with the Washington administration and personally with President Reagan. . . . Demanding the immediate withdrawal of the invading forces, Tass characterized the invasion 'as an act of open international banditry, of international terrorism' against a UN member-state." (*Washington Post*, 26 October 1983, A22)

ECONOMIC IMPACT

Observed Economic Statistics

April 1983: Airport's cost is estimated at $71 million; Cuba had pledged to pay 40 percent of that figure. (*Washington Post*, 21 April 1983, A1)

"Merchants say that state regulations force them to buy certain commodities from Cuba, such as sugar and cement, at uneconomic prices and that an agreement with Moscow for nutmeg [exports] has hurt income from that source. Farmers also complain about the regulations' effect on earnings from nutmeg, of which Grenada is one of the world's largest producers." (*New York Times*, 7 August 1983, A1)

"The decision to suspend air traffic will adversely affect the island's economy. . . . The island's economy is based on the export of bananas and nutmeg, and on tourism. The economic sanctions will hit shipments of the commodities, while tourists are expected to stay away because of the violence." (*Journal of Commerce*, 27 October 1983, 23B)

Within days after invasion, Reagan administration announces it will allocate $3 million in relief aid for Grenada. (*US News & World Report*, 14 November 1983, 25)

Calculated Economic Impact

Negligible, since sanctions were in force for only a few days before invasion.

Relative Magnitudes

Gross indicators of Grenadan economy	
Grenadan GNP (1980)	$80 million
Grenadan population (1983)	110,000
Annual effect of sanctions related to gross indicators	
Percentage of GNP	negl.
Per capita	negl.
Grenadan trade with US as percentage of total trade	
Exports (1979)	2
Imports (1979)	0
Ratio of US GNP (1980: $2,632 billion) to Grenadan GNP (1980: $80 million)	32,900

AUTHORS' SUMMARY

Overall assessment	Assigned scores
□ Policy result, scaled from 1 (failed) to 4 (success)	4
□ Sanctions contribution, scaled from 1 (none) to 4 (significant)	2
□ Success score (policy result *times* sanctions contribution), scaled from 1 (outright failure) to 16 (significant success)	8

Political and economic variables

□ Companion policies: J (covert), Q (quasi-military), or R (regular military)	R
□ International cooperation with sender, scaled from 1 (none) to 4 (significant)	3
□ International assistance to target: A (if present)	—
□ Sanctions period (years)	1
□ Economic health and political stability of target, scaled from 1 (distressed) to 3 (strong)	1
□ Presanction relations between sender and target, scaled from 1 (antagonistic) to 3 (cordial)	2
□ Type of sanction: X (export), M (import), F (financial)	F, X, M
□ Cost to sender, scaled from 1 (net gain) to 4 (major loss)	2

Comments

In this case a successful outcome was achieved entirely because of the military invasion. At most, the economic measures taken by the OECS nations helped persuade the US to initiate military action.

Other Publications from the Institute

POLICY ANALYSES IN INTERNATIONAL ECONOMICS

BOOKS

SPECIAL REPORTS

Promoting World Recovery: A Statement on Global Economic Strategy *by Twenty-six Economists from Fourteen Countries*/December 1982

Prospects for Adjustment in Argentina, Brazil, and Mexico: Responding to the Debt Crisis
John Williamson, ed./June 1983

Inflation and Indexation: Argentina, Brazil, and Israel
John Williamson, ed./March 1985